DATE DUE

ANCIENT AND MODERN MAN
IN SOUTHWESTERN ASIA

by

HENRY FIELD

University of Miami Press
Coral Gables, Florida
1956

Contents

List of Tables

List of Maps

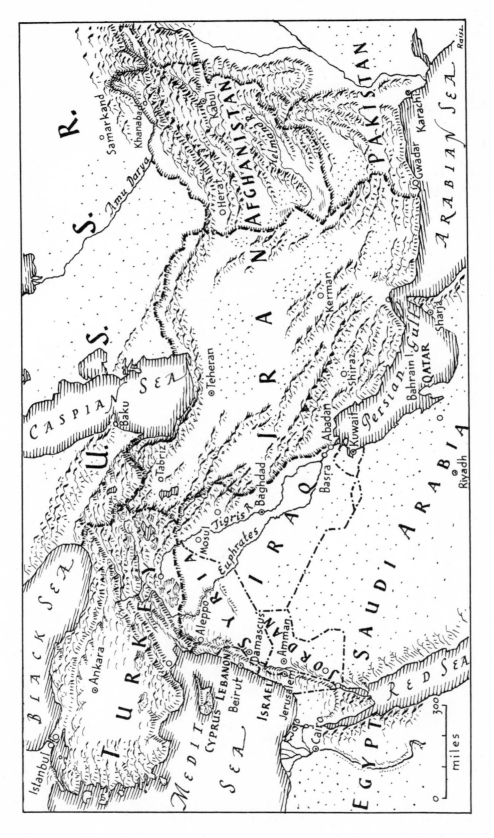

Approaches to Eastern Asia by Erwin Raisz

PREFACE

During the spring of 1952, I was invited to give the two Forbes Hawkes Lectures at the University of Miami.

The title selected was "Ancient and Modern Man in Southwestern Asia."

In 1952, an invitation was received from Mr. Ralph Lowell, Trustee of the Lowell Institute in Boston, to give eight Lowell Lectures during the following October. The same subject was chosen. Since there was more scope in this series, each lecture consisted of an introductory anthropogeographical section dealing with the geographical location, the land and the people, the climate, flora, fauna and latest population statistics, followed by a summary of information on Stone Age Man and his cultures and the racial elements among the living peoples based on anthropometric data.

The final lecture summarized our present knowledge of Ancient and Modern Man in each of the countries or areas ranging from the Suez Canal to West Pakistan border and from the central part of the Caucasus Mountains to the Arabian Sea.

In order to present the data upon which the 1952 Forbes Hawkes and the 1952-1953 Lowell Lectures were based, I have followed the same general outline with footnote references to important sources. However, the reader is presumed to have access to publications such as those by Bunak, Chantre, Coon, de Khanikoff, Garrod, Houssay, Kappers, Keith, Krogman, McCown, Murray, Muzaffer, Pantiukhov, Pittard, Shanklin, Bertram Thomas, Winifred Smeaton Thomas, Vallois, von Luschan, and other anthropologists, as well as to my publications[1] on Sinai, Iraq, Iran, the Caucasus and materials placed on microfilm[2] in the American Documentation Institute, c/o Photoduplication Service, Library of Congress.

With regard to the References, no attempt has been made to compile all those which deal with land and the people and with ancient and modern man, but rather they have been selected with the purpose of providing a general guide for the student or specialist.

The reader is referred to my "Bibliographies on Southwestern Asia" published during 1953, 1955 and 1956, by the University of Miami Press. In No. I, the 3,016 titles are divided into Anthropogeography and Natural History (Zoology and Botany). In the former are included Anthropology, Archeology, Geology, Agriculture, Medicine, Cartography, Astronomy, Art, Music and Poetry. In the introductory section is given a list of bibliographies and special area studies. No. II contains the following: Anthropogeography (nos. 1-1641) and Zoology (nos. 1642-3292) including groupings under General, Arthropods, Birds, Fish, Mammals, Mollusks and Reptiles, and Amphibians. No. III contains the following: Anthropogeography (nos. 1-3340) and Natural History (nos. 3341-6113) including Zoology (nos. 3341-4890) and Botany (nos. 4891-6113).

These three Bibliographies supplement each other. Each has an Author Index. Bibliography IV is now being compiled and should be distributed during March, 1957.

The reader is recommended to use "A selected and annotated Bibliography of Books and Periodicals in Western languages dealing with the Near and Middle East with special emphasis on Medieval and Modern times," pp. 1-137, edited by Dr. Richard Ettinghausen and published with Supplement, 1954. Originally published in 1952 under the auspices of the Committee on Near Eastern Studies of the American Council of Learned Societies, this new Supplement up to December, 1953, has been bound with the 1952 edition. The list of maps, archeological and anthropological references arranged by period and by country together with the author indexes are indispensable. In addition, the list of general periodicals dealing with the Near East, titles of publications on geography, geology and travel, including guide books, as well as bibliographical and reference works on the Ancient and Modern Near East should be consulted as background material. Specific references to Archeology and Anthropology may be easily found.

The reader is also referred to, "Yearbook of Anthropology," pp. 445-70, Wenner-Gren Foundation, New York, 1955. Since this excellent publication is readily available, no excerpts have been selected here. This anthropological review by Shevket Aziz Kansu, which summarizes the researches conducted during 1952-54, should be consulted by every specialist. There are references under each section, including Arabia, Iran, Iraq, Israel, Jordan, Lebanon, Syria, and Turkey.

My anthropogeographical interests in Southwestern Asia have included medical observations such as: the relation of diet and disease, especially in respect to the teeth; growth changes, primarily in stature, correlated with the quantity of calcium in the soil; the collection of useful plants and drugs with notes on their preparation and dosage; the compilation of medical data, from official and local sources and medical officers; and medical folklore.

In this study, the above information is presumed to be available to the reader by reference to my publications, including monographs and scientific papers.

The reader is referred to the important monograph on "Global Epidemiology: The Near and Middle East," Vol. 3, 1954, compiled under the direction of Brigadier James Stevens Simmons, Harvard University School of Public Health. The regional bibliographies are excellent. Many references are given in the footnotes. This volume should be consulted in connection with the study of the modern inhabitants of Southwestern Asia. By using the above sources and their references both the specialist and the student will be guided to the principal part of the literature in Western languages dealing with Anthropogeography in its widest aspects.

To return to the arrangement of the material--under each geographical heading there is a brief introductory section with the location, boundaries, physical features, climate, flora and fauna, historical outline and population estimate. This is followed by a chronological summary of evidence for Stone Age cultures and human remains, data on historical crania, and the physical anthropology, including some statistical tables.

Some comments on certain chapters are necessary.

The detailed list of Paleolithic sites in Lebanon and bibliographical references were compiled by my colleague, Dr. René Wetzel, geologist of the Iraq Petroleum Company, to whom I wish to express deep gratitude

The magnificent series of anthropometric data for males and females from Turkey outshines those for all other areas in Southwestern Asia. This should serve as a model for other countries.

With regard to the Caucasus, statistical tables on the living peoples have been compiled together with comparative data from the northwest in the Crimea, from the northeast in the Volga region, and from the east in Soviet Central Asia eastward into Tannu Tuva and northeast into Siberia. The reader is presumed to have ready access to my "Contributions to the Anthropology of the Caucasus," Peabody Museum, 1953. Unfortunately, I have been unable to obtain a copy of Victor Bunak's monograph on the Caucasus with long comparative tables, which I presume to be in print. I saw this large manuscript in the Museum of Anthropology, Moscow, during July, 1945.

The chapter on Iraq is relatively brief because I presume ready access to my anthropometric survey begun in 1925 and published finally in 1952.

The Arabian Peninsula was by far the most difficult chapter, for the material is scanty and widely scattered. The writings of Philby, Bertram Thomas, Thesiger, Caton Thompson, Twitchell and Sanger are readily available. Hence only brief descriptions of each country were considered desirable. Concentration was laid on the distribution of Stone Age sites, but in this great area where so little has been known for so long, selected notes on recent archeological data have been incorporated. Here my thanks to Mr. Karl Twitchell must be mentioned for allowing the first publication of his complete list of archeological sites, some from each of the four Provinces of Saudi Arabia, the Hejaz, Asir, Nejd, and Al Hasa. These have been included in Chapter X and added to Map 24.

In dealing with the Arabian Peninsula, the geographical arrangement is as follows: Saudi Arabia, Al Kuwait, the two Neutral Zones, Bahrain Island, Qatar Peninsula, Trucial Oman Coast, Muscat and Oman, Aden, including the Hadhramaut and the Eastern Protectorate, and Yemen.

The Chapter on Iran is short because in my two volumes entitled, "Contributions to the Anthropology of Iran," Field Museum of Natural History, Vol. 29, pp. 1-706, 1939, historical and modern references to ancient and modern man were presented and detailed repetition was therefore unnecessary here.

We have little information on Afghanistan, but the prospects for the discovery of Stone Age man and his cultures are excellent, since to the west, to the north and to the east we have evidence of ancient man.

Baluchistan, now part of West Pakistan, remains one of the principal lacunae; no data on the Old Stone Age and few anthropometric measurements are available.[3] This territory should be searched for surface Paleoliths and stratified deposits in caves and rockshelters because the Makran coast must have been an ancient migration route.

This concludes the regional survey.

In Chapter XIV, comparative tables of anthropometric data, arranged in ascending order by measurement and index, have been compiled from many sources. This shows that during the past 30 years more than 2,000,000 measurements, observations and indices have been recorded in Southwestern Asia.

Since the stature and cephalic index are among the most important racial criteria, tables for the entire area have been compiled. I have compiled and published lists of anthropometric data from Egypt, Israel (Palestine), Jordan (Trans-Jordan), Syria, Lebanon, Turkey (Anatolia), the Caucasus (Ciscaucasia and Transcaucasia), Kurdistan (Anatolia, Iraq, and Iran), the Persian Gulf (Bahrain Island) and the Arabian Peninsula (Saudi Arabia, Yemen and Oman) and Iran, Turkestan, Afghanistan, Baluchistan, West Pakistan and India; the reader is referred to these tables.

Certain important lacunae remain. Additional data is required on the people of the Arabian Peninsula, Iran, Afghanistan, Baluchistan, and some small groups such as: (a) the Chechens of Ras al-Ain in northeast Syria; (b) the Shebeks and Bejwans of northern Iraq; and (c) the dwellers in the Helmand of southeastern Iran.

In addition, considerable material remains unpublished or unavailable. For example, a series of measurements from Afghanistan eastward along the southern flank of the Himalayas has been recorded by Gordon Bowles. In the Caucasus and Central Asiatic Republics of Turkestan, Tadzhikistan, Uzbekistan and Khirghizia, including the Pamirs, Soviet physical anthropologists have measured thousands of individuals. The principal researches in the Caucasus are by V. Bunak, and those of Central Asia by L.V. Oshanin, V. Ginzburg, and the late IArkho. The greater part of this material remains unavailable.

In the final chapter a summary of our present knowledge of Stone Age Man and his cultures and the racial elements in the population has been compiled so that we can attempt to determine the position of ancient and modern man in Southwestern Asia in relation to Central Asia and India to the East, to Africa to the west and southwest, and to Europe to the northwest.

Gratitude must be expressed to the late Dr. E.A. Hooton, who assisted in planning the selection and arrangement of the material. His counsel and guidance from 1926-53 will be sorely missed. To Sir Arthur Keith, who encouraged and guided my anthropometric researches in Southwestern Asia from 1925-54, and to the Abbé Henri Breuil, who began my training in Prehistory in 1926, I record my sincere appreciation.

I am indeed grateful to the Governments of Egypt, Jordan, Lebanon, Syria, Iraq, Iran, U.S.S.R., Al Kuwait, Bahrain Island, Saudi Arabia, and West Pakistan for their generous assistance, special permits, and many local facilities placed at my disposal during the past 31 years.

In addition, three oil companies have made desert archeological reconnaissances possible in many areas, especially in difficult terrain:

(a) Iraq Petroleum Company in the Jazira of western Iraq, in Jordan, Syria, Lebanon, Qatar Peninsula and along the Trucial Oman Coast. These Expeditions were in 1928, 1934, and 1950.

(b) Anglo-Iranian Oil Company in Iran, 1934 and 1950.

(c) Arabian American Oil Company in Saudi Arabia, 1950 and 1955.

To these Companies I express deep gratitude for every type of assistance including permission to accompany trans-desert survey parties, transportation by car, boat and airplane, and guest privileges in base and desert camps.

In the preparation of the manuscript my thanks are due to the following: Miss Margaret Currier, Librarian of the Peabody Museum, Harvard; Mrs. K.C. Payne, who typed and checked the statistical tables and aided with the final revision; and to Miss Ruth Taffae, Edward Stys, and Mrs. Irving Levine, each of whom typed part of the text.

Dr. Claude T. Richards read the final text and suggested some editorial changes, which have been incorporated. I am grateful for his assistance.

My wife generously assisted in copy-reading part of the manuscript, especially the tables.

The greater portion of the IBM copy was proofread by Mrs. Ordella Ullom, Mrs. Frieda Johannes, and Miss Maryann Shelley. The corrections were stripped and inserted by Charles R. Allen and by Miss Shelley. Any Errata or Corrigenda are my sole responsibility since I read the final copy for the camera.

Throughout the text the place names conform to the spelling adopted by the U.S. Board of Geographical Names and the Permanent Committee on Geographical Names of the Royal Geographical Society of London. The majority of diacritical marks have been omitted.

Since I have published and placed on microfilm several thousand racial type photographs ranging from the Faiyum on the west to Iran on the east and from Ciscaucasia on the north to the Eastern Aden Protectorate, it was decided not to include photographs in this publication. The reader is also referred to Carleton S. Coon, "The Races of Europe," New York, 1939, and to Shanklin's photographs of Beduins (see References to Jordan).

Through the courtesy of Dr. Walter Kahoe, Director, Medical Department, J.B. Lippincott Company in Philadelphia, permission was granted to use 17 maps by Dr. Erwin Raisz drawn for "Global Epidemiology," Vol. 3. This series forms a welcome addition to the illustrative material.

The tribal map of Sinai has been copied from G.W. Murray, "Sons of Ishmael," p. 247, London, 1935.

The anthropometric zones in Anatolia are taken from Inan Afet, "Recherches anthropologiques sur 59,728 Turcs des deux Sexes," Archives Suisses d'Anthropologie Générale, Vol. 9, pp. 79-112, 1940.

PREFACE

The map of the archeological sites in Lebanon was sketched by René Wetzel and redrawn by Dr. Erwin Raisz.

The sketch maps showing the cephalic indexes in Southwestern Asia and in the Arabian Peninsula and the cranial indexes from Southwestern Asia were made by Dr. Winifred Smeaton Thomas and redrawn by Dr. Erwin Raisz.

Map 24 locating 100 archaeological sites in Southwestern Asia, primarily in the Arabian Peninsula, was compiled by the author and superimposed by Dr. Erwin Raisz on his "Landforms of Arabia."

Since the University of Miami Press has published my "Bibliographies on Southwestern Asia: I-III," 1953-56, with 12,421 references in 30 languages from books and 1,500 scientific Journals, the References in this monograph may be considered as complementary to these lists of titles from the same area.

The composition of the copy for photo offset by Edwards Brothers, Ann Arbor, Michigan was prepared on an IBM electric typewriter by Mark Grant, who was granted leave of absence from the American Council of Learned Societies for this project by Mr. Mortimer Graves. Mr. Grant worked with me on preparing the final copy in Coconut Grove, Florida. This required conferences with Mr. Grant and myself on format and standardization of style, which, in general, conformed to that used in the Near East Translation Project Series of the American Council of Learned Societies.

In conclusion, my gratitude must be expressed to Mr. Mortimer Graves for his assistance, to Mr. Mark Grant for his recommendations on format and for his technical skill, to Mrs. Forbes Hawkes for her University of Miami Lecture Series, and to Mr. Malcolm Ross for his general supervision of this study.

HENRY FIELD

June 20, 1956
Coconut Grove,
  Florida

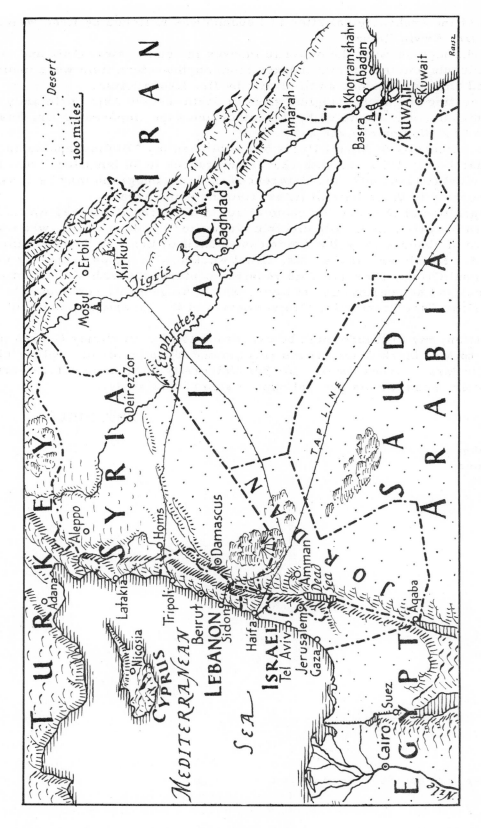

The Near East by Erwin Raisz

I. THE LAND

Southwestern Asia is almost completely bounded by water.

To the north lie the Black Sea and Caspian Sea. To the west is the eastern end of the Mediterranean and the Red Sea. The southern shore is lapped by the Arabian Sea, including the Gulf of Oman and the warm and shallow Persian Gulf.

The northern boundary is also formed by the central part of the high Caucasus Mountains, an arbitrary line dividing Ciscaucasia and Transcaucasia. Here toward the mid-point rise the superb, snow-covered peaks of Mt. Elbrus (18,468 feet) and Mt. Kazbek (16,545 feet).

Running east the boundary follows the frontier between Iran-Afghanistan and Soviet Turkestan and southwestward along the Afghan-Pakistan border to the Gulf of Oman.

This territory of Southwestern Asia, sometimes called the Near East or the Middle East, includes the following countries: Sinai (Egypt), Israel, Jordan, Lebanon, Syria, Turkey, the Caucasus, Iraq, the Arabian Peninsula (Saudi Arabia, Al Kuwait, the two Neutral Zones, Bahrain Island, Qatar Peninsula, Trucial Oman Coast, Muscat and Oman, Aden and Protectorates, and Yemen, Iran, Afghanistan, and Baluchistan in West Pakistan.

Here live about 65 million people on 2.8 million square miles.

Within these crossroads of three continents there is almost every range of physical features and climate.

To the northwest are the Taurus Mountains. In the center, plunging like a dagger through this heartland, strike the Zagros Mountains. To the north the central massif of the Caucasus forms a geographic barrier. In the northeast the Paropamisus-Hindu Kush Mountains merge into the high Pamir chain.

Southwestern Asia has spawned five deserts:

(a) The great Rub'al Khali (1,000 x 500 miles), the "Empty Quarter", dividing Saudi Arabia from Yemen, Aden and its Eastern Protectorate (including the Hadhramaut), Oman, and the Trucial Oman Coast.

(b) The Dahana (400 x 30 miles), a crescentic zone linking the southeast corner of the Great Nefud with the north central extension of the Rub' al Khali.

(c) The Great Nefud (400 x 200 miles), forming a protective shield to the north central part of Saudi Arabia.

(d) The salty Dasht-i-Kavir (250 x 100 miles), southeast of Tehran.

(e) The Dasht-i-Lut (150 x 75 miles), southeast of the Dasht-i-Kavir.

In addition, there are thousands of square miles of wilderness or steppe, ranging from the Syrian-Turkish border to the Rub' al Khali, and from western Syria and Jordan to Makran and Kalat in former Baluchistan, now part of West Pakistan.

The greater part of Southwestern Asia is mantled with hard sand and gravel through which struggle low bushes and camelthorn until the spring rains encourage great areas to bloom with a green carpet interspersed with multicolored plants.

Another physical feature is the Harrat-ar-Rajil, the great lava bed (100 x 60 miles), protecting southwestern Syria and northeastern Jordan. Thirty years ago the Royal Air Force pioneered a car track through this fearsome basalt-strewn region. With crowbars the boulders were forced aside to give 10-foot clearance for the wheels. The Nairn Overland Desert Mail drivers aptly called this "The Bay of Biscay"--often rough for mariners. Eight miles covered by a convoy in one hour was considered "good going" on my first trip across the Harrat-ar-Rajil in 1925.

Naturally, there is a wide climatic range from sub-zero on top of Demavend (18,600 feet), Elbrus and Kazbek to scorching blasts sweeping over the burning sands of the Rub' al Khali and the salt wastes of the Dasht-i-Kavir and Dasht-i-Lut.

In general, during the winter months the climate[1] is pleasant, with cool nights and warm days. The contrast between noon and midnight makes the nights feel cold.

Sandstorms often rage for several grim days at a time. The constant scratching of the rough particles of sand is hard on the nerves. The hot wind, bearing oceans of sand, requires calm and patience, for it is far easier to become angry at a sand-storm than at mountainous waves or driven snow.

The incessant heat, the prevailing wind, and the frequent gusts of sand are a constant burden even to the Beduin, his head wrapped in a headcloth.

The summers are very hot except high in the mountains or beside the deep blue shore of the Mediterranean. From June-September only foreigners work regular, long hours, thus shortening their lives and probably reducing their productive capa-city for the other eight months. However, many offices open early and reopen in the evening, remaining closed during the almost unbearable heat of the day. In June, 1950, at Badanah along Tapline in Saudi Arabia the thermometer registered 122° F. in the shade accompanied by a 50-mile per hour furnace-blast wind. It was hard to collect scientific specimens under those conditions, which are normal for this re-gion at this time of year.

At the other extreme, snow and hail are sometimes seen in the central belt of Southwestern Asia.

Heavy spring rains cause the wadis to roar like mountain torrents and turn the stony desert (Hamad) into a sea of mud. On several occasions our convoy has been bogged down to the axles. Thirty to fifty hours later the wind and sun evaporate the water. After heavy digging and much pushing, the convoy resumes its journey, al-ways avoiding dark-colored patches in order not to resume one of the trials and tribulations of desert travel by wheeled vehicle.

To summarize, the majority of dwellers in Southwestern Asia are accustomed to sun and sand, sand and sun. Theirs is a constant struggle against Nature, a constant struggle for water.[2]

No one who has not lived in a desert or wilderness away from civilization can imagine the constant and unceasing quest for water, both for their families and for their camels and sheep. Nature is a stern mistress. A traveler in a desert region soon learns respect for Nature. The possibility of death with burning eyeballs, a thickened tongue and a parched throat is ever present.

There are numerous wells, but the quality of the water is little improved by a not uncommon Beduin trick of hurling a dying she-camel down the shaft to discourage the next drawers of water--if they be enemies.

In the Syrian Desert the water table is about 75 feet below the surface, although in northern Saudi Arabia I have seen wells 190 feet deep. Surface pools occur at numerous localities; for example, at the Ain el-Asad near the Roman fortress of Qasr el-Azraq and at Amri in northeastern Jordan. The great Wadi Sirhan has a large lake near Kaf (Qaf). Southern Iraq has many lakes and marshes.

Large bodies of water include the Dead Sea, Lake of Tiberias, several lakes in southwestern central Turkey, Lake Tuz south of Ankara, Lake Van in eastern Ana-tolia, Lake Rezaiyeh (formerly Urmia) in northwestern Iran, Lake Habbaniya west of Baghdad, Lake Gokcha in Armenia, four small lakes near Shiraz, and a few scat-tered bodies of water, including the Helmand, along the central portion of the Iran-Afghan border.

Despite these lakes and the very long coastline, drinking water is an ever present problem. Alexander Graham Bell wrote in his diary that the two greatest reflections on man's inventiveness were that he could not fly like a bird and that he could die of

thirst when surrounded by water. Supersonic jets are the answer to the former, de-
salinating units (mechanical, chemical or thermal) to the latter.

Alpine flora abound in the Caucasus and on the high ranges and peaks from Mt.
Ararat (16,915 feet) to Mt. Kazbek, on Mt. Demavend, on Kuh-i-Taftan (13,091
feet) in southeastern Iran, and from Herat to the Pamirs. Except for the other
mountainous areas, including the mountains of Lebanon (from Homs to Mount Her-
mon), the Taurus, eastern Anatolia, the Zagros and Elburz and western Afghanistan,
the area tends to consist of a flat alluvial plain or low-rolling hills.

In the two latter regions the flora is typically xerophytic or drought-resistant.
The great areas of wilderness support scattered low bushes. The Shatt-al-Arab
above Basra is one of the important date-producing regions of the world. Here grow
the delicious Khastawi and Halawi dates. Date palms (Phoenix dactylifera) from Iraq
flourish at Indio, California.

Among other cultivated plants are wheat, barley, rice, cotton, lucerne (alfalfa),
maize, linseed, millet, sesame, coffee, tobacco. In Iran poppies are grown for
opium.

Agriculture is practiced with every device ranging from modern U.S. equipment
to the most primitive type of plough.

Irrigation for the most part is by water lift, water wheel or canal, including the
subterranean channels (Qanats) in Iran.

Many trees, in addition to the varieties of palms, grow in the watered areas.
The most famous through the centuries are the Cedars of Lebanon, still preserved
like the trees of our redwood parks. Willows and poplars flourish in many regions.

In certain areas, such as along the Mediterranean shoreline, in the Rowanduz
(Rowandiz) Gorge of northeastern Iraq, beside the Shatt-al-Arab, in Mazanderan
and in the subtropical zones of Transcaucasia, the flora is rich.

For convenience, the fauna will be divided into wild[3] and domestic. Among the
former are the ibex, moufflon and bear in the mountains, and elsewhere the gazelle,
fox,[4] jackal, hyena, badger, cheetah and wild boar. There is a wide range of
snakes, lizards, frogs, tortoises and turtles. Few snakes are poisonous; among
these is the dangerous horned viper (Ar. Abu Gurain = "father of two horns" Pseudo-
cerastes fieldi).

Insects abound in the towns, villages and encampments. Apart from vectors of
disease, such as malaria, dysentery and fevers (sandfly, etc.), locusts are the
principal enemy. Because of their destructiveness, Moslems believe them to be the
revenge of Allah. Several species of ants damage the crops.

In the lakes, rivers, streams and canals fish may be caught. In the Greater Zab
of northern Iraq swims a very large, coarse fish. According to report these fish
(Bizz) are so long that borne across the back of a small donkey the head rests on
the ground on one side, the tail on the other. Excellent trout-fishing may be obtained
north of Tehran. The Red Sea and Persian Gulf support considerable fish industry.
As to big-game fishing, larger than world-record specimens of sailfish have been
caught in the Arab nets of the southern part of the Persian Gulf. In the Caspian the
famed sturgeon yield tons of the most delicious caviar.

More than 400 species of birds have been recorded from Iran. In Mazanderan
snipe, woodcock, pheasants and ducks are abundant. Some wilderness areas are inhabited by thousands of sandgrouse. There are also turkey bustards, partridges and
storks, the latter considered sacred and called Hajji Luglug, "the bird which makes
the pilgrimage to Mecca."

The five most interesting animals in Southwestern Asia are: (a) the Arabian
ostrich, now almost extinct; (b) the Arabian oryx, probably the Biblical unicorn;
(c) the Mazanderan tiger; (d) the tiny wild horse (Ar. Wahash) last seen by Lady
Anne Blunt about 1870 between Damascus and the Euphrates, some may still live in
an unexplored corner of the Arabian Peninsula; and (e) the tahr (Ar. Wial) in Oman.

Turning now to domestic animals, the list includes camels, sheep, goats, horses, donkeys, oxen and dogs. In the desert and wilderness zones the camel is the sole means of transport. The Beduin is the slave of his camels, for he must move to grazing and water regardless of his own wishes.

The close cropping by the sheep, and more especially by the goats, destroys the budding spring vegetation. On mountain sides and hill slopes this constant cropping causes erosion and denudation and increases the action of geological agents. Throughout Southwestern Asia desiccation is taking place, always with renewed acceleration as dust bowls spread, as rivers tend to become dry from irrigation, as man-made and animal-encouraged erosion develop.

Soil conservation, large irrigation projects, reforestation, restricted charcoal-burning, and rotated areas of spring grazing would make large areas "blossom like a rose."

Six thousand years of cutting down the trees, making charcoal, using and re-using part of the land without any fertilizer, close cropping of the spring vegetation, no soil conservation--all these combined with the climatic conditions have impoverished the soil to the maximum as the population has increased out of all proportion. This land, this "Fertile Crescent," was one of the principal centers of civilization.

From its sandy soil sprang great thinkers, poets, mathematicians, astronomers, architects, engineers, craftsmen, sailors, warriors.

Southwestern Asia nurtured two of the great religious teachers, Jesus Christ and Mohammed.

With revenue from oil and foreign technical assistance, this region looks steadfastly toward the future.

II. SINAI, LAND-BRIDGE OF ASIA AND AFRICA

Sinai[1] lies between the Suez Canal and Israel. Shaped like an inverted isosceles triangle with a base of 100 miles and sides of 160 miles, this peninsula flies the Egyptian flag. Geographically, however, Sinai belongs to Asia rather than Africa.

This area of 23,000 square miles is bounded on the north by the Mediterranean and on the south by the Gulf of Suez and the Gulf of Aqaba, which meet off Ras Muhammad. At Aqaba intersect the three frontiers of Israel, Jordan and Saudi Arabia. The peninsula of Sinai may be divided arbitrarily into two zones:

1. The northern square with 100-mile sides bounded on the south by the great escarpment fringing the Plateau of El Tih. To the north from Port Fuad to Gaza the Mediterranean coast is mainly sand dunes. The principal dry stream bed with scattered water holes is the Wadi el-Arish, which meanders southwest past Bir Hasana and divides on the white limestone escarpment just north of Nekhl, the central point in Sinai. The Wadi el-Arish was fed by two streams from the central part of the Egma Plateau.

2. The southern equilateral triangle composed of a central mountain massif is bounded by a narrow sandy shoreline from Abu Zeneima to Ras Muhammad and from Aqaba southwest to this same cape. This region consists of range after range of multicolored granite mountains with red predominant; these give the name to the Red Sea. The southwestern coast, irregular in contour, is extremely picturesque.

Geology

The Wilderness of Tih consists of a bare, sandy waste with characteristic drought-resistant plants. There are low hills, sometimes in chains. South of this great expanse covered by sand and gravel, red sandstones shelve toward the escarpment south of Nehkl and far beyond to the vast plutonic mountain complex leading to the triple-peaked triangle of Jebel Musa (7,359 feet), Jebel Serbal (6,734 feet) and Jebel Katarina (8,527 feet).

In the middle of the southern triangle the Ancient Egyptians mined turquoise at Serabit el-Khadem (2,650 feet) and from rockshelters at about 1,100 feet on Jebel el-Magharah. Copper was also mined in the Wadi Nasr and associated with iron and manganese in the Wadi Khaliq. A dike, rich in copper, traverses syenite for nearly two miles in the Wadi Sened. The port used by the Ancient Egyptians was at Merkhah, a few miles south of Abu Zeneima on the Red Sea coast midway between Suez and Ras Muhammad. This point of debarcation and embarcation, in service about 1500 B.C., was discovered[2] in 1948 by W.F. Albright and the writer.

Climate

In general, the climate is healthy; February-April and November-December are the best months. However, during the rainy season violent floods occur in the mountains. In the central massif the air is usually very dry and dustless and the sky is clear. There is a marked difference in temperature between day and night, the latter often cold by marked contrast. Dew is common in the early morning. Snow is rare except on peaks. In the late spring and summer the Khamsin (= lit. 50-day wind) blows occasionally from the southeast along the unprotected shoreline.

In the spring there is abundant vegetation, mainly scrub and tamarisk trees, some of which exude a kind of manna. Meteorological observations recorded at El Arish, Nekhl and Tor have been recorded on ADIM[3] No. 3226.

Water Supply

The plateau is waterless except for permanent springs at Magdhaba, Bir Hasana,

Jebel el-Halal and Nekhl. This flat area is drained northward toward the Mediterranean by numerous watercourses but primarily by the great Wadi el-Arish. The mountains to the south are traversed by many wadis and contain springs and fertile oases.

Vegetation

The range of flora is relatively abundant. Chichester Hart described 509 species, 33 being particular to Sinai. Hume collected 650 species. Daumas (1951, pp. 20-23) gives a list with the Latin and Arabic names, a brief description of each plant, and the range. We saw date palms (Phoenix dactylifera) at El Arish, Nekhl, Suez, just north of Abu Zeneimeh and at Feiran (anc. Pharan). Several acres in the Wadi Feiran produce corn and tobacco.

Fauna

There is abundant marine life along the shores of the Gulf of Suez and the Gulf of Aqaba. Fishing is very profitable, but there is constant danger from barracuda, sharks and rays. The sand mackerel run up to 45 pounds.

Domestic animals form the basic method of transportation in Sinai. Camels, a few horses, and many sheep and goats predominate.

Animals,[4] including birds, are rare. Among those recorded by Jarvis and Daumas are: leopard (nimr), lynx or caracal, wildcat, fox (Abu el-Hussein or husseini), jackal (wawi), striped hyena (dhaba), gazelle (ghrazal), ibex (tetel or beden), hare (arnab), hyrax (Biblical coney) and hedge-hog (gumfut).

Among reptilia are a horned viper, called locally Abu Genabia ("the Father-of-going-sideways") because it moves by raising its coils laterally. There are many lizards, but always hard to catch; those in the sandy areas are dun-colored, those in the plutonic are dark.

According to Jarvis[5] the avifauna are mainly birds of prey, such as eagles, hawks, and vultures. The indigenous birds include the crested, sand and bifasciated larks, mourning chats, partridges and the Crowned, Senegal and Imperial sand grouse, the lesser and Arabian bustard, and quail.

Natural Resources

Along the Sinai coast south of Suez one million metric tons of crude oil were produced during 1951 at Sudr (lat. 29º 34´ N., Long. 32º 44´ E.) and at Asl 10 miles south of Sudr and 40 miles south of Suez.

Manganese is mined at Umm Bogma by the Sinai Mining Company with headquarters at Abu Zeneima.

Ancient Man

In this section we shall refer to all available records from 1871-1948 ranging from the Paleolithic to the historical period. However, since at this stage of our knowledge of the Stone Age cultures of Sinai it is impossible to assign all surface finds to definite Paleolithic, Neolithic, Chalcolithic or later periods, we shall proceed with a chronological account based on the year of discovery or publication.

After a reconnaissance survey has been completed, combined with at least one stratified deposit, probably in a cave or rockshelter, it may well be possible to assign deeply patinated flints to their correct periods. Hence we shall begin with the earliest record found in the literature.

1871. E.H. Palmer mentions flint implements found on hillsides in the Wilderness of Tih.

1906. Currelly (in Petrie, 1906, p. 127) described typologically Paleolithic flints from a small wadi bed in the Gaa Desert as follows:

"I soon chanced upon a very good implement. We picked up many others, all of which were much the worse for wear. One of the men came upon four flakes about

five inches long that fitted together; the edges were unrubbed, and they lay within a
few yards of each other. Sir John Evans considers that these could not possibly be
called Paleolithic, but that no one could say they were not, as the patina was very
rich... What I saw later confirmed me in the view that there had practically been
no climatic change during the period in which the Neolithic man had been in Sinai."

Currelly (in Petrie, p. 267) describes how on the Plateau of Tih, "are thousands
of flakes and implements from Paleolithic times. The flint seems to be good, and
there are quantities of large pieces; yet the implements are all small and of decidedly
poor workmanship. The majority have the orange patina well-known on Libyan flints.
One or two flints were of the regular celt pattern, but the majority were small
scrapers. Flakes that would join together were by no means rare, and it looked as
if the surface had remained undisturbed since they had been struck."

1906. The following exerpts are from Petrie:

1. In the valley [Wadi Useyt] there is a thickness of about 20 feet of river
gravels; and these are cut through by a small stream-bed, for in recent times
the rainstorms only form a narrow channel. The greater gravels apparently
belong to the fluvial period, when the current filled the whole breadth of the
valley. In these old gravels I found a flint scraper, which is certainly of human
work; thus it is clear that man was here in the great Pluvial age (p.15).

2. Before the Suez Canal was cut, great caravans of pilgrims from Egypt
came across the Tih from Aqaba, on their way to Mecca. A rough road was
made for them, and near Aqaba a bridge was built. The plateau of the Tih is
dreary in the extreme. During our journey across we did not see a single tent
or a beast grazing; but everywhere the long, level line of the upper chalk cliffs,
broken here and there, but again returning to the same level. The ground is like
the Libyan plateau, covered with chocolate-colored flints that have settled into
a hard pavement. The upper chalk as it wore away left behind it great masses of
flint nodules, and these have split up in the sun to the small flakes that form the
pavement, which is so level that it has almost the appearance of being rolled.

3. Now in the [Wadi Tayibeh] bed of large rolled flints I found an excellent
long thin flake of skilled Neolithic work (fig. 162, no. 6) and this with parallel
flaking (fig. 162, no. 5). The Pluvial age, in which these gravels were rolled
down by a strong and wide current, must then be contemporary with well-developed Neolithic Man. The same result is shown by a well-marked flake (fig.
162, no. 3) found by Mr. Porch at 15 feet in the old filling of Wadi Magharah,
which is composed of granite sand and blocks. The later stream has cut through
this filling, and so exposed a section of it. Other flakes were found 2 feet down
in the gravel of Seir Sidreh, shown in fig. 162, nos. 2 and 4. All these agree
with the flaked flints which I found in the old high gravels of the Nile Valley
(Naqada, p. 5, pls. 69,76),though these are perhaps mainly of an older type.

4. In the Wadi Ahmar we came to a little spur that runs out into the valley.
This had been made use of for a smelting place. The wind, blowing either up or
down the valley, would give a good draught, and along the crest of the hill some
smelting had been done by the aid of pits. These were sunk usually from 18 - 25
inches deep, and stones were built into a rough low wall around the edge of the
holes. The size of these holes varied, some being a few feet across, others
larger. The form also varied very much. I could see little indication of a defi-
niteness in their form. The crest of the little spur was covered with a thick
layer of ashes, but we found only one bit of slag. We carefully cleaned out and
planned the pits. Great numbers of flints of good workmanship lay about in the
ashes: and a considerable quantity of quartz and pieces of stone hammers were
found at intervals. The quartz showed the bulb of percussion, a mark of intentional

fracture; and some shell fragments, and one unfinished shell bead, made one think that bead manufacture had been done on the site. A short distance from the spur, in a little valley at right angles to the Wadi Ahmar, is an open pit from which a quantity of copper ore had been dug. This ash bed was very hard to understand. If these were pits for making test-smeltings for copper, it would be intelligible; but in that case, what was the use of the flints? In the middle of the site there was a cairn of stones, piled over the body of a man. Two beads were found, and proved to be ordinary Egyptian beads, well-known after the Nineteenth Dynasty. One was of round glass, with the two ends of the glass thread showing plainly, and the other was a double-eye bead. The illustrations (nos. 170, 171) show the good workmanship of the flints. The drills in particular are slender and long in the point, and the triangular drills are very even along their sides. Some are certainly arrowheads, and it is probable that the leaf-shaped implements may have served a similar purpose (pp. 239-40).

5. In the temple at Serabit el-Khadem, Petrie (p. 136) found a flint knife (fig. 144, no. 1) in an enclosure south of the hanafiyeh. He describes it as of the type well-known to belong to the Twelfth Dynasty, and was published from Kahun (see Illahun, vii, 7; xiii, 6). The straight edges of the handle end were covered by a wrapping fiber to protect the user's hand, as was found in the one at Kahun.

6. Near the turquoise mines in the valley of the Wadi Magharah, Petrie (p. 50) describes two large waste heaps that lay on the valley side, about half-way up to the main mines, A and B on Map 2 (opp. p. 38). These were turned over, and he found hundreds of flint flakes in them, many of which had been used. The commonest were long, stout flakes, which were entirely rounded at the edges and point, evidently from having been used for grubbing in the sand-stone. A common type with these was a flake chipped in at both sides of the end, so as to give a point. These were seldom or never worn down by grubbing, and hence were probably for some other purpose than for working on the sandstone. The principal types of these flakes are given in fig. 60. The great rarity or absence of any such flakes in the waste-heaps of the Egyptian galleries shows that we cannot attribute this abundance of flakes to the regular Egyptian work. Probably they were the tasks of the native Bedawyn, who extracted the turquoises in various ages since prehistoric times, when they supplied them to the Neolithic Egyptians, down through any period when the mines were not worked by more civilized people.

7. In addition to the large stone tools, there were many thousands of flints found near the mines. These have been collected also by previous travelers, and a wild notion has been formed that they were set in wooden handles, and used as chisels, struck with a mallet. To make any cuts in the sandstone, such as the chisel-marks, would soon snap a flint; yet there were very few broken ones, compared with the large number found. The real use of these flints is shown by the wearing and smoothing of the ends, due to grubbing against sand-stone. In fig. 60 are the various types which we found. In the top line the first six are all entirely rounded at the point by wear in the sandstone: this was probably done when scoring round the nodules of turquoise to get them out of blocks of rock. Next are five examples of the pointed flints, which are seldom worn much, and seem as if intended for some work not in sandstone.

Lastly are two of the long fine flakes, which were rather common. There seems to be some relation between the pointed forms and the worn flints. They were found at Magharah principally in three places: A, a heap of chips at 60 feet, above the valley, and 270 feet down the valley from Sahura's tablet; B, a heap of chips at the same level, and 160 feet down the valley from Sahura; and

R, scattered flints on the hill-side below Ra. n. user's tablet. In these places we found at: A, Flints largely worn, 1 in 8 pointed; B, Flints less worn, 1 in 20 pointed; and R, Flints little worn, 1 in 30 pointed.

These numbers depend partly on the selection made at Magharah. It seems that the proportion of pointed flints increases where they were most used for working in the sandstone.

The large flints were apparently used for working the rock, as many of them are worn. In the lower part there are portions of well-flaked tools, which belong probably to early times, as they were found on the surface and have no connection with the mining. The last three flints are heavily worn by working in sandstone. Now, these worn flints were found mainly in the heaps A and B at Magharah, and no black stone crushers or large tools were with them.

On the contrary, scarcely any flints occurred where the crushers and picks were found, below the mines of Sa. nekht and Tahutmes III at Magharah, and below the mines of Amenemhat II and the well-worked mines at Serabit. Also, there is no trace of working with flints in the rock surfaces of the mining of the Egyptians. The conclusion, then, seems to be that the large stone crushers and picks were used by Egyptian workers, and the flints were used by Bedawy grubbers of all periods to scrape the turquoises out of the rock without regular mining (pp. 160-61).

1911. H. W. Seton-Kerr picked up a flint handaxe and some crude flakes 15-20 miles south of El Arish. These are on exhibition in the Geological Museum, Cairo.

1913-1914. Leonard Woolley and T. E. Lawrence made a six-week archeological reconnaissance survey of northeastern Sinai, especially in the Ain Kadeis area. The following passages have been quoted or summarized from their pp. 18-38.

1. In writing the history of northern Sinai we are at once met by a great difficulty, the absence of significant references to the country in early records. This, of course, in its not very satisfactory way, gives an exact indication of the importance of the country in that time. It was a roadway at best, and a very unpleasant one. Travelers passing from Egypt to Syria by land all had to traverse it, and they went, as they do today, by the El Arish road if the governments were favorable, and by the Hebron-Beersheba-Muweilleh roads in other cases.

The Egyptians, the Patriarchs, the Jews, the Romans, the Crusaders and the Arabs all passed over these tracks, and they have given us place-names and no more. Probably in their eyes the country was too detestable to merit further reference, and by their default our notes on the history of the desert have to be compiled from the remains of occupation preserved in the country itself. By good fortune Sinai lends itself to such research, for everything that has even been made in the desert is kept forever for all to see. The careless traveler who piles up four stones in a heap by the roadside here erects an eternal monument to himself.

In the books of our predecessors, the Prehistoric age is the most fertile in material remains in the Negeb. They made constant reference to flint implements, and to cairns and graves and dwelling-houses of the Stone Age. Palmer even saw in the stone-heaps of Muweilleh a great city of the prehistoric period, and has no hesitation in describing as Neolithic the stone circles of Ras Seram and other places. Holland traced excellent roads across the desert by the heaps of flint arrowheads lying on either side. Only Lord Kitchener thought that some of the cairns must be of comparatively recent and Arab origin.

Now we have searched for stone implements over the whole face of the country, and have found very few. We brought away the four or five we found, and also a representative collection of flints so chipped that they might well be mistaken for results of human industry, while, in fact, they were found in circumstances which made any but a natural origin ludicrous.

The land is a land of flints: on all hill-slopes the exposed edges of the limestone have been eaten away by the wind, and the flints of the alternate layers have slipped forward until the slopes are red with them. The nodules in these strata are usually cracked into numberless pieces that still cling together; others have been splintered and scattered before the stone formed around them. On every yard of ground, and even out of the broken nodules that still hold together in their matrices, one can pick up what might well pass as worked flints.

We chose our selected pieces carefully from such impossible places, and in England have succeeded in deceiving with them several good authorities on flints by presenting these, so to speak, without context. Were these genuine, a little patience only would be required to collect from any one hill-side such an array of primitive weapons as would sink a battleship. It was this abundance of nature, rather than the extravagance of primitive man, which made ancient roads so easy for Mr. Holland to follow. Of the four or five real stone implements which we found, one came from Wadi Ain el-Guderat near the threshing floor, and all the others from Tell el-Seram, a conspicuous natural hill in the middle of a wadi south of Auja.

We have no means of dating the Guderat flint, but those from Tell el-Seram were found in and about the drift-sand which filled stone hut-ruins on the hill-top, together with quantities of broken pottery of the Byzantine period. Everything points to the potsherds and flints being contemporary. The peasants of the Byzantine Age were presumably as resourceful as those of today, and today throughout all Syria flint instruments are freely used. The teeth of chaff-cutting instruments are always small pointed flakes of flint properly struck from a core. Oval "scrapers" are used by shepherd-boys to shear the sheep, ousting, in many cases the iron shears to which European commerce gave a brief vogue, and straight heavy knives, often a foot or more in length, are made in any emergency for hacking to pieces a dead animal.

Zeyd, Mr. Holland's guide, knapped a flint when he wanted to trim his toe nails, and sometimes a flint razor is still used for shaving the head. In all cases the implement is used upon the one occasion and then thrown away. To date such castaways is difficult, for the brown patina of Sinai takes only a few years to produce; flints lying on modern Arab graves are a beautiful brown on the exposed side and quite white underneath.

Any man at any period may knap and use a flint, especially when there is such profusion of raw material, and one cannot from the casual product of his industry argue a Stone Age in the exclusive sense of the term. In our opinion all flint evidence tends to show that man had emerged from the historic Stone Age long before he tried to live in the Negeb.

Great quantities of stone circles and cairns still exist in Sinai. In our part they are not equally distributed, but are most common between El Auja and Wadi Lussan, and in the hill country to the south of Beersheba. They are rare to the south of a line drawn from Wadi Lussan to Jebel Harun. Of all sorts and sizes, they are built of rough unshaped boulders or blocks of limestone, interspersed with large lumps of flint, and they are nearly always placed upon rising ground, often upon the tops of the most prominent hills.

We have visited a great number of these and dug out a fair number, and the conclusion at which we have arrived is that in all probability none of them go back to the Prehistoric Stone Age; that a small number of them, in certain districts, are as old as the middle of the second millennium B.C.; that from that date to the present time such monuments have been erected by the nomad population of the country, and that of those now existing few are older than the Byzantine period, and the vast majority are comparatively modern.

Believing these conclusions to be correct we must nonetheless put in a word of caution regarding them. These structures conform to a tradition, as will be shown later, singularly consistent; their workmanship is primitive in character, and their material is necessarily identical at all periods. Even with careful examination it is generally difficult and often impossible to fix the approximate date of any one cairn.

2. Stone monuments were classified (pp. 21-23) as follows: ring graves, rectangular graves, chamber tombs, round shelters, rectangular shelters or houses, sheep pens, Dead Man's piles (Makatal), memorial heaps (Shehadat), ritual heaps, roadside heaps, boundary or guide heaps, and "trigpoints" of survey under Captain [now Colonel] F.S. Newcombe. Woolley and Lawrence (p. 27) conclude:

We, therefore, believe that the Stone Age proper has left no monuments in the country, which in that remote period was uninhabited. The first signs of human occupation that we find are the shelters and graves of the poverty-stricken nomad folk that huddled round the scanty water of the Muweilleh springs. Their houses seemed never to have been rebuilt, and by the look of the remains they had been inhabited only for a short period. Some unknown local conditions must have persuaded people to live here for a little while.

In fact, roughly speaking, the dawn of history in the southern part at least of this district seems, so far as its remains go, to coincide with the first efforts of Egypt to conquer Syria. The Tells that dot the northern fringe of the country with which our survey is concerned may well go back to a date far more remote than this; the way from Hebron by Raheiba and the spring of Muweilleh down to Egypt was a path well-worn by the patriarchs long before the Pharaohs of the Eighteenth Dynasty marched to the Philistine plains; but only when the relations of Egypt and Syria had already established a steady stream of traffic along the northern desert routes do there appear the least traces of permanent dwellings in the inhospitable south.

From Ceylon and the Indian ports and South Arabia came cargoes of spices and emeralds and silks to Aila and the other Red Sea ports, and passed thence by land over the desolate hills of our part of Sinai, either to Gaza for shipment to Greece or to the opulent cities of North Syria. And this latter route was at once cheaper and more secure than the long northern journey over the Mongolian desert.

In consequence at various times (notably in Justinian's reign) we find the Byzantine government fostering this trade, whose effects are still plainly visible along the road.

1917. Van Riet Lowe, now Director of the Archeological Survey, Johannesburg, wrote me in a letter dated November 18, 1948: "I was a soldier in that area and collected handaxes in both the Wadi el-Arish and the Wadi el-Ghazze, which runs into the sea just south of Gaza."

1931. Jarvis (p. 102) wrote:

Flint arrowheads, scraping-knives, etc. lie thick all over the plateau of Central Sinai, so thick, in fact, that one may gather a sackful in a day's march; and it was this extraordinary profusion that convinced the Palestine Exploration Party of 1913-1914 that 99 out of 100 were naturally chipped by the action of the weather and that the remaining one per cent were of present-day origin, as the Arab, if he has forgotten his knife, will always knap a flint to skin and cut up an animal, and also shapes and maintains a supply with which to light his pipe.

1935. The Abbé Henri Breuil collected deeply patinated surface flint implements in the El Kossaima area of northeastern Sinai. His surface sites were at El-Fallak, Tell Umm Khuraiba, Aqbat el-Sabha and Ain Qudairat. Through the courtesy of Mr. Harper Kelley I examined these unpublished specimens on November 12, 1947, in the Musée de l'Homme in Paris. This series was similar to those I have found in eastern Jordan, western Iraq and northwestern Saudi Arabia (Tell el-Hibr and Umm Wual).

1947-1948. The University of California African Expedition made a surface reconnaissance[6] during December and January. The following results were obtained relative to the use of stone tools ranging from the Lower Paleolithic to Ancient Egyptian.

1. On December 16 near Kilometer 115, east of Ismailia and north of the paved road leading to Israel, S.A. Huzayyin and I found, near the western end of Jebel Magharah, a splendid series of microlithic crescents bearing delicate retouches. These lunates, picked up within 30 square feet, indicated a Mesolithic workshop. They probably served as tips for reed arrows. The range of implements from this station was from Natufian to Predynastic. However, the cultural affinities were with the Nile Valley rather than with Asia. This was exactly what we had predicted for this land-bridge.

2. After searching in the stream-bed and along the low banks of the Wadi el-Arish near Magdaba (Maghdaba) midway between El Arish and Abu Aweiqileh (pron. Aweigileh), I found several rolled and a few unrolled flint flakes.

3. At Er Rawafi (El Rawafa), 2 miles east of Abu Aweiqileh, we located a superb Paleolithic station. Here on a low hill facing south above a water pool we collected hundreds of flakes and many flint implements darkly patinated with characteristic desert varnish. On the western slope beside and in the bed of a small gully lay dozens of yellowish-white handaxes, many of dehydrated flint. This is one of the finest surface stations in Southwestern Asia, ranking with Barda Balkha between Kirkuk and Sulaimaniya in northeastern Iraq.

During 1935 the Abbé Breuil had found deeply patinated implements in the El Qusaima (El Kossaima) region some 15 miles to the southeast.

4. On December 19, 1947, W.F. Albright found a Neolithic station 2 miles south of Kilometer 156 on the Ismailia-Abu Aweiqileh paved road and on the track toward Bir Hasana. The flint blades, two-edged knives, and a tanged spearhead lay in a small area on a gravel-covered surface of the low rolling plain between patches of sand. A few deeply patinated flints were also found.

5. A few miles north of Bir Hasana some chocolate-colored flint flakes were collected during my brief visit.

6. Two air miles northwest of Bir Hasana on the track leading to the Wadi el-Letheili on a flint-covered crest of a low hill south of the track I found many heavily patinated flint flakes, scrapers and cores.

7. Along the desolate tracks from Bir Hasana to Nekhl, former capital of Sinai, we found a few scattered flakes in the Wadi Jidil and the Wadi el-Bruq.

8. At Mile 57 in the Wadi Bir Hisn east of Jubeil Hisn from Nekhl toward the Suez Canal, I collected on the surface a typologically Acheulian handaxe together with some sherds and a blue bead. Nearby was a well with plenty of good water in regular use by the Beduins.

9. In southwestern Sinai south of Abu Zeneima near the broad entrance to the Wadi Feiran on a low chain of black mounds bordering the Wadi Khreizeh (Khraiza) I found a good series of flints covered a low hill bisected by a narrow wadi. On both sides, especially on the southern slope, a fine series of large, heavily patinated scrapers and flakes was collected. These were reminiscent of the Abbé Breuil's series from Ain Qudairat in northeastern Sinai, my series from the Rutba area in western Iraq, from the Wadi Rutga in southeastern Syria, and from Tell el-Hibr in northwestern Saudi Arabia.

10. In a rockshelter on the northern side of the Wadi Khreizeh, a tributary of the Wadi Feiran, I found a small hoe (or an adze), scrapers and hammerstones. Outside lay a round basalt pounder of the type used by the Ancient Egyptian miners. Trial trenches revealed neither tools nor pottery beneath a thick crust of stalagmite, but only charred débris indicating occupation of this shelter from Chalcolithic to recent times.

11. Albright (1948, pp. 9-10) writes:

"Such finds in a region where wide stretches of sand are interspersed with smaller areas of exposed rolling plain, strewn with gravel and flint, suggest the following explanation. During the millennia which have elapsed since the end of the Paleolithic Age, the sand shifted hither and thither over the plain, now exposing one tract, now another. Such exposed sites as were suitable for the manufacture of flint artifacts were used for the purpose. In the following periods they might be covered again with sand and could not be used for this purpose any longer. Hence we find the curious phenomenon of transitory use of suitable sites in this region. After the displacement of flint by copper for use in weapons and tools during the course of the Chalcolithic and Early Bronze, characteristic flint artifacts became increasingly rare. Hence the flint criterion of age becomes practically useless for later periods, though it still retains some value in the south, for special reasons (use of stone picks and gouges for mining turquoise, etc.)."

12. At Serabit el-Khadem (Lat. 29° 1′ 14″, Long. 33° 27′ 28″; alt. 735 meters) in a small wadi leading from the northern end of the temple I collected rolled picks and scrapers used by the Egyptian miners of turquoise for several centuries from about 1500 B.C. Following a visit and some correspondence, G.W. Murray wrote in a letter dated January 27, 1948: "On the surface of the coating of gravel covering the so-called 'lake terraces' in Wadi es-Sheikh (the upper lot near Tarfet el-Gidarein) in 1934 Stanhope White, then a Cambridge undergraduate with one of my expeditions in Sinai, found a 'Neolithic adze' which Mr. Henri Munier, formerly librarian of the Cairo Museum, called similar to some found at Beirut."

In addition to the notes on stone monuments referred to above by Woolley and Lawrence, special attention must be drawn to the circular stone buildings referred to as nawamis.

For example, Petrie (1906, p. 244) mentions one of the beehive tombs (nawamis, sing. namus) near the entrance to the Wadi Nasb and describes some arrowheads of the flat, chisel-shaped type, not particularly well-made. Petrie (1906, pp. 171-72) describes the nawamis[7] as buildings of dry stone.

In the Wadi Solaf above Feiran Oasis two nawamis were examined. One capstone was removed in order to measure 19 crania and calvaria, all belonging to basic Mediterranean types (see Field, 1952 b, Appendix B, pp. 122-26).

Crania[8]

In 1904 Ugo Giovannozzi brought to Florence[9] a small series of skulls from Sinai.

On January 7, 1948, a series of 19 crania were measured,[10] described,[11] and photographed. These were removed from one of the beehive tombs on the left bank of the upper part of the Wadi Solaf; the crania were replaced and the capstone set back in place. The location of this monument is given on the 1:1,000,000 Feiran sheet as Lat. 33° 45′ E. and Long. 28° 38′ N.

No. 12 was a child; Nos. 18 and 19 were adolescents. Since these 16 crania included several females and some whose sex could not be determined, no valid statistical means were possible. The measurements and indices are given in Tables 1-3.

However, since the cephalic index ranged from 66.7 - 77.6, this group was entirely dolichocephalic with ten in the hyperdolichocephalic (X-70) category.

I believe these crania belonged to direct ancestors of the modern Towara Beduins. During this same Expedition (1947-48) we visited St. Catherine's Monastery at the foot of traditional Mount Sinai. Here there is an ossuary (45 x 20 x 15 feet) with hundreds of bleached skulls and long bones arranged like cordwood. The racial mixture of these former monks renders them valueless for anthropometric study. The bones of the archbishops are segregated in small wooden boxes arranged in tiers.

During the return journey to Suez on the right side of the valley leading away from Pharan (modern Feiran) were some small tombs (7 x 8 x 4 feet) hewn into the living rock. In one were two male dolichocephalic skulls, one with a persistent metopic future, and one right femur--all bleached. Another tomb held the skeleton of a young longheaded adult in a supine position. A solitary male dolichocephalic skull with worn teeth lay in a partly sealed tomb nearby. These few crania from southern central Sinai indicate a small-boned, dolichocephalic people, probably very similar to the modern Beduins of the twentieth century.

Modern Inhabitants

According to the 1947 Census, the population[12] of Sinai, exclusive of nomads, was 20,602 males and 17,295 females.

The excellent study by Murray (1935) on the tribes, their origin and history, is presumed to be available to the reader. Here we shall outline some of the pertinent information together with our anthropometric data. The tribal distribution has been compiled by Murray (1935). This is given on Map 3 so that the reader may see at a glance the range of each of the main tribes.

In the northern part of Sinai live the following:

1. Ayaida (300 persons) in an area extending eastward from Ismailia. The subdivisions are Salatna, Fawaida, Geraba and Qawaila. Their wells are at Abul Uruq, Maqeibra, and Murra. Formerly, they cultivated gardens in the Wadi Solaf and Wadi Feiran.

2. Badara (30 tents) live near Jebel Ekma. Once affiliated with the Laheiwat, they now are under the protection of the Tiaha (Tiyaha).

3. Huweitat[13] (225 persons) live in Jebel Raha, south-southeast of Suez. They claim water rights in Gharandel, Mabuq, Eggidi, and Mareirat. The main sections of this large tribe live in eastern and southeastern Jordan, where I have camped with Mohammed Abu Tayi and his cousin Ibn Jazi.

4. Laheiwat, formerly of the Masaid division of the Beni Atiya, is now a single tribe. They range from Nekhl to Aqaba, but according to tradition originated in Nejd. They claim wells at Kuntilla, Heisi, Themed, and Ghadian in Wadi el-Araba; and in the west, Ain Sudr and Jifjaffa.

5. Masaid, (100 persons) part of the Laheiwat, live east of Kantara.

6. Qatawiya are ten small tribes living in the rich palm gardens of Qatia; only two are pure Arabs.

7. Suwarka (4,000 persons), the largest tribe in Sinai, live along the Mediterranean coast from Bir el-Abd to the eastern frontier with Israel.

8. Terabin (sing. Terbani) are part of this great tribe from southern Israel. In Sinai there are about 600 persons divided into Shubeibat, Gubeilat, and Husabila. One isolated clan, El Utut, lives near Eggidi; another, the Seraia, on the coast north of Nuweiba. The Terabin range from Jebel el-Magharah through Magdhaba and Wadi Amr to the Israeli frontier north of El Qusaima (Kosseima).

9. Tiaha (sing. Tihi) are part of the large tribe living east of Beersheba in Israel. They range from Jebel el-Halal to Naqb er-Rakna and from Nekhl to Jubeil Hasan

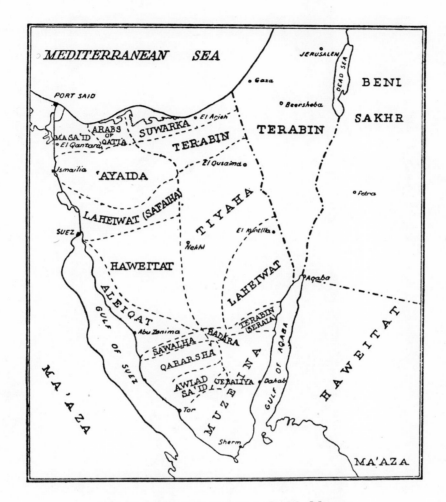

Bedouin Tribes of Sinai by G. M. Murray

(Hisn). Their sections are: Awarma, Baneiat, Bareikat, El Imur, Naghamsha, Qedeirat, Shatiyat, and Sibabha.

For the south, Murray (pp. 256-57) gives the following list:

1. The Towara (sing. Turi) with about 750 tents are united not by blood but by community of interests. They are divided into Sawalha (Awarma, Qararsha, and Wilad Said), Aleiqat and Muzeina.

2. The Jebeliyeh[14] are the descendants of Bosnian and Wallachian serfs, given by Justinian (A.D. 483-565) to St. Catherine's Monastery,[15] where they have always been employed as servants. Their Sheikh was Awda Masaud, with the following tribal subdivisions: Wilad Masaud, Wilad Musaad, Wiheibat, Wilad Salim, Heimat, and Wilad Gindi.

––––––––––––

During December, 1947 - January, 1948 I measured the following 225 Beduins and Jebeliyeh: Aleiqat (3), Badara (1), Billi (1), Ferayin (2), Heiwat (1), Jebeliyeh (73), Laheiwat (3), Muzeina (23), Nekhlawis (3), Qararsha (29), Sawalha (30), Terabin (23), Tiaha (22), and Wilad Said (11). In 1934 G.W. Murray measured the following 63 Towara Beduins: Aleiqat (13), Hamada (5), Huwaitat (1), Muzeina (18), Tabana (8), and Wilad Said (16). He very kindly allowed me to publish his results.[16] In order to present our data, Table 4 was compiled.

Summary

From these relatively few data we may deduce that the Beduins of Sinai are close in physical characters to the ancient Proto-Mediterraneans of Southwestern Asia.

Here on this land-bridge between Asia and Africa[17] the modern Beduins appear as the basic Mediterranean type. As one might expect, these Beduins form a relatively pure "island" of population, the main extraneous racial element being Negroid, probably from the adjoining Arabian Peninsula.

When we compare the measurements and indices of the Beduins of Sinai with the modern Egyptians (Field, 1952b, pp. 35-52) we see that the former are medium tall (166.0) within the stature range of 162.0 for the Huwaitat of Matarieh to 173.0 for the Harabi of the Faiyum. The majority of the 4,688 men recorded in Egypt are close to the 166.0 mean.

The cephalic index of the Sinai Beduins is about 72.5, being near the lowest point in the scale which ranges to 79.0 among the Bichariet measured by Ammar. From Egypt there exist data on 7,351 men. The majority are in the 75.0 - 77.0 group.

The Beduins of the Western Desert measured by Murray (Field, 1952b, pp. 53-55) are slightly taller (168.85), but with a hyperdolichocephalic index (69.27).

To the east the Beduins of Jordan and Saudi Arabia are also medium in stature and dolichocephalic, so that the Beduins of Sinai belong to the central zone of the basic Mediterranean types extending from the Western Desert of North Africa and the Nile Valley on the west to the western shore of the Persian Gulf on the east.

The Stone Age cultures from surface sites indicate continuous occupation since Lower Paleolithic times. There were culture contacts between the inhabitants of the Nile Valley extending at least as far southwest as Kharga Oasis to the west and the dwellers along the Mediterranean coast to Athlit on Mount Carmel and beyond.

To the south there must have been similar culture contacts with the Stone Age inhabitants of the Wadi el-Fau area of central Saudi Arabia and to the northeast with those who drank the waters of the Wadi el-Arabah, the Wadi Sirhan, the Wadi Hauran, and the Wadi Rutga.

At this stage it is impossible to determine whether the main migrations were from

Asia into Africa or the reverse. However, in passing we must observe that our scanty evidence indicated that the nearer to the Nile Valley the closer were the cultural resemblances and the nearer to the Jordan Valley, the closer were those of Western Asia.

During Stone Age times the Wadi el-Arish and the Wadi Feiran and its confluents flowed with water. Game was plentiful, hunters few. As desiccation began, this important land-bridge became less used for migrations. By the time of Moses and the Exodus (circa 1500 B.C.) Sinai was known as the great Wilderness of Tih, a place of wandering.

From the point of view of the physical anthropologist, the modern dwellers in Sinai belong to the basic Mediterranean type. Thus, from our two extremes of approach, Sinai forms the true land-bridge between Asia and Africa. In addition, anthropometric data on 500 Beduins should show the true racial trends, although my prediction is that they will be similar to those already obtained.

Further work is necessary, especially in an attempt to find a stratified deposit, probably in a cave or rockshelter, and a Paleolithic skull (or several) to determine whether the makers of the handaxes at Ar-Rawafi were Proto-Neanderthalers, direct ancestors of <u>Homo sapiens</u>, or a mixture.

From the time when the flint-knappers worked on the pleasant slopes of Ar-Rawafi to the Exodus may have been 100,000 years, not time for the face of the country to change, but plenty of time for the skin to become so dry and parched and windswept that only the Beduins, their camels, their flocks and herds may now exist. Here in Sinai the cycle is complete: a few Paleolithic hunters, now a few Bedu.

References

No attempt has been made to compile all the references to Sinai, but rather to include selected titles bearing on Anthropogeography with special emphasis on Prehistory and Physical Anthropology and to include certain titles omitted from Field 1948 a, pp. 479-93, 1952 b and 1953. The reader is also referred to the 6,518 titles on Egypt in Lorin, 1928-29 and to all volumes of BSEHGIS, especially Vol. 4, pp. 175-219, 1951-52, and Vol. 5, pp. 10-21 and 123-53, 1954; attention is also called to their Memoir series, especially Vol. 2, pp. 1-238, Cairo, 1955. For the best recent data on Sinai, see Murray (1935) and Daumas (1951). See also: "Encyclopaedia of Egyptian Affairs" published by Egyptian Book House, Cairo; Bulletins of the (Fouad I) Desert Institute of Egypt, Rue Sultan Hussein, Heliopolis, Cairo; and medical and zoological publications of U.S. Naval Medical Research Institute No. 3, known as NMRU-3, c/o U.S. Embassy, Cairo.

———————

Abel, F.M.
  1939-40. Les confins de la Palestine et de l'Egypte sous les Ptolémées. RB, Vol. 48, no. 2, pp. 207-36; no. 4, pp. 530-48; Vol. 49, no. 1, pp. 55-75; nos. 2-4, pp. 224-39.
Aghion, H.
  1940. Sur les terrases fluviatiles dans le Wadi Araba. BFS, no. 21, pp. 19-35.
  1946. Kosseir. RE, June 9.
Aimé-Giron, N.
  1939. Adversaria Semitica I: Graffiti "Sinaitiques" d'Egypte (en Nabatéen). ASAE, Vol. 39, pp. 343-51.
  1941. Adversaria Semitica III: Baal Saphon et les dieux de Tahpanhes dans un nouveau papyrus phénicien. ASAE, Vol. 40, pp. 433-60.
Albright, W.F.
  1948. Exploring Sinai with the University of California African Expedition. BASOR, no. 109, pp. 5-20.
Andrew, G.
  1938-39. The greywackes of the Eastern Desert of Egypt. BIE, Vol. 21, pp. 153-90.
Attia, M.E.
  1948-49. A new mode of occurrence of iron deposit in the Eastern Desert of Egypt. BIE, Vol. 31, pp. 49-68.
Awad, Hassan
  1951. La montagne du Sinai central. SRGE.
Bachatly, Charles
  1942. Bibliographie de la Préhistoire égyptienne. SRGE.
Badr, A.M. and Crossland, C.
  1939. Topography of the Red Sea floor. PMBSG, no. 1, pp. 13-20.
Ball, J.
  1939. Contributions to the geography of Egypt. MFE.
  1942. Egypt in the classical geographers. MFE.
Band, M.
  1950. Egypte. GB.
Bouchard, P.F.X.
  1945. Journal Historique: la chute d'El-Arish en 1799. RC.
Bruyère, B.
  1949-50. Un monument de Ramses II à Serapeum. BSEHGIS, Vol. 3, pp. 57-74.
  1950. Un ex-voto d'Isis au Musée d'Ismailia. ASAE, Vol. 52, pp. 515-22.

Cleland, W. Wendell
  1936. The population problem in Egypt. SP.
  1944. A population plan for Egypt. MMFQ, Vol. 22, no. 4, pp. 409-23. See also
      EC, Vol. 30, pp. 461-84, 1939.
Cooke, H.B.S., see Phillips, Wendell.
Cooke, Hedley V.
  1952. Challenge and response in the Middle East. New York.
Crossland, C., see Badr, A.M.
Crossland, Cyril
  1939a. Some coral formations. PMBSG, no. 1, pp. 21-35.
  1939b. Narrative and list of stations visited by R.R.S. "Mabahith," 1934-35.
      PMBSG, no. 1, pp. 3-11.
Daumas, Jacques
  1942. Sur les traces effacées de Moise. RACE.
  1948a. Notes sur l'Attaqa. BSEHGIS, Vol. 11, pp. 21-24.
  1948b. Nouvelle carte des massifs cristallins culminants de la péninsule du
      Sinai. Three sheets: Oum Shomer; Feiran-Serbal; and Monastery of St.
      Catherine. Scale 1:100,000. ASIF.
  1951. La Péninsule du Sinai. RACE.
  1952a. Le Gebel Gharib. BSEHGIS, Vol. 4, pp. 3-12.
  1952b. Commentaires sur le Codex Sinaiticus. BSEHGIS, Vol. 4, pp. 81-83.
  1954a. Le Gebel Shayib el-Banat. BSEHGIS, Vol. 5, pp. 9-21.
  1954b. Vestiges chrétiens des montagnes Sinaitiques. BSEHGIS, Vol. 5, pp. 123-
      53.
Daumas, Jacques and Laroche, Charles
  1947. Ascension du Gebel Lharam, point culminant du massif montagneux du
      Galala El Bahariya ou Galala Nord. BSEHGIS, Vol. 1, pp. 33-40.
Debono, F.
  1948. Pics en pierre de Serabit el-Khadim (Sinai) et d'Egypte. ASAE, Vol. 46,
      pp. 265-85.
Deloro, E.C.
  1939. Dans le désert arabique: la tribu bédouine des Ababda. BE, April 15.
Farag, I.
  1948. Deux nouveaux gisements du Bathonien fossilifère sur la rive occidentale
      du Golfe de Suez. SGF, no. 6, pp. 109-11.
Fedden, Robin
  1939. The land of Egypt. London.
Field, Henry
  1948a. The University of California African Expedition: I, Egypt (Faiyum and
      Sinai). AA, Vol. 50, pp. 479-93.
  1948b. Sinai sheds new light on the Bible. NGM, pp. 795-816. December.
  1952a. The Peabody Museum Harvard Expedition, 1950. BSEHGIS, Vol. 4,
      pp. 1-2.
  1952b. Contributions to the Anthropology of the Faiyum, Sinai, northern Sudan
      and Kenya. University of California Press. See Bibliography on Sinai, pp.
      140-61.
  1953-56. Bibliography of Southwestern Asia: I-III. UM.
Fontaine, A.L.
  1947a. Daphnae. BSEHGIS, Vol. 1, pp. 41-57.
  1947b. Régions et sites anciens intéressant de la Société d'Etudes Historiques
      et Géographiques de l'Isthme de Suez. BSEHGIS, Vol. 1, pp. 21-32.
  1948. Localisation d'Heracleopolis Parva et canaux pélusiaques du nord de
      l'Isthme de Suez. BSEHGIS, Vol. 2, pp. 57-73.

Fontaine, A.L.
   1952. Enquête sur Péluse. BSEHGIS, Vol. 4, pp. 17-80.
   1955. Monographie cartographique de l'Isthme de Suez, de la Péninsule du Sinai, du nord de la chaîne arabique suivie d'une catalogue raisonné sur les cartes de ces régions. MSEHGIS, Vol. 2, pp. 1-238.
Fontaine, A.L. and Goby, J.E.
   1948-50. Chronique de l'Isthme de Suez. BSEHGIS, Vol. 2, pp. 9-19; Vol. 3, pp. 1-15.
Forskal, Petrus
   1950. Resa till Lycklige Arabien, 1761-63. Uppsala.
Goby, Jean Edouard
   1942. Les monts d'Attaqa. BSRGE, Vol. 20, pp. 393-420.
   1943. Une mission scientifique danoise en Egypte et en Orient au dix-huitième siècle. RC, Vol. 10, pp. 181-96.
   1947. Les Bibliographies égyptiennes de l'Isthme de Suez. BSEHGIS, Vol. 1, pp. 85-87.
   1952. Histoire des nivellements de l'Isthme de Suez. BSEHGIS, Vol. 4, pp. 100-170. See Bibliography, pp. 165-169.
Goby, J.E., see Fontaine, A.L.
Gohar, H.A.F.
   1940a. The development of some Xeniidae (Alcyonaria) with some ecological aspects. PMBSG, no. 3, pp. 27-78.
   1940b. A revision of some genera of the Stolonifera with an amended system of classification and the description of two new species. PMBSG, no. 3, pp. 3-23.
   1940c. Studies on the Xeniidae of the Red Sea: their ecology, taxonomy, and phylogeny. PMBSG, no. 2, pp. 25-118.
   1948a. Commensalism between fish and anemone with a description of the eggs of Amphiprion Bicinctus Roppell. PMBSG, no. 6, pp. 35-55.
   1948b. A description of some biological studies of a new Alcyonarian species Clavularia Hamra Gohar. PMBSG, no. 6, pp. 3-33.
Hart, H. Chichester
   1891. The fauna and flora of Sinai, Petra, and Wady Arabah. London.
Hellstrom, B.
   1950. The Israelites' crossing of the Red Sea. Stockholm. English translation of a Swedish monograph, 1924.
Hickson, S.J.
   1940. The species of the genus Acabaria in the Red Sea. PMBSG, no. 2, pp. 3-22.
Hoogstraal, Harry, see Wassif, Kamil
Issawi, Charles
   1949. Population and wealth in Egypt. MMFQ, Vol. 27, no. 1, pp. 98-113.
Jansen, J.M.A.
   1947-1950. Bibliographie égyptologique annuelle. Leiden.
Jarvis, C.S.
   1931. Yesterday and today in Sinai. London.
Jomier, R.P.J.
   1949-50. Ageroud, un caravansérail sur la route des pélerins de la Mekke. BSEHGIS, Vol. 3, pp. 33-56.
   1952. Les graffiti "Sinaitiques" du Wadi Abou Darag. BSEHGIS, Vol. 4, pp. 171-73.
Jungfleisch, M.
   1944-45. La résurrection de la Mer Morte: son importance agronomique, BIE, Vol. 27, pp. 81-87.

Keldani, E.H.
    1941. A Bibliography of geology and related sciences concerning Egypt, up to
        the end of 1939. Government Press, Cairo.
Kiser, Clyde V.
    1944. The demographic position of Egypt. MMFQ, pp. 97-122.
Laroche, Charles, see Daumas, Jacques A.
Lawrence, T.E., see Woolley, C.L.
Lorin, Henri
    1928-1929. Bibliographie géographique de l'Egypte. SRGE.
Lucas, A.
    1941. The battle of Megiddo. BSRAA, no. 34, pp. 74-80.
Mihaeloff, S.
    1938-1939. Etude chimico-biologique de l'eau de la source chaude sulfureuse
        "Hammam Faraoun," Sinai. BIE, Vol. 21, pp. 25-29.
Mochi, Aldobrandino
    1907. Sulla antropologia degli Arabi. AAE, pp. 411-28.
Montet, Pierre
    1950. Les énigmes de Tanis. Paris.
Mortensen, Th.
    1939. Two new deep-sea Echinoderms from the Red Sea. PMBSG, no. 1, pp.
        37-46.
Moscatelli,
    1947. Péluse, ville oubliée. RE, May 18.
Munier, H.
    1937-43. Bibliographie géographique de l'Egypte. BSRGE, Vol. 20, pp. 369-91;
        Vol. 21, pp. 69-82.
Murray, G.W.
    1935. Sons of Ishmael. London.
    1945-46. A diorite quarry of the Roman period in Wadi Barud, Eastern Desert.
        BIE, Vol. 28, pp. 43-48.
    1953. The land of Sinai. JRGS, Vol. 99, pt. 2, pp. 140-54.
Nagaty, H.F.
    1942. Trematodes of fishes from the Red Sea: Pt. 3, on seven Allocreadiid
        species. PMBSG, no. 4, pp. 1-27.
Naklady, S.E.
    1948-49. The foraminiferal fauna of the Esna shales of Egypt. BIE, Vol. 31,
        pp. 209-47.
Nasr, A.H.
    1939. Algae. PMBSG, no. 1, pp. 47-76.
    1939-40. The chorography of the marine Algae inhabiting the northern part of
        the Red Sea coast. BIE, Vol. 22, pp. 193-219.
    1943-44. Some new Algae from the Red Sea. BIE, Vol. 26, pp. 31-42.
    1945-46. The biological forms of some marine Algae from Ghardaqa. BIE, Vol.
        28, pp. 203-13.
    1947. Synopsis of the marine Algae of the Egyptian Red Sea coast. BFS, no. 26.
Palmer, E.H.
    1871. The desert of the Exodus. Cambridge.
Peet, T.E.
    1915. Primitive stone building in Sinai. Man, no. 87, pp. 151-58.
Pesta, O.
    1941. Die Arten der Copepodengattungen (Candacia Dana und Calanopia Dana)
        aus dem Roten Meer. AKAW, Vol. 1, p. 150.

1943. Die Arten der Copepodengattungen (Rhincalanus Dana, Euchoeta Philippi, Centropages Kroeyer, Temosa Baird und Tortanus) giesbrecht aus Roten Meer. AKAW, Vol. 3.

Petrie, W.M. Flinders

1906. Researches in Sinai. London.

Phillips, Wendell and Cooke, H.B.S.

1948. Recent discoveries in Egypt and Sinai. SAS, Vol. 1, no. 11, pp. 204-207, July.

Rabino, H.L.

1938. Le Monastère de Sainte-Catherine du Mont Sinai. RACE.

Said, R., see Shukri, N.M.

Servin, A.

1947. Kantarah. Aperçus historiques. BSEHGIS, Vol. 1, pp. 59-68.

1949. La tradition judéo-chrétienne de l'Exode. BIE, Vol. 31, pp. 315-55.

1949-50. Stèles de l'Isthme de Suez: stèles persanes. BSEHGIS, Vol. 3, pp. 75-97.

Seton-Kerr, H.W.

1924. Paleolithic implements from Sinai. Man, Vol. 24, p. 32.

Shabetai, J.R.

1940. Plants collected from Sinai in April, 1937. BMAE, no. 243.

1948. Il y a des tulipes dans le désert. Images, March 20.

Shafei, Aly

1948. Irrigation of the wilderness of Etham. BSRGE, Vol. 22, pp. 151-55.

Shukri, N.M. and Said, R.

1944-45. Contribution to the geology of the Nubian sandstone: I, field observations and mechanical analysis, BFS, no. 25; II, mineral analysis. BIE, Vol. 27, pp. 229-64.

Stiasny, G.

1940. Gorgonaria aus dem Roten Meer. PMBSG, no. 2, pp. 121-92.

Tackhölm, Vivi

1939. The drug plants of the Sinai Peninsula. HREHS, Vol. 27, no. 101.

Tackhölm, Vivi and Drar, Mohammed

1942. Some new Egyptian plants. SBT, Vol. 36, nos. 2-3.

Tondrian, J.T.

1948. Un thiase dionysiaque à Péluse sous Ptolémée Philopator. BSRAA, no. 37, pp. 3-11.

Tromp, S.

1951. Preliminary compilation of the macro-stratigraphy of Egypt. BSRGE, Vol. 24.

Wassif, Kamil and Hoogstraal, Harry

1954. The mammals of South Sinai. PEAS, Vol. 9, pp. 63-79.

Wiet, G.

1944-45. La chute d'El-Arish. RC, Vols. 7-8, November, 1944-July, 1945.

Woolley, C.L. and Lawrence, T.E.

1915. The Wilderness of Zin. PEFQ, London.

III. ISRAEL

The State of Israel came into being on May 15, 1948. The present frontiers are defined by the Armistice agreement based on the military front.

Israel, formerly Palestine, is bounded on the north by Lebanon, on the northeast by Syria, on the east by the Hashemite Kingdom of the Jordan and on the south by the Sinai Peninsula of Egypt. The most southerly point of the inverted isosceles triangle, known as the Negeb (Negev), touches the Gulf of Aqaba. The so-called "Gaza strip," a littoral band 25 miles long, is now occupied by Egypt. The area of Israel is 8,050 square miles. In the north the Lebanon Mountains shade imperceptibly into the Galilee uplands (4,000 feet), which fall away steeply on the east to the Jordan Valley, on the west to the narrow littoral, and on the south to the Vale of Esdraelon. Further south an upland limestone plateau extends for nearly 100 miles. In the extreme south, the Negeb, comprising almost half of Israel, is mainly steppe or semi-desert which irrigation may develop. Beside the Mediterranean a coastal plain extends from Haifa to Gaza.

The geology[1] of Palestine is of especial interest.

Climate[2]

The summers are hot and dry with a maximum of 100° F. and the winters are mild and rainy. Snow falls on the hills, occasionally on the lowlands. In general, Israel has a typically "Mediterranean" climate, although those regions below sea-level may become extremely hot and humid. Rainfall[3] varies from 40 inches in Galilee to 10 or less in the Negeb. The prevailing wind is from the southwest off the Mediterranean.

Flora[4]

Because of the wide range in climatic conditions, there is considerable variety. For example, on the coastal plain the typical Mediterranean littoral flora abound. In the Jordan Valley a semi-tropical vegetation occurs. The mountains are also rich in many varieties.

Agriculture[5]

The total cultivated area in 1952-53 was 3,550,000 dunums, the principal crops being wheat, barley, maize and durra, hay, straw, green fodder, potatoes, and grapes. Citrus products in 1952-53 were 8.9 million cases.

Fauna[6]

About 600 species of vertebrate animals are still found. Among the rare mammals are: ibex, wild cats, cheetahs and leopards; other include hyena, fox and jackal. I saw two wolves in 1934 just east of Tiberias; they are now extremely rare. Among birds may be mentioned eagles, vultures, owls, and partridges. In 1953 there were 61,000 sheep, 36,000 cows, 437 bulls, 22,448 calves, 8,016 heifers, and 2.2 million laying hens.

Population[7]

On December 31, 1953 there were about 1,670,000 persons, [8] including 186,000 Moslems, Christians, and others. For comparison, a few figures are given: in 1900 there were 50,000 Jews; in 1922, 83,790 Jews out of a total population of 752,048; in 1946, 608,225 Jews out of 1,912,112; and in 1950, 1,203,000 Jews out of 1,370,-000. The highest year of immigration was 1949 when 239,076 Jews arrived, mainly from Yemen, Turkey, Poland, the Balkans, and Central and Western Europe.[9]

Development Plans[10]

Ever since 1914 when the Ottoman Government granted a concession to a Syrian Company, plans have been formulated for the reclamation of Lake Huleh and adjacent

Israel by Erwin Raisz

marshes by large-scale drainage. In 1934 the Palestine Land Development Company purchased this concession.

Ancient Man[11]

History. For an outline from Prehistory to Greco-Roman times, the reader is referred to Albright (1951) and to Reifenberg (1953) for the period circa 4,000 B.C. to the year 1917.

1864. Louis Lartet and Abbé Richard found the first flint implements in Palestine. The former recognized their antiquity because 17 years previously Boucher de Perthes had published an account of shaped flints found by him in the Somme gravels near Abbeville, northern France. In addition, Edouard Lartet had published in 1860 a monograph on Massat and Sévigné grottoes in France, where prehistoric engravings on bone had been found.

1908. Zumoffen found handaxes and scrapers in the caves of Adlun, midway between Tyre and Sidon, and from weathered breccias at Ras el-Kelb.

1905-17. A summary of archeological discoveries during this period has been compiled by Paul Karge.

1920-26. Typologically Paleolithic flint implements were found at numerous sites and a few cave soundings.

1925-26. Francis Turville-Petre[12] excavated Mugharet el-Emireh and Mugharet ez-Zuttiyeh at the north end of the Sea of Galilee. Here he found the first stratified deposits in Palestine; in one were Mousterian artifacts associated with a Neanderthal skull, thus establishing the same correlation between similar racial types and cultures in Western Europe. This was the first proof of the existence of Neanderthal Man in Southwestern Asia.

In Mugharet ez-Zuttiyeh handaxes of Acheulian type were abundant, but the flake industry contained a large number of Levalloisian types.

1928a. René Neuville began work at Mugharet Umm Qatafa[13] in the Judean desert. He found three Upper Acheulian levels.

1928b. Dorothy Garrod, assisted by George Woodbury excavated the cave of Shukbah in the Wadi en-Natuf of Western Judea.[14] Here was unearthed a stratum containing many microliths without any pottery. This level was superimposed on an eroded breccia of Levalloiso-Mousterian type. Miss Garrod termed this new microlithic industry Natufian.

1928c. Charles Lambert in behalf of the Department of Antiquities dug three trenches in Mugharet el-Wad ("Cave of the Valley"). He never reached an undisturbed stratum but he proved this as a significant Prehistoric site. The most important object was a naturalistic carving of a young deer on a piece of long bone, probably the end of a sickle-shaft. This sculpture is attributed by Dorothy Garrod to the Lower Natufian because some sculptures found by Turville-Petre at Al-Kebarah and by Neuville at Umm Zuetina were Lower Natufian.

1932a. René Neuville and Moshe Stekelis made a sounding in Mugharet Umm Qatafa. Below the Acheulian lay an industry of small irregular flakes named by Breuil "Tayacian," the oldest industry so far found in any Palestine cave.

1932b. Neuville described an early Levalloisian stage from the lowest levels of Irq el-Ahmar, a rockshelter 2 kilometers west of Umm Qatafa in the Judean desert.

1934. Neuville made soundings in the caves of Abu-Sif and Sahba in the Judean desert. He found an industry characterized by long narrow points, many with plain striking-platform, with a few handaxes similar to those from the Lower Levalloiso-Mousterian of et-Tabun.

1929-34. During this period Dorothy Garrod and staff spent almost two years excavating the caves of the Wady el-Mughara ("Valley of the Caves") at the western end of Mount Carmel.[15] Extensive work was conducted in the Mugharet el-Wad, et-Tabun and in the Mugharet es-Skhul, a small rockshelter 120 meters east of Mugharet el-Wad. The diagrammatic section of the Wady el-Mughara deposits reveals the following cultural sequence: Tayacian, Upper Acheulian, Levalloiso-Mousterian, Lower Aurignacian, Middle Aurignacian, Atlitian, and Natufian. A detailed description of the fossil fauna from the Wady el-Mughara caves together with climatic inferences has been published by the late Dorothea M.A. Bate (1937b).

The fauna from the oldest horizon suggests a warm and damp, probably tropical, climate. Gradually the climate grows drier, but perennial water is present, for in the Lower Levalloiso-Mousterian hippopotamus remains were present. In the Upper Levalloiso-Mousterian there is evidence of a great faunal break; from now on the animals are of modern type. There is abundance of the Persian fallow deer (Dama mesopotamica), indicating considerably increased rainfall. During the Aurignacian period the faunal assemblage is of modern type with such new arrivals as wolf, badger, marten, hare, etc. A much drier climate is indicated. Gazelles, a large ox, a hartebeest, a true horse (Equus caballus), as well as a wild "half ass," roamed the country.

By the time we reach the Natufian, the fauna appears to be of modern type, but still shows important differences from that of the present day. Gazelle remains are very plentiful, those of the fallow deer rare. This suggests a condition of aridity. The almost complete skull of a large dog is the first evidence of the domestication of animals in Southwestern Asia. However, there was no evidence that the domestication of either the sheep or goat was practiced by the Natufians in Palestine at this period.

The fragmentary Galilee skull from Mugharet ez-Zuttiyeh, about 35 miles from Mount Carmel, appears to have belonged to the Tabun type, although the frontal bones were like those of Neanderthal Man.

In 1939 McCown and Keith rejected the theory of a mingling of two peoples or races on the slopes of Mount Carmel in mid-Pleistocene times in favor of an evolutionary divergence. They proposed a revision in the nomenclature and in the scheme of classification of fossil man: Palaeoanthropus heidelbergensis (Mauer jaw), P. ehringsdorfensis (Weimar), P. Neanderthalensis (Neander Valley and La Chapelle-aux-Saints), P. krapinensis (Croatia) and P. palestinensis (Mount Carmel and Galilee).

Since 1939 new discoveries have been made in Southwestern Asia. Human remains have been found by Coon in northern Iran and by Solecki at Shanidar cave in northeastern Iraq. Just outside our area, Okladnikov found a Neanderthaloid child at Teshik-Tash near Tashkent, Soviet Central Asia.

These new finds have not yet been correlated into the general picture of the ancient inhabitants of Southwestern Asia.

1952a. Dorothy Garrod published[16] an important paper as a result of detailed studies on the flint implements from Layers F and G in the Mugharet el-Wad (Garrod and Bate, 1937, pp. 22-27). Studies have convinced Dr. Garrod (p. 129) that:

...we have in Syria and Palestine a culture which is truly intermediate in type between the Levalloiso-Mousterian and the blade-industries of the Upper Palaeolithic. Within the culture itself, we find an absence of forms transitional from one to the other. The striking of true blades (probably by the use of a punch) appears rather as a new discovery than as an evolution from the older flake technique. This is particularly noticeable in the cores, where not only are there no genuine intermediate forms between the double-ended Levallois core, from which flake-blades could be taken, and the narrow prismatic blade core, but where in two cases, as we have seen, a discoidal Levallois core and a true blade

core are found side by side on the same piece of flint. Typologists might claim
that in this industry we have a perfect case of culture contact. I would suggest,
on the contrary, that here is a case of the invention of a new technique within an
industry of old tradition, a possibility which, I think, we prehistorians have
neglected too much in our search for origins, although we have known in theory
that it must more than once have occurred.

It is, perhaps, significant that precisely in the area where we find this industry with old and new characters intermixed, we have, in the preceding
Levalloiso-Mousterian stage, a human type which is morphologically intermediate between Neanderthal and modern man (Turville-Petre and Keith, 1927; and
McCown and Keith, 1939). The scanty human remains from the Aurignacian of
Palestine, on the other hand, are definitely those of Homo sapiens. It will be interesting to see whether the man of the Emireh stage, if he is ever found, will
fill the evolutionary gap between the two.

It remains to consider what name we are to give to this industry whose peculiar characters entitle it to a separate status. The label Lower Aurignacian
which I chose under a misapprehension in 1937 is now seen to be unsuitable, but
any kind of portmanteau word would be even clumsier than the Levalloiso-Mousterian, which would have to be one of its components. I suggest that the usual
practice is followed, and that we name it Emiran, from the site in which it was
first found in place, and in which its special characters, afterwards misunder-
stood for more than twenty years, were first recognized by Francis Turville-
Petre.

1953. Charles E. Snow at the Peabody Museum, Harvard, reconstructed one of
the skulls, known as Skhūl V, excavated on Mount Carmel. He observes (p. 7) that
Skhūl V "is truly a remarkable combination of modern and archaic features. The
general vault contours, as well as the newly-formed face, seen both from above and
from the side, convey the definite impression of a 'classic Neanderthaloid' character. The flat-sided molars and nasal morphology bear out this appearance. On the
other hand, characteristics commonly found in modern man are suggested by the
well-formed median chin eminence, the developed mastoid processes, the occipital
contours, and the height of the vault. Is this Mt. Carmel group, then, of hybrid nature and origin? It is relevant to mention here the obscure but corroborative find
at the cave of Djebel Kafseh near Nazareth recovered by Neuville in 1934-35. This
illustrated calvarium combines again the peculiar and characteristic morphology of
both 'Neanderthal' and modern forms of man." The following selected measurements
and indices are based on Snow's reconstruction on Skhūl V, a male aged 30-35 years
(see Table 5).

The stature was estimated by applying formulae to the length of the femur: 178.76
(70.4 in.) with the Pearson formula; and 183.31 (72.2 in.) by Dupertuis and Hadden.

Clark Howell comments[17] that, "the Skhūl V mid-facial maxillary region is
definitely not 'Classic Neanderthal' (i.e., like La Chapelle-aux-Saints, La Ferrassie,
La Quina, etc.) . . . . . The resemblance to the face of the skull from Saccopastore and
to Krapina is not too remote."

Modern Man[18]

From 1919-1953 there were about 1,280,000 Jewish immigrants into Palestine
and Israel. For a period of several months there were as many as 30,000 per month.
However, by 1953 the stream had slowed to 10,350 persons annually.

Lawrence (pp. 57-58) gives the following estimates:

(a) Settled non-Jewish population as of December 31, 1946, about 736,000.

(b) 105,000 Beduins.

(c) The net out-migration of the non-Jewish population from January 1, 1947 -
May 15, 1948 was about 250,000.

The main wave of Jews came from Poland with lesser streams from Romania,
Germany, and Iraq. Minor waves came from Czechoslovakia, Morocco, Algeria,

Libya, Turkey, Yemen, and Aden. Thus, Israel would form an excellent locus for an anthropometric study of these Jews from widely divergent areas.

From a demographic standpoint, Israel is of particular interest because it is now so densely populated as a result of mass immigration. For example, in 1900 there were 50,000 Jews; in 1953 the estimate was 1.5 million.

The population growth and every phase of demographic study have been so well analysed[19] that further details here are unnecessary.

With regard to the Arabs, the only study which would prove valuable would be that of the Beduins of the Negeb. They will probably be similar to the Beduins of Sinai with slight admixture. The Arabs would show many facets of the Mediterranean types. However, since Palestine has always been astride the main crossroad between Southwestern Asia and Africa, many racial elements occur in the present population. All four divisions of the White Race, the Mediterranean, Iranian Plateau,[20] Nordic and Alpine are present, the two former being dominant. Except among a very small proportion of the Beduins, there is almost no Negro blood. Similarly, there are few Mongoloid traces. For statistical comparisons[21] it would be desirable to group Israel, Jordan, Lebanon, and Syria.

Here we shall give a summary of the work of Pierre-André Gloor under the auspices of the International Red Cross, 1949-50. He measured and observed 331 men and 33 women (see Table 6). The men were from the following: 31 in CICR Hospital at Bethany; 45 Arabs from CICR Delegation in Bethlehem; and 255 from refugee camps in Dheshé and Ain el-Arrub, south of Bethlehem.

The main geographical origins were from the following districts: Hebron (115); Jerusalem-Bethlehem (83); and Gaza (78). These included 276 Moslems and 55 Christians.

The mean age of the 331 males was 31.75, range 18-75.

Gloor (1951, pp. 110-32) breaks these 331 Palestinians into eight series, divided into five racial groups: Mediterraneans (Homo meridionalis); Alpines (Homo alpinus); Armenoids (Homo dinaricus); Nordics (Homo europaeus or nordicus); and Negroes. He estimates the following percentages: Mediterraneans (15-20), Alpines (25-30), Armenoids (30-40), Nordics (10) and Negroids (5-10).

In conclusion, Gloor estimates that 60 per cent of the population is brachycephalic, the remainder dolicho-mesocephalic.

With regard to sexual differences, Gloor (1952, pp. 9-12) observes that among the 33 females all the means are smaller and there is less range of variation than among the males. His measurements and analysis of growth changes (1952, pp. 12-15) deserve examination.

Summing up his observations on the evolution of Palestinian craniology, Gloor (1952, pp. 15-17) analyzes the data on the cephalic index with the following comments.

According to Sauter (1945), craniological material obtained in Palestine included 563 skulls ranging from the Neolithic to the nineteenth century of our era. Gloor examined eight crania; two excavated in 1949 from a tomb in El Gib (Gabaon) attributed to the Second Iron Age (first millennium B.C.); and six skulls from the ossuary of the Convent of Mar Saba, which contains the remains of hundreds of monks martyred in the year 614 at the time of the Persian invasion.

Among the former, one is a 10-year old child with a cephalic index of 73.86; the other a mesocephal of 25-30 years of age with a cephalic index of 75.29. These two skulls could be attributed to a population whose origin was Amorite living in Gabaon until the reign of David.

The other series are probably of diverse origin and included the following cephalic indices: 72.91, 74.21, 75.42, 84.23, 85.96, and 87.93.

Attention is called to the fact that Palestine belongs to those countries wherein the number of brachycephals increased during the centuries. Prior to the second millennium B.C., this round-headed element is absent, and the 28 skulls of this period are all dolichocephalic. From the second millennium B.C. we possess 204 crania, including 19 brachycephals (9.00 per cent). From the first millennium there are only 13 brachycephals out of 320 (4.00 per cent). Among the series from Mar Saba are nine brachycephals out of 19 crania (46.0 per cent). When we include the series studied by Kappers and the Samaritans measured by Genna, making a total of 553 Palestinians, there are 221 brachycephals (39.0 per cent).

The population has then changed very markedly during the last 20 centuries, a factor which is not astonishing when we consider the Diaspora.

Palestine later became a land of immigration and the brachycephals migrated from the Lebanese massif. However, the immigrants from Syria, Lebanon, and Turkey were far more numerous than those from Egypt or Jordan. Gloor comments (1952, p. 16) that the phenomenon referred to as "progressive brachycephalization" is far more easily explained by demographic changes than by some hypothetical evolutionary process. However, the Jewish immigrants were themselves brachycephalic and the Arab refugees moved into Egypt, Jordan or even into Syria or Iraq, where they tended to increase the cephalic index. It is significant that since the Jewish colonization in the Negeb (Negev) right down to the Gulf of Aqaba, the Mediterranean Race for the first time is bisected in this area.

There should be considerable interest in anthropometric researches in Israel[22] which now constitutes a new people. A particularly important phenomenon which already has been observed is the curious transformation which occurs in two or three generations as a result of the immigration of European Jews from agricultural colonies, the recent generation being particularly rich in men of tall stature, robust, and with light eyes. Gloor was astonished by the rarity of dark eyes in this population, which is entirely abnormal from what we know from the anthropology of the Jews.

Therefore, further anthropometric researches are most desirable.

Abel, F. -M.
    1938. Géographie de la Palestine. Paris.
Aharoni, J.
    1930. Die Säugethiere Palästinas. ZS, Vol. 5, pp. 327-43.
Albright, W.F.
    1935. Palestine in the earliest historical period. JPOS, Vol. 15, pp. 212-13.
    1946. From the Stone Age to Christianity. Baltimore.
    1951. The Archaeology of Palestine. Penguin Books.
Allen, G.M.
    1915. Mammals obtained by the Phillips Palestine Expedition. BMCZ, Vol. 59,
        no. 1, pp. 1-14.
Anati, Emmanuel
    1955. Rock engravings in the Central Negev. Archaeology, Vol. 8, no. 1, pp. 31-
        42.
Anonymous
    1953. Quest for settlement. REC.
Ashbel, D.
    1942. Rainfall map of Palestine, Transjordan, southern Syria, and southern
        Lebanon. 3rd ed. Jerusalem.
Ashkenazi, Touvia
    1938. Tribus semi-nomades de la Palestine du Nord. EESE, Vol. 2, pp. 1-286.
Avnimelech, Moshe
    1950. Contribution to the knowledge of the Quaternary oscillations of the shore-
        line in Palestine. RSP, Vol. 5, pp. 44-56.
    1950-51. The geological history of the Yarkon Valley and its influence on ancient
        settlements. IEQ, Vol. 1, no. 2, pp. 77-83.
    1951. On the finding of Elephas-bones in a boring near Yavneh, Israel. EGH,
        Vol. 43, no. 2 (1950), pp. 265-68.
    1952b. Late Quaternary sediments of the coastal plain of Israel. BRCI, Vol. 2,
        no. 1, pp. 51-57.
    1952c. Les Mollusques du Désert de Judée. JC, Vol. 92, pp. 77-79.
Avnimelech, Moshe, see Picard, L.
Bancroft, Helen
    1937. Report on charcoal fragments. In D.A.E. Garrod and D.M.A. Bate, "The
        Stone Age of Mount Carmel," p. 129. Oxford.
Bate, Dorothea M.A., see Garrod, D.A.E.
Bate, Dorothea M.A.
    1927. Report on fauna. In F. Turville-Petre, "Researches in Prehistoric Gali-
        lee, 1925-26," London.
    1932a. A note on the fauna of the Athlit caves. JRAI, Vol. 42, pp. 277-78.
    1932b. A new fossil hedgehog from Palestine. AMNH, Vol. 10, pp. 575-85.
    1933. A note on the fauna of the Athlit caves. JRAI, Vol. 62, pp. 277-79.
    1934a. A fossil wart-hog from Palestine. AMNH, Vol. 13, pp. 120-29.
    1934b. Two additions to the Pleistocene cave-fauna of Palestine (Trionyx and
        Crocodilus). AMNH, Vol. 14, pp. 474-78.
    1937a. New Pleistocene mammals from Palestine. AMNH, Vol. 20, pp. 397-400.
    1937b. The fossil fauna of the Wady el-Mughara caves. In D.A.E. Garrod and
        D.M.A. Bate, "The Stone Age of Mount Carmel," pp. 136-225. Oxford.
    1947. The Pleistocene mammal faunas of Palestine and East Africa. CPAP,
        pp. 38-39.
Blake, G.S.
    1939. Geological map of Palestine, scale 1:250,000. Survey of Palestine.

Blanckenhorn, M.
　1921. Die Steinzeit Palästina-Syriens und Nordafrikas. Berlin.
Bodenheimer, F.S.
　1935. Animal life in Palestine. Jerusalem.
Boesch, Hans
　1940. Der Einfluss des geographischen Faktors auf die Verhältnisse in Palästina. SG, nos. 2-3, pp. 1-12.
Boyko, H.
　1953. A short plant-ecological guide for the Excursion. DRP, pp. 631-635.
Braidwood, Robert J.
　1943. Note on the age of the Galilee and Mt. Carmel skeletal material. AA, Vol. 45, pp. 642-43.
Braidwood, Robert J. and Linda
　1953. The earliest village communities of Southwestern Asia. JWH, Vol. 1, pp. 278-310.
Brammall, A.
　1937. Report on samples of matrix from the Mughâret es-Skhul and et-Tabun. In D.A.E. Garrod and D.M.A. Bate, "The Stone Age of Mount Carmel," Vol. 1, pp. 126-27. Oxford.
Buzy, D.
　1928. Une Industrie mésolithique en Palestine. RB, Vol. 38, p. 558 et seq.
Carleton, Earle J.
　1941. Stone industries of Palestine-Syria; a study of material from 52 sites. Thesis for Honors, Harvard.
Clifford, M.H.
　1937. Report on the vegetable and other remains embedded in layer Eb, et-Tabun. In D.A.E. Garrod and D.M.A. Bate, "The Stone Age of Mount Carmel," pp. 130-31. Oxford.
Cooke, H.B.S., see Phillips, Wendell
Cooke, Hedley V.
　1952. Challenge and response in the Middle East. New York.
Coon, Carleton S.
　1948. The races of Europe. New York.
De Leeuw, A.
　1953. Experimental reservoirs in the Negev, DRP, pp. 498, 502.
De Vaumas, Etienne de
　1952a. Sur la morphométrie du massif palestinien. CRAS, Vol. 235, pp. 1410-12.
　1952b. Sur la morphométrie du massif galiléen. CRAS, Vol. 235, pp. 1146-47.
　1953a. La Palestine; etude morphométrique. IEJ, Vol. 3, no. 2, pp. 80-93, 178-190.
　1953b. Le Negeb: étude morphologique. BSGE, Vol. 26, pp. 119-63, August. See Bibliography and list of maps, pp. 119-20.
De Vaux, R.
　1946. La préhistorie de la Syrie et de la Palestine d'après les recherches récentes. RB, Vol. 53, pp. 99-124.
Dothan, M.
　1952. An archaeological survey of the Lower Rubin River. IEQ, Vol. 2, no. 2, pp. 104-17.
Elath, Eliahu
　1953. Population problems in Israel, JRCAS, Vol. 40, pt. 1, pp. 22-36.
Ettinghausen, Richard
　1952. Bibliography dealing with the Near and Middle East. See also 1954 Supplement. MEI.

Field, Henry
  1939. Contributions to the anthropology of Iran. FMNH, Vol. 29, pp. 1-706.
  1953-56. Bibliography on Southwestern Asia: I-III. UM.
Fohs, F. Julius
  1946. Development and land settlement potentialities of Palestine. Houston.
Garrod, D.A.E.
  1928. Excavation of a Palaeolithic cave in western Judaea. QST, p. 182 et seq.
  1929. Excavations in the Mugh-aret el-Wad, near Athlit, April - June, 1929.
    QST, p. 220 et seq.
  1930a. Note on three objects of Mesolithic Age from a cave in Palestine. Man,
    Vol. 30, p. 77 et seq.
  1930b. Fouilles paléolithiques en Palestine. BSPF, Vol. 27, p. 151 et seq.
  1931a. Excavations in the Mugh-aret el-Wad, 1930. QST, p. 99 et seq.
  1931b. Fouilles préhistoriques au Mont Carmel, 1930-31. CPF-X, p. 60
    et seq.
  1931c. Excavations in the caves of the Wady el-Mughara, 1929 and 1930. BASPR,
    no. 7, p. 5, et seq.
  1931d. Excavations in the Wady el-Mughara, 1931. QST, p. 46 et seq.
  1932a. A new Mesolithic industry: the Natufian of Palestine. JRAI, Vol. 62,
    pp. 261, 263, 265.
  1932b. Neuvos descubriementos prehistóricos en Palestina. Investigación y
    Progreso, Vol. 6, p. 62 et seq.
  1932c. Excavations in the Wady el-Mughara, 1931. BASPR, no. 8, p. 6, et seq.
  1934a. The Stone Age in Palestine. Antiquity, pp. 133-50, June.
  1934b. Excavations at the Wadi el-Mughara, 1932-33. BASPR, no. 10, p. 7 et
    seq.
  1934c. Excavations at the Wady el-Mughara, 1932-33. QST, p. 85 et seq.
  1935. Excavations in the Mugh-aret et-Tabūn, 1934. BASPR, no. 11, p. 54 et
    seq.
  1936. A summary of seven season's work at the Wady el-Mughara. BASPR, no.
    12, p. 125, et seq.
  1943. Excavations at the cave of Shukbah, Palestine, 1928...with an Appendix
    on the fossil mammals of Shukbah, by Dorothea M.A. Bate. PPS, Vol. 8,
    pp. 1-20.
  1952. A transitional industry from the base of the Upper Palaeolithic in Palestine
    and Syria. JRAI, Vol. 81, pp. 121-30.
Garrod, D.A.E. and Bate, D.M.A.
  1937. The Stone Age of Mount Carmel, Vol. 1, Oxford.
Gloor, Pierre-André
  1951-52. Recherches anthropologiques en Palestine méridionale: I, Enquête sur
    les Arabes (série masculine); II, série feminine; III, La croissance; IV, Evo-
    lution de la craniologie palestinienne. ASAG, Vol. 15, no. 2, pp. 108-42; and
    Vol. 17, no. 1, pp. 1-17.
Glueck, Nelson
  1934-51. Explorations in eastern Palestine. 4 vols. Baltimore.
  1935. Explorations in eastern Palestine. BASOR, Vol. 15.
  1946. The river Jordan. Philadelphia.
  1947. An archeologist looks at Palestine. NGM, Vol. 92, pp. 739-53.
  1953. Explorations in Western Palestine. BASOR, no. 131, pp. 6-15.
Guy, P.L.O.
  1953. The Kurnub catchment area as a Negev experimental reserve. DRP, 496-
    7.
Haas, G., see Stekelis, Moshe

Hinden, Rita
  1940. The fertility and mortality of the population of Palestine. SR, Vol. 32,
    nos. 1-2, pp. 28-49.
Issawi, Charles and Dabezies, Carlos
  1951. Population movements and population pressure in Jordan, Lebanon, and
    Syria. MMFQ, Vol. 29, pp. 385-403.
Ives, R.L.
  1950. The Palestinian environment. AS, Vol. 38, no. 1, pp. 85-104.
Izzeddin, Nejla, see Shanklin, W.M.
Johns, C.N.
  1948. Discoveries in Palestine since 1939. PEFQ, Vol. 80, pp. 81-101.
Jurkat, Ernest, see Notestein, Frank W.
Kallner, Amiran, D.H.
  1950-1951. Geomorphology of the central Negev highlands. IEJ, Vol. 1, no. 2,
    pp. 107-20.
Karge, Paul
  1917. Rephaim. Paderborn.
Keith, (Sir) Arthur
  1927. A report on the Galilee skull. In F. Turville-Petre, "Researches in Pre-
    historic Galilee." London.
Keith, (Sir) Arthur and McCown, T.D.
  1937. Mount Carmel Man: his bearing on the ancestry of modern races. BASPR,
    no. 13, p. 5.
Keith, Sir Arthur, see McCown, T.D.
Kirk, G.E.
  1946. Archaeological activities in Palestine and Transjordan since 1939. PEFQ,
    Vol. 78, pp. 92-102.
Langerhaus, P.
  1873. Ueber die heutigen Bewöhner des heiligen Landes. AAB, Vol. 6.
Lawrence, Norman
  1952. Israel: Jewish population and immigration. U.S. Bureau of the Census,
    ser. P-90, no. 2, pp. 1-58.
Lowdermilk, Walter C.
  1944. Palestine, land of promise. New York.
  1953. Floods in deserts. DRP, pp. 365-74.
Luschan, Felix von
  1892. La posizione antropologica degli Ebrei. AAE.
McCown, T.D.
  1932. A note on the excavation and the human remains from the Mugharet es-
    Sukhūl (Cave of the Kids), season of 1931. BASPR, no. 8, p. 12 et seq.
  1933. Fossil men of the Mugharet es-Sukhūl. BASPR, no. 9, p. 9 et seq.
  1934. The oldest complete skeletons of Man. BASPR, no. 10, p. 13 et seq.
  1936. Mount Carmel Man. BASPR, no. 12, p. 131 et seq.
McCown, T.D. and Keith (Sir) Arthur
  1937-39. The Stone Age of Mount Carmel. 2 vols. Oxford.
Movius, Hallam L., Jr.
  1953. Old World Prehistory: Paleolithic. In A.L. Kroeber, "Anthropology To-
    day," pp. 163-92. University of Chicago.
Neuville, René
  1930. Note de Préhistoire palestinienne. JPOS, Vol. 10, p. 205 et seq.
  1931. L'Acheuléen supérieur d'Oumm Qatafa. L'Anthropologie, Vol. 41, p. 13
    et seq., 249 et seq.
  1932. Statuette animale du Mésolithique palestinien. L'Anthropologie, Vol. 52,
    p. 546 et seq.

1933. Statuette érotique du désert de Judée. L'Anthropologie, Vol. 43, p. 558.

1934a. L'outillage en silex de Teleilat Ghassoul. Rome.

1934b. Le Préhistorique de Palestine. RB, Vol. 43, p. 237 et seq.

1934-35. Les débuts de l'agriculture et la famille préhistorique en Palestine. JJPES, p. xvii et seq.

1949. Trouvailles dans la Grotte d'Oumm-Qatafa (Israël). BSPF, Vol. 46, nos. 7-8, p. 234.

1951. Le Paléolithique et le Mésolithique du désert de Judée. AIIP, Memoir 24, pp. 1-270.

Notestein, Frank W. and Jurkat, Ernest

1945. Population problems of Palestine. MMFQ, Vol. 23, no. 4, pp. 308-52.

Perrot, Jean

1952a. Les industries lithiques palestiniennes de la fin du Mésolithique à l'Age de Bronze. IEQ, Vol. 2, no. 2, pp. 73-81.

1952b. Têtes de flèches du Natoufian et du Tahounien (Palestine). BSPF, Vol. 49, no. 8, pp. 439-49.

1953. La découverte en Palestine par René Neuville d'une petite pointe en os à base fendue. BSPF, Vol. 50, nos. 1-2, p. 14.

Petrbok, J.

1937. Die Bedeutung des Campignien von der Karmelspitze für die stratigraphische chronologie des palästinischen Quartär. ZDPV, Vol. 60, p. 139 et seq.

Pfannenstiel, Max

1949. Klimatisch bedingte Spiegelschwankungen des Mittelmeeres im Qartär und die paläolitischen Kulturen. MGGW, Vols. 36-38 (1943-45), pp. 257-63.

1952. Das Quartär der Levante. Pt. 1, Die Küste Palästina-Syriens. AAWL, no. 7, pp. 375-475.

Phillips, Wendell and Cooke, H.B.S.

1948. Recent discoveries in Egypt and Sinai. SAS, Vol. 1, pp. 204-207.

Picard, L.

1933. Zur post-miocänen Entwicklungsgeschichte der Kontienalbecken Nord-Palästinas. NJMGP, Vol. 70, pp. 93-115.

1937. Inferences on the problem of the Pleistocene climate of Palestine and Syria drawn from flora, fauna, and stratigraphy. PPS, Vol. 3, pp. 58-70.

1943. Structure and evolution of Palestine, with comparative notes on neighboring countries. HUGD.

1953. The history of groundwater exploration in Israel. DRP, pp. 583-90.

Picard L. and Avnimelech, M.

1937. On the geology of the central coastal plain. BGHU, no. 4, pp. 1-45.

Ravikovitch, S.

1953. The aeolian soils of the northern Negev. DRP, pp. 404-52.

Reifenberg, A.

1937. Chemical analyses of samples of matrix from et-Tabun. In D.A.E. Garrod and D.M.A. Bate, "The Stone Age of Mount Carmel," p. 128, Oxford.

1953. The struggle between the "Desert and the Sown." DRP, pp. 378-89.

Risdon, D.L.

1939. A study of the cranial and other human remains from Palestine excavated at Tell Duweir (Lachish) by the Wellcome-Marston archaeological research expedition. Biometrika, Vol. 31, pp. 99-166. London.

Sauter, Marc-R.

1945. Les races brachycéphales du Proche-Orient, des origines à nos jours. ASAG, Vol. 11, pp. 68-131.

1952. Les races de l'Europe. Paris.

Seltzer, Carl C.
   1940. Contributions to the racial anthropology of the Near East; based on data
      collected by Henry M. Huxley. PMP, Vol. 16, no. 2, pp. 1-62.
Shalem, N.
   1953. La stabilité du climat en Palestine. DRP, pp. 153-76.
Shanklin, W.M. and Izzeddin, Nejla
   1937. Anthropology of the Near East female. AJPA, Vol. 23, no. 3, pp. 381-415.
Skutil, Josef
   1952. Beth Galim, a Stone Age station in Palestine. AO, Vol. 20, pp. 214-25.
Snow, Charles E.
   1953. The Ancient Palestinian: Skhul V reconstruction. BASPR, no. 17, pp. 5-
      10.
Stekelis, Moshe
   1935. Les monuments megalithiques de Palestine. Paris.
   1942. Preliminary report on soundings in prehistoric caves in Palestine. BASOR,
      no. 86, pp. 1-10.
   1944a. Excavations in Palestine and Trans-Jordan, 1940-41: prehistoric caves.
      PDAQ, Vol. 11, pp. 115-18.
   1944b. Note on some flint implements from the seven wells (Saba Biyar). PDAQ,
      Vol. 11, pp. 44-46.
   1947. Rephaim-Baqa: a Palaeolithic station in the vicinity of Jerusalem (with an
      Appendix by P. Solomonica). JPOS, Vol. 21, pp. 81-97.
   1950-51. A new Neolithic industry: the Yarmukian of Palestine. IEJ, Vol. 1,
      no. 1, pp. 1-19.
   1952. Le progrès des recherches préhistoriques en Palestine. CIMPP, pp. 44-
      46.
Stekelis, Moshe and Haas, G.
   1952. The Abu Urba Cave (Mount Carmel). IEJ, Vol. 2, no. 1, pp. 15-47.
Thomas, O.
   1917. A new vole from Palestine. AMNH, Vol. 19, pp. 450-51.
   1919. A white-toothed shrew of Palestine. AMNH, Vol. 3, no. 13, p. 32.
   1920. A new shrew and two new foxes from Asia Minor and Palestine. AMNH,
      Vol. 5, no. 25, pp. 119-22.
Turville-Petre, F.
   1927. Researches in Prehistoric Galilee. London.
   1932. Excavations in the Mugharet el-Kebareh. JRAI, Vol. 62, p. 271 et seq.
Vaufrey, Raymond
   1940. Paléolithique et Mésolithique palestiniens. L'Anthropologie, Vol. 49, pp.
      616-20.
   1944. De prehistoria palestiniana: las culturas del Paleolitico y Mesolitico.
      AMS, Vol. 19, pp. 85-110.
Wright, G. Ernest
   1951. An important correlation between the Palestinian and Syrian Chalcolithic.
      BASOR, no. 122, pp. 52-55.
Yeivin, S.
   1952. Archaeological news: Israel. AJA, Vol. 56, no. 2, pp. 141-43.
Zaitschek, D.V.
   1953. Some useful plants of therapeutic value from desert regions in Israel.
      DRP, pp. 350-52.
Zohary, M.
   1952. Ecological studies in the vegetation of the Near East. IEJ, Vol. 2, no. 4,
      pp. 201-15.
Zumoffen, G.
   1900. La Phénicie avant les Phéniciens. Beirut.
   1908. L'âge de pierre en Phénicie. Anthropos, Vol. 3, p. 431 et seq.

IV. JORDAN

The Hashemite Kingdom of the Jordan[1] (formerly Trans-Jordan) came into existence during 1947. Three years later Samaria and part of Judea were included. Jordan is bounded on the west by Israel, on the north by Syria, on the northeast by Iraq
and on the east and north by Saudi Arabia.

Prior to the inclusion of parts of former Arab Palestine in 1950, Jordan was 225
miles in length and from 90-200 miles in breadth. The present area, including 3,700
square miles west of the Jordan River, is estimated[2] at 38,000 square miles.

The greater part of the country is formed by a plateau, ranging from 2,000 -
3,000 feet above sea level. This plateau possesses no natural boundaries between
its frontiers with Syria, Iraq, and Saudi Arabia. However, on Jebel Anaiza (Enaze)
Jordan, Iraq, and Saudi Arabia meet. It is these southeastern slopes that give birth
to the great Wadi Hauran. In March, 1928, I was privileged to accompany the Iraq
Petroleum Company's Survey Party to Jebel Anaiza where our cairn became this
famed tri-focal boundary point.

To the southeast stretches the Wadi Sirhan, now dry except for wells, such as
those we visited[3] at Qaf in June, 1950, and occasional water holes.

Sandstone[4] hills dominate the southwestern part of Jordan. Petra, "the rose-red
city half as old as time" is carved from sandstone, multi-colored[5] by the infiltration
of iron oxides.

After the spring rains the grazing is sufficient to support the camels, sheep, and
goats belonging to the Beduins who summer in the western highlands and winter in
the Wadi Sirhan and the deep valley, known as the Ghor, in which lie the Jordan
River and the Dead Sea.

Climate

In summer the shade temperature seldom reaches 100° F., although high on the
plateau and in the Jordan Valley 120° F. has been recorded. The nights are usually
cool, anyhow by contrast with the maximum daily temperature. In winter it is cold
on the uplands with a constant wind blowing across the sand and gravel. Rain falls
only from November to March. During the winter the climate in the Ghor and at
Aqaba is mild. On the plateau frost and some snow occur.

Pastoral nomadism is the only way of life on the plateau because of the little rainfall[6] (8 inches or less). However, three times that amount falls on the hills overlooking the lower Jordan Valley.

The 40,000 Beduins, mainly Huwaitat (Hawaitat) and Beni Sakhr, maintain flocks
of sheep and goats, which increase the erosion by cropping the young shoots which
push through the soil after the spring rains. They also breed some camels.

Flora

Except following the spring rains the greater part of Jordan is typical wilderness
with low xerophytic plants. The area west of the railway includes high hills and
slopes leading down to the Dead Sea. In this part there is a rich spring flora with a
great variety of leguminous plants.

Agriculture

Subsistence farming forms the basic support of the rural population. In 1947 only
1.2 million acres were cultivated. The principal crops are wheat, barley, millet,
maize, lentils, beans, peas, and vetches. A little tobacco and sesame are also
grown. Irrigation[8] would greatly increase productivity.

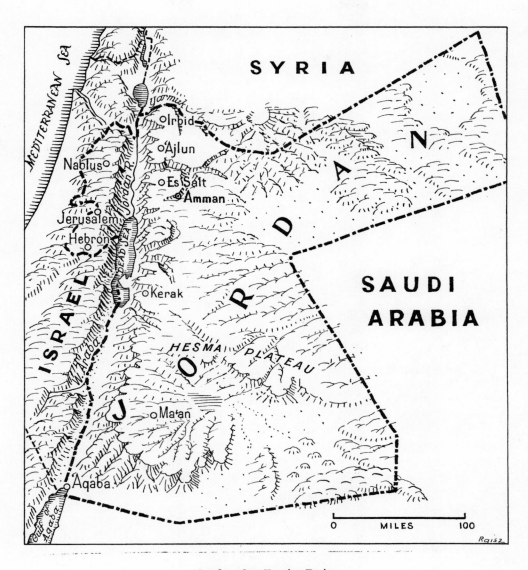

Jordan by Erwin Raisz

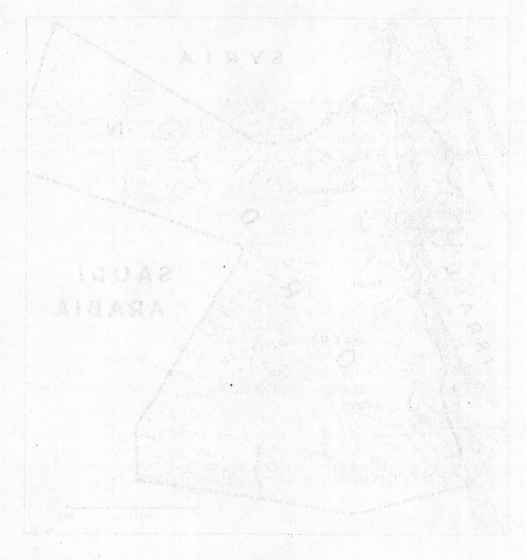

Fauna[9]

There are relatively few wild animals left in Jordan. Among those I have seen are gazelle, fox, jackal, hyena, and the turkey bustard (Houbara). The advent of roads, a railroad, wheeled vehicles, and highpowered rifles have taken their toll of animals, so that few remain. For this reason I have turned to Tristram (1873) who records the following: ibexes, gazelle, foxes, cheetahs, wolves, jackals, wild cats (Felis caligata), hares, gerbilles with squirrel-like tail, and root-eating mole-rats (Spalax typhlus).

The last lion reported was shot about 50 years ago while drinking at Ain al-Asad (= the "Lion's Pool") just south of the Roman fortress of Qasr el-Azraq.

Among the birds Tristram lists the following with some of their Latin names: Imperial eagle, spotted eagle (Aquila noevia), griffon vulture, lammergeyer (Gypaëtus barbatus), falcons and hawks, bimaculated ducks (hybrid between mallard and pintail), two partridges (Ammoperdrix heyi and Caccabis saxatilis), whistling raven (Corvus affinis), great spotted cuckoo, Alpine swift (Cypselus melba), hoopoe, Indian turtle-dove (Turtur risorius), sand-grouse, sun-bird (Cinnyris oseoe), wheat-ear (Saxicola monacha), black-throated warbler (Sylvia melanothorox), red-winged grakle (Amydrus tristrami), and the Moabite sparrow (Passer moabiticus).

In November, 1927 I saw two Arabian ostriches tethered to tent poles in the camp of Mohammed Abu Tayi at Al Jafar east of Maan. These had been captured by the Sulubba (Sleyb) in the Laha Depression midway between Bayir Wells and Jebel Enaze (Anaiza).

Population

The estimate of the Census Department in January, 1953 was 1,600,000 persons.[10] After the annexation of Arab Palestine in 1949, 280,000 refugees were included in this total. However, Issawi and Dabezies give the much lower figure for 1949 of 400,000 population with 70,000 in the towns of Amman, Irbid, Es Salt, and Kerak. Of the remainder 150,000 are settled, 140,000 are semi-nomadic, and 40,000 Beduins. Doreen Warriner estimated the total cultivated area in 1948 as 400,000 hectares, of which 26,000 are irrigated.[11]

Development Projects[12]

In 1926 Sir Ernest Dowson studied means of improving agricultural taxation and the planning of a land register with a view to settling the nomads or at least to restricting their migrations. In 1938 the infant mortality had declined to 181 per 1,000 from 242 per thousand four years before. Two Projects were proposed:

1. To develop the Wadi Zerka watershed area with dams and canals on the eastern side of the Jordan.

2. A similar plan was suggested for the Wadi Qilt area on the western side of the Jordan in territory annexed during 1949.

Ancient Man[13]

The earliest references to Men of the Old Stone Age in Jordan is the following account by Doughty (Vol. 1, p. 74):

"Walking in the torrent bed at Maan my eyes lighted upon, --and I took up, moved and astonished, one after another, seven flints chipped to an edge; we must suppose them of rational, that is an human labour. But what was that old human kindred which inhabited the land so long before the Semitic race?"

In another place Doughty (Vol. 1, p. 68) writes: "I have found in it (the gravel bed near Mt. Seir or Jebel Sherra) such wrought flint instruments as we have from some river and lake gravels and loams of Europe."

These specimens are now in the University Museum at Oxford.

1925. In December L.H. Dudley Buxton and the writer were on their way to join the Field Museum - Oxford University Joint Expedition to Kish, Iraq. After leaving Amman we proceeded eastward in a three-car Nairn convoy across the rough "Bay of Biscay," the name given to that 50-mile band of the Harrat ar-Rajil, the great lava bed. Just after dawn we halted on a large mudflat known as R.A.F. Landing Ground "H". Here Buxton found the first flint flaked by prehistoric man ever collected between the Jordan and the Tigris-Euphrates Valley. This was the beginning of my North Arabian Archeological Survey, a monograph still unpublished.

Other flint implements and flakes were found on this mudflat and at other enforced halts eastward to Rutba Wells.

1926. On January 11-12 Buxton and I collected a series of implements and flakes between Rutba Wells and Landing Ground "H", thereby establishing the fact that prehistoric man roamed across this great wilderness. Prior to our discoveries, the North Arabian or Syrian Desert had long been considered a geographic barrier to ancient migrations. The types of implements ranged from Mousterian to modern Beduin strike-a-lights.

1927. During November, while leader of the First Field Museum North Arabian Desert Expedition, I found typologically Paleolithic flint implements on numerous surface sites. The first was near Ziza south of Amman. Others were collected along the traverse from Al Qatrani-Bayir Wells-Shediya-Maan-Amman. At Bayir Wells[14] I dug in the face of a gravel bed in the wadi just south of the Qasr. Here at a depth of 11 feet 6 inches, a rolled and water-worn handaxe of Upper Acheulian type was unearthed. This was the first Lower Paleolithic implement found in situ east of the Hejaz railroad in Jordan.

Returning to Amman we continued eastward past Qasr el-Azraq across the "Bay of Biscay" to R.A.F. Landing Ground "M" where we found hundreds of implements and flakes, then southeast 22 miles to Umm Wual (= "The Mother of Ibexes") on whose peak (3,200 feet above sea level) we collected a series of typologically Mousterian implements before continuing northeast to Rutba Wells. Umm Wual later proved to be in Saudi Arabia, but at that time the boundaries between Jordan, Iraq, and Saudi Arabia had not been set by our survey cairn on the summit of Jebel Enaze (Anaiza).

1928. Continuing this archeological surface reconnaissance from March-June the following year as guests of the Iraq Petroleum Company's Desert Survey Party under William E. Browne, I found a chain of surface sites along the traverse from Rutba Wells to Amman and at such places as: Habeiba mudflats northeast of Amman, near Hammam-as-Sarakh, Qasr Hallabat and Umm Jemal. Thus, we were able to establish definitely the existence of ancient man in Jordan.

1929. The wilderness area of Jordan east of Amman is broken by the vast basalt-strewn region known as the Harrat ar-Rajil. Here in this most inhospitable region were found many traces of former habitation; the first stone implements had been collected on the surface near R.A.F. Landing ground "H" by Buxton and Field in December, 1925. During 1926-28 Group-Captain L.W.B. Rees[15] located ancient dwelling and camp sites, cairns, stone circles,[16] inscriptions,[17] camel brands[18] (sing. wasm), and graffiti. In November, 1927, Rees showed me many of these in eastern Jordan from Qasr el-Azraq to Bayir Wells. His publication[19] deals with these discoveries and calls particular attention to curious long, long walls which occur throughout the Harrat ar-Rajil and in areas adjoining this lava bed. To these Rees gave the name "kites" since they reminded him of "a small boy's kite--a more or less hexagonal head with the string and tail springing out of it."

I have followed some of these "kite" walls on the ground for 18 miles. From the air the outlines are clearly visible; on the ground these low walls would usually remain unnoticed. In passing, I suggest these "kites" were game, probably gazelle, traps.[20]

1932. During December a joint expedition of the Transjordan Department of Antiquities and the American School of Oriental Research, Jerusalem, under the direction of Mr. and Mrs. George Horsfield and Dr. Nelson Glueck, discovered prehistoric rock-drawings at Kilwa in southwestern Jordan near the Saudi Arabian border.

1934. Hans Rhotert and assistants spent November and December studying the rock-drawing at Kilwa. An ibex, 50 centimeters high, is one of the finest examples; Breuil believes that this may represent a wounded animal because two lines from its mouth suggest blood. On the back of the ibex appears a small human figure with arms outstretched. This figure is probably much later.

There are other animals represented, another ibex and a narrow-headed, horned ox and a seated pair of human beings in close embrace.

Recent analysis by Glueck of the photographs published by Rhotert assigns the Kilwa rock-drawings "to a period considerably later than the Mesolithic."

Rhotert and his staff collected more than 5,000 stone implements from 27 sites in the Kilwa area. The series ranged through Chellean, Acheulian, Levalloisian, Mousterian, Upper Paleolithic, Tahunian, Ghassulian, to the new "Kilwa-Culture," assigned by Glueck to the Mesolithic or later. The reader is referred to Rhotert's monograph on Jordan, especially his Bibliography.

1937-38. Waechter found eight implements both inside and outside a hut circle (25 meters) in the Wadi Dhobai. Each was retouched on both faces, the flaking being irregular. Similar types were collected by Rhotert near Jebel Tubaiq in southeastern Jordan.

1952. Stekelis excavated a late Neolithic human skull at Shaar Hagolan beside the Yarmuk River near the point where Syria and Jordan meet on Israel's frontier. This period was termed Yarmukian.

Summary

The Chellean and Acheulian handaxes from Kilwa are similar to those from: (a) the Wadi Araba and in situ at Bayir Wells in Jordan; (b) Ar-Rawafi in northeastern Sinai; (c) many surface sites in Israel; (d) Deraa in southwestern Syria; and Barda Balkha in northeastern Iraq. The large handaxe from Dawadami in central Saudi Arabia shows an evolved technique. However, the above sites indicate the range of handaxes in Southwestern Asia. Levalloiso-Mousterian cultures are far more widespread, extending from the Wadi Baaba in southwest Sinai to northeastern Iran. In Jordan near Thlathakhwat (= "The Three Sisters") I found typologically Mousterian implements and again to the east on Umm Wual in Saudi Arabia.

Surface sites with implements rejects and flakes, ranging from Upper Paleolithic to Mesolithic, occur widespread all throughout this region. Some of the principal localities east of the Jordan are: Deraa and the Wadi Rutga in Syria; Rutba and Jebel Enaze (Anaiza) in Iraq (also the boundary with Jordan and Saudi Arabia); and Tell el-Hibr in northwest Saudi Arabia.

No stratified deposit has yet been excavated. No cave or rockshelter has been located east of the Amman-Maan Railroad, although shelters used by shepherds have been visited. For example, about 500 paces east of Qasr Hallabat I sunk a trial trench in the floor of a small rockshelter; bedrock was encountered at a depth of 18 inches.

The stratigraphy of Jordan will have to be correlated with the excavations on Mount Carmel, although local cultural facies exist in the North Arabian or Syrian Desert. For example, I found Y-shaped implements (cf. Rhotert, p. 150, fig. 2) in northeastern Jordan and western Iraq.

The most recent stone implements picked up on the surface are Beduin strike-a-lights. Mohammed Abu Tayi of the Huwaitat demonstrated lighting a piece of cloth with flint and steel outside his black tent at Al Jafar.

Jordan has been inhabited more or less continuously from Lower Paleolithic times to the twentieth century.

Crania

Kappers recorded the cephalic index of a Beduin skull as 73.92.

Modern Man[21]

The anthropometric data (Table 7) on Jordan have been compiled by William H. Shanklin of the American University in Beirut.

The Beduins belong to the Mediterranean Race with the characteristic long and narrow heads with a dolichocephalic to mesocephalic index (see Table 8). However, the tribesmen and villagers living in the north and northwestern Jordan possess a higher cephalic index ranging from 79-81.

Shanklin has measured the only important series (791 males) in Jordan. However, in his first he recorded only the head length, head breadth, and cephalic index.

Shanklin sent me on April 20, 1954, his original tabulation sheets of raw data. Two corrections have therefore been made in his published[22] figures (1934): the cephalic index of the Huweitat was 74.6 not 74.2; and that of the Nuaimat villagers was 78.6 not 78.8. These corrections change the mean cephalic index for 791 males from Jordan from 77.3 to 77.4. The unclassified tribesmen were villagers, not Beduins, and the Kutum villagers belonged to the Kutum or Shitum tribe.

Shanklin, who continued his anthropometric studies in Jordan, sent the following information on the groups and his published references to the series in Table 8.

1. The Huwaitat Beduins were studied in the Kerak region.

2. The Beni Sakhr Beduins were measured near Amman.

These Beduin tribes migrate eastward to the Wadi Sirhan in Saudi Arabia. Another section lives in Sinai and moves westward into the area between Cairo and Suez.

3. The Maualy, Akeydat and Rwala (Ruwalla) Beduins[23] were measured in the Syrian Desert in the general area north of Palmyra, south of Aleppo, and east of Hama. The Rwala were studied on two trips: in the headquarters of Nuri ibn Shaalan and his son Fawaz near Salamieh east of Homs; and near Hidjaneh south of Damascus. The Rwala migrate across very wide areas, even far beyond the limits of the Syrian Desert. In general, they do not go north of the Palmyra area.

4. The Bekaa are Sunni Moslem villagers living on the Bekaa Plain between the Lebanon and Anti-Lebanon Mountains.

5. The Mitwali are Shiite Moslems living in the mountains of Lebanon. They were measured in the southern towns of Bint Jebail and Nabatiyyeh in Lebanon.

6. The Alouite belong to an Islamic secret sect. Some were recorded in the Alouite Mountains west of Hama, others in the villages of the plains east of the mountains.

7. The Hama series are Sunni Moslems living in and around Hama (Biblical Hamath).

8. Mhardeh, a Christian village, lies about 10 miles west of Hama in Syria.

9. Hafar is a Christian village east of Nebkh and west of Karyatein on the Damascus-Palmyra road in Syria.

10. Hidjaneh is a village of Sunni Moslems south of Damascus, Syria.

Tables 9-12 present the measurements and indices on 2,084 men.

Females[24]

The 70 Akeydat Beduin women were measured by Mrs. M. Krischner and the 100 Alouite and 103 Mitwali women by Shanklin (see Table 13).

Summary

Stone implements, ranging from the Lower Paleolithic to contemporary Beduin strike-a-lights, have been found in Jordan. At Bayir Wells between Maan and the Saudi Arabian Frontier typologically Paleolithic implements were found in situ in a gravel bed. Many surface sites have yielded typologically Middle and Upper Paleolithic, Mesolithic and Neolithic implements, rejects and flakes. Regarding the strike-a-lights, one of the Huweitat Beduins in Mohammed Abu Tayi's camp at El Jafar demonstrated the use of flint and steel for lighting a piece of cloth. Around these tents I saw many flint flakes which had thus originated. A few microlithic nuclei also resulted from this modern technique. These tiny nuclei resembled those from deep in "Y" trench at Kish (circa 3,000 B.C.) and similar forms from the Vindyha Hills in India.

The Beduins of Jordan, mainly Huweitat and Beni Sakhr, are slightly shorter than the apparent mean (165.00) for Southwestern Asia. The head is long and narrow with a cephalic index of about 75.0. The forehead is narrow (105.0), the face medium wide (131.0) across the zygomatic arches, the mandible narrow (104.5), the total face short (117.5), the upper face short (68.0) and the nose short (52.0) and narrow (33.60).

It is, therefore, clear that the Beduins of Jordan belong to the basic Mediterranean group of Southwestern Asia with a very minor admixture of Negroid blood, a customary element in Beduin encampments.

References

Ashbel, D.
    1942. Rainfall map of Palestine, Trans-Jordan, southern Syria and southern
        Lebanon. 3rd ed. Jerusalem.
Boyd, William C.
    1939. Blood groups. TB, Vol. 17, p. 2. 1939.
Boyd, William C. and Lyle G.
    1938. The blood groups of the Rwala Bedouin. JI, Vol. 34, no. 6, pp. 441-46.
Canaan, T.
    1930. Studies in the topography and folklore of Petra. Jerusalem.
Clark, J.G.D.
    1933. Paleolithic implements from southwestern Jordan. Man, Vol. 33, pp. 147-
        49.
Cooke, Hedley V.
    1952. Challenge and response in the Middle East. New York.
Crawford, O.G.S.
    1932. Paleolithic axes from Transjordan. Antiquity, Vol. 6, pp. 216-17.
Dapples, E.C.
    1941. Surficial deposits of the deserts of Syria, Trans-Jordan, Iraq, and west-
        ern Iran. SP, Vol. 11, no. 3, pp. 124-41.
Doughty, Charles M.
    1936. Arabia Deserta. 2 Vols. London.
Feinbrun, Naomi and Michael Zohary
    1955. A geobotanical survey of Transjordan. BRCI, Vol. 5 D, no. 1, pp. 5-36.
        December.
Field, Henry
    1929. Early man in North Arabia. NH, Vol. 29, pp. 34-44.
    1931. Among the Beduins of North Arabia. OC, Vol. 45, no. 905, pp. 577-95.
    1934. Sulle caratteristiche geografiche dell'Arabia settentrionale. BRSGI, Ser.
        6, Vol. 12, pp. 3-13. January.
    1952. Camel brands and graffiti from Iraq, Syria, Jordan, Iran and Arabia.
        JAOS, Supplement no. 15, pp. 1-41.
    1953-56. Bibliography on Southwestern Asia: I-III. UM.
Fohs, F. Julius
    1943. Development and land settlement potentialities of Transjordan. Houston.
Glueck, Nelson
    1936. Christian Kilwa. JPOS, Vol. 16, pp. 9-16.
    1937. An aerial reconnaissance in southern Transjordan. BASOR, no. 66, pp.
        27-28; no. 67, pp. 19-26.
    1939. Kilwa: a review. Antiquity, pp. 416-24, December.
    1940. The other side of the Jordan. New Haven.
    1944a. The geography of the Jordan. NGM, Vol. 86, pp. 719-44.
    1944b. Wadi Sirhan in North Arabia. BASOR, no. 96, pp. 7-17.
Grimme, H.
    1937. Altsinaitische Forschungen,epigraphisches und historisches. Paderborn.
Hart, Henry Chichester
    1891. Some account of the fauna and flora of Sinai, Petra and Wady Arabah.
        London.
Hayne, W. Amherst
    1873. On the flora of Moab. In H.B. Tristram,"The land of Moab." New York.
Horsfield, Agnes
    1943. Journey to Kilwah. GJ, Vol. 102, pp. 71-77.

Horsfield, G. and Glueck, Nelson
    1933a. Prehistoric rock-drawings in Transjordan. ILN, June 3.
    1933b. Prehistoric rock-drawings in Transjordan. AJA, Vol. 37, pp. 381-86,
        529.
Huxley, Julian
    1954. From an antique land. London.
Ionides, M.G.
    1946. Jordan Valley irrigation. Engineering, September 13.
Issawi, Charles and Dabezies, Carlos
    1951. Population movements and population pressure in Jordan, Lebanon, and
        Syria. MMFQ, Vol. 29, pp. 385-403.
Izzeddin, Nejla, See Shanklin, W.M.
Jusatz, H.J.
    1936. Blutgruppenzugehörigkeit der Rwala-Beduinen. ZFR, Vol. 3, p. 315.
Konikoff, A.
    1946. Transjordan: an economic survey. Jerusalem. See Supplementary Bibliog-
        raphy, pp. 1-16.
Merrill, Selah
    1881. East of the Jordan: a record of travel and observation in the countries of
        Moab, Gilead, and Bashan. London. See Bibliography, pp. 533-36.
Neuville, René
    1931. L'industrie lithique de Teleilat Ghassoul. BSA, Vol. 2, pp. 55-56.
Post, George E.
    1930. The geology of Edom. In G.L. Robinson, "The sarcophagus of an ancient
        civilization: Petra, Edom and the Edomites." New York.
Rees, L.W.B.
    1929. The Transjordan Desert. Antiquity, Vol. 3, pp. 389-407.
Rhotert, Hans (ed.)
    1938. Transjordanien: vorgeschichtliche Forschungen. Stuttgart. See Bibliography,
        p. 2.
Robinson, George Livingston
    1930. The sarcophagus of an ancient civilization: Petra, Edom and the Edomites.
        New York.
Seltzer, Carl C.
    1940. Contributions to the racial Anthropology of the Near East; based on data col-
        lected by Henry M. Huxley. PMP, Vol. 16, no. 2, pp. 1-62.
Shanklin, W.M.
    1934. The anthropology of the Transjordan Arabs. PNB, nos. 3-4, pp. 1-12.
    1935a. The anthropology of the Rwala Bedouins. JRAI, Vol. 65, pp. 375-90.
    1935b. Blood groupings of the Rwala Bedouin. JI, Vol. 29, no. 6, pp. 427-33.
    1936a. Anthropology of the Akeydat and the Maualy Bedouin. AJPA, Vol. 21, pp.
        217-52.
    1936b. Blood groupings of the Maualy and Akeydat Bedouin. AJPA, Vol. 21, pp.
        39-48.
    1946. Anthropometry of Transjordan Bedouin with a discussion of their racial
        affinities. AJPA, Vol. 4, pp. 323-75.
Shanklin, W.M. and Cummins, Harold
    1937. Dermatoglyphics in Rwala Bedouins. HB, Vol. 9, pp. 357-65.
Shanklin, W.M. and Izzeddin, Nejla
    1937. Anthropology of the Near East female. AJPA, Vol. 22, pp. 381-415.
Stein, (Sir) Aurel
    1939. Une récente exploration en Transjordanie. CRAIB.
    1940. Surveys on the Roman frontier in Iraq and Trans-Jordan. GJ, Vol. 95,
        no. 6, pp. 428-38.

Tristram, H.B.
    1873. The land of Moab. New York.
Waechter, John
    1947a. Some surface implements from Transjordan. PPS, Vol. 13, pp. 178-80.
    1947b. The excavations at Ala Safat, Transjordan. JPOS, Vol. 21, pp. 98-103.
Warriner, Doreen
    1948. Land and poverty in the Middle East. Oxford.

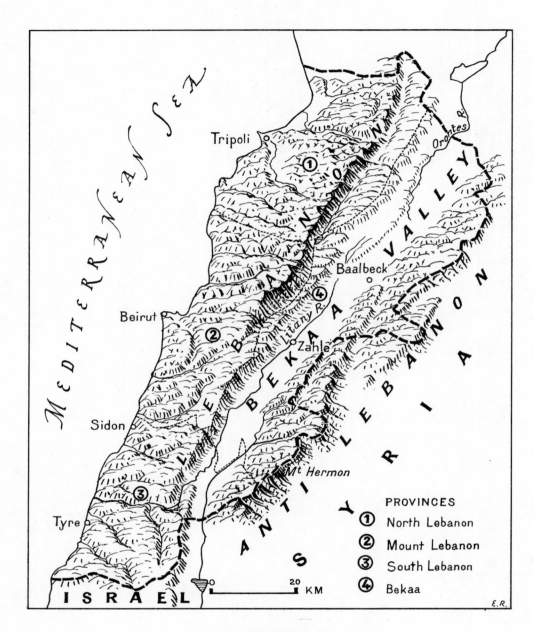

Lebanon by Erwin Raisz

V. LEBANON

The Lebanon,[1] bordering the Mediterranean, has been an independent Republic since November 26, 1943. To the north and east lies Syria. The southern boundary marches with Israel. The area is given[2] as 3,977 square miles with a maximum length of 125 miles and a maximum breadth of 40 miles. The central massif,[3] known as the Lebanon Mountains, runs in a northeast-southwest direction almost the full length of the country. Between the mountains and the Mediterranean there is a narrow, broken coastal strip. The highest peak is Qurnat as-Sawda (11,024 feet) to the southeast of Tripoli. A parallel range, the Anti-Lebanon Mountains, follows the Lebanese-Syrian border. Between these two ranges lies a valley known as the Bekaa (70 x 10 miles). Here rise the Orontes and Litani rivers.

The mean annual temperature[4] for Beirut is 68° F. with a maximum recorded range of 107° - 29° F. The average annual rainfall for Beirut during a 41-year period was 35.9 inches.

A few miles eastward on the mountains there is heavy winter snow which remains from December to May. The Bekaa is hot in summer with some frost and snow in winter. In the mountains about 50 inches of rain falls annually with one-third less on the coast. The rainy season lasts from October to April. Naturally, there is a wide range of vegetation from the typical Mediterranean varieties to the stunted oaks, junipers and dwarf bushes near the peaks.

From the Mediterranean to east of the Khabur River there are three zones of vegetation:

(a) the coastal plain and lower part of mountains support typical Mediterranean flora. Here grow wheat, barley, millet, maize, onions, garlic, cucumbers, tomatoes, potatoes, tobacco, figs, olives, dates, grapes, bananas, and citrus fruits.

(b) Conifers, including firs and cedars, flourish on the highest portions of the Lebanon and Anti-Lebanon Mountains. Hitti (1951, p. 50) writes:

"The most magnificent and renowned among the trees of Lebanon is the cedar (Cedrus libani), whose virtues of strength (Ps. XXIX:5), durability (Jer. XXII:14), majesty (2 Kings XIV:9) Zech, XI:1-2) and suitability for carving (Isaiah XLIV:14-15) were sung by ancient poets, prophets, and historians. The cedar provided the early Lebanese with the finest timber for constructing their sea-faring ships and attracted kings from the Tigro-Euphrates and the Nile valleys, where no large trees could flourish. Unfortunately today it does not constitute as much of the glory of Lebanon as it anciently did (Isaiah XXXV:2; LX:13). It survives only in small batches--bouquets on the bare breast of Lebanon--the best known of which is that above Bisharri, where upward of 400 trees, some perhaps 1,000 years old, still grow. The highest is about 80 feet. They are popularly referred to as Arz al-Rabb, the cedars of the Lord."

(c) The canyon-like trough and the plateaus of eastern Syria form the third zone where the small rainfall produces the characteristic xerophytic plants.

The alpine flora is more closely related to Oriental plants than to the glacial flora of Europe and northern Asia. Fruit-growing is the basic activity, but wheat, maize, and barley are raised. The citrus crop for 1950-51 was 77,000 tons.

The fauna is similar to that of Syria, but wild animals are on the decrease as the country is opened up with roads, and no real conservation exists.

Thirty years ago the population[5] of the State of Great Lebanon was 628,863.

In 1950 the estimate[6] was raised to 1,257,000 with the following urban-dwellers:

43

Beirut, 247,000; Tripoli, 78,000; Sidon, 78,826; and Zahleh, 78,031. The mixed population is basically Mediterranean, but there are several blond elements. On a religious grouping the Maronites, a Uniate sect of the Roman Church are the largest community with 337,734 in 1946. They live in the old territory of Mount Lebanon east of Beirut. There are also 244,307 Sunnis, 217,520 Shias, 113,197 Greek Orthodox, 77,023 Druze, 66,542 Greek Catholics, and 61,000 Armenian Orthodox. Arabic, French, and English are the principal languages.

De Vaumas (1953, pp. 68-75) gives a brief historical outline of the exploitation of the forest (from the beginning of the second millennium B.C. to the second century of the Christian Era) and the occupation of Lebanon (second century to the Middle Ages). Special attention is called to his map of the distribution of villages and to the table (p. 75), giving the Districts (Cazas) number of villages, area, and population.

Ancient Man[7]

De Vaumas (1953, pp. 67-68) published his "Introduction to the Human Geography of the Lebanese Republic" beginning with the Prehistoric period. The earliest inhabitants dwelt beside the littoral, where their traces are abundant. They also lived in the mountainous region. Evidence of Paleolithic occupation has been found at Tartige (1300 meters) near Jebel Jaje, at Mayrouba (1100 meters) and at Beskinta (1500 meters) on the edge of the high pleateaus, at Bikfaya (1000 meters), at Broummana (750 meters) and Beit Méri (720 meters) above Beirut, and also at Djezzine (1000 meters) in western Lebanon.

Since these sites must be far from a complete list, we must conclude that the prehistoric hunters roamed through these mountains high above the great forest.

Attention is called to the fact that in Galilee, Lower Paleolithic implements were found on Khallet el-Hamra (800 meters) and Acheulian at Ain Ebel and at Tibnin (600 meters).

Thus, we see that prehistoric man lived in the same regions from the most ancient times down to the twentieth century. Here they hunted game, now completely disappeared, but whose presence is clear from texts of the Middle Ages. The question is, did the prehistoric hunters lives at these sites, or did they use them as bases for hunting? In the Bekaa, where the forest was less dense or even absent, the following prehistoric sites have been located: Deir el-Ahmar (Paleolithic)-Serain (Mousterian)-Mejdel Anjar (Acheulian)-Dakoué (Acheulian); and Kefr Aya (Levalloisian)-Qaroun (Acheulian).

In the Qalamoun there are many surface stations, the majority being along the Damascus-Homs road: Breijé (Eneolithic), Qara (Chellean), Deir Attiyé (Lower Paleolithic), Nebek (Acheulo-Chellean), Yabroud and district (Levalloiso-Acheulian-Chellean), Maaloula (Levalloisian), Doummar (Neolithic), Mezzé, and Qatana (Upper Acheulian).

Now to turn to the more general picture of Prehistoric man in Lebanon.

The oldest implements were collected by Wetzel and Haller on the 55.0-60.0 meter terraces and in the alluvial gravels of the first Pluvial period. Paleolithic implements were found by Zumoffen in the caves of Adlun, midway between Tyre and Sidon, Nahr Ibrahim, Nahr el-Kelb (al-Kalb) and Antelias.

Lower Paleolithic implements were found by Wetzel and Haller at Strombes on the terraces from +14.50 to -6.0 meters.

During the Middle Paleolithic, a long pluvial period, the prehistoric hunters lived in the rockshelters of Nahr al-Jawz near al-Batrun and Nahr Ibrahim according to evidence obtained by Zumoffen. According to Wetzel and Haller, Middle and Upper Paleolithic and Mesolithic implements correspond to the second Pluvial period and occur on the +6.0 meter levels.

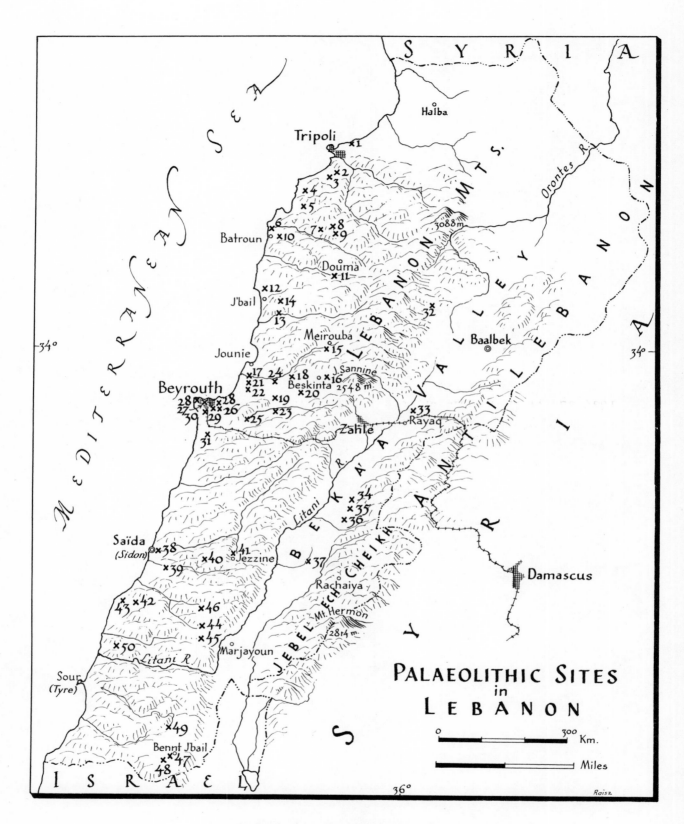

PALAEOLITHIC SITES
in
LEBANON

Archeological Sites by René Wetzel

Desiccation increased during the Upper Paleolithic with alternating warm and cool Mediterranean climates. During this period the cultures correspond to the Aurignacian of Western Europe; according to Zumoffen these occur in the caves of Antelias and Nahr el-Kelb. Since 1938 J. Franklin Ewing has excavated at Ksar Akil near Antelias. Here Aurignacian skeletons and implements have been found with bones of deer, hyenas, rhinoceroses, foxes, and goats.

In order to obtain the location and distribution of Paleolithic sites in Lebanon, I invited my colleague, Dr. René Wetzel, to compile a list and prepare a sketch map of localities. The following table, Map 7, and the list of references[8] were received during February, 1954.

PALEOLITHIC SITES IN LEBANON

(After Wetzel)

No.	Name	Altitude (in meters)	Location	Site	Typology
1	Ras Lados[9]	35	5 Km. N.E. of Tripoli	E	Mousterian
1	Ras Lados[10]	6	In railway cutting	E	Mousterian or Aurignacian (?)
2	Bahras[11]	50	3 Km. S.W. of Tripoli	E	Tayacian
2	Abou Halqa[12]	15	4 Km. S.W. of Tripoli	E	Aurignacian
3	Qalmoun[13]	100	1 Km. E. of village; 6 Km. S.W. of Tripoli	E	Mousterian
4	Enfeh[14]	15	N.E. of village	E	Levalloisian (?)
5	Chekka[15]	15	Km. 20 on Tripoli-Beirut road near cemetery quarry	E	Levalloiso-Mousterian
6	Ras Qoubba[16]	15	1 Km. N. of Batroun Cave	E	Levalloisian
7	Nahr el-Joz[17]	200	12 Km. E. of Batroun between Kafer Hay and Reifoun	E	Lower Paleolithic
8	Dar Baachtar[18] (Bejderfeld)	550	20 Km. S. of Tripoli; 4 Km. N.W. of Deir Billa on right bank of Nahr el-Joz	E	Levalloisian
9	Deir Billa[19]	550	20 Km. S. of Tripoli; Al Doudou Cave, 100 meters S. of Deir Billa village	E	Levalloisian
10	Batroun[20]	50	N. and N.E. of town	S	Lower Paleolithic
11	Tartege[21]	1300	18 Km. N.E. of Jubail (anc. Byblos), between Jej and Douma	S	Paleolithic
12	Amchit[22]	100	3 Km. N. of Jubail, Saleh Cave, 1 Km. E. of village	S	Levalloisian
13	Nahr Ibrahim[23]	50	Km. 25 on road Beirut-Tripoli, 1 Km. from viaduct	E	Moustero-Levalloisian
14	Moghara Abou Saheb[24]	100	Wadi Soubha, 2 Km. E. of Jubail	S	Aurignacian (?)
15	Meirouba[25]	1100	14 Km. E.N.E. of Jounie	S	Levalloisian
16	Beskinta[26]	1500	40 Km. E. of Beirut; 2 Km. E. of village	S	Levalloisian

No.		Altitude (in meters)	Location	Site	Typology
17	Nahr el-Kelb[27]	15	7 Km. N.E. of Beirut; 200 meters S. of bridge near Km. 156 of railway line	E	Levalloisian
18	Djaita[28]	500	13 Km. N.E. of Beirut in Nahr el-Kelb; 7 Km. E. of bridge on Beirut-Tripoli road; 3 caves near springs	E	Capsian and Neolithic
19	Bikfaya[29]	950	25 Km. E. of Beirut	S	Upper Levalloisian
19	Bikfaya[30]	1050	25 Km. E. of Beirut	S	Lower Mesolithic
20	Dour Choueir[31]	1200	40 Km. E. of Beirut	S	Upper Paleolithic
21	Dbaye[32]	250	Km. 15 on road Beirut-Tripoli	S	Acheulian
22	Antelias[33]	250	10 Km. N.E. of Beirut, two caves 2 and 2-1/2 Km. (Ksar Akil) E. of Antelias	E	Upper-Middle Paleolithic (Aurignacian)
23	Broumana[34]	750	15 Km. E. of Beirut; 2 Km. E. of village	S	Upper Paleolithic
24	Dik el Mahdi[35]	500	17 Km. N.E. of Beirut	S	Acheulian
25	Beit Mery[36]	720	10 Km. E. of Beirut; Nahr Beirut Valley	S	Acheulian
26	(Derkuene[37]	150	5 Km. S.E. of Beirut	S	Acheulian
	(Sin el-Fil[38]	60	3 Km. S.E. of Beirut; right bank of Nahr Beirut	S	Acheulo-Mousterian
27	Beirut[39]	50	Left bank of Nahr Beirut, near bridge to Tripoli	S	Levalloisian
27	Beirut[40]	10	Minet el-Hosn	S	Mousterian
28	Ras Beirut[41]	8-52	Raised beaches at 15,40/45 and 50/52 m. near the "Grotte aux Pigeons"	E and S	Lower Levalloisian-Acheulian
29	Beirut[42]	150	Furn el-Chebak	S	Chelleo-Acheulian
29	Beirut[43]	75	Nar Elias	S	Mesolithic
29	Beirut[44]	65	Mar Elias el-Tifeh	S	Levalloisian
30	Bir Hassan[45]	59	2.2 Km. S.S.E. of St. Elie; 5 Km. S. of Beirut	S	Acheulian
30	Borj el-Brajni[46]	70	Between Bir Hassan and Khalde radio station	S	Mousterian
31	Khan Khalde[47]	60	Km. 12 on Beirut-Haifa road	S	Paleolithic
32	Deir el-Ahmar[48]	1100	15 Km. N.N.W. of Baalbek	S	Paleolithic
33	Serain[49]	1000	6 Km. N.E. of Rayak	S	Mousterian
34	Mejdel Anjar[50]	1000	14 Km. S.S.E. of Zahle; 400 meters N.W. of Mejdel Anjar	S	Acheulian
35	Dakoue[51]	1000	16 Km. S.E. of Zahle	S	Acheulian
36	Kafer Aya[52]	1000	25 Km. S.S.W. of Zahle	S	Levalloisian
37	Qaraoun[53]	900	35 Km. S.S.W. of Zahle; 9 Km. N.W. of Rachaya	S	Acheulian
38	Saida[54]	50	Near church	S	Acheulian
39	Kafer Hattor[55]	250	5 Km. S.E. of Saida	S	Acheulian
40	Kafer Melki[56]	400	8 Km. E. of Saida	S	Levalloisian
41	Jezzine[57]	1000	20 Km. E. of Saida	S	Levalloiso-Acheulian
42	Akbie[58]	50	Km. 12 on Saida-Haifa road; N.E. of Ain el-Kantara	S	Acheulian
43	Aldoun[59]	50	Km. 17 on Saida-Haifa road; cave east of road	E	Acheulian
44	Tell Habouche[60]	400	Km. 25 on Saida-Merjayoun road	S	Acheulian
45	Nabatiye[61]	500	Km. 28 on Saida-Merjayoun road	S	Acheulian
46	Jbaa[62]	500	14 Km. N.W. of Merjayoun	S	Acheulian
47	Khalet el-Hamra[63]	800	30 Km. E. of Nakoura; between Bent Jubail and Ain Ebel	S	Lower Paleolithic
48	Ain Ebel[64]	500-1000	28 Km. E. of Nakoura; 3 Km. S.W. of Bent Jubail	S	Acheulo-Levalloisian
49	Tibnin[65]	800	Km. 18 Sour-Bent Jubail road	S	Acheulian
50	Wadi Abou Chahine[66]	?	Sidoun-Sour region (not determined)	S	?

Crania[67]

Vallois (1937) described a series of 17 skulls from the Aeneolithic (fourth-third millennia B.C.) cemetery at Byblos.[68] Among these, eight were dolichocephalic and two mesocephalic; seven were deformed, but originally of the same Mediterranean type. Kappers mentioned a thirteenth century mesocephalic skull from Byblos.

From Phoenician and Greek sarcophagi, attributed to the fifth and fourth centuries, Chantre (1894) and Kappers recorded 2 dolichocephals, 14 mesocephals, and 7 brachycephals (80.0 and 84.0 - 87.0). Among the Phoenicians the skull of King Tabnit was mesocephalic, that of his wife brachycephalic. Kappers and Seligman wrote that second to fourth century tombs at Palmyra yielded 4 dolichocephals and 3 mesocephals.

Modern Man[69]

The most significant factor in dividing the inhabitants of Lebanon is religious because they are predominantly Christian, an unique circumstance among the Arab States. As a direct result and because of Western contacts by sea, Lebanon has modernized rapidly.

Shanklin has measured 451 Lebanese composed of 149 Bekaa villagers from the plain and 302 Mitwali mountaineers, who are Shias. These two groups (see Table 14) are similar with the following ranges (the Bekaa villagers first): stature (165.42 - 166.96); head length (177.72 - 176.04); head breadth (150.64-152.82); cephalic index (86.90 - 87.38).

The mean cephalic index is given by Coon (p. 623) as 86.0. In both groups the forehead was narrow, the face medium wide, the upper facial heights long, and the nose short and narrow.

Coon (pp. 623-24) described the Lebanese as of a little more than moderate European stature (167.0); their bodily proportions are medium but they are thicker than the Beduins and incline to corpulence. Still quoting Shanklin's data, Coon writes that most of the Lebanese have brunet-white unexposed skin color, although in about 20.0 per cent the skin is as light as that of northern Europeans. Half of them possess black hair, the remainder dark brown. About 80.0 per cent have dark brown eyes but there is a green brown element. About 5.0 per cent have either blue or nearly pure blue eyes.

The hair is wavy, of fine texture and often heavy on the beard and body. The nose is convex (53.0 per cent) with rarely compressed wings. Occipital flattening is often present. The Lebanese are Mediterraneans mixed with roundheaded Alpines.

Summary

Lebanon has been occupied since Lower Paleolithic times. This coastal territory with its superb geographical location and natural caves overlooking the Mediterranean was an obvious home of Prehistoric Man and his descendants.

Along the Mediterranean littoral have migrated wave after wave of ancient peoples. In early historic times the Canaanites, called Phoenicians by the Greeks, became the first international traders.

Since the seaports have attracted seamen and merchants from all over the world, the racial medley, especially in Beirut, is almost complete. However, the mountains retain some important racial elements. In general, the Lebanese are Mediterraneans with Alpine admixture, for the majority are roundheaded.

Anthropometric data on some of the isolated groups would be of value.

References

Bergy, A.
    1932. Le Paléolithique ancien stratifié à Ras Beirut. MUSJ, Vol. 16, p. 169 et
        seq.
Braidwood, Robert J. and Braidwood, Linda
    1953. The earliest village communities of Southwestern Asia. JWH, Vol. 1, pp.
        278-310.
Burkhalter, L.
    1949a. Bibliographie préhistorique. BMB, Vol. 8, pp. 129-53.
    1949b. Inventaire des stations préhistoriques du Proche-Orient. BSPF, Vol. 46,
        pp. 363-65.
Chantre, E.
    1894. Crânes de la nécropole de Sidon. BSAL, Vol. 13, p. 12.
Combier, Charles
    1945. Aperçu sur les climats de la Syrie et du Liban. Beirut.
Cooke, Hedley, V.
    1952. Challenge and response in the Middle East. New York.
Coon, Carleton S.
    1948. The races of Europe. New York.
Day, Alfred E.
    1930. Geology of Lebanon. Beirut.
Delcourt, L.
    1927. Observations sur l'abri de Ksar Akil. BSPF, Vol. 24, p. 56 et seq.
De Vaumas, Etienne
    1947. Les terrasses d'abrasion marine de la côte libanaise. BSRGE, Vol. 22,
        pp. 21-85.
    1949a. Sur la structure de la Galilée libanaise et de la dépression du Houlé.
        CRAS, Vol. 229, pp. 943-46.
    1949b. Sur la surface d'érosion polycylique du Liban. CRAS, Vol. 228, pp. 257-
        59.
    1953. La répartition de la population au Liban. BSGE, Vol. 26, pp. 5-75.
Dubertret, Louis
    1945-46. Géologie du cité de Beyrouth. Avec carte géologique au 1:20,000. DGFL,
        Section Géologique.
    1946a. Géologie et morphologie de Beyrouth (Liban). CRAS, Vol. 222, pp. 1008-
        1009.
    1946b. Sur le Quaternaire côtier libanais et les oscillations du niveau de la mer
        au Quaternaire. CRAS, Vol. 223, pp. 431-32.
    1949a. Carte géologique au 50,000^e. Feuille de Saida. RLMTP.
    1949b. Carte géologique au 200,000^e. Feuille de Tripoli. RLMTP.
Ewing, J. Franklin
    1947a. Egbert revisited. America, Vol. 77, pp. 263-65.
    1947b. La vie de l'homme préhistorique à la lumière des fouilles de Ksar Aqil
        près d'Antélias (Liban). In Arabic. Al-Machriq, Vol. 41, no. 2, pp. 218-43.
    1947c. Preliminary note on the excavations at the Paleolithic site of Ksar Akil,
        Republic of Lebanon. Antiquity, Vol. 21, pp. 186-96.
    1948. Ksar Akil in 1948. Biblica, Vol. 29, pp. 272-78. Rome.
    1949. The treasures of Ksar Akil. TFUQ, Vol. 24, no. 93, pp. 255-88.
    1955. Ksar Akil, a Paleolithic site in Lebanon. BPAS, Vol. 9, no. 1, pp. 6-7.
Field, Henry
    1951. Reconnaissance in Southwestern Asia. SJA, Vol. 7, no. 1, pp. 86-102.
    1953-56. Bibliography on Southwestern Asia: I-III. UM.

Fish, W.B.
  1944. The Lebanon. GR, Vol. 34, pp. 235-58.
Fleisch, Henri
  1946a. Découverte d'une industrie à éclats du niveau de 45 m. à Râs-Beyrouth (Liban) et la position relative du Levalloisien. CRAS, Vol. 223, pp. 249-51.
  1946b. Levalloisien du niveau +15 mètres à Râs-Beyrouth (Liban). BSPF, Vol. 43, pp. 7-9.
  1946c. Position de l'Acheuléen à Râs-Beyrouth (Liban). BSPF, Vol. 43, pp. 1-7.
  1949. Anciens depôts de plage à Râs-Beyrouth. L'Anthropologie, Vol. 53, pp. 154-55.
  1950. Un ancien rivage -50 m. à Râs-Beyrouth. SGF, no. 15, pp. 275-77.
  1954. Nouvelles stations préhistoriques au Liban. BSPF, Vol. 51, nos. 11-12, pp. 564-68.
  1955. Le rhinocéros de Merck dans la grotte levalloiso-moustérienne de Ras el-Kelb. L'Anthropologie, Vol. 59, nos. 1-2, pp. 169-70.
Frass, O.
  1878. Geologie aus dem Libanon. JNK, Vol. 34, pp. 257-391.
Fritsch, K.
  1893. Die Funde des Herrn Pater Gottfried Zumoffen in den Höhlen am Fusse des Libanon. ANGH, Vol. 19, pt. 1, pp. 1-41.
Haller, Jean
  1943. Notes de préhistoire phénicienne: l'abri de Abou-Halka (Tripolie). BMB, Vol. 6, pp. 1-20.
Haller, Jean and Wetzel, René
  1940. Notes de préhistoire phénicienne: la carrière d'argile de la Société des Ciments Libanais à Chekka (Liban). BMB, Vol. 4, pp. 55-67.
  1941. Notes de préhistoire phénicienne: le gisement levalloisien d'Amrit. BMB, Vol. 5, pp. 31-33.
  1945. Aperçu sur la préhistoire de la Syrie et du Liban en 1945. DGFL, Notes et Mémoires, Vol. 4, pp. 49-58.
Hitti, Philip K.
  1951. History of Syria including Lebanon and Palestine. New York.
  1953. Lebanon. EA, pp. 169-71.
Hourani, A.K.
  1946. Syria and Lebanon. Oxford.
Kappers, C.U. Ariens
  1934. An introduction to the anthropology of the Near East. Amsterdam.
Keller, A.
  1934. Le Miocène du Liban. NMHCF, Vol. 1, pp. 155-72.
Pervès, Maurice
  1946-48. La préhistoire de la Syrie et du Liban. RS, Vol. 25, nos. 1-2, pp. 109-29.
Sauter, Marc.-R.
  1945. Les races brachycéphales du Proche-Orient des origines à nos jours. ASAG, Vol. 11, pp. 68-131. See Bibliography, pp. 119-31.
Seligman, C.G.
  1917. The physical characters of the Arabs. JRAI, Vol. 47, pp. 214-37.
Vaufrey, Raymond
  1949. Les fouilles américaines de Ksar Akil (Liban). L'Anthropologie, Vol. 53, pp. 340-41.
Warriner, Doreen
  1948. Land and poverty in the Middle East. New York.

Wetzel, René and Dubertret, L.
    1951. Carte géologique au 50,000ᵉ. Feuille de Tripoli. SGFF.
Wetzel, René and Haller, Jean
    1944. Sur le Quaternaire côtier de la region de Tripoli (Liban). EFI, no. 6, pp. 34-49.
    1945. Le Quaternaire de la région de Tripoli. DGFL, Section Géologique, Notes et Mémoires, Vol. 4, pp. 1-48. See Bibliography.
Wright, H.E., Jr.
    1951. Geologic setting of Ksar Akil, a Paleolithic site in Lebanon; preliminary report. JNES, Vol. 10, pp. 115-19.
Zumoffen, G.
    1926. Géologie du Liban. Paris.

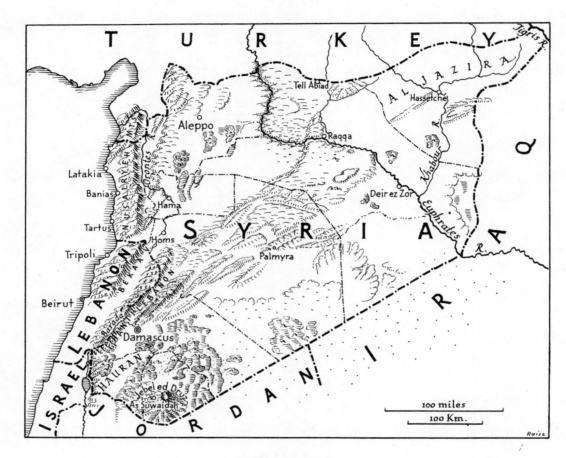

Syria by Erwin Raisz

VI. SYRIA

In Roman times Syria[1] extended from the Mediterranean to the Euphrates and from Sinai to southern Turkey. Prior to 1918 Syria included modern Syria, Lebanon, Israel, and Jordan. Today the northern frontier with Turkey is delimited by the single-track railway. To the east and southeast lies Iraq. The southern boundary marches with Jordan and Israel. The western boundary is divided into a northern area bordering on the Mediterranean and the southern section, which is the Lebanon. Syria consists of two principal zones: a narrow mountainous strip, the eastern part of the Anti-Lebanon Mountains; and the open wilderness sloping eastward and cut diagonally by the Euphrates Valley. To the southwest rises Jebel Druze, an area formed by broken volcanic sheets and cones. The geology[2] is of especial interest.

The climate[3] of the narrow littoral belt is temperate, but the eastern wilderness shows considerable range with hot summers and cold winters with frequent night frosts. Rainfall of 30-40 inches occurs in the west, but the greater part of Syria has less than 10 inches of annual precipitation. Thus, the littoral, or ancient Phoenicia, and the small deltas, such as Latakia (Laodicea), are the only highly productive areas without irrigation.

In Syria meet the Mediterranean and western Asiatic steppe flora. Syria is an agricultural country with only one-third urban-dwellers. Cereals, olive-oil, tobacco and wool are exported. In 1946 only 284,000 hectares were under irrigation.

Wild animals[4] include the isabelline bear, hyena, fox, jackal, gazelle, badger, pole-cat, ermine, roe, deer, fallow deer, Syrian squirrel, pouched marmoset and gerbil. Wolves and leopards are now very rare. The oryx, ostrich and lion are extinct. Two snow leopards were shot in 1950 east of Station T-2. Snakes, lizards, and scorpions are common in southern Syria. The commonest birds[5] are the eagle, vulture, turkey bustard, owl, partridge, sand grouse, and lark. In addition to the geological agents, the sheep and goats increase erosion by cropping young vegetation on hillsides. According to Hitti (1951, pp. 52-53) the first known reference to the camel in literature is given in the Bible (Judges VI:5) where the Midianite invasion of Palestine during the eleventh century B.C. is described. The earliest known drawings of the camel were found on Jebel al-Tubaiq in southeastern Jordan by George and Agnes Horsfield and were published in detail by Rhotert. These pictographs represent the small one-humped Arabian camel.

The fat-tailed sheep, referred to in the Bible (Exodus XXIX:22 and Lev. III:9), was introduced from Central Asia.

History.[6] Waves of immigration have swept into Syria for many millennia: the Canaanites and Phoenicians in the third millennium B.C., the Hebrews and Arameans in the second, and for many centuries Beduins from Arabia. The Egyptians, Assyrians and Hittites invaded Syria before the Roman conquest during the first century B.C. Later came the Persians and Macedonian Greeks. The kingdom of Palmyra was destroyed by Aurelian in A.D. 272.

Special attention is called to northwestern Syria,[7] which was one of the cultural links of the ancient world.

In 1922 the population was given as 1,198,829, excluding Jebel Druze (Jebel ed-Druz) with 50,328 inhabitants.

The area of the modern Republic of Syria in 1953 was estimated[8] at 66,000 square miles. The population[9] in 1950 was given as 3,228,000 including 288,400 Beduins. The number of inhabitants of the principal cities in 1950 was: Aleppo, 339,000; Damascus, 303,000; Homs, 106,000; and Hama, 75,000.

In addition to the Sunnis, there are many religious minorities: Moslem Shias in Salamiya, whose spiritual leader is the Aga Khan; the Druze; the Nusairis or Alouites (Alawites) of Jebel Ansarieh; and many Christian sects. The health[10] of the population is summarized in GE, 1954, pp. 145-57.

There are numerous development possibilities[11] in Syria.

Ancient Man[12]

Paleolithic Man lived in Syria, although as yet no stratified deposit containing human remains and a cultural sequence has been found.

The most probable localities for caves or rockshelters would be on the flanks of the Anti-Lebanon, deep in the Jebel Druze, or on Jebel Abdul Aziz west of Hassetché (Hasseké) in the Jazira.

The following sites have yielded specimens now in the Musée de l'Homme in Paris where I examined[13] them in 1950:

1. Levalloiso-Mousterian at Abou Afsa and Ain Arus (Arouss) near the source of the Balik River, 70 kilometers east of the Euphrates and 6 kilometers south of the Turkish border.

2. Upper Paleolithic at Palmyra (anc. Tadmor).

3. Miscellaneous cultures including: (a) obsidian implements from Tell Abiad near Raqqa; (b) Madamié south of Damascus; (c) Koneitra and Catana southwest of Damascus; (d) Mezzé, Hameh, and Plage de es-Saa near Damascus; (e) Moumbata, Tarryé, Sasnyé, Hama, Kalaat Yahmour, Slenfé, 50 kilometers east of Latakia and near Deir ez-Zor; and (f) Bac de Soussa near Abu Kemal on the right bank of the Euphrates.

During the Peabody Museum Expedition[14] to the Near East, 1950, I found flint implements at the following surface sites:

(a) Rejim Rouhaibé on Damascus-Palmyra road

(b) Tell el-Wusta (75 feet) between Airoud and Aatné

(c) Near Iraq Petroleum Company's Telegraph Pole 335/9

(d) Mile 13 east of T-3 toward T-2

(e) Mile 20 east of T-3

(f) Mile 22.7 east of T-3

(g) Mile 37.5 east of T-3

(h) 3 miles northeast of T-2, including a delicately flaked spearpoint

(i) Mile 20 from north of T-2 toward Deir-ez-Zor

(j) Mile 31.3 north of T-2

(k) Mile 32.0 south of Deir-ez-Zor toward T-2

(l) Two mounds 6 and 10 miles from Hassetché toward Jebel Abdul Aziz

(m) Tell Mejdal (100 feet) with flints and one microlithic obsidian nucleus

(n) Mile 15.0 above Wadi Swaab

(o) Mile 35.0 from T-2 on 50 foot escarpment drained by Wadi Rutga

(p) At the point where the track from T-2 to Abu Kemal climbs onto a plateau with the Wadi Rutga on the right, a fine series of flint implements, including a handaxe, many large nuclei, choppers, scrapers, and blades. Within a 5-acre area on this bluff overlooking the now dry Wadi Rutga the Paleolithic flintknappers must have sat. This is one of the richest sites in Southwestern Asia. The quality and deeply patinated condition of the flint is reminiscent of that from the Rutba area in western Iraq, Jebel Thlathakhwat in southeastern Jordan, and Tell el-Hibr in northwestern Saudi Arabia.

The wide range of distribution of surface flint implements from Koneitra to the Khabur and from Ain Arus to Abu Kemal prove that man in various Paleolithic, Mesolithic, and Neolithic cultural phases dwelt in Syria.

Crania[15]

Fifteen skulls from Ras Shamra,[16] attributed to the nineteenth-sixteenth century, were described by Vallois as mesocephalic. A fourteenth century skull was of Armenoid brachycephalic type.

In 1873 Langerhaus[17] measured six skulls of the Beni Adwan and Beni Sakhr tribesmen: these proved to be five dolichocephals and one mesobrachycephal.

Kappers recorded the cephalic index of a Hauran Beduin skull as 73.4.

Modern Man

In addition to the urban-dwellers, the Beduins form a minority element, but their territory extends from the juncture between the sown and the desert all the way north to the Turkish border and eastward to the common frontier with Iraq.

The townspeople show many racial elements, ranging from the true Mediterranean to blond Nordic-like group, probably the Circassian traces resulting from Caucasian invasions. There are many Mediterranean admixtures from the gracile to the coarse types and a certain degree of Negro blood introduced through the Beduin tent-dwellers.

There are some excellent publications[18] on the Beduins of Syria.

In the "Supplement to Report of the Peabody Museum-Harvard Expedition to the Near East, 1950" I have placed on Microfilm No. 3956, pp. 1-161, in ADI the following lists:[19]

1. Non-Tribal persons (pp. 1-52).
2. Tribesmen with the names of tribe, sub-tribe, and section (pp. 53-92).
3. Villages including location, population, religion, Mukhtar, notables, landowners, water resources, Government (or other) institutions, and notes (pp. 93-160).

Shanklin measured 1,598 Syrians divided into five groups of 1,032 villagers and three series of 566 Beduins (see Table 15).

The stature of the former ranges from 163.08-168.02. However, the Beduins show a wide range from 161.89-170.12, the latter figure being unusually high for a Beduin group. In head length the villagers range from 178.74-184.38, but the Beduins are more consistently longer-headed, range 190.42-191.68. In breadth there is more uniformity in both groups: the villagers ranging from 142.54-148.50; and the Beduins 143.63-147.06. The forehead is medium broad except for the narrow Hidjaneh villagers (103.46) and Ruwalla (Rwala) Beduins (103.78). The face is medium wide except for the Hidjaneh and Rwala. In both series the bigonial breadth is narrow, the face long, the nose short and narrow. The Hama villagers are brachycephalic (83.24), the remainder being mesocephalic (range 75.00-79.81).

The Beduins are the closest to the basic Mediterranean type; the villagers show some admixtures.

A fine series of blood groups has been recorded with the majority in the O category (see Boyd, pp. 180-81 and 234-35).

Some unpublished data[20] on 38 Syrian Beduins[21] may be included here.

While in Beirut on March 30, 1934, I visited some Beduin tents, which were pitched on the edge of the market place within a few hundred paces of the river. The Sheikh stated that they belonged to the same Beduin stock as those who lived at de Kouani above Beirut. After some difficulty, permission to measure and photograph the men (Nos. 1594-1599 and 1616-1630) was obtained from the Sheikh, who offered himself, somewhat unwillingly, as the first subject. These Beduins were born in various localities in northeastern Syria, on the border of the Syrian Desert, but they did not appear to owe allegiance to any great desert chieftain, such as the late Nuri ibn Shaalan, Paramount Sheikh of the Ruwalla tribe.

During the same afternoon I visited a large Beduin encampment at de Kouani near Beirut. It was strange to see Beduins living on the wooded slopes of the Lebanon foothills amid plenty of verdure and water. In the winter they wander down from northern Syria and return to near Homs during the summer months.

Provenance. Nos. 1594, 1595, 1616, and 1628-1630 were from Beirut; Nos. 1596-1611, and 1620-1622 from Homs; Nos. 1614, 1619, and 1626 from Damascus; Nos. 1612 and 1623 from the Lebanon; No. 1615 from near Samaria; Nos. 1613 and 1625 from near Sidon; No. 1617 from Rakka; No. 1624 from Hama; and No. 1627 from Tripoli. Nos. 1594-1615 were examined near de Kouani above Beirut. Nos. 1616-1630 were examined in Beirut market place.

Age. (See Table 16). The mean age was 37.41, range 18-70.

Vital Statistics. (See Table 17). Unreliable as these figures must be, there was an equal number of sons and daughters and the size of the families appears to be small. Every Beduin examined at de Kouani was married with the exception of seven men. No. 1596 boasted four wives. It is customary among Beduins and Arabs not to refer to deceased sons or daughters and to treat them rather as though they had never existed. Thus, despite my questioning on the subject of vital statistics, there was not a single admission of infant mortality, which always runs high among these groups. The figures, therefore, indicate the number of children living in each family with no reference to deceased children.

In the group observed in the Beirut market place 11 individuals were unmarried. No. 1619 had been married six months, No. 1618 only four months and No. 1620 had three boys and two girls living and No. 1623, two boys and one girl living.

Morphological Characters of Syrian Beduins

Skin. The color was dark olive brown, tanned by exposure to the elements. It was similar to that of the Beduins of the North Arabian or Syrian Desert but No. 1626 had a particularly dark skin although he exhibited no traces of Negro blood.

Hair. (See Table 18). The hair color was dark brown in every case with the exception of Nos. 1618 and 1628 who had gray hair as a result of age. No. 1630 had extremely dark hair which was almost black in color. There was no trace of submerged blondism.

Eyes. (See Table 19). The eye color was dark brown with the exception of No. 1626 who appeared to have blue-brown eyes. No. 1628 (aged 70) had very bad eyes which were light blue in color.

Teeth. (See Table 20). The average condition of the teeth[22] was good with but two exceptions. The upper and lower incisors of No. 1630 were widely spaced.

Musculature. Three men were recorded as having good musculature; one was in the excellent category.

Health. Eight men were in good health,[23] one in fair, and No. 1627 in poor condition from apparent undernourishment.

Tattooing.[24] (See Table 21). The majority (63.16 per cent) were tattooed extensively and only one man bore no tattooed marks.

Eighteen out of the 23 Beduins examined in Beirut bore tattooed marks, some of which were relatively complex in character and in design. No. 1610 had three spots arranged in an equilateral triangle on the left temple near the eye; Nos. 1597-1602, 1606-1608, and 1613 on back of right hand; Nos. 1594, 1605, and 1612 on back of left hand; No. 1595 a small circle above three spots on each temple, also two spots on each side of the nasal bridge at eye level; No. 1602 a circle surrounded by seven spots on each temple; No. 1596 spot on the nasal tip; No. 1615 a single spot on the thumb and on the fourth finger, also special design like six-toothed comb (Misht) on each wrist; and No. 1612 single spot on each temple. Nos. 1603, 1604, 1609, 1611, and 1614 bore no tattooed marks.

In the group examined at de Kouani six men were tattooed: No. 1622 on the back of the right hand "purely for decoration"; No. 1624 spot on the nasal tip and a straight line on the left hand; No. 1623 on the right hand; No. 1626 spot on the nasal tip and on the center of the right cheek; No. 1617 a single spot on the nasal tip, on the chin and on the right cheek "as identification marks"; and No. 1629 a fish on the right hand as a "tribal mark." This last is a most important statement because of the possibility that this may be a trace of ancient totemistic[25] survival.

Henna. Henna was used by three individuals; No. 1622 on the palms of the hands "to celebrate a feast"; No. 1620 on hands and feet "to make them beautiful"; and No. 1617 on nails "for decoration." No. 1607 had henna on both palms of the hands; otherwise this custom was not observed except among the older women.

Measurements and Indices

This small Beduin series consists of 37 males of adult age; the males range from 17-70 years.

While the few recorded observations on pigmentation of hair and eyes, in addition to the general impression obtained, indicate a relatively homogeneous group, it must be stated that these Beduins, who dwell on the western fringe of the North Arabian or Syrian Desert, are undoubtedly less homogeneous than the true nomads of the interior.

Examination of the measurements, averages, indices and graphs reveals the fact that this group of 37 Beduins conform in general to series obtained by other anthropologists, mainly Shanklin and Kappers. The cephalic indices indicate that the majority of individuals are as follows: dolichocephalic 26; mesocephalic 9; and brachycephalic 2. The average was 73.0 per cent and appears on the low side compared to the 103 Syrian Beduins recorded by Kappers,[26] whose average cephalic index is 77.2 (±0.97) with a variation spread of 3.24. In view, however, of the small number of individuals in my two groups this is not surprising. Seligman (pp. 214-37) states that the Beduin tribes of North Arabia, including the Syrian Desert, are the modern relatives of the Palmyrenes and Phoenicians, who lived at the beginning of the Christian Era.

There are 21 individuals in the age group from 19 - 35 while only eight men were more than 50 years of age.

The statistics are given in Table 22. In practical anthropology there are always certain difficulties and not only can the younger members of the group be ordered by the tribal elders, but they are more ready to submit to measurement especially when accompanied by a small financial reward. The result is that the majority of individuals recorded belonged to the younger age groups, although in a large series I have tried to obtain a wide range of ages to get a more reliable mean.

While the graphs of the cephalic indices revealed three peaks at 69.0, 73.0, and 76.0, this is undoubtedly due to the paucity of examples; but it is worth noting that among the 37 individuals there is a very wide range of variation from 68.1 - 82.4.

Shanklin recorded a single peak at 76 - 76.9 for 791 Transjordan tribesmen and villagers. The Howeitat (Huwaitat) main peak was at 73 - 73.9 and that of 136 Egyptians of the Kena and Girga districts about 73.0. These averages show that while the Beduins measured by the writer belong to the northern "desert border population," they do not fit in with the people living along the western border of the Syrian Desert whose average cephalic indices range from 80 - 80.9.

The Beduins of the Syrian Desert are Mediterranean dolichocephals with some admixtures from town-dwellers such as those in Damascus, Homs, Hama, Aleppo, Deir-ez-Zor, Hassetché (Hasseké) and Ras-al-Ain on the Turkish border.

The Druze,[27] who inhabit the isolated Jebel Druze, are brachycephalic with dark brown hair and eyes and heavy beards and considerable body hair. They form one of the main roundheaded groups in Southwestern Asia and for this reason the brachy-cephalic Bakhtiari tribesmen (see under Iran) in Khuzistan were once suggested to be their close relatives.

Summary

Middle and Upper Paleolithic implements prove the presence of Prehistoric Man in Syria, but no stratified deposit shows the earliest cultural relationships with the inhabitants of Anatolia, Kurdistan, the Iranian Plateau, Israel, and the Arabian Peninsula.

The Beduins belong to the Mediterranean race with slight Negroid admixture. On the western fringe of the wilderness or steppe, known as the Syrian Desert, these Beduins are naturally less pure because of easy access to Damascus, Homs, Hama, and Aleppo.

The Druze are a roundheaded group living in the Jebel Druze.

Certain series of anthropometric data are most desirable: villagers along the Syrian-Turkish border; Chechens at Ras-al-Ain; and several groups of Beduins from the Jazira such as the Shammar and the Baqqarah (pron. Baggara).

References

Ashkenazi, Touvia
  1948. The Anazah tribes. SJA, Vol. 4, no. 2, pp. 222-39.
Blankenhorn, Max
  1914. Handbuch der regionalen Geologie, Vol. 4, pt. 4, Syrien und Mesopotamien.
    Heidelberg.
Boyd, William C.
  1939. Blood groups. TB, Vol. 17, pt. 2, pp. 113-240. See Bibliography, pp.
    236-40.
Braidwood, Robert J.
  1940. Test diggings in Syria. Asia, Vol. 40, pp. 47-52.
  1952. The Near East and the foundations for civilization. Condon Lectures. Ore-
    gon State System of Higher Education, Eugene, Oregon.
Braidwood, Robert J. and Braidwood, Linda
  1953. The earliest village communities of Southwestern Asia. JWH, Vol. 1, pp.
    278-310.
Charles, R.P.
  1939. Tribus moutonnières du Moyen-Euphrates. DEO, Beyrouth (Beirut).
Clawson, M. Don
  1938. Prevention and treatment of chronic endemic dental fluorosis (mottled
    enamel). TADS, pp. 7-11.
Clawson, M. Don and Perks, A.J.
  1938. New endemic areas reported from Western Asia (3 Iraq, 2 Jordan, 2
    Syria, 1 Bahrain, 2 Trucial Oman Coast and 1 Palestine). TADS, pp. 11-15.
    See Bibliography.
Cooke, Hedley V.
  1952. Challenge and response in the Middle East. New York.
De Boucheman, A.
  1934. Note sur la rivalité de deux tribus moutonnières de Syrie: les Mawali et
    les Hadidiyn. REI.
  1935. Matériel de la vie bédouine. DEO, Beyrouth (Beirut).
  1939. Une petite cité carvanière: Soukhné. BEO, Beyrouth (Beirut).
De Vaumas, Etienne
  1946. Sur les terrasses d'abrasion marine de la région de Lattaquié (Syrie).
    CRAS, Vol. 223, p. 150.
  1953. Sur les terrasses d'abrasion marine des régions de Djeblé et de Tartous
    (Syrie). CRAS, Vol. 237, pp. 1343-44.
Dubertret, Louis, et al.
  1933. Contributions à l'étude géologique de la Syrie septentionale. Paris.
  1949. Carte géologique, au 50,000e. Feuille de Zebdani. RSMTP.
Ewing, J. Franklin
  1946. Aurignacian man in Syria. AJPA, Vol. 4, pp. 252-53.
Field, Henry
  1947a. Contributions to the Anthropology of Syria. ADIM 3956, pp. 1-161.
  1947b. Anthropometry of 38 Syrian Beduins. ADIM 2417, pp. 1-71.
  1951. Reconnaissance in Southwestern Asia. SJA, Vol. 7, pp. 86-102.
  1955. A Reconnaissance in the Near East, 1950. PMP, Vol. 48, pp. 5-10.
  1953-56. Bibliography on Southwestern Asia: I-III. UM.
Fohs, F. Julius
  1946. Development and land settlement potentialities of Syria and Iraq. Houston.
Harden, D.B.
  1949. Tomb-groups of glass of Roman date from Syria and Palestine. Iraq, Vol.
    11, pt. 2, pp. 151-59.

Haut-Commissariat de la République Française
  1930. Les tribus nomades et semi-nomades des Etats du Levant placés sous
    Mandat français. Service des Renseignements du Levant. Beyrouth (Beirut).
Hitti, Philip K.
  1951. History of Syria including Lebanon and Palestine. London.
Huxley, Henry M.
  1902a. Preliminary report of an anthropological expedition to Syria. AA, Vol. 4,
    no. 1, pp. 47-51. New York.
  1902b. Syrian songs, proverbs and stories. JAOS, Vol. 23, pp. 175-288. New
    Haven.
  1915. The Samaritans: Anthropology. JE, Vol. 10, pp. 675-76.
  1955. International Bank for Reconstruction and Development. The Economic Develop-
    ment of Syria. Baltimore.
Issawi, Charles and Dabezies, Carlos
  1951. Population movements and population pressure in Jordan, Lebanon, and
    Syria. MMFQ, Vol. 29, pp. 385-403.
Izzeddin, Nejla
  1934. On the anthropology of the Druzes. CIAES-I, pp. 131-32. See Shanklin, W.M.
Kappers, C.U. Ariens
  1930. Contributions to the anthropology of the Near East. Proceedings, KAWA,
    Vol. 1. Amsterdam.
Khalifah, E.S.
  1938. Chronic endemic dental fluorosis (mottled enamel). TADS, pp. 1-6.
Krogman, Wilton M.
  1949. Ancient cranial types at Chatal Hüyük and Tell Al-Judaidah, Syria, from
    the late fifth millennium B.C. to the mid-seventeenth century A.D. TTKB,
    Vol. 13, pp. 407-77.
Langerhaus, P.
  1873. Ueber die heutigen Bewohner des heiligen Landes. AAB, Vol. 6.
Mackay, Dorothy
  1949. The jewelry of Palmyra and its significance. Iraq, Vol. 11, pt. 2, pp. 160-
    87. See Bibliography pp. 186-87.
Mallowan, M.E.L.
  1947. Excavations at Brak and Chagar Bazar. Iraq, Vol. 9, pt. 2, pp. 89-259.
    1947.
McEwan, C.W.
  1937. The Syrian Expedition of the Oriental Institute of the University of Chicago.
    AJA, Vol. 41, no. 1, pp. 7-16.
Montagne, Robert
  1947. La civilization du désert. Paris.
Muller, V.
  1936. En Syrie avec les Bédouins. Paris.
Nasrallah, Joseph
  1950. A carding comb from the Chalcolithic of Syria. Man, Vol. 50, pp. 28-30.
Nehring, A.
  1890. Ueber Spalax fritschi aus der Antelias Höhle am Libanon. SBGNF, pp. 77-
    85.
  1902. Ueber Mustela foina Syriaca n. sub. sp. und Mustela nalaesyriaca n. sp.
    SBGNF, pp. 146-47.
Perks, A.J., See Clawson, M. Don
Rialle, Girard de
  1866. Crânes syriens. BSA, Ser. 2, Vol. 1, pp. 563-72.

Rust, A.

1933. Beitrag zur Erkenntnis der Abwicklung der vorgeschichtlichen Kultur-
perioden in Syrien. PZ, Vol. 24, p. 205 et seq.

1950. Die Hohlenfunde von Jabrud (Syrien). VUSHM, n.s., Vol. 8.

Sauter, Marc-R.

1945. Les races brachycéphales du Proche-Orient des origines à nos jours.
ASAG, Vol. 11, pp. 68-131.

Seligman, C.G.

1917. The physical characters of the Arabs. JRAI, Vol. 47, pp. 214-37.

Seltzer, Carl C.

1936. The racial characteristics of Syrians and Armenians. PMP, Vol. 13, no.
13.

1940. Contributions to the racial anthropology of the Near East. PMP, Vol. 16,
no. 2, pp. 1-62.

Shanklin, William M.

1935a. The anthropology of the Rwala Beduins. JRAI, Vol. 65, pp. 375-90.

1935b. Blood groupings of the Rwala Bedouin. PSEBM, Vol. 32, pp. 754-55.

1936a. Blood groupings of the Maualy and Akeydat Bedouin. AJPA, Vol. 31,
pp. 39-48.

1936b. Anthropology of the Akeydat and Mitwaly Bedouin. AJPA, Vol. 31, pp.
217-52.

1936c. Blood groupings of the Rwala Bedouin. JI, Vol. 29, pp. 427-33.

1938. Anthropometry of Syrian males. JRAI, Vol. 68, pp. 379-414.

Shanklin, W.M. and Cummins, H.

1937. Dermatoglyphics in Rwala Bedouins. HB, Vol. 9, pp. 357-65.

Shanklin. W.M. and Izzeddin, Nejla

1937. Anthropology of the Near East female. AJPA, Vol. 22, pp. 381-415.

Snodgrasse, Richard M.

1945. Some comments upon recent Arabs from northwest Syria. CASB, Vol. 1,
p. 6.

Vernier, Bernard

1938. Qédar: carnets d'un Méhariste syrien. Paris.

Warriner, Doreen

1948. Land and poverty in the Middle East. New York.

Woolley, (Sir) Leonard

1942. North Syria as a cultural link in the ancient world. JRAI. Huxley Memorial
Lecture.

VII. TURKEY[1]

This country is bounded on the north by Greece, Bulgaria and the Black Sea, on the east by the Soviet Union and Iran, on the west by the Aegean and Mediterranean Seas, and on the south by Syria and Iraq.

Here we shall not be concerned primarily with Thrace or European Turkey, but rather with the large peninsula of Asia Minor,[2] two-thirds of which is surrounded by the waters of the Black, Aegean, and Mediterranean Seas.

Asia Minor or Anatolia consists of a ring of mountains enclosing a series of land plateaus. The eastern border is dominated by high mountains, the highest peak being Mount Ararat (16,915 feet). In the west the mountains are lower but the highest peak, Mount Eriyas (Argaeus) is more than 13,000 feet high. Large areas remain almost uninhabited because of wide sterile lava sheets. The climate[3] may be divided into three categories:

(a) Pontic with cold winters and humid summers, along the wooded coastal strip from the Troad to just west of Batumi; (b) Mediterranean from the Troad southward along the Ionian coast to Antalya and Mersin; and (c) Continental from Mamisa to Kars.

Rainfall ranges from 100 inches annually along the Black Sea coast to 10 inches on the central desert between Kutahya and Kaisarieh.

In Asia Minor, where rainfall is abundant, the mountains are covered with forests[4] of Quercus, Fagus, Ulmus, Acer, Carpinus and Corylus and some conifers. Along the northern coast grow apple, pear, cherry, and plum trees. In the sheltered southern valleys the orange, lemon, citron, sugar cane, and date palm flourish.

Turkey has become self-sufficient in foodstuffs as a result of the recent increase of cultivated areas. Cereals, mainly wheat and barley, are the main crops on the plateau. Tobacco was the important export crop until 1951; the Izmir district is the center. Cotton has led the export crops. Beet sugar, fruit and oil seeds are also grown in quantity.

Wild animals[5] include the bear, boar, chamois, deer (fallow, red, and roe), gazelle, hyena, ibex, jackal, leopard, lynx, moufflon, wild sheep, and wolf. Among domestic animals are the buffalo, Syrian camel and a mule camel bred from a Bactrian sire and a Syrian dam. Many sheep and Angora goats are raised on the central plateau; horses are bred on the Uzan Yaila; and small, hardy oxen are bred for transport and plowing.

The rivers and lakes are well stocked with fish.

The area of Thrace is 23,485 and that of Anatolia 743,634 square kilometers. According to the 1950 Census[6] the total population was 20,934,670 with the following number of urban-dwellers: Istanbul, 1,100,022; Ankara, 286,781; Izmir, formerly Smyrna, 230,508; Adana, formerly Seyhan, 117,799; Bursa, 100,007; and Eskisehir, 88,459. The Turkish people are Moslems, mainly Sunnis. The two per cent of non-Moslems include Greek Orthodox, Armenian Christians, and Jews who live in Istanbul.

The Turkish language, which is of Central Asiatic origin was introduced by the Seljuks. Kurdish (Kermanji) is spoken along the southern boundary marching with Syria and Iraq. French, German or English is spoken by most educated Turks.

History.[7] Assyrian texts, attributed to the second millennium B.C., reveal the existence of their trading colonies in Cappadocia. Later in this same period ruled

Turkey by Erwin Raisz

the Hittites at their capital city of Hattushash. This Empire flourished from circa 1600-1200 B.C. Iron was first worked in the Near East in Anatolia by the Hittites; this gave them an important monopoly. Then Asia Minor was split up into dynasties and peoples, among them the Phrygians, Cimmerians, and Lydians. There are three important dates: (a) the Persian conquest in 546 B.C.; (b) the conquest of Alexander in 334 B.C.; and (c) the constitution of the Roman province of Asia in 133 B.C.

Ancient Man[8]

We shall present the evidence in chronological sequence.

1894. J.E. Gauthier found an Acheulian handaxe at Birecik near Urfa.

1907. Arne found worked flints between Nisile and Djerablous.

1910. At Uzagil near Ankara, Campbell Thompson discovered Mousterian remains. He also collected Paleolithic implements at Soganlidere near Kayseri.

1927. At Pirun near Adiyaman, Eugène Pittard located an Aurignacian site.

1928. Pittard began the first Paleolithic survey by finding implements near Malatya.

1930. Hans Henning von der Osten found a good series at this same locality near Malatya.

1931. Levalloiso-Mousterian implements were collected by Kurt Bittel at Maltepe near Ankara.

1936. The Institute of Anthropology moved to Ankara and Shevket Aziz Kansu and his student and colleagues, Muine Atasayan, Inan Afet, Kilic Kökten, Muzaffer Senyürek and others, began their researches at that time.

During the past 20 years, the following chronology of the Stone Age cultures has been established.

Lower Paleolithic

Chellean. These surface finds include biface handaxes from: (a) Uzagil near Ankara by Campbell Thompson; (b) near Istanbul by Atasayan; and (d) at Dülük and Metmenge near Gaziantep by Kökten.

Chelleo-Acheulian. Kökten found a handaxe at Susuz outside Kars.

Acheulian. Handaxes have been found: (a) at Birecik near Urfa by Gautier; (b) in a riverbed near Antakaya by Mureddin Can; (c) at Tekeköy near Samsun by Kökten; (d) at Keysun and Adiyaman near Malatya by Kökten; and (e) at Dülük and Metmenge near Gaziantep by Kökten.

Upper Acheulian (Micoquian). At a depth of 1.30 meters under the sands of Altindere near Antakya, Mureddin Can collected two small handaxes. Kansu found Levalloiso-Mousterian implements at a depth of 3.10 meters in the terraces of Çubuksuyu near Ankara. Two small Micoquian handaxes were also found by Kökten: one at Güdül near Ankara; the other at Bozova near Urfa.

Clactonian. A tool of this type was collected on the surface at Dülük near Gaziantep by Atasayan.

Middle Paleolithic

Levalloiso-Mousterian. In Pleistocene terraces at Etiyokuşu near Ankara, Kansu found typical specimens. In other Pleistocene terraces near Ankara other flints of this period were found at the following localities: near Ergazi, Maltepe, Yüksek Ziraat Enstitüsü and Gazi Egitim Enstitüsü. Kansu also found Clactonian implements in central Anatolia at Gölköy near Kastamonu and at Gemerek near

Sivas. In this same region Halil Hasedemir found similar implements near Neveşehir and Nigde; Kökten found others in the Muratsuyu terraces near Elâzig, around Liz near Muş, and on the plain between Hilâr and Geyik near Diyarbekir.

<u>Mousterian</u>. At Adiyaman near Malatya, in the valleys of Tereköy near Samsun, and those at Borluk near Kars, Kansu obtained a large series of implements. In 1946 Kökten excavated Mousterian tools in Karain Cave at Yagçakoy near Antalya.

Upper Paleolithic

<u>Aurignacian</u>. This industry is as rich as the Levalloiso-Mousterian. Beside Pirun bridge at Adiyaman (Malatya), Pittard collected on the surface some implements of this type. In 1944 in a cave deposit at Bozanönü near Isparta, Kansu, Senyürek and Kökten found implements in a stratified deposit. No Upper Paleolithic cave art or statuettes have been found. However, some rock-engravings of wild mountain goats were recorded in 1938 at Adiyaman (Malatya) by Pittard, Koşay, and Kansu; those resemble Upper Paleolithic rock-engravings from North Africa and Spain.

In 1940 Kansu and Kökten began a regional survey of ancient sites worthy of soundings: Samsun (1940); Kars, Sivas, Baburt, Erbaa and Kelkit Valley to Samsun (1941-42); Samsun to Rize and Ankara (1943-44); and Antalya-Diyarbekir-Urfa-Gaziantep (1946). In these areas the caves, rockshelters, settlements, tumuli, mounds, towers, flint and obsidian quarries, rock monuments, and historical ruins have been mapped.

The Staff of the Institute of Anthropology, under the direction of Kansu, has compiled the following summary:

1. The Turkish Historical Society has located 10,000 natural and artificial caves; 512 were investigated, and trial trenches have been sunk in 20 caves.

2. No remains of fossil man have been unearthed. Bones of Quaternary fauna are not abundant.

3. The Neolithic is represented by: (a) a pressure-flaked lancepoint from near Sivas; (b) cromlechs from an island in Lake Çildir near Kars; and (c) dolmens and menhirs (?) at Ilica near Ankara. In the lower strata of Pilar mound in Lake Hafik small flints of Campingnian type were found associated with wooden platforms and piling.

4. Mesolithic, Chalcolithic and later periods are represented in the Samsun and Kars regions and along the river Aras.

5. Settlements have been mapped along natural lines of migration from Kars to the northwest, west, southeast, and south.

Summary

Anatolia has been inhabited since the Lower Paleolithic, but the correlations in chronology and techniques with Western Europe, the Caucasus and Southwestern Asia have not been determined. Hundreds of caves and rockshelters remain to be examined.

We can predict the discovery of <u>Homo anatoliensis</u> from a cave or rockshelter, but his physical type remains to be seen. Presumably, Neanderthal Man also lived in Anatolia for his skeletons and implements have already been found at Krapina to the northwest, on Mount Carmel to the south, in Shanidar Cave to the southeast, and at Teshik-Tash near Tashkent to the east.

The physical relationship of the Paleolithic hunters in Anatolia to those who dwelt beside the southern shore of the Caspian and to the ancient inhabitants of the caves near Khurrumabad in Luristan remains to be determined.

There has been a continuous occupation of Anatolia in Paleolithic, Neolithic, Mesolithic, Chalcolithic, Protohistoric, and historical times.

Crania[9]

Considerable work has been done on crania excavated in Anatolia. For this reason I have made a selection of the material to summarize here. The principal researches have been conducted by Kansu, Krogman, and Senyürek. Since Krogman's publications are easily available, I have concentrated on the Turkish publications by Kansu and Senyürek.

At the University of Ankara from 1935-52 Shevket Aziz Kansu and Muzaffer Suleyman Senyürek have studied many crania from the Hittite and later periods (see References).

1935. The first study by Kansu based on 375 Hittite crania, reveals a mean cephalic index of 84.07, range 76.19--98.70 (see Table 23) with more than one-third of the series hyperbrachycephalic.

Table 23 (Kansu, 1935a, pp. 106-107) shows that these 375 crania are leptorrhine (47.23 per cent) and hypsicephalic (77.65) indicating an Alpine type. There is no disharmony between the cranial and facial indices. The orbital index is mesoseme. The face is orthognathous. The cranial capacity is estimated at 1460.85 cubic centimeters.

Kansu (p. 106) comments that these brachycephals of true Alpine type, who lived on the plateaus of Anatolia, were the Turks of Anatolia with some infusion of Mongoloid blood.

1936-37. At Alishar Hüyük, from a level attributed to the third millennium B.C., 3 skeletons (2 males, 1 female) were excavated by members of the Turkish Historical Society. Kansu (1937a, p. 25) comments that these 3 fragmentary skeletons probably belonged to the Hittite or Proto-Hittite period. The crania are brachycephalic (82.12 and 83.43 for the males), spheroid and with no massing of bone at glabella. The mean stature, based on 2 humeri and 2 femora, was 159.0; if the left humerus of one male (No. 3) is omitted, the stature was 164.86.

1937. Afet summarizes Kansu's craniological data on 394 skulls from the Neolithic (1) to the Ottoman (375) periods (see Table 24) for comparison with Afet's series of 200 Turkish women.

1945. Sauter (pp. 76-102) summarizes the finds in Anatolia as follows:

1. Five skulls from the Aeneolithic site of Ahlatlibel near Ankara were one brachycephal (probably Alpine), two mesocephals and two dolichocephals. (See Kansu, 1939a).

2. At Kusura Winifred Lamb found 2 dolichocephals and one brachycephal (81.18) in a Chalcolithic stratum. (See Kansu and Atasayan.)

3. At Alaca Hüyük the Proto-Hittite level yielded two brachycephals (82.0 and 83.0), of Alpine type. (See Kansu, 1937a).

4. At nearby Alishar Hüyük 10 skulls were found: one dolichocephal from the Chalcolithic period (up to 3000 B.C.); three dolichocephals and four mesocephals of the Copper Age (3000-2500 B.C.); and one dolichocephal and one brachycephal (83.4) from the Early Bronze period (2500-2000 B.C.). Krogman classifies the roundhead as an Alpine. (See Krogman, 1937.)

5. At Hissarlik (City II, circa 2500 B.C.), Virchow in 1882 found a female brachycephal (82.5).

6. At nearby Kum-Tepe in a Neolithic (or possibly Chalcolithic) level a female brachycephal (82.7).(See Kansu, 1937b.)

7. At Alishar Hüyük in Hittite (2000-1300 B.C.) levels one dolichocephal, five mesocephals and five brachycephals (80.0-85.0) of Alpine type were excavated. (See Krogman, 1937.)

8. From Hittite levels at Kusura came one mesocephal and one brachycephal (83.0) of Alpine type. (See Kansu and Atasayan.)

9. At Hissarlik (City III, circa 2000 B.C.) three hyperdolichocephals were found. (See Virchow, 1882.)

10. Hanay Tepe (circa 2000 B.C.) yielded one hyperdolichocephal.

11. At Böz-Hüyük near Eskisehir two brachycephals (one with 88.0) may have belonged to the Armenoid group. (See Virchow, 1896.)

12. At Alishar-Hüyük from the Phrygian level came four dolichocephals. (See Krogman, 1937.)

13. Hanay-Tepe yielded seven dolichocephals and seven mesocephals from Stratum A, tenth-eighth centuries B.C. (See Virchow, 1882.)

14. From the Perso-Hellenistic levels, seventh to first century B.C., at Alishar came a dolichocephal and a mesocephal. (See Krogman, 1937.)

15. Virchow described a sixth or fifth century mesocephal from ancient Ophrynion in Troy. (See Virchow, 1897.)

16. From Roman and Byzantine levels of the first-eleventh centuries at Alishar Hüyük were unearthed three dolichocephals, two mesocephals, and two brachycephals (84.0). (See Krogman, 1937.)

17. From the upper level at Alishar Hüyük, attributed to the eleventh-eighteenth centuries (Seljuks and Osmanli Turks), came four hyperbrachycephals. Krogman (1937) described them as part of the first wave of Armenoids.

18. Kansu studied 375 crania with 334 brachycephals (89.1 per cent) and 41 mesocephals. (See Kansu, 1935a.)

19. Noureddine Bey and colleagues measured 500 skulls in Istanbul with 348 brachycephals (69.6 per cent). (See Noureddine Bey, Nechet Omer Bey, Mouchet, and Sureya Bey.)

1946. Senyürek published in Turkish a study on seven crania from Masat Hüyük.

1947. At Kara Hüyük, 10 miles northwest of Elbistan in Maras Vilayet, the Turkish Historical Society excavated strata belonging to the Roman, post-Hittite and Hittite periods. Senyürek (1949d) studied two post-Hittite skeletons belonging to the period attributed to the end of the second to the first half of the first millennium B.C. One skull was Mediterranean, the other Alpine. Another skull from Arslan-Tepe in Malatia, attributed to the Neo-Hittite period, was brachycephalic of Alpine type. (See Kansu, 1939b.)

Senyürek (1949d, pp. 17-18) comments that the crania (see Table 25) from Kara Hüyük are evidence for at least two racial elements in the post-Hittite population. He adds that during the Chalcolithic and Copper Ages the inhabitants of Anatolia were dolichocephals of Eurafrican and Mediterranean types and that the brachycephals were at that time in the minority. During the succeeding Hittite period, the brachycephals increased and from this Senyürek concludes that the Hittites were invaders of predominantly Alpine type. However, during this period there were also dolichocephals, so that during the post-Hittite period of this region of Anatolia there existed roundheaded and longheaded elements.

1949a-d. Senyürek has published[10] four dental studies: (a) the intensity of attrition increased with age; (b) taurodontism[11] occurred among the ancient inhabitants of Anatolia; (c) report on two fossil teeth from Karain cave; and (d) report on the ancient inhabitants of Kara Hüyük.

1949d. Four skeletons, excavated in 1934 at Kum-Tepe near Troy, were studied by Kansu (1937b). Years later Senyürek (1949e, pp. 300-304) reexamined them (see Table 26) with the following observations: No. 1 is mesocephalic; No. 2 from the latest level is brachycephalic and Alpine in type; No. 3 from the earliest level is definitely dolichocephalic and of Eurafrican type; and No. 4 also from the earliest level is probably dolichocephalic.

The earliest inhabitants of Kum-Tepe and of this region were dolichocephalic, the brachycephals having come in later probably by invasion and infiltration. Senyürek (1949e, p. 304) concluded that the majority of the inhabitants prior to the Chalcolithic were dolichocephals.

1950. Three skulls (Nos. II, III and VIII) were found in the Copper Age stratum of Alishar Hüyük during the 1936 season. Senyürek (1950a, p. 71) suggests that an earthquake killed these individuals. The last two crania are brachycephalic, the first mesocephalic (see Table 27).

1950b. A Chalcolithic skeleton was excavated by Senyürek in June, 1949, at Kala-Tepe near Büyük Güllücek, 12 miles northeast of Alishar Hüyük. This skeleton belonged to the period from the last part of the fourth to the early centuries of the third millennium B.C. A copper lance-point lay beneath the occiput; nearby was a fragment of deer antler. This male was about 30 years old. After detailed measurements (see Table 28) and examination, Senyürek concludes (1950b, p. 303) that, "the Büyük Güllücek skeleton represents an individual of the dolichocephalic Eurafrican type present amongst the Chalcolithic and Copper Age inhabitants of Anatolia."

1951a. Two male and three female crania and the long bones of six persons were excavated in 1948 at Seyh Hüyük. Their provenance, Stratum IX, corresponds to VIII and IX at Tell Arapachiyah, contemporary with the Chalcolithic of Tell Halaf (first half of fourth millennium B.C.) in northeastern Syria.

According to Senyürek and Tunakan (1951, p. 442) the crania (see Table 29) are of Eurafrican racial type. However, the three female crania show artificial cranial deformation of Aymara type; these are the first artificially deformed Chalcolithic skulls from Anatolia. Estimates of stature were as follows:

No. 1 ranged from 164.69-172.80; No. 2 from 161.77-163.48; No. 3 from 146.36-148.62; No. 4 from 150.74-156.84; and No. 5 from 145.37-149.08.

1951b. Senyürek (1951a, pp. 447-68) studied the average longevity of the Chalcolithic and Copper Age inhabitants of Anatolia. He concluded (1951a, p. 458) that most of them died before age 40 and only a few lived beyond 60 years. Some interesting comparisons of distributions of deaths according to sex among various ancient people were made (1951a, Table 9, p. 467).

1951c. Human remains from Alishar Hüyük were reexamined by Senyürek. A Chalcolithic skeleton of a 25 year old male, medium in stature (estimates ranging from 156.51-157.91), and mesocephalic with a pentagonoid calvarium.

Senyürek concluded (1951b, p. 48) that, "in the sum total of his characters, this individual falls within the limits of the Mediterranean Race."

The skeleton of a male child, aged 11-12, was found in the Copper Age stratum. No racial deductions can be valid on a sub-adult.

1951d. After completing studies on 68 adult and 10 children's crania from 16 sites in Anatolia, Senyürek (1951d, pp. 614-15) examined the fluctuation of the cranial index[12] in Anatolia.

1952a. At Kül-Tepe near Kayseri in Central Anatolia Tahsin Ozgüc excavated during 1948-50 a series of skeletons. This site was an Assyrian trading colony established at the beginning of the second millennium B.C.

According to Senyürek (1952a, p. 327, see also footnotes to this article); Nos. 9, 11, 12, 2A and 6b are adult males. Nos. 10, 13, 4 are adult females. The remainder are juveniles (Nos. 14 and 15) or subadult females (Nos. 7, 2B and 6a).

The estimated stature for the male was 165.24, for the females, range 152.23 - 156.26.

The crania (see Table 30) belong either to the Eurafrican type, represented by the large-headed dolichocephalic skulls from Level III, or to the Alpine type, represented by the brachycephalic female from Level II.

1952b. A study of the dentition of 17 crania from Alishar Hüyük was made by Senyürek (1952b, pp. 153-224). These ranged from the Chalcolithic (4) to more recent than Early Bronze Age (11) with the majority (11) attributed to the Copper Age.

Summary

Senyürek (1951d, pp. 614-15) concludes[13] that "the majority of the Chalcolithic and Copper Age inhabitants of Anatolia were dolichocephals of mainly Eurafrican and Mediterranean types, and that the brachycephals, probably representing the invaders, were rare in these periods. This study has further supported the conclusion that the earliest inhabitants of Anatolia were longheaded, and that the brachycephals came in subsequently.

"The craniological evidence indicates that an invasion of brachycephals into Anatolia took place during the Chalcolithic period and that it was followed by a second invasion, bringing in the brachycephalic elements to Alaca Hüyük and other Copper Age sites, probably at about the middle of the Copper Age. The next invasion of brachycephals, which was more important and extensive than the previous ones, occurred at about 2000 B.C. This was made by the Hittites who were predominantly of the classical Alpine type."

Modern Man

The detailed anthropometric survey of 1937, together with previous data, present a clear picture of the metric and racial characters of the inhabitants.

Afet (1937) compiled the data on 2,945 Turks available up to that time (see Table 31). This material was published in conjunction with her anthropometric study on 200 Turkish women.[14] Additional measurements and indices on Turks were compiled in Field (1939).

Turkey is the only country in Southwestern Asia where a detailed and regional anthropometric survey[15] has been made. By order of Mustapha Kemal Ataturk, 39,465 males and 20,263 women were measured and observed in ten regions during July - November, 1937.

This survey, involving 9,090 work-days by 83 specialists, was directed by Shevket Aziz Kansu in accordance with a classificatory system developed by Eugène Pittard, University of Geneva. The tabulations were calculated in the Central Statistical Office, Ankara. The ten regions (see Table 32) ranged from west to east with No. I series from Thrace and Nos. IX and X those from Eastern Anatolia.

I have compiled four tables (nos. 32-35) from the statistical survey for the males and four for the females (nos. 36-39) so that the main trends may be seen.

Males

Stature (see Table 32). The mean is 165.28 range 164.41 - 166.80 with the shorter peoples in Thrace (164.44) and beside the Aegean (164.41). The tallest (166.80) live in Central Anatolia.

Head Measurements and Indices (see Table 32). The head length is 182.3, range 180.7 - 184.0; the breadth is 151.9, range 146.8 - 156.5; and the cephalic index is 83.28, range 79.78 - 86.29.

The shortest heads (180.7) are in Eastern Anatolia, ranging from Tokat to the Iran-Iraq frontier. The longest (184.0) are in Southern Anatolia, an area extending from the Mediterranean coastal region due south of Ankara along the Syrian border to a few miles east of Nusaybin.

The cephalic index is 83.28, range 79.78--86.29. The most brachycephalic (86.29) group live in Northwest Anatolia, ranging from the Sea of Marmora along the northern coastline to Amasya northwest of Tokat. The other ultrabrachycephals (85.41) live in Central Anatolia.

The only mesocephals (79.78) live in Southern Anatolia along the Syrian frontier.

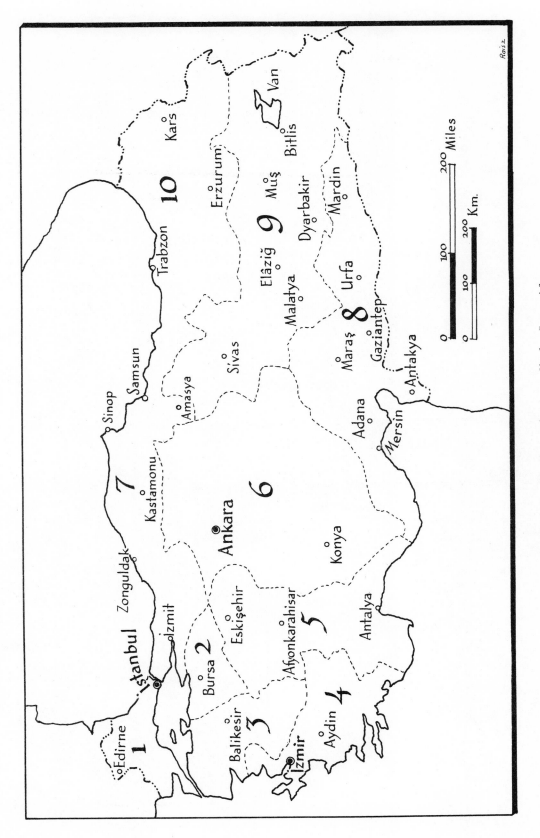

Anthropometric Zones in Anatolia by Inan Afet

With the above three exceptions, there is remarkable uniformity in head form, the range for 28,643 Turks being 81.07 - 84.53.

For comparison with my previously compiled and published anthropometric data ranging from Kharga Oasis in Egypt to Turkestan and from the Anatolia-Caucasus region to the Red Sea-Arabian Sea littoral, Table 33 has been compiled.

Observations in Southwestern Asia have revealed that in addition to the stature, head form and cephalic index, the nasal profile and eye color are the most significant criteria. I have, therefore, excerpted two tables to examine the trends based on percentages.

Nasal Profile (see Table 34). The largest groups of convex noses occur in widely separated areas I and IX. The highest percentage (57.15) is in Eastern Anatolia in the mountainous territory ranging in an inverted crescent from Tokat through the high Hakkari Mountains to the Iranian frontier. Here dwell the Kurds and prior to World War I the Assyrians (Upper and Lower Tiyari, Baz, Diz, Tkhuma, Supna, and other tribes). The lowest percentage (6.40) occurs in area VIII along the Syrian frontier from Silifke to Nusaybin. The mean for 39,465 males shows approximately one-third in the convex and straight categories and slightly less in the wavy group. Only 7.64 per cent were recorded as concave.

Eye Color (see Table 35). In every area (I-X) there occur light eyes, the largest percentages (42.20, 41.81 and 41.23) being in areas VII, V and I respectively. These three areas, Northwest Anatolia, the interior of Western Anatolia and Thrace, reveal a roughly inverted isosceles triangle except for area II, where the percentage is only 35.76. The lowest percentage (11.66) is in area X, Northeast Anatolia bordering the Black Sea and Soviet frontier.

The percentage of dark eyes is highest in area X of Northeast Anatolia, but in the Tokat-Van area of IX the percentage drops to 7.68 per cent, a remarkable change. Five groups (areas I, II, III, VII and VIII) have less than 3.5 per cent in the dark category.

This table (p. 164) indicates that there is a considerable percentage of light eyes in Anatolia; this is also true of the Caucasus.

Females

Stature (see Tables 36-37). The mean is 151.25, range 151.25-154.11 with the shortest peoples in Thrace. In Eastern Anatolia, from Tokat to the Iran-Iraq frontier, and along the Aegean coastline live the other shorter groups 151.68-151.97.

The tallest (154.11) are in Northeast Anatolia with Erzurum as the center. This region is bounded on the north by the Black Sea, on the east by the Caucasus and northwestern Iran.

Head Measurements and Indices (see Tables 36-37). The head length is 175.1, range 173.2-176.8; the breadth is 146.7, range 140.8 - 151.8; and the cephalic index 83.75, range 79.86 - 86.92.

The shortest heads (173.2) are found along the Black Sea littoral from Thrace to west of Ordu and continue (173.6) southeast across Eastern Anatolia to the Iran-Iraq frontier.

The longest heads (176.0-176.8) occur in three widely scattered areas from Western, Southern, and Northeast Anatolia.

The broadest heads (151.8) are in Central Anatolia ranging from northwest to northeast along the Black Sea coast (150.4). The narrowest (140.8) occur in Northeast Anatolia.

The cephalic index is 83.75, range 79.86-86.92. The mesocephals occur in Northeast Anatolia. The ultrabrachycephals (86.30-86.92) live in Northwest Anatolia and from the western Black Sea littoral across Central Anatolia almost to the Mediterranean coast.

Certain differences between the distribution of headform among the males and females appear. For example, the male mesocephals live in Southern Anatolia, but the females are in Northeast Anatolia. On the other hand, the ultrabrachycephals show a remarkable uniformity, for the males (86.29) and females (86.92) live in Northwest Anatolia, ranging from Thrace along the Black Sea coast to an arbitrary point west of Ordu.

Nasal Profile (see Table 38). The highest percentage (62.50) of convex noses occurs in area IX of Eastern Anatolia, the same area where the males also had the highest percentage (57.15). Regionally, the women have the highest percentages of convex noses in the same three areas as the men (IX, V and I). Nasal convexity is less dominant among the women with slightly more than one-quarter in this category compared to one-third of the men. Among the women one-third are in the straight category and one-quarter in the wavy division. There are double the number of women with concave noses (16.06 per cent) to 7.64 for the men.

Eye Color (see Table 39). The Turkish women also possess a marked percentage (23.78) of light eyes. The largest groups occur in areas II, IV, and VII with 30.95, 29.72, and 29.42 per cent respectively. This shifts the concentration to a crescent from the Aegean littoral through Bursa-Bilecik to the western half of the Black Sea coast. On the other hand the greatest number (65.13 per cent) of dark eyes occurs in area X of Northeast Anatolia, the same region as the men.

The majority (59.14) of women possess mixed eyes with one-quarter of the 20,263 women in the light-eyed category.

In general, there is a general similarity of percentage dispersal among the women and men.

Summary

Since we are dealing with 39,465 males and 20,263 females obtained by a well-planned regional survey, it is advisable to consult the original publication (in Turkish and French), wherein the material has been analyzed in great detail. Hence only a few comments here are necessary.

The Turkish men are medium short with long, broad heads and a brachycephalic index. The nose is straight or convex. The eyes are mixed with many light-eyed groups.

The women are short with short and broad heads and a brachycephalic index. The nose is straight, convex or wavy. The eyes are mixed with many light-eyed groups.

There is a general uniformity in the large series of male and female Turks measured and observed.

References

Afet, Inan (Afet Uzmay)
   1937. Une étude anthropométrique sur 200 femmes Turques "en Turquie." Istan-
      bul.
   1939. L'Anatolie, le pays de la "race" turque: recherches sur les caractères an-
      thropologiques des populations de la Turquie; enquête sur 64,000 individus.
      Geneva.
   1940. Recherches anthropologiques sur 59,728 Turcs des deux sexes. ASAG,
      Vol. 9, pp. 79-112.
Angel, J.L.
   1939. The Babaköy skeleton. AFO, Vol. 13, nos. 1-2, pp. 28-32.
   1951. Troy: the human remains. UC, Monograph, no. 1.
Atasayan, M., see Kansu, Shevket Aziz
Aygen, N.
   1939. Etude sur les valeurs angulaires des crânes turcs. RTA, Vol. 15, pp. 212-
      38.
Barker, James M.
   1951. The economy of Turkey. IBRD.
Bilge, A.
   1939. Rapports entre les sutures craniennes et de la morphologie du crâne sur
      50 crânes turcs. RTA, Vol. 15, pp. 101-65.
Braidwood, Robert J., see Perkins, Ann
Bump, Gardiner
   1951a. The Chukor Partridge (Alectoris graeca) in the Middle East with observa-
      tions on its adaptability to conditions in the southeastern United States. USFWS,
      mimeographed report.
   1951b. "Operation Sand Grouse" in the Middle East.
Caskey, J.L.
   1947. Archaeological Digest: Turkey. AJA, Vol. 51, pp. 444-45.
Çetin, Ismail
   1953. Turkey's geography. In Turkish. U.S. Army Language School, Monterey,
      California.
Çinar, N.
   1939. Recherches anthropométriques sur 24 garçons et 201 filles, élèves d'une
      école primaire d'Ankara. RTA, Vol. 15, pp. 65-79.
Cooke, Hedley V.
   1952. Challenge and response in the Middle East. New York.
Coon, Carleton S.
   1948. The races of Europe. New York.
Dellenbach, M.
   1937. Documents pour l'histoire anthropologique des Turcs. CTH, p. 11.
Dönmez, Ahmet and Brice, W.C.
   1951. A flint blade workshop near Gaziantep, south Turkey. Man, Vol. 51, pp.
      76-77.
Ehrich, Robert W.
   1940. Preliminary notes on Tarsus crania. AJA, Vol. 44, no. 1, pp. 87-92.
Erguvanli, Kemal
   1946. Gaziantep-Narli Arasinda Buluman Paleolitik Aletler Hakkinda Bir Not. In
      Turkish. TTKB, Vol. 10, pp. 375-79.
Ettinghausen, Richard
   1952. Bibliography of books and periodicals in Western languages dealing with
      the Near East. See 1954 Supplement. MEI.

Field, Henry
    1939. Contributions to the anthropology of Iran. FMNH, Vol. 29, pts. 1-2, pp.
        1-706.
    1940. The "Mongoloid spot" in Turkey and Iraq. AJPA, Vol. 27, pp. 119-26.
    1953-56. Bibliography on Southwestern Asia: I-III. UM.
Giuffrida-Ruggeri, V.
    1908. Contributo all' antropologia fisica delle regione dinariche e danubiane e
        dell' Asia anteriore. AAE, Vol. 38, pp. 127-80.
Gögüs, Sabahat, see Waechter, J.
Gökcül, N.
    1939. Recherches anthropologiques sur les élèves de deux sexes d'une école
        primaire d'Ankara. RTA, Vol. 15, pp. 36-48.
Güler, H.
    1939. Sur les relations entre les indices craniens, faciaux, frontaux et fronto-
        sagittaux de 221 crânes turcs. RTA, Vol. 15, pp. 49-66.
Güngör, K.
    1939. Recherches anthropométriques sur les Yörüks. RTA, Vol. 15, pp. 189-
        212.
Hauschild, M.W.
    1920-1921. Die kleinasiatischen Völker und ihre Beziehungen zu den Juden. ZE,
        Vols. 52-53, pp. 518-28.
Hauschild, M.W. and Wagenseil, F.
    1931. Anthropologische Untersuchungen an anatolischen Türken. ZMA, Vol. 29,
        pp. 193-260.
Istatistik Umum Müdürlügü [Central Statistical Office]
    1937. Enquête anthropométrique turque faite sur 59,728 individus de deux sexes.
        Ankara.
Kansu, Shevket Aziz
    1930a. Note sur l'indice du prognathisme des crânes turcs. RTA, Vol. 6, pp. 5-
        18.
    1930b. Türk Kadin ve Erkeginin Mukayeseli Sefalometrisi kakkindu bir muhtara.
        In Turkish. RTA, Vol. 6, pp. 44-49.
    1930c. Sur la morphologie des crânes trouvés dans un hüyük (tell) d'Anatolie:
        contribution à l'étude craniologique des Hittites. RTA, Vol. 10, pp. 3-17,
        25-30.
    1931. Recherches anthropométriques sur les turcs d'Anatolie et de Roumélie.
        RTA, Vol. 6, pp. 98-110; and Vol. 7, pp. 3-15, 17-19, 22-39.
    1932. Sur la tache bleue congénitale chez les nouveau-nés et les enfants turcs.
        RTA, Vol. 8, pp. 34-47.
    1934a. Deuxième contribution à l'étude craniologique des Etis (Hittites). RTA,
        Vol. 10, pp. 105-109.
    1934b. Craniologie de l'Anatolie. CIAES-I, pp. 376-79.
    1935a. Craniologie de l'Anatolie. L'Anthropologie, Vol. 45, nos. 1-2, pp. 105-
        107.
    1935b. Craniologie de l'Anatolie. In Turkish. RTA, Vol. 11, pp. 65-67. Same
        text as 1934b.
    1935c. Contribution à l'étude anthropologique du métopisme. L'Anthropologie,
        Vol. 45, pp. 376-79. See also text in Turkish in RTA, Vol. 11, pp. 68-72.
    1937a. Etudes anthropologiques de quelques squelettes d'Alaca Höyük. In
        French and Turkish. BABOA, pp. 15-25.
    1937b. Etude anthropologique sur les ossements de Kum-Tepe (Troade). TTKB,
        Vol. 2, pp. 557-69, 70, 82.
    1937c. Etudes anthropologiques sur quelques squelettes trouvés à Alaca Höyük.
        BABOA, Vol. 1, pp. 570-82.

1938. Recherches sur les angles de la base du crâne chez les Turcs. CIAES-I, pp. 146-49.

1939a. Les ossements d'Ahlatibel (Age du Cuivre). RTA, nos. 19-22, pp. 22-35.

1939b. Etude anthropométrique d'ossements d'Arslan-Tépé (Malatya). RHA, Vol. 5, pp. 77-84.

1939c. Recherches anthropométriques sur les enfants turcs des deux sexes. CIAES-I, pp. 149-50. See also, in Turkish, BABOA, Vol. 3, pp. 81-91.

1943. A first anthropological study on the Seljuk Turks and its results. THS, Ser. 9, no. 2, pp. 443-44, 46.

1945a. Hatay'da (Antakya) bulunan üst aşöleen (Micoque) ve nigde-Nevşehir çevrelerinde toplanan Levalloisien aletter hakkinda bir not. In Turkish with English summary. TTKB, Vol. 9, pp. 293-98.

1945b. Isparta, Burdur illeri çevresinde T.T.K. adina 1944 haziraninda yapilan prehistorya araştirmalarina dair ilk rapor. In Turkish with English summary. TTKB, Vol. 9, pp. 277-87.

1947. Stone Age cultures in Turkey. AJA, Vol. 51, pp. 227-32.

Kansu, S.A. and Atasayan, M.

1938. Contributions à l'étude sur l'histoire raciale de l'Anatolie. CAIES-I, pp. 142-45.

1939. Recherches sur les squelettes de l'âge du Cuivre de Kusura aux environs de Afyon Karahissar. RTA, Vol. 15, pp. 272-313.

Kansu, S.A. and Tunakan, S.

1935. L'omoplate chez les Turcs. RTA, Vol. 11, pp. 3-18.

1938. Etude anthropologique des squelettes datant des époques Hittite et Phrygienne et de l'Age Classique, provenant des fouilles du Hüyük de Karaoglan, 1937-38. TTKB, Vol. 12, no. 48, pp. 759-78.

Kinay, M.

1939. De la croissance chez les élèves de sexe masculin d'une école secondaire d'Ankara. RTA, Vol. 15, pp. 176-88.

Kökten, K.

1939. Recherches anthropométriques sur les élèves des écoles primaires de Samsun. RTA, Vol. 15, pp. 247-71.

1947. Bazi prehistorik istasyonlar hakkinda yeni gozlemler. In Turkish with French summary. TCFD, Vol. 5, pp. 223-36.

1949. Yili Tarihöncesi Araştirmalari Hakkinda kisa Repor. [Recherches de Préhistoire faites en 1949]. In Turkish with French summary. TTKB, Vol. 13, no. 52, pp. 813-31.

Krogman, Wilton M.

1933. The cranial types. In: E.F. Schmidt, "Alishar Hüyük, 1928-29," pt. 2, OIP, Vol. 20, pp. 122-38.

1937. Cranial types from Alishar Hüyük and their relations to other racial types, ancient and modern, of Europe and Western Asia. In Hans Henning von der Osten, "Alishar Hüyük, 1930-32," pt. 3, OIP, Vol. 30, pp. 219-93.

Lamb, Winifred

1949. New developments in early Anatolian archaeology. Iraq, Vol. 11, pt. 2, pp. 188-202.

Mantran, Robert

1952. Histoire de la Turquie. Paris.

Maringer, J.

1946-49. Das Paläolithikum in der Turkei. Anthropos, Vol. 41-44, pts. 4-6, pp. 875-76.

Musters, Chaworth, J.L.

1932. A contribution to our knowledge of the mammals of Macedonia and Thessaly. AMNH, Vol. 9, pp. 166-71.

Nourredine Bey, Nechet Omer Bey, Mouchet and Sureya Bey
    1928. Craniologie des Turcs. RA, Vol. 38, pp. 321-25.
Nourreddine, Omer O.
    1937. Les groups sanguins chez les Turcs. CRSB, Vol. 124, p. 6.
Ozden, Osman
    1946. Türk Altetleri üzerinde antropometrik arastirmalar. In Turkish with
        French summary. Ankara.
Ozgüc, T.
    1948. Ausgrabungen in Kul-Tepe. Ankara.
Peake, Harold
    1916. Racial elements concerned in the first siege of Troy. JRAI, pp. 154-72.
Perkins, Ann and Braidwood, R.J.
    1947. Archaeological News: the Near East. AJA, Vol. 51, pp. 191-202, 419-31.
Pfannenstiel, Max
    1941. Die altsteinzeitlichen Kulturen Anatoliens. Istanbuler Forschung, Vol. 15.
Pittard, Eugène
    1933. La "race" turque. CIAAP, pp. 89-95.
    1911. Contribution à l'étude anthropologique des Turcs. Osmanli. BSB, pp. 500-
        44.
    1935. La valeur de l'indice skélique chez 210 Turcs d'Anatolie. Volume published
        in honor of Dr. Wateff, Sofia, pp. 2-8.
    1950. Examen d'outillages préhistoriques recueillis en Anatolie: II, les perçoirs.
        ASAG, Vol. 15, pp. 3-11.
Pittard, Eugène and Donici, A.
    1929. Contribution à l'étude anthropologique des Turcs d'Asie-Mineure. RTA,
        Vol. 5, pp. 1-29.
Sauter, Marc-R.
    1945. Les races brachycéphales du Proche-Orient des origines à nos jours.
        ASAG, Vol. 11, pp. 68-131.
Senyürek, Muzaffer Süleyman
    1941. A craniological study of the Copper Age and Hittite populations of Anatolia.
        TTKB, Vol. 5, no. 19, pp. 219-35 and 237-54.
    1946. Study of the skulls from Maşat Hüyük, excavated under the auspices of the
        Turkish Historical Society. In Turkish. TTKB, Vol. 10, no. 38, pp. 231-42.
    1949a. The attrition of molars in the ancient inhabitants of Anatolia: a prelimi-
        nary report. TTKB, Vol. 13, pp. 229-44.
    1949b. The occurrence of taurodontism in the ancient inhabitants of Anatolia: a
        preliminary report. TTKB, Vol. 13, pp. 215-27.
    1949c. A short preliminary report on the two fossil teeth from the cave of Karain,
        excavated under the auspices of the Turkish Historical Society. TTKB, Vol.
        13, pp. 835-36.
    1949d. Study of the skulls from Kara Hüyük excavated under the auspices of the
        Turkish Historical Society. TTKB, Vol. 13, no. 49, pp. 1-20.
    1949e. A note on the skeletons from Kum-Tepe in the vicinity of Troy. TCFD,
        Vol. 7, no. 2, pp. 295-99, 300-304.
    1950a. A note on three skulls from Alaca Hüyük. TTKB, Vol. 14, no. 53, pp. 71-
        84.
    1950b. Study of the skeleton of a Chalcolithic Age warrior from Büyük Gullücek.
        TCFD, Vol. 8, no. 3, pp. 290-310.
    1951a. The longevity of the Chalcolithic and Copper Age inhabitants of Anatolia.
        TTKB, Vol. 15, no. 60, pp. 447-68.
    1951b. A note on the human skeletons in the Alaca Hüyük Museum. TCFD, Vol.
        9, nos. 1-2, pp. 43-61.
    1951c. A note on three skulls from Alaca Hüyük. TTKB, Vol. 14, no. 53, pp.
        57-84.

1951d. Fluctuation of the cranial index in Anatolia, from the fourth millennium B.C. to 1200 B.C. TTKB, Vol. 15, no. 60, pp. 593-615.

1951e. Two cases of premature suture closure among the ancient inhabitants of Anatolia. TTKB, Vol. 15, no. 58, pp. 247-62.

1951f. A study of the human skulls from Polath Hüyük. AST, Vol. 1, pp. 63-71.

1952a. A study of the human skeletons from Kul-Tepe excavated under the auspices of the Turkish Historical Society, 1948. TTKB, Vol. 16, no. 16, pp. 323-43.

1952b. A study of the dentition of the ancient inhabitants of Alaca Hüyük. TTKB, Vol. 16, no. 62, pp. 153-224.

1953. "Southwest Asia." In IDAI, pp. 79-88.

Senyürek, Muzaffer Süleyman and Tunakan, Seniha

1951. The skeletons from Seyh Hüyük. TTKB, Vol. 15, no. 60, pp. 438-45.

Seton-Williams, Veronica, see Waechter, J.

Seven, B.

1939. Etude de la région pterique chez 200 crânes turcs. RTA, Vol. 15, pp. 80-100.

Thomas, O.

1906. New Insectivores and voles collected by Mrs. A. Robert near Trebizond. AMNH, Vol. 17, pp. 415-21.

Tunakan, Seniha, see Kansu, S.A. and Senyürek, Muzaffer Süleyman

Vallois, H.V.

1950. Un homme de Néanderthal en Turquie? L'Anthropologie, Vol. 54, p. 359.

Virchow, Rudolf

1882. Alttrojanische Gräber und Schädel. KAWB, Vol. 2, pp. 1-133.

1896. Funde aus dem nordwestlichen Phrygien und von Salonik. VBG, pp. 123-26.

1897. Uber die Schädel von Ophrynion. VBG, p. 137.

Von Luschan, F.

1911. The early inhabitants of Western Asia. JRAI, Vol. 41, pp. 221-44.

Waechter, J., Gögüs, Sabahat and Seton-Williams, Veronica

1951. The Sakce Gözü cave site, 1949. TTKB, Vol. 15, no. 58, pp. 193-201.

Warriner, Doreen

1948. Land and poverty in the Middle East. New York.

Weisbach, A.

1873. Die Schädelform der Türken. MAGW, Vol. 3, pp. 185-245.

Zaborowski, A.

1881. Sur seize crânes d'un tombeau grec d'Asie-Mineure. BSA, pp. 234-38.

VIII. CAUCASUS

The Caucasus[1] is the region between the Black Sea and Caspian--a borderland between Europe and Asia.

The North Caucasian steppe joins the flat, black earth of the Ukraine. The central part of the Caucasus is the great mountain chain dividing Ciscaucasia and Transcaucasia.

The Greater Caucasus consists of a system of ranges joining the Taman and Apsheron Peninsulas. To the south lies a large valley through which flow the Kura and Riani rivers. Still further south rise the Lesser Caucasus Mountains and high tablelands bordering on Anatolia and Iran.

The central mountain range is 900 miles long and from 30 - 140 miles in width. There are many peaks about 15,000 feet, including Mount Elbruz (18,465 feet) and Mount Kazbek (16,545 feet). The perpetual snowline oscillates on the southern slopes from 9,000 - 11,000, and on the northern slopes from 11,000 - 13,000 feet. As a result of the general dryness and the summer heat, the Caucasian peaks are far less covered with snow and ice than those of the Alps.

The climate of Caucasia and Switzerland have a common mean, although the absence of snow in the Caucasus produces a corresponding lack of glaciers. However, between the Jumantau and the Kaltver glaciers, ice stretches almost continuously for 120 miles. The lowest glacier is Kalchidon (7,000 feet), which drains from the Adaikhokh into the Upper Urukh Valley. The most famous glacier is the Devdoraki, one of eight frozen streams which decorate Mount Kazbek; the glacier advanced 770 feet from 1865-1876.

The climate has great variation, ranging from that on the mountain peaks to sea level. The greatest temperature range is at Yerevan (formerly Erivan), the capital of Armenia, where at 3,230 feet there is a January average of 14.9° F. and an August average of 78.8°. At Sukhumi on the Black Sea the same range for the corresponding months is 48° and 76.1°. The highest mean annual temperatures are those of Lenkoran (60.3°) and Sukhumi (58.0°), and the lowest (38.6°) at Gudaur (7,245 feet), a few miles south of Kars. At Tbilisi (formerly Tiflis), the capital of Georgia standing at 1,490 feet, the mean annual temperature is 55° with a temperature in January of 32° and in August of 76.5°.

The rainfall may be divided conveniently into two zones: (a) the wet region typified by the Black Sea Coast with 53-93 inches annually; and (b) the steppes north of Pyatigorsk and the Armenian highlands where less than 12 inches fall annually.

Our principal interest in the Caucasus lies south of the imaginary notochord of the mountainous Caucasian backbone. For to the north lies Europe, to the south Transcaucasia, which I include in Southwestern Asia.

The flora presents unusual diversity but links to Anatolia. The vegetation centers of Georgia, northern Iran, Anatolia and Armenia lay originally in Transcaucasia, which during the Tertiary was an island with a mild oceanic climate. The flora survived the Glacial period, the regression and reduction of the Arcto-Tertiary type of forest, and the appearance of the grassy types. Then followed climatic changes caused mainly by the merging of islands into extensive land tracts. Thus evolved desert and semi-desert vegetation.

It is, therefore, clear why there still exists such a diversity of flora ranging from the high altitude forests to the cultivated trees and shrubs in coastal regions.

The fauna[2] is similar to that of the mountainous areas of Central Europe except in the southeast where the links are to southern Asia. The latter are represented by the tiger (only in Lenkoran), leopard, hyena, and jackal. The Carnivora include the bear, wolf, lynx, wild cat, fox and wild boar, the latter near Borzhom. There are also red, roe and fallow deer, goats, chamois, moufflon, and Asiatic wild sheep or argali (Ovis ammon).

Among the 400 species of birds are pheasants, grouse, blackcock, quail, and partridges. The birds of prey include the sea eagle, griffon vulture, lammergeier, hawks and owls. Large flocks of northern water birds winter on the steppes of eastern Transcaucasia.

In the seas and rivers about 190 species of fishes have been determined; of these, 115 are Mediterranean, 30 are common to the Caspian Sea, and the remaining species are peculiar to the Black Sea. The most useful economically are sturgeon, herring, trout, barbel, chub, bream, ray, sea dace, carp and anchovy.

The original Socialist Soviet Republics of Transcaucasia were: Georgia, Armenia, and Azerbaidzhan. However, in January, 1932, five "Autonomous Units" were created,[3] as given in Table 40.

In 1933 the area of the Transcaucasian SFSR was 185,000 square kilometers with a population of 6,888,000, consisting mainly of Georgians, Armenians, and Turks, the latter in Azerbaidzhan. The capital, Tbilisi, had a population of 414,000. In 1926 the minorities included South Osetes (96,796), Russians (96,085), Abkhazians (56,847) and Greeks (54,051).

Ancient Man[4]

The Caucasus has been inhabited continuously since Upper Paleolithic times.

During the past 30 years the principal research has been done by G.K. Nioradze and S.N. Zamiatnin.

A number of caves[5] have been excavated and many open-air sites[6] located.

The following caves or rockshelters were partly excavated from 1914-36. For convenience, the sites have been arranged chronologically:

1914. P.P. Schmidt and L. Kozlovskii found two sites in Imeretia: (a) late Mousterian and Upper Paleolithic implements in Khergulis-Klde near Chiaturi. The fauna included bear, wild horse, and Bos.

(b) Upper Paleolithic implements in Bartashvili Peshchera (= cave) near Kutaisi in Imeretia.

1916-17. S.A. Krukovskii excavated the Azilian cave of Gvardzhilas-Klde near Chiaturi in Imeretia. Geometric microliths, small crude axes and tools of bone and horn, including a harpoon of Azilian type, were found. Among fauna represented were Ursus arctos, Ursus spelaeus, Bison bonasus, and Bos taurus.

1918. S.A. Krukovskii found Mousterian and Upper Paleolithic implements and bone points in Taro-Klde cave near Chiaturi in Imeretia.

1926-28. Nioradze excavated the Upper Paleolithic cave of Devis-Khvreli above the Chkherimela River in Imeretia. Bone tools, mainly awls and compressors, were found. The fauna consisted of wild boar, wild goat, and bear. A fragmentary human mandible and two molars were unearthed.

1934. Near Chiaturi in Imeretia, Zamiatnin found Upper Paleolithic implements in the following caves: (a) Tsirkhvali; (b) Bnele-Klde; and (c) Mgvimevi. Near Rockshelter No. 5 a row of linear geometric signs were seen on a rock.

1936. (a) Nioradze found Upper Paleolithic flint implements in Virchow Peshchera near Kutaisi in Imeretia. Many geometric microliths and nuclei-shaped flint tools were excavated. Among fauna were mineralized cave bear bones.

(b) Zamiatnin found traces of an Upper Paleolithic site in Darkveti cave above the Kvirila River in Imeretia.

(c) Zamiatnin also excavated Upper Paleolithic implements in the upper part of Navalishenskaia Peshchera in the Adler Raion.

(d) L.N. Solovev found Tardenoisian flint implements, many of geometric forms, in Planta cave near the confluence of the Amtkel and Kodor rivers in Abkhazia.

————————

From 1926-1936 A.N. Kalandadze located the following Upper Paleolithic open-air sites in Mingrelia:

(a) Dafnari near Lapchkhuti.

(b) Liia on the Ingur River terrace near the Zugdidi-Dzhvari highway.

(c) Odishi in the Zugdidi Raion.

(d) Rukhi II six kilometers from Zugdidi.

(e) Supsa-Shroma.

(f) Motsviari on the right bank of the Sefa River.

(g) Kheti on the slopes of Urta Mountain. Fragments of a human calvarium, flint flakes, and animal bones were found.

(h) Entseri on the left bank of the Ingur. In Abkhazia, Kalandadze found typologically Upper Paleolithic flint implements at:

(i) Atap.

(ii) Gali on the 80-meter terrace.

(iii) Zakharovka above the Amtkel River.

(iv) Tabachnaia on the 100-meter terrace near Sukhumi.

(v) Tsebelda.

(vi) IAshtukh near Sukhumi.

(vii) Abazinka six kilometers upstream from Old Matsesta in Sochi Raion.

(viii) Semenovka near the Matsesta River in Sochi Raion.

During the past decade a great deal of research has been conducted in Paleolithic, Mesolithic, and Neolithic cultures. Eventually the racial and Paleolithic cultural links between the Caucasus region and Southwestern Asia will be established.

Crania

In this section Table 41 has been compiled in order to present the data on crania from the Caucasus. We find that 141 out of 255 crania are in the X - 80.0 group, the remainder within the range 80.0 - 88.4.

In order to compare the cephalic indices of crania with those obtained on the living, Keith suggests the addition of two points to the former.

When we look at the Osete crania, we see that they range from 76.59 - 88.4, which, according to the above formula, should be considered as 78.59 - 90.4, figures which compare relatively well with the table of Osete cephalic indices. As among the living, there appear to be dolichocephalic and brachycephalic crania, indicating the presence of two elements even in early historic times.

Modern Man[7]

Within the Republics of Georgia, Azerbaidzhan and Armenia there live many racial groups conversing in more than 40 languages, most of them mutually unintelligible.

The Caucasus is one of the richest areas in the world for diversity of peoples, for many "islands of population" exist in the mountain fastnesses.

Here dwell Caucasians, Mediterraneans, Mongolians, and Ural-Altaians with many subdivisions.[8]

In this section we shall examine part of the anthropometric data[9] available on the Caucasus, including Ciscaucasia and Transcaucasia.

The indication of some general trends may prove helpful, especially since I shall discuss in footnotes 9-35 the relationship of the Osetes to some of the groups from Southwestern Asia, including Iran, Iraq, Arabia, Jordan, Palestine (now partly Israel), Syria, Anatolia, Kurdistan, Afghanistan and Baluchistan, and India as listed in my Iran Report (Field, 1939, pp. 436-89).

Special attention has been paid to the compilation of data on stature and cephalic index. In the latter case, in addition to the Caucasus and Turkestan figures I have included some groups from the Crimea to the west, the Volga to the northeast, and Central Asia, Tannu Tuva and Siberia to the east and northeast. These supplementary figures were selected by Mr. Eugene V. Prostov from relatively recent Soviet publications, not readily accessible. A few comparative figures obtained on females have also been given.

In Tables 42-74 I have not attempted to compile every series of anthropometric measurements available for the Caucasus and adjacent territories, but rather to include those series wherein the technique is less apt to vary from modern standard anthropometric measurements.

The anthropometric data will be treated in the following order of measurements and indices: stature, sitting height (trunk length), relative sitting height, head length, head breadth, cephalic index, minimum frontal diameter, bizygomatic breadth, bigonial breadth, total facial height, upper facial height, fronto-parietal index, facial index, nasal height, nasal breadth, and nasal index. Wherever considered desirable, the number of individuals in a series has been given in parentheses. For convenience, each series has been arranged in ascending order. In some cases the number of individuals within a group was not available; these have been omitted. Each group with nine or less individuals has been relegated to the footnotes.

Stature[10] (see Table 42). Among the 7,543 men we see a wide range from the Kubin Jews of Azerbaidzhan (162.2) to a selected group of 20 Osetes (180.0) in the central mountain complex of the Caucasus. The largest concentration ranges from 164.5 - 167.0, the latter being close to the mean for Southwestern Asia.

The small series of 177 women (see Table 43) showed a small range from 152.4 - 159.39.

I was able to compile measurements of stature on 20 groups of 1,298 Osetes[11] (see Table 44) with a range of 164.7 - 171.8. The 20 selected tall Osetes, aged 21 - 25, were 180.5.

The 107 women were considerably shorter, range 157.3 - 159.39.

Since there may well be racial affiliations to the East, I have compiled measurements on some groups from Soviet Turkestan[12] in Table 45. The range of 15 groups of 1,842 men is 163.70 - 171.90 with the majority about 166.5, the apparent mean for Southwestern Asia.

Sitting Height - Trunk Length (see Table 46). Comparative data[13] are relatively few. Some observers, such as Gilchenko, employed an outmoded technique. As a result, their measurements cannot be listed. The range for nine groups of 274 men is 84.64 - 86.90.

The Osetes and Yezidis show a remarkable degree of homogeneity. There appears to be a markedly small range of variation in relative sitting height throughout Southwestern Asia.

Relative Sitting Height (see Table 47). The range of 49.92 - 53.39 for 274 males shows considerable homogeneity.[14]

Head Dimensions. Since these are among the most important racial criteria, we shall examine the head length, head breadth, and cephalic index of the peoples of the Caucasus as well as some groups in the Crimea, Volga region, Turkestan, Central Asia, Tannu Tuva, Siberia, and India.

Head Length (see Table 48). There is considerable range[15] (181.9 - 193.6), the majority being in the category 187.0 - 190.0.

Only three groups of 154 women were found. The head length in Table 49 showed remarkable uniformity with the range 182.0 - 183.0.

Head Breadth (see Table 50). Among the 26 groups of 3,355 men the head breadth[16] ranged from 145.0 - 161.8 which is considerable; the maximum concentration is in the range 152.7 - 156.6.

Cephalic Index[17] (see Table 51). We now come to one of the most important racial criteria. For comparison with the cephalic index on the living, some crania from the Caucasus have been added. I have also compiled Tables 52-59 for the Osetes of Georgia and the peoples of the Crimea, Volga Region, Soviet Central Asia, Tannu Tuva, and Siberia.

Among the 94 groups of 9,192 individuals, there are 41 below 82.0 and 54 above 83.0. It must, however, be noted that there are 28 groups between 81.0 - 83.9. The entire range for the series is 75.6 - 91.07. In general, the dwellers in the Caucasus are brachycephalic or ultrabrachycephalic. In the latter category, attention must be called to artificial cranial deformation by the use of the cradleboard.

At this point it seems desirable to interject a request for standardization of these divisions of cranial indices, since there already exist the Broca, Topinard, Martin, Keith, and Harvard systems. I naturally put in a strong plea for the Harvard system, which is now being used widely throughout the world.

Among the 17 Osete[18] groups of 1,536 individuals, the range was 80.5 - 85.53, showing them all to be brachycephalic (see Table 52).

The seven groups of 246 women (see Table 53) showed a range of 76.4 - 85.6, with three groups of Kurds, presumably from the Lake Goktcha area, in the mesocephalic category.

To the northwest in the Crimea (see Table 54) the five groups of 973 individuals showed a range of 82.9 - 85.3, all brachycephals.[19]

In the Volga region (see Table 55) to the northeast the 13 groups of 1,805 individuals showed a range of 79.5 - 86.0. Only one group, the 122 Mishari Tatars of Chistopol, were in the mesocephalic (75.0 - 79.9) category; the remainder were brachycephals.[20]

Due east across the Caspian the 21 groups[21] of 2,268 males in Turkestan (see Table 56) ranged from 75.16 - 85.84. However, only six groups were mesocephalic.

Further still to the east and northeast in Soviet Central Asia (see Table 57) the 20 groups[22] of 5,360 males ranged from 75.2 - 87.1. There were only two groups of Turkomans in the mesocephalic category. Seven groups were hyperbrachycephalic (85.0 - X).

From the little-known mountainous territory of Tannu Tuva[23] (see Table 58), we have data on four groups with 288 men, all brachycephals with a range of 80.5 - 84.2.

For comparison we have assembled data[24] on 14 Siberian groups (see Table 59) with 2,181 males. The range is from 79.2 - 84.5. Only two groups in the Khakass AA are mesocephals, the remainder brachycephals. The Yagnobians[25] are considered part of the Mountain Tajiks (Tadzhiks).

Summary

The brachycephals predominate among the following peoples: the mountain peoples of the Caucasus region, including the Osetes, the Yezidis, Kurds, Chechens, Circassians, Adighe, Georgians, Kabardins, Lezghians, Nogais, Kumyks, Tats, Karachais, Lazes, Mountain Jews, and Armenians; the Bakhtiari of southwestern Iran; the Chaldeans of northern Iraq; the peoples of Anatolia, especially the formerly resident Assyrians; the Druze of Syria; the majority of South Arabs from Yemen to Oman; some Turkomans, Afghans (75.16 - 84.77), Baluchis (75.59 - 89.0), and Siberian tribesmen (79.2 - 84.5): and according to Guha some groups in Bombay, Hathiamar, Baroda, Mysore, southern Bengal, and Burma.

Dolichocephals and mesocephals predominate on the Iranian Plateau, on the plains of Iraq, and westward through Jordan and Israel into the Nile Valley. In India dolichocephaly prevails in Kashmir, Tammu, Punjab, United Provinces, Rajputana, Bihar, Orissa, eastern Hyderabad, the Madras States, and eastward into Assam. In the south the majority are dolichocephalic to mesocephalic (72.51 - 77.36).

In my Iran Report (1939) I have drawn attention to the Mediterranean type which extends from Morocco on the Atlantic Ocean, through the central part of Southwestern Asia, south of the Himalayan chain and eastward to the shores of the Pacific. There also appears to be a brachial extension of this type into the Pamirs.

Minimum Frontal Diameter (see Table 60). The forehead width has been studied in the Caucasus and for comparison[26] a few means for Turkestan are given.

The 12 Caucasian groups of 651 males show a wide range of 94.4 - 120.06. It is probable that von Erckert's group of 16 Osetes with a minimum frontal diameter of 94.4 is far from correct.

The five groups of 553 males in Turkestan (see Table 61) ranged from 103.0 - 109.0.

Fronto-Parietal Index (see Table 62). The ten groups[27] with 434 males showed a range of 68.24 - 77.05.

Bizygomatic Breadth (see Table 63). Our 34 groups[28] with 4,463 males showed a wide range of 136.0 - 147.6.

From Turkestan (see Table 64) we have ten groups of 1,047 men with a range of 129.0 - 142.1.

Bigonial Breadth (see Table 65). The ten groups[29] with 380 men in the Caucasus showed a range of 108.63 - 119.38.

From Turkestan (see Table 66) we have six groups of 604 men with a wide range of 107.89 - 118.00.

Upper Facial Height (see Table 67). Eight groups[30] of 256 men show a range of 70.85 - 76.61.

Total Facial Height (see Table 68). The 15 groups[31] of 1,377 men show a range of 120.2 - 130.24 with the majority in the 126.0 - 128.0 category.

The nine groups of 1,030 males in Turkestan (see Table 69) range from 115.42 - 132.90.

Total Facial Index (see Table 70). The 15 groups[32] of 1,377 males show a range of 85.50 - 91.70.

Nasal Length (see Table 71). The 18 groups[33] with 1,680 males show a range of 51.00 - 60.00.

Nasal Breadth (see Table 72). The 19 groups[34] of 1,786 males show a range of 30.40 - 37.96.

Nasal Index (see Table 73). The 39 groups[35] of 3,448 males show a wide range of 56.60 - 75.30. The majority of groups fall between 63.0 - 66.5

Among the six groups of 184 women (see Table 74) the range is 59.78 - 70.20 with the majority in the 62.6 - 64.8 category.

Summary

The Caucasus has been inhabited at least since Upper Paleolithic times. Further cave exploration will yield earlier cultures linking Neanderthal Man with Western Europe and with the inhabitants of Mount Carmel to the southwest, of Shanidar Cave on Jebel Baradost in northeastern Iraq, of Hotu Cave overlooking the southeastern corner of the Caspian, and of Teshik-Tash near Tashkent.

The Caucasus is the most complex racial area in the world.

Here is the home of the Caucasian Race.

References

Baschmakoff, Alexandre
  1937. Cinquante siècles d'évolution ethnique autour de la Mer Noire, Vol. 1,
    Paris.
Field, Henry
  1939. Contributions to the anthropology of Iran. FMNH, Anthropological Series,
    Vol. 29, nos. 1-2, pp. 1-706.
  1948. Contributions to the anthropology of the Soviet Union. SMC, Vol. 110, no.
    13, pp. 1-244.
  1953a. Contributions to the anthropology of the Caucasus. PMP, Vol. 48, no. 1,
    pp. 1-154. See Bibliography, pp. 122-32 and our 101 references to Soviet
    Archeology and Anthropology, 1936-52, pp. 117-19.
  1953b-1956. Bibliography on Southwestern Asia: I-III. UM.
Formosov, A.N.
  1926. Notes on the mammals of the North Caucasus. BSIER, Vol. 1, pp. 73-90.
Gilchenko, V.V.
  1890. Materials on the Anthropology of the Caucasus. In Russian. Trudy, IAE,
    Vol. 16, no. 2.
Ginzburg, V.V.
  1940. IAgnobtsi v Antropologicheskom otnotsenu. SE, no. 3, pp. 89-91. Moscow.
Minorsky, Vladimir
  1953a. Studies in Caucasian history. Cambridge Oriental Series, no. 6, pp. 1-
    169.
  1953b. Bibliography. BSOAS, Vol. 15, Pt. 3, pp. 669-81.
Movius, Hallam L., Jr.
  1948-55. Old World Bibliography, nos. 1-8. Peabody Museum, Harvard.
Pantiukhov, I.I.
  1893. Anthropological observations in the Caucasus. In Russian. Zapiski Kav-
    kazskogo Otdiela, Vol. 15. Tiflis.
Satunin, K.A.
  1909. Beiträge zur Kenntnis der Säugetierfauna Kaukasiens und Transkaspiens.
    MKM, Vol. 6, pp. 286-300.
Slonim, Marc
  1937. Les onzes Républiques soviétiques. Paris.
Vereschagin, N.K.
  1953. On the history of the landscape of pre-Caucasia in the Quatenary. In Rus-
    sian. IVGO, Vol. 85, no. 2, pp. 200-201.
Ward, Lauriston
  1947. Reference list of the archeology of the Soviet Union. Peabody Museum,
    Harvard. Mimeographed.

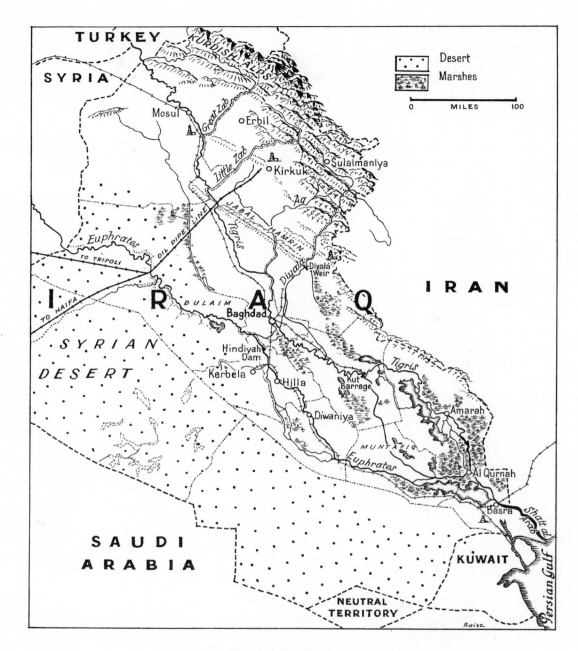

Iraq by Erwin Raisz

IX. IRAQ

Iraq,[1] formerly Mesopotamia (= "land between the rivers"), is bounded on the north by Anatolia, on the east by Iran, on the south by the Persian Gulf and Al Kuwait, on the southwest by Saudi Arabia and the small, rhomboidal western Neutral Zone, and on the west by Syria and Jordan.

The country may be divided into seven zones:

(a) The Kurdistan highlands forming a mountainous crescent from Faishkhabur on the Tigris to Khanaqin. This region, constituting the northeastern part of Iraq, marches with Iran.

(b) The uplands including the greater part of northern Iraq.

(c) The alluvial plain delimited by the ancient shoreline of the Persian Gulf which extended about 6,000 B.C. as far north as Samarra and Hit.

(d) The southern marshes between the Tigris and the Euphrates and between Amara and the foothills of the Pusht-i-Kuh in Iran.

(e) The Jazira (Gezireh) or northern island forming a rough square between the Euphrates and the Syrian border.

(f) Western Iraq, a wilderness region covered with gravel and sand, being part of the Syrian or North Arabian Desert.

(g) The Shamiya or southwestern wilderness between the Euphrates and the borderland with Saudi Arabia, the western Neutral Zone and Al Kuwait.

The climate[2] is arduous, ranging from extremely hot and humid in summer--the range is 120° F. in the shade--to severe frost in winter. Rainfall is scanty except on the northern uplands where 15 - 25 inches fall annually. Spring flooding by the Twin Rivers is normal, extensive areas of the alluvial plain being covered by water. The Tigris can rise at the rate of one foot per hour and a maximum of 27 feet was recorded up to 1949. In Lower Iraq vast areas are inundated every year. Irrigation[3] control has improved conditions.

The greater part of the year winds[4] sweep across the barren wilderness.

In plant[5] life Iraq is a bridge between Asia and Africa. In the northern and eastern regions the flora reflects the continental character of Asia and in the southern and western parts the flora is strictly African. Zohary (1950, pp. 188-89) determined the following phytogeographical groups: (a) 204 species in the Mediterranean; (b) 968 species in the Irano-Turanian; (c) 118 species in the Saharo-Sindian; (d) 23 species in the Eurosibero-Boreoamerican; and (e) 600 species in the bi-and pluri-regional.

Iraq is primarily an agricultural economy based on adequate rainfall on the higher ground to the north and northeast. The alluvial plain requires irrigation. The principal crops[6] are barley, wheat, rice, dates, cotton, and tobacco.

The wild animals[7] include bear, ibex, gazelle, cheetah, wolf, fox, jackal, hyena, boar, badger, and jerboa. Among birds may be listed the chukhor partridge, sand grouse, pelicans, turkey bustards, larks, and many water-fowl in the southern marshes, especially in the Hor al-Hawiza east of Amara.

In 1950[8] there were 7,490,000 sheep, 184,000 horses, 413,000 donkeys, 130,000 water buffaloes, and 52,000 mules. In 1945 the number of camels was estimated at 307,000.

The area of Iraq is 175,000 square miles, only half of which is at present habitable except by Beduins. The census of November, 1947, recorded[9] a population of 4,799,500 with 2,253,170 males, and the principal urban-dwellers as follows: Baghdad, 552,047; Mosul, 340,541; Basra, 206,302; and Kirkuk, 148,349.

Arabic is spoken everywhere, but the minority groups use Kermanji, Persian, and Turkish.

Ancient Man[10]

During the past 30 years evidence of Prehistoric Man, ranging from Lower Paleolithic to Neolithic, has been found.

1925. At dawn on December 15 in eastern Trans-Jordan (now Jordan) near Royal Air Force Landing Ground[11] "H," which lies 403 air miles west of Baghdad, L.H. Dudley Buxton and the writer collected on the surface of the large mudflat (circa 100 acres), surrounded by low hills (50 - 75 feet), the first typologically Paleolithic implements ever found between Amman and the Tigris River. The reason for this camp-site was later found to be because of its proximity to a peculiar crater-like depression containing a mud flat within its circumference. This may be seen from a considerable distance.

About noon we picked up similar deeply-patinated flint implements, flakes, and rejects, on the surface near R.A.F. Landing Ground "R," (800 feet above sea level); this is 295 air miles from Baghdad on the now disused Rutba-Amman track.

Later that same day near Rutba Wells we found similar heavily-patinated worked flints.

This desert series was divided and presented to the Iraq Museum (Case No. 1) and Field Museum of Natural History, now Chicago Natural History Museum.

1926. From January 12 - 13 Dudley Buxton and the writer searched[12] the Landing Ground "H" area and collected[13] a representative series of typologically Middle and Upper Paleolithic flint implements, flakes, and rejects.

1927. During the First Field Museum North Arabian Desert Expedition the writer collected worked flints in eastern central Jordan and subsequently along the Amman-Rutba track.[14] A most interesting series was found in the Rutba area, showing a long range of occupation near the great Wadi Hauran.

1928 a. Dorothy Garrod[15] collected rolled and waterworn typologically Lower and Middle Paleolithic implements from the river gravels of Kirkuk.

1928 b. Dorothy Garrod (1930 and 1938) excaved two caves near Sulaimaniya from October - December. The results proved the presence of both Middle and Upper Paleolithic man in this region. The cave of Zarzi contained Upper Aurignacian industry of a Grimaldian type, although the type Station--La Grotte des Enfants-- lies more than 2,000 miles westward. The cave of Hazar Merd contained a Levalloiso-Mousterian culture resembling closely that of the Mount Carmel caves in Israel.

1928 c. During the Second Field Museum Desert Expedition, I continued to locate numerous prehistoric surface sites along Iraq Petroleum Company traverses[16] within the isosceles triangle, whose apex is Rutba Wells and whose base is formed by the western boundary of Iraq, the line running north from Jebel Enaze[17] (Anaiza) to Jebel Tenf (Jebel et-Tinf). Among the richest sites was Jebel Enaze, the low hills forming the common boundary between Iraq, Jordan, and Saudi Arabia. The southeastern slopes of this Jebel gives birth to the Wadi Hauran, which meanders northeastward past Rutba to the Euphrates just south of Haditha. Other rich sites were: (a) the now-barren slopes of Tellul Basatin (= "The Hills of Gardens") lying about midway on the Jebel Enaze - Jebel Tenf traverse and close to our Rutba - Qasr el-Burqu traverse; and (b) the glistening black basalt peaks of Jebel Tenf (Jebel et-Tinf) on the Iraq-Syrian border.

1928 d. In the Kirkuk gravels I also found water-worn flint implements of Lower and Middle Paleolithic types.

1934. During the Field Museum Expedition to the Near East I located many surface sites[18] in desert area not previously searched. We followed the Iraq Petroleum Company's southern line (H for Haifa line) and returned along the northern (T for Tripoli) line.

Later I searched near Zakho, Rowanduz (Rowandiz), Aqra, and Sulaimaniya--the four mountain passes leading to and from the Iranian Plateau. At all of these localities typologically Paleolithic implements were found on the surface.

On the lookout rock above Diyan Cave (3,500 feet) on Jebel Baradost near the Rowanduz Gorge, I collected typologically Aurignacian flint implements indicating Paleolithic inhabitation of this cave.

1949a. Naji al-Asil (pp. 205-206), Director-General of Antiquities, and his assistant, Fuad Safar, made a surface collection of handaxes at Barda Balka[19] just east of Chemchemal on the Kirkuk-Sulaimaniya road. This was the first Lower Paleolithic site in Iraq.

1949b. Carleton S. Coon (1950, pp. 91-92) investigated the eastern cave of Hazar Merd near Sulaimaniya. The base was reached at 90 centimeters. No evidence of Paleolithic occupation was discovered. The pottery was Neolithic.[20]

1950a. In March-April the Peabody Museum-Harvard Expedition[21] (Henry Field, leader) and the Iraq Department of Antiquities (Fuad Safar, representative) jointly made soundings in Diyan and Pastun (Bastoon) Caves high on Jebel Baradost near Rowanduz in northeastern Iraq. Trial trenches reached the base at less than 15 feet. No Paleolithic evidence was obtained. The lowest levels revealed the earliest stages of agriculture, presumably a late Neolithic phase, and pottery of Hassuna and al-Ubaid types (see Safar). On the scree slope outside Havdian Cave at the foot of Jebel Baradost within view of Havdian village, Fuad Safar and I collected microlithic flints resembling those from the lowest levels at Kish[22] and suggesting cultural affinities with the ancient inhabitants of the Caucasus (cf. Gvardzhilas-Klde in Imeretia) and of the Vindyha Hills of India.

In the Qaara Depression north of Rutba Wells on the southern slopes of Tell el-Afaif typologically Paleolithic implements were collected. At Barda Balka, east of Chemchemal on the Kirkuk-Sulaimaniya road, Fuad Safar and I collected a fine series of handaxes. This Lower Paleolithic site is linked culturally to the site on the escarpment overlooking the Wadi Rutga west of Abu Kemal in southeastern Syria and to sites in Lebanon, Israel, and in the Wadi Arabah near Petra and the Wadi Bayir in Jordan.

1951a. The Oriental Institute of the University of Chicago Expedition (Robert J. Braidwood,[23] leader) worked east of Chemchemal in Palegawra Cave. Here Bruce Howe excavated flint artifacts, including "extended Gravettian" blade-tools and microliths, attributed by Robert Braidwood (1952, p. 26) to 10,000 B.C. or later. The wild animals killed by the Palegawra hunters were sheep, goat, pig, gazelle, and deer, a similar faunal assemblage to those we had found in Diyan and Pastun caves high on Jebel Baradost.

At nearby Karim Shahir, a temporary two-acre encampment of about 6,000 B.C., were unearthed chipped stone axes showing polished surfaces, mortars, and millstone fragments associated with beads, pendants and bracelets (see Robert Braidwood, 1952, p. 26).

At Barda Balka, Bruce Howe and Herbert E. Wright Jr.[24] removed from a gravel bed typologically Acheulian handaxes, flake and pebble tools of coarse flint and limestone and remains of fossil elephant and rhinoceros.

1951b. Ralph S. Solecki of the University of Michigan Expedition[25] (George G. Cameron, leader) made four examinations of Shanidar Cave (In Kermanji, Shkaft Mazin Shanidar [="Cave Big Shanidar"]), located near Lat. 36°50′ N. and Long. 44°13′ E. At an altitude of 2,100 feet this limestone cave overlooks the juncture of the Greater Zab and the Rowanduz rivers.

Four levels were identified: (a) modern to Neolithic; (b) Mesolithic with intrusive elements; (c) typologically Aurigacian flints; and (d) Upper Mousterian artifacts (see Solecki 1952 b, pp. 127-92).

1952-53. Solecki[26] (1953 b, pp. 229-32) continued work in Shanidar Cave, where he found an infant's skeleton in the Mousterian level at a depth of 26 feet. This is the first Paleolithic skeleton found in situ in Iraq.

Other Neanderthal (or Neanderthaloid) children have been found: (a) in Forbes Quarry, Gibraltar;[27] (b) at La Quina[28] in the Charente District of France; and (c) at Teshik-Tash[29] near Tashkent in Soviet Central Asia.

1954-55. Bruce Howe reports that Palegawra was further excavated to insure adequate sampling of stone industry and fauna. This reinforced the impression that here was a late state of the Zarzi terminal food-gathering horizon and furnished an excellent collection of fauna as well as somewhat more hopeful samples for C14 analysis.

Reconnaissance and sounding in the Erbil-Rowandiz quarter of the Greater Zab drainage revealed several rockshelters with some version of the Zarzi horizon and two with Mousterian horizons. No suitable C14 samples were obtained, and these sites remain geologically largely unfixed. Since the Zarzi horizon repeatedly proved to be the last Stone Age one in these caves (and also in those reported by others), it begins to seem that this, in various forms, may be the only stone-working tradition of the terminal food-gathering stage in caves in this quarter of Iraq and that this negative evidence suggests that open-air sites like Karim Shahir will eventually provide the remaining stages approaching the fully settled village one.

This second season's work was again an ASOR adjunct to the main enterprise of early village excavations elsewhere.

Further excavation may well reveal adult crania, possibly skeletons, which will indicate racial relationships between these early inhabitants of Iraq with the former dwellers on the pleasant slopes of Mount Carmel to the west, and those in Iran, the Caucasus, and Turkestan.

We now know that man has lived in Iraq from the Lower Paleolithic to modern times.

Crania[30]

In addition to the Shanidar skeleton referred to above, there is a good series of crania from historical periods[31] mainly from Kish,[32] especially those excavated by Buxton and the writer in Babylonian Mound "W."

1. The earliest historical crania (hyperdolichocephalic) are from Jemdet Nasr, 18 miles northeast of Kish[33] and those from "Y" trench at Kish.[34]

2. From the fourth millennium B.C. levels at El-Obeid nine dolichocephals, one mesocephal and one brachycephal (80.0) were excavated.[35] The roundhead is definitely not Armenoid, possibly Alpine.

3. Keith measured seven dolichocephals from the "Tomb Mound" (1900-1700 B.C.) at Ur of the Chaldees.

4. Lebzelter measured one dolichocephal and one Armenoid brachycephal (83.0) from Basra.

5. Other more recent levels yielded crania from Nuzi[36] and four skulls from Seleucia[37] dated 100 B.C. - 200 A.D.

6. Penniman described 14 crania from "Y" trench at Kish as being two brachycephals (80.5 and 80.7), eight dolichocephals (Eurafrican), two Armenoids, and

two mixed. Sauter (p. 78) disagrees with these classifications and from the cranial profiles places four crania in the Alpine group.

7. Buxton and Rice studied 26 crania from "A" trench (circa 2500 B.C.); among these were 18 dolichocephals, six mesocephals, and two brachycephals (82.0 and 89.0). These last are Armenoid; Sauter disagrees, regarding the cranium with cephalic index of 82.0 as Alpine.

8. Buxton and Rice measured four neo-Babylonian (eighth-fifth centuries B.C.) crania: three hyperdolichocephals and one brachycephal (81.0).

9. According to Buxton and Rice (pp. 67-73) there are three cranial types:

(a) The majority of the crania are longheaded and hypsicephalic, the extra height being the result of scaphocephaly, an Eskimo and Australian aboriginal trait. The ill-filled cranial box is characteristic. The general contour of this type of Kish skull is strongly reminiscent of the Combe-Capelle calvarium, except that the Kish crania are much smaller. The forehead is retreating, the browridges are always prominent, and the cheekbones rather wide. The nose is broad, in some cases inclining to extremely platyrrhine, although the face has seldom survived. This is the type described by Sergi, Giuffrida-Ruggeri and Fleure and named the "Eurafrican" type, which Fleure compares to Combe-Capelle.

(b) These crania are also dolichocephalic with rounded, not angular, contours when viewed from above. The eyebrow ridges are nearly absent. The occiput is very prominent. The orbits are usually horizontal. These belong to Elliot Smith's "Brown Race."

(c) The minority are brachycephalic with a flattened occiput. These are Armenoids.

10. Buxton and Rice (pp. 68-81) studied 26 Kish crania (see Table 75). They grouped them into Mediterranean, Eurafrican (17), and Armenoid (4) types. The differences between the longheadedness of the Mediterranean and Eurafrican and the brachycephalic Armenoid are so conspicuous as to be unmistakable, but the distinction between the Mediterranean and Eurafrican is less obvious, though it may be equally important. There were no traces of either Negroid or Eastern Asiatic blood, nor at Kish was there any skull of Nordic type, although some late crania from Nineveh found by Campbell-Thompson suggest a Proto-Nordic type.

11. Buxton and Rice (p. 79) concludes that "the inhabitants of the Kish region have not altered to any great degree within the last 5,000 years."

12. Doris Ray Swindler published in 1956 a study of the cranial and skeletal material from Nippur near Afaq (pron. Afej), central southern Iraq. (See references.)

13. Our detailed field notes[38] on the large series of Kish crania and long bones have been placed on Microfilm No. 2345, pp. 1-118 in the American Documentation Institute (ADI). (See Table 76.)

The greater part of these skeletal remains were brought to Field Museum of Natural History, now Chicago Natural History Museum.

Years later, after they had been cleaned and repaired under my direction by T. Ito, they were taken for study by Dr. Gerhardt von Bonin of the University of Illinois. His report has never been published.

I recorded the following measurements at Kish:

Field No.	Provenance, Notes and Measurements
210	From 8.5 meters. Found with No. 211 above stone doorsocket. GOL 192. GB 130. CI 67.71. Slightly prominent parietal eminences.

Field No.	Provenance, Notes and Measurements
212	From north-south railway trench. Depth 7.5 meters. Complete adult mandible. Third molars show some wear. Height of ascending ramus 54. Big. B. 75. Bicondylar breadth 105. Breadth of ascending ramus 43. Height of body of mandible 32. Right clavicle length 136.
215-216	Calvaria from north-south railway trench. Extreme thickness of bone suggests pathological condition in both cases.
319	From Z1 trench depth 10.5 meters. GOL 184. GB 141. Cl 76.63.
331	From Trench Z2 at 11.0 meters. GOL 189. GB 135. Cl 71.43.
345	From B Trench at 6.0 meters. GOL 180. GB 132. Cl 73.3
346	From B Trench at 7.0 meters near No. 345. Aged male calvarium, probably Hammurabi period. GOL 177. GB 126. Cl 71.24. Left OB 43. Height left OB 33.01 82.5. MFD 87. Big. B. 115.
387	From B3 Trench at 4.0 meters. GOL 177. GB 134. Cl 75.7. A narrow minimum frontal diameter and large parietal bosses. Probably Hammurabi period. Found near No. 388.
388	From B3 Trench at 4.0 meters. Cranium suggests hyperdolichocephaly. Probably Hammurabi period.
389	From B3 Trench at 4.0 meters west of Nos. 387 and 388. Almost complete brachycephalic cranium. GOL 158. GB 130. Cl 82.3. MFD 96. Interorbital width 29. Big. B. 111 (?). OH 29. OB. 31. Ol 93.5.

The majority were dolichocephalic with marked parietal bosses, a characteristic element among the early inhabitants of Kish. Few individuals possessed rugose characters; the supraorbital crest tended to be poorly developed and the muscular attachments were undeveloped giving a gracile appearance to the skulls.

The minority brachycephals, usually associated by language specialists to the Sumerians, also revealed these same gracile qualities.

At Jemdet Nasr,[39] a low mound 18 miles northeast of Kish, the Field Museum-Oxford University Joint Expedition conducted excavations in 1926 and 1928. On January 6, 1926 I accompanied Professor Stephen H. Langdon, Director of the Expedition, and Ernest Mackay, field Director, to Jemdet Nasr.

A Beduin, who had brought to our Kish camp some painted sherds, guided us to this site, which lies west of Tell Bargouthiat ("the Hill of the Flea") about midway between the Euphrates and Tigris rivers in the Hilla Liwa.

This site, destroyed by fire more than 5,000 years ago, yielded polychrome pottery, pictographic tablets in linear script and many other archeological treasures, so important that this tiny mound (150 x 30 x 3 meters) has given its name to a period in Mesopotamian chronology.

In March, 1928 I returned for two weeks with Louis Charles Watelin, field director, Eric Schroeder and 120 Arab workmen from the Kish area. My primary interest was to search for human skeletons associated with early types of painted pottery and tablets.

Six skeletons were excavated, but owing to the poor condition of the bones, only fragmentary parts of the skeleton could be preserved.

At Jemdet Nasr the floors of the small rooms were reached at an average depth of from 0.50 - 2.0 meters. The following notes were recorded:

No. J.N. 1. Fairly complete skeleton found at a depth of 3/4 meter at the eastern end of the mound. The skull and long bones were badly crushed. The grave furniture consisted of one unpainted pottery vessel.

No. J.N. 2. A fragmentary skull found at a depth of 50 centimeters. The skull was badly crushed and no observations were possible. Grave furniture consisted of two badly broken painted pots and a number of individual beads.

No. J.N. 3. A flattened skull found at a depth of 3/4 meter slightly east of J.N. 1. Grave furniture consisted of a painted kettle and two unpainted pottery jars.

No. J.N. 4. A complete skull found at the western side of the Tell at a depth of 1-1/4 meters. The skull was slightly crushed, but the following observations were possible before removal from the surrounding earth.

The sutures appeared to have been closed during life, which suggests that the individual was of middle age. The inion was markedly prominent, but there were no parietal eminences. This latter observation is of particular interest, since the majority of Kish crania show the development of these bosses to a marked degree. The supraorbital ridges were not very pronounced, and from the general lack of roughness due to muscular attachments, and from the sharpness of the ridges in the orbital sockets, I was inclined to believe that this individual was a female. The pelvis, however, was lacking and the long bones were beyond the power of preservation, so that accurate determination of sex was impossible.

The most important observations were on the length and breadth of the skull, which was measured with standard head callipers. It was impossible to obtain accurate measurements, but the greatest occipital length was approximately 195-8 millimeters. There was apparently little distortion in the actual length of the skull, but lateral pressure had undoubtedly caused some slight changes in the original width, which I estimated to have been about 100-15 millimeters.

It will readily be seen that the cephalic index based on these figures must have been between 60 and 65. This index is extremely low even for a hyper-dolichocephalic individual, and from personal observation during excavation I am confident that this individual belonged to a dolichocephalic group. Furthermore, there was no possibility of this having been an intrusive burial, since the archaeological objects found in the immediate neighborhood belonged to the early period, and there was no evidence of disturbance in the superimposed strata.

No grave furniture was found with this skull, but fragments of broken painted and unpainted jars were closely associated with these human remains.

J.N. 5. A fragmentary skull found near J.N. 4 at a depth of 1-1/4 meters. There was no grave furniture.

J.N. 6. A very fragmentary skeleton found in the center of the Tell at a depth of 3/4 meter. There was no grave furniture.

Since one skull (J.N. 4) is the only complete specimen yet found associated with this particular culture, it is of considerable importance to be able to assert that it was extremely dolichocephalic in form.

Thus, we see that racially the earliest inhabitants of Mesopotamia (now Iraq) were longheaded Mediterraneans; at least there existed a dolichocephalic element.

According to my theory[40] these were the direct descendants of the Proto-Mediterraneans, the ancestors of the modern Beduins and of the basic population of the Tigris-Euphrates alluvial plain from Baghdad south to Basra. The brachycephals were invaders who conquered the Mediterraneans and built the city states.

We have so far been unable to recognize the Mongoloid and Negroid elements among the crania. However, we can spot these racial elements among the present inhabitants. We are, therefore, faced with longheaded crania representing every gradation of the Mediterraneans and a roundheaded element which seems to have been correlated with the conquering invaders. Naturally, racial admixtures occurred during the past 200 generations and new elements were introduced, but these latter were very much in the minority.

Modern Man

Living Peoples. Since my volumes on Iraq contain all then available published[41] and unpublished anthropometric data, there is no need to recapitulate statistical tables and deductions here.

Similarly, each of the six sections of "The Anthropology of Iraq" contains many bibliographical references; the reader is referred to Field (1953a, 1955, 1956a). Attention is also called: (a) to the anthropometric data on 553 male Assyrians[42] measured at Habbaniya Camp during 1950; (b) reports[43] on the hair, teeth, "Mongoloid spot," blood groups and on the intensity of ultra-violet radiation; (c) articles[44] on special groups; and microfilmed articles.[45]

In order to present statistical differences between our groups measured in Iraq from 1925-1950, tables have been calculated and presented here (see Tables 77-95) for the first time.

Buxton (pp. 81-94) gives a brilliant summary of the ethnic relations between Mesopotamia (now Iraq) with the Near and Middle East extending eastward into India.

He warns against relying solely on averages because of the considerable mixing of races. For example, where a brachycephalic stock has mixed with dolichocephals, the resultant mesocephalic index will be misleading unless the variation from the average is examined. In a pure racial group, this variation will be small.

In the Near East there are the dolichocephalic Brown-Eurafricans and the brachycephalic Armenoids.

The question of the brachycephals[46] is of especial interest. Throughout the entire littoral of the Eastern Mediterranean the roundheads form a dominant element. In the Near East, especially in Mesopotamia, the population of roundheads is commoner in modern than in more ancient times. At Kish the Neo-Babylonian skulls show a greater proportion of roundheads, than do those of Early Sumerian times. At Kish they form an insignificant part of the population, but in the West the Armenoids are always very important. This type is widespread along the great upland arc to the north and east of Mesopotamia.

When the ethnic relations between Mesopotamia and India are examined, Buxton (pp. 84-94) writes that the basal population, as at Kish, is entirely longheaded, although several elements are represented. On the top of the basal population occur roundheads, as at Kish. As far as the cephalic index is concerned, the really pure types fall into two groups and the resultant hybrid: the Indo-Aryan and Dravidian; and the hybrid Indo-Dravidian. The Rajputs and the Chuda of the Punjab represent relatively pure types. The Turko-Iranians show considerable variation resulting from a fusion between dolichocephals and brachycephals.

The dolichocephals fall into distinct groups: the broad-nosed Proto-Indians, the narrower-nosed Chersiots, and the tall, narrow-nosed peoples whom Haddon has called Indo-Afghans. Their relationships are hard to trace. Haddon groups the Proto-Indians with the Australians and includes in his Pre-Dravidian group (Buxton's "Proto-Indians") the Sakai of the Malay Peninsula, the Veddas, the Indian jungle tribes, and some of the primitive peoples of the Dutch Indies. Evidence for the existence of this type in the Near or Middle East appears doubtful. At Kish no crania of this type were found. However, there does exist in the Near East a type with heavy browridges and occasionally a broad nose.

Buxton (p. 93) concluded that: "I cannot agree with those who would see in certain types of skulls found in Mesopotamia and others found in India or elsewhere proof of any association of these peoples in historic times...the physical type seems to me, to go back to a much remoter period, contemporary with the great 'Völkerwanderung, no doubt extending over a very long period of time, which culminated in an extension of longheaded people of a definite type all along the southern face of the great Eurasiatic massif. This community of physical type, possibly already disturbed, was finally altered by the spread of the Armenoid type and of peoples akin physically to men of that type, who penetrated from the highlands into the lowlands at a period in Asiatic history yet to be determined, and who by hybridizing in different degrees with their predecessors brought about that welter of physical types which confront every student of ethnology of the region stretching from Cape Cormorin to Kurdistan. It is to this mixed people that we owe, as it would appear, the development of great civilizations of the ancient world of whose origins we know so little, but of whose fine flower recent excavators have given us such striking examples."

Summary

Iraq has been occupied,[47] perhaps continuously, since Lower Paleolithic times.

We have archeological evidence,[48] including large handaxes from Barda Balka; Mousterian artifacts and a Neanderthal child from Shanidar Cave; Aurignacian flint implements from Shanidar; Mesolithic and Neolithic objects and vast quantities of historical materials from Kish, Jemdet Nasr, Ur of the Chaldees, Tell Asmar, Khafaje, Warka, Telloh, Nuzi, Nineveh, Babylon, Eridu, Samarra, Tell Hassuna, Jarmo, Matarrah, etc.

With regard to the modern inhabitants, the Beduins and Arabs belong to the Mediterranean race with every possible range of variation. There are two types of dolichocephals, one straight-nosed, the other with large convex noses. The brachycephals dominate the northeastern mountainous area.

As a result of the past 30 years of concentrated work in excavation of historical sites, preliminary cave exploration in Kurdistan, and my anthropometric survey, we are now in a position to determine the cultural and racial position of Iraq in relation to adjoining regions. As a result of further studies these pictures will come more clearly into true focus and perspective.

References

Al-Asil, Naji
    1949. Barda Balka. Sumer, Vol. 5, no. 2, pp. 205-206.

Allouse, Bashir E.
    1950. Hand list of the birds of Iraq. INHM, no. 1.
    1953. The avifauna of Iraq. INHM, no. 3, pp. 1-163. See Bibliography, pp. 147-
        51.
American Geographical Society
    1954. Iraq in "Focus," Vol. 4, no. 5, pp. 1-5. AGS.
Amschler, Wolfgang
    1936. Die ältesten Funde des Hauspferdes. Unter erstmaliger Benutzung der von
        Dr. Henry Field (Chicago, U.S.A.) in Kish ausgegraben Knochenmaterialen.
        WBKL, Vol. 4, pp. 497-516.
    1953. Goats from Ur and Kish. ADIM, no. 3926, pp. 10-14.
Anonymous
    1929. Paleolithic discoveries in northern Iraq. Science, Vol. 69, no. 1776, Sup-
        plement, p. x.
    1946. An introduction to the past and present of the Kingdom of Iraq, Baltimore.
        See Bibliography, pp. 112-18 and map.
Arutinov, A.A.
    1903. Ein Beitrag zur Anthropologie der Aissoren. JRA, Vol. 3.
Awad, Gurgis
    1952. Bibliography relating to excavations in Iraq, 1947-51. Sumer, Vol. 8, no.
        1, pp. 90-100.
    1953. Arabic publications on historical geography of Iraq. In Arabic. Sumer,
        Vol. 9, no. 1, pp. 63-97; no. 2, pp. 295-316.
Baqir, Tahir
    1952-53. The trees and plants of Ancient Iraq. In Arabic. Sumer, Vol. 8, no. 1,
        pp. 3-36; Vol. 9, no. 1, pp. 3-44; and no. 2, pp. 193-239.
Barth, Fredrik
    1952. A preliminary report on studies of a Kurdish community. Sumer, Vol. 8,
        no. 1, pp. 87-89.
Bashir, Francis and Awad, Gurgis
    1952. Historical notes on geographical names in Iraq. In Arabic. Sumer, Vol. 8,
        no. 2, pp. 236-80.
Basmachi, Faraj
    1950. The pottery of the eastern cave at Hazer Merd. Sumer, Vol. 6, no. 1, pp.
        104-105.
Bate, Dorothea M.A.
    1930. Report on fauna. In D.A.E. Garrod, "The Palaeolithic of southern Kurdis-
        tan." BASPR, no. 6, pp. 8-43.
Batten, Dennis J.
    1951. Cave exploration on Jebel Baradost, Iraq. BNSS, no. 13.
Bawden, Edward
    1944-45. The Marsh Arabs of Iraq. GM, Vol. 17, pp. 382-83.
Boesch, Hans
    1939. El-Iraq. EG, Vol. 15, no. 4, pp. 325-61.
    1947. Das Klima des Nähen Ostens: Qaiyarah. Zürich.
    1949. Beiträge zur Morphologie des Nähen Ostens. EGH, Vol. 42, pp. 23-33.
        See Bibliography, p. 33.

Boyd, William C.
   1939. Blood groups. TB, Vol. 17, pt. 2, pp. 174 and 233.
Boyd, William C. and Boyd, Lyle G.
   1941. Blood groups and types in Baghdad and vicinity. HB, Vol. 13, pp. 398-404.
Braidwood, Linda
   1951. The Jarmo flint and obsidian industry. Sumer, Vol. 7, no. 2, pp. 105-106.
   1952. Early food producers: excavations in Iraqi Kurdistan. Archaeology, Vol. 5, pp. 157-64.
   1953. Digging beyond the Tigris. New York.
Braidwood, Robert J.
   1951a. A preliminary note on prehistoric excavations in Iraqi Kurdistan, 1950-51. Sumer, Vol. 7, no. 2, pp. 99-104.
   1951b. From cave to village in prehistoric Iraq. BASOR, no. 124, pp. 12-18.
   1952. The Near East and the foundations for civilization. Condon Lectures, Oregon State System of Higher Education, Eugene, Oregon. See plates, maps and Bibliography, especially chapters 3-4, pp. 22-43.
   1955a. The Iraq-Jarmo Project of the Oriental Institute of the University of Chicago, 1954-55, Sumer, Vol. 10, no. 2, 1954, pp. 120-138, especially pp. 1-3, 5-9, 11-14.
   1955b. Early Man in Iraq, Archaeology, Vol. 8, no. 4, pp. 281-82.
Braidwood, Robert J. and Braidwood, Linda
   1950. Jarmo: village of early farmers in Iraq. Antiquity, Vol. 24, no. 96, pp. 189-95.
   1953. The earliest village communities of Southwestern Asia. JWH, Vol. 1, pp. 278-310, Paris. See footnote references and table 1 and especially pp. 278-87.
Brooke, V.
   1875. On a new species of deer from Mesopotamia. PZS, pp. 261-66.
Buxton, P.A. and Dowson, V.H.W.
   1922. The Marsh Arabs of Lower Mesopotamia. IA, Vol. 50, pp. 289-97, 1921.
Buxton, P.A., Pitman, C.R.S., et al
   1920-22. Survey of Iraq fauna by members of Mesopotamia Expeditionary Force, 1915-19. JBNHS, Vols. 27-28.
Buxton, L.H. Dudley
   1924. On the human remains excavated at Kish. In S.H. Langdon, "Excavations at Kish," Vol. 1, pp. 115-25. Paris.
Buxton, L.H. Dudley and Rice, David Talbot
   1931. Report on the human remains found at Kish. JRAI, Vol. 61, pp. 57-119.
Cameron, George C.
   1952. The cradle of civilization revisited. MAQR, Vol. 58, no. 21, pp. 324-30.
Christian, V.
   1938. Semites and Sumerians in Mesopotamia. Research and Progress, Vol. 6.
Clawson, M. Don
   1936. The Shammar Bedouin dental survey. DMOT, Vol. 53, nos. 2-3, pp. 3-36.
   1953. Dental survey of Iraq. ADIM, no. 3926, pp. 19-45.
Cooke, Hedley V.
   1952. Challenge and response in the Middle East. New York.
Coon, Carleton S.
   1948. The races of Europe, pp. 412-13. New York.
   1950. The eastern cave at Hazer Merd. Sumer, Vol. 6, no. 1, pp. 91-92.
Crawshay, R.U.E. de B.
   1923. Prehistoric man in Mesopotamia. Man, Vol. 23, p. 111.
Dodge, Bayard
   1940. The settlement of the Assyrians. NES, no. 10.

Dowson, V.H.W., see Buxton, P.A.

Drower, E.S.

1953. The Haran Gawaita and the baptism of Hibil-Ziwa. BAV.

1956. Water into wine: a study of ritual idiom in the Middle East. London.

Ehrich, Robert W.

1939. Late cemetery crania. In R.F.S. Starr, "Nuzi," Vol. 1, pp. 570-90. Cambridge, Massachusetts.

Falcon, N.L., see Lees, G.M.

Field, Henry

1929. Early Man in North Arabia. NH, pp. 33-44, January-February.

1931. Modern Arabs of the Kish area. FMN, Vol. 2, no. 11, p. 1. November.

1932a. Ancient wheat and barley from Kish, Mesopotamia. AA, Vol. 35, pp. 303-309.

1932b. Fish at Jemdet Nasr and Kish. FMN, May.

1932c. Human remains from Jemdet Nasr, Mesopotamia. JRAS, pt. 4, pp. 967-70.

1935. Arabs of central Iraq, their history, ethnology, and physical characters. FMNH, Anthropological Memoirs, Vol. 4, pp. 1-474.

1936a. The Arabs of Iraq. AJPA, Vol. 21, no. 1, pp. 49-56.

1936b. Fish in Mesopotamian "Flood" deposits. Man, Vol. 36, no. 75, March.

1937a. Jews of Sandur, Iraq. Asia, Vol. 36, pp. 709-10, October.

1937b. Oryx and ibex as cult animals in Arabia. Man, Vol. 37, no. 69, p. 56.

1940a. The anthropology of Iraq. Pt. 1, No. 1 - The Upper Euphrates. FMNH, Anthropological Series, Vol. 30, pp. 1-224.

1940b. The "Mongoloid spot" in Turkey and Iraq. AJPA, Vol. 27, no. 1, pp. 119-26.

1949a. The anthropology of Iraq. Pt. I, No. 2 - The Lower Euphrates-Tigris region. FMNH, Anthropological Series, Vol. 30, pp. 225-426.

1949b. Some notes on the Al bu Muhammad of Iraq. JRCAS, Vol. 36, pts. 3-4, pp. 274-77.

1951a. The Anthropology of Iraq, Pt. II, No. 1 - The Northern Jazira. PMP, Vol. 46, no. 1, pp. 1-116.

1951b. Mountain peoples of Iraq and Iran. AJPA, Vol. 9, no. 4, pp. 472-75.

1951c. Caves and rockshelters in Southwestern Asia. BNSS, no. 13, pp. 14-18.

1951d. Reconnaissance in Southwestern Asia. SJA, Vol. 7, no. 1, pp. 86-102.

1952a. Assyrian males measured at Habbaniya, Iraq. ADIM, no. 3617, pp. 1-277.

1952b. Photographs of Yezidis, Sulubba, Shammar and Turkomans. ADIM, no. 3603, pp. 1-58.

1952c. Anthropometric data from Southwestern Asia: Nippur workmen, Kurds of Iran, and the Beharna of Bahrain. ADIM, no. 3602, pp. 1-75.

1952d. The Anthropology of Iraq. Pt. II, No. 2 - Kurdistan and No. 3 - Conclusions. PMP, Vol. 46, nos. 2 and 3, pp. 1-174. See Bibliography.

1953a. Bibliography on Southwestern Asia: I. UM.

1953b. The Track of Man. New York.

1953c. Jebel Anazeh in Jordan, Iraq and Saudi Arabia. Antiquity, Vol. 26, pp. 312-13.

1955. Bibliography on Southwestern Asia: II. UM.

1956a. Bibliography on Southwestern Asia: III. UM.

1956b. A reconnaissance in Southwestern Asia, 1950. PMP, Vol. 48, no. 2, pp. 1-119, 1956.

Fisher, W.B.

1950. The Middle East: a physical, social and regional geography. Chapter 15, The Tigris-Euphrates Lowlands, pp. 339-70. New York.

Fohs, F. Julius
   1946. Development and land-settlement potentialities of Syria and Iraq. Houston.
Friederich, J.
   1932. Arier in Syrien und Mesopotamien. In "Reallexicon der Assyriologie,"
      Vol. 1, pp. 144-48. Berlin.
Furlani, G.
   1930. Antropologia della Mesopotamia antica e sepolture partiche. AAE, Vol. 64,
      pp. 202-208.
Garrod, D.A.E.
   1928. Notes on some Mousterian finds in Spain and Iraq. PPS, Vol. 5, pp. 268-
      72.
   1930. The Palaeolithic of southern Kurdistan: excavations in the caves of Zarzi
      and Hazer Merd. BASPR, no. 6, pp. 9-43.
   1938. The Upper Palaeolithic in the light of recent discovery. PPS, Vol. 4, pp.
      1-26.
Guest, Evan
   1932. Notes on trees and shrubs of Lower Iraq. DA, no. 26.
   1933. Notes on plants and plant products with their colloquial names. DA, no. 27.
Gunther, Albert
   1874. A contribution to the fauna of the River Tigris. AMNH, Vol. 14, pp. 36-38.
Hamy, E.T.
   1894. Documents pour servir à l'anthropologie de la Babylonie. NAM, Vol. 6.
Hooper, David and Field, Henry
   1937. Useful plants and drugs of Iran and Iraq. FMNH, Botanical Series, Vol. 9,
      no. 3, pp. 71-241.
Howe, Bruce, see Wright, H.E., Jr.
International Bank for Reconstruction and Development
   1952. The economic development of Iraq. Washington.
Ireland, Philip W.
   1937. Iraq. London.
Ivanovskii, A.A.
   Ezidy. In Russian. RAZ, Vol. 1, no. 3, pp. 100-103.
Jawad, Jasim
   1945. The social structure of Iraq. Iraq Government Pamphlet. Baghdad.
Kayssi, A.I.
   1949. The Rh blood groups of the population of Baghdad. AJPA, Vol. 7, pp. 549-
      51.
Kayssi, A.I., Boyd, William C. and Boyd, L.G.
   1938. Blood groups of the Bedouin near Baghdad. AJPA, Vol. 23, no. 3, pp. 295-
      98.
Keith, (Sir) Arthur
   1927. Report on the human remains. In: Hall and Woolley "Ur Excavations," p.
      214 et seq. Oxford.
   1935. Introduction. In Field, 1935, pp. 11-76.
Kennedy, Walter P.
   1935a. The polynuclear count in an Iraq population. RSTMH, Vol. 28, no. 5,
      pp. 475-80.
   1935b. Further studies on the polynuclear count in Iraq. RSTMH, Vol. 29, no. 3,
      pp. 291-98.
   1938. Intensity of ultra-violet radiation from the sky of Iraq. QJRMS, Vol. 64,
      pp. 489-94.
Kennedy, Walter P. and MacFarlane, James
   1936. Blood groups in Iraq. AJPA, Vol. 21, pp. 87-89.

Khadduri, Majid
    1951. Independent Iraq. New York. See map.
Kherumian, R.
    1951. Génétique et anthropologie des groupes sanguins. Paris.
Krischner, Harald and M.
    1932. The anthropology of Mesopotamia and Persia. AKAW, Vol. 35, pp. 205-
        27 and 399-410.
Krogman, Wilton M.
    1940. A study of four skulls from Seleucia-on-the-Tigris dating from 100 B.C.
        to 200 A.D. HB, Vol. 12, pp. 313-22.
Laufer, Berthold
    1931. Tamed deer in ancient times. FMN, Vol. 1, no. 3, p. 1.
Laurence, Barbara
    1956. Cave fauna from Iraq and Qatar. In: Field, Henry, "An anthropological
        reconnaissance in the Near East, 1950," PMP, Vol. 28, no. 2, pp. 80-81.
Lebon, J.H.G.
    1953. Population distribution and the agricultural regions of Iraq. GR, Vol. 43,
        no. 2, pp. 223-28.
Lees, G.M. and Falcon, N.L.
    1952. The geographical history of the Mesopotamian plains. GJ, Vol. 118, pt. 1,
        pp. 24-38.
Libby, W.F.
    1954. Chicago radiocarbon dates: IV. Science, Vol. 119, no. 3083, pp. 135-40.
Longrigg, S.H.
    1925. Four centuries of modern Iraq. Oxford.
    1953. Iraq, 1900-1950. A political, social and economic history. Oxford. See
        references, pp. 401-12.
MacFarlane, James, see Kennedy, Walter P.
Macfayden, W.A.
    1938. Water supplies in Iraq. Iraq Geological Department Publication no. 1.
        Baghdad.
Main, Ernest
    1935. Iraq from mandate to independence. London.
Müller, G.
    1938. Rassebilder in Irak. ZE, Vol. 70, pp. 47-51.
Penniman, T.K.
    1930. A note on the inhabitants of Kish before the Great Flood. In: Watelin,
        Louis Charles and Langdon, Stephen, "Excavations at Kish," Vol. 4, pp. 65-
        72. Paris.
Peters, James L.
    1956. Birds from Station T-3, Syria. In: Field, Henry, "An anthropological
        reconnaissance in the Near East, 1950." PMP, Vol. 28, no. 2, pp. 78-79.
Peters, S.P.
    1933. Vertical extent of north-westerly winds over Iraq in summer. MON, no. 64.
Rice, D.T., see Buxton, L.H. Dudley
Safar, Fuad
    1950. Pottery from caves of Baradost. Sumer, Vol. 6, no. 2, pp. 118-21.
Sanborn, Colin C.
    1956. Bats collected by the Peabody Museum-Harvard Expedition. In: Field,
        Henry, "An anthropological reconnaissance in the Near East, 1950," PMP,
        Vol. 28, No. 2, p. 77.
Sarkis, Yakub
    1941. Tobacco in Iraq: its existence and cultivation a little before 300 years ago.
        In Arabic. MBC.

Sauter, Marc-R.
   1945. Les races brachycéphales du Proche-Orient des origines à nos jours.
      ASAG, Vol. 11, pp. 68-131. See excellent Bibliography, pp. 119-31.
Seligman, C.G.
   1917. The physical characters of the Arabs. JRAI, Vol. 47, pp. 214-37.
Shiriaev, G.
   1956. Plants from Lebanon, Syria, Iraq, Iran, Kuwait, Bahrain and Trucial
      Oman Coast. In: Field, Henry, "An anthropological reconnaissance in the
      Near East, 1950," PMP, Vol. 28, no. 2, pp. 71-76.
Simmonds, S.
   1953. Economic and commercial conditions in Iraq. OES, July. See Appendixes
      I-X and map.
Smeaton, Winifred
   1934. A preliminary report on an anthropometric survey of peoples of Iraq.
      CIAES-I, p. 132. London.
   1937. Tattooing among the Arabs of Iraq. AA, Vol. 39, no. 1, pp. 53-61.
   1940. Individuals measured in Royal Hospital, Baghdad. In Field, 1940a, pp.
      131-55.
Solecki, Ralph S.
   1952a. Cave sites in the Rowanduz District. Sumer, Vol. 8, no. 1, pp. 37-48.
   1952b. Shanidar cave, a Paleolithic site. Sumer, Vol. 8, no. 2, pp. 127-92.
      See Bibliography, pp. 159-60.
   1953a. Shanidar cave, a Paleolithic site. Sumer, Vol. 9, no. 1, pp. 60-93.
   1953b. Shanidar cave. Sumer, Vol. 9, no. 2, pp. 229-32.
   1954. The Shanidar child. IP, Vol. 3, no. 8, pp. 4-7, March.
   1955. The Shanidar child: a Paleolithic find in Iraq. Archaeology, Vol. 8, no. 3,
      pp. 169-75.
Sousa, Ahmed
   1944. Irrigation in Iraq, its history and development. Iraq Government Pamphlet.
      Baghdad.
Speiser, E.A.
   1930. Mesopotamian origins: the basic population of the Near East. Philadelphia.
Standley, Paul C.
   1940. Plants collected by the Field Museum Expedition, 1934. In Field, 1940,
      pp. 165-97.
Stein, (Sir) Aurel
   1940. Surveys of the Roman frontier in Iraq and Trans-Jordan. GJ, Vol. 95,
      pp. 428-38.
Swindler, Doris Ray
   1956. A study of the cranial and skeletal material excavated at Nippur. Univer-
      sity Museum, Philadelphia.
Trotter, Mildred
   1936. The hair of the Arabs of central Iraq. AJPA, Vol. 21, pp. 423-28.
U.S. Department of State
   1953. Facts about Point 4 in Iraq. TCA. March.
Von Oppenheim, Max (Freiherr)
   1952. Die Beduinen. Vol. 3, pt. 2, pp. 175-495. Edited by Werner Caskel. Wies-
      baden.
Warriner, Doreen
   1948. Land and poverty in the Middle East. New York.
Watelin, Louis Charles
   1929. Notes sur l'Industrie lithique de Kish. L'Anthropologie, Vol. 39, pp. 65-
      76.

Watelin, L.C. and Langdon, S.H.
  1934. Excavations at Kish, pp. 65-72. Paris.
Weber, Neal A.
  1952. Observations on Baghdad ants. CASP, no. 1, pp. 1-30.
Weissenberg, S.A.
  1911. Die Mesopotamischen Juden in anthropologischer Beziehung. AAB, Vol. 7,
    nos. 2-3, pp. 233-39.
Willcocks, (Sir) William
  1911. The irrigation of Mesopotamia. London.
Wright, H.E., Jr.
  1952. The geological setting of four prehistoric sites in northeastern Iraq. BASOR,
    no. 128, pp. 11-24.
Wright, H.E., Jr. and Howe, Bruce
  1951. Preliminary report on soundings at Barda Balka. Sumer, Vol. 7, no. 2,
    pp. 107-17.
Zohary, M.
  1941. The flora of the desert south and west of Basra. LSP, Vol. 153, pt. 1,
    August.
  1950. The flora of Iraq and its phytogeographical subdivision. Government Press,
    Baghdad. See Bibliography, pp. 189-95.

Arabian Peninsula by Erwin Raisz

X. THE ARABIAN PENINSULA

In previous chapters we have traced Stone Age Man and his cultures and studied the physical characters of the modern inhabitants in Sinai, Israel, Jordan, Syria, Turkey, and Iraq--all countries adjoining the area which may be defined as the Arabian Peninsula.

We shall, therefore, include in this Chapter[1]: Saudi Arabia, Al Kuwait, the two Neutral Zones, Bahrain Island, Qatar Peninsula, Trucial Oman Coast, Muscat and Oman, Aden (including the Hadhramaut and the Eastern Protectorate), and Yemen.

The Arabian Peninsula is bounded on the west by Jordan and the Red Sea, on the north by Jordan, Iraq, the two Neutral Zones and Al Kuwait, on the east by the Persian Gulf and the Gulf of Oman, and on the south by the Indian Ocean.

This area includes about 1,000,000 square miles, of which nine-tenths is in Saudi Arabia. There is a gradual slope from west to east; the mountainous belt along the Red Sea coast tilts eastward to the flat littoral beside the Persian Gulf. The highest peaks, rising to 14,000 feet, lie in the Yemen. The desert areas are the Nefud in the north and the great Rub'al Khali in the south. Two great ancient river-systems, the Wadi Sirhan and the Wadi Hadhramaut, may be followed for hundreds of miles. The climate is characterized by dry winds, cloudless skies, and great extremes of temperature ranging from 120° F. in summer to severe frost in winter. Near the coast the humidity is very high. Rainfall in the north is limited to 4 - 8 inches annually.

The flora ranges from high altitude types in the western highlands and Oman to the xerophytic forms in the wilderness, steppe or desert areas.

The fauna also shows considerable divergence, but in the greater part of the area the principal wild animals are: the gazelle, wolf, hyena, jackal, fox, and cheetah. Among birds are the turkey bustard, eagle, falcon, hoopoe, and sand grouse. A few ostriches may survive in inaccessible regions. The oryx and tahr are rare.

For convenience, we shall summarize the data by political[2] divisions.

SAUDI ARABIA[3]

This country covers an estimated area of 93,000 square miles. Saudi Arabia is bounded on the north by Jordan, Iraq, Kuwait and the two Neutral Zones, on the west by the Gulf of Aqaba and the Red Sea down to Yemen, on the south by Aden Protectorate and Muscat and Oman, and on the east by the Persian Gulf, the Qatar Peninsula and the Trucial Oman Coast. Many boundaries remain undefined, but for our purpose these general areas will suffice.

There are four Provinces[4]:

1. The Hejaz, a plain 10-40 miles in width, along the Red Sea Coast from Aqaba to the northern boundary with Asir. On the eastern edge rise high mountains up to 8,000 feet.

2. Asir, between the Hejaz and Yemen, is also a coastal plain up to 40 miles wide and about 200 miles long. The eastern fringe is bounded by rugged mountains up to 9,000 feet.

3. Nejd, a large sedimentary plateau about 200 miles wide, is the seat of Riyadh, the capital. The southern boundary is the great "Empty Quarter," known as the Rub' al Khali.

4. Hasa extends along the Persian Gulf from Kuwait and the Neutral Zones to the Rub' al Khali. Here lie the oil fields.

Saudi Arabia by Erwin Raisz

Since three excellent accounts, including anthropogeographical data, of Saudi Arabia have been published[5] recently, further details here are unnecessary, so we shall concentrate on our two objectives.

Ancient Man. We shall attempt to trace the discoveries chronologically, except for Twitchell's list which for convenience appears under 1954.

1928. In March we collected[6] typologically Mousterian heavily patined flint implements on the summit of Umm Wual[7] in the northwest between Tapline and Jebel Enaze[8] (Anaiza), the tri-focal point of Saudi Arabia, Jordan, and Iraq. A fine series of Paleolithic implements was obtained on the highest point and slopes of Jebel Enaze.

On the eastern part of the great mudflat, which extends to the north and northwest of Umm Wual, I saw a large block of white, finely-grained limestone. This conspicuous object was surrounded by flint flakes, a large flint nucleus[9] and a flint hammerstone. The flakes fitted the nucleus. This limestone block had served as an anvil for the Paleolithic flint-knapper. [10]

1932. A flint arrowhead was found by Bertram Thomas[11] lying on the Sanam[12] sands.

1945. Cornwall[13] obtained a large Paleolithic handaxe from Duwadami (24° N. and 44° E.) in central Saudi Arabia.

1948. During December O.A. Seager[14] collected typologically Neolithic flint, quartzite and obsidian implements at Irq el-Kudnah (Lat. 19° 51´ N. and Long. 45° 24´ E.) and in the Wadi el-Fau area from Qaryah (19° 47´ N. and 45° 09´ E.) northwest to Jebel Tuwaiq.

1949. Don Holm[15] in October found a superb quartzite spearpoint (24.0 x 7.5 x 0.75 cm.), with broad pressure flakes on one side, from 65 kilometers east of Sulaiyil[16] (20° 30´ N. and 46° 15´ E.)

1950a. During January-February Holm and Clements of Aramco collected a series of flint implements[17] from Tell el-Hibr to Jebel Umm Wual.[18]

1950b. From June 7-17 along Tapline between Hafar al-Batin and Tell el-Hibr on the Saudi Arabian-Jordan frontier, I collected[19] surface flint implements at 15 sites; these ranged from Middle Paleolithic to Neolithic or later.[20]

Special attention is called to Tell el-Hibr. On the southern slopes of this series of low hills lie millions of flints, hundreds of them being scrapers, points, flakes, hammerstones and rejects ranging from Middle Paleolithic to Neolithic and later; presumably, modern Beduin strike-a-lights will also be found there.

The flint of Tell el-Hibr has a flaking quality unparalleled in the area from the Jordan River to the Iranian Plateau. This must have been the source of supply for the weapons and tools of many of the ancient flint-knappers and was probably used as one of the first mediums of exchange or barter in Southwestern Asia. There is a parallel in Western Europe; flint from Grande-Pressigny[21] in France has been found widely scattered throughout Europe.

1951-54. The staff of Aramco continued to collect surface specimens on archeological sites; this material was obtained by several desert survey parties.

1953. Mr. George Colley, International Bechtel Corporation, called my attention to the following archeological sites and caves: (a) ruins 10 miles northwest of Badana; (b) cave south of Duwaid; (c) depression, resembling sinkhole, encircled by an escarpment (125 feet high), with good grazing, used by Beduins; (d) caves near Ansab Wells; (e) sinkhole or meteor crater (300-400 feet in diameter) west and five miles south of Jauf Wells; and (f) inscriptions on low hill 1.5 miles north of (e).

1954. Karl S. Twitchell[22] has compiled the following notes on archeological sites[23] arranged by Province.

A. Hejaz

Three watering places for the use of pilgrims between Baghdad and Mecca constructed by order of Queen Zobeida, consort of Haroun al-Rashid, were visited. This trans-desert route is known as the Darb ez-Zobeida.[24]

Darb ez-Zobeida

1. Four wells at Thunthaba, 34 kilometers south of El Birka.
2. Cistern and many recent ruins at El Birka, 197 kilometers northeast of Jidda.
3. Cistern at Mislah, 30 kilometers north of El Birka.

Wadi Fatima and Jidda Vicinity

4. Ruins of Hadda and adjacent gardens on north bank of Wadi Fatima and 40 kilometers east of Jidda.
5. Scattered ruins and water tunnels along the Wadi Fatima from Hadda to Ain Jimun.

Medina Vicinity

6. Ruins of Alemat village about 30 kilometers east of Medina on pilgrim road to Hail (Hayil) and Baghdad. Nearby stand ruins of a flood-water catchment basin (200 x 150 feet), a well (18 feet in diameter), and a cut stone cistern.
7. The fort of Qaalat es-Surah (elevation 2,200 feet) on the pilgrim road to Damascus. A Turkish inscription bears the date A.H. 1073. Outside is a cistern (55 feet square), a well (36 feet in diameter and 70 feet deep).
8. Southeast of the present town of Khaibar (elevation 2,200 feet) and on top of the lava flow stands a large ruined village reported to be of Jewish origin.
9. Fifteen miles southeast of Khaibar lies Sud Haseed (elevation 2,380 feet). This dam (28 feet high, 182 feet along the base and 270 feet at the crest), was built

about 1,500 years ago in two stages. The walls are of well-dressed basalt courses.

Al Ula Vicinity

10. Three miles north of Al Ula on the Hejaz Railroad stand the extensive ruins of Horaiba (elevation 2,110 feet). Amid the rubble was a stone tank (5 x 5 x 5 feet). In the adjacent sandstone cliffs to the south are many hand-cut caves. Some of these could have served as dwellings, others were just large enough for a coffin; all seen had been opened for many years.

11. At Medain Salih (elevation 2,240 feet) are many large tombs cut out of the gray sandstone cliffs and hills. There are many well-carved eagles, men's faces, snakes, urns, gables, and steps. Inside the large rooms are many niches for bodies. Every tomb seen had been opened and robbed. However, in some rooms there was a hollow sound, suggesting tombs or rooms still unopened.

12. At the junction of the Wadi Ula and the Wadi Jizal (elevation 1,440 feet) stand ruins (180 x 200 feet) with many sherds, lava fragments, and sandstone and granite grinding stones. Upstream are ruins of large buildings, probably houses. Twitchell found a gold coin and a hammerhead. Thirty-four miles down the Wadi Jizal are many ruined buildings and water tunnels indicating intensive cultivation. Ten miles beyond this point is a ruined fortress containing many kiln-fired bricks. Nine miles further lie ruins of fortresses, villages, and water tunnels (elevation 1,010 feet). Ahmad Fakry observed that early Arab historians refer to the fertility and civilization of the Wadi Jizal. At the present time there are no inhabitants.

13. Near An Najal in the bed of the Wadi Aeis ancient walls were seen.

14. At Al Darr in the Wadi Yenbu sherds cover the ground. Coins and statuettes were reported, but none were found. This great valley has been under cultivation for centuries.

Midian

15. On May 8, 1931, the ruins of a Roman (?) temple, lying on the south bank of the Wadi Hamdh, were visited. This appeared to be a small temple with steps leading to the river. Many delicately carved gypsum fragments are now used as headstones for Beduin graves. A column and a fragment of a base were seen.

16. From the air three stone circles (200 feet in diameter), each with a tail extending about 200 feet, were seen in 1937 on hilltops between the Wadi Hamdh and Umm Lej.

17. The Umm Garayat mine, which lies 14 kilometers east of Wej, is believed to have been worked by the miners of King David. There are several ancient mines in this area.

18. El Gala fortress near Wej, on the pilgrim road to Mecca. This is one of the outposts built by the Egyptian Government to protect the pilgrims. Another fortress lies about 25 miles distant.

19. At Bedaa, near Dthiba, 60 miles east of Wej, tombs similar to those at Horaiba (No. 10) were reported but not visited.

B. Asir

20. Ruins of buildings and a water system were seen at Al Garia about 60 miles south of Khamaseen on the Wadi Dawasir and about the same distance from the western edge of the Rub' al Khali. Himyaritic inscriptions were seen on stones cleared from a well. Sherds lay scattered on the surface.

21. At Najran are two superimposed cities. Many walls, bearing Himyaritic inscriptions, still stand. Three grinding stones (4-1/2 feet in diameter and 14 inches thick) were seen as well as a large mortar.

22. The Mufija dam site near Najran shows expert cutting of granite for sluiceways, some of which had lime-concrete lining.

23. The Tariq el-Feel ("Road of the Elephants") is a ruined paved road from Najran to Suq el-Ahad. This construction is attributed to the Abyssinians about A.D. 570.

24. Eleven kilometers north of Tureeb (elevation 5,360 feet) stand low walls and inscriptions. There is also a pavement (100 feet long) and a semi-circular wall (38 feet in diameter).

C. Nejd

25. At Faid (elevation 2,550 feet) are ruins (1,000 x 900 feet). Legend attributes the founder as Faid bin Sami bin Noah, the grandson of Noah. The walls were built of mud and lava. A column and a sarcophagus were seen. Beads and sherds are scattered on the ground.

26. At Garara stands a cistern (126 feet in diameter) of well-dressed stone.

27. At Haleet, southwest of Dawadami, lie ruins of a mining town. Sherds, bearing a green slip, and grinding stones were seen.

28. At Mahad Dahab (Lat. 23° 29′ 52″ N. and Long. 40° 52′ 45″ E.), which lies 246 miles northeast of Jidda toward Hail, are ruins of a gold-mining town. Here may be seen ancient workings. On the surface lie sherds with a green slip, mortars and grinding stones of lava. Modern mining operations have been continuous here since 1936. Gold, silver, copper, lead, and zinc have been produced.

29. Other ancient mines have been located at Nogra and Najady, about 100 miles northeast of Mahad Dahab (No. 28). About 15 miles south of Nogra stand ruins (one kilometer square) and two cisterns. In 1949 six other ancient mines were discovered about 276 miles east of Jidda.

30. At Alameera (elevation 2,800 feet) are ruins and a cistern (18 x 133 feet) with lime-concrete mortar walls. Four other cisterns were recorded. About 1,000 paces south a dam runs diagonally across a small wadi. This rubble masonry is nine feet wide for 50 feet, then 4.8 feet for 1,000 feet.

31. At Shaib Buqqar, 39 kilometers south of Almeera, stands a cistern (90 x 90 x 5 feet). The original depth is masked by drifted sand. There are two 9-foot pilasters on the east and west sides and three on the north. The well-dressed, granite walls are 4.5 feet thick with good lime mortar, one-quarter inch thick, lining the cistern.

About 1.5 kilometers south of Shaib Buqqar is another cistern (200 feet in diameter and 10 feet deep to the drifted sand). There is a sand-box (150 x 50 feet). Stairs lead down into the cistern. Gold coins (circa A.D. 1300) are reported to have been found here. Four ruins lie to the west. Near two tombs (?), about 600 feet to the west, a few sherds with a blue slip and glass fragments were seen.

32. Extensive ruins of mud-brick buildings were visited at Jubaila during 1931. This town, recorded by Arab historians, has now been partially rebuilt.

33. Gerald de Gaury reports ruins at Daraya on the Wadi Hanifa. This ancient capital of Nejd lies about one hour west of Riyadh.

34. At Aflaj (elevation 1,650 feet), 214 miles south of Riyadh toward Laila, are five immense water pits. There exists evidence of former extensive cultivation. At the edge of one of these pits there are traces of three irrigation ditches, the largest being the upper (eight feet wide). The present water level is 27 feet below at this point. Several other ditches and water tunnels radiate from these pits.

Ten miles south of Laila stand three mud-brick forts (?). The one visited had walls eight feet thick and measured 40 x 40 x 35 feet, the latter being higher in ancient times. A typical room measured 8 x 9 x 7 feet. Sherds, bearing a green slip similar to those from Mahad Dahab (No. 28) and attributed to a period not earlier than the tenth century, lay on the surface. In addition, red sherds with a brownish-gray slip were seen. Coins were reported but none were found.

At Harafa, six miles west of the pit called Shughaib, relatively recent ruins were visited.

D. Al Hasa

35. Numerous mounds covered with sherds lie north of Sofwa near Al Qatif.

36. At Umm as-Saih near Al Khobar are many burial mounds, similar to those on Bahrain. In 1950 Field collected pottery and glass fragments here.

37. There are ruins at Oqair (Ojair) along the coast from the present Customs pier. In March, 1955 Dr. and Mrs. Field collected sherds from this chain of low mounds.

38. Ruins of mud-brick buildings and numerous sherds were seen on the western side of Jabrin Oasis (elevation 710 feet), which lies 161 miles south by west of Hofuf. Jabrin covers an estimated 7,500 acres. More ruins are reported to the south.

Crania

In view of the strict religious precepts of the Moslems, particularly the Wahhabi, the data available are extremely few.
few.

1. Mochi (pp. 411-28) measured some crania from the Hejaz in the Museum of Anthropology in Florence. The cephalic index ranged from 71.3 - 86.0.

2. Near Tell el-Hibr in a small rockshelter (5 x 4 x 3 feet) partly closed by a wall lay a bleached human skeleton. The skull was dolichocephalic[25] (C.I. circa 72.0) with marked parietal bosses,[26] massing of bone at glabella and with rounded orbital margins. Sex male. Aet. 40. This typically Mediterranean skull, probably that of a Beduin, was reverently replaced.

Modern Man

The population is estimated[27] at 7,000,000; no census has been taken. The urban-dwellers are given as follows: Mecca, 200,000; Riyadh and Mubarraz, 60,000 each; and Medina and Jidda, 50,000 each.

The location of the principal tribes is given by Lebkicher, Rentz, and Steineke (p. 53) with the Howeitat (Huwaitat), Anaiza, Sherarat, Ruwalla, and Southern Sham-mar in the northwestern sector. In the center live the Harb, Ataiba, Subai, and Suhul. The southeast is dominated by Al Manasir, who range northeast into the Qatar Peninsula. In the Rub' al Khali and on its northern fringe wander Al Murra, the famous desert trackers who have black, very curly hair and are dark-skinned.

A brief description of the peoples in each of the four Provinces is now given:

Hejaz. Since the holy cities of Mecca and Medina draw tens of thousands of pil-grims annually, some remain permanently. These pilgrims have drawn tradesmen from all over the world, so that an anthropometric study of this region would be of little value. For example, Moslems from China, India, Java, and Turkestan in Soviet Central Asia as well as Negroes from Africa, intermarried to some extent with Medi-terraneans, provide a racial medley. Coon (1948a, p. 409) writes that many mem-bers of the old Hejazi families may be grouped into a type where "the men are of medium to tall stature, broad shouldered, long-bodied, heavy of weight, and of a constitutional type which tends to an excess of both muscle and fat. Their heads are large and mesocephalic to brachycephalic, their faces are both broad and long, their noses frequently large-tipped and fleshy. The chin is prominent and the mandible strong. Their hair is dark brown to black, the beard heavy, and the eye character-istically brown, although light eyes are by no means uncommon. Although this Alpine-looking Hejaz type may not yet be established on a scientific basis, its existence will be confirmed by readers who are acquainted with the people of this region."

Mochi[28] recorded measurements and indices on 12 men from Jidda (see Table 96). The mean stature was 168.0, cephalic index 79.4, bizygomatic breadth 132 and nasal breadth 37.

Nejd. No anthropometric data are available on this region, but they undoubtedly belong to the basic Mediterranean type, of which the Southern Shammar are an ex-cellent example, with some Negro admixture.

Hasa. This area, bordering on the Persian Gulf, has a mixed population as a result of maritime trade for at least 6,000 years. In the interior there are Beduins of relatively pure Mediterranean types with some Negro admixture.

Asir. Coon (1948a, p. 409) writes that no anthropometric data are available, but that the inhabitants probably resemble the Mediterraneans of the Yemen highlands.

No anthropometric survey has yet been made; the political and religious objections are at present almost insuperable.

In June, 1950, I had an opportunity to study the racial types of several hundred Southern Shammar Beduins along Tapline. These men belong to the basic Mediterranean type, being far less mixed than their cousins, the Northern Shammar[29] of Iraq. The Southern Shammar, originally from the area of Jebel Shammar in northwestern Saudi Arabia, possess long, narrow heads, medium wide foreheads and faces, long total and upper faces, and straight or convex, narrow noses. The hair is dark brown with low waves, although there is some submerged blondism. The eyes are large, clear, and dark brown. The skin color is medium brown, the exposed portions being darkened by wind and sun. The unexposed portions are light brown similar to that of the Northern Shammar. The teeth appeared to be in good condition, sugar being relatively rare and expensive.

Although some Negro blood is evident, this appeared to be less infiltrated among these tent-dwellers. In other words, there were a few almost full-blooded Negroes, but almost no Negroid admixture, undoubtedly because of the tribal restrictions and penalties enforced. This is not so true among the Northern Shammar[30] where there has been considerable admixture.

To summarize, the Beduins of northern Saudi Arabia belong to the basic Mediterranean Race.

Comparing the Southern Shammar with the Beduins of Sinai,[31] the former are taller, larger-boned and more muscular.

Summary

Saudi Arabia has been inhabited since Lower Paleolithic times, although the present evidence for the entire Stone Age is very limited and widely scattered. The assemblage of the archeological mosaic has begun, but the general picture remains undefined. Ancient man left traces of his passing from the Wadi el-Fau in the south central portion northward to the northern half of Tapline area, or to be more specific from Irq el-Kudnah to Jebel Enaze and from Qaf to Duwadami.

The later periods are represented by scattered finds along the eastern periphery of Hasa, especially in the Hofuf area and from Medain Salih to Nejran[32] in the Hejaz.

Anthropometric data are not available, so that no racial analysis is possible. However, the Mediterraneans appear to be dominant with a darker, curly-haired element along the northern undemarcated border in the Rub' al Khali. The latter is represented by the great trackers, Al Murra tribesmen.

It is to be hoped that a National Museum of Arabia[33] will be founded at Riyadh with branches in Jidda and Dhahran, so that archeological, botanical and zoological collections may be made and research, including an anthropometric survey, with scientific publications may begin in the near future.

AL KUWAIT[34]

This independent tribal state is bounded on the west and north by Iraq, on the east by the Persian Gulf, and on the south by Saudi Arabia and the eastern Neutral Zone, jointly owned by Kuwait and Saudi Arabia; this borders on the Persian Gulf.

In area[35] Kuwait covers about 20,000 square miles. The population[36] has been estimated at 500,000 with 70,000 in Kuwait town.

The climate[37] is very hot (116° F. in July - August) in summer, with often a strong wind from the northwest, and cool (36° F. in January - February) in winter. The annual rainfall ranges from 2.5 - 6.0 inches. Sandstorms are frequent.

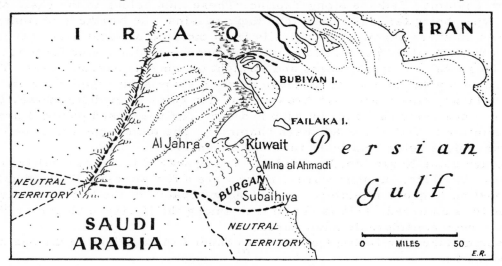

Kuwait by Erwin Raisz

Ancient Man

No Paleolithic evidence is available. A search should be made along the Wadi al-Batin,[38] which slices in a northeasterly direction across the western edge of Kuwait. It is possible that caves and rockshelters occur in this area. The two lines of migration were along the coast or beside the Wadi al-Batin.

Neolithic or later flint implements[39] of light color and poor quality were found by Colonel and Mrs. H.R.P. Dickson on the slopes of Jebel Burghan and Jebel Gurain.[40]

At Madaniyat, three miles west of Magwa, we visited[41] two stone-walled enclosures, the stones being flush with the ground. A few worked flints were collected. Trial trenches would determine the purpose and possible date of these small (10 x 12 feet) enclosures. The history of Kuwait remains to be written; this is of special interest because of the excellence of the harbor indicating an early sea-borne trade with India, Africa, and the Orient.

Modern Man

Few anthropometric data are available.

Coon (1948a, pp. 413-14) measured 40 Kuwaiti sailors in Aden Harbor. They show closer relationships, in many respects, with Iraq than Arabia. The average stature is 165.0, but the body build is often heavy and thickset. The shoulders are especially broad, the sitting height great. A mean relative span of 106 far exceeds that of all known Arabs and the relative sitting height of 52.5 approaches average European and Iraqi proportions. The Kuwaiti head is about the same size as that of the Yemenis, but is usually shorter and broader with a cephalic index of 79.6. The faces and noses of the Kuwaitis are much longer than those of the Yemenis. The upper facial height is 73.5 and the total facial height of 128.2 is almost as long as any in Iraq. The upper facial index is 56.0, the total facial index 96.4. The nasal length is 56.0 and breadth of 36.0 with an index of 64.7.

We see, therefore, that these 40 Kuwaitis are high mesocephals, leptoprosopic, leptene, and leptorrhine. The hair is straight or low wavy in equal proportions. The beard and head hair are usually heavy. The head hair is black but the beard ranges from brown to gold and red in one-third of the series. A high ratio of 18.0 per cent of red beards was recorded. About one-quarter of the group possessed mixed eyes, so that from the eye and beard colors we see evidence of submerged blondism.

Coon (1948a, p. 414) concludes that the Kuwaitis are straighter-haired, darker-skinned, heavier-nosed, and longer-faced than the rest of the inhabitants of Arabia and that the racial connections lie to the northeast into the Tigris-Euphrates Valley.

The Beduins of the interior belong undoubtedly to the basic Mediterranean type.

In Kuwait town there are Saudi Arabians, Persians (Iranians), Baluchis, Indians, and many individuals with varying degrees of Negroid features. This medley of races would render any random sampling, such as a hospital series, entirely worthless.

However, there is one group which would repay careful investigation; this is the Sulubba[42] or Sulaib, Sleyb, and other variant spellings.[43]

Encamped outside the west gate of Kuwait on May 21, 1950, I saw at least 100 Sulubba families in reed mat huts. This is by far the largest concentration of Sulubba I have ever seen, for there are usually only one or two well-patched black tents attached to each large Beduin encampment.

Summary

Man has lived in Kuwait since late Neolithic or early historical times.

Little is known about the early inhabitants, but there must have been cultural and racial links with Mesopotamia, Saudi Arabia, and along both shores of the Persian Gulf and beyond the seas.

The racial elements are basic Mediterranean and every variation of a vast medley of seafaring folk, whose dhows sailed the Persian Gulf, Indian Ocean, and Arabian Sea.

NEUTRAL ZONES

These two small areas are owned jointly by Saudi Arabia and Iraq and Saudi Arabia and Al Kuwait.

(a) The diamond-shaped western Neutral Zone is bounded on the west by Ansab, on the south by Uqubah and on the east by the Wadi al-Batin.

No evidence of Ancient Man is available. The modern inhabitants are Beduins.

(b) The eastern Neutral Zone is bounded on the west and south by Saudi Arabia, on the north by Al Kuwait, and on the east by the Persian Gulf.

No evidence of Ancient Man is available, but since worked flints have been found on Jebel Gurain near the northern border, we may presume other sites will be found on the highest points in the Neutral Zone.

The oil geologists of the American Independent Oil Company (Aminoil) reported but few Beduins in this territory.

PERSIAN GULF[44]

At Aden, Coon (1948a, pp. 414-15) measured 21 men from Lenja across the Persian Gulf from Aden. They are shorter (161.0) than Omanis (164.8) and built like the Kuwaitis. The cephalic index of the Lenja sailors is 81.0; they seem to bear a strain of the same brachycephalic maritime element found in Oman and along the Yemen littoral. The Lenja men are broad and stocky, lighter-skinned than the Kuwaitis, exclusively straight-haired, tend to baldness and very heavy beards. They have black hair and reddish-brown beards. Three-quarters of the group possess dark brown eyes, the remainder some light eyes. These Lenja sailors had more than the usual fourth of partial blondism, especially in beard color. The nasal profile is convex (43.0 per cent), straight in most of the others. The nasal tip, usually horizontal, is of moderate thickness. The wings are often flaring and the integumental thickness of the lips higher than in most Arabs, but with thin membranes and relatively little lip eversion.

BAHRAIN ISLAND

Bahrain,[45] an independent Arab State ruled by Sheikh Sulman bin Hamed al-Khalifah, consists of an archipelago of small low-lying islands about 20 miles off the Saudi Arabian coast.

There are five principal islands covering 231 square miles; the largest is Bahrain (30 x 8-10 miles) linked by a causeway to the northern island of horseshoe-shaped Muharraq.

Except for a narrow cultivated strip of Bahrain, the land is barren and the landscape consists of low, rolling hills with many rocky cliffs and shallow wadis.

In the center of the northern part of Bahrain rises Jebel el-Dukhan[46] (450 feet and 250 feet above plain level).

The climate[47] may be divided into three seasons: cold in December to March; pleasant in April-May and October-November; and hot and humid from June-September. During the greater part of the year the wind blows from the northwest and west. The annual rainfall is less than three inches.

Hence only xerophytic flora[48] exist except in cultivated areas where date palms (Phoenix dactylifera), pomegranate, banana and fig trees are irrigated by springs and artesian wells. Belgrave states that 200 species of desert plants have been determined.

There is little wild life. Mongoose and jerboa live in the cultivated and desert areas. On Umm as-Nasaan island live gazelle, black buck and hare. The lesser bustard (Ar. houbara) is hunted with falcons. Other game birds such as ducks, snipe and sand grouse are rare. Among the many local birds are bulbuls, hoopoes (Ar. hidhid) and escaped parrots. There are many sea birds, especially tern and cormorant, as well as herons, flamingoes and numerous shore birds.

The 1950 Census[48] gave Bahrain 109,650 inhabitants from 30 nations, with an estimated increase to 115,000 in 1952.

Ancient Man

Stone Age implements were found in 1954 for the first time by T.G. Bibby.[49]

Bahrain is famous for the 50,000 tumuli which are concentrated in three areas: (a) the largest group covers the plain between Aali and the Rifaas; (b) between Jidhafs and Diraz; (c) and a few dozen graves north of Suq al-Khamis Mosque. The

origin and dating of these burials[50] remain undetermined, although Mackay who
opened 34 tumuli attributed them to 1500-1200 B.C.; Cornwall and Albright assigned
them to the second millennium B.C. During 1950 Sir Charles Belgrave, T.G. Bibby,
and the writer opened a medium-sized tumulus[51] near Aali.

During 1954, the Danish Archeological Bahrain Expedition[52] located 12 surface
sites yielding rough flint flakes and chips, as well as cores with various degrees of
flaking and retouching. Blades are rare. Professor P.V. Glob describes these finds
of 300 implements and about 3,000 flakes, assigning them to the period ranging from
the Mousterian to Neolithic.

Professor Glob, again accompanied by T.G. Bibby, plans to return to Bahrain
to continue excavations during 1956.

Modern Man

Bahrain has been a focal point for seafaring people for at least 4,000 years, hence
the racial medley is unsurpassed.

Under the classification of Nationalities, there were recorded in the 1950 Census
the following: Bahrainis, 91,179; Persians (Iranians), 6,934; Indians, Pakistanis
and Goanese, 3,043; Saudi Arabs, 2,526; Omanis and Muscatis, 2,466; Americans
and Europeans, 2,208; other foreigners, 1,264; and total, 109,650.

Many races form the Bahrainis. The Beharna (Baharna), the original inhabitants,
are believed to be descendants of Arabs taken by Nebuchadnezzar (circa 550 B.C.)
into Mesopotamia (now Iraq); later they fled south and settled on Bahrain. They are
Shias living mainly in villages and certain quarters of Manama. Formerly, they
were second-class citizens, content to farm and work for their masters.

During the eighteenth century and later, Sunnis arrived. The Al-Khalifah, present
ruling family, belong to this religious group. There are many Negroes of the Sunni
sect; they are former slaves or descended from freed slaves, who have escaped
from other parts of the Persian Gulf.

No anthropometric survey has been made, nor would one be practical, because
the racial mixtures would yield little of statistical value.

However, at the suggestion of Sir Charles Belgrave in May, 1950, I measured
45 Beharna [53] males in the village of Jidhafs. Table 97, which gives the measurements and indices for these Beharna, reveals that these descendants of the aboriginal
inhabitants of Bahrain possess the following characters: a long, narrow head with
dolichocephalic index; a narrow forehead, relatively wide face with a very narrow
lower jaw; a short upper and total face; a narrow, short nose with a leptorrhine index.

Since tradition derives the origin of the Beharna from the Hilla Liwa of central
Iraq, this small series should be compared with the Kish Arabs, although to my
eyes they appeared to be similar yet distinctly different. For example, of the few
Beharna measured or the hundreds seen in Jidhafs, very few could pass as Arabs
of central Iraq.

QATAR PENINSULA[54]

This independent Sheikhdom of about 8,000 square miles has been ruled by Sheikh
Ali bin Abdullah bin Qasim al-Thani since August 20, 1949.

The coastline is rugged and the interior is sandy, windswept and barren. A few
scattered wells, such as at Umm el-Kahab, northeast of Dukhan, afford limited
water for the few Beduin, mainly Beni Hajar, Al Manasir and Al Naim.

The climate is blazing hot and extremely humid in summer and relatively cold in winter. The annual rainfall is about 4 - 5 inches. A strong wind usually sweeps across this inhospitable land.

The population in 1954 is estimated at 25,000,[55] with about 20,000 in Doha, the administrative town on the east coast.

The flora consists of low hardy, xerophitic species with mile after mile of camels'-thorn (Ar. hatab).

The following animals were listed[56] by Sheikh Mansur, blind for 20 years, who was described as the best informed man on the Qatar Peninsula: fox, hare, gazelle, wolf, hyena, jackal, jerboa, black mouse, brown and white desert mouse, horned viper, desert monitor, large lizard with spiny tail, small lizards and hedgehog. The birds[57] include eagle, turkey bustard, small bustard, vulture, hawks, hoopoe and many shore and sea birds.

In 1953 the population[58] consisted of Qataris in Doha[59] and Beduins,[60] and about 3,600 employees of Petroleum Development (Qatar) Limited,[61] including 226 Europeans, Qataris, or immigrants from Pakistan, Iran and Baluchistan.

Ancient Man. No evidence of Stone Age Man or his cultures is available.[62]

It is probable that when Sargon of Agade (Akhad), who reigned during the third millennium B.C., conquered Bahrain (Niduk-ki), his emissaries landed on the Qatar Peninsula, but we have as yet no archeological evidence. This inhospitable, barren, hot and windswept peninsula was not inviting to ancient or recent[63] settlers. Hence, apart from Doha and a few peripheral fishing villages, there are no settled communities, excepting the Dukhan and Umm Said oil centers.

Modern Man. The inhabitants may be divided into three groups: Beduins,[64] workmen at Dukhan and Umm Said, and Doha townspeople. The few Beni Hajar and Al Manasir seen had the characteristic long, narrow head and face; they were short in stature, with small bones, hands and feet. The hair and eyes were uniformly dark brown. They belonged to the basic Mediterranean Race with very little Negroid admixture.

The workmen at Dukhan and Umm Said were racially mixed, ranging from some very dark brown, deep wavy haired South Arabian[65] types to almost three-quarters Negro plus Arab. In Doha there was also a high percentage of Negro blood, the remainder being South Arabian, Persian, Baluchi, Indian, and other stocks.

Thus, anthropometric data on the main Beduin tribes, who live on the Qatar Peninsula or migrate there from Saudi Arabia, would prove of value. Since there are no large encampments, this would be a formidable task.

My general impression was that these Beduins are smaller and slighter in build than the Northern[66] or Southern Shammar and in these characters resemble the Beduins of Sinai.[67]

Summary. No Stone Age evidence exists. The modern Beduins belong to the basic Mediterranean stock. The Doha townspeople are Arab with considerable Negro and other admixtures from beyond the seas.

TRUCIAL OMAN COAST[68]

The seven Sheikhs[69] of this narrow strip, which follows an indentation of the Persian Gulf and across to Oman on the east, rule their own territories.

This area of about 6,000 square miles, known for generations as the Pirate Coast, extends from just north of Ras al-Kheima south and west to an undefined border toward the southern end of the Qatar Peninsula.

The Persian Gulf littoral is low and sandy with occasional salty areas (Sabkha sing. Sabkh). The shoreline is cut by salt creeks and lagoons, forming mangrove swamps. Many islands lie offshore. The central area is mountainous, forming a

backbone from Ras as-Shaam to east of Bireimi (Buraimi) Oasis; in the north these
highlands run down to the Gulf of Oman.

The climate is very hot from May - October, with 115° F. and 90-98 per cent
humidity. During the rest of the year the days are pleasantly cool and the nights often cold. A steady wind in summer makes the climate almost unbearable. The annual rainfall is 4 - 5 inches. The mud huts (Barasti), thatched with palm, are special
for this area.

In 1951 the population was estimated at 80,000 with about 8,000 Beduins. The inhabitants are Wahhabi Arabs with considerable Negro admixture and some groups of
Baluchis, Iranians and a few Hindus. The two largest communities are Dubei (20,000)
and Sharjah.

The flora is xerophytic except for mountainous areas, where herbarium specimens should be collected. The fauna is similar to that of Qatar, but rare animals,
including the tahr (Ar. Wial), and birds are reported from the mountains to the east.

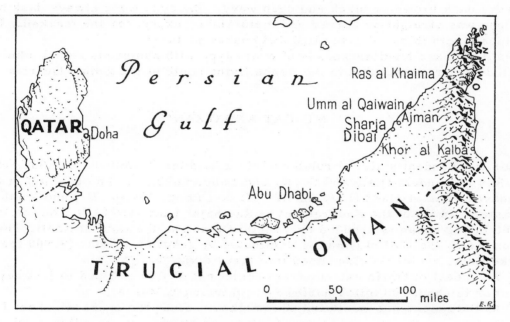

Trucial Oman by Erwin Raisz

Ancient Man. No traces of Stone Age sites were reported from the IPC survey
parties.[70] However, the coastal areas and caves in the mountains should be searched.
Portuguese ruins are reported near Ras al-Kheima and along the extreme part of
the northwestern shoreline.

Early in June, 1950, I collected[71] coarse, unpainted sherds on the summit and
slopes of Jebel Ali south of Dubei; this is the highest point (about 190 feet above sea
level and visible from afar) along the shore. No flint was found, but the gypsum
fragments on the surface added to the difficulty in the short time at my disposal.

At Ras al-Kheima a ruin with buildings was described; pottery and coins have
been found. This area would repay excavation.

On Umm Munar island, due east of Abu Dhabi, extensive ruins, possibly Megalithic, are reported; no photographs were available.

Modern Man. In Sharjah and Dubei the population appeared to be extremely mixed.
In the suqs the Arabs revealed considerable Negro admixture. There were also
Beduins from Oman and Saudi Arabia, Iranians, Indians, Baluchis and Muscatis and
other elements.

An anthropometric survey would prove valueless; however, samples of the Beduins (Beni Kitab, Beni Kaab, and Al Naim), dwellers in Bireimi Oasis, and the Shahu, a wild tribe living in caves near the shore northeast of Ras al-Kheima, would be important but exceedingly difficult.

Summary

No Stone Age evidence exists. The modern inhabitants along the shoreline are mixed because of the two ports of Dubei and Sharjah. No anthropometric data are available. My visual impression of hundreds in these two towns was that the racial elements linked to South Arabia rather than to North Arabia. For example, I saw no Beduin who looked like a Shammar from northwestern Saudi Arabia or northern Iraq. No Beduin looked like the Towara or Terabin of Sinai.

In general, the Beduins of the Trucial Coast appeared medium tall, thickset for these nomads, with larger hands and feet than their northern relatives. The hair was very dark brown or black and deep wavy. The eyes were always dark brown. The nose was straight or curved and leptorrhine, except for the markedly Negroid individuals with thick, everted lips and coarse features.

The Arabs are Mediterraneans of every type with numerous racial admixtures. The Beduins are more akin to the Arabs living south of the Empty Quarter.

MUSCAT AND OMAN[72]

This independent state,[73] ruled by Saiyid Said bin Taimur since 1932, extends from Ras Musandam (Lat. 26° 23′ N. and Long. 56° 32′ E.) on the Gulf of Oman southeast to Ras al-Hadd (Lat. 22° 32′ N. and Long. 59° 48′ E.) and southwest to the eastern limits of the Hadhramaut at Ras Sajar (Lat. 16° 8′ N.) on the Indian Ocean. Inland Oman is bounded by Trucial Oman and the Rub' al Khali. The northern portion facing the Gulf of Oman is dominated by Jebel el-Akhdar (9,900 feet).

Like Gaul, we may divide Oman into three divisions:[74]

1. The coast of Oman extends from southwest of Ras al-Hadd to just beyond Ras al-Hamar to about 100 miles northwest and includes Muscat.

2. Al Batina extends westward and northwest along the coast for about 140 miles from Hail al-Amair (Umair) almost to Khatmat Milaha, three miles north-northwest to Al Murair. There are many small towns and villages, each with a fort.

3. Ruus[75] al-Jibal is a mountainous promontory situated on the western side of the entrance of the Persian Gulf. At the northern end stands the Musandam peninsula. The coast is precipitous. In the rocky mountains live wolves, leopards, hyenas, and foxes. Here dwell herdsmen and fisherfolk.

Other areas are under the jurisdiction of the Sultan of Muscat: (a) the Province of Dhufar,[76] 700 miles southwest of Muscat; and (b) the town and port of Gwadar on the Makran Coast of Baluchistan, now West Pakistan.

The climate[77] is tropical with a mean annual temperature of 80° F., or more.

The vegetation includes tamarisks, oleanders, kafas, euphorbias, the milbush, rhamus, and acacias.

The population estimated at 500,000 is concentrated in Al Batina plain, where live 100,000-200,000 people, and in Dhufar, with 50,000-100,000.

Muscat was in Portuguese hands from 1508 to the middle of the seventeenth century. In 1741 Ahmed bin Said, a descendant of Yemenite Imams, consolidated Arab power in Zanzibar and on the East African coast. His family has ruled Oman ever since. Muscat is protected on the east and south by steep hills, the remainder by a wall. In 1952 the population[78] was estimated at 5,500 and the nearby town of Matrah, 8,500-10,000, for this has become the terminus for trade with the interior. The commercial and cultural ties are more with Iran and India than with Arabia.

Muscat and Oman by Erwin Raisz

Ancient Man. No evidence of Stone Age occupation is available, probably because so little of the area has been searched. Caves in the mountains overlooking the Gulf of Oman may well yield ancient man and his cultures. Wilfred Thesiger brought to London two little polished nephrite axes[79] from a few miles northeast of Salala in Dhufar. Just north of the Qara Mountains and due north of Salala on the coast, Bertram Thomas (1932b, pp. 126-29) came to Ba Musgaiyif near Qarn Hanun, where he found small megalithic[80] monuments consisting of aligned triliths bearing inscriptions and graffiti,[81] one representing a camel. Thomas found other ancient monuments, probably graves, and inscriptions in the Wadi Dhaghaub and Wadi Dhikur.

Crania. Thomas excavated a pre-Islamic skull, with mandible missing, from a rock tomb at Hasik near Ras Nus in Dhufar. Keith and Krogman (1932, pp. 312-14) describe the skull[82] as follows: probably 25-30 year-old male; forehead smooth, with glabella only slightly accentuated; mastoids small; palate very small and narrow; brachycephalic; orthocephalic; face low; and orthognathous; mesorrhine; and mesoconchic.

Keith and Krogman (1932, pp. 313-16) described an Omani skull,[83] complete with mandible, in the Royal College of Surgeons Museum for comparison with a South Arabian skull brought back by Bertram Thomas.

This is an adult male aged about 25. The supraorbital crest and inion are not strongly marked, the mastoids are rather small but glabella is fairly prominent. The skull is markedly round and hypsicephalic. The most prominent feature is the strongly flattened occiput, so that the post-auricular length is but 45.0 per cent of the total length. The face is long. The zygomatic arches are strong, but do not give high cheekbones. The nose is leptorrhine, the orbits hypsiconchic. The palate tends to be U-shaped and of average depth. The teeth are small, particularly the third molar. The face is orthognathous.

Modern Man. The Omanis are mainly Arabs of mixed origin with a strong Negro element, especially in Muscat, once a slave-trading center. There are also Baluchi communities, as well as others from Pakistan and India.

Few anthropometric data are available. Three Omanis were measured by Bertram Thomas.[84] Table 98 gives those few, but important, data. The mean stature is given by Leys and Joyce[85] as 164.8, the heads of moderate size with a meso-cephalic index. In addition to Mediterranean types, there are brachycephals.

Keith and Krogman (p. 310 and figs. 2-3) describe an Omani viewed in profile: the head above the ears seems lofty; its occiput rises steeply from the neck; the ears are planted very near the back of the head as in shortheaded peoples. The cephalic index was 82.7. The nose is long, prominent and aquiline. The lips are full and prominent. There is little beard under the lower lip and on the upper checks. The hair is black with no tendency to curl. The face is long and sallow brown. The stature is 5 feet 6-1/2 inches.

This Omani is compared in profile to an Armenian of Asia Minor and a Madrasi with a flattened occiput. Although there are resemblances, there are also differences. The Omani appears closer in type to the Madrasi than to the Armenian.

Keith and Krogman (p. 311) therefore postulate that there was an early trade migration from Persia (Iran) or an adjacent country along the Persian Gulf. Discoveries in the Indus Valley have established the fact that the peoples of northwestern India (now Pakistan) traded with the earliest dwellers in Lower Mesopotamia. They suggest that Pamir-Levant brachycephals broke southward and "implanted their predominant traits at various points on the Persian Gulf and further afield."

A series of measurements and photographs[86] of Arabs from the interior would prove of especial interest.

Summary[87]

No Stone Age evidence exists. The Omanis are Mediterraneans with a brachycephalic element. Considerable Negroid blood has infiltrated into the coastal population. Because of the seaport capital of Muscat, there is a medley of racial types including Iranians, Pakistanis, Indians, and Negroes.

SOUTH ARABS

It has been difficult to know where to include the anthropometric data recorded by Bertram Thomas[88] on the South Arabs, because his subjects ranged in origin from the Western and Eastern Aden Protectorates to Muscat and Oman and northward into the Rub' al Khali.[89]

Hence geographical assignment to present ill-defined political areas seemed impractical.

After careful consideration it was decided to include the data here at the close of the Muscat and Oman section rather than to place them in the Hadhramaut or in Saudi Arabia.

In any event, in order to accentuate the racial differences between the North and South Arabs, observations and deductions by Sir Arthur Keith and W.M. Krogman on racial and cultural relationships between the South Arabs and Africa on the west and India on the east should be placed apart from the sections dealing with the North Arabs.

Thomas (1932b, pp. 323-26) recorded age, stature, head length, head breadth, and cephalic index on 37 male adults and 5 children. These 42 subjects were divided among 10 tribes, so that the deductions may only be very tentative except to note that all except the 6 Somalis were brachycephalic.[90] Table 99 presents [91] the measurements and indices on 33 males, whose homes were widely scattered across South Arabia.

Keith and Krogman (pp. 301-33) present Bertram Thomas' limited anthropometric data, relate them to previous observations, and summarize their conclusions.

Seligman[92] discovered that the Southern Arabs were markedly roundheaded, a surprising discovery, for the peoples of Africa from the fellahin of Egypt to the Bushmen of the Kalahari Desert are longheaded. The Northern Arabs are longheaded, as were the earliest inhabitants of Jemdet Nasr, Kish and Ur of the Chaldees in Mesopotamia.

Bertram Thomas also proved that the Southern Arabs measured by him are amongst the most brachycephalic of peoples.

For comparative data he presents[93] in Table 100 the head length, head breadth, and cephalic index of nine groups covering a very wide range of territory.

Keith and Krogman (pp. 318-19) quote Bertram Thomas as stating that the Sultan of Muscat contended that "the affinities of the South Arabs are with the races of northeast Africa rather than with those of Northern Arabia."

However, Keith and Krogman conclude that the South Arab presents a strange blend of characters, for his fuzzy hair, often almost beardless face, very dark complexion and some of his facial features are reminiscent of races in adjacent Africa (Somali, Danakil, Hadendoa) and Egyptians from Predynastic to modern times.

On the other hand, many other features are Caucasian: the large dark eyes; the facial features and expression; and the nose and lips.

Other features, especially among sub-adults, resemble those of natives of southern India.

The Beduin of North Arabia is entirely Caucasian. The South Arab is half-Caucasian and half-Hamitic or Dravidian.

Keith and Krogman (pp. 320-21) proposed a new theory to account for these new data. At one time a Proto-Negroid belt crossed the ancient world from Africa to the Malay Archipelago. In the intermediate areas this belt became transformed "giving rise to the Hamitic peoples of Africa and to their cousins the Dravidian and brown-skinned peoples of India."

Thus, the Arabian Peninsula was once occupied by a people intermediate to the Somalis on one hand and to the Dravidian peoples of India on the other.

The Caucasian stock, at an unknown date, broke southward from north of the Anatolian-Himalayan highlands into the Arabian Peninsula and the lands which link Mesopotamia to the Punjab, Baluchistan, Afghanistan, and Iran.

Regarding the origin of South Arabian brachycephaly, Keith and Krogman (p. 322) conclude that, "it is not to Armenia but to Baluchistan and Persia that we would seek for the originals of the roundhead of South Arabia."

Keith and Krogman (pp. 229-30) continue that the South Arabians are small-brained with a cranial capacity grouped into three categories: below 1325 cc.; 1325-1475 cc.; and above 1475 cc. The majority are in the smallest category with none in the large (1475+) division.

The conclusion is that there exists in South Arabia a relatively unique brachycephaly; a wide, short skull of medium height but with non-Armenoid dimensions (i.e., post-auricular height).

The Hamitic influence may be traced as far east as the Mahra Qara-Shehera groups. The fuzzy hair, chin tufts, hair and skin pigmentation and the general facial picture are all Hamitic. Bertram Thomas noted that one of the Qara looked like a Bisharin. In addition, the Mashai give a strong hint of the Dravidian i.e., Tamil or Singhalese. The photographs of the Shehera and Kathiri children have an East Indian appearance.

In conclusion, Keith and Krogman (p. 333) write that, "the South Arabs represent a residue of Hamitic population which at one time occupied the whole of Arabia. To account for their roundheadedness and certain Caucasian traits we have had to postulate migration and miscegenation... The dark-skinned indigenes of South Arabia may have been roundheaded and, at a later date, Hamites from Africa and roundheaded Caucasians may have invaded their land and their marriage beds. For aught we know, many racial waves may have spread southwards or northwards in long past times. As already said, the clues to such problems lie buried in the sands of Arabia."

In conclusion, we shall quote excerpts from the two other writers.

The South Arabs differ from those of the north in being roundheaded, with curly to frizzly, black hair and a different caste of countenance.

A clear summary is given by Major-General Maitland, Political Resident in Aden, who wrote:

"The people of Arabia belong to two distinct and apparently quite different races. The common idea of the Arab type...is a tall, bearded man with a clean-cut, hawk-like face. The Arabs of South Arabia are smaller, darker, coarser featured and nearly beardless. All authorities agree that the Southern Arabs are nearly related by origin to the Abyssinians. Yet strange to say it is the Egypto-African race who are the pure Arabs, while the stately Semite of the north is Mustrab... Arab by adoption and residence rather than by descent."

Coon (1948a, pp. 402-403) divides the inhabitants of Arabia into two general groups: Arabs proper; and the aboriginal inhabitants of Hadhramaut,[94] Dhufar and the island of Socotra. The former are almost without exception of Mediterranean Race.

Summary

With regard to the South Arabs, there are racial connections to the west into East Africa, to the northwest into the Nile Valley, and eastward to Oman.

In addition, certain Caucasian features exist as well as Hamitic or Dravidian elements.

We must, therefore, postulate a people intermediate between the Somalis and Indians mingled with the invading Caucasians from the north and northeast.

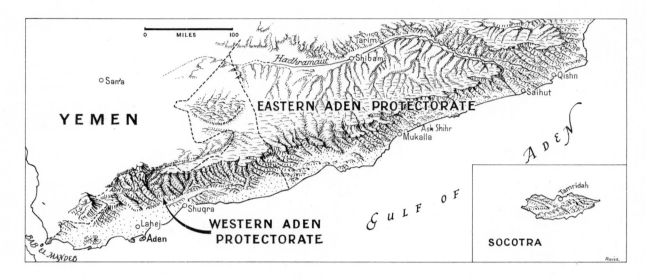

Aden Colony and Protectorate by Erwin Raisz

ADEN COLONY AND PROTECTORATES[95]

The area of Aden Colony is 75 square miles, that of the Western and Eastern Aden Protectorates about 112,000 square miles.

These three regions are bounded on the north by Yemen and the Rub' al Khali, on the east by Dhufar Province of Muscat and Oman, and on the south by the Gulf of Aden and the Arabian Sea. The northern boundaries remain undemarcated.

Since we are surveying the ancient and modern inhabitants from east to west along the shores of the Indian Ocean and the Gulf of Aden to Perim Island, we shall begin with the Eastern Aden Protectorate, including the Hadhramaut.

Hadhramaut. This region on the south coast of Arabia is bounded on the east by Dhufar Province in western Oman, on the north by the Empty Quarter, and on the west by Yemen and Aden.

According to Philby[96] the name of Hadhramaut occurs in Genesis as Hazarmiveth and Hadoram, sons of Joktan. Greek accounts refer to Adramytta and Chodramotites. Numerous ruins occur in Wadi Duwan and Adim.

The general features of the country are well-known from von Wissman's map[97] and from the air reconnaissance of Squadron-Leader Cochrane and Flight-Lieutenant A.R.M. Rickards.[98] A recent aerial survey has been completed. Up to 1938 Mr. and Mrs. W.H. Ingrams[99] were the only Europeans who had traveled from end to end of the Wadi Hadhramaut.

The geology of the coastal region around Mukalla has been described by Little.[100] A description with photographs of the geological reconnaissance has been published by Miss Elinor Gardner.

Ancient Man[102]

During the winter of 1937-38 Miss Gertrude Caton Thompson, Miss Freya Stark, and Miss Elinor Gardner explored the Hadhramaut with four objectives.

1. To bridge the gap in Paleolithic distribution maps between East Africa and Asia.

2. To test it as an area of possible contact with the Makran Coast, Mesopotamia, and India.

3. To investigate the material culture of its pre-Islamic inhabitants and to attempt to establish an absolute or relative chronology.

4. To study Quaternary physiography, former climatic conditions, and to compare local Pleistocene conditions with those of a typical desert area such as Kharga Oasis and the Libyan Desert. These were Miss Gardner's objectives.

In 1936-37 Caton Thompson and Gardner (1939, pp. 29-31) obtained Quaternary Paleoliths at the following localities: (a) on the Mukalla plain; (b) on the spurs of the jol near the south edge overlooking the Wadi Hadhramaut above Tarim; (c) on and in cliff screes of the Wadi Hadhramaut and the Wadi Amd; and (d) in the 10-, 5-, and 3-meter gravel terraces of the Wadi Amd near Hureidha, and in the somewhat earlier eolian silt of the valley's main filling.

Previously, Mr. and Mrs. Ingrams had found surface Paleoliths.[103]

The technique of the implements is Levalloisian but almost uniformly crude compared to African, North Arabian and Palestinian specimens of similar types. This may be due in part to the very bad quality of the chert, in part to the absence of culture contacts with advanced Stone Age technicians of East Africa.

No handaxe was found either by Miss Caton Thompson or by Huzayyin[104] during a brief visit in 1936.

Thus, a crude flake industry of Levalloisian type would seem alone to represent

Paleolithic Man in the Hadhramaut. No Chalcolithic evidence was found.

In the pre-Islamic ruins at Sune in the Wadi Adim south of Tarim were collected microlithic obsidian flakes in geometric forms--trapezoids, triangles, rectangles and crescents,[105] neatly retouched on their later edges. In 1935 Miss Freya Stark[106] had found similar obsidian tools on the ruin-field of Gheibun near Meshed in the Wadi Duan. The year before Mr. and Mrs. Ingrams[107] had also found some of these at Gheibun. In 1936 Huzayyin collected obsidian microliths there and felt assured their date was that of the ruins. From the surface of a small pre-Islamic mound, three kilometers west of Shibam, obsidian implements were also found.

From the tombs and Moon Temple at Hureidha, obsidian implements were excavated by Miss Caton Thompson (1944, pp. 134-36 and Pls. 58-59) who has summarized her study of 260 obsidian microliths, including four large and 20 smaller cores[108] as well as a quantity of waste and core residuals, from these four surface sites.

Miss Caton Thompson (1939, p. 32) suggests that "these little trapezoids were used as arrow-tips of a form well-known in prehistoric Denmark at least 6,000 years ago and common (whether in flint, chert, chalcedony, or obsidian is immaterial) over large parts of Europe and the Mediterranean, including Predynastic and Dynastic Egypt, at various dates down to 2000 B.C., or in the Sudan over a thousand years later. In Mesopotamia Sir Leonard Woolley has recorded a variant of this type in the royal tomb of Meskalamdug at Ur of the Chaldees."

The recorded connection of these obsidian tools with pre-Islamic sites thus covers a large area in the Hadhramaut, and we may deduce that they still formed the normal equipment of everyday life a few centuries or less before the Christian era. They were absent at the old Arab sites of Usaila near Aden, Senahiye, and Maryama in the Wadi Hadhramaut, and at Andal in the Wadi Amd.

The obsidian probably came from the southwestern region.

In conclusion, Miss Caton Thompson (p. 136) writes that there was no evidence of blade industries in the Paleolithic flake implements, apart from a single endscraper in the 10-meter (Levallois) gravels of the Wadi Amd. The true parentage of these obsidian and chert microliths lies in East Africa.

Crania

Morant (in Caton Thompson, pp. 107-11) described the human remains, including 14 incomplete crania, excavated by Miss Caton Thompson at Hureidha.

They were discovered in artificial caves, which had probably been used as sepulchers for a considerable period, and are attributed to the last few centuries before the Christian era. The bones were in a bad state of preservation.

Of these 14 crania, two were immature, eight adult male, and four adult female. The oldest was probably less than forty. Qualitatively, this series appeared to be unusually homogeneous; they are remarkable on account of the small size, feeble muscular development and low cephalic index, the average being 70.3 for the five males, 70.7 for the two females and 69.5 for the two juveniles.

The calvarial and facial measurements and indices have been published.[109]

The most significant factor with regard to these 2500 year-old crania is that they are typical dolichocephals with but two exceptions.

Several crania exhibit developed parietal bosses characteristic of the earlier inhabitants of Kish. The hyperdolichocephaly of most of this series is similar to that of the Jemdet Nasr calvarium which I measured in situ in March, 1928.

Modern Man

Coon (pp. 402-403) divides the varied population into four social and ethnic groups:[110]

1. Beduin, who live in the smaller side valleys and in the valleys between the Hadhramaut proper and the Gulf of Aden. They are slender, small-headed men, with ringlet hair, and facial features which relate them partly to the Veddoids. Their affiliation to the White racial stock is of borderline quality.

2. Tribesmen in Hadhramaut valley proper, who trace their ancestry to Yemen and other parts of Arabia. Their ancestors seem to have arrived during pre-Islamic times.

3. Artisans from different parts of the Arabic-speaking world.

4. Sayyids who form a priestly aristocracy.

Thus, in the Hadhramaut there are Veddoid and Mediterranean elements with Negroid admixture.

The origin of these non-Mediterranean, partly Veddoid, people is obscure. Culturally, they possess many primitive traits relating them to the food-gathering economy of the Veddas and Australians and to the cattle culture of the Todas in India and of the Hamites and Bantu in East Africa.

Western Protectorate.[111] The terrain is very rugged ranging from the littoral to the interior plateau (5000-8000 feet).

One of the best descriptions of the land and the people is given by the late Squadron-Leader A.R.M. Richards, who published[112] a sketch map from Nisab to the Wadi Marib.

Ingrams[113] described his explorations in Aden Protectorate.

Aden Colony.[114] In this area of 75 square miles the population[115] based on the 1946 census was 80,500. Since then there have immigrated into Aden about 2,000 Indian traders and clerks and many Arabs from Yemen. About 2,000 Aden Jews have emigrated to Israel. The population is estimated for 1950 as follows: Arabs, 79,500; Somalis, 6,500; Moslems, 8,000; Hindus, 3,500; and Jews, 1,500.

Summary

Stone Age Man lived in the Aden Protectorates, although no Lower Paleolithic tools have yet been found. The culture contacts seem to link with East Africa rather than eastward toward the Persian Gulf, but that may well be because of the lack of research. When I examined[116] Miss Caton Thompson's flint and chert implements from the Hadhramaut, there was a marked resemblance in technique and desert patina with some of my North Arabian Desert series, especially those from Rutba Wells[117] in western Iraq and those from the escarpment above the Wadi Rutga in southeastern Syria.

Furthermore, since stone implements have now been collected from central southern Saudi Arabia, in the Wadi el-Fau and Irq el-Kudnah, northward to Tell el-Hibr,[118] Umm Wual and Jebel Aneza (Enaze or Anaiza), the tesserae in the mosaic begin to form a pattern.

It seems probable in the light of our present knowledge that south of an arbitrary line drawn across the Arabian Peninsula fringing the lower margin of the great sands of the "Empty Quarter," Stone Age Man dwelt and migrated: (a) eastward along the coastal zone through to eastern Oman and around to the Persian Gulf; (b) westward across the Strait of Bab el-Mandeb into the Somalilands and Ethiopia (Abyssinia) and on down to the delightful uplands of Kenya and Tanganyika; and (e) northward past Marib, Nejran and up the western fringe of Saudi Arabia into Sinai, Israel, and Jordan.

The movement of these migrations was probably in both directions, although the numbers involved were undoubtedly small because of the rugged nature of the terrain.

YEMEN[119]

Yemen lies in the southwest corner of the Arabian Peninsula. It is bounded on the west by the Red Sea, on the north by Asir Province of Saudi Arabia, on the east by an undefined border near Marib in the western fringe of the Rub' al Khali, and on the southeast and south by Aden.

The ruler is the Imam Ahmed ibn Yahya Nasir, who became king on March 14, 1948.

Yemen is a rugged and mountainous country of about 74,000 square miles. The coastal plain varies in width from 20 - 100 miles, giving place to a high central plateau with peaks ranging up to 13,000 feet. To the east there is a tableland which loses itself in the great sands.

The climate naturally shows great variation from the extremely hot coastal strip, where the annual rainfall is three inches, to the capital at Sanaa (7,100 feet), where the temperature ranges from 60° - 85° F. and the rainfall 14 - 16 inches annually.

Fauna. The animals are mainly of African origin. Legends about lions and giraffes persist. There are gazelle, jackals, hyenas, baboons, hyraxes, and several kinds of rodents. Numerous birds are seen: storks, gray hornbills, pelicans, gray shrikes, green bee-eaters, fly catchers, Abyssinian rollers, hawks, and falcons. There are also some snakes and lizards.

Flora. This is also principally of African derivation, although in the highlands also flourish Asiatic, European and Mediterranean plants. Mocha coffee and Sanaa dates are famous.

The population may be divided[120] into: (a) the Sayyids of Ashraf, the religious aristocracy; (b) the Kabail, tribesmen belonging to the Qahtanic or South Arabian stock, who form the majority of the population; (c) the trading class; (d) a mixed group of African descent; and (e) 1,000 Jews, about 50,000 having migrated recently to Israel.

The total population is unknown; it is estimated[121] at 4 - 5 millions.

Hoogstraal (pp. 213-44) published photographs of Yemenis. Those in Faizz seemed like Arabs with yellowish-brown skins, very dark hair and eyes, and heavy eyebrows.

The mountaineers (p. 237) have narrow heads and faces with high cheekbones and slightly convex noses. A Mabari had a long, narrow, oval face with a thin-tipped, convex nose and recurved alae. The city-dwellers, especially in Sanaa, refer to these mountain-dwellers as Beduins, although they are a settled agricultural people.

In Sanaa an army group (p. 239) showed considerable racial admixture, the majority being short with oval to wide faces but with several tall men, one of whom on the right looking like a Kurd from northeastern Iraq.

Ancient Man. No evidence of Stone Age man and his cultures exist. However, there is every reason to believe that man lived there because of the discoveries of stone implements in Central Saudi Arabia and the Hadhramaut and across the Strait of Bab el-Mandeb in East Africa.

Further research in Yemen is most desirable to establish another link in the chain of Prehistoric evidence. In historic times[122] Yemen controlled the frankincense route through the old Minaean and Sabaean kingdoms.

Crania. Mochi (pp. 411-28) measured 15 crania from Yemen in the Museum of Anthropology in Florence. The cephalic index ranged from 74.4 - 88.4 and the nasal index from 55.6 - 77.8. Six measurements and two indices are given in Table 101.

Modern Man. Coon (1948a, pp. 403-408) gives a detailed description of the Yemenis based on 400 adult males measured in 1933-34. He considers the plateau Yemenis as forming, "the purest nucleus of the Mediterranean race in Arabia which has yet been studied."

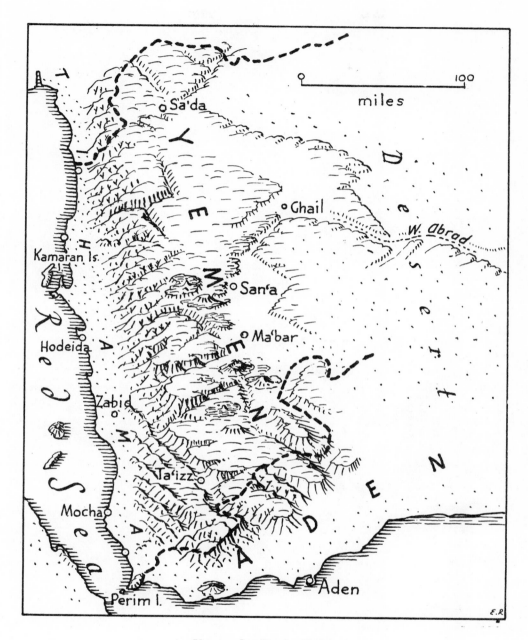

Yemen by Erwin Raisz

The men belong, with few exceptions, to a homogeneous Mediterranean type. The mean age was 33. The stature of 164.0 is typical of the smaller group of the Mediterraneans; although short, they are relatively long-legged. Table 102 gives the means for this series.

Thus, these Yemenis are medium in stature, mesocephalic, with a narrow forehead and face with moderate height and long upper face. The nasal height is similar to that of most Nordic groups and the nasal breadth is narrow. The face is leptoposopic and leptene, showing a disharmony. The nose is leptorrhine.

The skin color is medium brown. The hair is low wavy with 20.0 per cent in the curly category. In form the hair consists of wide, open ringlets and is the same in the dominant form found among the Veddoid aborigines of the Hadhramaut. There is no Negroid hair in this group. The hair is black but there appears to be submerged blondism, for 12.0 per cent had golden brown beards and rufous hair was not uncommon.

In addition, one quarter of the group have light and mixed eyes, although dark brown is the principal color. Not a single case of pure blue or pure gray eyes was seen in the Yemen.

The nasal index is convex in half of the group and 47.00 per cent possess straight noses, the remainder being concave.

Near Yermin, Ibb, and Taiz, a mixture between this Mediterranean strain and the nearby Veddoid type was recorded. The coastal Yemenis are naturally far more mixed since they represent Negroid farmers, introduced as agricultural serfs, as well as Malay and Indonesian elements from overseas. However, Coon (1948a, pp. 407-408) observed that the coastal Yemenis are shorter (160.0) than the plateau Mediterraneans. They are smaller-headed, with a head length of 177.0, height of 122.0 and cephalic index of 84.0. The face is broader and very short (118.0). The nasal index is 64.0. They often have coarse and straight hair. The skin color tends to be darker, their faces fuller, and the ears more prominent and slanting than the plateau-dwellers.

These sea-borne coastal people have little racial connection with the dwellers in the highlands. Among the sheikhs and army officers, there are tall, very longheaded and long-faced Atlanto-Mediterraneans. The Nordic-looking people are usually confined to the social stratum from which civil officers and religious men are drawn. The latter, who are lighter and blonder, may be descendants of early post-Islamic holy families from the Hejaz.

Summary

We have no Stone Age evidence from Yemen, although it may be presumed to await discovery.

The modern peoples appear to be mesocephalic Mediterraneans with some Veddoid admixture. On the coast there is a racial medley of seafaring folk. These include brachycephalic Mediterranean, Nordic, Negro, and Malay elements.

References

Belgrave, James H.D.
  1953. Welcome to Bahrain. Stourbridge, Worcestershire, England.
Bowen, Richard Le Baron Jr.
  1949. Arab dhows of eastern Arabia. AN, Vol. 9, pp. 87-132.
Brzezinski, A., Gurevitch, J. and Hermoni, D.
  1952. Blood groups in Jews from the Yemen. AE, Vol. 16, pp. 335-37.
Caton Thompson, Gertrude
  1944. The tombs and Moon temple of Hureidha (Hadhramaut). SA, no. 13, pp. 1-
    191. See map, plates, and Bibliography.
  1953. Some Palaeoliths from South Arabia. PPS, Vol. 19, Pt. 2, pp. 189-217.
    See maps and plates.
Caton Thompson, Gertrude and Gardner, Elinor W.
  1939. Climate, irrigation and early man in the Hadhramaut. GJ, Vol. 93, no. 1,
    pp. 18-38.
Cipriani, Lidio
  1938. Arabi dello Yemen e dell'Higiaz. AAE, Vol. 68, pp. 115-77.
Clark, Harlan B.
  1947. Yemen--southern Arabia's mountain wonderland. NGM, November.
Coon, Carleton S.
  1948a. The races of Europe. New York.
  1948b. Southern Arabia: a problem for the future. PMSAO.
Cornwall, Peter Bruce
  1942. Arabia awaits the outcome. Asia, Vol. 42, pp. 275-78.
  1943. The tumuli of Bahrein. Asia and the Americas, Vol. 43, pp. 230-34.
  1944. Dilmun: The history of Bahrein Island before Cyrus. MS.
  1945. An Arab state at the dawn of history. AW, Vol. 1, pp. 27-33.
  1946a. Ancient Arabia: explorations in Hasa, 1940-41. GJ, Vol. 107, pp. 28-50.
  1946b. On the location of Dilmun. BASOR, no. 103, pp. 3-10.
  1946c. A lower Palaeolithic hand-axe from Central Arabia. Man, Vol. 46, p. 144.
  1948. In search of Arabia's past. NGM, Vol. 93, pp. 492-522.
Deflers, A.
  1889. Voyage en Yemen. Paris.
Dickson, H.R.P.
  1951. The Arab of the desert. 2nd ed. London, 1951.
Dougherty, Raymond P.
  1932. The sealand of Arabia. New Haven.
Durand, Captain
  1880. The sepulchral tumuli of Bahrain. JRAS.
Dyson, Robert H. Jr.
  1955. The status of Archeology in the Persian Gulf. BPAS, Vol. 9, no. 1, pp.
    1-7, November.
Ettinghausen, Richard
  1952. Bibliography of books and periodicals in Western languages dealing with
    the Near and Middle East. See 1954 Supplement. MEI.
Field, Henry
  1929. Early man in North Arabia. NH, Vol. 29, no. 1, pp. 33-44.
  1931. Among the Beduins of North Arabia. OC, Vol. 45, pp. 577-96.
  1932. The ancient and modern inhabitants of Arabia. OC, Vol. 46, pp. 847-72.
  1934. Sulle caratteristiche geografiche dell' Arabia settentrionale. BRSGI,
    Ser. 6, Vol. 11, pp. 3-13.
  1936. Racial types from South Arabia. OC, Vol. 50, pp. 33-34, January. Chicago.

1937. Oryx and ibex as cult animals in Arabia. Man, Vol. 37, no. 69, March. London.

1941. Climatological data from Southwestern Asia. BAMS, Vol. 22, no. 7, pp. 299-300, and ADIM, no. 1591, pp. 1-20.

1943. The Yezidis of Iraq. GSA, no. 10, pp. 5-13.

1947. Near East travel bibliography. ADIM, no. 2392, pp. 1-60.

1948. The University of California African Expedition: I, Egypt. AA, Vol. 50, pp. 479-93.

1951a. Reconnaissance in Saudi Arabia. JRCAS, Vol. 38, Pts. 2-3, pp. 185-97.

1951b. The anthropology of Iraq, Pt. 2, no. 1, the Northern Jazira. PMP, Vol. 46, no. 1, pp. 1-116.

1951c. Reconnaissance in Southwestern Asia. SJA, Vol. 7, no. 1, pp. 86-102.

1952a. Camel brands and graffiti from Iraq, Syria, Jordan, Iran and Arabia. JAOS, Supplement no. 15, pp. 1-41.

1952b. Contributions to the anthropology of the Faiyum, Sinai, Northern Sudan and Kenya. UCP, pp. 1-352.

1953a. Bibliography on Southwestern Asia: I, pp. 1-122. UM.

1953b. Jebel Anazeh in Jordan, Iraq and Saudi Arabia. Antiquity, Vol. 26, pp. 212-13.

1955a. Bibliography on Southwestern Asia: II, pp. 1-144. UM.

1955b. New Stone Age sites in the Arabian Peninsula. Man, Vol. 55, no. 145, pp. 136-38.

1956a. Bibliography on Southwestern Asia: III, pp. 1-258. UM.

1956b. An anthropological reconnaissance in the Near East, 1950. PMP, Vol. 48, no. 2, pp. 47-63.

Glaser, E.

1890. Geschichte und Geographie Arabiens. Berlin.

Glubb, John Bagot

1943. The Sulubba and other ignoble tribes of Southwestern Asia. GSA, no. 10, pp. 14-17.

Gordon, Edmund I.

1955. The inscribed stone "foot" at Bahrain. BPAS, Vol. 9, no. 1, pp. 7-8, November.

Gurevitch, J., see Brzezinski, A.

Hamann, J.

1933. Les types constitutionnels chez les Arabes. L'Anthropologie, Vol. 43, pp. 313-22.

Harris, W.B.

1893. A journey through Yemen. London.

Hermoni, D., see Brzezinski, A.

Hogarth, D.G.

1904. Penetration of Arabia. London.

Hoogstraal, Harry

1952. Yemen opens door to progress. NGM, pp. 213-44. February.

Howe, Bruce

1950. Two groups of rock engravings from the Hijaz. JNES, Vol. 9, no. 1, pp. 8-17.

Huzayyin, S.A.

1937. Egyptian University Scientific Expedition to Southwest Arabia. Nature, Vol. 140, pp. 513-14.

1939. Some anthropometrical studies in southwest Arabia. CRICAE, pp. 156-57. Résumé.

Ingrams, Doreen
    1941. Excursions into the Hajr province of Hadhramaut. GJ, Vol. 98, pp. 121-34.
    1949. A survey of social and political conditions in the Aden Protectorate. Asmara.
Ingrams, W.H.
    1935. House building in the Hadhramaut. GJ, Vol. 85, pp. 370-72.
    1936a. Aden Protectorate; a report on the social, economic and political conditions of the Hadhramaut. HMSO.
    1936b. Hadhramaut: a journey to the Seiar country and through Wadi Maseila. GJ, Vol. 88, pp. 524-51.
    1936c. Unexplored regions of the Hadhramaut. JRCAS, Vol. 23, pp. 378-412.
    1937. A report on the social, economic and political condition of the Hadramaut. See Bibliography, pp. 176-77. CO, Paper no. 123. London.
    1938a. Peace in the Hadhramaut. JRCAS, Vol. 25, pp. 507-41.
    1938b. The exploration of the Aden Protectorate. GR, Vol. 28, pp. 638-51.
    1938c. The Hadhramaut: present and future. GJ, Vol. 92, pp. 289-312.
    1942. Arabia and the Isles. London.
    1945a. From Cana (Husn Ghorab) to Sabbatha (Shabwa): the South Arabian incense road. JRAS, pp. 169-85. October.
    1945b. Life in ancient Hadhramaut. Antiquity, Vol. 19, no. 76, pp. 187-91.
    1945c. Southwest Arabia: today and tomorrow. JRCAS, Vol. 32, pp. 135-55.
    1946. A journey in the Yemen. JRCAS, Vol. 33, pp. 58-69.
Ingrams, W.H. and Ingrams, Doreen
    1945. The Hadhramaut in time of war. GJ, Vol. 105, pp. 1-27.
Keith, (Sir) Arthur and Krogman, W.M.
    1932. The racial characters of the southern Arabs. In: Thomas, Bertram, "Arabia Felix," pp. 301-33.
Khadduri, Majid
    1951. Iran's claim to the sovereignty of Bahrayn. AJIL, Vol. 45, no. 4, pp. 631-47.
Lane, Arthur and Serjeant, R.B.
    1948. Pottery and glass from the Aden littoral, with historical notes. JRAS, pp. 108-33.
Lebkicher, Roy, Rentz, George, and Steineke, Max
    1952. The Arabia of Ibn Saud. New York.
Leys, N.M. and Joyce, T.A.
    1913. Notes on a series of measurements from East Africa. JRAI, Vol. 43, pp. 195-267.
Little, O.H.
    1925. The geography and geology of Makalla. Cairo.
Mackay, Ernest
    1929. Bahrain and Hemamieh. BSAE, Vol. 47.
Manzoni, R.
    1884. Il Yemen. Rome.
Melamid, A.
    1953. The political geography of Trucial Oman and Qatar. GR, Vol. 43, pp. 192-206.
Mochi, Aldobrandino
    1907. Sulla antropologia degli Arabi. AAE, pp. 411-28.
Modi, J.J.
    1920. The physical characters of the Arabs: their relations with the Persians. JASB, Vol. 11, pp. 724-68.

Musil, Alois
  1928. Northern Nejd, pp. 188-89. AGS, 1928.
Niebuhr, Carsten
  1774. Travels and description of Arabia. Amsterdam.
O'Shea, Raymond
  1947. The sand kings of Oman. London.
Philby, H. St. J.B.
  1923. The heart of Arabia. London.
  1928. Arabia of the Wahhabis. London.
  1930. Arabia. New York.
  1933. The Empty Quarter. New York.
  1934. Harun al Rashid. New York.
  1938. The land of Sheba. GJ, Vol. 92, pp. 1-21, 107-32.
  1939a. African contacts with Arabia. RASJ, Vol. 38, pp. 33-46.
  1939b. Sheba's daughters. London.
  1946. A pilgrim in Arabia. London.
  1947. The background of Islam. Alexandria.
  1948. Arabian days. London.
  1949a. South Arabian chronology. Muséon, Vol. 62, pp. 229-49. Louvain.
  1949b. Two notes from Central Arabia. GJ, Vol. 113, pp. 86-93.
  1950a. Golden jubilee in Saudi Arabia. JRCAS, Vol. 36, pp. 112-23.
  1950b. Motor tracks and Sabaean inscriptions in Najd. GJ, Vol. 116, pp. 211-
    15.
  1950c. Notes on the last kings of Saba. Muséon, Vol. 63, pp. 269-72. Louvain.
  1951. The lost ruins of Quraiya. GJ, Vol. 117, pp. 448-58.
  1952. Arabian highlands. Cornell University Press.
Rentz, George
  1950. Recent literature on the kingdom of Saudi Arabia. MEJ, Vol. 6, pp. 244-
    49.
  1951. Recent literature on the Hadhramaut. MEJ, Vol. 5, pp. 371-77. Wash-
    ington.
Rickards, A.R.M.
  1931. An air reconnaissance of the Hadhramaut. GJ, Vol. 77, pp. 209-16.
Sanger, Richard H.
  1954. The Arabian Peninsula. Cornell University. See Bibliography.
Scott, Hugh
  1941. The peoples of south-west Arabia. JRCAS, Vol. 28, pp. 146-51.
Segall, Berta
  1955. The arts and King Nabonidus. AJA, Vol. 59, no. 3, pp. 207-14.
Seligman, C.G.
  1917. The physical characters of the Arabs. JRAI, Vol. 47, pp. 214-37.
Sergi, G.
  1902. Crani arabi. ASRA, Vol. 8, no. 2, p. 11.
Steineke, Max, see Lebkicher, Roy
Stark, Freya
  1936. The southern gates of Arabia: a journey in the Hadhramaut, p. 166. New
    York.
Swauger, James L.
  1951. Report from Qataban. CMP, pp. 156-58. May.
Swayne, H.G.C.
  1935. Rock of Aden. NGM, December.
Thesiger, Wilfred
  1938. Empty Quarter of Arabia. The Listener, p. 971. London.

1946. A new journey in southern Arabia. GJ, Vol. 108, pp. 129-45.

1947. A journey through the Tihama, the Asir and the Hijaz mountains. GJ, Vol. 110, pp. 188-200.

1948. Across the Empty Quarter. GJ, Vol. 111, pp. 1-21.

1948-49a. Sands of the Empty Quarter. GM, Vol. 21, p. 312.

1948-49b. Studies in the southern Hejaz and Tihama. GM, Vol. 21, p. 8 et seq.

1948-49c. Wolves of the desert; the Saar tribe at the watering place. GM, Vol. 21, pp. 394-400.

1950a. The Badu of southern Arabia. JRCAS, Vol. 37, pp. 53-61.

1950b. Desert borderlands of Oman. GJ, Vol. 116, pp. 137-71.

Thomas, Bertram

1929a. Among some unkown tribes of South Arabia. JRAI, Vol. 59, pp. 97-111.

1929b. The south-eastern borderlands of Rub' al Khali. GJ, Vol. 73, pp. 193-215.

1931a. Alarms and excursions in Arabia. London.

1931b. A journey into Rub' al Khali, the southern Arabian desert. GJ, Vol. 77, pp. 1-37.

1931c. Some anthropological observations on South Arabians. Man, Vol. 31, p. 229.

1932a. Anthropological observations in South Arabia. JRAI, Vol. 62, pp. 83-103.

1932b. Arabia Felix; across the "Empty Quarter" of Arabia. New York.

1937. The Arabs; the life story of a people who have left their deep impress on the world. London.

1938. Arab rule under Al Bu Said dynasty of Oman, 1741-1937. PBA, Vol. 24, pp. 27-53.

Twitchell, K.S.

1933a. In the Queen of Sheba's kingdom. Asia, Vol. 33, pp. 4-9, 63-67.

1933b. More experiences in Arabia Felix. Asia, Vol. 33, pp. 106-12, 130-31.

1944. Water resources of Saudi Arabia. GR, Vol. 34, pp. 365-86.

Twitchell, K.S. and Jurji, E.J.

1952. Saudi Arabia. 2nd ed. Princeton.

Twitchell, Nora

1944. Arabia. AW, Vol. 1, pp. 41-47.

U.S. Department of Commerce, Office of International Trade

1948. Arabian Peninsula areas, summary of economic information: Aden, Bahrain, Kuwait, Musqat and Oman, Qatar, Trucial Oman and Yemen. IRS, Vol. 5, no. 92, November.

Van den Berg, L.W.C.

1886. Le Hadhramaut et les Colonies arabes dans l'Archipel Indien. Batavia.

Van der Meulen, D. and Wissmann, H. von

1932. Hadramaut: some of its mysteries unveiled. Leiden.

Weissenberg, S.A.

1909. Die jemenitischen Juden. ZFE, Vol. 41, pp. 309-26.

Zeuner, F.E.

1954. "Neolithic" sites from the Rub' al Khali, southern Arabia. Man, No. 209, pp. 133-36. See Bibliography, p. 136.

Zwemer, S.M.

1900. Arabia. Edinburgh.

Iran by Erwin Raisz

XI: IRAN

Iran,[1] formerly Persia, is bounded on the north by Transcaucasia, the Caspian Sea, and Turkestan; on the east by Afghanistan and West Pakistan; on the south by the Persian Gulf and the Gulf of Oman; and on the west by Anatolia and Iraq.

Iran may be divided into four zones:

(a) The saucer-shaped Iranian Plateau, with an average height of 4,000 feet above sea level, is bounded on the north by the Elburz Mountains, on the west and south by the Zagros range, and in the east by Afghanistan and Baluchistan. The Elburz chain is dominated by snow-capped Mt. Demavend (19,000 feet), northeast of Tehran. The Zagros runs northwest to southeast for 800 miles with many peaks rising 9,000 - 10,000 feet.

(b) The coastal plain between the Elburz and the southern shore of the Caspian. This is a narrow fertile band with an annual rainfall up to 80 inches.

(c) The humid littoral plain beside the Persian Gulf.[2]

(d) The two large desert areas of Khurasan are the Dasht-i-Kavir and the Dasht-1-Lut.

The greater part of Iran has an arid and semi-arid climate[3] with freezing temperatures in winter and hot summers. Tehran (4,002 feet) has recorded a maximum range of 104° and -5° F. with an annual daily average of 62°. During the summer the wind blows constantly from the north. The vegetation[4] tends to be limited except along the fertile band from the Caspian shore to an altitude of 3,000 feet, where the flora is Mediterranean with extensive forests of alder, beech, boxwood, elm, hornbeam, juniper, maple, oak, walnut, plane, poplar, and willow trees. In other areas flourish the Euphrates poplar, the blackberry, willow, tamarisk, and licorice.

About one-third of Iran is desert and wasteland with less than 15.0 per cent under cultivation. The main agricultural areas are the Caspian provinces, Azerbaijan and Khurasan. The principal crops are wheat, barley, cotton, rice, tea, sugar beet, tobacco, fruit and vegetables, and lucerne for animal feeding. Irrigation[5] is mainly by qanat.

Iran may be divided into five zoological zones: the Iranian Plateau, the Caspian littoral, the territory west of Shiraz, Khuzistan, and the Persian Gulf shoreline. The fauna[6] of the Plateau is Palearctic with a prevalence of desert forms. Beside the Caspian the animals are similar to those of southeastern Europe except for the rare tiger still seen in Mazanderan. Wild asses live in the salt deserts. Ibex, moufflon, and bears are found in the mountains. There are also wild boar, badger, fox, jackal, and hare. Game birds are plentiful, including snipe, woodcock, pheasant, and duck in Mazanderan. Amphibians and reptiles are relatively rare.

Sheep (18,000,000) are raised for meat and for wool for carpets. Karakul sheep are kept for lambskins. In 1951 there were 7,000,000 goats and 3,900,000 head of cattle.

The area of Iran is estimated at 628,000 square miles with a population[7] in 1950 of 18,772,000 comprising the following urban-dwellers: Tehran and district, 1,010,-000; Tabriz, 272,000; Isfahan, 192,000; and Meshed, 191,000.

Persian, an Indo-Aryan language[8] related to those of Western Europe, is spoken everywhere. However, Kurdish is widely spoken in the northwest, and the Lurs, Bakhtiari, Qashqai and Baluchi (in southeast) speak their own languages.

With regard to religion,[9] the majority are Shia Moslems but there are some Sunnis. There are also about 10,000 Parsees or Fire-Worshipers, the remnants of the great Zoroastrian sect. Jews and Armenians in Isfahan, Assyrians near Urmia, Uniates and Latin Christians are found. Although we are not concerned primarily with the historical period, some references[10] are given.

Ancient Man

1933a. W.E. Browne[11] collected typologically Middle Paleolithic implements 27 miles from Lake Niriz, southeast of Shiraz, at 8,000 feet above sea-level in sparsely wooded country with nearby large springs. This may well have been a sweet-water lake in Paleolithic times.

1933b. Browne collected Neolithic flint implements on the shore of Daryacheh-i-Maharlu,[12] a shoe-shaped lake (8 x 3 miles) lying 10 miles southeast of Shiraz. The 20-foot raised beaches suggest that the lake level may have been lowered suddenly.

1934a. Browne and Field visited[13] Maharlu and examined two limestone rock-shelters (18 x 10 x 14 feet), each with an outside platform and scree slope. Here we collected hundreds of small flints, including many microliths. These rockshelters are located 10 - 15 meters above the level of the valley, which leads down to the present shoreline of the lake, about 1,000 paces distant. These rockshelters would repay further research.

1934b. Fabri searched for Stone Age traces in Iranian Baluchistan.

1949a. Carleton S. Coon[14] excavated Belt Cave[15] at the southeast corner of the Caspian. Four cultural horizons were found:[16] (a) a mixed deposit with Neolithic, Iron Age, Islamic, and modern materials; (b) a true Neolithic horizon with pottery and domestic animals in upper level and domestic sheep and goats but no pottery below; (c) a Mesolithic culture in which the principal food was supplied by a grassland or desert-animal, Gazella subguttarosa jacovlev, still found on the Turkoman plain; and (d) an earlier Mesolithic during which Belt Cave was a flint factory and the principal food was a small seal and many water birds. Below was sterile clay and at the bottom the limestone cave floor.

1949b. Coon also examined nearby Hotu Cave which gave indications of yielding deeper deposits.

1949c. At Tamtama, 13 miles northwest of Lake Rezaiyeh (Lake Urmia) at 5,000 feet, Coon excavated some animal bones and one Neanderthaloid femur associated with 23 crude implements and cherty flakes.

1949d. In a small cave at Bisitun (anc. Behistun), 30 miles east of Kermanshah on the main road from Baghdad to Tehran, Coon excavated about 1,100 implements and many animal bones.

1950. During the Peabody Museum-Harvard Expedition[17] a reconnaissance survey was conducted in Khuzistan and Luristan. Flint implements were found at: (a) Manouchcharabad, southwest of Dizful; (b) Papila (Papileh) on the Wadi Kahunak, southeast of Dizful; (c) Sareb-Darreh, seven miles southwest of Khurrumabad; and (d) two rockshelters overlooking Khurrumabad. At Konji rockshelter (50 x 60 x 25 feet) 300 feet above the valley floor near Khurrumabad, we sank a small trial trench. Typologically Upper Paleolithic implements were found. This rockshelter deserves excavation.

1951a. Coon returned with an expedition[18] to Belt Cave. Excavation confirmed the four levels found in 1949, particularly the pre-ceramic Neolithic. Four skeletons were unearthed.

1951b. Work was begun in nearby Hotu Cave, sealed since about 700 B.C., to a depth of 14.0 meters to a point where the walls were sloping in, and where the underlying deposit consisted of an homogeneous mass of nearly fluid kaolin. The deposits were divided[19] into "Iron Age, Neolithic, and putatively Pleistocene." The Neolithic specimens began with the software of the Upper Neolithic of Belt Cave and continued into a transition to painted pottery similar to Sialk II.

The Pleistocene deposit revealed a sequence of four gravels and three intervening sands above a succession of three complexes of red gravels and sands and an underlying black humus. The fauna showed an alternation of wet and dry forms: the former represented by ox and pig; the latter by gazelle, seal, mole-vole and thrush. Sheep were found in both climatic phases.

The flint assemblage included cores, flakes, flake-blades and blades, some of Aurignacian type.

In the lowest gravel bed the skeletons of a man and two women were found. The man was robust, belonging to the general Crô-Magnon category. Female No. 1 was short, mesocephalic and had arthritis; her face resembled that of No. 2, who was tall and slender, with a long, narrow, high-vaulted skull, a large brain, an orthognathous face, a pointed chin and small modern-type teeth.

These females seem to represent a dry-lands adapted form of Upper Paleolithic man, with no trace of the Neanderthaloid characters shown by the two Mesolithic skeletons from Belt Cave.

1951c. In Khunik rockshelter in southern Khurasan Coon collected patinated Mousterian implements on the surface. Early Islamic pottery was excavated. Evidence of an earthquake was recorded.

Summary

Paleolithic man lived in Iran ranging[20] from Lake Urmia southeast across the Zagros Mountains to Lake Niriz southeast of Shiraz and from the southeastern corner of the Caspian to southern Khurasan.

We now have evidence from deep in Hotu Cave of Upper Paleolithic man and his local cultural facies.

Other sites, mainly in the limestone caves and rockshelters of Luristan, indicate many potential sites for excavation. The triangular region from Shiraz to Meshed to Zahidan (formerly Duzdab) deserves reconnaissance[21] for caves and rockshelters. Similarly, the prehistoric racial and cultural connections between southeastern Iran and Pakistan along the Makran Coast should be investigated.

Historical Crania

From excavations at Tepe Hissar, Hamadan (anc. Ecbatana), Shah Tepe, Tepe Jamshidi and Tepe Bad-Hora (Luristan), Tureng Tepe and Rayy (anc. Rhages) skeletal material has been studied. A summary of these has been published[22] so that detailed recapitulation here is unnecessary. However, a few notes will prove helpful.

Tepe Hissar. Level I yielded four crania with two dolichocephalic types: a small, gracile Mediterranean; and a large Proto-Nordic type. In Hissar II 16 crania were found: seven male and seven female Mediterraneans and two male Proto-Nordics. Hissar III (circa 2000 - 1500 B.C.) revealed the following males: Mediterranean (51), Proto-Nordic (39), Alpine (3), Asiatic plus (?) Alpine (1) and Negroid (11) and 32 females, all Mediterranean. Six crania were identified by Krogman as Pseudo-Australoid. The minority brachycephals from Hissar III or Islamic levels were identified as Alpine, Armenoid, and Asiatic or Mongoloid types. The Negroids were probably imported slaves. Krogman gives comparative statistical tables (Field, 1939, pp. 259-60).

Hamadan. Nine crania were grouped by Lebzelter as: (a) Eurafrican, possibly Nordic; (b) a brachycephalic, high-vaulted type, with a wide nose; (c) a dolichocephalic type, with a primitive face and a broad nose, forehead and occiput of Eurafrican appearance with many morphological characters of Australiform type.

Shah Tepe. Near Asterabad T.J. Arne found 29 crania (17 males, 8 females, and

4 children), in levels ranging from 3000 - 2000 B.C. — A.D. 700-900. Arne wrote, "the people who lived on the steppe during the Copper Age belong to a relatively homogeneous race, dolichocephalic or mesocephalic."

Luristan. At Tepe Jamshidi a skull was found by Ghirshman associated with painted pottery attributed to the first half of the second millennium B.C. This skull was probably male, aged 20-30, mesocephalic, and orthocephalic, with a cranial capacity of about 1384 cubic centimeters.

At Tepe Bad-Hora near Asadabad a female skeleton holding a baby in her arms was unearthed by Ghirshman. This skull, aged 20-30, was mesocephalic with a brachycephalic tendency, head height low, chamaecephalic and tapeinocephalic with an estimated cranial capacity of 1236 cubic centimeters.

Vallois, who studied these two crania, describes No. 1 as Mediterranean but with an Armenoid face and slight occipital flattening. No. 2 is Mediterranean and Armenoid, with a slight predominance of the latter.

Tureng Tepe. The date of these eight crania is uncertain, probably only several centuries. The cephalic indices are: 78.3, 81.8, 82.3, 82.5, 84.0, 85.0, 86.7, and 89.0.

Rayy. James H. Gaul measured a series of 11 male and four female crania in a Drum House (Nakhareh khana), a twelfth century Seljuk tower base near Shah Abdul Azim, a few miles south of Tehran. They were grouped as follows: dolichocephals (three males); mesocephals (four males, three females); and brachycephals (four males, one female). The cephalic indices of two males were 83.52 and 86.66, and for one female 86.14.

Modern Man[23]

The physical anthropology of Iran has been discussed in some detail (Field, 1939, pp. 287-507 and 1940). In addition, I searched the literature for comparative anthropological and anthropometric data as well as recorded observations or theories proposed on the origins and physical relationships of the peoples of Iran.

These excerpts (Field, 1939, pp. 36-158) were arranged chronologically from Herodotus (circa 445 B.C. to Herzfeld and Keith 1938). In order to facilitate the use of this material, an index to the tribes and racial groups with brief summaries from the various authors was compiled (pp. 601-51). This shows at a glance the principal anthropometric data and the several theories of origin for each tribe or racial group.

In a third section (pp. 439-88) the anthropometric data for Iran have been compared with those of Iraq, Jordan, Palestine, Syria, Anatolia, the Caucasus, Kurdistan, Turkestan, Afghanistan, Baluchistan, and India in order to show the racial position of the inhabitants of Iran.

In 1950 I measured[24] 150 Bakhtiari tribesmen, 52 Lurs from between Khurrumabad and Dorud in Luristan, and 50 Kurds from the Sinneh district of Kurdistan. For comparison with the mountain peoples of Iraq,[25] Table 103 was compiled.

The following observations on Table 103 should be noted:[26]

(a) These mountain peoples are all related to some degree, although the Assyrians probably belong to a different racial stock with links in the Caucasus.

(b) The Assyrians are the tallest, the Bakhtiari the shortest. Among the Kurds those of northwestern Iran are the tallest, but the 646 Kurds fall close to the mean of 1665 for the peoples of Southwestern Asia. The Lurs of Pusht-i-Kuh are short, but their relatives in the Khurrumabad area are considerably taller.

(c) The Lurs of central Luristan have the longest heads, the Kurds of Sulaimaniya the shortest. In breadth the Lurs of Khurrumabad are the narrowest, the Assyrians the widest. The Assyrians are hyperbrachycephalic, the Lurs of Khurrumabad

mesocephalic. The Kurds and Bakhtiari are brachycephalic. The Lurs are dolichocephalic and the fact that the Kurds of the Sinneh (Iran) district are mesocephalic is
probably explained by their intermarriage with Lurs. The dolichocephalic element
among the Bakhtiari is probably caused by intermarriage with the Lurs, which is in
accord with their oral tradtion.

(d) The nasal profile is one of the most important racial criteria in Southwestern
Asia, with particular emphasis on the convex and straight categories. For example,
more than two-thirds of all Kurds of Iraq and Iran, the Lurs of Pusht-i-Kuh and the
Baktiari tribesmen possessed convex noses. About half of the Assyrians and the Lurs
of central Luristan had straight noses.

(e) The majority of all the Kurds of Iraq and Iran and most of the Lurs and Assyrians (97.17 per cent) were leptorrhine. Very few platyrrhine individuals were
recorded or seen. The Bakhtiari are divided into mesorrhine (49.66 per cent) and
leptorrhine tribesmen. Their convex nasal profile links the Bakhtiari with the
Iranian Plateau Race and upholds my observations that this convexity is concentrated
among the peoples of western Iran. Eight of the nine groups are leptorrhine with near
uniformity among the Assyrians, many of whom are fair-haired, light-skinned, and
possess blue eyes.

(f) The blond element in those four groups is linked either to the peoples of the
Caucasus or to the dwellers in the Altai or Pamirs. In 1934 I saw many blonds among
the North Osetes[27] near Dzhaudzhikau (formerly Ordzhonikidze, formerly Vladikavkaz) on the northern flank of the Caucasus.

Additional anthropometric data and racial type photographs from southeastern
Anatolia, the Caucasus (especially the Kurds near Lake Goktcha), and the peoples
along the southern periphery of Soviet Central Asia from the Murghab River to the
Tien Shan Mountains, will provide the necessary links in the chain of racial evidence.

Summary

In general, the population is Mediterranean, although there is a slight admixture
of brachycephaly, particularly in the northwestern (Kurdistan) and northeastern areas,
where roundheaded invaders have left their imprint on the modern population.

Non-Mediterranean elements, such as Mongoloid, Armenoid, Nordic, and Alpine
were observed, but with the anthropometric data at present available no indication of
probable percentages of these elements is possible.

However, as a result of statistical analyses[28] and impressional types, Dr. Hooton
and I divided the modern peoples of Iran into:
1. Iranian Plateau Dolichocephals
    (a) Large, convex-nosed, leptorrhine, leptoprosopic hyperdolichocephals
with abundant hair.
    (b) Straight-nosed, square-jawed, long-faced dolichocephals of Mediterranean
type.
    (c) Straight or concave, rather broad-nosed, square-jawed, short-faced doli-
chocephals of primitive Mediterranean type.
    (d) Mixtures of (a) and (b), possibly Proto-Nordic.
2. Iranian Plateau Brachycephals
    (a) Concave – or straight-nosed, square-jawed people with globular heads;
possibly Proto-Alpine.
    (b) Markedly convex-nosed, with high-vaulted head and flattened occiput;
Armenoid type.
    (c) Convex-nosed, long-faced hypsicephals, possibly derived from Turkestan
brachycephalic admixture with (a).

In addition to these basic elements in the population, we recognized a new racial type which does not fit into the regular divisions of the White Race, namely Nordic, Mediterranean, and Alpine.

To this we have given the tentative name of "Iranian Plateau Race" with the following characters: Stature, medium; body, light and slender; skin color, light to medium brown; head hair, dark brown and wavy; beard, medium, heavy; body hair, strongly developed; head, long and narrow and extremely dolichocephalic; forehead, high and sloping; brow ridges, strongly marked; face, elongated and narrow; facial structure, long and prominent; eyes, brown; malars, prominent; nose, large, high, moderately broad and convex; nasal tip, depressed, thin to medium broad; alae, strongly recurved; jaw, often square; and chin, prominent and strong.

A good example of the Iranian Plateau race has been published;[29] this aged Lur of Pusht-i-Kuh has a magnificent profile.

The relationship of this Iranian Plateau type to peoples to the east and northeast may only be determined when adequate representative anthropometric data are available in Baluchistan, Afghanistan and the Soviet areas ranging northeast into the Altai[30] Mountains.

An anthropometric survey of Iran, as proposed in 1934 to the Prime Minister and President of the Majlis, and discussed in 1950 with the late General Ali Razmara, should be put into effect by the Government of Iran. This is now all the more desirable since the surveys of Turkey and Iraq have been made.

References

Angel, J. Lawrence
   1952. The human remains from Hotu Cave, Iran. PAPS, Vol. 96, no. 3, pp. 258-
      69.
Anonymous
   1942. Persian Gulf Pilot comprising the Persian Gulf and its approaches, from
      Ras al-Hadd, in the southwest, to Cape Monze, in the east. Ninth ed. HDA.
Arne, T.J.
   1935a. La steppe turkomane et ses antiquités. Hyllnings-skrift tillägnad Sven
      Hedin, pp. 28-43. Stockholm.
   1935b. The Swedish Archeological Expedition to Iran, 1932-33. ACA, Vol. 6,
      pp. 1 et seq.
   1939. Preface to C.M. Fürst and J.W. Amschler on Shah Tepé. See under Fürst.
Arutinov, A.A.
   1902. Anthropology of the Aissors. In Russian. RAZ, Vol. 3, no. 4, pp. 88-100.
Beckett, Philip
   1953. Qanats around Kirman. JRCAS, Vol. 40, pt. 1, pp. 47-58.
Brown, T. Burton
   1948. Excavations in Azerbaijan. London.
   1950. Recent archaeological work in Azerbaijan. JIS, Vol. 1, no. 1, pp. 17-22.
Cooke, Hedley V.
   1952. Challenge and response in the Middle East, pp. 233-58. New York.
Coon, Carleton S.
   1949. Cave explorations in Iran, 1949. UPMM, pp. 1-124.
   1952a. Excavations in Hotu Cave, Iran, 1951; a preliminary report. PAPS, Vol.
      96, no. 3, pp. 231-49.
   1952b. The excavations at Hotu Cave. TNYAS, Ser. 2, Vol. 14, pp. 179-80.
Crowfoot, Joan
   1942. The flint industry. In: Alexander Longsdorff,"Tall-i-Bakun A, 1932," OIP,
      Vol. 59, pp. 76-80.
Dupree, Louis
   1952. The Pleistocene artifacts of Hotu Cave, Mazanderan, Iran. PAPS, Vol. 93,
      no. 3, pp. 250-57.
Elwell-Sutton, L.P.
   1952. A guide to Iranian area study, pp. 1-235. See chapter references and
      Bibliography, pp. 162-235. ACLS.
Ettinghausen, Richard
   1952. A selected and annotated Bibliography of books and periodicals in Western
      languages dealing with the Near and Middle East with special emphasis on
      Medieval and modern times. See 1954 Supplement. MEI.
Fabri, C.L.
   1934. On the track of Stone Age man in Persian Baluchistan. Asia, Vol. 34, pp.
      468-73, New York.
Field, Henry
   1939. Contributions to the anthropology of Iran. FMNH, Anthropological Series,
      Vol. 29, pp. 1-706.
   1940. The Iranian Plateau race. Asia, Vol. 40, pp. 217-21, New York.
   1951a. Reconnaissance in Southwestern Asia. SJA, Vol. 7, no. 1, pp. 91-92.
   1951b. Caves and rockshelters in Southwestern Asia. BNSS, no. 13, pp. 14-18.
   1951c. Mountain peoples of Iraq and Iran. AJPA, Vol. 9, no. 4, pp. 472-75.
   1953a. Bibliography on Southwestern Asia: I. UM.
   1953b. Contributions to the anthropology of the Caucasus. PMP, Vol. 48, no. 1,
      pp. 1-154.

1955. Bibliography on Southwestern Asia: II. UM.

1956a. Bibliography on Southwestern Asia: III. UM.

1956b. An anthropological reconnaissance in the Near East, 1950. PMP, Vol. 48, no. 2, pp. 27-46.

Fortescue-Foulkes, J.

1953. Season breeding and migrations of the desert locust (Schistocerca gregaria Forskal in South-Western Asia. ALRCM, no. 5, pp. 6-9, especially map 1.

Fürst, Carl M.

1939. The skeletal material collected during the excavations of Dr. T.J. Arne in Shah Tepé at Astrabad-Gorgan in Iran. Sino-Swedish Expedition. Pub. 9, Stockholm.

Ganji, M.H.

1955. The climates of Iran. BSGE, Vol. 28, pp. 195-299, September. See references.

Hayes, Guy S., see Mashayekhi, M.B.

Houssay, Frederic

1887. Les peuples actuels de la Perse. BSAL, Vol. 6, pp. 101-46.

Krogman, Wilton M.

1937. Cranial types from Alishar Hüyük and their relations to other racial types, ancient and modern. In H.H. von der Osten "The Alishar Seasons 1930-32." OIP, Vol. 30, pt. 3, pp. 213-93.

1939. Racial types represented at Tepe Hissar from the mid-fourth to the mid-second millennium B.C. Ms.

1940a. Racial types from Tepe Hissar, Iran, from the late fifth to the early second millennium B.C.; a chapter in the protohistory of Asia Minor and the Middle East. KAWA, Afdeeling Natuurkunde, Section 2, Vol. 39, no. 2.

1940b. The peoples of early Iran and their ethnic affiliations. AJPA, Vol. 26, pp. 269-308.

Lebzelter, Viktor

1931. Schädel aus Persien. ANMV, Vol. 45, pp. 137-57.

Mashayekhi, M.B., Mead, P.A., and Hayes, G.S.

1953. Some demographic aspects of a rural area in Iran. MMFQ, Vol. 31, no. 2, pp. 149-65.

McCown, D.E.

1942. The comparative stratigraphy of early Iran. SAOC, no. 23.

Mead, Pauline A., see Mashayekhi, M.B.

Mecquenem, R. de

1924. Contribution à l'étude des outils en pierre trouvés dans les ruines de Suse. L'Anthropologie, Vol. 33, pp. 469-74.

Mehdevi, Anne Sinclair

1953. Persian adventure. New York.

Minorsky, V.

1945. The tribes of western Iran. JRAI, Vol. 75, pp. 73-80.

Morant, G.M.

1938. A description of nine human skulls from Iran excavated by Sir Aurel Stein. Biometrika, Vol. 30, pp. 130-33. London.

Popov, G.

1953. Investigations of suspected outbreak areas of the desert locust (Schistocerca gregaria Forskal) in Iran. ALB, no. 14.

Saba, Mohsen

1951. Bibliographie française de l'Iran; bibliographie méthodique et raisonnée des ouvrages français parus depuis 1560 jusqu'à nos jours. 2nd edition. Tehran.

Schmidt, Karl P.
   1952. Diagnoses of new reptiles and amphibians from Iran. CASNHM, no. 93,
      pp. 1-2.
Simmons, J.S., Whayne, T.F., Anderson, G.W., and Horack, H.M.
   1954. GE, pp. 178-204. See Bibliography, pp. 202-204.
Skrine, C.P.
   1931. The highlands of Persian Baluchistan. JRGS, Vol. 78, pp. 321-40.
Sykes, (Sir) Percy
   1897. Recent journeys in Persia. JRGS, Vol. 10, pp. 568-97.
   1902. Ten thousand miles in Persia. London.
Vallois, H.V.
   1935a. Notes sur les têtes osseuses. In Contenau, "Fouilles de Tépé Giyan."
      Musée du Louvre, Série Archéologique, Vol. 3, pp. 119-34. Paris.
   1935b. Notes sur les têtes osseuses des fouilles de Tépé-Giyan, Iran. In
      Coutenau and Fhirshman, "Fouilles du Tépé Giyan," Musée du Louvre, Vol. 3,
      pp. 119-34.
Wulsin, Frederick R.
   1932. Excavations at Tureng Tepe near Asterabad. Supplement to the Bulletin
      of the American Institute of Persian (later Iranian) Art and Archaeology.
      New York.

XII. AFGHANISTAN

This country,[1] about the size of Texas, is bounded on the north by Soviet Turkestan, on the west by Iran, on the east by Kashmir and Pakistan, and on the south by Baluchistan, now part of West Pakistan.

In the northern area there are extremes of climate[2] ranges from 120° F. in the shade to -12° F. in the winter. The atmosphere is dry with brilliant sunshine and bright clear nights. During the summer heat there are frequent dust storms. In Kabul snow lies for two or three months. The southwest monsoon brings rain only to the valleys leading down toward the Indus.

On the mountain ranges from 6,000 - 10,000 feet grow large trees, mainly conifers, yew, hazel, juniper, walnut, wild peach, and almond. From the 3,000 - 5,000 foot level grow wild olive, wild privet, acacias, and mimosas. On the Kandahar tableland flourish camel's-thorn and other xerophytic flora.[3] The chief cultivated trees are the mulberry, willow, poplar, ash, and occasionally the plane.

In most parts of the country there are spring and autumn crops. The former yields wheat, barley and lentils, the latter rice, millet, sorghum, maize, tobacco, beets, and turnips. Near the towns melons and watermelons form an important crop. Sugar-cane and cotton grow on rich plains. Poisonous and medicinal plants[4] are found in some areas.

Wild animals[5] include the tiger in the north, the common leopard, wolves, jackals, foxes and hyenas, goats, sheep, gazelle, deer, markhor and ibex, boar, and asses (Equus onager). Among domestic animals are the one-humped camels, the yabu (an indigenous horse about 14 hands high), fat-tailed indigenous sheep and goats.

The area of Afghanistan is approximately 250,000 square miles with an estimated population of 12,000,000, represented by 53.0 per cent Afghans, 36.0 per cent Tajiks and 11.0 per cent Mongolians and other minorities. The urban-dwellers are distributed as follows: Kabul, 206,000; Kandahar, 77,000; Herat, 76,000; and Mazar-i-Sharif, 42,000. The Afghan government recognizes the independence of Pukhtunistan (Pushtunistan), a 10,000 square mile area in West Pakistan.

The religion is Mohammedan with 90.0 per cent Sunnis, the rest Shiah.

The official language is Pushtu, but many speak Persian.

Ancient Man[6]

No evidence of Paleolithic man has been found, but there is every probability that in the mountains overlooking both banks of the Helmand River, in the mountain chain extending from northwest of Herat to the Hindu Kush, and in the highlands from Kandahar to Kabul, Paleolithic man and his cultures will be found.

To the west at the southeastern corner of the Caspian in Hotu Cave[7] and in southern Khurasan, we now have evidence of Paleolithic occupation and to the north at Teshik-Tash near Tashkent in Uzbekistan, a Neanderthaloid child, associated with a Mousterian assemblage, was unearthed.[8]

Furthermore, to the east in West Pakistan, Lower Paleolithic artifacts, known as pre-Soan (Sohan), and Soan industries, have been found. From Chauntra in West Punjab, Lower Paleolithic handaxes of Abbevillio-Acheulian types are known. No Paleolithic fossilized human bone has been found in West Pakistan.

Thus, we have evidence of Paleolithic cultures in Iran to the west, in Uzbekistan to the north and in West Pakistan to the east.

Afghanistan by Erwin Raisz

Hence, the discovery of Prehistoric Man and his cultures in Afghanistan may be safely predicted.

During the past four years historical researches[9] have been conducted.

Modern Man[10]

Bellew (pp. 13-16) lists the principal nationalities as Afghans, Pathans, Ghilzais, Tajiks, and Hazaras, as well as Uzbeks on the southern bank of the Oxus and Kafirs on the southern slopes of the Hindu Kush.

With regard to the origin[11] of the Afghans, there are several theories:

1. Tradition refers Afghans to Syria according to Bellew (pp. 13-16), who adds that they are representatives of ancient Indian inhabitants; their true home was in the Kandahar and Arghanab valleys (pp. 109-110).

2. Finn (pp. 32-33), Ripley (pp. 442-52), and Ujfalvy (p. 44) state that the Afghans are Iranians.

Afghanistan is essentially the homeland of the Indo-Afghans who have been described[12] as possessing: black wavy hair; very light transparent brown complexion; stature variable, 161.0 - 174.8; dolicho-mesocephalic index (71.3 - 77.5); face long, features regular, nose prominent, straight or convex, usually leptorrhine and finely chiseled; and dark eyes.

In the north, the ancient Paropamisus, live the tall Hazara (168.4) with a cephalic index of 85.0 and a nasal index of 80.5.

As the Pamiri[13] (Homo alpinus of Lapouge) have a leptorrhine (62.6-72.0) nose, these distinctly mesorrhine people must be regarded as of "Mongol" stock, as indeed their features proclaim; they are said to have been placed there by Genghis Khan during the first quarter of the thirteenth century. Among other tribes may be mentioned the Afridi (Haparytae of Herodotus), who originally occupied the entire Sufed Khoh range and adjacent country; at an early period it was encroached on by Turki tribes. The Tajiks are widespread. Haddon (p. 103) concludes that the term Pathán is wrongly applied to various tribes for it really belongs to the Pukhtún.

Anthropometric data on the peoples of Afghanistan are rare, the largest series being those as yet unpublished by Gordon Bowles,[14] who recorded data on 172 Afghans in Table 104:

These Afghans were dolichocephalic to mesocephalic with a stature range of 164.0 - 170.0.

In order to determine resemblances and dissimilarities between the peoples of Iran as represented by photographs of my small series from Iran (Field, 1939) and the peoples of Afghanistan, I invited Gordon Bowles to examine the photographs and write his comments[15] which follow:

On the basis of individual photographs of the four Iran groups, it is difficult to be certain that the country even in the areas or groups from which these samples have been drawn is adequately represented. Assuming this to be the case, however, there are a few significant factors which seem to be quite clear in the relationships between these groups and the various peoples of eastern Afghanistan and northwestern India. In the first place, not one of the groups can be considered to be very close to the Pathans, who speak Pashto (Pustu), or to the peoples of the Punjab. The inference to be drawn from this is that there seems to be a large number of dissimilar physical factors, although these are in many cases of such a nature as to characterize local morphological types rather than to distinguish fundamental racial differences. In general, Iran and Indo-Afghanistan contain the same basic racial elements. Secondly, there do occur in the Indo-Afghan area occasional individuals who strongly suggest individuals in the Iran series.

On the whole, however, these are accidental in distribution and are to a great extent atypical. It might be more accurate to say that whereas a few examples do occur in the Indo-Afghan area, which are similar to individuals in the Iran series, these are very sporadic and would suggest a slight infiltration rather than a basic fundamental similarity between the main bulk of peoples of the two areas.

Thirdly, there do seem to be more of these occasional examples of similar types in the western Pahari-speaking areas of the mountainous slopes of the northern States, especially in Chambra State, Kangra Provinces, the northwestern part of the Punjab and eastern Afghanistan.

Fourthly, there are a few examples also of peoples who are found in concentration in the western Pahari regions of the northern Punjab who do occur sporadically in Iran. The subgroups especially concerned are the Lahuli of Lahul, the Gaddi or Brahmauri and Churahi of Chamba and to a certain extent the Dogri, Mirpuri, Punchi of southern Kashmir State and the Plains Punjabi between the Indus and the Sutlej and especially along the base of the Siwalik hills.

In order to define these areas more closely: Chamba State is in the northwestern part of the Punjab just east of Kashmir State; the western Pahari live only in the foothills of the Himalayas, a region which includes Chamba State as far east as the Sutlej; and central Pahari from the Sutlej to the border of Nepal. Of the four Iran series the Kinareh and the Yezd-i-Khast seem to be most affected.

In conclusion, only occasional and very few individuals would fit into the non-Jewish Afghan, Pathan, or northwestern area of India. My deductions were that in general these Afghans appear to have definite racial affinities with Iran rather than toward the Indus Valley. The majority could pass for inhabitants of the region between Tehran and Shiraz and in some cases for Arabs of Central Iraq. On the other hand, several men would be classified as belonging to India rather than to Iran.

As a tentative suggestion based on scanty evidence, it appears that the physical features of certain groups of Afghans are linked with the Iranian Plateau rather than with India. Furthermore, among our photographic series from Iran few if any individuals would pass for peoples of India, although from an anthropometric standpoint individuals who dwell along the west coast of India from Ras Pishkan to Cape Comorin may differ little from our Iranian series.

Thus, there appears to be a dividing line somewhere in eastern Afghanistan, probably the Hindu Kush, sometimes called Paropamisus or Caucasus Indicus, with its loftiest peak, Tirach Mir, rising to 25,420 feet.

Additional anthropometric data, compiled from three sources,[16] appear in Table 105.

Supplementary anthropometric data are given by several recorders:

1. De Khanikoff (pp. 59, 63) gives the mean cephalic index of 76.2 and observed that the stature of 140.0 - 150.0 is more frequent than 160.0 - 170.0.[17] He placed the Afghans between the Turkomans and Mongols since they are not only brachycephalic as the latter but also prognathous (pp. 55-56).

2. Houssay (p. 110) writes that the Afghans are Aryans with cephalic indices ranging from 73.15 - 76.19.

We require additional series of representative samples of the population in order to draw valid deductions on the measurements, indices, photographs, and racial types of the Afghans and to compare these series with the peoples of Iran, Soviet Central Asia, and West Pakistan.

Summary

No evidence of Paleolithic man exists, although I believe this will be found in the near future. Adequate anthropometric data are also lacking for establishing general trends.

References

Anonymous
 1951. Point Four: Near East and Africa. DS.
Bacon, Elizabeth E.
 1951. An inquiry into the history of the Hazara Mongols of Afghanistan, SJA,
  Vol. 7, no. 3, pp. 230-47.
Bellew, H.W.
 1880. The races of Afghanistan, being a brief account of the principal nations inhabiting that country. Calcutta.
Davis, J. Barnard
 1873-75. A description of three Siah Posh Kafir skulls. Anthropologia, Vol. 1,
  pp. 441-43, London.
De Khanikoff, Nicholas
 1866. Mémoire sur l'ethnographie de la Perse. MSGP.
Dupree, Louis
 1951. Preliminary field report on excavations at Shamshir Ghar, Koh-i-Duzd,
  and Deh Morasi Ghundai. Afghanistan, Vol. 6, pt. 2, pp. 22-31; pt. 3, pp. 30-
  35.
Ettinghausen, Richard
 1952. A selected and annotated Bibliography of books and periodicals in Western
  languages dealing with the Near and Middle East with special emphasis on
  medieval and modern times. ACLS. With Supplement, 1954.
Fairservis, Walter A., Jr.
 1950a. Exploring the Desert of Death. NH, Vol. 59, no. 6, pp. 246-53.
 1950b. Archaeological research in Afghanistan. TNYAS, Vol. 12, no. 5, pp. 172-
  74.
 1951. Afghanistan. AJA, Vol. 55, pp. 97-98.
 1952. Preliminary reports of the Prehistoric archaeology of the Afghan-Baluchi
  areas. AMNH, no. 1587, pp. 1-39.
 1953. Future archaeological research in Afghanistan. SJA, Vol. 9, no. 2, pp.
  139-46.
Field, Henry
 1939. Contributions to the anthropology of Iran. FMNH, Anthropological Series,
  Vol. 29, pp. 1-704.
 1953-56. Bibliography on Southwestern Asia: I-III. UM.
Finn, Alexander
 1914. Some reminiscences of a stay in Persia. Lectures delivered to the Persia
  Society, 1913-14, pp. 23-42. London.
Fortescue-Foulkes, J.
 1953. Seasonal breeding and migrations of the desert locust (Schistocerca gregaria Forskal) in Southwestern Asia. ALRCM, no. 5.
Frye, Richard N.
 1954. An epigraphical journey in Afghanistan. Archaeology, Vol. 7, no. 2, pp.
  114-18.
Garson, J.G.
 1888. On skulls from the Hindu Kush district. JAI, Vol. 18, pp. 20-26.
Guha, B.S.
 1938. The racial composition of the Hindu Kush tribes. Twenty-fifth Indian Science Congress, pp. 247-66, Calcutta.
Haddon, A.C.
 1924. The races of man and their distribution. Cambridge, England.

Herrlich, Albert
   1942. A contribution to the anthropology of the Hindu Kush Kafirs. JRAI, Vol. 2,
      pp. 51-99.
Houssay, Frédéric
   1887. Les peuples actuels de la Perse. BSAL, Vol. 6, pp. 101-48.
Khanikoff, Nicolas de
   1866. Mémoire sur l'ethnographie de la Perse. MSGP.
Rainey, Froelich
   1953. Afghanistan. BUM, Vol. 7, no. 4, pp. 41-56.
Ripley, William Z.
   1899. The races of Europe. London.
Stenz, E.
   1946. The climate of Afghanistan, its aridity, dryness and divisions. New York.
Ujfalvy de Mezö-Kövesd, Károly Jenö
   1896. Les Aryens au nord et au sud de l'Hindou-Kouch. Paris.
Vavilov, N.I. and Bukinich, D.D.
   1929. Agricultural Afghanistan. In Russian. Leningrad.
Wheeler, R.E.M.
   1947. Archaeology in Afghanistan. Antiquity, Vol. 21, no. 82, pp. 57-65.

XIII. BALUCHISTAN

This country, now within the borders of West Pakistan, extends from the Gomal River to the Arabian Sea and from the borders of Iran and Afghanistan to those of the Punjab and Sind. Formerly, Baluchistan[1] was divided into a British Zone, comprising 9,000 square miles, and three subdivisions: areas directly administered, native states and tribal areas. The former included 36,000 square miles, the remainder 87,000 square miles.

The central portion of the Suliman range dominates the northern part of the country with the peak of Kaisargarh (Takht-i-Sulaiman)[2] at 11,300 feet. The parallel ranges of the Sulimans end eastward in the high ridge of the Siwaliks facing the Indus plains.

The central area is dominated by an alluvial desert, Kach Gandava, a land of dust-storms and strong winds where the thermometer never sinks below 100° F. in summer and drops below freezing-point in winter.

The mountain folds of southern Baluchistan open fanwise from the Kalat Plateau draining either to the Arabian Sea or to the central swamps of Lora and Mashkel.

West Pakistan,[3] which includes Baluchistan, has a brisk, cool season from November - March with a mean temperature of 60° F. and an extremely warm period from April-November with an average mean of 85° F. The average rainfall is about 10 inches, of which Sind may receive as little as 6.3 inches.

Remains of forests[4] in areas now desiccated indicate marked climatic changes. For example, in the highlands traces of Arab irrigation and cultivation in now desert regions prove climatic variations.

In addition, within historical record there have been compressions resulting in a relative rise of the ground, over the crests of anticlinal folds.

One of the principal lines of migration from the Indus Valley into southeastern Afghanistan lies along the Mula River, which carries the floods of the Kalat highlands through magnificent gorges into the Gandava basin.

With regard to the history of Baluchistan, Herodotus refers[5] to the Mykians-- the Maka of the Behistun inscription in Iran--as being included in the fourteenth satrapy of the Persian Empire organized by Darius in the sixth century B.C. Makran, which probably signifies "the land of the Maka," was traversed by Alexander the Great in 325 B.C. after his victories in India.

During the Sassanian dynasty, Bahram Gur (fifth century of the Christian Era) occupied Makran on the way to India and is believed to have brought back to Persia thousands of dancers, the ancestors of the gypsies in Southwestern Asia.

George C. Cameron[6] (pp. 15-16) wrote:

"So far as it is possible to determine, in ancient times there were longheaded races in Iran preceding the Nordic peoples. The basis for this belief is found in the appearance, in Mesopotamia, of a brown Eurafrican type of man. Our present evidence concerning him is indeed scanty, but seems to suggest a remote physical connection with India.[7] It is possible that these longheads themselves were Sumerians,[8] or were related to them, for it has been said that one can still trace the ancient Sumerian face eastward among the peoples of Afghanistan and Baluchistan, even to the valley of the Indus.[9] Two centuries later the Arabs overthrew the Persian Empire. In A.D. 707 Mohammed bin Kasim captured strongholds in Makran and established Muslim power in the Indus Valley. The Arabs ruled Baluchistan from Khuzdur in Jhalawan until the tenth century. From 1595-1638 Baluchistan formed part of the Mogul Empire."

The Baluchis, comparatively newcomers, conquered western Makran, but not the Brahuis of the Kalat uplands.

In 1921 the population,[10] largely nomadic, was estimated at 799,625, with 733,-477 Sunnis, 51,348 Hindus, 6,693 Christians, and 7,741 Sikhs. The chief languages are vernaculars of Baluchistan, Pushtu, Punjab, Urdu, and Sindhi. The Baluchi language belongs to the Iranian branch of the Aryan sub-family of the Indo-European family.

Ancient Man[11]

Paleolithic Man lived in India as evidenced by his stone implements, but to date no Paleolithic skeleton has been found.

Three recent accounts of Stone Age Man have been summarized:

1. Zeuner[12] (1951, pp. 18-19) observed that the pebble tools are very common in the gravel beds of Indian rivers and are always associated with typologically Acheulian handaxes. The evidence from Gujerat, Dharwar, Bellary, Nellore, Madras, Mayurbhanj, and Kota shows that man had reached the Middle Acheulian stage of technological evolution when he made these implements in such abundance.

Blade industries of Upper Paleolithic type are almost completely absent in India. They may be present in caves in the Kurnool District and in the Nandi-Kanama Pass. However, the microlithic stage is found in abundance, especially in sandy districts and on the peaks of riverside hills. These little artifacts, mainly of quartz, or agate, or other white or conspicuously colored stones, are easy to find. In India the Microlithic[13] phase lasted into the Neolithic.

2. Piggott (1952, pp. 27-28) writes that in the Upper Miocene deposits of the Siwalik Hills remains of fossil apes have been discovered. These seem to have occupied a place in the evolution of the common stock from which man and the contemporary anthropoids eventually sprung.

Piggott (1952, p. 29) continues that the earliest indication of tool-making men in Pleistocene India appears to be during the last phase of the Second Glaciation or at the beginning of the Second (Great) Interglacial. In these deposits in Northern India, in the Potwar (Rawalpindi) region, and perhaps again in Central India, in the Upper Narbada Valley (Hoshangabad, Jubbulpore District) large rough flake-tools have been found. These should belong to the last phases of the Lower Pleistocene, contemporary with the earlier Pithecanthropoids of Java.

The last account is given more fully in order to present the picture from western Baluchistan on the Iranian border into India.

3. Sahni (pp. 130-31) summarizes the evidence for the antiquity of man in India.

Paleolithic. In 1863 Bruce Foote picked up the first implement at Pallavaram near Madras. This has been followed by a host of new finds in the Indian States of the Punjab, Uttar Pradesh, Vindhya Pradesh, Madhya Bharat, Bihar, Orissa, Bombay, Madras, and other parts of peninsular India. The Paleolithic industries of Southern India are grouped under the term Madrasian.

In Pakistan various stone industries are represented in the West Punjab, Sind, and Baluchistan.

Sahni (pp. 134-38) continues with the statement that West Pakistan was the home of the distinctive Paleolithic industry, known as the Soan (or Sohan) after the local river.

These artifacts, which occur in the Soan and Indus valleys, consist mainly of quartzite pebble tools and some flake tools classified as follows:

1. Pre-Soan. These implements have been found in the boulder conglomerate at Kallar in the western Punjab of Pakistan and as far east as Jammu in Kashmir. These are the earliest implements found on the Indian continent.

2. Early Soan. In Terrace I of West Punjab, attributed to the Second Interglacial, were found choppers and Abbevillio-Acheulian handaxes. These tools, struck from flat, oval or rounded quartzite pebbles, had their cutting edge on one side. However, some were flaked on both sides; these represent the most advanced types. Flakes and cores occur. These types, without prepared striking platforms, resemble the early Clactonian.

3. Late Soan. These pebble tools show improved workmanship divided into: (a) finely-worked pebble tools together with flake tools of Levalloisian technique occur in the basal gravels of Terrace II, attributed to the Third Glacial; and (b) flakes and blades resembling evolved Levalloisan techniques with core and pebble tools in the minority.

In the Potwar region of Pakistan the Soan choppers and chopping tools are found with the Abbevillio-Acheulian handaxes of Madras type.

At Chauntra in West Punjab both Soan and Acheulian tools have been collected. In this locality appear Abbevillian, Middle and Late Acheulian forms. This admixture did not happen until the Third Interglacial. The center of origin of the Soan industry lay in Pakistan. However, attention must be called to the meeting grounds of the Soan pebble-tool and Madras handaxe industries: these are the basin of the Rihand in Uttar Pradesh, Mayurbhanj in Orissa, the Sabarinati Valley in Gujerat (Bombay) and even in the southern part of Madras.

In passing we might mention the Paleolithic culture of Upper Burma, called Anathian (Burmese an-ya-tha = an Upper Burman) by Movius. Here handaxes entirely replace pebble handaxes.

Mesolithic. Even less is known of this period than the Paleolithic. Microliths for hafting were fashioned from agate, carnelian, jasper, quartz or other siliceous forms. They were shaped into points, crescents, triangles, blades, and also include small cores and beads. The principal complication is that microliths range from the late Paleolithic to the Neolithic periods, with some contemporary peoples using beer bottle glass.

Microliths are distributed widely in India, Pakistan, and Ceylon (see Sahni's map).

In Pakistan microliths occur in Jamalgarhi (Peshawur District), near Karachi, and in Shahpur District.

The Mesolithic industry of the Indo-Pakistan region resembles closely the Capsian industry of the Mediterranean area. Sahni (p. 143) suggests that the makers of microliths in these widely separated areas might well belong to the same racial type, for recent work by Sankalia and Iravati Karve disclosed ancient human crania possessing Hamitic or Negroid affinities. He postulates, therefore, an influx of northeast Africans or Proto-Egyptians into India during Mesolithic times.

Proto-Neolithic. In Sind this period constitutes a special phase of the Mesolithic, distinct from the normal microlithic. In it probably lay the roots of the Harappa and Mohenjo-Daro stone industries, forerunners of the Indus Valley civilization.

The distinctive tools were long, slender blades and nuclei, the latter resembling the fluted cores from Sanganakallu in West Pakistan; similar cores and blades have been found near Sukhur and Rohri. In addition, they occur as far south as Raichur in Hyderabad with no intervening links. This period is also represented at Pampur and Sombur near Srinagar, Kashmir. Sahni (p. 144) refers to his discovery of a factory site on the flat-topped hills east of Khairpur in Sind. A nearby cave deserves exploration. The presence of cores and blades at Mohenjo-Daro, similar to those from the Sukhur and Khairpur areas, leads some archeologists to attribute them to a relatively recent date.

Neolithic. The distinctive implement is the polished stone axe, usually of basalt. Other types include adzes, hammerstones, fabricators, picks, chisels, etc. The transition from the Mesolithic, Proto-Neolithic into the Neolithic remains undetermined. In Pakistan, Neolithic implements have been found at Shadipur in the Attock district of the North-West Frontier Province and other localities.

Protohistoric. The Neolithic cultures merge imperceptibly into this period.

Within the Protohistoric period belong the cultures found at Kulli and Shahi Tump in Makran. During this period agriculture and the domestication of animals encouraged small villages such as Kulli and Shahi Tump. Later large urban settlements, such as Mohenjo-Daro and Harappa, and others near Ropar in Ambala district and Rangpur in the Limbdi district of Saurashtra in India. These belonged to a culture known as the Indus Valley civilization,[14] which extended westward as far as Sumeria in Mesopotamia, now Iraq. Racially, the ancient dwellers in the Indus Valley were dolichocephalic.

Sir Aurel Stein (1934, pp. 189-90) writes that at Nal, in the upper valley of the Hingol, Chalcolithic remains had first come to light about the turn of the century. In 1925 Hargreaves cleared a small necropolis finding many fine, painted vessels as well as fractional burials. This pottery, which shows a distinct type of its own found only at a few other sites in Makran, appears to be later than the ceramic prevalent at the Chalcolithic sites of Baluchistan, especially Makran. Stratigraphic evidence from Stein's excavations at the Shahi Tump mound in Kej prove this point. However, a new ethnic element may have appeared and introduced this type of pottery into prehistoric Gedrosia.

Sahni (pp. 165-66) described a skeleton found at Nal. The dolichocephalic cranium, with a cubic capacity of about 1,450 cubic centimeters, possessed a fine, long nose similar to that of the modern inhabitants of northeastern Baluchistan. The body was flexed on the left side, a method employed during the Copper Age. However, the typical pottery resembled that from the upper levels at Mohenjo-Daro on the Indus and Harappa between the Ravi and Sutlej rivers. Sahni (p. 166) comments that the Nundara phase at Nal dates back to the Harappa culture of about 4,500 years ago.

Sewell (Guha, pp. 35 and 56) writes that the Nal skull, attributed to the first Copper Age, is identical in conformation with that of the Sumerians of Ur of the Chaldees in Lower Iraq.

At Nundara, 100 miles south of Nal, Stein (1931, p. 190) sank trial trenches into the high mound overlooking a side valley draining into the Hingol River. In this stone-built township painted pottery of the Nal type was found in abundance. Neither stone implements nor "Mother Goddess" and bull figurines, chracteristic of the influence of Indian cult, came to light. The surrounding desert appearance suggests a climatic change.

We can, therefore, follow in outline a sequence[15] of cultures in Pakistan from the Paleolithic to early historic times.

Modern Man

There is a remarkable medley of racial groups.[16] The Muhammadani nomads occupy the central mountainous region known as the Kir;[17] these are the most numerous of the desert people, called Rekis.

To the south of these highlands lie the Mashkel and Kharan deserts inhabited by the Naushirwanis, an Iranian group who immigrated within historical times. They appear to be identical with the Tahuki (Tahukani), who lived in Irano-Baluchistan.

Between the Naushirwanis and the fish-eating population (Icthyophagi of Arrian) of the Makran-Las Bela coast dwell many tribes, some ancient, some modern arrivals. The Tajiks are widespread; among these are the Dehwars (Dehkans) and the Durzadas who extend throughout Makran.

The Arabs once occupied southern Baluchistan and Sind, where they remained until the twelfth century. The Kalmats of the Makran coast once dominated Bela and Sind, west of the Indus.

In the mountains south of Kharan and in the eastern hills are the Brahuis of Dravidian stock represented by the Kambaranis and Mingals (Mongols).[18]

The Boledi, who are mentioned by early writers, were once the ruling groups of southern Baluchistan (anc. Boledistan).

The Sajidis (Sajittae) and Saka (Sacae) are others of the more ancient peoples. The Gitchkis have been dominant since the seventeenth century in Panjgur and Kej, when they drove out the Boledis.

The Gadaras of Makran, formerly Gedrosia, are now represented by Sidi half-castes.

The Marri and Bugti tribes, who occupy the most southern buttresses of the Suliman Mountains, are Rind Baluchis, almost certainly of Arab extraction, and claim to be Quraish.

Regarding the origin of the Baluchis,[19] Brahuis, Tajiks, and Negroids, there are several theories, which have been summarized here.

1. Prichard (p. 171) described the "Beludjs" as Aryans close to but not belonging to Persians.

2. De Khanikoff (p. 108) observed that they are similar to the Bakhtiari tribesmen.

3. Deniker (p. 508) stated that the Baluchis (Biloch) belong to the Indo-Afghan race, mixed with Arabs in the south, with Jats and Hindus in the east, with Turks in the northwest, and with Negroes in the southwest. The Rind of Makran, said to be pure Baluchis, are only Arabs of the Katratan tribe.

4. Ivanov (p. 162) commented that the nomadic Baluchis, who are of Iranian origin, differ from Persians and Kurds. They are generally much smaller, with not as regular features and a very sharp facial angle.

5. Haddon (p. 103) writes that the Baluchi (Baloch) are generally akin to the Afghan, but the latter is essentially dolichocephalic, whereas the former are on the borderline of mesocephaly and brachycephaly, and so it may be advisable to call their type Indo-Iranus, comprised of the Baluchi, Achakzai-Pathans, Pani-Pathans and Kakar-Pathans, Tarin, Dehwar, and Brahui. The stature range is 164.2 - 172.2, the cephalic index from 80.0 - 82.8, and the nasal index from 67.8 - 74.3. This may be regarded as an intermediate or mixed type.

The Brahui (stature 165.9, CI 81.5, and NI 70.9) speak a Dravidian language, but in physical measurements and appearance they are Baluchi. The Chuta and Bandiya are more brachycephalic than the Hazara, but their nasal indices are leptorrhine (58.0 and 58.9 respectively) and they are therefore of Pamiri stock.

5. Sykes (pp. 342-43) writes that the Brahui tribe was dark, of Dravidian origin; darker, shorter and thicker-set than the Baluchi. See also Bray.

6. Deniker (pp. 505-506) observes that the Tajiks also occur in western Afghanistan, northwestern Baluchistan, Afghan Turkestan, right up to and even beyond the Pamirs (Galtcha). Similar to the Tajiks are the Polus, north of the Kuen-Lun, the Sarts of Soviet Turkestan and some two million Azerbaidzhanis in the Caucasus, where they were introduced by the Persians during the seventeenth century.

7. With regard to Negroid characters in the modern population, von Eickstedt (pp. 311-12) observed that these were believed to have existed among the modern populations of Susiana and southern Baluchistan, indicating "the presence of an ancient Veddoid and non-Negroid element."

8. Anthropometric data on the inhabitants of Baluchistan have been published[20] and appear in the statistical Tables 107 and 122 in this study. Hence, recapitulation here is unnecessary except for a few passing observations. The following ranges

were recorded: Stature, 164.25-168.51; head length, 174.2-186.24; head breadth,
139.42-153.43; cephalic index, 76.50-87.00, on 931 males; bizygomatic breadth,
129.75-135.39; bigonial breadth, 99.49-109.02; total facial height, 114.43-119.35;
and nasal index, 69.4-70.9.

Summary

Evidence has been found to establish that Baluchistan, now part of West Pakistan, has been inhabited since Proto-historic times. Although the pre-Soan and Soan industries occur in West Pakistan to the east, these have not yet been identified in former Baluchistan.

Since the Paleolithic hunters lived in Luristan and Kurdistan to the northwest and to the east and southeast in India, Baluchistan must have been on the line of migration.

With regard to the modern inhabitants, there is considerable variation because of the various racial elements present. Since no adequate anthropometric survey[21] has been completed, no valid deductions may now be drawn.

References

Blanford, W.T.
    1883. Geological notes on the hills in the neighborhood of the Sind and Punjab
        frontier between Quetta and Der Ghazi Khan. MGSI, Vol. 20, pt. 2.
Boyd, William C.
    1939. Blood groups. TB, Vol. 17, Pt. 2, p. 171.
Bray, Denys de Saumarez
    1913. The life history of a Brahui. London.
Buxton, L.H. Dudley and Rice, David Talbot
    1931. Report on the human remains found at Kish, Iraq. JRAI, Vol. 61, pp. 57-
        119.
Cameron, George C.
    1936. History of early Iran. Chicago.
Cappieri, Mario
    1955. The Mediterraneans in connection with the prehistoric populations. Ms.
Census of India
    1921. Baluchistan. Delhi.
Chaudri, I.M., Ilkin, E.W., Mourant, A.E., and Walby, J.A.E.
    1952. The blood groups of the people of northwest Pakistan. Man, pp. 168-69.
Curzon, G.N.
    1892. Persia and the Persian question. 2 vols. London.
Das, Gupta Arunendu
    1952. Economic geography of India and Pakistan. 3rd ed. Calcutta.
De Cardi, Beatrice
    1950. On the borders of Pakistan: recent exploration. JRAPCS, Vol. 24, pp. 52-57.
De Khanikoff, Nicholas
    1866. Mémoire sur l'ethnographie de la Perse. MSGP, pp. 108, 133-39.
Deniker, Joseph
    1926. Les races et les peuples de la terre. Paris.
De Terra, H. and Patterson, T.T.
    1939. Studies on the Ice Age in India and associated human cultures. CI, no. 493.
Eichstedt, Egon von
    1934. Rassenkunde und Rassengeschichte der Menschheit. Stuttgart.
Ettinghausen, Richard
    1952. A selected and annotated Bibliography of books and periodicals in Western
        languages dealing with the Near and Middle East with special emphasis on
        mediaeval and modern times. ACLS.
Field, Henry
    1939. Contributions to the Anthropology of Iran. FMNH, Anthropological Series,
        Vol. 29, pp. 1-706.
    1953-56. Bibliography on Southwestern Asia: I-III. UM.
Frankfort, Henri
    1932. Archaeology and the Sumerian problem. SAOC, no. 4, pp. 1-72.
Guha, B.S.
    1952. A brief survey of Indian anthropological literature, 1946-47. BDA, Vol. 1,
        pp. 154-59.
Haddon, A.C.
    1924. The races of man. Cambridge, England.
Hargreaves, H.
    1929. Excavations in Baluchistan, 1925. MASI, no. 35, pp. 1-90.
Hedin, Sven
    1910. Zu land nach Indien durch Persien, Seistan, Baluchistan. Leipzig.

Holdrich, T.H.
　　1901. The Indian borderlands. London.
Ilkin, E.W., see Chaudri, I.M.
Ivanov, W.
　　1926. Notes on the ethnology of Khurasan. JRGS, Vol. 67, pp. 143-58.
Karve, Irawati
　　1948. Anthropometric measurements of the Marathas. DCMS, no. 7, pp. 1-71.
Keith, (Sir) Arthur
　　1927. In Hall and Woolley, "Ur Excavations," Vol. 1, p. 216. Oxford.
Longworth-Dames, M.
　　1904. The Baloch race. RASM, no. 4.
　　1907. Popular poetry of the Baloches. RAS, 2 vols.
Mackay, Ernest
　　1938. Further excavations at Mohenjo-Daro, Vol. 3, New Delhi.
　　1943. Chanhu-Daro excavations. New Haven.
Majumdar, W.G.
　　1934. Explorations in Sind. MASI, no. 48, pp. 1-167.
Marshall, (Sir) John, et al.
　　1931. Mohenjo-Daro and the Indus civilization, Vols. 1-3. London.
McCown, Donald A.
　　1946. In E.J. Ross, "A Chalcolithic site in northern Baluchistan." JNES, Vol.
　　　　5, p. 284.
McMahon (Sir) A.H.
　　1897. The southern borderland of Afghanistan. GJ, Vol. 10.
Mourant, A.E., see Chaudri, I.M.
Patterson, T.T., see De Terra, H.
Piggott, Stuart
　　1943. Dating the Hissar sequence--the Indian evidence. Antiquity, Vol. 17, pp.
　　　　169-82.
　　1946. The chronology of prehistoric northwest India. AI, no. 1, pp. 8-26.
　　1947. A new prehistoric ceramic from Baluchistan. AI, no. 3, pp. 133-36.
　　1952. Prehistoric India. Pelican Books no. A205. London.
Pithawalla, M.B.
　　1948. Introduction to Pakistan; its resources and potentialities. Karachi.
Prichard, James Cowles
　　1843. The natural history of man. London.
Ross, E.J.
　　1946. A Chalcolithic site in northern Baluchistan. JNES, Vol. 5.
Sahni, M.R.
　　1952. Man in evolution. Bombay. See excellent Bibliography, pp. 259-66.
Sankalia, H.D.
　　1951. Ancient and prehistoric Maharastra. JBNHS, Vol. 27, pp. 96-106.
　　1953. The Godvari Palaeolithic industry. DCMS, no. 10, pp. 1-59.
Sankalia, H.D., Subbarao, B. and Deo, S.B.
　　1953. The archaeological sequence of Central India. SJA, Vol. 9, no. 4, pp. 343-
　　　　56. See map with Stone Age sites.
Santapau, H.
　　1952. Contributions to the Bibliography of Indian Botany. JBNHS, Vol. 50, no.
　　　　3, pp. 520-48 and Vol. 51, no. 1, pp. 205-59.
Shafer, Robert
　　1954. Ethnography of Ancient India. Wiesbaden. See Bibliography, pp. 171-73.
Stein, (Sir) Aurel
　　1929. An archaeological tour in Waziristan and northern Baluchistan. MASI, no.
　　　　37, pp. 1-93.

1931. An archaeological tour in Gedrosia. MASI, no. 43, pp. 1-211.

1934. The Indo-Iranian borderlands: their prehistory in the light of geography and of recent explorations. JRAI, Vol. 64, pp. 179-202.

Subbarao, B.

1953. Baroda through the ages. Baroda.

See Sankalia, H.D.

Sykes, (Sir) Percy

1902. Anthropological notes on southern Persia. JAI, Vol. 32, pp. 339-52.

Tate, G.P.

1896. Kalat, a Memoir. Calcutta.

1897. Perso-Baluch boundary. GJ, Vol. 9.

1909. The frontiers of Baluchistan. London.

Vats, M.S.

1940. Excavations at Harappa. New Delhi.

Vredenburg, E.

1901. A geological sketch of the Baluchistan desert and part of eastern Persia. MGSI, Vol. 31, pt. 2.

1904. On the occurrence of a species of Halorites in the Trias of Baluchistan. RGSI, Vol. 31, pp. 162-66.

Walby, J.A.E., see Chaudri, I.M.

Wheeler, R.E.M.

1947. Harappa, 1946: the defences and cemetery. BASI, no. 3, pp. 58-130.

Zeuner, Frederick E.

1950. Stone Age and Pleistocene chronology in Gujarat. DCMS, no. 6, pp. 1-48. See Bibliography, pp. 45-48.

1951. Prehistory in India. DCHS, no. 1, pp. 1-30. Poona.

XIV. COMPARATIVE DATA

Anthropometric measurements and observations have been recorded in Southwestern Asia since 1880 when Chantre, von Erckert, and others began their work in the Caucasus.

During the next two decades racial studies continued on a modest scale, for the difficulties of travel and the natural reticence of the individuals made the task extremely difficult. Political tensions and World War I and its aftermath increased the difficulties, so that few data were recorded from 1900-25.

However, during the last thirty years a wealth of anthropogeographical data has been recorded and published.

As a result, within the area from Suez to Afghanistan and from Anatolia and the Caucasus to the Arabian Sea, we can now determine the racial elements in each large region and the general relationship of the peoples of Southwestern Asia to those of North and East Africa, southeastern Europe, Soviet Central Asia (Turkestan, Kazakhstan, Kirghizia, and Uzbekistan), and India. As more data are published the details of this giant mosaic become clearer.

The principal areas where detailed anthropometric studies have been compiled are: Turkey, Egypt, Iraq, Jordan, and the Caucasus. The regions still least known from the anthropometric viewpoint are the Arabian Peninsula, Afghanistan, and Baluchistan. Representative series have also been studied in Sinai (Egypt), Palestine, Syria, and Iran.

The principal work has been done by: Chantre (Egypt and the Caucasus); Myers, Ammar, and Mitwally (Egypt); Murray and Field (Sinai); Shanklin (Jordan, Lebanon and desert border of Palestine and Syria); Gloor (Palestine); Huxley and Kappers (Syria); Shevket Aziz Kansu, Afet, and collaborators as part of the Government survey (Turkey); Buxton, Field, Smeaton, and Kappers (Iraq); Chantre, Krischner, Danilov, Deniker, and Field (Iran); Chantre, von Erckert, Bunak, Pantiukhov, Gilchenko, Nasonov, Topinard, Riskine, Dzhawachischwili and Field (Caucasus); Matsievskii and Poiarkov (Afghanistan); Leys and Stein and Field (Baluchistan); Field (Bahrain Island); and Leys and Joyce, Bertram Thomas and Coon (Arabian Peninsula).

Important results remain unpublished (or unavailable): Soviet data from the Caucasus, especially the comparative tables compiled by Bunak; and Gordon Bowles' series from Afghanistan eastward along the southern limits of the Himalayas.

Additional measurements are required from every region, the principal lacunae being Saudi Arabia, Yemen, Aden, Hadhramaut, Oman, Iran (southern, southeastern, and eastern, especially the Helmand area of Seistan), and Afghanistan.

Looking back, during the past 30 years we have assembled anthropometric measurements, observations and photographs, medical statistics and notes (including blood grouping, the incidence of the tache mongoloide, body weight, rates of pulse and respiration, hair samples, the identification and medicinal purpose of useful plants and drugs), tribal maps showing migrations, and historical records on tribal origins and racial admixture.

The most elaborate anthropometric survey has been conducted by the Turkish Government under the direction of Shevket Aziz Kansu and Afet. The country was divided into ten zones (Map 10) and teams were assigned to conduct the survey. A total of 39,465 males and 20,263 females were studied. Since these data were recorded by a team of anthropologists, no name could be placed under recorder. In order to present the statistical data on Southwestern Asia, I have compiled tables from many sources.

149

Furthermore, in the tables I have compiled all available data not published previously in my anthropometric lists.

The measurements and indices have been arranged in ascending order. As in my previous tables,[1] each series under stature and cephalic index with nine or less individuals has been relegated to the footnotes. Certain problems arose in presenting the figures. For example, in recent years geographical boundaries have been changed; this is so in respect to Palestine (now Israel), Jordan, Syria, and Lebanon. The locality, given wherever possible, should assist the student to locate the area where a group has been studied. For example, Beduins migrate across present political boundaries; the Huweitat (Howaitat) range from the Wadi Sirhan in northwestern Saudi Arabia westward across Jordan, Sinai to the area just west of Suez. On the other hand, the Northern Shammar are restricted to northwestern and western Iraq, and their cousins, the Southern Shammar to northern Saudi Arabia. However, Sections of Al Manasir in the Qatar Peninsula migrate into Saudi Arabia.

In view of the range of migration of these tribes, the reader must remember that in the following tables the country where the group was studied does not necessarily indicate their limited range.

Another example concerns displaced persons such as the Assyrians examined in Hinaidi (Baghdad) and Habbaniya Camp for Royal Air Force Levies in Iraq. The Assyrian homeland prior to World War I was the Hakkari Mountains of southeastern Anatolia with other groups living on the plain near Lake Urmia in northwestern Iran.

Other factors are the change of political boundaries, the creation of new kingdoms, and the change of names for countries. For example, when Henry M. Huxley, a member of the Howard Crosby Archeological Expedition,[2] 1900-1901, recorded data on 634 males and 46 females in Syria, this country included what are now known as Lebanon and Jordan.

Since World War I two Kingdoms and one State have been created: Iraq (1932), Jordan (1947), and Israel (1948).

The name changes have been Mesopotamia to Iraq, Persia to Iran, and Trans-Jordan to Jordan. In addition in Israel, Turkey and the Caucasus the names of some towns have been changed. For example, in the Caucasus we now have Yerevan for Erivan, Tbilisi for Tiflis, Dzaudzhikau for Ordzhonikidze formerly Vladikavkaz, and minor changes by Georgianizing most cities in Georgia e.g., Kutaisi for Kutais, Batumi for Batum.

Finally, from Palestine (now Israel and part of western Jordan) no attempt has been made to determine the racial elements within the present population since the influx of Jews from Central and Eastern Europe, the Yemen, Iraq, etc. has complicated the racial picture.

Despite the foregoing qualifications, the large body of anthropogeographical data reveals the principal racial elements within each area and their general relationship with each other.

Although to the trained observer and analyst the statistical tables, arranged in ascending order for each measurement or index, reveal details and trends at a glance, it has seemed desirable to make some comments for the non-specialist. Furthermore, in selecting the materials for presentation certain arbitrary rules have been followed. All series without the number of individuals observed have been omitted. All series with plotted peaks in graphs, such as those by Kappers, have not been included, but see Appendix C.

The standard measurements of stature, sitting height, head length, head breadth, minimum frontal diameter, bizygomatic diameter, bigonial diameter, total facial height, upper facial height, nasal height, nasal breadth and ear length and ear breadth have been included. In a few cases other measurements, such as span and head height, have been added. Among indices I selected relative sitting height, cephalic, total facial, upper facial, nasal and ear, with a few figures on the length-height, breadth-height, fronto-parietal, cephalo-facial, zygo-frontal, and zygo-gonial indices.

The main purpose in the selection of the measurements and indices is to choose directly comparable series in order to eliminate false deductions. Since we are dealing with many observers and recorders, this factor must always be considered. Furthermore, we are dealing with millions of statistical computations, many hand-sorted and not tabulated electrically; hence errors must exist despite checking and rechecking calculations. In conclusion, original measurements do not become more accurate by the addition of decimal points to the means, despite their more impressive eye-appeal. Similarly, the larger the series by the same observer, the more valid becomes the mean.

Measurements and their corresponding indices illuminated with graphs and the percentages of descriptive observations, especially on the color of the skin, hair, and eyes, and the shape of the nasal profile, present only one side of the racial criteria. Front and profile photographs, when accompanied by careful sortings, reveal the dominant and minor racial elements in a group or population.

For example, within each Mediterranean group we find a wide range from the gracile to the coarse types with every shade of intermediate variation. The Negroid and Mongoloid elements may readily be distinguished. The hirsuteness of the Yezidis and Subba of Iraq and the paucity of facial and body hair among the Beduins of the Jazira in Sinai, Jordan, Syria, Iraq and the Arabian Peninsula north of the Rub' al-Khali, are also distinguishing secondary sexual characters.

Submerged blondism in the color of the hair and/or eyes indicates racial admixture with a blond element. The characteristic Iranian Plateau convex nose, even in its less accentuated form, appears to be dominant over straight, concave or wavy noses. The stature, nasal profile, together with stature and head form, are the principal criteria in Southwestern Asia.

For statistical tabulations by country on each measurement and index as well as general deductions, the reader is referred to my Iran Report (1939, pp. 440-89). Here comparative tables were compiled to indicate the racial position of the peoples of Iran in relation to their neighbors. The tables of these figures appear in the following geographical order: Iran, Iraq, Arabia, Jordan, Palestine (Israel), Syria, Turkey (Anatolia), the Caucasus, Kurdistan (Anatolia, Iraq, and Iran), Soviet Turkestan, Afghanistan, and Baluchistan (now West Pakistan). Some data from India have been included.

There is no need to repeat these deductions here, for this volume is readily available.

In order to show the relative wealth of anthropometric data now available on the males of Southwestern Asia, Table 122 has been compiled to show that the maximum number of 348 groups of cephalic indices have been calculated. By counting the number of males in each of the 25 measurements and indices, we arrive at a total of 1,040,649.

When we add the females, we can see that the anthropometric data now available from Southwestern Asia form a splendid array upon which some statistically valid deductions may be drawn.

To the statistician and physical anthropologist, the tables speak for themselves and the significant implications stand out crystal clear. However, for the non-professional demographer we shall call attention to the general trends with special emphasis on stature and cephalic index.

Attention is called to the number of individuals within each group. Naturally, the large groups of Turks from each area are the most representative series.

Stature (see Table 107). The 206 groups of 62,367 individuals show a very wide range from 159.4 - 186.6. We believe the mean for Southwestern Asia to be about 166.5 and in this table we see that there are 34 groups from 166.0-166.98. The mean for 39,465 Turks is 165.28, which is close to our theoretical mean for the entire area.

In looking at the groups below 166.0, we find the desert nomads (Ruwalla, Beni Sakhr, Huwaitat, and those of Sinai), the fellahin of Egypt, 11 series of Jews, Georgians of the Caucasus, the Total Turks (I-X), the Druze of Syria and others. Above the theoretical mean of 166.5, there is a wider range with 62 groups from 167.0 - 168.9. In the upper part of the series (1700+), we find Osetes of the Caucasus, Assyrians (originally from the Hakkari Mountains of southeastern Anatolia), Kurds from Anatolia and Lurs of Pusht-i-Kuh of western Iran.

The wide stature range does not permit the deduction of significant trends except that the dwellers on the plains tend to be shorter than the mountaineers.

Since it has been suggested that the higher the proportion of calcium in the soil and water, the taller are the people, this correlation may well apply in Southwestern Asia. Researches in Iraq appear to confirm this theory. To summarize, 148 out of 206 groups are with two points each side of our theoretical mean of 166.5. This tends to confirm our mean since the great majority of all series measured fall between 164.0 and 168.0. Small groups[3] have been omitted.

Outside Southwestern Asia to the northeast in Turkestan the stature ranges from 163.8 - 171.9 with the greatest concentration in the 166.3 - 166.8 group. In Baluchistan the range of 393 men was 164.3 - 168.5. To the east in India from Rajputana to Bengal, we have Guha's range of 162.8 - 168.0. Haddon[4] observes that the pre-Dravidians were short (157.5); this is close to the mean for 30 Sheher Arabs of South Arabia.

Thus, in Southwestern Asia we see a wide range of stature with the mean about 166.5. The taller elements are in the central mountain complex, the shorter toward the periphery.

Sitting Height (see Table 108). Although only 57 groups have been compiled, the total number of individuals is 46,126. The wide range is from 77.07 - 93.03. The 39,465 Turks (I-X) had a trunk length of 84.71. The Beduins tended to be shorter, although the 273 Northern Shammar were 88.1. The Syrian villagers were medium and the Iraqi groups longer in trunk length. The 38 Samaritans of Palestine measured by Genna possessed very long trunks, 93.03--a doubtful figure.

Head Measurements. The head length and head breadth and the resultant cephalic index are significant racial criteria, so that special attention should be paid to them. In Southwestern Asia artificial cranial deformation with the use of the cradleboard (Ar. mehed, Assyrian, darjushta) does exist, especially among the Assyrians, Armenians, the Yezidis of Sheikh Adi district (Bahsany, Bashiqa and the neighboring villages), and certain groups in the Caucasus. Care should, therefore, be used in recording these peoples as brachycephalic or even hyperbrachycephalic (85.0+). We shall discuss the cephalic index in some detail in its proper place.

Head Length (see Table 109). These 122 groups of 49,850 males range from 167.16 - 201.0. The Syrian and Lebanese series possess the shortest heads, the Beduins the longest. The 39,465 Turks (I-X) have a mean of 182.3 with a range of 180.7 - 184.0. The Beduins, who are close to the Mediterranean mean for this area, have a wide range from 185.0 - 194.0, but the majority are in the upper half of this category. When these new data are compared with those quoted by Field,[5] we see that the range is 167.16 for 91 Syrian Greeks to 201.0 for 22 Kurds of northern Iraq.

Outside Southwestern Asia in Soviet Turkestan the range is 180.69 - 189.0.

To summarize, the shortest heads are in western Syria and Lebanon, the longest in the North Arabian or Syrian Desert.

Head Breadth (see Table 110). These 123 groups of 50,153 males range from 135.85 - 157.0. Attention is again called to certain groups who practise artificial cranial deformation (see under head length), for the use of the cradleboard also affects the head breadth. The narrowest heads occur among Beharna of Bahrain and some Beduins, the widest being the Druze of Syria, the Lebanese of Beirut, the Turks of Western Anatolia, the Armenians of Lebanon, and Chantre's Kurds of northern Iraq. The mean for 39,465 Turks (I - X) was 151.9.

Outside Southwestern Asia in Soviet Turkestan the range is 145.0 - 155.4. Attention is called to the small series of 44 Beharna, descendants of the aboriginal inhabitants of Bahrain Island in the Persian Gulf, who possess the narrowest heads (135.85) and to the Turks of Northwest Anatolia (Group VII) with the broadest (156.6) heads represented by a large series (4,161).

To summarize, the Beduins of the Jazira have the narrowest, the Druze and Turks of Central and Western Anatolia, the widest heads.

Head Height (see Table 111). Because of the extreme difficulty in recording this measurement, few data have been compiled. I have never attempted to insert the instrument into the ears, fearing to cause a riot. All the measurements were obtained by Shanklin and Huxley. These 21 groups of 2,798 males ranged from 122.76 - 140.22. The Beduins of Syria and Jordan measured by Shanklin have the lowest, the Druze, Maronites, and Samaritans the highest heads.

Minimum Frontal Diameter (see Table 112). The 76 groups of 48,037 men ranged from 100.7 - 117.06. The narrowest foreheads occur among the peoples of Western Anatolia (Group III) and among the Beduins of Syria and Jordan. The mean for 39,465 Turks was 108.0, which is about the midpoint of the total range. The majority of the Turks are in the 108.0 - 110.7 category. The wider foreheads occur among the Kurds of northwestern Iran, the Bakhtiari tribesmen of Khuzistan in Iran, and the Assyrians, whose homelands were the Hakkari Mountains of southeastern Anatolia and the Urmia plain of northwestern Iran.

Among the Armenians of the Caucasus the marked degree of brachycephaly caused by artificial shortening and broadening of the head did not result in an equivalent widening of the forehead.

Outside Southwestern Asia in Soviet Turkestan the range is 104.97 - 109.0. In India the foreheads appear to be extremely narrow (101.54 - 105.23).

To summarize, there is considerable variation in forehead width; the Kurds of Western Anatolia and the Beduins of Syria and Jordan have the narrowest foreheads. The Turks are in the center of the range. The Lurs, Kurds, Bakhtiari, and Assyrians possess the widest foreheads.

Bizygomatic Breadth (see Table 113). The face width of 75 groups with 47,628 men ranged from 124.39 - 151.0. The Beduins of Iraq, Syria, Jordan, and Sinai possessed narrow faces; the 44 Beharna of Bahrain had the narrowest (124.39). The 39,465 Turks had a mean of 139.0, ranging from 136.1 - 141.6. The broadest faces occur among the Turks of Central and Northwest Anatolia, the Druze of Syria, the Assyrians, and Chantre's Kurds of northern Iraq.

Outside Southwestern Asia in Soviet Turkestan the range is 129.0 - 142.1, even greater than in our area. In India the range is given by Guha as 132.0 - 134.0; this is close to the mean for Iran.

To summarize, the peoples of the western part of Southwestern Asia have the narrowest zygomata and the mountain-dwellers of Jebel Druze and southeastern Anatolia (Assyrians) and the peoples of Central and Northwest Anatolia possess the widest faces.

Bigonial Breadth (see Table 114). The range for 64 groups of 47,088 men is 96.0 - 115.59. G.W. Murray, who is not a physical anthropologist, recorded 97.4 on 163 Towara (Tuarah) Beduins of Sinai; this measurement is probably too low.

The Sulubba, Anaiza, and Baij Beduins have the narrowest jaws. The mean for 39,465 Turks is 107.2, although the nine Turkish groups show considerable divergence from 102.7 - 110.21. The Beduins also show a wide range (100.38 - 108.10). The widest mandibles occur among the three same groups with wide foreheads, the Bakhtiari tribesmen, the Kurds of northwestern Iran and the Assyrians, formerly dwellers in the southeastern Anatolian highlands.

To summarize, the narrowest mandibles are found among the peoples of Syria, Jordan, Sinai, and Israel, and the broadest in a crescent from southeastern Anatolia to Khuzistan in southwestern Iran.

Upper Facial Height (see Table 115). These 72 groups of 48,005 males range from 60.56 - 79.10. The Beduins of Sinai and Jordan and the Arabs of the Kish area possess the shortest upper faces. The peoples of Syria and Lebanon appear in the center of the series. The 39,465 Turks have a mean of 73.3 with a range of 71.0 - 75.1. The Turks of Western and Central Anatolia, the Kurds of Iranian Kurdistan, the Samaritans of Nablus, and the Assyrians have the longest upper faces.

To summarize, the western Beduins have the shorter faces and the Turks of Western and Central Anatolia and the Assyrians the longer upper facial heights.

Total Facial Height (see Table 116). The 80 groups of 48,496 men range from 114.30 - 138.11. The peoples of Iraq and Syria tend to have short total facial heights corresponding to their short upper faces. The Samaritans, Moslems and Christians measured in Palestine possess the longest faces. The mean for 39,465 Turks is 122.4 with a range of 120.8 - 124.0. Outside Southwestern Asia in Soviet Turkestan the range is 115.42 - 124.66.

To summarize, the mountain peoples tend to have longer faces than the dwellers on the plains, particularly the Beduins of the Jazira in Syria, Jordan, Iraq, Saudi Arabia, and Sinai.

Nasal Height (see Table 117). These 78 groups of 48,182 males range from 45.0 - 63.10. The 276 Moslems in Palestine measured by Gloor, and the Turks living in the interior of Western Anatolia had short noses. The Iraqi series possessed long noses. The 39,465 Turks had a mean of 52.0 with a range of 48.1 - 52.8.

Outside Southwestern Asia, Guha's figures for India range from 51.18 - 54.61.

To summarize, the Turks of the interior of Western Anatolia have short noses and the peoples of northern Iraq long noses.

Nasal Breadth (see Table 118). These 78 groups of 48,133 men had a range of 32.4 - 39.0. The Turks of Northeast and Eastern Anatolia, the Jews of Sandur in northeastern Iraq and the Beni Sakhr Beduins of Jordan had the narrowest noses. The Druze and Maualy Beduins of Syria and the Bakhtiari tribesmen of Khuzistan had the widest noses. The Druze had no Negro blood. The Maualy, living on the borderland between the desert and the sown, may well have had Negro blood introduced by the descendants of former slaves in the Arabian Peninsula.

The 39,465 Turks had a mean of 34.0 with a range of 33.4 - 35.0, thereby showing remarkable homogeneity for such a large and representative series.

To summarize, the Turks (34.0) seem to approach the theoretical mean for Southwestern Asia. The Beduins show considerable variation (33.38 - 36.82). The narrower noses occur in Northeast, Eastern, and Southern Anatolia and the wider in Jebel Druze, the Syrian Jazira, and Khuzistan.

Ear Length (see Table 119). These 62 groups with 46,997 men had a wide range of 35.29 - 68.21. The shortest ears were those of the Northern Shammar Negroes and the Jebeliyeh, who were imported from Bosnia and Wallachia by Justinian during the sixth century to St. Catherine's Monastery at the foot of Mount Sinai. The next shortest groups are the Turks from the interior of Western Anatolia and those of Southern Anatolia. The longest ears were those of Christian villagers in Syria, the Maronites, and small Christian and Samaritan groups in Palestine.

The 39,465 Turks had a mean of 59.9 with a range of 57.6 - 60.9.

Attention must be called to the fact that since the ear lengthens with age, the mean age of each group should be consulted before more valid deductions may be drawn.

To summarize, the people with the shortest ears seem to live in the interior of Western and Southern Anatolia, and those with the longest in Syria, but these figures on small groups may well be statistically unreliable.

Ear Breadth (see Table 120). These 62 groups of 46,995 men range from 32.06 - 52.53. Again caution is necessary, for age widens the ears. The narrowest are those of the Alouites and Beduins of Syria and Jordan and the Al bu Muhammad Marsh Arabs of southeastern Iraq. The widest ears occur among the Lurs of Khurrumabad, the Kurds of northwestern Iran, and the Bakhtiari of Khuzistan, all living in an arc of western Iran.

The mean for the 39,465 Turks is 34.6 with a range of 33.0 - 37.6.

To summarize, the narrowest ears occur in Syria, Iraq, and Jordan, and the widest in western Iran from Kurdistan to Khuzistan.

Relative Sitting Height (see Table 121). These 42 groups of 6,079 men range from 47.44 - 53.68. The Lurs of Khurrumabad, the Arabs of the Hilla Liwa, and Assyrians of Iraq, the Kurds of northwestern Iran, and the Bakhtiari tribesmen of Khuzistan are shortest in relative sitting height. The Beduins of western Iraq (Northern Shammar and Anaiza) had the longest trunk lengths.

Cephalic Index (see Table 122). This is the most important single racial criterion and for this reason all available indices have been compiled.

These 348 groups of 70,485 men have a range of 71.91 - 91.07.

The 39,465 Turks have a mean of 83.28 with a range of 82.61 - 85.41, showing remarkable uniformity for such a large and representative series.

According to the Keith fivefold categories, we find the following number of groups: no hyperdolichocephals (X - 70), 54 dolichocephals (70.1 - 75.0), 126 mesocephals (75.1 - 79.9), 113 brachycephals (80.0 - 84.9) and 55 hyperbrachycephals (85.0 - X). To recapitulate, we find 180 groups in the category X - 79.9 and 168 from 80.0 - X. However, while there were no hyperdolichocephals, there were 55 groups of hyperbrachycephals.

The most dolichocephalic groups are the Beduins and fellahin of the central western part of Southwestern Asia extending westward into the oases west of the Nile Valley.

By contrast, the most brachycephalic groups are the Armenians of the Caucasus, the Assyrians of southeastern Anatolia and northwestern Iran, the Druze of southwestern Syria, and the Bakhtiari tribesmen of Khuzistan in southwestern Iran.

The mean for 39,465 Turks is 83.28 with a range of 82.61 - 85.41, again revealing a remarkable uniformity for this large series.

Outside Southwestern Asia in Soviet Turkestan the range for 16 groups of 1,982 men is 75.16 - 85.84.

From India Guha gives us a series of 14 groups with 995 men with a range of 72.48 - 80.84.

Attention must again be called to artificial cranial deformation by cradleboard which causes occipital flattening and broadening of the head, and by rope cradle (among the Yezidis of the Jebel Sinjar district of northwestern Iraq) which elongates the cranium, sometimes making a permanent visible band just behind bregma. The former is practised by the Armenians, Assyrians, and some groups in the Caucasus, and by the Yezidis of the Sheikhan district of northeastern Iraq. For some references see Field.[6]

To summarize: the nomads, and many villagers of the western part of our area including western Egypt, are dolichocephalic; the Egyptians of the northeastern part of the Delta, some Beduins of Jordan and Syria, the Kurds of Anatolia, the Caucasus and Iran, the Subba and Marsh Arabs of southeastern Iraq, and the Jat of Baluchistan, are mesocephals. The Pani of Baluchistan, the Osetes of the Caucasus, my 148 Bakhtiari tribesmen, the Jews of Iraq, the Cypriots, the Turks of Western and Eastern Anatolia, Thrace and the Aegean area, and the total Turks (I - X), are brachycephals. In the highest category, the hyperbrachycephals (85 - X) include the Sheikhan Yezidis, Mountain Jews of Daghestan, Assyrians, Armenians of the Caucasus, Turks of Central and Northwest Anatolia, Alouites and Mitwali of Lebanon, Druze and some Bakhtiari tribesmen of Khuzistan in southwestern Iran. Groups with nine or less individuals have been omitted[7] from Table 122.

Length - Height Index (see Table 123). These 20 groups of 39,884 men have a range of 64.07 - 79.28. The 39,465 Turks have a mean of 68.87 with a wide range of 65.40 - 74.76. The Beduins of Jordan have the lowest, the Druze, Maronites and Nusairiyeh of Syria the highest index.

Breadth - Height Index (see Table 124). These nine groups with 419 men have a range of 84.98 - 95.78. The Beduins of Jordan are the lowest, the Turkomans of the Aintab area of Syria the highest index.

Fronto - Parietal Index (see Table 125). These 71 groups of 45,871 men have a wide range of 66.42 - 80.89. The 39,465 Turks have a mean of 71.25 with a range of 66.42 - 73.46. The lowest are the Turks of Western and Northwest Anatolia and the highest are the Northern Shammar, Dulaimis and Yezidis of Jebel Sinjar in Iraq.

Cephalo - Facial Index (see Table 126). These 20 groups with 2,146 men range from 78.22 - 95.70. The lowest are the Syrian gypsies, Lebanese of Beirut, and Maronites of Syria; the highest are the Kurds of northwestern Iran, the Lurs of Khurrumabad, and the Turkomans of the Aintab area of Syria.

Upper Facial Index (see Table 127). These 66 groups of 46,216 men range from 49.34 - 72.00. The mean for 39,465 Turks is 52.66, range 51.19 - 53.96. The Turks of Northeast and Eastern Anatolia, the Howeitat Beduins of Jordan, and the Al Sawaad Marsh Arabs of Halfayah in southeastern Iraq, are the lowest; the highest index includes the Kurds of northern Iraq, the Samaritans of Nablus, and the Syrian gypsies.

Total Facial Index (see Table 128). These 76 groups with 47,951 men have a range of 76.02 - 96.20. The mean for 39,465 Turks is 87.78 with a range of 85.76 - 90.82. The lowest include three groups from Palestine (38 Samaritans from Nablus, 276 Moslems and 55 Christians), one series of Kish Arabs, the Druze, and the Turks in the interior of Western Anatolia. The highest series include the Sulubba (Sleyb) of the Jazira, the Kurds of northwestern Iran, the Turkomans of northern Iraq, and the Beharna of Bahrain Island.

Zygo - Frontal Index (see Table 129). These 62 groups of 45,300 men have a wide range from 72.31 - 92.72. The mean for 39,465 Turks is 77.57, range 72.31 - 80.31. The lowest are the Turks of Western and Northwest Anatolia; the highest index includes the Beharna of Bahrain Island, the Nippur workmen from Afaq (pron. Afej) in central southern Iraq, the Maronites of Syria, and the Samaritans of Nablus in Palestine.

Nasal Index (see Table 130). These 80 groups of 47,384 men range from 51.74 - 80.60. The 39,465 Turks have a mean of 65.39 with a range of 61.72 - 68.01. The lowest include three series from northern Iraq and the small group of Baij Beduins living in the Hilla Liwa between the Euphrates and Tigris rivers. Among the highest are the Towara (Tuarah) Beduins of Sinai, Moslems in Palestine, and the Northern Shammar Negroes.

Ear Index (see Table 131). The 56 groups of 46,362 males range from 50.02 - 74.04. The mean for the 39,465 Turks is 59.04, range 54.44 - 62.44. The lowest are Al Sawaad Marsh Arabs of the Amara Liwa in southeastern Iraq, and the Beduins and villagers of Syria and Jordan. The highest include the Turks of Thrace and the interior of Western Anatolia, the Bakhtiari tribesmen of Khuzistan in southwestern Iran, and the Northern Shammar Negroes of Iraq.

Comparative Data on Females

In this section I have compiled all data available including the 565 Iraqi women already published (PMP, Vol. 46, pp. 127-34, 1952).

In Tables 132-152 we are dealing with a maximum number of 21,981 women, of whom 20,263 are from Turkey arranged in 10 groups. Since the Turkish series were recorded by a team of anthropologists under Shevket Aziz Kansu, no name could be placed in the right-hand column. By counting the number of individuals in each of the 25 measurements and indices, we arrive at a total of about 525,000 statistical records.

Statistical tables for the measurements and indices have been compiled for comparison with those on the males and to attempt to determine trends.

Stature (see Table 133). The 35 groups of 21,981 women range from 146.7 - 159.4. The 20,263 Turks range from 151.2 - 154.1. The Jews of Yemen and Iraq, the Turks of Thrace, and the Assyrians are the shortest. The tallest are the Osetes of the Caucasus and the Samaritans of Palestine.

Sitting Height (see Table 134). These 29 groups of 21,145 women range from 77.05 - 85.08. The 20,263 Turks had a mean of 78.89, range 77.99 - 79.84. The shortest are the Jews of Iraq, the Assyrians, and the Turks of the Aegean area, Eastern and Western Anatolia. The longest are Turkomans of northern Iraq, the Druze of Syria, and the Samaritans of Palestine.

Head Length (see Table 135). These 35 groups of 21,438 women ranged from 169.10 - 184.77. The 20,263 Turks have a mean of 175.1, range 173.2 - 176.8. The shortest heads are among the Mitwali of the Lebanon Mountains, the Alouites and Druze of Syria, and the Sheikhan Yezidis who use the cradle-board. The longest are possessed by the Northern Shammar Beduins of Iraq and the Yezidis of Jebel Sinjar, where the head is elongated by the camel's-hair cradle employed.

Head Breadth (see Table 136). These 33 groups with 21,275 women range from 136.0 - 151.8. The mean for 20,263 Turks is 146.7, range 140.8 - 151.8. The narrowest heads are among the Sulubba (Sleyb), the Yezidis of Jebel Sinjar, and the Beduins of Syria and Iraq. The broadest heads occur among the Turks of Northwest and Central Anatolia and 25 Armenians of Istanbul.

Minimum Frontal Diameter (see Table 137). These 28 groups of 21,082 women range from 98.90 - 113.20. The mean for 20,263 Turks is 104.9, range 101.1 - 108.0. The narrowest foreheads are those of the Sulubba (Sleyb) and the Yezidis of Jebel Sinjar and Sheikhan. The widest foreheads occur among the Turks of Bursa-Bilecik and the Assyrians, whose homelands were either the Hakkari Mountains of southeastern Anatolia or the Urmia Plain of northwestern Iran.

Bizygomatic Breadth (see Table 138). These 28 groups of 20,961 women range from 117.50 - 131.9. The mean for 20,263 Turks is 130.6, range 128.4 - 131.9. The narrowest faces are among the Sulubba (Sleyb), the Beduins of Syria, and the Subba of central southern Iraq. The widest faces occur among the Turks of Northwest, Western, and Central Anatolia.

Bigonial Breadth (see Table 139). These 24 groups of 20,970 women range from 94.16 - 107.52. The mean for 20,263 Turks is 100.4, range 96.0 - 106.4. The narrowest mandibles are those of the Kurds, Subba, and Northern Shammar and Aqaidat Beduins of Iraq. The widest are among the Turks of Northeast and Western Anatolia and the Assyrians.

Upper Facial Height (see Table 140). These 27 groups of 21,060 women range from 62.00 - 73.92. The 20,263 Turks have a mean of 68.7, range 66.8 - 70.3. The shortest are among the Alouites of Syria, the Sulubba (Sleyb) and the Jews of Sandur, Iraq, and the Turks of Northeast and Southern Anatolia. The longest upper faces occur among the Maronites of Syria, the Subba of Iraq, and the Assyrians.

Total Facial Height (see Table 141). These 28 groups of 20,967 women range from 107.60 - 118.66. The 20,263 Turks have a mean of 111.8, range 110.2 - 114.0. The shortest faces occur among the Turks of Western Anatolia, and the longest among the Alouites of Syria and the Assyrians.

Nasal Height (see Table 142). These 28 groups of 21,069 women range from 46.18 - 54.95. The 20,263 Turks have a mean of 48.4, range 46.6 - 51.4. The shortest noses occur among the Yezidis of Jebel Sinjar and the Turks of Thrace. The longest are found among the Turks of Western Anatolia, the Alouites of Syria, and the Assyrians.

Nasal Breadth (see Table 143). These 28 groups of 21,066 women range from 30.2 - 36.60. The 20,263 Turks have a mean of 31.0, range 30.2 - 32.3. The narrowest noses occur among the Turks of Western, Eastern, and Northwest Anatolia, the broadest among the Jews of Iraq and the Alouites and Beduins of Syria.

Ear Height (see Table 144). These 24 groups of 20,878 women range from 54.5 - 62.22. The 20,263 Turks have a mean of 56.8, range 54.5 - 58.6. The shortest ears occur among the Turks of the interior of Western Anatolia, and of Southern and Eastern Anatolia. The longest ears were found among the Jews and Subba of Iraq.

Ear Breadth (see Table 145). These 25 groups of 20,960 women range from 30.8 - 35.5. The 20,263 Turks have a mean of 32.8, range 30.8 - 35.5. The narrowest ears occur among the Turks of Eastern and Central Anatolia, and the Alouites of Syria; the widest among the Assyrians and the Turks of Thrace.

Cephalic Index (see Table 146). These 43 groups of 21,538 women range from 74.70 - 88.1. The 20,263 Turks have a mean of 83.75, range 79.86 - 86.92.

The only two dolichocephalic groups are the Sulubba (Sleyb) and the Sinjar Yezidis of northwestern Iraq.

The 13 groups of mesocephals (75.1 - 79.9) include the Northern Shammar and Aqaidat Beduins, the Turkomans of Iraq, and the Turks of Northeast Anatolia.

The 17 groups of brachycephals include the Subba, Kurds, Assyrians and northern Jews of Iraq, the Turks of Eastern, Western, and Southern Anatolia and of the Aegean area, Thrace and Bursa-Bilecik, and the North Osetes of the central Caucasus.

Among the 11 groups of hyperbrachycephals (85-X) are Sheikhan Yezidis of northeastern Iraq, Armenians of Lebanon, Turkey, and the Caucasus, the Alouites and Mitwali of Syria, and the Turks of Central and Northwest Anatolia. Attention is called to the dominant roundheadedness among these 21,538 females.

Fronto-Parietal Index (see Table 147). These 26 groups of 21,520 women range from 67.61 - 78.12. The 20,263 Turks have a mean of 71.50, range 68.65 - 74.83. The lowest are Turkomans of Iraq, the Turks of Northwest and Central Anatolia; the highest are the Turks of Northeast and Eastern Anatolia and the Assyrians.

Zygo-Frontal Index (see Table 148). These 26 groups of 21,531 women range from 76.86 - 86.80. The 20,263 Turks have a mean of 80.14, range 76.92 - 83.52. The lowest are the Sheikhan Yezidis of northeastern Iraq and the Turks of Western and Northwest Anatolia; the highest are the Turks of Bursa-Bilecik, the Sulubba (Sleyb), and the Assyrians.

Upper Facial Index (see Table 149). These 26 groups of 20,892 women range from 50.99 - 56.28. The 20,263 have a mean of 52.36, range 51.36 - 53.49. The lowest are the Turkomans and Sandur Jews of northern Iraq and the Turks of Northeast Anatolia; the highest are the Beduins of Syria, the Subba of central southern Iraq, and the Assyrians.

Total Facial Index (see Table 150). These 28 groups of 21,070 women range from 83.65 - 94.50. The 20,263 Turks have a mean of 85.18, range 83.65 - 87.46. The lowest are the Turks of the interior of Western Anatolia and Bursa-Bilecik; the highest are the Assyrians, the Aqaidat Beduins of Syria, and Sulubba (Sleyb).

Nasal Index (see Table 151). These 28 groups of 21,065 women range from 58.28 - 72.90. The 20,263 Turks have a mean of 63.91, range 60.38 - 67.00. The lowest are the Alouites of Syria, the Turks of Western Anatolia and the Assyrians; the highest are the Jews and Jebel Sinjar Yezidis of Iraq.

Ear Index (see Table 152). These 23 groups of 20,833 women range from 52.30 - 63.05. The 20,263 Turks have a mean of 58.18 with the maximum range 54.80 - 63.05. The lowest are the Jews and Jebel Sinjar Yezidis of northern Iraq; the highest are the Assyrians and Turks of the interior of Western Anatolia and Thrace.

XV. THE NURSERY OF MODERN MAN

Prehistoric man lived in Southwestern Asia.

Across this heartland of Asia, Africa, and Europe (Eurafrasia) he migrated backwards and forwards always in search of pleasanter living and more security. In caves and rockshelters he and his family took refuge from the storm. With a fire near the entrance no wild animal would dare approach.

The principal prehistoric evidence is revealed by the discovery of stone implements either of flint or quartzite, for these are almost indestructible by geological agents.

In most areas of Southwestern Asia flint is rare locally, but was undoubtedly available by barter from certain regions.

For example, in the North Arabian or Syrian Desert between the Harrat ar-Rajil lava bed and Rutba Wells occur wide bands of flint shimmering in the sunlight. Concentrations of surface flint also occur in eastern Jordan in the rectangle formed by Amman-Maan, Maan-Bayir Wells, Bayir Wells-Qasr el-Azraq, and westward to Amman.

Other flint-covered areas are between Rutba Wells and the Saudi Arabian frontier, and certain localities such as: near the Wadi Baaba in southwestern Sinai, Jebel Thlathakhwat in eastern Jordan; Tell el-Hibr in northwestern Saudi Arabia; Jebel Enaze (Anaiza or Aneza), the trifocal point of Saudi Arabia, Jordan, and Iraq; Tellul Bastin on the Iraq-Jordan frontier; Jebel et-Tinf in central southern Syria; Tell el-Afaif in the Qaara Depression northeast of Rutba Wells in Iraq; and the escarpment overlooking Wadi Rutga in southeastern Syria.

Bands of platy flint occur in the eastern bank of the Wadi Bayir just south of Bayir Wells in southeastern Jordan.

To summarize, surface flint was abundant in this extensive region of Southwestern Asia.

Quartzite, suitable for flaking into handaxes and cleavers, is far less abundant, although pebbles do occur in many wadi beds, such as the Wadi el-Arish in Sinai, the Wadi Araba and Wadi Bayir in Jordan, the Wadi Hauran and Zab rivers in Iraq, and the Wadi Rutga in Syria. Naturally, stone implements have been found in all these regions close to the sources of raw material.

Scattered on the surface of the sandy desert and wilderness areas lie thousands of flint flakes and chips, the rejects from his tools. Occasionally, perfect implements reward the searcher.

In some localities a flint workshop is found with large nuclei, hammerstones, and flakes. Here, tens of thousands of years before Christ, prehistoric flint-knappers struck these nuclei and trimmed the flakes to their will. Flint fractures like glass; when a blow is struck, a flake is detached. Trial and error enable the skilled worker to produce standard results. Pressure-flaking with a bone gives delicate retouches to the sharp edge. Implements include large handaxes, cleavers, hammerstones, nuclei, knives, scrapers, gravers, and other types.

In the greater part of this area the flints remain uncovered by sand. However, each flint is deeply patined and often greasy to the touch; this is called "desert varnish." In some regions the flint has turned white through dehydration.

Thus, cultural evidence of ancient man has been found during the past 30 years in caves, rockshelters, wadi beds, gravels, on hill-tops, near wells, and on the low-rolling surface of the ground.

The piecing together of this story is like a giant mosaic: each new site is plotted on the map, and finally, the pattern appears. In some cases certain areas yield no evidence; these, then, remain blank. For example, no typologically Paleolithic implements have been found in Iraq south of Baghdad. Presumably, the waters of the Persian Gulf extended northward covering the alluvial plain now watered by the Tigris and Euphrates rivers.

The reader may wonder how easy or difficult it is to find these surface implements, flakes or rejects. The method I have evolved is to drive along and to imagine that we are looking for a spot to pitch camp. Naturally, we choose the highest point for protection. In addition, a mound with a wadi nearby forms additional security from sudden attack by marauding Beduins always anxious for rifles and ammunition and the prized field glasses.

In many cases, on the slope of the mound or hill facing south beside a dry wadi, flints flaked by the prehistoric hunters will lie.

Another near certainty are the tops of high hills, especially those which dominate the plain, for example, Tell el-Hibr and Umm Wual in northwest Saudi Arabia or Jebel Thlathakhwat (the "Three Sisters") in western Jordan. These peaks formed excellent protection from direct attack and from their summits warnings could be given.

The earliest record (1875) of Stone Age implements was given eloquently by Doughty in his "Arabia Deserta" (new ed., 1937, Vol. 1, pp. 68, 75-78). In the Wadi Araba, which meanders through Petra, "the rose-red city half as old as time," Doughty leaned down amid the rolled and water-worn boulders to pick up the first Lower Paleolithic implements in Southwestern Asia.

Years later in 1927 I also found similar tools in this winding and desolate streambed. A few days earlier in southwestern Jordan I was fortunate to excavate with a pickaxe from the side of the gravel bed of the Wadi Bayir a typologically Acheulian, quartzite handaxe.

To the west in Israel thousands of Paleolithic handaxes, mainly of flint, have been collected from numerous surface sites. To the southwest at Ar-Rawafi in northeastern Sinai we found in 1948 a Lower Paleolithic workshop with several hundred handaxes of dehydrated white flint.

In Syria near Deraa I found similar white flint handaxes in 1928. There are also numerous Lower Paleolithic surface sites in Syria, extending northeastward to the Wadi Rutga near Abu Kemal. Similar implements have been found in Lebanon, near Ankara in Anatolia, and eastward to Abkhazia in the Caucasus.

In Iraq there is the famous open-air site of Barda Balka east of Kirkuk. Here on the surface surrounding a standing monolith (still worshipped today by sterile women), we saw in 1950 hundreds of large quartzite handaxes and cleavers. This is the richest Paleolithic site yet found in Iraq.

In Anatolia Lower Paleoliths have been collected.

From Iran no Lower Paleoliths have been found, although there is every reason to believe they exist in that country.

To the south, almost in the center of Saudi Arabia, a perfect flint handaxe was found near Dawadami.

Thus, we see that Lower Paleolithic implements have been found in Israel, Jordan, Syria, Lebanon, Iraq, the Caucasus, and Saudi Arabia.

Outside Southwestern Asia Lower Paleolithic implements occur to the west in the Nile gravels and into North Africa, including the Sahara, and to the southwest in the Somalilands, Ethiopia, and Kenya into Tanganyika, the Rhodesias, and the Union of South Africa.

To the northwest their Paleolithic relatives ranged through the Balkans and across Western Europe from the Iberian Peninsula into France, England, Belgium, Germany, and the Soviet Union.

To the east we have evidence from the Soan gravels of West Pakistan and many sites in India ranging eastward into Burma.

Thus, we see that Lower Paleolithic Man roamed from the head waters of the Tagus in southern Spain to the swiftly-flowing Terek in the central Caucasus, southward up the Nile to Cape Elizabeth and eastward at least to the Irawaddy. The only continents where they may not have arrived are the Americas and Australia.

In the Middle Paleolithic period lived Neanderthal Man and his cultures which are termed Mousterian. In Southwestern Asia Neanderthal (or Neanderthaloid) remains have been found in Israel, Turkey, Iraq, and Iran.

The chance of finding fragile human bones of this period are extremely improbable. They must have been buried in a cave or rockshelter under ideal conditions for fossilization, with no disturbances from burrowing animals, and the good luck to be unearthed under trained eyes and by scalpels and brushes guided by expert fingers.

Fortunately, Neanderthal (or Neanderthaloid) human remains have been excavated: (a) the Galilee skull by F. Turville-Petre; and (b) several skeletons from large rockshelters on Mount Carmel by Dorothy Garrod and assistants. Associated with the latter were a rich industry and many animal bones. Later studies on the skeletons by Sir Arthur Keith and Theodore W. McCown indicated that here beside the Mediterranean littoral lived a racial mixture of Neanderthalers and Homo sapiens.

I had always been taught that Homo sapiens, represented some 30,000 years ago in Western Europe by the Aurignacians, never mated with the brutish Neanderthal girls. Another theory, reflecting less on their physical attributes, suggested that Neanderthal men and women were wiped out by malaria or plague or some other dread disease before the arrival of the Aurignacians.

The discoveries on Mount Carmel by Miss Garrod disprove these theories, for there a mixed type was found.

In recent years a new discovery was made: the excavation by Ralph Solecki of a Neanderthal (or Neanderthaloid) child in Shanidar Cave high on Jebel Baradost in northeastern Iraq, associated with a Mousterian culture. Outside our area, Neanderthal Man has been found from Gibraltar to Tashkent in Soviet Central Asia.

Regarding the latter, the Neanderthaloid child was unearthed by A.P. Okladnikov in Teshik-Tash rockshelter. These ancient human bones were associated with a Mousterian culture. It was a great day when I held this delicate skull in my hands in the Moscow Museum in June, 1945; for here was the eastern end of the Neanderthal chain ranging from Devil's Tower rockshelter on Gibraltar to Soviet Uzbekistan --and both the skulls were of children.

The Neanderthalers inhabited the pleasant slopes and valleys of Iran. While driving through Luristan in 1950 I saw from the road many caves or rockshelters, many of which should have trial trenches sunk in them.

Typologically Mousterian implements occur in Sinai, Israel, Jordan, Syria, Lebanon, Turkey, Iraq, the Caucasus, Saudi Arabia, the Hadhramaut, and Iran.

I have picked up excellent Mousterian implements on the summits of Jebel Thlathakhwat in eastern Jordan, Tell Hibr and Umm Wual in northwestern Saudi Arabia. From many surface sites in former Palestine, Syria, Lebanon, Turkey, the Caucasus, and 8,000 feet above Lake Niriz near Shiraz, in Iran, typologically Mousterian implements have also been collected.

Outside Southwestern Asia the range is also extremely widespread: to the northwest from Gibraltar, Spain, France, Britain, Italy, Germany, Moravia, Poland, the Crimea, through Turkestan and across into Siberia.

To the west from the Nile Valley into Tunisia, Algeria, and Morocco and as far south as Timbuktu, Mousterian implements have been found. To the south the range extends across the Somalilands into Kenya and into South Africa.

To the east the Neanderthalers migrated into India and probably all the way to the China Sea.

Thus, we see that Neanderthal Man roamed widely throughout Europe, across most of Asia south of about Latitude 52°, and the greater part of Africa. In other words, he was master of Eurafrasia some 500 centuries ago.

Now we come to the Upper Paleolithic Period with the direct ancestors of modern man and his Aurignacian cultures. This period was about 25,000 - 15,000 years ago.

Throughout the northern part of the "Fertile Crescent" wandered the Aurignacian hunters. From the Mediterranean to the southeast corner of the Caspian Sea his implements have been found. On numerous surface sites across the Syrian Desert, I have picked up typologically Aurignacian implements.

However, no traces of the bones of these ancient hunters came to light until Carleton Coon, of the University Museum, Philadelphia, found three skeletons in Hotu Cave in northeastern Iran. This momentous discovery in 1951 gives us for the first time direct evidence of the ancient racial type inhabiting this area. Preliminary observations reveal that the dwellers in Hotu Cave overlooking the Caspian Sea are of modern, not Neanderthaloid, type. These were close relations of our direct ancestors.

Upper Paleolithic Man and his cultures are also widespread throughout Southwestern Asia and Eurafrasia in general.

Men of the New Stone Age (Neolithic Period) also lived in Southwestern Asia. They preferred the Mediterranean littoral as we foreigners do today. They ranged south across the central part of Saudi Arabia leaving well-flaked flint arrowheads near the Wadi Dawasir just north of the great billowing sandy waste, the Rub' al Khali. Neolithic hunters chased game into the Empty Quarter.

This period has not received as much attention from Prehistorians as the Paleolithic, but again the tesserae of the mosaic are beginning to fit together.

To summarize, Stone Age Man lived in and migrated across Southwestern Asia for perhaps 100,000 years. During this long interval of time there were many climatic changes. For many generations the wadis flowed with water. This was a pleasant land. Forests covered the slopes. Grass was plentiful. Game abounded. Tools could be fashioned from the high-grade flint on Tell el-Hibr in northwest Saudi Arabia and the hundreds of square miles of flint beds, running mainly north and south across the Syrian Desert.

Here in Southwestern Asia occur the greatest number of species of domesticated animals and cultivated plants. Five other regions of the earth have similar concentrations: China, the Indus Valley, Ethiopia (Abyssiania), Central America, and Peru. These also were the homes of the great civilizations. It was not by chance that they evolved and developed in these regions from China to the Atlantic.

From another angle we see the bounties of our region for human development. Ellsworth Huntington became convinced that some 25,000 years ago Iran was one of the most ideal places in Eurafrasia for mankind. He postulates that the most ideal climatic conditions for conception and birth are 72° Fahrenheit. Iran was such a place.

Lastly, the oldest traces of Man or his cultures have been found near Peiping (Peking), on the island of Java, in southeast Africa, and near Ipswich in England. These four points lie on the periphery of the tricontinental land mass. It is, therefore, improbable that any of these points was the sole "Cradle of Man."

I was brought up to believe that Central Asia was the Cradle of Man. In the light of recent evidence from Africa, in the area from Nairobi to Johannesburg, it now seems probable that this region was also a Cradle of Man. After examining the wealth of material in Kenya and Tanganyika with Louis Leakey in 1948 and talking with Robert Broom in Washington, I cannot accept the old theory that Central Asia was the only Cradle of Man.

Thus, because of its geographical position, former pleasant climate and fertility, the abundance of species of domesticated animals and cultivated plants, I have termed Southwestern Asia the "Nursery of Man."

By this I mean the area of the Eastern Hemisphere where our direct ancestors (Homo sapiens) developed. Later migrations swept in every direction, northeast into Central Asia, along the Makran coast into India, southwest into Ethiopia and the Somalilands toward Kenya, west across Sinai into the Nile Valley, northwest into the Danube Valley, and north toward the Don and Volga rivers.

There were also counter migrations from most of these back into Southwestern Asia. Thus, the study of migrations is complex, still unsolved, but the fate of movements of population in many directions has now been established.

In passing, it must be observed that the physical characters of the basic population of the great river valleys including the Nile, Tigris-Euphrates, Indus, Irawaddy, and Yangtse, have remained unchanged for 200 generations, since the earliest record of the written word.

———————

We have, therefore, seen that Southwestern Asia has been inhabited more or less continuously for about 100,000 years.

From this soil sprang one of the greatest civilizations, extending from the Tigris-Euphrates alluvial plain to the Iranian Plateau. There were culture contacts with the Nile Valley to the west and the Indus Valley to the east.

Here in Southwestern Asia developed agriculture and many basic contributions to our twentieth-century civilization. For example, 500 years before the birth of Christ, at Kish the stars were plotted in their courses and the study of Astronomy began.

Here in ancient Mesopotamia the science of mathematics evolved; our Arabic numerals bear witness to this achievement. The culmination of the pioneer work of this great research center of 2,500 years ago is that devastating twentieth-century Einstein formula, known as the contributor to the H-bomb.

Racially, the earliest inhabitants of the greater part of Southwestern Asia bore a close resemblance to the modern peoples. This is especially true of the Mesopotamian Valley, where 5,000 years ago the basic population was similar to that of today. Conquerors came and went, and to quote the inscriptions on Sumerian tablets, "the land was smitten with weapons" time and time again.

However, these invaders left but little physical imprint on the general population. Today traces of non-Mediterranean elements may be recognized, particularly of the Mongol invasions by Genghis Khan, his grandson Hulagu Khan, and by Tamerlane (Timur-i-Lang). Occasionally, in central Iraq may be seen an Arab with straight black hair and high cheekbones, obviously with Mongoloid admixture.

When we come to modern peoples of Southwestern Asia, we find selected anthropometric criteria of classificatory value. For example, the most significant are stature, cephalic index, and nasal profile. In Southwestern Asia we find a considerable stature range with the mean about 166.5. The cephalic index ranges from hyperdolichocephalic to hyperbrachycephalic.

The Mediterraneans, including every possible combination from gracile to coarse types, are dolichocephalic. This is the basic element for the non-mountainous regions. The typical representatives are the medium short, small-boned longheaded Beduins of the Arabian Peninsula.

The roundheaded groups are principally the mountain peoples such as the Kurds Armenians, Assyrians, Bakhtiari, and the Druze.

The nasal profile tends to be either straight or convex, the highest percentage of the latter being recorded on the Iranian Plateau.

We conclude, therefore, that the modern inhabitants of Southwestern Asia may be classified as Caucasians divided into Mediterranean, Nordic, and Alpine elements.

Since a new element, exemplified by a longheaded group with a high head, dark brown hair and eyes, and a finely-chiseled convex nose, does not fit into the three customary divisions of the White Race, I have assigned these individuals to a new classification, the Iranian Plateau Race.

The question of blondism in Southwestern Asia also requires clarification. For example, among the Kurds, Assyrians and many mountain-dwellers in the Caucasus, fair hair and blue eyes have been recorded with widespread evidence of submerged blondism.

The homelands of the convex nose and this blond element may well prove to be the Pamir-Altai region and the Caucasus respectively. Further data are necessary before conclusions may be drawn.

In addition to members of the White Race, there are Mongoloids and Negroids, the latter introduced generations ago as slaves into the Beduin black tents. Among the great Beduin tribes of the Arabian Peninsula, such as the Rwala (Ruwalla), Northern and Southern Shammar, and Anaiza, there are almost pure Negroes as well as an obvious infiltration of Negroid blood despite severe penalties for infringements of their strict code.

In the eastern part of our area, the Brown Race has infiltrated westward.

Thus, as a result of 30 years of research, usually under the most adverse conditions of climate and deep reluctance on the part of the inhabitants to submit to the callipers and questions, we now can show the racial position of the peoples of Southwestern Asia in relation to the inhabitants of Europe, Africa, Central Asia, and India.

To summarize, Southwestern Asia forms the crossroad of Eurafrasia. Here dwell 60,000,000 people in 12 countries, forming the greatest medley of races, religions, and languages on earth.

Here developed one of the greatest civilizations, spurred by the beginnings of agriculture and the domestication of animals. Later came the invention of writing and the wheel, the discovery of brick-making and of the principle of the arched vault, and the development of mathematical research and astronomy.

Here dwelt Neolithic, Chalcolithic, and Paleolithic Man.

Here was the Nursery of Modern Man (Homo sapiens) in an area equidistant from our two hypothetical Cradles, one in Central Asia, the other in East-South Africa.

Here, because of geographical location in relation to Eurafrasia, climate, plants capable of cultivation, animals suitable for domestication, and the former fertility in many regions, mankind selected Southwestern Asia as their habitat.

Central Asia and Africa were the Cradles of all mankind.

Southwestern Asia was the Nursery of Man.

Appendix A: STATISTICAL DATA ON SOUTHWESTERN ASIA

Country	Area	Population	Religions	Languages
Aden Colony	75	80,516	Islam, few Hindus Jews, Zoroastrians and Christians	Arabic, Hindustani, English
Aden Protectorate	112,000	650,000	Islam (Shafai) few Jews	Arabic
Afghanistan	250,000	12,000,000	Islam (Hanafi) few Hindus and Jews	Pushtu, Persian
Iran	618,000	17,000,000	Islam (Shia), Parsis, Jews, Armenians and Assyrians	Persian, French, English
Iraq	116,000	4,800,000	Islam, few Christians, Armenians, Assyrians, Jews	Arabic, Kermanji, Persian English
Israel	7,200	1,500,000	Judaism, some Moslems, Christians	Hebrew, Arabic, English
Jordan	34,740	450,000	Islam, some Christians and Bahais	Arabic English
Saudi Arabia	927,000	6,000,000	Islam	Arabic
Syria	71,660	655,620	Islam (Sunni)	Arabic, French, English
Lebanon	3,977	1,180,000	Christians (Maronite)	Arabic, French, English
Turkey	296,185	18,790,174	Islam	Turkish, French, English, German
Totals...	2,366,837	63,106,310		

Appendix B: ANTHROPOMETRIC DATA ON SOUTHWESTERN ASIA

by

Winifred Smeaton*

This paper summarizes the data available up to 1932 on the physical types of the population of Southwestern Asia on the basis of the cephalic index. Attention has been focused on statistical evidence from the Arabian Peninsula, Palestine, Syria, and Iraq.

The fundamental human stocks in this part of Asia are Mediterranean and Armenoid. In ancient times, at least, there seem to have been two dolichocephalic varieties of Mediterranean types, the Eur-African, which is of considerable antiquity and survives in scattered places; and Elliot Smith's "Brown Race" (Haddon, pp. 24-26, and Buxton, 1925, pp. 69-71). The Eur-African skull is typically hypsicephalic, a characteristic which is usually accompanied by great development of the temporal muscles. At the same time, there is usually a small cranial capacity. On the other hand, the Brown-Mediterranean is of a more delicate skeletal construction, but is closely allied to the Eur-African, of which it may be another variety, or even a mutation.

The Armenoids, who are usually considered to be the eastern or Asiatic branch of Alpine man, are short-headed and high-headed, with a noticeable flattening of the occiput. The form of the nose is equally characteristic; a fleshy aquiline nose with wide tips is often referred to as an "Armenoid" nose. These divisions are entirely physical, and have little to do with the usual "racial" and national divisions into Armenians, Arabs, Kurds, Turks, and Persians. But it must be remembered that this division is simply a matter of convenience and that most individuals cannot be assigned arbitrarily to one group or the other.

There is, as a matter of fact, still another element in the population of Southwestern Asia, the Negro. An exact study of the amount of Negro admixture is not feasible, but slaves from Africa have at all times been imported into Arabia and the surrounding regions, and have left their mark on the physical type. Even today it is noted that among the Beduins, many sheikhs have bodyguards composed of Negroes or men with a strong infusion of Negro blood. The majority of towns on the sea coast, according to "The Handbook of Arabia" published by the British Government in 1920, have a small Negro population, and this element is also reported from some inland communities.

The following pages summarize the facts available up to 1932 concerning the physical types of the population of Southwestern Asia on the basis of the cephalic index. No single measurement or index can possibly give a true racial classification, since, as Morant (pp. 302-303) points out, a classification based on cephalic index, for example, has only a linear arrangement. Moreover, it is not known to what extent head and other measurements are affected by environment. Head measurements, however, have a distinct advantage in being applicable to the living and to the dead, and scant as the amount of material may be, it is nevertheless more extensive than that collected on any other measurements and observable traits. Therefore, the

---

*Now Mrs. Homer Thomas. Compiled during 1932 at Field Museum of Natural Natural History under the direction of Dr. Henry Field. Minor editorial revisions have been made to conform to our style.

available statistics have been gathered together in the form of tables, arranged geographically. In order to present the facts more graphically, three maps have been plotted of the distribution of headform in Southwestern Asia, both of the present and of the past population. Map 21 shows present-day groups in the northern area, including Syria, Palestine, Iraq (Mesopotamia) and the surrounding areas: Egypt, Asia Minor, Kurdistan, the Caucasus, and Persia (Iran). Map 22 shows present-day groups in Central and South Arabia and the adjacent parts of Africa. Map 23 gives the distribution of the headforms of the ancient population of the entire region, based, it must be remembered, on very small series of skeletal remains.

There are certain lacunae in the data owing to exclusion of material pertaining to people on the periphery of the area under consideration. The lack of data from Arabia is particularly to be noted. This is caused largely by the natural lack of friendly response to anthropometry and the difficulty of access to some groups. No theories are offered in the presentation of this material, but it is to be hoped that a realization of the need for more data will stimulate investigators to make the further necessary researches in order to build a firm foundation for theory.

In the attempt to discover the ethnic constituents of any people in Asia, it must be remembered that we are dealing with an essentially mixed population. An homogeneous group is the exception rather than the rule, for the process of mixture has been going on for at least 5,000 years. On Map 21 the distribution of headform in the northern area is a picture not of the actual population in the regions indicated but of the distribution of certain special groups which have been measured. Where the group numbers with accompanying symbols are reported from a definite locality, the group was measured in, or originated in, that locality; but in cases where the group number with accompanying symbol is enclosed in a large circle, the measurements were obtained from individuals within a large area. Many of the groups consist of males only, some list men and women separately, and some include both or do not specify; but in any case the status of the group is not affected.

A brief analysis of the groups measured may be made according to geographical location. Table 153 may be consulted for details as to mean index, size of group, observer, and bibliographical reference. Wherever it is practicable, groups with similar headform from a single location or from the same general area have been listed under one number, in order to eliminate as much confusing detail as possible. For example, in Mosul all the brachycephalic groups in the city are listed as 20a, 20b, and so on, and are indicated by the symbol used to denote brachycephaly.

Beginning with Syria and Palestine, groups No. 1 and No. 2 are found in the mountains along the Mediterranean coast north of Tripoli in Lebanon. The Ansaries (Noussariyah) form part of the population of the Alouite Mountains, but separate groups have been measured. Here, as may be observed, is a brachycephalic population, with a tendency toward hyperbrachycephaly. The Druze (No. 3), of whom 80 men were measured by Kappers, have a mean index of 87.26, which is hyperbrachycephalic. The distribution, however, is rather scattered, and runs from 75 - 97.

When we come to the Lebanese (No. 4), although the mean index is about 85, there is actually a subbrachycephalic admixture in the brachycephalic population, which is caused by the inclusion of individuals from Damascus, a town of 188,000 with a mixed population. This brings up the question of what Kappers calls the "desert border population" (No. 6) of which a series of 135 males was measured in Aleppo, Hama, Homs, Maalullah (not shown on the map), and Damascus. The mean index is 81.7.

Group No. 5, which consists of Armenians, is located in Beirut, although most of the group are students, and consequently come from various places. A group of Kurds measured in Syria by Chantre was found also to be brachycephalic, with a mean index of 85.2. This is not a typical Kurdish index, for the majority of Kurds

are slightly brachycephalic, but rather an index typical of Syria. Armenoid infiltration thus is seen to have been comparatively effective here. However, beyond the
mountains a difference is found, as shown by a group of 107 Syrian Beduins (No. 7)
from the districts around Aleppo, Palmyra, Selemiye, Deir-ez-Zor, and in the
Hauran. These are distinctly mesocephalic, and are presumably more like the population of Arabia proper.

Proceeding down through Palestine, we find several groups recorded, most of
whom are mesocephalic. First in order are the Samaritans (No. 8), who are a small
community living near Nablus, the direct descendants of the old population of Samaria.
Groups of them have been measured by several observers. The indices run from 76.2
(males) to 80.84 (females), but the entire group is definitely mesocephalic. Kappers
measured 139 Palestinian Arabs (No. 9) "north of the line Jaffa-Jericho," but the
exact location is not given. This group has a mean index of 81.6, which is subbrachycephalic. Smaller groups of fellahin measured by Weissenberg at Safed (No. 10) and
near Jaffa (No. 11) are low mesocephalic. Here we approach a truer Arabian index,
for in spite of the dearth of measurements from most of Arabia, it is known that a
large proportion of its population, the Adnan Arabs, are dolichocephalic or mesocephalic.

Kappers (1931b, pp. 121-4) suggests that the subbrachycephalic groups, that is,
the Palestinian Arabs and the "desert border population," may be related to the ancient non-Phoenician or the pre-Hebrew population of Palestine and Syria, especially
the Amorites, who settled in the country about 2600 B.C. The indices of these groups,
however, are too high for any Adnan (Phoenico-Palmyrene) group, and too low for
the brachycephalic Kohtan (Qahtan) Arabs. It must not be forgotten that a prevailing
index of 81.5 might result from a mixture of brachycephals and mesocephals, i.e.,
Hittite and Phoenico-Palmyrene groups. But until we know certainly whether an intermediate index actually results from such a mixture, or whether simply the range
of variations is increased, we can only advance this as a tentative explanation.

In this connection must be considered Kappers' series of Jews, both Sephardim
and Ashkenazim, although they are not located on the map, since three-quarters of
each group were measured in Amsterdam, and the rest in Syria and Palestine. The
Ashkenazim have an average index of 81.2 and the Sephardim of 78.6, a difference
which is rather significant. The Sephardim, who incidentally form only 8.0 per cent
of the present Jews, are considered by Weissenberg and Pittard to be closer to the
original Hebrews. However, since Kappers (1931b, p. 126) thinks the original
Hebrew index is about 80.82, he is inclined to agree with Szpidbaum that the Sephardim
are mixed with longheaded Arabs. Certainly the typical Phoenico-Palmyrene index,
77-78, agrees with that of the Sephardim. On the other hand, there seems to be a
similar relationship between the Ashkenazim and the Kohtan Arabs, either directly
or through the Assyrians (Krischner, 1932b, p. 226).

In considering Iraq next, an apparently curious situation is encountered. The
groups here are found to be concentrated for the most part in the cities, especially
Mosul, but this means simply that certain elements of the urban population were
accessible for observation. It is striking that of all the groups measured in or near
Mosul, only one is certainly mesocephalic, although Krischner's Moslem Arabs
(Nos. 20h and 20i) really should be so classed.

The mesocephalic group (No. 19) consists of those individuals, 38 in number,
with a cephalic index less than 81, out of a group of 102 Iraqi Arabs. If a similar
arbitrary division were made in Krischner's Moslems (No. 20h), a definitely mesocephalic group would likewise emerge, at least among the men. The frequency distribution curve of the women (No. 20i) shows a decided 82-83 peak (Krischner, 1932b,
p. 220) so that as a group the women are subbrachycephalic. This is, however, a
normal sex difference for a relatively longheaded population. The male curve has

several peaks, indicating that the general group is not homogeneous, but like Kappers' Iraqis, contains Adnan and Kohtan strains. Kappers' groups, (Nos. 19 and 20a) the mesocephalic and brachycephalic divisions of his Iraqis, will be found in Baghdad and Basra as well, for it is composed of individuals from all three cities.

The other Mosul groups, including Chaldeans from Karakosh (No. 18) and Tell Kaif (No. 20b), are indisputably brachycephalic, but appear to be mixed, for both 83 and 87 are prominent indices among them. Photographs of individuals from Karakosh, not measured, will be published by Field (1935).

In addition to the Chaldeans (Nos. 18, 20b and 20c), are the Suriani or Aissori (Nos. 20d and 20e), who claim to be direct descendants of the ancient Assyrians and who are often grouped together with the Chaldeans; the Christian "Arabs" of the vicinity (Nos. 20f and 20g), who are certainly not of the same stock as the other Arabs; and the Kohtan elements of Kappers' Iraqi group (No. 20a). Krischner's Yezidis and Christians from Bahsany and Beheschika (Bashiqa) should be included among these brachycephalic groups, but are not indicated on the map. It is a question whether one or both of the brachycephalic elements shown by the 83 peak and the 87 peak underlie the Kohtan Arabs and the Ashkenazim Jews. Generally, it is taken to be the 83 index group, because the Kohtans and the Ashkenazim are prevailingly subbrachycephalic. In Yemen also the prevailing element is subbrachycephalic. It is significant that even the 48 Kurds (No. 20j) measured in Mosul by Krischner (1932b, p. 224) are brachycephalic, being affected, as is pointed out, by Armenoid or Ponto-Zagrian influence. The only mesocephaly shown in northern Iraq is among the Arab groups.

In the regions north of Iraq and Syria, Map 21 indicates, as usual, only scattered groups, most of which are not definitely located but are assigned to countries or regions generally. A glance at this map shows both mesocephalic and brachycephalic populations. From Table 122 it is seen that all the mesocephalic groups in Anatolia, Kurdistan, and Caucasia are Kurds. According to Speiser, the ancestors of the Kurds, the ancient Guti or Qurti, were brachycephalic, part of the Zagros stock. It should be mentioned that the Kurds from Diarbekr and Mardin (No. 33) were measured in Damascus. Azerbaidzhan has another mesocephalic people in the Tatars (No. 38) who have a mean index of 77.6 for 207 individuals. This figure is quoted by Tschepourowsky (1905-1906b, p. 295) from the work of different observers. For the moment the study of Persia may be laid aside. In Anatolia two groups of Osmanli Turks measured by Elisieff and Chantre (Nos. 25a and 25b) have mean indices of about 84. Two Turkish groups in Lycia, the Bektachi and the Tachtadschy, measured by von Luschan, show indices verging on the hyperbrachycephalic (Nos. 26a and 26b).

All the Georgian groups (No. 34) including Osetes, Mingrelians and Circassians, are subbrachycephalic, except five "Kurds" (No. 31) measured by Chantre in Batum who, surprisingly, seem to be hyperbrachycephalic. However, these cannot be taken as typical Kurds and no doubt are not rightly so classified.

Various groups from the Caucasus were measured: Armenians (No. 27a); Kurds (No. 28); and two Caucasian tribes (Nos. 27b and 27c). The Kurds here are mesocephalic and the Caucasians subbrachycephalic, while the Armenians are hyperbrachycephalic. Forty-three Jews from Transcaucasia (No. 36) measured by Pantiukhov and reported by Tschepouowsky, are also hyperbrachycephalic, with a mean index of 87.5. The Kurdish group (No. 28) was measured in Kurdistan as well as in the Caucasus. Three distinct types thus are seen to exist in the general region of the Caucasus.

In Persia (now Iran) are also found various types. Only groups in northern and western Persia are shown on Map 21, although the tables give figures for other groups, especially Persians and Armenians in the neighborhood of Isfahan, and

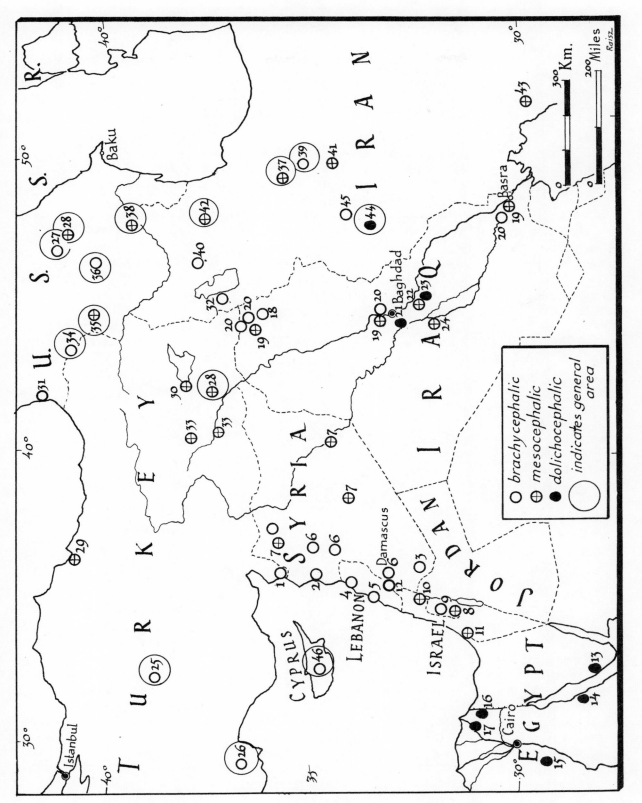

Cephalic Indices in Southwestern Asia by Winifred Smeaton Thomas

Zoroastrians from Yezd. A group of Armenians, men and women (No. 40), was measured in Tabriz by Krischner. The men show two prevailing indices, 84 and 86 - 87, while the women are prevailingly hyperbrachycephalic. This, in respect to the men at least, agrees with the results of Chantre's and Kappers' work on Armenians. (See group No. 5 for Kappers' Armenian students. Chantre's group, although listed in the table, is not shown on the map.) In other words, the Armenians are not homogeneous, but are a mixture of two groups, each with a characteristic cephalic index. (See Krischner, 1932a, p. 205.)

Buxton (1925, p. 95) writes that the true Armenians, in spite of being the prototype of Armenoid peoples, have an infusion of Mediterranean blood. The Mediterranean admixture would not account for the 83 - 84 index, but our biological knowledge of the inheritance of headform and the effect are discussed fully in Chantre (1904). A combined group of 188 Arab Beduins in Egypt is given by Chantre (1904, p. 307), their index being 73.96. Various other groups having affinities with the Egyptians are listed, but they lie rather outside the present field of interest.

Until recently very little has been known of the racial connections of the people of South Arabia, and even now comparatively little is known, in spite of the important work of Bertram Thomas in measuring South Arabian tribes, and the earlier work of Leys and Joyce and others. As may be seen from Table 153, the South Arabian groups measured are, with one exception, numerically so small that only tentative conclusions may be drawn as to the characteristic cephalic indices of the various tribes. And indeed even those whose work has thrown light on the South Arabian problem admit that the final solution is yet to be reached.

Nevertheless, the evidence is indisputable that the South Arabs, the true Arab, according to tradition and the native historians, are brachycephalic. At the same time, they show certain Hamitic or African traits in physiognomy and hair form, especially in the regions most open to African contacts. In this connection, attention is called to the similarity between South Arabs and certain African ("Hamitic") groups as shown by photographs. Chantre (1904, pp. 238-39) gives photographs of two Bisharin showing striking resemblances to some of the South Arabs measured by Thomas (see plates in Appendix I of "Arabia Felix"). Until the publication of Thomas' work with the discussion of the racial characters of South Arabs by Keith and Krogman (pp. 301-33), the only measurements were those collected by Seligman (1917, pp. 214-39).

African peoples from the Cape to the Nile delta are dolichocephalic (occasionally mesocephalic), and the most important element in North Arabia and Iraq is dolichocephalic. Therefore, the brachycephaly of South Arabia, lying between the two, is most surprising. As Keith and Krogman point out (p. 304), brachycephaly can be evolved independently, and an originally longheaded people in South Arabia may have become roundheaded. A more favored theory is that Armenoids found their way to the southern end of the Arabian Peninsula by way of Afghanistan and the Pamir highlands. Seligman (1917, p. 223) suggests an Armenoid admixture in the South Arabians, and attributes it to Mesopotamian influence. Individual instances are found of Armenoid traits, such as the convex nose and post-auricular shortness of the head. The occurrence of Armenoid traits is most noticeable in Oman. A study of the table of Thomas' measurements (Keith and Krogman, pp. 323-26) shows that the brachycephaly of the South Arabs is of a different type from that of most Armenoids, for the South Arabs are a relatively small-headed people with a small cranial capacity, whereas the typical Armenoids have large heads, with increased cranial capacity caused by unusual breadth and height. Bertram Thomas' data confirm Seligman's discovery of South Arabian brachycephaly, but contrary to Seligman, he also finds evidence of Hamitic blood. Likewise, there is evidence of Indian, that is, Dravidian connections. This should not cause any surprise, inasmuch as there are definite likenesses between the peoples of northeast Africa and the Dravidian stock in India, and South Arabia occupies an intermediate geographical position (Keith and Krogman, p. 304).

Map 22 shows the distribution of headform in South Arabia and the adjacent part of Africa. The sources for the data shown on this map are given in Table 153. In addition to the measurements of groups in Yemen, Hadhramaut, and Oman, there are included African "Hamitic" groups and "Arabs" from the Sudan. There is also included the only group from the central part of Arabia which has so far been measured a series of 12 men from Jidda. Beginning with the Jidda group (No. 47), it may be remarked that these are probably not typical Hejazi, for the number is small, and Jidda, moreover, is a coastal town whose population is undoubtedly very mixed. The mesocephalic index (79.37) of the group, while certainly not out of place in this part of Arabia, may nevertheless not be typical of the region. Most of the groups measured in Yemen (Nos. 48a, 48b, 48c, and 48d) are subbrachycephalic, except one group of 30 measured by Atkey in the mountains near Sanaa (No. 49), which is mesocephalic.

African Somalis (Nos. 51a, 51b, and 51c) are dolichocephalic, with one group approaching mesocephaly, but the group of six Somalis measured by Thomas in South Arabia (not shown on the map) have a mean index of 79.91, which is on the borderline between mesocephaly and brachycephaly. The six individuals, therefore, are probably not pure Somali. The combined groups of Kababish (No. 50), an Arab tribe from the Sudan, measured by Atkey and Seligman, are dolichocephalic, and the same is true of the Tigre from Abyssinia (No. 52) and the Beni Amer (No. 53). The Hadendoa (No. 54) and the Bisharin or Beja (No. 55), who are further north, are mesocephalic. However, none of these African tribes show any of the brachycephaly which is characteristic of South Arabia.

The Sheher (No. 56) who live in the country behind Aden, 82 of whom were measured by Leys and Joyce, have a low subbrachycephalic index. Proceeding eastward along the Hadhramaut coast, the tribes measured by Thomas (Nos. 57-61; see his end map and Table 99) seem in general to have an increasing index as the sphere of Hamitic influence recedes; at least this holds as far as Al Kathiri. Among the Bautahari and Harasi only one individual from each tribe was measured the Bautahari having a cephalic index of 79.12 and the Harasi of 83.33. Three Omanis (No. 62) measured by Bertram Thomas have an average index of 85.18, but a series of 31 men from Muscat (No. 63) recorded by Leys and Joyce are mesocephalic, with a mean index of 78.28. Whether Muscat as a seaport gives a heterogeneous series, it is difficult to say, but certainly the South Arabian series, although immensely important (in being all that we have) can only indicate what may be the results of additional measurements in the future.

Cranial Material

The cranial evidence for the headform of the former population of Southwestern Asia is, like that for the living, scattered and fragmentary. For the most part, the investigator must be content with the tentative evidence of single skulls or small groups found in various locations. Moreover, the skulls date from different periods, ranging from the immediate past to the beginning of the fourth millennium.

It will be noted, however, that the types bear a strong resemblance to each other, indicating that there has been little change in the racial constituents of the population, at least within historic times. For the sake of convenience the material will be taken in geographical rather than chronological order. Map 23 shows the range and distribution of the crania listed.

Beginning with the Phoenician sites, there are a number of crania including two

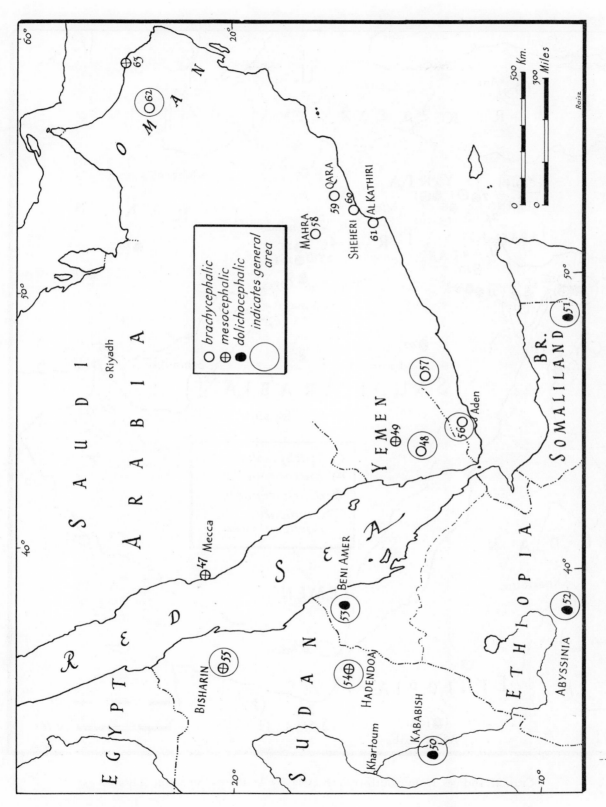

Cephalic Indices in Arabian Peninsula and Adjoining Areas by Winifred Smeaton Thomas

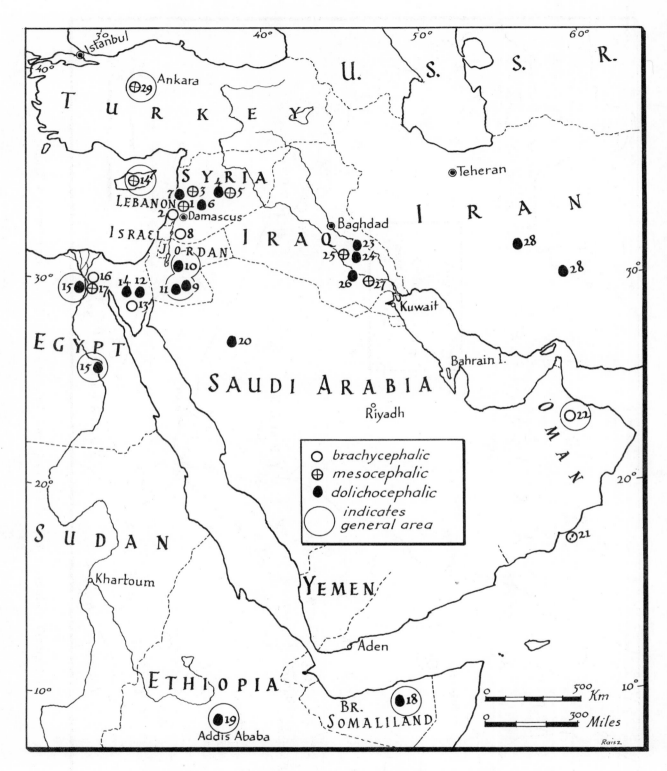

Cranial Indices from Southwestern Asia by Winifred Smeaton Thomas

which are probably not Phoenician (see Nos. 2a and b in Table 154). Phoenician skulls, as may be observed, are characteristically mesocephalic. One of these skulls (No. 3) was found at Byblos (modern Jebail) in a tomb of the thirteenth century B.C.; the remainder date from the fifth and fourth centuries B.C. The two brachycephalic skulls (Nos. 2a and 2b) Kappers (1931a, p. 108) infers may have belonged to Greeks or other foreigners, since at that period their influence was felt along the coasts.

Phoenician crania have been observed at Carthage and other Punic sites, but they belong to the period of Phoenician colonization after the ninth century B.C. The skull from Byblos thus is particularly interesting as being the oldest Phoenician skull yet observed. According to Kappers' description (1931a, p. 108), this skull is slightly platycephalic with "occiput en chignon," aquiline nose, rectangular orbits, and well-developed supraorbital ridges. The post-auricular length of the skull is 49.0 per cent of the total length. The Phoenician skulls of the later period agree in type with the Byblos skull.

The crania from Palmyra are next in order (Nos. 4 and 5). They belong to an Aramean population from about the second or third centuries of the Christian Era. Group No. 4a consists of five skulls: two were brought back by Burton (Blake, p. 312); the other three were collected by Cotsworth (Busk, 1874, p. 366). The average cephalic index of the five skulls is 73.96, which is dolichocephalic, but two of the skulls are actually mesocephalic. Of the other Palmyrene skulls listed, one is meso-cephalic (No. 5) and the others are dolichocephalic, that is, No. 4b is dolichocephalic and group No. 4c, consisting of six individuals, has a mean index of 73.6. The three indices, however, vary only by three points.

There is a great resemblance between the Phoenician skulls and those from Pal-myra both in measurements and observable characters, such as the development of the supraorbital ridges, rectangular orbits, and the shape of the occiput. Quoting from Kappers (1931a, p. 112), "there can be no doubt of the relationship of the Phoenician population B.C. with the Palmyrene Arameans...at the beginning of the Christian era."

An ancient skull found in the valley between the Lebanon and Anti-Lebanon (No. 6) seems to belong to the same type as the Palmyrene crania. It is dolichocephalic with an index of about 70. Another having the same characteristics is the Nabatean skull (No. 12a) from the southern part of Sinai, which was described by Busk (1879, p. 321). It also is dolichocephalic, the index being 72. The same type is also represented by a recent skull in the Anatomical Institute of the American University of Beirut (No. 7). The exact origin of this skull is not known, but it evidently is an Arab, not a Lebanese skull, since its index is 73.4, and the Lebanese are brachycephalic.

Another racial type is represented by the two skulls from Megiddo (No. 8), which belong to the time of Solomon (tenth century B.C.). Both are reckoned as subbrachy-cephalic, the indices being 79.57 and 81.38 with a mean value of 80.45, which lies on the borderline between mesocephaly and brachycephaly. Kappers (1931b, p. 121) writes that if these are male skulls, they would appear to approximate the original male Hebrew index, which he puts at about 80.5 on the skull, or 81.5 on the living. In this connection it must be observed that the group of Palestinian Arabs measured by Kappers (group No. 9 on Map 21), who are located north of the line between Jaffa and Jericho, have a comparable index of 81.6. All other Palestinian groups are mesocephalic, although possibly the group from Safed is too small to be entirely typical. Kappers also suggests that a larger group might have given a higher index.

Next is a group of six skulls from Yabrud in the north of Palestine. Of these, five are dolichocephalic and one is brachycephalic, with an index of 81.9. This latter, however, does not show the Armenoid characteristics of hypsicephaly and flattening of the occiput, and the increased head width is probably an individual variation (Seligman, 1917, p. 216). In spite of this brachycephalic individual, the group has an index of 74.8. Two other Palestinian skulls from south of Beersheba (No. 10) are also dolichocephalic. Crania from Midian and Sinai measured by Seligman (Nos. 9, 11, and 12b) are dolichocephalic. Five adult Sinai skulls have been measured by Giovannozzi (Nos. 13 and 12c), two of which are subbrachycephalic and three dolichocephalic. In other words, the dolichocephals are in the majority and represent a definite type which was spread widely across North Arabia, Palestine, and Syria. That the type still exists is shown by the measurements made by Chantre on the dolichocephalic Tuarah of southwestern Sinai (Group No. 13 of living peoples), as well as by observations of many travelers in North Arabia. Seligman (1917, p. 218) writes: "...the northern Semites were essentially longheaded and the Arabs of northern Arabia exhibited and still exhibit this characteristic."

The latest finds from Palestine [up to 1932] are those of the earliest inhabitants so far discovered in Southwestern Asia, Palaeanthropus palestinus. The joint expedition of the British School of Archaeology in Jerusalem and the American School of Prehistoric Research, under the direction of Dorothy Garrod, found a rich Mousterian deposit in the caves of Mount Carmel. The first discovery was made by Turville Petre in a cave on the west side of the Lake of Galilee, and consisted of three frontal bones of a type similar to that of Neanderthal man. During 1931 the skeleton of a child was found by Theodore McCown in the Mousterian stratum of Mugharet as-Sukhul. Finally, in March, 1932, while McCown was in charge of the excavation, eight fragmentary skeletons were found. From the preliminary studies made on these finds, Keith believed that the inhabitants of Palestine in Mousterian times were related to Neanderthal man in Europe, but had many traits like those of the most primitive of modern or Neanthropic races, especially the Australian aborigines.

The Field Museum North Arabian Desert Expeditions, 1927-28, under the leadership of Henry Field, have proved the existence of man in various Paleolithic phases of culture through the discovery of numerous flint implements scattered over the surface of the high desert or wilderness, which extends eastward to the river Euphrates. No limestone caves were discovered in the area visited, and it is improbable that human skeletal remains will be found, although geological and cultural evidence bear witness to the former fertility of this region, which is now inhabited only by nomadic Beduins.

The chain of surface sites extends as far east at Rutba Wells and again appears near Kirkuk where in 1927 Dorothy Garrod and in 1928 Henry Field found implements of Mousterian types in the river gravels. Dorothy Garrod also conducted archeological soundings in the Kirkuk and Sulaimaniya Liwas, proving that there is a continuous chain of Paleolithic and Neolithic stations from the Mediterranean to the western foothills of the Kurdistan Mountains.

In view of the recent discovery of Palaeoanthropus palestinus, it seems plausible to suggest that members of this race were spread over the area lying between Palestine and Kurdistan and that at some future date the racial connections between the early peoples of Asia and Africa may be proved by means of a detailed study of the earliest inhabitants of Southwestern Asia.

Bronze Age crania from Cyprus (No. 14a) were measured by Buxton. The 14, whose measurements are certain, have a mean index of 78.61, while the entire group of crania, including later specimens as well as those of Bronze Age (No. 14b), have a slightly higher average index of 78.93. It is evident that this is a different stock, and undoubtedly a mixed one, as far back as we have any traces, the elements being Armenoid and Mediterranean. The present male inhabitants of Cyprus have a mean index of 82.54, caused by an additional brachycephalic admixture in the population. Cretan skulls of the Minoan period have an average index of 73.4, which shows that the proto-Egyptian stock was widespread on the island.

For comparison, the indices of ancient Egyptian skulls (No. 15) have also been introduced. In Upper Egypt, the average index is 73, while in Lower Egypt an admixture in the population is shown by the prevalence of a 75.4 index (Group No. 15b), as well as an index of 73 (No. 15a). More detailed reports of groups from Egypt confirm the 73 index. New Empire crania from cemeteries at Shellal near Aswan show an average male index of 73.38 and an average female index of 73.73. Old Empire skulls from Naqada are similar, the male index being 72.99 and the female 74.19. These groups are not indicated on the map. The graves at Abusir-el-Meleq yielded skulls whose cephalic indices range from 68.69 - 79.77; 18 are dolichocephalic and 11 mesocephalic.

A subbrachycephalic group of crania were excavated from an "ancient Arab cemetery" at Abassieh near Cairo (No. 16) by Panceri; 13 crania, both male and female, have an average index of 85.3. Seligman (1917, p. 231) suggests that they belonged to immigrants from South Arabia. Four other skulls from Cairo (No. 17) measured by Mochi have been indicated on the map as mesocephalic; actually, one is dolichocephalic, two are mesocephalic, and one brachycephalic. One group of 12 males and females from Tripoli in Libya are dolichocephalic and four males are brachycephalic, but Tripoli in Libya is too far afield for our investigation. Similar isolated groups of brachycephals are found all along the North African coast, but the typical North African is dolichocephalic. A series of ten Somalis reported by Puccioni (No. 18) have an average index of 72.2, while seven Uallega and Qoram crania (No. 19) are also dolichocephalic with a slightly higher index (73.86).

Central and South Arabia has so far contributed very little to our knowledge of their former population. The single skull reported from Central Arabia comes from Kheybar in the Hejaz (No. 20), a dolichocephalic female skull whose index is 72.8. Bertram Thomas found one skull (No. 21) at Hasik, an island off the coast of South Arabia. Its dimensions are small, the head length being 171 mm., breadth 137 mm. and height 133.5 mm. The cephalic index is 80.12, which is subbrachycephalic. A comparison of this skull with the one from Oman (No. 22) is most interesting, for the latter shows a markedly different type of brachycephaly. The Omani skull is a good example of the Armenoid type, being not only very brachycephalic, but also hypsicephalic, with a higher cranial vault and marked flattening of the occipital region. The index given in Table 154 was obtained by Keith and Krogman, but it should be mentioned that this skull was formerly measured by Seligman (1917, p. 220), who obtained a slightly different figure.

The crania from Kish (Nos. 24 and 25) are interesting and important. Of the material published by Buxton (1924) in a preliminary report, one skull (No. 23a) is brachycephalic, with an index of 82.08, and the others (No. 24a) are extremely dolichocephalic. As may be seen from Table 154, the indices of two are uncertain; the average index of the four whose measurements are certain is 68.27. On Map 23 the brachycephalic skull is indicated separately, as are also the four dolichocephalic crania. Finally, in 1931 Buxton and Rice published the results of measurements on all the skeletons from graves in the "A" Cemetery at Kish (No. 24b). Twenty-five skulls have an average index of 71.54, although two individuals are brachycephalic. Of the four measurable Neo-Babylonian skulls from Mound "W", one is brachycephalic (No. 23b) and the others (No. 24d) are dolichocephalic with a mean index of 69.89.

The skeletal remains from Jemdet Nasr described by Field date from the early part of the fourth millennium B.C. The only skull which could be measured (No. 24c) was found to be extremely dolichocephalic. Field suggests that it belonged to the Proto-Mediterranean stock.

Excavations at Ur of the Chaldees made by Woolley have thrown considerable light on the ancient physical types as well as material culture. Two groups of skeletons from widely different periods were unearthed. The first come from an ancient cemetery at al-Ubaid four miles west of Ur of the Chaldees dating from the early part of the fourth millennium. The remains of 17 individuals were found, but it was possible to measure only nine of them with accuracy. Six male crania (No. 26a) have a mean cephalic index of 72.6, and three female crania (No. 27) have a mesocephalic index of 77.6. These represent a population which may be contemporary with that of the Jemdet Nasr crania. The second group were found under the "Tomb Mound" at Ur, and are of the period 1900-1700 B.C., according to Woolley. The physical type represented here is different from that of al-Ubaid, but it is still a long-headed people. In fact, the type seems to have been modified by an infusion of people with even narrower heads than the previous population. This long, narrow and high-headed people is more likely to have come from Arabia than anywhere else. Of the seven individuals found here, not one is of the Armenoid type. The three males (No. 26b) have the remarkably low average index of 69.8, and the three females (No. 26c) whose measurements are certain have a mean index of 72.2. Part of the length of these skulls results from well-developed supraorbital ridges.

Material from peripheral areas adds more detail to the picture of the former population of Southwestern Asia. A Greek cemetery of the third century of the Christian Era in Asia Minor yielded 15 skulls (No. 29), whose average cephalic index is 76.56, which is mesocephalic. Of the skulls from Troy II and nearby places reported by Virchow, one is brachycephalic (No. 31). Three skulls from Troy III (No. 30a) and one less ancient skull from Khanai Tepe (No. 30b) are dolichocephalic. The skulls from Ophrynion (No. 30c), dating from about 500 B.C., have a higher index (74.5) but are still dolichocephalic. Since Troy lies beyond the limits of the map, these crania cannot be shown.

In another region, Persia (now Iran), dolichocephalic crania are also found. De Khanikoff acquired five Zoroastrian skulls (No. 28), three from Yezd, and two from Kerman, which have an average index of 70.

In conclusion let me state that I have attempted to collect the available anthropometric data from Southwestern Asia with the hope that the lacunae* shown on Maps 21-23 will inspire physical anthropologists to obtain statistical measurements and racial type photographs of the peoples of the Near East.

---

*Since this material was compiled during 1932, measurements on many thousands of males and females have been made, so that the racial position of the inhabitants of Southwestern Asia in relation to the peoples of Asia, Africa, and Europe is now clearer. (H.F.)

References

Blake, C.C.
  1871. Notes on human remains from Palmyra. JRAI, Vol. 1, pp. 312-20.
Brooks, C.E.P.
  1930. Climate. New York.
Busk, G.
  1874. Notes on some skulls from Palmyra. JRAI, Vol. 4, pp. 360-67.
  1879. Notes on a skull termed Nabathean. JRAI, Vol. 8, pp. 321-23.
Buxton, L.H. Dudley
  1920. The anthropology of Cyprus. JRAI, Vol. 50, pp. 183-235.
  1924. Human remains excavated at Kish. In: Stephen Langdon, "Excavations at
      Kish," Vol. 1, pp. 115-25. Paris.
  1925. The peoples of Asia. London.
Buxton, L.H. Dudley and Rice, David Talbot
  1931. Report on the human remains found at Kish. JRAI, Vol. 61, pp. 37-119.
Chantre, E.
  1885-1887. Recherches anthropologiques dans le Caucase. Lyons.
  1904. Recherches anthropologiques dans l'Afrique orientale. Lyons.
De Castro, L.
  1911. Contributo alla craniologia dell'Etiopia. AAE, Vol. 41, pp. 327-39.
Elliot Smith, G. and Wood Jones, F.
  1910. The archaeological survey of Nubia, 1907-08, Vol. 1, Report on the human
      remains. Cairo.
Field, Henry
  1932. Human remains from Jemdet Nasr, Mesopotamia. JRAS, pt. 4, pp. 967-
      70.
  1935. The Arabs of Central Iraq, their history, ethnology and physical characters.
      FMNH, Anthropology Memoirs, Vol. 4, pp. 1-474.
Garrod, Dorothy
  1932. A new species of fossil man. ILN, p. 36, July 9.
Giovannozzi, U.
  1904. Crani arabi del Museo Antropologia di Firenze. AAE, Vol. 34, pp. 343-
      53.
Giuffrida-Ruggieri, R.
  1917. Prime linea di un Antropologia sistematica dell'Asia. AAE, Vol. 47, pp.
      165-249.
Haddon, A.C.
  1935. The races of man. New York.
Hrdlicka, Ales
  1913. The natives of the Kharga Oasis. SMC, Vol. 59, no. 1, pp. 1-118.
Kappers, C.U. Ariens
  1930a. Contributions to the anthropology of the Near East: no. 1, The Armenians.
      KAWA, Vol. 33, no. 8, pp. 792-801.
  1930b. The spread of the brachycephalic races. KAWA, Vol. 33, no. 8, pp. 802-
      808.
  1931a. Phoenician and Palmyrene skulls. KAWA, Vol. 34, no. 1, pp. 106-15.
  1931b. The Semitic races. KAWA, Vol. 34, no. 1, pp. 116-30.
  1931c. Kurds, Circassians and Persians.
      KAWA, Vol. 34, no. 4, pp. 531-41.
  1931d. Turks and Greeks. KAWA, Vol. 34, no. 8, pp. 1085-98.

Keith, (Sir) Arthur
    1927. The human remains from Ur. In: H.R. Hall and C.L. Woolley, "Ur Exca-
        vations," Vol. 1, Ch. 10. Oxford.
    1932. A new link between Neanderthal man and primitive modern races: Palae-
        anthropus of Palestine. ILN, pp. 34-35, July 9.
Keith, (Sir) Arthur and Wilton M. Krogman
    1932. The racial characters of the southern Arabs. In: Bertram Thomas, "Ara-
        bia Felix," Appendix 1, pp. 301-33. New York.
Krischner, Harald and M.
    1932a. The anthropology of Mesopotamia and Persia: Armenians, Khaldeans,
        Suriani (or Assyrians) and Christian "Arabs" from Irak. KAWA, Vol. 35,
        pp. 205-17.
    1932b. Jesidis (Yezidis) and (Moslem) Arabs from Irak with some remarks on
        Kurds and Jews. KAWA, Vol. 35, pp. 218-27.
    1932c. The anthropology of Persia. KAWA, pp. 399-410.
Langerhaus, P.
    1873. Ueber die heutigen Bewohner des heiligen Landes. AAB, Vol. 6, pp. 39-
        58.
Leys, N.M. and Joyce, T.A.
    1913. Notes on a series of measurements from East Africa. JRAI, pp. 195-267.
MacMichael, H.A.
    1910. The Kababish: some remarks on the ethnology of a Sudan Arab tribe.
        JRAI, pp. 215-31.
Mochi, A.
    1907. Sulla antropologia degli Arabi. AAE, Vol. 37, pt. 3, pp. 411-28.
Morant, G.M.
    1928. Preliminary classification of European Races based on cranial measure-
        ments. Biometrika, Vol. 20-B, pp. 301-75.
Müller, F.W.
    1915. Die anthropologischen Ergebnisse des vorgeschichtlichen Gräberfeldes
        von Abusir el-Meleq. Leipzig.
Owen, R.
    1879. Note on skulls sent by Richard F. Burton. JRAI, Vol. 8, pp. 323-24.
Puccioni, N.
    1911. Ricerche antropometriche sui Somali, AAE, Vol. 41, pp. 295-326.
Seligman, C.G.
    1910. The physical characters of the Nubia of Kordofan. JRAI, Vol. 40, pp. 141-
        63.
    1913. Some aspects of the Hamitic problem in the Anglo-Egyptian Sudan. JRAI,
        Vol. 43, pp. 593-705.
    1917. The physical characters of the Arabs. JRAI, Vol. 47, pp. 214-39.
Speiser, Ephraim
    1930. Mesopotamian origins. University of Pennsylvania, Philadelphia.
Talbot, P.A.
    1916. Notes on the anthropometry of some central Sudan tribes. JRAI, Vol. 46,
        pp. 173-83.
Tschepourkowsky, E.
    1905-1906a. A quantitative study of the resemblance of man and woman. Bio-
        metrika, Vol. 4, p. 165.
    1905-1906b. Contribution to the study of interracial correlation. Biometrika,
        Vol. 4, pp. 293-95.

Tucker, A.W. and Myers, C.S.
   1910. A contribution to the anthropology of the Sudan. JRAI, Vol. 40, pp. 141-
      63.
Virchow, Rudolf
   1891. Description of two skulls from Palestine: Wadi Asluj and Rekhameh. ZE,
      Vol. 23, pp. 578-82.

Appendix C: ANTHROPOMETRIC DATA RECORDED BY KAPPERS

These data were received from Dr. A.J. van Bork-Feltkamp, Indisch Institute, Amsterdam, following my request for a copy of the raw data tables compiled by the late Professor C.U. Ariens Kappers, who published peaks of curves rather than means. All doubtful measurements and all individuals aged seventeen or less have been omitted. These omissions will account for minor differences in the results published by Kappers and L.W. Parr in "An Introduction to the Anthropology of the Near East," Amsterdam, 1934, and subsequent papers by Kappers. I have placed the complete raw data on ADIM 2419, pp. 1-92, in the American Documentation Institute c/o Photoduplication Service, Library of Congress, where a copy may be purchased. These new tabulations were machine-calculated by Mrs. Lowe, statistician of Coconut Grove Bank, Florida. Table 156 now present Kappers' data so that the means may be compared directly with our previously published tables and the compilations in this study.

The material has been presented according to his arrangement (see Tables 155 and 156).

Appendix D: LIST OF 100 ARCHAEOLOGICAL SITES

These 100 archaeological sites (Map 24) have been superimposed on the Raisz map of the Landforms of Arabia.

The reader is also referred to my map entitled, "North Arabian Desert Archaeological Survey," drawn by Dr. Erwin Raisz and published by the Peabody Museum - Harvard during April, 1956. This will supplement my Report to be published by the Peabody Museum, Harvard.

During the completion of these data, Mr. Karl S. Twitchell very generously sent notes on a series of sites ranging from near Wej in Midian to Najran in Asir. His notes have been included under the Arabian Peninsula and for convenience repeated here, with the site numbers changed to conform to our clockwise arrangement.

A few references to publications have been given to guide the researcher.

Abbreviations

ADIM--American Documentation Institute, c/o Photoduplication Service, Library of Congress
AJA--American Journal of Archaeology
GJ--Journal, Royal Geographical Society
ILN--Illustrated London News
JRCAS--Journal, Royal Central Asian Society
PMP--Peabody Museum Papers, Harvard
PPS--Proceedings, Prehistoric Society
SJA--Southwestern Journal of Anthropology

---

1. Several rolled and a few unrolled flakes were found during December, 1947 in the bed of the Wadi el-Arish near Magdhaba, between El Arish and Abu Aweiqileh in northeast Sinai. In 1917 Van Riet Lowe collected handaxes in the Wadi el-Arish.
Reference: Field, Contributions to the Anthropology of the Faiyum, Sinai, Northern Sudan and Kenya, p. 136, footnote 43, University of California Press, 1952.

2. At Er Rawafi (El Rawafa), two miles east of Abu Aweiqileh, a superb Lower Paleolithic station was found by Huzayyin, Albright, and Field. This is one of the most important surface stations in Southwestern Asia.
Reference: Field, ibid., p. 87, 1952.

3. Two air miles northwest of Bir Hasaneh, and on a flint-covered crest south of the Bir Hasaneb-Wadi el-Letheili track, Field found a station rich in heavily patinated flakes, scrapers, and cores.
Reference: Field, ibid., pp. 87-88, 1952.

4. At El Qusaima the Abbé Henri Breuil found deeply patinated surface flint implements in 1935.
Reference: personal communication.

5. In the Wadi el-Ghazze just south of Gaza, Van Riet Lowe in 1917 collected handaxes in this area.
Reference: personal communication.

6. Beersheba. Many surface finds in this area and in other regions of the Negeb to the south.
References: many publications by Nelson Glueck.

7. E. Anati in 1954 discovered rock drawings in the central Negev (Negeb).
References: Shem, pp. 245-54, 1954; Luchot, pp. 11-12, 1954; Palestine Exploration Quarterly, p. 49 et seq., 1955; and Archaeology, Vol. 8, pp. 31-42, 1955.

8. Typologically Lower Paleolithic handaxes from Wadi Seir were collected by Doughty in 1875, and by Field in 1927.
References: "Arabia Deserta," Vol. 1, p. 68; and Field, "Early Man in North Arabia," Natural History, pp. 34-44, New York, 1929.

9. About five miles northeast of El Jafar on the track to Bayir Wells some flint flakes were collected by Field in 1927.
Reference: Field, ibid., pp. 34-44, 1929.

10. Bayir Wells where a typologically Lower Paleolithic handaxe was found in situ during November, 1927.
Reference: Field, ibid., pp. 34-44, 1929.

11. Jebel Thlathakhwat, where typologically Mousterian implements deeply patinated, chocolate brown, were collected on top of each peak.
Reference: Field, ibid., pp. 34-44, 1929.

12. Qasr el-Azraq, where many flint flakes were found in the neighborhood of this Roman fort, particularly to the northwest toward Hammam as-Sarakh.
Reference: Field ms.

13. Jebel Tubayq, where Prehistoric rock-drawings were discovered by George and Agnes Horsfield and described by them and Nelson Glueck.
References: Agnes Horsfield, GJ, Vol. 102, pp. 71-77, 1943; George Horsfield and Nelson Glueck, ILN, June 3, 1933 and AJA, Vol. 37, pp. 381-86, 529, 1933.

In 1938 Hans Rhotert found a number of Prehistoric sites in these mountains.
Reference: Rhotert, Transjordanien vorgeschichtliche Forschungen, Stuttgart, 1938.

14. Ten miles northeast of Kaf (Qaf) on the track to Turaif (Tapline Station VI at Km. 1263) flint implements were collected by Field and Don Holm on June 16, 1950.
References: Field, Reconnaissance in Saudi Arabia, JRCAS, Vol. 38, Pts. 2-3, pp. 192-93, 1951; also PMP, Vol. 48, no. 2, 1956.

15. On Tell el-Hibr, a source of flint in Paleolithic and Neolithic times, Field and Holm collected on June 16, 1950 many hundreds of implements and flakes.
References: Field, ibid., pp. 191-92, 1951; also PMP, Vol. 48, no. 2, 1956.

16. Qasr Dauqara, at the southwestern end of the Khabra Dauqara, just south of the Roman fort, flint implements were collected by Field and Holm on June 16, 1950.
References: Field, ibid., p. 189, 1951; also PMP, Vol. 48, no. 2, 1956.

17. On Jebel Agrin flint implements were found by Field and Holm on June 16, 1950.
Reference: Field, ibid., p. 190, 1950, and PMP, Vol. 48, no. 2, 1955.

18. Near Km. 1284 northwest of Turaif, flint implements were collected and inscriptions recorded by Field and Holm on June 16, 1950.
Reference: Field, ibid., p. 192, 1951, and PMP, Vol. 48, no. 2, p. 63, 1955.

19. On Jebel Umm Wual, Field collected typologically Mousterian implements in December, 1927.
Reference: Field, "Early Man in North Arabia," Natural History, pp. 34-44, 1929.

20. On Jebel Aneiza (Anaize, Enaze) Field collected in March, 1928, many flint implements.
Reference: Field ms.

21. On Jebel Rijlat al-Asdah, south of Tapline and northwest of Km. 1163, Field and Holm collected flint implements in June, 1950.
Reference: Field, ibid., p. 192, 1951, and PMP, Vol. 48, no. 2, 1955.

22. Ruins northwest of Badana reported in 1953 by George Colley, International Bechtel Corporation.
Reference: private communication in 1950.

23. At Kish, eight miles east of Babylon, ancient city excavated by Field Museum-Oxford University Joint Expedition, 1923-34, flint implements were found from Babylonian levels down to just above virgin soil.
References: Louis Charles Watelin, "Notes sur l'industrie lithique de Kish (Iraq)," L'Anthropologie, Vol. 39, pp. 65-76, Paris; see also Anne H. Fuller on ADIM, no. 4469, pp. 96-116.

24. Cave south of Duwaid reported during 1953 by George Colley, International Bechtel Corporation.
Reference: personal communication in 1950.

25. On Jebel Umm el-Rijm about 70 kms. north-northwest of Rafha, Charles Rock of Aramco found several heavily patinated, dark brown scrapers.
Reference: personal communication in 1950.

26. Flints were collected in 1953 by George Colley, International Bechtel Corporation, in a depression, resembling a sinkhole, encircled by an escarpment (125 feet) with good grazing; in the Spring the Beduins drive their camels to this area.
Reference: personal communication in 1950.

27. At Ur of the Chaldees, excavated by the University of Pennsylvania-British Museum Expedition, flint implements were found from the Babylonian down to the lowest levels.
Reference: Sir Leonard Woolley.

28. At Eridu (Abu Shahrain) above Basra on the former shore of the Persian Gulf the Iraq Department of Antiquities found flint implements in the lower levels.
References: articles in Sumer.

29. In 1953 George Colley, International Bechtel Corporation, reported caves near Ansab Wells in the southwest corner of the Neutral Zone.
Reference: personal communication in 1950.

30. At Madaniyat, three miles west of Magwa, stand two stone-walled enclosures, the stones being flush with the ground. Nearby are other ruins.
Reference: Field, SJA, Vol. 7, no. 1, p. 92, 1951.

31. Colonel H.R.P. Dickson found many flint implements due south of Warah near a roughly circular tar pit (250 feet) just north of Burghan Hills, Southern Kuwait.
Reference: Field, SJA, Vol. 7, no. 1, p. 92, 1951.

32. On Jebel Gurain on the southern boundary between Kuwait and the eastern Neutral Zone, light-colored, worked flints, probably Neolithic or later, were found by Field on May 21, 1950.
Reference: Field, SJA, Vol. 7, no. 1, p. 93, 1951.

33. In 1953 George Colley, International Bechtel Corporation, reported a sinkhole or meteor crater (300-400 feet in diameter) south of Jauf Wells west of Ras al-Mishab. A few worked flints were collected.
Reference: personal communication in 1950. See no. 36.

34. At Faid (elevation 2,550 feet) are ruins (1,000 x 900 feet). Legend attributes the founder as Faid bin Sami bin Noah, the grandson of Noah. The walls were built of mud and lava. A column and a sarcophagus were seen. Beads and sherds were scattered on the surface.
Reference: Twitchell.

35. At Garara stands a cistern (126 feet in diameter) of well-dressed stone.
Reference: Twitchell.

36. In 1953 George Colley, International Bechtel Corporation, reported inscriptions on low hill 1.5 miles north of No. 33.
Reference: private communication in 1950.

37. Inscriptions were reported by an Aramco employee from near some wells due northwest of Saddah.
Reference: private communication in 1950.

38. Near Duwadami a magnificent handaxe was found by an Aramco geologist.
References: Peter B. Cornwall, Man, Vol. 46, p. 144; GJ, Vol. 107, pp. 28-50, 1946.

39. On Armah Plateau (25° 00´ N. and 47° 10´ E.) northeast of Riyadh about 40 miles southwest of Rumiyan, a square kilometer is covered with chert nodules (up to 0.5 meters in diameter), with many flaked by human hands. This was reported by an Aramco surveyor.
Reference: personal communication in 1955.

40. Extensive ruins of mud-brick buildings were visited at Jubaila during 1931. This town, recorded by Arab historians, has now been partially rebuilt.
Reference: Twitchell.

41. Gerald de Gaury reported ruins at Daraya on the Wadi Hanifa. This ancient capital of Nejd lies about one hour west of Riyadh.
Reference: personal communication.

42. Numerous mounds covered with sherds lie north of Sofwa near Al Qatif.
Reference: Twitchell.

43. 30 Kms. west of Dhahran, Don Holm, Aramco geologist, collected rolled and worn, dehydrated, white chert tools.
Reference: personal communication in 1955.

44. At Umm as-Saih near Al Khobar are many burial mounds, similar to those on Bahrain, also shell-middens. Field and Willard C. Beling of Aramco in June, 1950 collected a series of sherds and glass bracelets.
References: Field, JRCAS, Vol. 38, Pts. 2-3, p. 186, 1951.

45. On Bahrain Island surface flint implements have been collected by P.V. Glob, Director of the Danish Archeological Expedition.
References: Glob, Kuml, pp. 92-105, 142-53, 164-69, Aarhus. 1954. Pp. 178-93, 1955.

46. Hofuf, an ancient city which still requires trial trenches. Pottery, coins, etc. have been found.
Reference: Twitchell.

47. There are ruins at Oqair (Ojair or Al Uqayr) along the coast from the present Customs pier. Pottery in profusion and flint flakes.
References: Twitchell; and Field, 1955.

48. At the southwestern edge of Duhail in 1950 Field and T.G. Bibby visited a sinkhole (100 x 30 feet). A small cave (35 x 15 feet) contained thousands of well-preserved animal bones as well as three fragmentary human dolichocephalic skulls.
Reference: Field, SJA, Vol. 7, no. 1, p. 98, 1951.

49. Aramco surveyors reported during 1955 at Jafurah el-Jiban (24° 20´ N. and 50° 10´ E.) quartzite bifaces from gravels 10-20 meters above level plain.
Reference: Field, Man, Vol. 55, no. 145, p. 137, September, 1955.

50. Jal as-Sahban (24° N. and 50° 15´ E.). Southeast of Selwa and just north of the old Wadi Sahaba which lies about 60 miles across sabkha, a finely grained, buff-colored quartzite with rolled and worn arêtes was found.
Reference: Field, Man, Vol. 55, no. 145, p. 137, September, 1955.

51. Ruins of mud-brick buildings and numerous sherds were seen on the western side of Jabrin Oasis (elevation 710 feet), which lies 161 miles south by west of Hofuf. Jabrin covers an estimated 7,500 acres. More ruins are reported to the south.
Reference: Twitchell.

52. Near Awaifa in Wadi Amairi D.M. Morton, area geologist of the Qatar Petroleum Company, found flint implements during March-April, 1955 at Ral al-Galaa at the east end of Natih. Triliths are known from Boy and Nafun. Of unknown significance

and date, two large stone cairns (3.0 meters in diameter and 1.0 meter high) have been noted at the east end of Fahud, five or six at the northern flank of Natih, and several in the Wadi Amairi near Awaifa.
Reference: Field, Man, Vol. 55, no. 145, p. 137, September, 1955.

53. At Es Shalfah (21° 50′ N. and 49° 42′ E.) Aramco surveyors and geologists collected many flint implements.
Reference: Field, Man, Vol. 55, no. 145, p. 137, September, 1955.

54. During the spring of 1955, Z.R. Beydoun, geologist for Petroleum Concessions Limited, found the Stone Age site of Nahrit (17° 01′ N. and 50° 40′ E.) in the northern Hadhramaut. Two flint implements were collected near a circle (14.0 meters) of upright rock slabs up to five feet six inches in height.
Reference: Field, Man, Vol. 55, no. 145, p. 137, September, 1955.

55. Aramco camp, known as G-2554 (18° 18′ N. and 49° 46′ E.), where 19 blades of "Solutrian" type lay arranged in a circle 1.0 meter in diameter. The largest specimen, with the finest pressure-flaking technique, measured 13.5 x 4.25 x 0.75 centimeters; the next in size being 12.0 x 5.0 x 0.5 centimeters. This excellent quality flint is laminated with marked concentric circles. Several of these specimens would pass for the finest Solutrian feuilles-de-laurier, almost matching in skill of craftsmanship the work of the Solutrian, Dynastic Egyptian or Danish flint-knappers, with the exception of certain ceremonial Egyptian knives, the hafted blade from Solutré and the Fünen dagger.
Reference: Field, Man, Vol. 55, no. 145, p. 137, September, 1955.

56. Near Aramco camp (48° E. and 18° N.) a rich haul of flint implements was made by geologists and surveyors.
Reference: Field, Man, Vol. 55, no. 145, p. 137, September, 1955.

57. Near Tarim surface Paleoliths were found by Miss Caton Thompson.
Reference: Gertrude Caton Thompson, PPS, Vol. 19, pt. 2, pp. 189-218, 1953. See Fig. 6.

58. Paleoliths from near Shiban beside the Wadi Hadhramaut were collected by Miss Caton Thompson.
References: Gertrude Caton Thompson, PPS, Vol. 19, Pt. 2, pp. 189-218, 1953. See Fig. 7. For obsidian and chert microliths, see Caton Thompson, "The Tombs and Moon Temple of Hureidha (Hadhramaut)." Reports of the Research Committee of the Society of Antiquaries of London, No. 13, Plate 60, Oxford, 1944.

59. Post-Paleoliths, probably Neolithic, were collected by Miss Caton Thompson from the surface of Harshiat gravels near Mukalla.

60. Paleolithic implements were found by Miss Caton Thompson from the Wadi Amd in the Hureidha area.
References: Gertrude Caton Thompson, GJ, Vol. 93, no. 1, pp. 18-38, 1939; PPS, Vol. 19, Pt. 2, pp. 189-218, and Figs. 2-3, 1953. For obsidian and chert microliths and obsidian cores from Hureida, see Caton Thompson, "The Tombs and Moon Temple of Hureidha (Hadhramaut)." Reports of the Research Committee of the Society of Antiquaries of London, No. 13, Plates 58-59, Oxford, 1944.

61. At Shabwah Major T.A. Altounyan led an Iraq Petroleum Company survey party into the Hadhramaut during December, 1949 and January, 1950. He obtained a flint point, shiny with "desert varnish," from the wadi bed near Shabwa as well as a series of seals. He purchased from a Beduin a suberb Spartan bronze figurine from the Wadi Jurdhan southwest of Shabwa.
References: personal communication from Major Altounyan; regarding figurine, see Berta Segall, AJA, Vol. 59, no. 3, pp. 207-14, 1955; see also Caton Thompson, "The Tombs and Moon Temple of Hureidha (Hadhramaut)," pp. 150-51 and footnote 12, London, 1944.

62. Aden area.

References: W.H. Ingrams.

63. Marib.

References: Articles by W.F. Albright and Staff of Expedition sponsored by the American Foundation for the Study of Man, New York.

64. At Shaqqat el-Khariyta three "Neolithic" sites were found by D.G. Bunker and G. Popov of the Anti-Locust Survey.

Reference: F.E. Zeuner, Man, Vol. 54, no. 209, pp. 133-36, 1954.

65. At Najran are two superimposed cities. Many walls, bearing Himyaritic inscriptions, still stand. Three grinding stones (4-1/2 feet in diameter and 14 inches thick) as well as a large mortar were recorded.

References: Twitchell; and Philby.

66. The Mufija dam site near Najran shows expert cutting of granite for sluiceways, some of which had lime-concrete lining.

Reference: Twitchell.

67. The Tariq el-Feel ("Road of the Elephants") is a ruined paved road from Najran to Suq el-Ahad. This construction is attributed to the Abyssinians about A.D. 570.

Reference: Twitchell.

68. Eleven kilometers north of Tureeb (elevation 5,360 feet) stand low walls and inscriptions. There is also a pavement (100 feet long) and a semicircular wall (38 feet in diameter).

Reference: Twitchell.

69. At Aramco campsite at Jiladah (18° 48′ N. and 46° 18′ E.) many flint implements have been collected.

Reference: Field, Man, Vol. 55, no. 145, p. 137, September, 1955.

70. Ruins of buildings and a water system were examined at Al Garia about 60 miles south of Khamaseen on the Wadi Dawasir and about the same distance from the western edge of the Rub' al Khali. Himyaritic inscriptions were seen on stones cleared from a wall. Sherds lay scattered on the surface.

Reference: Twitchell.

71. From east of Sulail (20° 3′ N. and 46° 15′ E.) Don Holm of Aramco collected during October, 1949 the finest specimen I have ever seen from Southwestern Asia --a quartzite spearpoint (24 x 7.5 x 0.75 cms.) with large broad pressure flakes on one side.

Reference: Field, JRCAS, p. 195, 1951.

72. In the Wadi Dawasir area Aramco surveyors and geologists have collected many surface implements.

Reference: personal communication from Aramco Staff in March, 1955.

73. Along Wadi Thalith (alt. 2,772 feet) Aramco surveyors and geologists have found surface implements.

Reference: personal communication from Aramco Staff in March, 1955.

74. At Aflaj (alt. 1,650 feet), 214 miles south of Riyadh toward Laila, are five large water pits. There exists evidence of former extensive cultivation. At the edge of one of these pits there are traces of three irrigation ditches, the largest being the upper (eight feet wide). The present water level is 27 feet below at this point. Several other ditches and water tunnels radiate from these pits. Ten miles south of Laila stand three mud-brick forts (?). The one visited by Twitchell had walls eight feet thick and measured 40 x 40 x 35 feet, the latter being higher in ancient times. A typical room measured 8 x 9 x 7 feet. Sherds, bearing a green slip similar to those from Mahad Dahab (No. 81) and attributed to a period not earlier than the tenth century, lay on the surface. In addition, red sherds with a brownish-gray slip were seen. Coins were reported but none were found. At Harafa, six miles west of

the pit called Shughaib, relatively recent ruins were visited.
Reference: Twitchell.

75. Ruins of Hadda and adjacent gardens on the north bank of Wadi Fatima and 40 kilometers east of Jidda.
Reference: Twitchell.

76. Scattered ruins and water tunnels along the Wadi Fatima from Hadda to Ain Jimun.
Reference: Twitchell.

77. Four wells at Thunthaba, 34 kilometers south of El Birka, on the Darb ez-Zobeida.
References: Twitchell. For notes on the Darb ez-Zobeida, see Musil, "Northern Nejd," pp. 188-89, New York, 1928.

78. Cistern and many recent ruins at El Birka, 197 kilometers northeast of Jidda, on the Darb ez-Zobeida.
Reference: Twitchell.

79. Cistern at Mislah, 30 kilometers north of El Birka, on the Darb ez-Zobeida.
Reference: Twitchell.

80. At Haleet, north of Dawadami, lie ruins of a mining town. Sherds, bearing a green slip, and grinding stones were seen.
Reference: Twitchell.

81. At Mahad Dahab (Lat. 23° 29′ 52″ N. and Long. 40° 52′ 45″ E.), which lies 246 miles northeast of Jidda toward Hail, are ruins of a gold-mining town. Here may be seen ancient workings. On the surface lie sherds with a green slip, mortars and grinding stones of lava. Modern mining operations have been continuous here since 1936. Gold, silver, copper, lead, and zinc have been produced.
Reference: Twitchell.

82. At Shaib Buqqar, 39 kilometers south of Alameera, stands a cistern (90 x 90 x 5 feet). The original depth is masked by drifted sand. There are two nine-foot pilasters on the east and west sides and three on the north. The well-dressed, granite walls are 4.5 feet thick with good lime mortar, one-quarter inch thick, lining the cistern.

About 1.5 kilometers south of Shaib Buqqar is another cistern (200 feet in diameter and 10 feet deep to the drifted sand). There is a sand-box (150 x 50 feet). Stairs lead down into the cistern. Gold coins (circa A.D. 1300) are reported to have been found here. Four ruins lie to the west. Near two tombs (?), about 600 feet to the west, a few sherds with a blue slip and glass fragments were seen.
Reference: Twitchell.

83. At Alameera (alt. 2,800 feet) are ruins and a cistern (18 x 133 feet) with lime-concrete mortar walls. Four other cisterns were recorded. About 1,000 paces south a dam runs diagonally across a small wadi. This rubble masonry is nine feet wide for 50 feet, then 4.8 feet for 1,000 feet.
Reference: Twitchell.

84. Other ancient mines have been located at Nogra and Najady, about 100 miles northeast of Mahad Dahab (No. 81). About 15 miles south of Nogra stand ruins (one kilometer square) and two cisterns. In 1949 six other ancient mines were discovered about 276 miles east of Jidda.
Reference: Twitchell.

85. Ruins of Alemat village about 30 kilometers east of Medina on prilgrim road to Hail (Hayil) and Baghdad. Nearby stand ruins of a flood-water catchment basin (200 x 150 feet), a well (18 feet in diameter), and a cut stone cistern.
Reference: Twitchell.

86. At Al Darr in the Wadi Yenbu sherds cover the ground. Coins and statuettes were reported, but none were found. This great valley has been under cultivation for centuries.
Reference: Twitchell.

87. Near An Najal in the bed of the Wadi Aeis ancient walls were seen.
Reference: Twitchell.

88. Fifteen miles southeast of Khaibar lies Sud Haseed (alt. 2,380 feet). This dam (28 feet high, 182 feet along the base and 270 feet at the crest), was built about 1,500 years ago in two stages. The walls are of well-dressed basalt courses.
Reference: Twitchell.

89. Southeast of the present town of Khaibar (alt. 2,200 feet) and on top of the lava flow stands a large ruined village reported to be of Jewish origin.
Reference: Twitchell.

90. From the air three stone circles (200 feet in diameter), each with a tail extending about 200 feet, were seen in 1937 on hilltops between the Wadi Hamdh and Umm Lej. Cf. "kites" in Jordan.
Reference: Twitchell.

91. The fort of Qalaat es-Surah (alt. 2,200 feet) on the pilgrim road to Damascus. A Turkish inscription bears the date A.H. 1073. Outside is a cistern (55 feet square), a well (36 feet in diameter and 70 feet deep).
Reference: Twitchell.

92. At the junction of the Wadi Ula and the Wadi Jizal (alt. 1,440 feet) stand ruins (180 x 200 feet) with many sherds, lava fragments, and sandstone and granite grinding stones. Upstream are ruins of buildings, probably houses. Twitchell found a small gold coin and a hammerhead. Thirty-four miles down the Wadi Jizal are many ruined buildings and water tunnels indicating intensive cultivation. Ten miles beyond this point is a ruined fortress containing many kiln-fired bricks. Nine miles further lie ruins of fortresses, villages, and water tunnels (alt. 1,010 feet). Ahmad Fakry, who accompanied Twitchell, observed that early Arab historians refer to the fertility and civilization of the Wadi Jizal. At the present time there are no inhabitants.
Reference: Twitchell.

93. On May 8, 1931, the ruins of a Roman (?) temple, lying on the south bank of the Wadi Hamdh, were visited. This appeared to be a small temple with steps leading down to the river. Many delicately carved gypsum fragments are now used as headstones for Beduin graves. A column and a fragment of a base were seen.
Reference: Twitchell.

94. The Umm Garayat mine, which lies 14 kilometers east of Wej, is believed to have been worked by the miners of King David. There are several ancient mines in this area.
Reference: Twitchell.

95. Three miles north of Al Ula on the Hijaz R.R. stand the extensive ruins of Horaiba (alt. 2,110 feet). Amid the rubble was a stone tank (5 x 5 x 5 feet). In the adjacent sandstone cliffs to the south are many hand-cut caves. Some of these could have served as dwellings, others were just large enough for a coffin; all seen had been opened for many years.
Reference: Twitchell.

96. El Gala fortress near Wej, on the pilgrim road to Mecca. This is one of the outposts built by the Egyptian Government to protect the pilgrims. Another fortress lies about 25 miles distant.
Reference: Twitchell.

97. At Medain Saleh (alt. 2,240 feet) are many large tombs cut out of the gray sandstone cliffs and hills. There are many well-carved eagles, men's faces, snakes, urns, gables, and steps. Inside the large rooms are many niches for bodies. Every tomb seen had been opened and robbed. However, in some rooms there was a hollow sound, suggesting tombs or rooms still unopened.
References: Doughty; and Twitchell.

98. At Bedaa, near Dthiba, 60 miles north of Wej, tombs similar to those at Horaiba (No. 95) were reported but not visited.
Reference: Twitchell.

99. Ezion-geber (anc. *Elath, now Tell el-Kheleifeh) near Aqaba, the port and refinery center of Solomon (see I Kings IX:26). Here copper and iron were smelted, refined, and made into commodities for local and foreign markets.
Reference: Nelson Glueck.

100. Near El Kuntilla flint implements were collected in 1915.
Reference: Van Riet Lowe in private communication.

ABBREVIATIONS

AA--American Anthropologist, Menasha, Wisconsin.

AAB--Archiv für Anthropologie (now: Archiv für Anthropologie und Völkerforschung), Brunswick.

AAE--Archivio per l'Antropologia e l'Etnologia, Florence.

AAWL--Abhandlungen, Akademie der Wissenschaften und Literatur, Mainz.

ACLS--American Council of Learned Societies, Washington.

ADI--American Documentation Institute, c/o Photoduplication Service, Library of Congress.

ADIM--American Documentation Institute Microfilm, c/o Photoduplication Service, Library of Congress.

ADOG--Ausgrabungen der Deutschen Orientalischen Gesellschaft, Berlin.

AE--Annals of Eugenics, London.

AFO--Archiv für Orientforschung, Berlin.

AGP--Annales de Géographie, Paris.

AGS--American Geographical Society, New York.

AI--Ancient India, Archaeological Survey of India, New Delhi.

AIIP--Archives de l'Institut de Paléontologie Humaine, Paris.

AJA--American Journal of Archaeology, Cambridge, Massachusetts.

AJIL--American Journal of International Law, Washington.

AJPA, American Journal of Physical Anthropology, Philadelphia.

AKAW--Anzeiger der Kaiserlichen Akademie der Wissenschaften, Vienna.

ALB--Anti-Locust Bulletin, British Museum (Natural History). London.

ALRCM--Anti-Locust Research Centre Monograph, British Museum (Natural History), London.

AMNH--American Museum of Natural History, New York.

AMS--Actas y Memorias, Sociedad Espanola de Antropologia, Madrid.

AN--The American Neptune, Salem, Massachusetts.

ANGH--Abhandlungen der Naturforschenden Gesellschaft, Halle.

ANMV--Annalen, Naturhistorisches Museum, Vienna.

AO--Archiv Orientálni, Prague.

AS--American Scientist, New Haven, Connecticult.

ASAE--Annales du Service des Antiquités de l'Egypte, Cairo.

ASAG--Archives Suisses d'Anthropologie Générale, Geneva.

ASIF--L'Académie des Sciences de l'Institut de France, Paris.

ASRA--Atti della Società Romana di Antropologia, Rome.

AST--Anatolian Studies, Ankara.

AW--The Arab World, New York.

B.

BABOA--Belletenden Ayri Basim Olarek Alinmistir, Istanbul.

BAMS--Bulletin of the American Metereological Society, Easton, Pennsylvania.

BASI--Bulletin, Archaeological Survey of India, New Delhi.

BASOR--Bulletin, American Schools of Oriental Research, New Haven.

BASPR--Bulletin, American Schools of Prehistoric Research, Peabody Museum, Harvard.

BAV--Biblioteca Apostolica Vaticana, Rome.

BCAS--Boston College Anthropological Series, Boston.

BDA--Bulletin, Department of Anthropology, Government of India, Calcutta.

BE--La Bourse Egyptienne, Cairo.

BEO--Bulletin d'Etudes Orientales,
Institut Français de Damas et
Beyrouth (Beirut), Lebanon.

BFAUE--Bulletin of the Faculty of
Arts of the University of Egypt,
Cairo.

BFS--Bulletin of the Faculty of Sciences, Fouad I University, Cairo.
Now Cairo University.

BGHU--Bulletin of the Geological
Department, Hebrew University,
Jerusalem.

BGI--Bibliographie Géographique In-
ternationale, Paris.

BIE--Bulletin de l'Institut d'Egypte,
Cairo.

BIFAO--Bulletin de l'Institut Français d'Archéologie Orientale,
Paris.

BJVD--British Journal of Venereal
Diseases, London.

BMAE--Bulletin of the Ministry of
Agriculture, Cairo.

BMB--Bulletin du Musée de Beyrouth
(Beirut), Lebanon.

BMCZ--Bulletin of the Museum of
Comparative Zoology, Harvard.

BNSS--Bulletin of the National Speleo-
logical Society, Washington.

BPAS--Bulletin of the Philadelphia
Anthropological Society.

BRCI--Bulletin, Research Council
of Israel, Jerusalem.

BRSGI--Bollettino della Reale Società Geografica Italiana, Rome.

BSA--Bulletin de la Société d'Anthropologie, Paris.

BSAE--British School of Archeology
in Egypt, London.

BSAL--Bulletin de la Société d'Anthropologie de Lyons.

BSB--Bulletin de la Société Scientifique de Bucharest, Bucuresti.

BSEHGIS--Bulletin de la Société
d'Etudes Historiques et Géographiques de l'Isthme de Suez,
Ismailia.

BSGE--Bulletin de la Société Royale
de Géographie d'Egypte, Cairo.

BSGF--Bulletin de la Société Géologique de France, Paris.

BSIER--Bulletin of Scientific Exploration of the North Caucasus Vladi-
kavtz (later Ordzhonikidze, now
Dzaudzhikau).

BSOAS--Bulletin of the School of Oriental and African Studies, University of London.

BSPF--Bulletin de la Société Préhistorique Française, Paris.

BSRAA--Bulletin de la Société Royale
d'Archéologie d'Alexandrie.

BSRAC--Bulletin de la Société Royale
d'Archéologie Copte, Cairo.

BSRGE--Bulletin de la Société Royale
de Géographie d'Egypte, Cairo.

BUM--Bulletin of the University
Museum, Philadelphia.

C.

CASB--Bulletin, Chicago Anthropological Society.

CASNHM--Chicago Academy of Sciences Natural History, Miscellanea.

CASP--College of Arts and Science
Publications, Baghdad.

CHE--Cahiers d'Histoire Egyptienne,
Cairo.

CI--Carnegie Institution of Washington.

CIAAP--Fifteenth International Congress of Anthropology and Archaeology, Paris, 1931.

CIAES-I--First International Congress
of Anthropological and Ethnological
Sciences.

CIMPP--Acts of the First International
Congress of Mediterranean Prehis-
tory and Protohistory, Florence,
Naples and Rome, 1950.

CMP--Carnegie Museum, Pittsburgh.

CO--Colonial Office, London.

CPAP--Proceedings, First Pan-Afri-
can Congress on Prehistory, Nairobi. Published by Basil Blackwell,
Oxford.

CPF-X--Congrès Préhistorique de
France, Tenth Session.

CRAIB--Comptes Rendus, Académie
des Inscriptions et Belles-Lettres,
Paris.

CRAS--Comptes Rendus Hebdomaires
des Séances de l'Académie des
Sciences, Paris.

CRICAE--Comptes Rendus, Second
International Congress of Anthropological and Ethnological Sciences, Copenhagen, 1939.

CRSB--Comptes Rendus des Séances
de la Société de Biologie, Paris.

CSAB--Chicago Anthropological Society Bulletin.

CTH--Second Turkish Congress on
History, Istanbul, 1937.

D.

DA--Department of Agriculture Bulletin, Baghdad.

DCDS--Deccan College Dissertation
Series, Poona.

DCHS--Deccan College Handbook
Series, Poona.

DCMS--Deccan College Monograph
Series, Poona.

DEO-- Documents d'Etudes Orientales
de l'Institut Français de Damas.
et Beyrouth (Beirut), Lebanon.

DGFL--Délégation Générale de France
au Levant, Section Géologique,
Beyrouth (Beirut), Lebanon.

DMOT--The Dental Magazine and
Oral Topics, London.

DRP--Desert Research, Proceedings,
Research Council of Israel,
Jerusalem.

DS--Department of State, Washington.

E.

EA--Encyclopedia Americana Annual, New York.

EC--L'Egypte Contemporaire, Cairo.

EESE--Etudes d'Ethnografie, de
Sociologie et d'Ethnologie, Paris.

EFI--Ecole Française d'Ingénieurs
de Beyrouth (Beirut), Lebanon.

EG--Economic Geography, Concord,
New Hampshire.

EGH--Eclogae Geological Helvetiae,
Basle.

F.

FMN--Field Museum News, Chicago.

FMNH--Field Museum of Natural History, now Chicago Natural History
Museum.

G.

GB--Guides Bleus, Paris.

GBG--Gerlands Beiträge zur Geo-
physik, Leipzig.

GE--Global Epidemiology, Vol. 3,
New York, 1954.

GJ--Journal of the Royal Geographical Society, London.

GM--The Geographical Magazine,
London.

GR--Geographical Review, New York.

GSA--General Series in Anthropology,
Menasha, Wisconsin.

GSGS--General Staff Geological Survey, London.

H.

HB--Human Biology, Baltimore.

HCRF--Haut-Commissariat de la
République Française, Service
des Renseignments du Levant,
Beyrouth (Beirut), Lebanon.

HDA--Hydrographic Department,
Admiralty, London.

HMSO--Her Majesty's Stationery
Office, London.

HRAF--Human Relations Area Files,
421 Humphrey St., New Haven.

HREHS--Horticultural Review of the
Egyptian Horticultural Society,
Cairo.

HUGD--Hebrew University Geological
Department, Jerusalem.

I.

IA--Indian Antiquary, Mazgaon.

IAE--Institut Antropologii i Etnografii,
USSR Academy of Sciences, Leningrad.

IBRD--International Bank for Reconstruction and Development, Washington.

ICB--Imprimerie Catholique, Beyrouth
(Beirut), Lebanon.

IDAI--International Directory of Anthropological Institutions. Published by Wenner-Gren Foundation
for Anthropological Research,
New York.

IEJ--Israel Exploration Journal, Jerusalem.

IEQ--Israel Exploration Quarterly, Jerusalem.

ILN--Illustrated London News.

INHM--Iraq Natural History Museum, Baghdad.

IP--Iraq Petroleum, London.

IPA--Information Please Almanac, New York, 1954.

IPC--Iraq Petroleum Company.

IRS--International Reference Service, U.S. Department of Commerce, Office of International Trade, Washington.

IUM--Istatistik Umum Müdürlügü, Ankara.

IVGO--Izvestiia, Vsesoiuznogo Geografischeskogo Obshchestva, Moscow.

J.

JAI--Journal of the Anthropological Institute, later JRAI.

JAOS--Journal of the American Oriental Society, New Haven.

JASB--Journal of the Anthropological Society of Bombay.

JBNHS--Journal of the Bombay Natural History Society, Bombay.

JC--Journal de Conchyliogie, Paris.

JE--Jewish Encyclopedia, 1915.

JI--Journal of Immunology, Baltimore.

JIS--Journal of the Iran Society, London.

JJPES--Journal of the Jewish Palestine Exploration Society, Jerusalem.

JMLB--Journal de Médicine Libanais, Beyrouth (Beirut), Lebanon.

JNES--Journal of Near Eastern Studies, Chicago.

JNK--Jahreshefte Naturkunde, Württemberg.

JPOS--Journal of the Palestine Oriental Society, Jerusalem.

JRA--Journal Russe d'Anthropologie, Moscow.

JRAI--Journal of the Royal Anthropological Institute of Great Britain and Ireland, London.

JRAPCS--Journal of the Royal India, Pakistan and Ceylon Society.

JRAS--Journal of the Royal Asiatic Society, London.

JRCAS--Journal of Royal Central Asian Society, London.

JRGS--Journal of the Royal Geographical Society, London.

JTVI--Journal of the Transactions of the Victoria Institute, London.

JWH--Journal of World History, Paris.

K.

KAWA--Koninklijke Akademie van Wetenschappen te Amsterdam.

KAWB--Königliche Akademie der Wissenschaften, Berlin.

L.

LSP--Linnaean Society, Proceedings, London.

M.

MAGW--Mitteilungen der Anthropologischen Gesellschaft, Vienna.

MAQR--Michigan Alumnus Quarterly Review, Ann Arbor, Michigan.

MASI--Memoirs, Archaeological Survey of India, New Delhi.

MBC--Magazine of the Board of Commerce, Baghdad.

MEI--Middle East Institute, Washington.

MFE--Ministry of Finance, Survey and Mines Department, Cairo.

MFOB--Mélanges de la Faculté Orientale, Beyrouth (Beirut), Lebanon.

MGGW--Mitteilungen, Geologische Gesellschaft in Wien, Vienna.

MGSI--Memoirs, Geological Survey of India, New Delhi.

MGSP--Mémoires de la Société de Géographie, Paris.

MKM--Mitteilungen, Kavkazskii Musei, Tiflis (Tbilisi).

MMFQ--The Milbank Memorial Fund Quarterly, New York.

MON--Meteorological Office Notes. Baghdad.

MSEHGIS--Mémoire de la Société d'Etudes Historiques et Géographiques de l'Isthme de Suez, Cairo.

MSGP--Mémoires de la Société de
Géographie, Paris.
MUSJ--Mélanges de l'Université St.
Joseph, Beyrouth (Beirut), Leba-
non.

N.

NAM--Nouvelles Archéologiques du
Museum, Paris.
NES--Near East Service, Beirut.
NGM--National Geographic Magazine,
Washington.
NH--Natural History, American
Museum of Natural History, New
York.
NJMGP--Neues Jahrbuch für Miner-
alogie, Geologie und Paläontologie,
Stuttgart.
NMHCF--Notes et Mémoires, Haut-
Commissariat Français, Beyrouth
(Beirut), Lebanon.
NMSGB--Notes et Mémoires, Section
Géologique, Beyrouth (Beirut),
Lebanon.

O.

OC--Open Court, Chicago.
OES--Overseas Economic Surveys,
Her Majesty's Stationery Office,
London.
OIP--Oriental Institute Publications,
University of Chicago.
OPA--Office of Public Affairs, U.S.
Department of State, Washington.

P.

PAPS--Proceedings of the American
Philosophical Society, Philadel-
phia.
PAUB--Publications of the American
University of Beirut, Lebanon.
PBA--Proceedings of the British
Academy, London.
PDAQ--Palestine Department of An-
tiquities Quarterly, Jerusalem.
PEAS--Proceedings, Egyptian Aca-
demy of Sciences, Cairo.
PEFQ--Palestine Exploration Fund
Quarterly, London.

PMBSG--Publications of the Marine
Biological Station, Ghardaqa (Red
Sea).
PMP--Peabody Museum Papers,
Harvard University.
PMSAO--Peabody Museum Studies in
Anthropology of Oceania, Cam-
bridge, Massachusetts.
PNB--Psychiatrische en Neurolog-
ische Bladen, Amsterdam.
PPS--Proceedings of the Prehistoric
Society of East Anglia, Cambridge
(formerly Ipswich), England.
PSEBM--Proceedings, Society for
Experimental Biology and Medi-
cine, New York.
PZ--Prähistorische Zeitschrift,
Leipzig.
PZS--Proceedings, Zoological Society
of London.

Q.

QJRMS--Quarterly Journal of the
Royal Meteorological Society,
London.
QST--Quarterly Statement of the
Palestine Exploration Fund, London.

R.

RA--Revue d'Anthropologie, Paris.
RACE--Royal Automobile Club of
Egypt, Cairo.
RAS--Royal Asiatic Society, London.
RASJ--Journal of the Royal African
Society (now: African Affairs),
London.
RASM--Royal Asiatic Society Mono-
graph, London.
RAZ--Russki Antropologicheskii
Zhurnal, Moscow.
RB--Revue Biblique, Paris.
RC--La Revue du Caire, Cairo.
RCFO--Revue des Conférences Fran-
çaises en Orient, Cairo.
RE--La Rayon d'Egypte, Cairo.
REC--Refugee Economic Corporation,
New York.
REI--Revue des Etudes Islamiques,
Paris.
RGAG--Revue de Géographie Alpine,
Grenoble.

RGSI--Records, Geological Survey
    of India, New Delhi.
RHA--Revue Hittite et Asiatique.
RLMTP--République Libanaise,
    Ministère des Travaux Publiques,
    Damascus.
RS--Revue Syria, Damascus.
RSP--Rivista di Scienze Preistoriche,
    Florence.
RSMTP--République Syrienne, Minis-
    tère des Travaux Publiques,
    Damascus.
RSTMH--Royal Society of Tropical
    Medicine and Hygiene, London.
RTA--Revue Turque d'Anthropologie
    (Türk Antropologi Mecmuasi),
    Istanbul.

S.

SA--Society of Antiquaries, London.
SAOC--Studies in Ancient Oriental
    Civilization, Oriental Institute,
    University of Chicago.
SAS--South African Science, Johan-
    nesburg.
SBGNF--Sitzungsberichte der Gesell-
    schaft der Naturforschenden
    Freunde zu Berlin.
SBT--Svensk Botanisk Tidskrift, Up-
    psala.
SE--Sovetskaia Etnografiia, Moscow.
SG--Schweizer Geograph, Zürich
    University.
SGF--Société Géologique de France,
    Comptes Rendus, Paris.
SGFF--Service Géographique des
    Forces Françaises Libres, Bey-
    routh (Beirut), Lebanon.
SJA--Southwestern Journal of An-
    thropology, Albuquerque, New
    Mexico.
SMC--Smithsonian Miscellaneous
    Collections, Washington.
SNR--Sudan Notes and Records,
    Khartoum.
SP--Science Press, Lancaster,
    Pennsylvania.
SR--The Sociological Review, Lon-
    don.
SRGE--Société Royale de Géographie
    d'Egypte, Cairo.
SZ--Spolia Zeylanica, Colombo,
    Ceylon.

T.

TADS--Transactions of the American
    Dental Society of Europe, London.
TAPS--Transactions of the American
    Philosophical Society, Philadelphia.
TB--Tabulae Biologicae, The Hague.
TCA--Technical Coöperation Admini-
    stration, U.S. Department of State.
TCFD--Tarih-Cografya Fakültesi
    Dergisi, Ankara University.
TUQ--Thought, Fordham University
    Quarterly, New York.
THS--Turkish Historical Society,
    Istanbul.
TNYAS--Transactions, New York
    Academy of Sciences.
TTKB--Türk Tarih Kürümü, Belleten,
    Ankara.

U.

UC--University of Cincinnati Mono-
    graphs published by Princeton Uni-
    versity Press.
UCP--University of California Press,
    Berkeley.
UM--University of Miami, Coral
    Gables, Florida.
UPMM--University of Pennsylvania
    Museum Monograph, Philadelphia.
USFWS--U.S. Fish and Wildlife Ser-
    vice, Washington.

V.

VBG--Verhandlungen der Berliner
    Gesellschaft für Anthropologie,
    Ethnologie und Urgeschichte, Ber-
    lin.
VNGZ--Vierteljahrsschrift der Natur-
    forschenden Gesellschaft, Zürich.
VUSHM--Vor- und Frühgeschichtliche
    Untersuchungen aus dem Schleswig-
    Holsteinische Museum Vorgeschicht-
    licher Altertumer, Schleswig.

W.

WBKL--Wiener Beiträge zur Kultur-
    geschichte und Linguistik, Universi-
    tät Wien Institut für Völkerkunde,
    Vienna.

Z.

ZDPV--Zeitschrift des Deutschen
    Palästina-Vereins, Leipzig.

ZE--Zeitschrift für Ethnologie,
    Berlin.

ZFR--Zeitschrift für Rassenkunde,
    Stuttgart.

ZMA--Zeitschrift für Morphologie
    und Anthropologie, Stuttgart.

ZS--Zeitschrift für Säugertierkunde,
    Berlin.

NOTES

Introduction. The specific references have been placed for easy consultation under each of the geographical headings. In some cases the same title has been repeated in several chapters. For this reason no general Bibliography has been compiled. For convenience, some dates have been inserted in order to emphasize recent publications.

However, certain general titles must be called to the attention of the reader since
these should always be at hand, not only for special guidance but also for sources.
It is the author's desire that through the use of these Bibliographies listed here below, together with each of the chapter references and footnotes, the reader will thus
be guided to the most important material within our anthropogeographical scope.
Five recent Bibliographies include:

(a) Richard E. Ettinghausen, "A selected and annotated Bibliography of books and
periodicals in Western languages dealing with the Near and Middle East with special
emphasis on Medieval and Modern times," published by the Middle East Institute,
Washington, D.C. There are 1,719 titles (pp. 1-111) with a detailed Table of Contents
by subject and country and an Index of authors. This was completed during the summer, 1951, and published in 1952. A Supplement, bound in the same cover, completed during December, 1953, was published under the same auspices in 1954. This
contains 253 titles with an Index of authors.

(b) Henry Field, "Bibliography on Southwestern Asia: I," University of Miami
Press, Coral Gables, Florida, 1953. This anthropogeographical Bibliography of
3,016 selected titles has been compiled to serve the specialist and student of this
area ranging from Istanbul to the Hindu Kush on the north and from Aden to the
Makran Coast on the south, from the Suez Canal on the west to the eastern boundary
of Afghanistan and Baluchistan (now West Pakistan) on the east. Special effort was
made to include books and especially articles in 600 widely scattered Journals from
1940-1952. This Bibliography is divided into: (a) Anthropogeography (Nos. 1-1680)
including Anthropology, Archeology, Geology, Agriculture, Cartography, Astronomy,
Medicine, Art, Music, and Poetry; (b) Natural History divided into Zoology (Nos.
1681-2441) and Botany (Nos. 2442-3016).

(c) Henry Field, "Bibliography on Southwestern Asia: II," University of Miami
Press, 1955. This covers the same general area, arranged along similar lines,
with references to books and articles in 760 Journals. This Bibliography is divided
into: (a) Anthropogeography (Nos. 1-1641); and (b) Natural History grouped in
seven categories under Zoology (Nos. 1642-3292).

(d) Henry Field, "Bibliography on Southwestern Asia: III," University of Miami
Press, 1956. This also covers the same general area, arranged along similar lines,
with references to books and articles in 1,100 Journals. This Bibliography is divided
into: (a) Anthropogeography (Nos. 1-3340); and Natural History grouped in seven
categories under Zoology (Nos. 3341-4890) and Botany (Nos. 4891-6113).

(e) Hallam L. Movius, Jr., "Old World Bibliography," Nos. 1-8, 1948-55,
American School of Prehistoric Research, Peabody Museum, Harvard. In each
section under "Asia" are listed general references and by country.

The reader is also referred to Carleton S. Coon, "Races of Europe," New York, 1948. There is considerable detail on the physical anthropology of the peoples of Southwestern Asia with excellent racial type photographs. This volume shows the general racial connections and trends between the peoples of Europe and those of Southwestern Asia.

Attention is also drawn to C.U. Ariens Kappers and Leland W. Parr, "An Introduction to the Anthropology of the Near East," Amsterdam, 1934.

The principal recorders of anthropometric data are given in Chapter 14.

Special articles include the following: Arno C. Huth, "The Problem of Communications," Journal of International Affairs, Vol. 6, no. 1, pp. 65-75, 1952; Etienne de Vaumas, "La Structure du Proche-Orient," BSGE, Vol. 23, pp. 265-320, with Bibliography by countries, and "Montagnes du Proche-Orient, l'Amanus et le Djebel Ansarieh," étude morphométrique, RGAG; Bertil Lundman, "Geography of human blood groups (A,B,O system)," Evolution, Vol. 2, no. 3, pp. 231-37, 1948; Robert F. Spencer, "The Arabian Matriarchate: an old controversy," SJA, Vol. 8, no. 4, pp. 478-502 with Bibliography, 1952; Hallam L. Movius, Jr., "Old World Prehistory: Paleolithic," in A.L. Kroeber, ed.: "Anthropology Today," pp. 163-92 with Bibliography, University of Chicago, 1953; Robert J. Braidwood, "The Near East and the foundations for civilization," Condon Lectures, pp. 1-43 with Bibliography, Oregon State System of Higher Education, Eugene, Oregon, 1952; Robert J. and Linda Braidwood, "The earliest village communities of Southwestern Asia," Journal of World History, Vol. 1, pp. 278-310, Paris, 1953; Henry Field, "Caves and rock-shelters in Southwestern Asia," BNSS, no. 13, 1951; and F.S. Haddad and J. Moucadie, "The incidence of the "Rh" factor in the Middle East," JMLB, Vol. 4, pp. 200-205, 1952.

Special attention is called to "Global Epidemiology: a geography of Disease and Sanitation" by J.S. Simmons, T.F. Whayne, G.W. Anderson, H.M. Horack, and R.A. Thomas, Vol. 3, pp. 1-357, Philadelphia, 1954. Within our prescribed area, denoted as Southwestern Asia, there are chapters on Israel, Jordan, Lebanon, Syria, Turkey, Iraq, the Arabian Peninsula (Kuwait, Saudi Arabia, Bahrain Island, Qatar Peninsula, Trucial Oman Coast, Muscat and Oman, Aden and Yemen). Each chapter is arranged according to the following plan: Geography and Climate, Population and Socio-economic conditions (vital statistics, food and nutrition and housing), Environment and Sanitation (water supplies, waste disposal and fauna and flora), Health Services and Medical Facilities, Diseases and Bibliography. The reader is presumed to use this volume as a constant source of recent information on each of these countries.

Four important publications, which appeared during 1955, must be added at the last moment:

1. "Yearbook of Anthropology, 1955," edited by William L. Thomas, Jr., Wenner-Gren Foundation for Anthropological Research, 14 East 71 Street, New York. The section entitled, "Southwest Asia: an anthropological review for 1952-54" by Shevket Aziz Kansu, University of Ankara, includes sections with bibliographies in Arabia, Iran, Iraq, Israel, Jordan, Lebanon, Syria, and Turkey. The reader should consult these sections and lists of references, which should be considered as complementary to this study.

2. Foreign Affairs Bibliography, 1942-52, compiled by Henry L. Roberts assisted by Jean Gunther and Janis A. Kreslins, published for the Council on Foreign Relations by Harper and Brothers, New York, 1955. Attention is called to: Near East General, pp. 583-85; the Arab World, pp. 586-89; Turkey, pp. 589-92; Syria and Lebanon, pp. 592-93; Palestine (Israel and Jordan), pp. 594-601; Iraq, p. 601; Saudi Arabia, etc., pp. 601-602; Iran, pp. 602-604; and Afghanistan, p. 605.

3. "University of Pennsylvania Radiocarbon Dates: I" by Elizabeth K. Ralph, Science, Vol. 121, no. 3136, pp. 149-51, February 4, 1955. This paper includes dates assigned to samples excavated by Carleton S. Coon in Belt and Hotu Caves (Lat. 36° 20´ N. and Long. 53° 35´ E.) just east of Turujan near the Caspian shoreline in Iran. For Belt Cave, the dates of occupation range from 7,280±260 to 12,275 ± 825; for Hotu Cave, the range was 1,220±230 to 11,860±840.

4. A short annotated Bibliography relating to the sociology of Muslim peoples by Burton Benedict, Institute of Islamic Studies, McGill University, Montreal.

Preface

1. Contributions to the Anthropology of the Faiyum, Sinai, Sudan and Kenya, pp. 1-352, UCP, 1952. Arabs of Central Iraq, their History, Ethnology, and Physical characters, FMNH, Anthropological Memoirs, Vol. 4, pp. 1-474, 1935. The Anthropology of Iraq: Pt. 1, no. 1, pp. 1-224, The Upper Euphrates and Pt. 1, no. 2, pp. 225-426, and the Lower Euphrates-Tigris Region, FMNH, Anthropological Series, Vol. 30, 1940 and 1949; The Northern Jazira, Pt. 2, no. 1, pp. 1-116; and Kurdistan, Pt. 2, no. 2, pp. 1-106, and Conclusions, Pt. 2, no. 3, pp. 107-76 PMP, Vol. 46, 1951 and 1952. Contributions to the Anthropology of Iran, FMNH, Anthropological Series, Vol. 29, pp. 1-706, 1939. Contributions to the Anthropology of the Caucasus, PMP, Vol. 48, no. 1, pp. 1-156, 1953. Contributions to the Anthropology of the Soviet Union, SMC, Vol. 110, no. 13, pp. 1-244, 1948; Bibliography on Southwestern Asia: I, 1953; II, 1955; III, 1956, University of Miami Press. See also my "Bibliography, 1926-55" with 409 titles, multilithed and distributed privately during January 1956; and my "List of Microfilms, 1941-55" also multilithed and distributed privately during February, 1956.

2. See ADIM 1495, 1591, 2037, 2196, 2308, 2309, 2310, 2341, 2342, 2343, 2345, 2347, 2391, 2392, 2414, 2416, 2417, 2419, 2422, 2483, 2939, 2941, 3226, 3227, 3494, 3601, 3602, 3603, 3617, 3703, 3704, 3926, 3927, 3928, 3956, 3973, 3977, 3986, 3987, 4213, 4223, 4224, 4279, 4280, 4282, 4283, 4284, 4427, 4469, 4470, 4479, 4480, 4506, 4612, and 4786. Copies may be purchased from the Chief, Photoduplication Service, Library of Congress.

3. During March - April, 1955, Mrs. Field and I made a reconnaissance survey across Makran and Kalat in behalf of the Peabody Museum - Harvard. We recorded anthropometric data and racial type photographs on 275 male Baluchis and Brahuis. Microliths were excavated from a rockshelter near Big Kapoto, ten miles south of Kalat. This Report will be published in Peabody Museum Papers.

4. Plant Ecology: reviews of research published as Vol. 6, pp. 1-379, of the Arid Zone Research by Unesco, Paris, 1955. This contains brief descriptions of Afghanistan, Pakistan, Iran, Israel, Turkey, Iraq, Jordan, Lebanon, Saudi Arabia, Syria, and Yemen arranged in that order. Each section contains excellent Bibliographies which supplement my anthropogeographical and botanical references in "Bibliography on Southwestern Asia: I and III," University of Miami Press, 1953 and 1956. Special attention is drawn to Fig. 3, the schematic geobotanical map of Iran, Israel, and Turkey.

5. The following title has just been drawn to my attention: M. Akram, "Bibliographie analytique de l'Afghanistan," pp. 1-504. Centre de Documentation Universitaire, Paris, 1947.

6. As this study was going to press, I received a copy of my "An Anthropological Reconnaissance in Southwestern Asia, 1950," PMP, Vol. 48, no. 2, pp. 1-146, April 23, 1956. The reader is referred to this new publication, which contains data on Syria, Iraq, Iran, the Persian Gulf (Kuwait, Bahrain, Qatar Peninsula, and the Trucial Oman Coast) and Saudi Arabia. In addition to the anthropometric, archeological and tribal data (nb. tribal maps of Syria, p. 4 and Qatar, p. 54), there are included the following Appendixes:

A. Census (1947) and Surficial Area (1949) of Iraq.

B. Plants from Lebanon, Syria, Iraq, Iran, Kuwait, Bahrain and Trucial Oman Coast by G. Shiriaev.

C. Bats collected by the Expedition by Colin C. Sanborn.

D. Birds from Station T-3, Syria by James L. Peters.

E. Cave fauna by Barbara Lawrence.

Attention is called to the Bibliography, pp. 91-100. Since this publication is presumed to be readily available, all these references have not been included here.

Mention must also be made of the reason for not including photographs to illustrate racial types. Since large series have already been published by Coon, Field, Kappers, Shanklin, and others, the student is referred to their publications.

Chapter I: THE LAND

1. See D. Ashbel, "Rainfall map: Near East," Jerusalem, 1940; Hans Boesch, "Das Klima des Nähen Ostens," VNGZ, Vol. 86, pp. 8-60, 1941; and G. Bauer, "Luftzirkulation und Niederschlagsverhältnisse in Vorderasien," GBG, Vol. 45, pp. 381-548, 1945.

2. The anecdote about Hamoudi, the Arab foreman at the excavations at Carchemish on the Upper Euphrates, comes to mind. T.E. Lawrence took him to Oxford as his guest. He was fascinated by all the cars, the bicycles, the buildings, the stores, the unveiled women. When it was time to leave Lawrence offered him his choice of a present. The Arab begged for a water faucet. With such a miraculous gadget he would soon be a power in his homeland, for with a flick of his wrist clear, cold water always flowed.

3. See ADIM nos. 4470, 4480, and 4612.

4. Wolves have been reported in the Baalbek area of the Anti-Lebanon Mountains by James Myram, curator of Woburn Park, England. Mr. H. St. J.B. Armitage of Muscat in a private communication dated April 16, 1952, wrote: "wolves are found in these parts. They often come down from the western Hajar into the Batinah. Less than two years ago, one of the local askars here found five dead wolves and one live wolf cub on the Sih al-Ghaizain, which is the plain through which the Wadi Hawasinah reaches the coast. The five had died of thirst as did the survivor very soon after capture."

On April 11, 1931 The Children's Newspaper published in London reported as follows: "While they were held up by a storm in the Syrian Desert between Mosul and Deir-ez-Zor, some motorists were attacked by wolves. Four members of the party were killed."

Mr. H.C.H. du Boulay, Basrah Petroleum Company, wrote on March 29, 1954: "I would inform you that in February, 1947, I shot two animals that I believed were wolves about 15 miles west of Iraq Petroleum Company's H-3 Station to the north of the Haifa-Baghdad road. These animals were the size of a large Alsatian and gray in color and were in a party of four. That winter was a very dry one in that part of Iraq and the Beduins coming through had lost a lot of camels, etc. and I assumed that these wolves had followed the flocks down and had been living on the weaklings. I have heard of the odd wolf in the mountains of Lebanon and also in the Alawite Mountains, but I have not heard of any wolves around Basrah." For additional information on wolves in Southwestern Asia see P.N. Boratav, "Les histoires d'ours en Anatolie," pp. 1-46, Helsinki, 1955. During the Field Museum Anthropological Expedition to the Near East, 1934, I was presented with a wolf cub in Beled Sinjar. Later we were given a fox cub. These two cubs traveled in the cars with us for several weeks. For an article on wolves see The Field, Vol. 203, p. 703, 1954.

Attention must be called to the Tariq adh-Dhib ("the Wolf's Trail"), which lies northwest of Rutba Wells in Iraq. The district is Latitude 33° 10´ N. and Longitude

38° 21′ E. as given on Raisz' map of the North Arabian Desert with my traverses and the archeological sites; this four-color map was completed during April, 1956.

Chapter II: SINAI

1. For descriptions of the land and the people see Murray (1935 and 1953), Daumas (1951), and Field (1952b, pp. 67-161). See also ADIM No. 2939, pp. 1-72 and No. 3226, pp. 54-172 and the two sheets on 1:500,000 scale published by the Survey of Egypt: (a) North Sinai, 1945 (T/45/57); and (b) South Sinai, 1943 (T/43/327). For additional references see Lorin (1928-29) and my Bibliographies (Field 1952b, pp. 140-61 and 1953) and the following References: Abel, Aghion (1940 and 1946), Aimé-Giron (1939 and 1941), Albright, Andrew, Attia, Awad, Bachatly, Badr and Crossland, Ball (1939 and 1942), Band, Bouchard, Bruyère (1949-50 and 1950), Cleland (1936 and 1944), Crossland (1939a and b), Daumas (1942, 1948a-b, 1951, and 1952a and b), Daumas and La Roche, Debono, Deloro, Farag, Fedden, Field (1948a-b, 1952a-b and 1953), Fontaine (1947a-b, 1948, 1952 and 1955), Fontaine and Goby (1948-50), Forskal, Goby (1942, 1943, 1947 and 1952), Gohar (1940a-c and 1948a-b), Hart, Hellstrom, Hickson, Issawi, Jansen, Jarvis (see also nine references in Field 1952b, p. 151), Jomier (1949-50 and 1952), Jungfleisch, Keldani, Kiser, Lorin, Lucas, Mihaeloff, Montet, Mortensen, Moscatelli, Munier, Murray (1935, 1945-46 and 1953), Nagaty, Naklady, Nasr (1939, 1939-40, 1943-44, 1945-46 and 1947), Palmer, Peet, Pesta (1941 and 1943), Petrie, Rabino, Servin (1947, 1949 and 1949-50), Shabetai (1940 and 1948), Shafei, Shukri and Said, Stiasny, Täckholm, Täckholm and Drar, The Middle East (1953-55), Tondrian, Tromp, Wiet, and Woolley and Lawrence. For general data on population problems in Egypt, see Cleland (1936 and 1944), Issawi (1949) and Kiser (1944). For recent information on social and political conditions in Egypt, see H.V. Cooke (1952). For maps, see British War Office 18 sheets of North Sinai and 12 of South Sinai, scale 1:100,000 with the relief shown in hachures.

2. During the University of California African Expedition 1947-48. For description and map showing probable route of the Exodus, see Field, 1948b.

3. In the American Documentation Institute (ADI), c/o Photoduplication Service, Library of Congress.

4. See Wassif and Hoogstraal (1954, pp. 63-79 with 20 references in Bibliography). For list of fauna, see Field, 1952b, pp. 74-75 and footnote 10 with references.

5. For ten references to his publications, based on data obtained while Governor of Sinai, see Field, 1952b, p. 151.

6. See Field, 1952b, pp. 81-91 for additional information.

7. The most detailed accounts of these buildings are given by Peet (1915, pp. 151-58), Petrie (1906) and Murray (1935).

8. For comparative data on Egypt, see : Giufrida-Ruggeri, "I crani egiziani del Museo Civico di Milano," AAE, 1905. See also A. Batrawi, "The racial history of Egypt and Nubia: Pt. 1, the craniology of Lower Nubia from Predynastic times to the sixth century A.D.," JRAI, Vol. 75, Pts. I-II, pp. 81-101 with Bibliography. The racial affinities of ancient Nubian populations are discussed.

9. Quoted by Aldobrandino Mochi, "Sulla Antropologia degli Arabi," AAE, pp. 411-28, 1907.

10. I recorded these data during the University of California African Expedition, 1947-48.

11. See Henry Field, 1952b, pp. 122-26, 1948a, pp. 486-87.

12. Quoted from The Middle East, 1953.

13. The main sections of this tribe live in Jordan under Sheikh Mohammed ibn Abu Tayi and his cousin Ibn Jazi.

14. See Murray (1935, pp. 265-66) and Field 1952b, p. 92.

15. For a description, see Rabino (1938) and Daumas (1951).

16. See Field, 1952b, pp. 118-21.

17. For comparative anthropometric data to the west of Sinai, see Field, 1952b, pp. 35-66. These tables include our Beduins and Jebeliyeh from Sinai, so that their relative positions may be seen.

Chapter III: ISRAEL

1. For geology, see Abel, Picard (1937 and 1943), Blake and de Vaumas (1953a-b). For references, see de Vaumas (1952a-b, 1953b, pp. 119-20). For soil analyses of Athlit caves, see Brammall and Reifenberg (1937). For a description of the eolian soils of the northern Negeb with excellent soil maps and tables of mechanical and chemical composition of loess soils, see Ravikovitch, DRP, 1953, pp. 404-52.

2. For climatic summary, see GE, 1954, pp. 51-52, and Boesch. For Pleistocene climate, see Picard (1937). Attention is also called to Shalem (DRP, pp. 153-76) where he states that one can resolve the problem of climate by coördinating many scientific disciplines. Palestine, situated between the desert and the sown, has a rich literature demonstrating that it is Man who has been the climatic factor by controlling the water supply. Shalem denies Ellsworth Huntington's theories regarding the change of climate, commenting that the ancient Hebrew literature furnishes abundant proof of climatic stability.

3. For distribution of rainfall, see Ashbel. For description of floods in the Negeb, see Lowdermilk (1953, pp. 365-74). With regard to the water supply, see notes on the Kurnub catchment area, which lies across the main watershed of Israel, by Guy (1953, pp. 496-97). See also details of two experimental reservoirs built in the Negeb during 1951; one in Wadi Huzaiyil, the other in Wadi Sab, southwest of Beersheba. The latter is described by de Leeuw (pp. 498, 502). According to Picard (1953, pp. 583-90) prior to World War I borings were rare and unsuccessful. The German Army found little water in the coastal plain as a result of boring to an average depth rarely exceeding 60 meters. As recently as 1940 borings deeper than 200 meters in harder rocks could not be advised. Following the principle of fault traps and drilling in hard rocks from 1942-52 led to the development of deep bores as well as to a large increase of groundwater supply. Picard concluded that while prospecting in the Wadi Araba of the southern Negev is still in an exploratory stage, the finding of water in the Nubian sandstone may play a large rôle in the future groundwater exploration of Israel.

4. For recent data see GE,(1954, p. 63), and Boyko (pp. 631-35). For analyses of vegetal remains from Athlit caves, see Bancroft and Clifford. For a note on useful plants of therapeutic value from desert regions in Israel, see Zaitschek in DRP (1953, pp. 350-52).

5. See The Middle East, 1953, pp. 158-59.

6. For general references, see Aharoni, Bodenheimer and Allen. For new species, see Thomas (1917, 1919 and 1920). For fossil fauna, see Bate (1927, 1932a-b, 1933, 1934a-b and 1937a-b). For medical references, see GE,(1954, pp. 59-63). For data on Mollusca from Judean desert, see Avnimelech (1952c, pp. 77-79).

7. For data on the Jewish population and immigration, see Lawrence, Notestein and Jurkat (1945), and The Middle East, 1955. For recent data, see GE, (1954, pp. 53-55).

8. Quoted from Israel Office of Information, Bulletin, April, 1953, New York.

9. For a description of the European Jews, their ethnic and racial history and blood groups, see Sauter and Coon.

10. See Hedley V. Cooke, pp. 202-32.

11. For references from the Lower Paleolithic to the historical period with special attention to the Stone Age, see Albright (1935, 1946 and 1951, pp. 256-57),

Blanckenhorn, Braidwood, Braidwood and Braidwood, Buzy, Carleton, Coon, de Vaux, Garrod (1928, 1929, 1930a-b, 1931a-d, 1932a-c, 1934a-b, 1935, 1936, 1943 and 1952), Glueck (1934-51, 1935, 1946 and 1947), Ives, Johns, Karge, Kirk, McCown and Keith (Vol. 1, pp. 228-33 and Vol. 2, pp. 380-83), Neuville (1930, 1931, 1932, 1933, 1934a-b, 1949 and 1951), Perrot (1952a-b and 1953), Petrbok, Skutil, Snow, Stekelis (1935, 1942, 1944a-b, 1947, 1950-51), Stekelis and Haas, Vaufrey (1940 and 1944), Wright, Yeivin and Zumoffen (1900 and 1908). For a summary of the history from the earliest times to the British occupation, see "The Middle East," pp. 153-56, 1955.

12. See Turville-Petre (1927 and 1932).

13. See Neuville (1931, 1949 and 1951).

14. See Garrod (1928 and 1943).

15. See Garrod (1929, 1931a-d, 1932c, 1934b, 1935 and 1936), Keith and McCown, McCown (1932, 1933, 1934 and 1936) and McCown and Keith.

16. See Garrod (1952).

17. See BASPR, no. 17, p. 9.

18. For description of the semi-nomadic tribes of northern Palestine, see Ashkenazi. For population and immigration statistics, see Issawi and Dabezies, Lawrence and Notestein and Jurkat. For special articles, see Anati, Langerhaus, and Von Luschan. For settlement possibilities, see Anonymous, Fohs, and Lowdermilk (1944).

19. See Eliahu Elath, Hinden, Notestein and Jurkat, The Middle East (1953-55) and GE (1954).

20. For definition and description, see Field (1939).

21. For anthropometric data, see Gloor and Risdon.

22. For list of maps, see de Vaumas (1953b, p. 120) and map of Israel by Josine Manson, scale 1:500,000, issued by the Jewish National Fund of America, New York, 1950.

Chapter IV: JORDAN

1. For general references, see Canaan, Cooke, Field (1934 and 1953-56), Glueck (1944a), Konikoff, Merrill, Tristram, Warriner, The Middle East (1953), and GE (1954). For decisions rendered by U.S. Board on Geographic Names, see "Gazetteer of Jordan" with 11,000 entries, 1955. See also Archaeological map of the Hashemite Kingdom of the Jordan, Sheet no. 2 (Maan), no. 3 (Karak); Scale 1:250,000. See also Feinbrun and Zohary, especially soil map (p. 9), phytogeographical map (p. 15), vegetation map (p. 36), Figs. 1-22 and Bibliography (pp. 27-28).

2. Quoted from The Middle East (1953).

3. During the Peabody Museum-Harvard Expedition to the Near East, 1950.

4. For geological references, see Post and Dapples.

5. For excellent colored photographs, see Huxley.

6. For rainfall map, see Ashbel.

7. For a description of the flora: of Moab, see Hayne; of Petra and the Wadi Arabah, see Hart; of Jordan, see Tristram. For botanical references, see Feinbrun, Zohary and Field (1953 and 1956).

8. For a study of Jordan Valley irrigation, see Ionides.

9. For zoological references, see Field (1953-56). See also GE, pp. 93-95, 1954.

10. Quoted from The Middle East, 1955. See also GE (pp. 88-90).

11. See Ionides (1946). The Middle East (1953) gives a figure of 480,000 acres. N.B. 1 hectare = 2.471 acres.

12. See Hedley V. Cooke (1952) and Fohs (1943).

13. For references from the Lower Paleolithic to historical times, see Field (1929 and 1953-56), Glueck (1936, 1937, 1939, 1940 and 1944a-b), Grimme, Horsfield

and Glueck (1933a and b), Rhotert, Robinson, Stein (1939 and 1940) and Waechter (1947a and b). See also Clark, Crawford and Neuville.

14. See Field (1929).

15. Officer Commanding, Royal Air Force Trans-Jordan, headquarters in Amman. Group-Captain Rees, V.C., had an intimate knowledge of the desert and Harrat ar-Rajil both from the air and on the ground. A keen amateur archeologist, he searched continually and recorded every type of human construction and inscription or design. In November, 1927, he guided me to many sites.

16. Stone circles range from central Jordan eastward to the Rutba area of Iraq, southeastward to Al Kuwait and across northwest Saudi Arabia to the slopes of Tell el-Hibr and Jebel Anaiza (Enaze). I also recorded stone circles near the eastern limits of Jebel Aziz west of Hassetché (Hasseké) on the Khabur River in northeastern Syria. In 1947 I also recorded stone circles in central and southwestern Sinai: These few examples indicate the wide range of these stone circles in Southwestern Asia.

17. See Field (1952, Fig. 21 and references pp. 37-41).

18. For a collection of camel brands (wasms) and graffiti from Jordan, see Field (1952).

19. L.W.B. Rees, "The Transjordan Desert," Antiquity, Vol. 3, pp. 389-407, December 1929. Attention is called to the map and aerial photographs.

20. I shall discuss these in detail in my forthcoming, "Archeological Survey of the North Arabian Desert" to be published by the Peabody Museum, Harvard.

21. For anthropometric data, see Seltzer (1940), Shanklin (1934, 1935a, 1936a and 1946) and Shanklin and Izzeddin. For blood groups, see Boyd, W.C. and Lyle G. Boyd (1938), Jusatz, and Shanklin (1935b and 1936b). For dermatoglyphics among the Rwala Beduins, see Shanklin and Cummins, especially Bibliography.

22. In Psychiatrische en Neurologische Bladen, Nos. 3-4, pp. 1-12, Amsterdam, 1934.

23. For references to the Maualy, Akeydat and Rwala, see JRAI, Vol. 68, pp. 379-414, and Table 24, p. 408, 1938. For Maualy and Akeydat, see AJPA, Vol. 21, pp. 217-52, some discrepancies occur; use JRAI, Vol. 68, pp. 379-414 in preference to the earlier publication in AJPA, Vol. 21, pp. 217-52, and JRAI, Vol. 65, pp. 375-90.

24. These data were published by Shanklin and Izzeddin in AJPA, Vol. 22, pp. 381-415, 1937.

Chapter V: LEBANON

1. For general references, see Cooke, Field (1953-56), Fish, G.E. (1954), Hitti (1951 and 1953), Hourani (1946), The Middle East (1953) and Warriner. For a study of economic and rural life see Frances C. Rintz, "A frame for random sampling in three villages of the Lebanon: Istabl, Hawsh al-Harimah and Ghazzah" in Report on Current Research, Spring, 1956, published by the Middle East Institute, Washington, pp. 27-37 with map on p. 29.

2. According to The Middle East, 1953.

3. For geology, see Day, de Vaumas, (1947, 1949a-b, 1953), Dubertret (1945-46, 1946a-b, and 1949a-b), Frass, Keller, Wetzel and Haller (1944 and 1945a) and maps scale 1:200,000 (Tripoli sheet) and 1:50,000 (Hamidiyé, Batroun, Djbail, Sir ed-Danié, Qartaba and Baalbek sheets), Wright and Zumoffen. For list of Pleistocene fauna, see Fritsch.

4. See Combier.

5. For population statistics, see Hitti (1953, pp. 169-71) and de Vaumas (1953).

6. According to The Middle East, 1953. For 1948 figures, see GE, pp. 110-11. For density map, see de Vaumas (1953, Map 1).

7. For a Prehistoric bibliography, see Burkhalter (1949a-b). For Stone Age

references, see Bergy, Braidwood and Braidwood, Delcourt, de Vaumas (1953), Ewing (1947a-c, 1948 and 1949), Fleisch (1946a-c, 1949, 1950, 1954 and 1955), Haller (1943), Haller and Wetzel (1940, 1941 and 1945), Pervès, Vaufrey and Wright.

8. The references are to the special bibliography (pp. 586-92) furnished by Wetzel to accompany his list of sites (pp. 124-28). Minor editorial revisions were made in the table to conform to our style. In the table note under Site E refers to excavations, S to surface finds. Dr. René Wetzel, now recovering from a serious illness in southern France, is a geologist of the Iraq Petroleum Company. He has surveyed large areas in Lebanon, Syria and Iraq. During 1950 he invited me to accompany his Survey Party from Station H-2 to the Qaara Depression, a region in which I had long desired to search for stone implements. I found typologically Paleolithic flints and collected a new botanical species, Euphorbia fieldi. See under "Iraq" in SJA, Vol. 7, no. 1, pp. 86-102, 1951; and PMP, Vol. 48, no. 2, 1955.

9. No. 53, p. 35.

10. Nos. 37, 53. Some data remain unpublished.

11. In red soil below conglomerate terrace. No. 53.

12. Nos. 37, 38, and 53.

13. No. 53.

14. No. 53. Some data remain unpublished.

15. Nos. 35 and 53.

16. Nos. 53, 56, 57, 58, and 59.

17. Nos. 7, 29 (pp. 1-17), 39 (p. 73), 53 and 56 (p. 278).

18. No. 56.

19. No. 5.

20. Nos. 39 (p. 188) and 56 (p. 431).

21. No. 59.

22. No. 34.

23. Nos. 39, 43, 56 (p. 277), and 57.

24. No. 5.

25. No. 5. Behind Hotel Haifa.

26. Nos. 5 and 43.

27. Two caves have been cut by the railroad line. Nos. 7, 28, 39 (p. 67), 43, 49 (p. 10), 56 (p. 431) and 57 (p. 20).

28. Nos. 22 (p. 107), 39, 40 (p. 223), 41 (p. 655), 43, 49 (p. 10), 57 (pp. 92-106), 58 (p. 431), and 59 (p. 143).

29. This site lies 200 meters south of Beharsaf section and 150 meters west of Naas spring.

30. Midway between Bikfaya and Dour Choueir.

31. East of village. No. 5.

32. Two kilometers east of Beirut waterworks.

33. Nos. 2, 7 (p. 6), 8, 9, 10, 11 (p. 187), 12, 15, 16, 17, 18, 19, 23 (p.116), 29, 37 (p. 54), 39 (pp. 89, 110 and 114), 43, 44, 45, 47, 52 (p. 111), 54, 55, 56, and 58 (p. 431).

34. Nos. 5 and 34.

35-36. No. 5.

37. No. 11 (p. 209).

38. No. 11 (p. 207).

39. This is now a built-up area. Nos. 56 (p. 283) and 57 (p. 88).

40. No. 41.

41. Nos. 1, 3, 6 (pp. 226-27), 7, 8, 11, 13, 14, 21, 22, 23, 26, 27, 31, 32, 37, 39 (pp. 15, 161-67, 184-86, 88-91, 97-99 and 213-20), 40, 42 (p. 32), 48 (p. 203), 50, 51, 53 and 56 (p. 434).

42. In the south and southwestern suburbs. Nos. 1 (p. 206) and 7.

43. Nos. 6 (pp. 226-27), 7 and 56 (p. 434).

44. No. 1 (p. 200).

45. On road from Bir Hassan to Nebi el-Aoussay. No. 1 (p. 202).

46. Nos. 6, 7 (p. 115), 39, 42 (p. 32) and 59.

47. No. 5.

48. No. 39 (pp. 170-71).

49. No. 24.

50. Unpublished ms. by Bergy.

51. No. 58.

52. Nos. 39 (p. 73) and 58.

53. Between bridge and village. No. 13.

54. No. 34.

55. Unpublished ms. by von Heidenstamm.

56. No. 39 (p. 414).

57. No. 39.

58. Nos. 39, 43 (Vol. 3, p. 7), 56 (p. 275), 57 (p. 17) and 58 (p. 31).

59. Nos. 43 (Vol. 3, p. 6), 56 (p. 274), 57 (p. 4), 58 (p. 434).

60. Nos. 5 and 34.

61. Near Nabatiye el-Foka. Nos. 5 and 34.

62. No. 5.

63. Nos. 4 (p. 78), 39 (p. 43) and 43 (Vol. 3, p. 12).

64. No. 4 (p. 78), 39 (pp. 179-94).

65. No. 39.

66. Raised beaches with artifacts. No. 5.

67. Excerpted from Marc-R. Sauter (1945, pp. 81-91). See Tables I, II, IV, V, and VII.

68. Also spelled Jubail, Jubayl and Djebeil. This coastal village, 20 miles north of Beirut, was the ancient Byblos of the Phoenicians and Gebal of the Bible (see Ezekiel XXVII: 9). Excavations have revealed a temple, citadel, and tombs. From here papyrus was exported to Egypt, hence the Greek byblos = book, papyrus and English Bible. Quoted from Webster's "Geographical Dictionary," 1949.

69. For excellent Bibliography, see Sauter (1945, pp. 119-31).

REFERENCES TO LIST OF SITES

1. Bergy, R.P., 1932, Le Paléolithique ancien stratifié de Râs Beyrouth. MUSJ, Vol. 16, no. 5, pp. 169-214.

2. Blanckenhorn, Max, 1905, Ueber die Steinzeit und Feuerstein Artefakten in Syrien-Palästina. ZE, pp. 447-68.

3. Bourcart, J., 1940, Recherches stratigraphiques sur le Pliocène et le Quaternaire du Levant. BSGF, Vol. 10, pp. 177-86.

4. Bovier Lapierre, R.P., 1908, Stations préhistoriques du Beled Becharra (Haute Galilée). La Géographie, Vol. 17, pp. 77-79.

5. Burkhalter, L., 1949-1950, Bibliographie préhistorique. BMB, Vol. 8, pp. 129-53 and Vol. 9, pp. 8-51.

6. Chester, J., 1875, Notes on Ruad and adjacent places of northern Syria. PEFQ, pp. 226-27.

7. Dawson, J.W., 1882, Notes on prehistoric man in Egypt and the Lebanon. JTVI.

8. Day, A.E., 1926, L'abri-sous-roche de Ksar Akil près de la grotte d'Antélias. PAUB, July 1.

9. Delcourt, Mad., 1927, Observations sur l'abri de Ksar Akil. BSPF, Vol. 24, pp. 156-61.

10. Desribes, R., 1914, Harpons trouvés dans la brèche paléolithique d'Antelias. L'Anthropologie, Vol. 25, p. 213.

11. _____, 1921, Industries paléolithiques en Phénicie. MFOB, Vol. 7, pp. 189-210.

12. Doherty, R.P. and Ewing, R.F., 1939, Qsar Akil. BMB, Vol. 3, pp. 181-82.

13. Dubertret, L., 1940, Sur la structure de la platforme de Beyrouth et sur ses grès quaternaires. SGF, no. 8.

14. Dubertret, L., Vautrin, H., and Keller, A., 1937, La stratigraphie du Pliocène et du Quaternaire marins de la côte syrienne. NMSGB, Vol. 2, p. 119.

15. Ewing, R.F. and Franklin, J., 1946, Aurignacian man in Syria. AJPA, Vol. 4, pp. 252-53.

16. _____, 1947, Egbert of Ksar Akil. America, Vol. 77, pp. 43-44 and Vol. 78, pp. 263-65.

17. _____, 1947, Preliminary note on the excavations at the Paleolithic site of Ksar Akil. Antiquity, Vol. 21, pp. 186-96.

18. _____, 1947, The life of prehistoric man in the light of excavations of Ksar Akil near Antelias (Lebanon). Al-Machriq, Vol. 41, pp. 218-48. In Arabic.

19. _____, 1948, Ksar Akil in 1948. Biblica, July.

20. Fitzgerald, G.M., 1930, Some Stone Age sites recently investigated. PEFQ, pp. 85-90.

21. Fleisch, R.P., 1946, Découverte d'une industrie à éclats du niveau de 45 m. à Râs Beyrouth (Liban) et position relative du Levalloisien. CRAS, Vol. 223, pp. 249-51.

22. _____, 1946. Le Levalloisien du niveau 15 à Râs Beyrouth (Liban). BSPF, Vol. 43, pp. 299-301.

23. _____, 1946. Position de l'Acheuléen à Râs Beyrouth. BSPF, Vol. 43, p. 293.

24-25. No references.

26. _____, 1952, Préhistoire et brèche de pente du niveau de 45 m. à Râs Beyrouth (Liban). CIMPP, pp. 70-80.

27-28. No references.

29. Fraas, O., 1876, Drei Monate im Lebanon, pp. 25, 65-68. Stuttgart.

30. _____, 1878, Aus dem Orient: II. Geologische Beobachtungen am Libanon, pp. 107-26.

31. Garrod, D.A.E. and Gardner, E.W., 1935, Les dunes consolidées mousteriennes de Syrie et Palestine. La Nature, May 1.

32. Guigues, P.E. and Abbé Moulier, 1896, Les stations de la pierre polie au Liban. La Nature, July 25 and Cosmos, April 26.

33. _____, 1937, Les fouilles de Kafer Terra (Jebel en-Namous). BMB, Vol. 1, p. 60.

34. _____, Unpublished ms.

35. Haller, J., 1941, Notes de Préhistoire phénicienne: la carrière d'argile de la Société des Ciments Libanais de Chekka (Liban). BMB, Vol. 4, pp. 55-62.

36. _____, 1945, Notes de Préhistoire phénicienne: le gisement de Levalloisien d'Amrit. BMB, Vol. 5, pp. 31-33.

37. _____, 1945, Aperçu sur la Préhistoire de la Syrie et du Liban, au 1945. NMSGB, Vol. 4.

38. _____, 1946, Notes de Préhistoire phénicienne: L'abri de Abou Halga (Liban). BMB, Vol. 6, pp. 1-19.

39. Karge, P., 1915, Rephaim. Die Vorgeschichtliche Kultur Palästinas und Pheniciens. Paderborn.

40. Lartet, L., 1865, Notes sur la découverte de silex taillés en Syrie. BSGF, Vol. 22.

41. Lortet, G., 1884, La Syrie d'aujourd'hui. Voyage dans la Phénicie et la Judée. Paris.

42. Luppe, M. de, 1926, Silex taillés des environs de Beyrouth, BSPF, Vol. 23, p. 32.

43. Morgan, J. de, 1927, La Préhistoire orientale, Vol. 3, pp. 1-18. Paris.

44. Murphy, R.P. Joseph W., 1938, The method of prehistoric excavations at Ksar Akil. BCAS, Vol. 3, no. 1, pp. 272-75.

45. _____, 1939, Ksar Akil. BCAS, Vol. 4, pp. 211-17.

46. Neuville, R., 1933, Notes de Préhistoire syro-palestinienne. L'Industrie dite solutrienne de Minet el-Dhalie, (Liban). JPOS, Vol. 13, pp. 126-31.

47. Obermaier, Hugo, 1911, Der Mensch der Vorzeit, Vol. 1, pp. 170-74, 316-20, 537, and 542.

48. Pervès, M., 1945, Notes de Préhistoire syro-libanaise. BSPF, Vol. 42, nos. 10-12, p. 201.

49. Tristram, H.B., 1866, The land of Israel, pp. 10-13. London.

50. Vaumas, Abbé de, 1947, Les terrasses d'abrasion marine de la côte libanaise. BSRGE, Vol. 20, pp. 21-85.

51. _____, 1948, Les conditions de l'occupation humaine au Liban. AGP, no. 305, pp. 40-49.

52. Vaux, P. de, 1949, La préhistoire de la Syrie et de la Palestine d'après les recherches récentes. RB, Vol. 53, pp. 99-124.

53. Wetzel, R. and Haller, J., 1945, Le quaternaire côtier de la region de Tripoli (Liban). NMSGB, Vol. 4.

54. Zumoffen, G., 1893, L'homme préhistorique d'Antélias. La Nature, April 29.

55. _____, 1893, Notes sur la découverte de l'homme quaternaire de la grotte d'Antélias (Liban) Beyrouth.

56. _____, 1898, L'âge de la pierre au Phénicie, L'Anthropologie, Vol. 8, pp. 272-83 and 426-38.

57. _____, 1900, La Phénicie avant les Phéniciens. ICB.

58. _____, 1908, L'âge de la pierre en Phénicie. Anthropos, Vol. 3, pp. 431-45.

59. _____, 1926. Géologie du Liban, p. 149. Paris.

Chapter VI: SYRIA

1. For the best description of the land, the people, and their history from the Stone Age to the historical period, see Hitti (1951). For other general references, see Cooke, Field (1953-56) and Warriner. For most recent data, see International Bank for Reconstruction and Development (1955). See also, "The agricultural development of Syria," pp. 1-143, Ministry of Agriculture, Damascus, 1955.

2. For geological references, see Blanckenhorn, De Vaumas (1946 and 1953), and Dubertret et al. (1933).

3. See The Middle East (1953, p. 293) and GE, 1954, p. 137.

4. For special articles, see Nehring (1890 and 1902) and GE, 1954, pp. 143-45. The following article appeared in Science Service about 1925: "The wild ass and his sons still scamper and bray in the Syrian desert. And wild ostriches still make their nests about the ruins of the once proud Greco-Roman city of Palmyra. A recent expedition into the Syrian hinterland, sent out by the Hebrew University of Jerusalem, has determined that these animals still exist, and has brought back to headquarters a number of other species new to science. The scientific personnel of the expedition consisted of I. Aharoni, zoologist, M. Zohary, botanist, Miss F. Eckmann, parasitologist, and George Halil Tahan, hunter. It was found that although the wild ass, mentioned in the Bible, has become extinct over a large part of his former range, he may still be found on a long, narrow strip of territory stretching from Mosul

toward Persia. The Syrian ostrich was seen in the vicinity of Palmyra, and three of its eggs were purchased from an Arab. They were smaller than other ostrich eggs, and Mr. Aharoni is of the opinion that the birds may turn out to be a distinct subspecies. Another prize brought back by the expedition consists of two fine skeletons of the cheetah, or hunting leopard. This animal is domesticated and used like a hunting dog in some parts of Asia, but these particular specimens were hunting 'on their own' too near a flock of sheep. They were shot by a French official of the Syrian mandate, M. Paul Clerc, and presented by him to the Hebrew University. Many smaller animals were observed and collected. Of one rare species, the Syrian squirrel, three living and 13 dead specimens were brought in. Small birds were also investigated by the expedition. One occurrence vividly illustrated the literal accuracy of the verse in the Book of Proverbs: 'The eye that mocketh at his father...the ravens of the valley shall pluck it out.' A wounded magpie had been captured, and was placed near an owl, also injured. The magpie promptly tried to pluck out the owl's eye."

5. These have been determined by the late James L. Peters, Museum of Comparative Zoology, Harvard.

6. See The Middle East (1953, pp. 295-98).

See also Braidwood (1952), Harden (1949), Dorothy Mackay (1949), and Mallowan (1947).

7. See Woolley (1942).

8. In The Middle East, 1953. See also GE, 1954, pp. 137-38.

9. For population statistics and migrations, see Issawi and Dabezies, and Field (1956), especially Map 1 opposite p. 5 of Beduin tribes.

10. For a description of two areas with chronic endemic dental fluorosis, see Clawson (1938), Clawson and Perks (1938), and Khalifah (1938).

11. See Fohs (1946).

12. For Stone Age references, see Braidwood (1953), Field (1956), Ewing (1946), Hitti (1951), Nasrallah (1950), and Rust (1933 and 1950).

13. Through the kindness of Mr. Harper Kelley.

14. See Field (1951 and 1956). See also traverse report on ADIM 3977, pp. 3-16.

15. See Krogman (1949) and Rialle (1866). These notes have been excerpted from Sauter (1945, pp. 84-85, 98). See also: Blake, "Notes on human remains from Palmyra," JRAI, 1872; Busk, "Notes on some skulls from Palmyra," JRAI, 1875; and Duckworth, "Note on a skull from Syria," JRAI, 1899. For photograph of a burial at Chatal Hüyük, Period V (= Judeidah VI), see C.W. McEwen (1937, p. 8).

16. Ancient Ugarit near coast north of Latakia. The clay tablets of second millennium B.C., found in 1929, are of great significance.

17. See References.

18. See Ashkenazi (1948), Charles (1939), de Boucheman (1934, 1935 and 1939), Haut-Commissariat de la République Française (1930) on ADIM 3956, pp. 1-161, Montagne, Muller, Snodgrasse, and Vernier.

19. This material was selected from HCRF (1930), a rare copy being lent to me by former Premier René Pleven. The large tribal map in this publication should be consulted. See also ADIM 4506, pp. 1-230.

20. The raw data and pls. 1-52 have been placed on ADIM 2417, pp. 1-71.

21. For additional data, see Sauter (1945), Seltzer (1940) and Shanklin (1935a-b, 1936a-c) and Shanklin and Cummins (1937). See also Shanklin, in AJPA, Vol. 4, no. 3, pp. 323-71, 1946, esp. Bibliography.

22. For dental studies, see "Chronic endemic fluorosis (mottled enamel)" in TADS, 1938. The historical note (pp. 3-6) is by E.S. Khalifah. Observations on prevention and treatment (pp. 7-10) are given by M. Don Clawson and data on new endemic areas are reported from Southwestern Asia (pp. 11-14) by M. Don Clawson and A.J. Perks. There is a good Bibliography on p. 15.

23. For note on Bejel, see article by E.H. Hudson, BJVD, Vol. 27, pp. 174-76, 1951. For other references by Hudson, who lived many years in Deir-ez-Zor, see his references in Field, 1953, p. 23.

24. See my forthcoming "Body-Marking in Southwestern Asia," a monograph to be published in Peabody Museum Papers, Harvard.

25. See Field, in Man, Vol. 37, no. 69, 1937.

26. See Kappers, Vol. 1, Fig. 28.

27. From personal observation at Qasr el-Azraq in Jordan during 1928. For general information, see M. Hidayet Hosain, "The Druzes, their origin, manners and customs," Oriental Studies in honour of Cursetji Erachji Pavry, pp. 156-162, London, 1933. See also Nejla Izzeddin (1934) and Shanklin and Izzeddin (1937).

Chapter VII: TURKEY

1. For special articles, see (a) James M. Barker on "Backward Areas," a paper read at the Mid-Century Convocation of the Massachusetts Institute of Technology; (b) "Turkey: frontier of freedom" published in the Background Series, Office of Public Affairs, Department of State, June, 1952, see map on p. 3; (c) Turkish Information Office (444 E. 52 St., New York 22). Pamphlets Nos. 1, 2, 4, 5, 6, and 12 as well as "Facts on Turkey" and "The New Turkey"; (d) Senyürek (1953); (e) Çetin; and (f) Anatolian Studies, Journal of the British Institute of Archaeology at Ankara. For general references, see Ettinghausen (1952) and Field (1953-56). For medical data, see GE, 1954, pp. 205-32, with map and 76 references. For titles obtained too late to include in References see: (a) E.Y. Bostanci, "A research on the growth in sitting height and leg length of Turkish schoolchildren in Ankara" (in Turkish), Revue de la Faculté des Sciences de l'Université d'Ankara, (RLFHG), Vol. 13, nos. 1-2, pp. 69-136, 1955; (b) Shevket Aziz Kansu, "Sur les civilizations préhistoriques de la Turkie" (in French), Belleten, Vol. 19, no. 76, pp. 541-45, 1955; (c) Seniha Tunakan, "Etude statistique sur la fréquence des jumeaux en Turkie" (in Turkish), Review of the Faculty of Language, History and Geography, University of Ankara; and (d) Enise Yener, "Sur l'ancienne costume feminine" (in Turkish), RLFHG, Vol. 13, no. 3, pp. 27-37, 1955.

2. See The Middle East (1953), Hedley V. Cooke (1952, pp. 259-85) and Warriner (1948). For map, see "Turkey" published by the Turkish Information Service, New York.

3. See The Middle East (1953, p. 313) and GE (1954, p. 206).

4. For botanical references, see Field (1953).

5. For zoological references, see Field (1953-56), Musters (1932) and Thomas (1906). For special reports on the Chukhor partridge (Alectoris graeca Forskal) and the sand grouse, see Bump (1951 a and b).

6. Quoted from The Middle East, 1953. See also GE (1954, pp. 206-208). For the population density (per square kilometer), see map opp. p. 16, in International Bank for Reconstruction and Development Publication No. IBRD, 1951. 1, "The Economy of Turkey: an analysis and recommendation for a development program," Washington, 1951.

7. Excerpted from The Middle East (1953, p. 315). See also pp. 316-18, Barker (1951, pp. 3-9), Lamb (1949, pp. 188-202 and 2 maps), and Mantran (1952).

8. For Stone Age references, see Afet (1939), Caskey, Dönmez and Brice, Erguvanli, Field (1953), Shevket Aziz Kansu (1945a and b and 1947), Kökten (1947 and 1949), Lamb (1949), Maringer, Ozden, Perkins and Braidwood, Pfannenstiel, Pittard (1950) and Waechter, Gögüs and Seton-Williams. For references to ancient inhabitants of Anatolia, see Vallois (1950) and Muzaffer Süleyman Senyürek (1946 and 1949 a-c). These notes have been excerpted from the article by Shevket Aziz Kansu, in AJA, Vol. 51, pp. 327-32.

9. For references, see Afet (1937), Angel (1939 and 1951), Ehrich (1940), Kansu (1935a-b, 1937a-c, 1939a-b and 1943), Kansu and Atasyan (1939), Kansu and Tunakan (1938), Krogman (1933 and 1937), Ozgüc, Senyürek (1941, 1946, 1949a-c, 1950a-b, 1951a-f and 1952a-b), Senyürek and Tunakan, Virchow (1882 and 1896), and Von Luschan. Special attention is called to Krogman (1937) and Senyürek (1941 and 1951e). Senyürek (1952a, pp. 330-33) compares crania from Kul-tepe with those from Mesopotamia (Al-Ubaid, Kish, Ur, and Nuzi).

10. See Senyürek (1949a-c and 1952b).

11. Taurodontism, as defined by Sir Arthur Keith, is the condition where the pulp chambers were enlarged at the expense of the roots and were embedded in the dental alveoli; where the pulp chamber was small, this is termed cynodontism. See Senyürek (1949b, p. 222).

12. In this important paper Senyürek gives detailed footnotes which should be consulted.

13. See footnote references by Senyürek (1951d, pp. 614-15).

14. These data have been included in the comparative tables in Chapter XIV since the large series of 20,263 females were studied by the Government survey.

15. See Turkiye Antropometri Anketi [Enquête Anthropométrique Turque faite sur 59,728 individus de deux sexes], IUM, no. 151, pp. 1-165). For map showing regional divisions (1-X), see map 1 following p. 166. For methods employed in measurements, see Plates 1-2 at end. See also Afet (1939 and 1940). For incidence of the "Mongoloid spot" (Tache mongoloide) in Turkey, see Kansu (1932) and Field (1940). For description of Osmanli Turks, see Coon (1948, pp. 617-22 with footnotes; see also Index for references to Turks). For Physical Anthropology, see all references, many quoted from Sauter, under Afet, Angel, Aygen, Bilge, Çinar, Coon, Dellenbach, Ehrich, Field, Giuffrida-Ruggeri, Gökcül, Güler, Güngör, Hauschild, Hauschild and Wagenseil, Kansu, Kansu and Atasayan, Kansu and Tunakan, Kinay, Kökten, Krogman, Nourredine Bey, Ozgüc, Peake, Pittard, Pittard and Donici, Sauter, Senyürek, Senyürek and Tunakan, Seven, Vallois, Virchow, Von Luschan, Weisbach and Zaborowski.

Chapter VIII: CAUCASUS

1. The References to the Caucasus are few because the reader is referred to Field (1953, pp. 122-32) and to Vladimir Minorsky (1953a-b). The introductory section is based on Field (1953a), which was compiled from many Russian and other sources.

2. For additional references, see Formosov and Satunin.

3. See Marc Slonim (1937).

4. Excerpted from Field (1948). For additional references, see list of our 101 articles on Soviet archeology in Field (1953a, pp. 116-119) and ADIM no. 2308. See also Ward, Movius and Vereschagin.

5. See Field (1948, pp. 50-51).

6. See Field (1948, pp. 52-53).

7. The reader is presumed to have access to Field (1953a), where data on Ciscaucasia, Transcaucasia, Georgia and Osetia are published.

8. See Field (1953a, Table 5, p. 9, et seq.).

9. Since my principal interest in the Caucasus during the 1934 Expedition was to record the physical characters of the Osetes, I shall comment on their position in relation to some of the groups from Southwestern Asia. These observations have been relegated to the footnotes in order not to interrupt the text wherein general trends have been emphasized. Attention is called to the tables in Field (1953a), where other comparative data have appeared.

10. The seven Osetes from Ellis Island, New York, 170.26, Kennard; six non-enlisted Osetes from Osetia, 172.5, von Erckert.

11. The Osetes fall into the taller part of Table 45 and are conspicuously present near the maximum recorded stature. No Osete groups occurred in the lower half of this Table. The range (164.7-180.5) shows considerable variation, but the majority seem to fall between 169.0 and 170.0, a figure which places the Osetes in the medium tall classification. The Mountain Osetes tend to be taller than the dwellers on the plains. It must be noted that the blond and light-eyed groups are considerably shorter than the brunet series.

The frequency distribution of stature recorded by Gilchenko (p. 109) shows that 110 men were between 156.0 - 169.9, the majority being between 166.0 - 169.9, and 90 men between 170.0 - 190.0, half of whom had a stature of 170.0 - 174.9. Gilchenko observes that although the Alaghirs consider themselves of newest Osete origin, they show almost as great standard deviations as the Digors and Kurtatins. The average stature of the Alaghirs is somewhat higher than that of the general Osete average.

12. Table 45 shows that the Osetes are considerably taller than the majority of the Turkestan groups. However, the people of Ferghana and the Tatars approximate the Osete stature. When we compare the Osetes to the peoples listed in my Iran Report (Field, 1939), we obtain the following results: The dwellers on the Iranian Plateau are considerably shorter (165.0-166.0) with the exception of the peoples of northwestern Iran, who are as tall as the Osetes. In Iraq the Kish Arabs (359) are as tall as the blond groups of Osetes. The Iraq Army Soldiers (222) are of equal stature with the tallest groups of Osetes, always excepting the twenty selected tall men measured by Gilchenko. The Osetes are taller than my other Iraqi series, with the exception of the Assyrians (106). The Osetes are taller than the coastal peoples of South Arabia, the Syrians, the Turks from Anatolia, the Assyrians, the Armenians of the Caucasus, about equal in stature with some Beduins of Trans-Jordan, and the Kurds, and shorter than two small groups of Samaritans in Palestine. These new figures add some slight degree of confirmation to my theory (Field, 1939) that there is a general tendency for the mountain peoples to be taller than the inhabitants of the plains or the coastal regions.

13. Among my Osete groups the same individuals appear in different categories. Even bearing this in mind the range 84.97 - 85.15 is remarkably small. When these Osete figures are compared with my Table for Southwestern Asia, it appears that the Osetes possess longer trunks than the Jews of Isfahan (86) and the peoples living on the Iranian Plateau as represented by the Yezd-i-Khast (46) and Kinareh (74) villagers, but the Hassan Kuli Khan Lurs of Pusht-i-Kuh (52) are considerably larger (89.11). In Iraq the Kish Arabs (340) were shorter, the soldiers (222) about the same, but the small series of mixed Turkoman elements recorded by Ehrich were longer (88.00 - 90.22) in trunk length. In this measurement the Kurds, Armenians, and Syrians also seem to be longer, but the Beduins of Trans-Jordan approximate that of the Osetes.

14. The Osetes again show remarkably little variation (range 49.92 - 50.26). They are slightly taller than three of the Iran groups (range 48.16-49.74) and their relative sitting height is slightly higher, but the Lurs have a considerably greater index (52.84). The Lurs have very short legs (79.52) and long trunks (89.11) in contrast to the better proportioned Osetes. The Kish Arabs (49.08), the Iraq Army Soldiers (49.76), and the Akeydat and Maualy Beduins of Trans-Jordan (50.54) show little difference in relative sitting height from that of the Osetes. The majority of my other comparative series, including Syrians, Turks of Anatolia, Armenians, and Kurds, have an index ranging from 52.0 - 53.6.

15. The Iraq Army Soldiers (222) were shorter (186.24) in head length, the Kish Arabs (358) about the same (188.76) and the Baij Beduins (35) longer (191.31). The

only group of South Arabs (29) was considerably shorter (180.00). The Trans-Jordan Beduins (295) possessed longer heads (190.42-191.35). In Syria the Druze were considerably shorter (178.2), as were the Syrians (263) with a head length of 183.06, but the Rwala (Ruwalla) Beduins (270) were much longer (191.48). The Anatolian groups show that the Turks (1237) are shorter (180.1-185.4) and the Assyrians (22) even shorter (173.9). The Kurds (203) show great variation (181.31-193.0), the majority being shorter than the Osetes. The greater number of the Turkestan groups are shorter headed, especially the Arabs (183.66). The 18 Afghans are also shorter (185.0). All 15 groups in Baluchistan (927) are shorter headed (174.42-186.24), the majority (457) having a range of 177.96 - 179.67. In general, the Osetes tend to have longer heads than the average group in Southwestern Asia, Turkestan, or Baluchistan. Among the 32 groups, ranging from 181.9-204.0, the Osetes fall into the upper half of the series. My Osetes show little variation (187.68-188.04), but the 300 Osetes measured by Riskine possessed slightly longer heads (190.0). The Mountain Osetes seem to have slightly shorter heads than those of the plains. Gilchenko's figures indicate that artificial cranial deformation shortened their heads. The measurements given by Chantre seem to be out of all proportion, although it is hard to see how he could have made any serious error unless he did not take the glabello-occipital length in the median line. Gilchenko (pp. 161-62) recorded a head length of 188.2 for 82 artificially deformed heads and 190.3 for 118.2 undeformed. Among the 200 Osetes 10 (5.0 per cent) possessed a head length of 200-204, and 93 (46.5 per cent) 190-199, and 82 (41.0 per cent) 180-189. The Armenians (719) have much shorter heads (168.0-186.39) as have the Georgians (900) with a head length of 185.0, but the Turkomans (59) have much longer heads (193.0). When we examine the position of my Osetes in relation to the groups listed in the Iran Report, (Field, 1939), we find that they fall about midway between the villagers of Kinareh (187.02) and those of Yezd-i-Khast (192.51). The 46 Persians measured by Danilov (188.00) had the same head length as the Osetes.

16. The Osetes possess very broad heads (155.5-168.0), possibly accentuated to this marked degree by artificial cranial deformation. Among my groups the Mountaineers possess the broadest heads, the Plainsmen the narrowest. All Caucasian groups, including the Armenians, tend to have narrower heads. Turning to Southwestern Asia we see that the Osetes have broader heads than all groups in Iran (140.68-146.0) and in Iraq (139.93 - 153.1), as well as all other groups from South Arabia, Jordan, Palestine, Syria, Anatolia, Kurdistan, Turkestan, Afghanistan, and Baluchistan except the Ansaries of Antioch (164.0) in Syria. To summarize, out of about 120 groups, including some 7,500 individuals, the Osetes possess the broadest heads of all but three groups, including 383 individuals.

17. During the compilation of the cephalic indexes among the peoples of the Caucasus I have used Baschmakoff (pp. 29-31), Rudolph Martin, Gilchenko, Pantiukhov, Tschepourkowski, IArkho, Coon, Seltzer, and figures quoted in my Iran Report (Field, 1939). The measurements given by Pantiukhov (pp. 26-28) were obtained on recruits. The following groups contained nine or less individuals: Persian Ajemis (6), 76.64, Chantre; Ingushes (3), 80.49, Chantre; Gurians (4), 80.58, Chantre; Khevsurs (2), 80.79, Chantre; Karachais (5), 81.5, von Erckert; Chechens (8), 82.95 Chantre; coastal Abkhazians (4), 83.0, Chantre; Kabardins (4) 84.54, Chantre; Assyrians (5), 85.00, von Erckert; Assyrians (5), 85.1, von Erckert; Mountain Jews (4), 85.3, von Erckert; Turkomans (4), 85.56, Chantre; Nogais (4), 85.7, Chantre; Georgians (7), 85.85, Chantre; Lezghians (3), 85.9, von Erckert; Avars (5), 86.45, Chantre; and Osetes (2), 87.6, von Erckert. In addition, the above number of individuals was not recorded in the following sources quoted. For general trends the following groups have been added in ascending order: Azerbaidzhanis, 78.1, Deniker; Circassians, 78.5, Chantre; Kurds, Transcaucasia, Tats, Azerbaidzhan, 79.0, Deniker, Azer-

baidzhanis, 79.4, von Erckert; Chechens, 80.4, Chantre; Gurians, 80.5, Chantre; Khevsurs, 80.7, Chantre; Abazes, North Abkhazia, Chantre; Imeretians, 80.9, Chantre; Kalmyks, 80.9, von Erckert; Kalmyks, 81.0, Rossikov; Karachais, 81.1, Chantre; Circassians (Adighe), 81.4, Deniker; Kurds, 81.6, Chantre; Galgaevtsi, 81.9, Rossikov; Circassians, 81.9, von Erckert; Kabardins (Kuban), 82.0, Chantre; Circassians (Shapsug), 82.1, Chantre; Circassians (Beslins), 82.2, Chantre; Osetes, 82.7, Deniker; Circassians (Temirgais), 83.0, Chantre; Mountain Tatars, 83.6, Deniker; Kabardins, 83.6, Deniker; Kumyks, 84.0, Chantre; Plains Osetes, 84.2, Bunak; Chechens, 84.2, von Erckert; Georgians, 84.3, Chantre; Mountain Chechens, 84.4, Rossikov; deformed Kurds, 84.6, Chantre; Lezghians, 84.6, Deniker; Nogais, 85.0, Chantre; Kumyks, 85.0, Chantre; Lezghians (Avars), 85.1, von Erckert; Lezghians, 85.5, von Erckert; Nogais, 85.8, Deniker; Nogais, 86.0, Chantre; Lezghians, 86.2, Deniker; Nogais, 86.4, von Erckert; Lezghians, 86.7, Rossikov; Lazes, 86.8, Deniker; Mountain Jews (Daghestan), 87.0, Deniker; Lazes, 87.3, Chantre; Lezghians (Avars), 87.6, von Erckert; and Assyrians, 88.7, Deniker. See Field (1939).

18. Within the 17 groups of 1,536 Osetes with a range of 80.5 - 85.53, the majority being about 82.0. Within my small groups (range 84.06 - 85.53) the Plainsmen are the least, the Mountaineers the most brachycephalic. On the other hand, Bunak obtained reverse results: a cephalic index of 83.8 for Mountain Osetes; and 84.2 for Plains Osetes. Examination of this table suggests that within my five series the use of the cradleboard shortened and broadened the heads, thus artificially raising the cephalic index. This is especially true when Gilchenko's 82 deformed heads fall only slightly below (0.27) the figures for my Osete Plainsmen. Deformed heads were recorded by Gilchenko (59.0 per cent), Chantre (53.0 per cent), and von Erckert (43.75 per cent). There is some question as to which Osete cephalic index should be accepted for comparison with other groups in the Caucasus and other areas. I have selected the cephalic index of 82.0 as probably being the most representative for undeformed Osetes. The Tatars appear to be more dolichocephalic than the Osetes, but the Armenians tend to have rounder heads. The Osetes are definitely in the brachycephalic division. However, at this point it will be advisable to examine Gilchenko's measurements arranged in frequency tables. According to Broca's classificatory system there were two dolichocephals (x-75.00), 12 sub-dolichocephals (75.01-77.77), 32 mesocephals (77.78-80.00), 72 subbrachycephals (80.01-83.33), and 82 brachycephals (83.34-x). Gilchenko recorded a range of 72.00-94.18. In another table Gilchenko gives the frequency distribution for his subbrachycephals and brachycephals, following the Broca system. Out of 152 Osetes 108 were between 80.01-85.00, the majority (72) being below 83.33. On the other hand, special attention must be drawn to the fact that 44 Osetes had cephalic indices ranging from 85.01-94.18. In this hyperbrachycephalic division 29 men were within the range 85.01-88.00. At the same time the fact that there were 15 men with cephalic indices above 88.01 points to extreme artificial cranial deformation by means of the cradleboard. In direct contrast were the 14 men with cephalic indices below 77.77, and the 32 from 77.78-80.00. Since the raw data are not available, it is impossible to group the individuals according to the Harvard Anthropometric Laboratory system, but at least 90 individuals (45 per cent) would have fallen into the brachycephalic division (82.6-x) and very few among the dolichocephals (x-76.5). The majority of the Osetes would therefore have been classed as mesocephals with a marked brachycephalic tendency. Turning to the south we see that the Osetes are considerably more brachycephalic than my basically Mediterranean types (73.50-76.35) in Iran. A group of 20 Bakhtiari tribesmen had a mean index of 88.38 (cf. the Druze in Syria). The Osetes are also rounder headed than the 359 Kish Arabs (75.33) or the 222 Iraq Soldiers (76.62). Nineteen Chaldeans from Qaraqosh near Mosul had an index of

86.01. The figures from Arabia indicate dolichocephalic and brachycephalic elements, the latter approximating the Osete index. The Trans-Jordan Beduins are longer headed as are all the listed Palestine groups. In Syria there are numerous non-Beduin brachycephalic groups, including 48 Ansaries (84.43), 182 Lebanese (84.88), 265 Syrians (85.11), 136 Alouites (85.66), and 80 Druze (87.26). The Turks of Anatolia (range 81.80-87.20) seem to be more brachycephalic than the Osetes but less than the Assyrians (88.70-89.50). The Kurds seem to be distributed in a manner similar to the Osetes with both dolichocephalic and brachycephalic groups. In passing I must comment on the fact that there is a blond element among the Kurds.

19. Taking the undeformed Osetes as possessing a cephalic index of 82.0, we see that they are slightly less roundheaded than the Crimean groups.

20. The undeformed Osetes (82.00) fall well within the upper range of this series from the Volga Region, which seems to be populated with brachycephals.

21. I have selected some figures obtained recently by Soviet physical anthropologists in Central Asia. However, these do not include long series of unpublished data which Bunak showed me in Moscow during June, 1945. Some of Oshanin's data on Iranian tribes in the Western Pamirs have been included. In addition, three Goranis with C.I. of 93.5, 83.3 and 75.6 were recorded by Oshanin.

22. The majority are more brachycephalic than the Osetes.

23. Tannu Tuva, located between the Tanna and Sayan Mountains of northern Central Asia, forms geographically part of Outer Mongolia.

24. Some recent figures from Siberia have become available through the work of IArkho and Schreiber. However, Debets is now collecting anthropometric data in northwestern Siberia and many new figures should be available before the end of 1956.

25. Ginzburg (pp. 89-91) writes that the Yaghnobians do not constitute a separate anthropological group from their neighbors, the Mountain Tajiks. He assigns them to the "Sub-Pamirian Europeoid" type. Among the 21 individuals the mean head length was 183.29, the head breadth 153.05 and the cephalic index 83.52.

26. The Osetes show remarkable variation (94.4-120.6) in the width of the forehead. My own measurements, which tend to be high, indicate that Osete foreheads are broad. Gilchenko's measurements give an average of 111.2, but in his frequency distribution table for 200 Osetes he groups them as follows: 97-99 (2); 100-109 (79); 110-118 (102); 120-127 (16); and 133 (1). Thus, more than half of his Osetes fall into the 110-118 class, 17 (8.5 per cent) into the 120-133 class and 81 (40.5 per cent) show as a small minimum frontal diameter (97-109). This suggests that there are narrow and broad forehead groups among the Osetes. When we compare the minimum frontal diameter of the Osetes with external groups, we find that they are broader than all my Iran (111.90-114.50) and Iraq (106.42-114.10) series. They also have broader foreheads than the 29 South Arabs (107.72), 62 Samaritans (103.0-104.3), 572 Syrians (106.82-115.0), 312 peoples of Anatolia (105.0-113.28), Kurds (100.0-116.0), Turkestan groups (103.0-109.0), and some of Guha's series from India (101.54-105.23). The only peoples, who appear to approximate the forehead width of the Osetes are the 120 Akeydat Beduins (117.64) and the 175 Maualy Beduins (118.50), both of Trans-Jordan, now Jordan.

27. The differences between my Osete groups is infinitesimal (74.41-74.74). However, there are considerable variations among my Iran (77.77-81.19) and Iraq series, for we see that their fronto-parietal index is greater than the 152 Kurds (62.89-73.89) and the 29 South Arabs (72.59).

28. The North Osetes are well grouped together, ranging from 143.95-144.45, in the upper part of the Table. Their faces are considerably broader than those of the Yezidis and also of all the groups measured in Turkestan.

29. The North Osetes tend to have very broad lower faces, range 116.46-119.38. This is considerably higher than all groups tabulated in my Iran Report (Field, 1939),

except the figure of 118.0 for 29 Arabs of Turkestan measured by Maslovskii.

30. In upper facial height the North Osetes appear to possess relatively short upper faces, range 70.85-71.75.

31. In total facial height the North Osetes, range 122.35-124.50, fall well within the central part of the table in the Iran Report (Field, 1939).

32. In total facial index the North Osetes, range 85.50-86.85, tend to be low for all areas listed in my Iran Report (Field, 1939), except Anatolia.

33. The size and shape of the nose is one of the most important racial criteria in Southwestern Asia and adjoining areas. The nasal length of the North Osetes, range 52.06-53.38, tends to be short in relation to the group in my Iran Report (Field, 1939).

34. The nasal breadth of the North Osetes, range 32.78-33.41, tends to be narrow in comparison with the groups in my Iran Report (Field, 1939).

35. Several groups contained nine or less individuals, so they are listed here: Osetes from Koban (7), 66.03, Chantre; Chechens (8), 66.46, Chantre; Kabardins (4), 66.49, Chantre; Abkhazians (4), 66.66, Chantre; Imeretians (4), 66.70, Chantre; Avars (5), 69.65, Chantre; Georgians (7), 69.65, Chantre; Nogais (4), 70.00, Chantre; Turkomans (4), 70.50, Chantre; Gurians (4), 72.54, Chantre; Ingushes (3), 74.82, Chantre; and Khevsurs (2), 75.78, Chantre. The nasal index of the North Osetes shows considerable variation, range 62.62-74.20. My series of 105 males range from 62.62-65.18. This great variability makes it impossible to formulate any conclusive grouping of the North Osetes in relation to the series in the Iran Report (Field, 1939).

Chapter IX: IRAQ

1. Since I have published six sections of a detailed anthropogeographical survey and numerous articles (see references), this Chapter on Iraq will be brief as I presume this material will be readily available. In each section of the survey there is a list of bibliographical references, so that only a few are given here. Special attention is called to the following, arranged alphabetically: American Geographical Society, Anonymous, Awad (1952 and 1953), Bashir and Awad, Boesch (1939), Cameron, Cooke (1952), Field (1953a), and Fisher (1950), GE, International Bank for Reconstruction and Development, Ireland, Jawad, Khadduri, Lees and Falcon, Longrigg (1925 and 1953), Main, Simmonds, The Middle East, U.S. Department of State Technical Coöperation Administration (1953) and Warriner. Attention is also called to Field (1956b, pp. 11-26) where details of my 1950 reconnaissance survey are given. This includes: (a) Reconnaissance survey for surface sites with flint or quartzite implements in western Iraq, particularly in the Qaara Depression, and in the Rowandiz and Kirkuk-Chemchemal regions. (b) Making soundings in two caves on Jebel Baradost above Rowandiz Gorge. (c) Searching for recent historical sites east of Kish in Hilla Liwa. (d) Recording anthropometric data on 533 Assyrian men and 126 women at the Royal Air Force Headquarters, Habbaniya and 41 workmen at the Nippur excavations in Ad Diwaniya Liwa. (e) Collecting zoological and botanical specimens. For data on cranial and skeletal material from Nippur for comparison with my anthropometric measurements on 41 local Arabs see Swindler. See also References in Field 1956b, pp. 91-100. While this study was being processed Sumer, Vol. 11, no. 2 (1955) was received. Attention is called to the following articles: (a) "Geological aspects of the Archaeology of Iraq" by H.E. Wright, Jr., pp. 83-90; (b) "Archaeological reconnaissance of Jebel Sinam and Old Basra in southern Iraq" by Ralph S. Solecki, pp. 122-23; (c) "A postscript to the Shanidar Cave Report, 1955" by Solecki, p. 124; (d) "Archaeological survey of the ancient canals in Iraq" by Albrecht Goetze, pp. 127-28; and (e) "Statement concerning Archaeology and soil survey in Mesopotamia (Iraq)" by M.A. Beek and P. Buringh, pp. 143-44.

2. See Boesch (1939, 1947, and 1949).

3. See MacFayden (1938), Sousa (1944), and Willcocks (1911). For development possibilities, see Fohs (1946). On April 21, 1955 King Faisal II inaugurated the Samarra dam and a few days later the Habbaniya dam--both part of the great Wadi Tharthar Project.

4. See Peters (1933).

5. See Baqir, Field (1932a and 1953a), Guest (1932 and 1933), Hooper and Field, Shiriaev (1956), Standley (1940) and Zohary (1941 and 1950). For reference to trees and plants of Ancient Iraq, see Baqir. For references to tobacco, see Sarkis. See also Sister Mary Alverna de Bozy, "A selected bibliography of plant life in Iraq and neighboring countries," M.S. Thesis, Catholic University, Washington, August, 1953. Early in 1956 Dr. Nicholas Polunin of the Gray Herbarium, Harvard University, arrived in Baghdad to work with Evan Guest in the Iraq Department of Agriculture in the compilation of "The Flora of Iraq."

6. See The Middle East (1953, p. 128).

7. See Allouse (1950 and 1953), Brooke, P.A. Buxton, Pitman et al. (1920-22), Buxton and Dowson, Field (1937b and 1953a), Gunther, Lawrence, Peters, Sanborn, and Weber. For entomological references, see Wiltshire, in Field (1952d and 1953a). For references to fauna in ancient time, see Amschler (1936 and 1953), Baqir, Bate, Field (1932b and 1936b) and Laufer. The following Memorandum was received from Dr. Louis Hussakof, American Museum of Natural History, regarding fish bones excavated by me at Kish in March, 1928, while attached to Field Museum-Oxford University Joint Expedition: "The material consists of fragments broken out from a layer or stratum of hardened clay. The fragments vary in thickness--from about 7/8 to 1-7/8 inches; this variation proves that they are derived from where the layer thins out toward its margin or end. On one flat surface of the clay there are numerous spines and bones of small fishes. They are apparently confined to this one surface and do not occur throughout the thickness of the clay. In some of the clay fragments the fish remains are exceedingly numerous, forming a compact layer about half an inch thick, distinguishable from the rest of the clay by its darker brown color. The large quantity of these fish bones indicates that a great number of fishes in that body of water died from some sudden catastrophic cause. Such an occurrence, though rare in nature, is of course known to occur. It is not conclusively shown by the fragments in hand whether the fish remains lie above or below the layer of clay; that is to say, whether they died and fell to the bottom before the clay was deposited, or after it already formed the bottom. My impression, based on the mode of weathering of the fish layer, is, that the fish remains probably lie above the clay. By sifting the material through a wire sieve, the small fish bones were separated out for examination. They belong to small fishes (i.e., fishes probably under ten inches in length) and comprise: (1) vertebrae; (2) fin-spines; (3) small pharyngeal bones (bones bearing teeth found in the throat of some fishes); and (4) small, isolated bones of the skeleton. Although the fish remains are numerous, they represent (in the material examined) only three or four genera. Conspicuous among the remains are the pharyngeal bones of fishes belonging to the family with very many genera, of which the carp, goldfish, and minnows may be mentioned as examples."

My reply on June 3, 1929, was as follows: "I quite agree with your suggestion that the fish died from some catastrophic cause. It seemed to me that this small room in which the skeletons were found must have been the last to dry up following the abatement of the flood which took place about 3400 B.C. The fish all swarmed into this room, and when the water evaporated the skeletons of the fish were covered with silt, and remained buried for over 5,000 years until we uncovered the room in 1928. I am very grateful to you for the information that most of the remains belong to the family Cyprinidae."

These fish were drowned in the Flood, believed to be the Biblical Deluge, and preserved in the alluvial silt. In 1934 I collected fish in the main canal near Tell el-Uhaimir (anc. Kish). These were identified as Cyprinidae.

8. Quoted from The Middle East (1953, p. 129).

9. Quoted from The Middle East (1953, p. 128). See also Lebon (1953) and Field (1940a, pp. 103-105 and 1956b, pp. 67-70).

10. See Al-Asil, Batten, Robert J. Braidwood (1951a-b), Robert J. and Linda Braidwood (1950 and 1954), Coon (1950), Crawshay, Field (1951c-d, and 1952d), Garrod (1930 and 1938), Libby, Safar, Solecki (1952a-b and 1953a-b), Stein, Watelin, Wright and Howe.

11. These landing grounds from Amman to Ramadi were marked out by the Royal Air Force during 1921-22 at 20 mile intervals. The landing grounds from Amman to El Jidd were lettered eastward consecutively "A" to "R" (with the omission of "I" and "O"); those from Ramadi to El Jidd were given Roman numerals I-XI westward. See R.A.F. "Pilot's Handbook of the Cairo-Baghdad Route," Government Press, Cairo, 1923 and Field (1929 and 1952d, p. 137).

12. Through the assistance of Miss Gertrude Bell, Director of Antiquities, and the cordial coöperation of Air Vice Marshal Sir John Higgins, who allowed us to accompany a R.A.F. armored car patrol on January 11, 1926 from Baghdad to Landing Ground "H."

13. In October, 1926, Buxton published a preliminary report on these discoveries in the Antiquaries Journal, London.

14. These specimens and a chain of surface sites in Jordan, Syria, Iraq, and Saudi Arabia will be described in my forthcoming "Archeological Survey of the North Arabian Desert" based on surface reconnaissances in 1925, 1926, 1927, 1928, 1934, and 1950. Dr. Erwin Raisz completed on April 9, 1956, a four-color map showing the location of these sites.

15. In the spring of 1928 Miss Dorothy Garrod came to Kish to discuss with me the search in Iraq for Paleolithic man and his cultures in the area 42° - 48° Longitude East. Her selection was north of Latitude 34° and the Kirkuk-Sulaimaniya region where many limestone caves were reported. See Garrod (1928). See ADIM, no. 4612, pp. 14-34.

16. By special arrangement we were granted permission as an independent unit to accompany an Iraq Petroleum Company (IPC) survey party under Major A.L. Holt and W.E. Browne.

17. See Field (1953b, pp. 212-13 and 1 Plate).

18. These will be published in my forthcoming Report, together with a map drawn by Dr. Erwin Raisz showing the archeological sites along my traverses. See No. 14.

19. See also Robert Braidwood (1952, pp. 23-24).

20. See Basmachi (pp. 104-105).

21. For preliminary summary of results, see Field (1951d, pp. 89-91 and see also "A Reconnaissance in Southwestern Asia, 1950," PMP, 1956.

22. See Watelin (pp. 65-76).

23. For references, see Robert and Linda Braidwood (1950 and 1953), and Robert Braidwood (1951a-b, 1952, pp. 24, 26, and 1955a-b). Following my request Bruce Howe sent the following notes on his work: In 1951 the Oriental Institute Expedition concentrated on the Chemchemal-Sulaimaniya area near the Lesser Zab drainage. The main project was the early village of Jarmo. An adjunct to this was my ASOR-sponsored work on terminal food-gathering sites, an effort to fill in the transitional sequence from Paleolithic to Neolithic. This included surface reconnaissance, soundings and fuller excavation.

Soundings at Barda Balka in behalf of the Directorate General of Antiquities of Iraq showed a combined hand-axe, pebble-tool and small flake assemblage, including

Acheulian types. This, in situ in fluvial gravels, lay at the base of the "Jarmo Silts." They constitute the last major aggradation cycle in the Chemchemal Valley and are tentatively correlated with the last, or Würm, glaciation.

A sounding at the small cave of Palegawra showed a final Paleolithic or Mesolithic type blade industry marked by geometric microliths, backed blades and bladelets, burins, scrapers. An apparently late phase of the Zarzi horizon originally discovered earlier by Garrod, this stage remains geologically unfixed. No suitable C14 samples were collected there in 1951.

Excavations at Karim Shahir revealed an extensive hill-top one-level occupation site containing an assemblage composed, on the one hand, of a blade industry marked by microliths, crude scrapers and burins having affinity with the terminal food gathering cave stages and, on the other, of chipped celts, rare polished bracelets and beads and simple clay figurines pointing toward early village community assemblages like Jarmo. This site, like Jarmo, rests on the surface of the "Jarmo Silts," the same aggradation cycle whose base contains the Barda Balka horizon. However, there is no closer dating yet possible, and there are no suitable C14 samples.

Typologically, Palegawra and Karim Shahir contain general similarities, but do not represent a continuum. They seem separated from each other and from the Jarmo stage by as yet missing industrial assemblages. Whether the series will turn out to be a sequence of successive evolving stages or a group of nearly contemporaneous, but differentiated, stages is not yet clear.

24. See Wright and Howe (pp. 107-11). Howe also comments in a private communication received in March, 1956: "For details of the latter in 1950-51 and 1954-55 consult Braidwood, Matson, Reed, Helbaek and Wright. All the findings outlined in above Footnote 23 are to be considered preliminary reports, tentative, subject to change as the full body of material is analyzed in detail. This work is proceeding now in: Chicago, Minneapolis, State College, Pennsylvania, Cambridge, Massachusetts, Copenhagen and Vienna." See ILN, no. 6099, Vol. 228, pp. 410-11, April 28, 1956. See also H.E. Wright, Jr., "Geological aspects of the Archaeology of Iraq." Sumer, Vol. 11, no. 2, pp. 83-91, 1955. This was received on June 10, 1956 too late for inclusion in References.

25. The first survey was made with Dr. Mahmud el-Amin of the Iraq Directorate-General of Antiquities. Excavation in Shanidar Cave was a joint expedition. For references, see Solecki (1952a-b, 1953a-b, 1954 and 1955).

26. Solecki, then a Fulbright Research Scholar, and leader of the Expedition, financed by the Smithsonian and the Directorate-General of Antiquities, was assisted by Mr. Hussein Azzam of the Iraq Museum.

27. By Dorothy Garrod. This child is known as Gibraltar II or familiarly as "Abel."

28. By Dr. Henri-Martin. Nearby were adult Neanderthalers and beside them three limestone balls, possibly used as bolas.

29. By A.P. Okladnikov.

30. For crania, see Robert and Linda Braidwood (1950), Buxton (1924), Buxton and Rice, Ehrich, Field (1932c), Furlani, Keith (1927), Krogman, Penniman, Swindler, Watelin and Langdon, and Weissenberg.

31. For early historical references, see Awad (1952 and 1953), Friederich (1932), Safar, and Speiser. For recent popular descriptions of archeological expeditions, see Linda Braidwood and Field (1953b).

32. Buxton and Rice (1931, pp. 60-63) described the physical setting of Kish.

33. See Field (1932c, pp. 967-70).

34. See Penniman (pp. 65-72).

35. Quoted from Sauter (pp. 77-78).

36. See Ehrich (pp. 570-90).

37. See Krogman (pp. 313-22).

38. By L.H. Dudley Buxton and Field for 1925-1926 notes and by Field for 1927-1928.

39. Excerpted from Field (1932c).

40. Proposed in Baghdad Times, January 6, 1926.

41. For anthropometric data, see Coon (1948), Field (1931, 1935, 1936a, 1940a, 1949a, 1951a-b, 1952a-d, 1953a and 1956b), Hamy, Keith (1935), Krischner, Müller, Sauter, Seligman, and Smeaton (1934 and 1940). The statistical data on stature and cephalic index have been incorporated into the comparative tables. However, all the other tables will be found in Field (1952d, pp. 110-34). For 21 manuscripts microfilmed on 3,451 pages in ADI, see Field (1952d, pp. 145-46). For a description of the Arabs of Iraq in relation to adjacent areas, see Keith (1935). For tribal data on the Beduins of Iraq, see von Oppenheim. For data on the polynuclear count see Kennedy (1935a-b).

42. During the Peabody Museum-Harvard Expedition to the Near East (Field, 1956b). The Assyrians are refugees from Turkey, the result of Christian persecution after World War I (see Dodge). Although studied in Iraq, their homeland for many centuries was from the high mountain area of southeastern Anatolia eastward to the Urmia plain of northwestern Iran. They are listed under Iraq because this is one of their present locations; another group lives in Syria beside the Khabur River. For old references, see Arutinov. See also my "An Anthropological Reconnaissance in the Near East, 1950," PMP, Vol. 48, no. 2, 1956.

43. For reports: on hair, see Trotter; on tattooing, see Smeaton (1937); on teeth, see Clawson (1936 and 1953); on the "Mongoloid spot," see Field (1940b); on the polynuclear count, see Kennedy (1935); on blood groups, see Boyd, Boyd and Boyd, Kayssi, Kayssi, Boyd and Boyd, Kennedy and MacFarlane, Kherumian; and on the intensity of ultra-violet radiation, see Kennedy (1938).

44. See Barth, Bawden, Buxton and Dowson, Dodge, Drower, Field (1937a, 1949b, and 1951b).

45. See ADIM Nos. 2416, 2483, 2941, 3227, 3926, 3977, 4213, 4279, 4284, 4427, 4469, 4612, and 4809 in American Documentation Institute (ADI), c/o Photoduplication Service, Library of Congress.

46. See Sauter.

47. For a summary of the inhabitation of Iraq, see Field (1952d, pp. 38-41).

48. See Field (1951b and 1952d).

Chapter X: THE ARABIAN PENINSULA

1. A few general and specific references will be given; no attempt at compiling a detailed bibliography is desirable, for the reader is presumed to be familiar with or to have ready access to such standard works as those of the following arranged alphabetically: Carruthers, Cheesman, de Gaury, Dickson, Doughty, Hogarth, Philby, Stark, Thesiger, Thomas and Twitchell. For references, see: The Middle East (1954, pp. 49-50); Ettinghausen (pp. 65, 70-71 and 77); Field (1953a, 1955a and 1956); GE, (1954, pp. 252-53, 265, 278, 286, 310, 315, and 329); and The Arabian Peninsula: a selected and annotated list of periodicals, books, and articles in English, pp. 1-111, Library of Congress, 1951.

For a list of Stone Age sites and recent archeological notes, see Field 1951a, pp. 185-71. See also my published archeological map of the North Arabian Desert, based on reconnaissance surveys of 1925, 1926, 1927, 1928, and 1950, drawn by Dr. Erwin Raisz. This will accompany my Report to be published in Peabody Museum Papers.

For additional references see the forthcoming Bibliography on the Arabian Peninsula to appear on June 30, 1956 as three monographs on Saudi Arabia, Eastern and

Southern Arabia. This is being compiled by Dr. Harry W. Hazard, American Geographical Society, in coöperation with the Human Relations Area Files (HRAF), 421 Humphrey Street, New Haven, Connecticut.

For special articles on Arabs, see Hamann, Modi, and Sergi.

2. Since many boundaries remain undefined, this arrangement is not entirely satisfactory. However, the most logical arrangement has been attempted. For example, Bertram Thomas' anthropometric data and a summary of observations on the physical characters of the South Arabs have been placed under Oman, because this seemed a more logical place for this discussion which includes possible relationships with northeast Africa on the west and India on the east. A line drawn across the northern fringe of the Rub' al Khali appears to divide the North and South Arabs. This is all the more complex because Bertram Thomas left from Dhufar in Oman, crossed the Empty Quarter in Saudi Arabia and arrived at Doha on the east coast of the Qatar Peninsula.

3. In 1932 by Royal Decree, Saudi Arabia was created instead of "Nejd and Its Dependencies"; quoted from Twitchell and Jurji (1952, pp. 6-7). For general references, including background of Arabia and the Middle East, the Government, the people and the land and the culture and customs of the Arabs with excellent maps of ancient and modern Arabia and superb photographs also special sections on geology (pp. 114-17 and 124), climate, flora, fauna, religion, etc., see Lebkicher, Rentz and Steineke, "The Arabia of Ibn Saud." However, the Stone Age and physical anthropology are omitted because of lack of data. See also books selected for further reading, pp. 170-72. For another excellent account of the characteristic features, including geology, topography and climate, social and political development and the position of Saudi Arabia in world economy, see Twitchell and Jurji. See also Solon T. Kimball, "American Culture in Saudi Arabia," TNYAS, Vol. 18, no. 5, pp. 469-84, March, 1956. For the most recent and extremely readable account of the Arabian Peninsula with good photographs, see Sanger.

4. Details summarized from Twitchell and Jurji, (pp. 4-7).

5. See Lebkicher, Rentz and Steineke, Twitchell and Jurji and Sanger.

6. During Field Museum North Arabian Desert Expedition, 1928, of which I was leader. Accompanying an Iraq Petroleum Company Survey Party under W.E. Browne, we made a broad 150-mile sweep from R.A.F. Landing Grounds "K" to "R," halting at Umm Wual (= "the Mother of Ibexes") and passing well south of Jebel Enaze (Anaze, Anazeh, or Anaiza) for which we were searching. At that time the Jordan-Saudi Arabian boundary was not defined, so that we presumed we were still inside Jordan and Iraq.

7. Formerly written Umm Muwal. This low black peak, rising about 50 feet above plain level, overlooks a large mud flat creased with many cracks.

8. See Henry Field (1953b). The great Wadi Hauran, which used to carry water across to the Euphrates near Haditha, originated on the southeastern slope of the Jebel Enaze. Our surveyor's cairn, built of yellow limestone blocks (many of them bearing camel brands (wasms) hammered into the soft stone) is the official tri-focal boundary point. See Field (1952a).

9. The flint was from Tell el-Hibr, about 50 miles due west near the Saudi Arabian-Jordan frontier. I visited Tell el-Hibr in June, 1950, and deduced that this was one of the principal sources of flint for prehistoric man.

10. The last of the skilled flint-knappers was Fred Snare of Brandon, Suffolk, England. At the suggestion of Mr. Henry Balfour, I visited him several times during 1928-30 to watch him at work. He used a wooden block as an anvil, his left knee

protected by a leather pad for pressure flaking. His direct ancestors were employed by William the Conqueror to repair flint walls of buildings; the reference is given in Domesday Book. I purchased a complete set of his working tools for FMNH.

11. See Thomas (1932b, p. 207).

12. These sands, northwest of Umm Quraiyin, lying in the Rub' al Khali, the "Empty Quarter," were crossed by Thomas on his great trans-desert camel ride from the Arabian Sea to the Qatar Peninsula. He writes (p. 207) that he was given a perfect flint arrowhead and a spearhead from the white and rolling sands of Sanam (approx. Lat. 21° N., Long. 51° 20′ E.). Thomas commented that flints are sometimes used as strike-a-lights in the Rub' al Khali. For large map of Rub' al Khali, see Thomas (1932b).

13. See Cornwall, (1946a, c and 1948).

14. O.A. Seager, Manager, Exploration Department, Arabian American Oil Col (Aramco) and his survey party.

15. This is the finest specimen I have seen from Southwestern Asia. The workmanship compares favorably with the techniques developed in Ancient Egypt and by Danish draftsmen, for quartzite is much more difficult to flake than good quality flint.

16. In Field (1951a, p. 195) I gave the locality as east of Sulail (20° 3′ N. and 46° 16′ E.). This new correction now stands.

17. These were from 12 surface sites. The best specimens were presented to the Peabody Museum, Harvard. See Field, (1951a, p. 194-95).

18. See note 6.

19. During the Peabody Museum-Harvard Expedition to the Near East. As a guest of Aramco, I was driven along Tapline to Turaif with excursions to search for traces of ancient man and his cultures (see Field, 1951a, pp. 185-97 and 1956b, pp. 58-63).

20. For additional data on stone ruins, catchment basins (mahfur, pl. mahafir), tumuli and graves, inscriptions, wasms (pl. wusûm or wasmat), graffiti and localities where pottery was collected, see Field (1951a, pp. 185-97, 1952a, 1953b, and 1956b). See also Philby, Bertram Thomas, Dickson, Doughty, Wilfred Thesiger, et al. In the Aramco files at Dhahran, George Rentz and his colleagues are compiling data on monuments, inscriptions, pottery, glass, etc. as well as flint implements and tribal information. In due course studies will be published. In 1929 Mr. and Mrs. W.E. Pearson of Aramco collected on the surface of large ruins west of Al Qatif many sherds, pottery, spindle whorls, Chinese and other copper coins, glass bracelets, many beads and several ostrich egg fragments. The distribution of stone circles and other monuments remains to be plotted and dates assigned.

21. This honey-colored flint occurs in large nuclei, up to ten inches in length; the excellent quality made flaking easy and as a result beautiful weapons and implements were manufactured near the quarry and carried far and wide across Europe. The nuclei are termed in French livres de beurre (= "pounds of butter") because of their color. Grande-Pressigny flint was one of the earliest forms of commerce.

22. As a supplement to my article (1951a), Twitchell generously gave me these notes for inclusion here.

23. For many references, see Doughty, Philby's publications, Twitchell and Jurji (pp. 75-78) and Sanger (pp. 25-26, 138-39).

24. See Musil (1928), and Field (1951a). Note: nos. 32-35 are from central and southern Nejd.

25. From observation as I did not want to touch it in order to respect Wahhabi wishes.

26. A characteristic feature of Kish crania.

27. Quoted from The Middle East, p. 29, 1953. However, in Lebkicher, Rentz and Steineke, p. 95, very different estimates are given: total for Saudi Arabia 3.5 millions with Al Hasa, Nejd and the Rub' al Khali 2.0 millions, the Hejaz 1.0 million and Asir 500,000 persons. The cities show a wide range of estimates: Mecca, 400,000-800,000; Hofuf, 150,000-200,000; Riyadh, 30,000-80,000; Jidda, 30,000-50,000; and Al Qatif, 20,000-30,000.

28. Excerpted from Mochi. Quoted from Coon (1948a, p. 409, notes 5-6).

29. See Field (1951b, pp. 13-27) and the tribes and sub-tribes, figs. 1-2.

30. For data on Northern Shammar Negroes, see Field (1951a, pp. 27-29).

31. See Field (1952b, pp. 92-133).

32. Near Nejran oasis (17° 30´ N. and 43° 45´ E.) on the western fringe of the Rub' al Khali, Philby (1949b) recorded many graffiti, including human figures, men on camels and possibly oryx.

33. In London on September 2, 1938, I had an audience with H.R.H. the Emir Saud, now King of Saudi Arabia. H.E. Sheikh Hafiz Wahba acted as interpreter. The purpose of this audience was to propose to King Ibn Saud an outline for The National Museum of Arabia. At the Emir Saud's suggestion, the following Plan was carried to the King at Riyadh:

Arabia holds the key to many scientific mysteries. Through the might and wisdom of His Majesty Ibn Saud, Arabia has once again become united as the bearer of the flaming torch of Mohammed. He has placed Arabia among the Council of Nations. The sands of the desert contain scientific treasures--facts upon which History and Prehistory can be re-written. Whence the Beni Hilal? Whence indeed? The searcher after truth must be encouraged. There is no area of the habitable globe, which is as little known as the vast peninsula of Arabia. In ancient times the great wadis of the Gezireh carried life-giving water through the now barren tracts of wilderness. Stone implements, fashioned by the skillful hand of Prehistoric Man tens of thousands of years ago, have been found from Kurdistan to the Mediterranean. As leader of three Field Museum Expeditions (1927, 1928, and 1934), I found hundreds of flint implements from the gorges of Zakho, Aqra, Rowandiz, and Sulaimaniya in northeastern Iraq, westward from Rutba Wells to Damascus, southward from Damascus to Maan, and eastward to the Wadi Bayir and Al Jafar, home of Mohammed Abu Tayi of the Huwaitat. In my opinion the Wadi Sirhan and Central Arabia must contain further evidence of Prehistoric Man. Arabia lies on this great route linking Southwestern Asia with Africa. Who are the modern inhabitants of Arabia? How does the basic element in Arabia compare to those of their neighbors? What is the true position of the Arab in relation to the peoples of Asia, Africa, and Europe? Arabia holds the answer to these questions. In addition, the study of Anthropology in Arabia would reveal the following and other data: (a) the history of each tribe; (b) the genealogy of each important Sheikh; (c) the names of the tribes and sub-tribes with distribution maps showing winter and summer quarters; (d) the physical relationships of the tribes; (e) the variations in language and dialect; (f) the important folk songs, especially those accompanying the rababa; (g) primitive medicine and its folklore; and (h) whence the Beni Hilal?

Zoology. The remarkable collections made by H. St. J. Philby and Bertram Thomas reveal the wide diversity of animal genera and species in Arabia. Furthermore, the peculiar adaptation of these animals to desert life and conditions make them of great scientific interest and importance. Among mammals, the oryx, gazelle, wolf fox, jackal, leopard and hyena are the most important. In addition, however, a study of the reptiles, amphibians and fishes will undoubtedly yield many new species and some new genera. A special study of the horse would also be of value for the sake of comparison with ancient and modern horses in adjoining countries. No detailed study of the Arabian camel has yet been made. Near Rutba Wells in 1934 I collected 18 camel skulls. This series proves to be of considerable scientific value. The birds, especially the ostrich and insects, particularly locusts, will prove important as already shown by the collections of Philby and Thomas. The exact relationships between the animals of Southwestern Asia and Africa can only be determined after Arabian collections become available. Arabia also holds the answer to these questions.

Botany. The flora shows many peculiarities and special adaptations to wilderness and true desert conditions. A collection of herbarium specimens with native names should be made so that accurate determinations, together with distribution maps, can be published. Useful plants and drugs should also be obtained. Arabia also holds the key to these problems.

Geology. There are many special desert phenomena which should be photographed and illustrated with specimens. This has no relation to oil and minerals. Arabia will yield many of these specimens.

Plan. In view of the foregoing outline I beg leave to suggest to your Majesty the foundation of The National Museum of Arabia at Riyadh. A house with six rooms would suffice for the purpose. Each room would be devoted to one branch of scientific research, namely, Anthropology, Zoology, Botany, Geology. There would also be a Library and an Office, thus requiring six rooms in all. In order to train your personnel to maintain this Museum I suggest that you select three intelligent young men to take over the duties. They could be sent to the University of Chicago, where they could be trained in these subjects and by spending part of their time in Field Museum of Natural History, also in Chicago, they could learn not only how to collect the specimens but also how to organize them in your National Museum. As a precedent, the Governments of Iraq and Iran already have students at the University of Chicago. After the three "Saudi Arabian Fellows" have received their training, they will return to Riyadh to begin collecting specimens and data. The Fellows will accompany the specimens to Field Museum of Natural History, where they will learn how to identify them and prepare their reports for publication. Some specimens, notably the insects, will have to be sent to the British Museum for identification. As usual the type specimens will be retained by the identifier, but a duplicate set will be returned to The National Museum of Arabia for the permanent collections. The question of the publications will have to be determined later, but an English as well as an Arabic text must be given.

Conclusion. To summarize briefly, I believe that a program of this general character would contribute markedly to the study of the Natural Sciences and thus advance the sum total knowledge of mankind. As sponsor of this project Your Majesty would receive the everlasting gratitude of scientific workers throughout the world. Arabia would at long last reveal some of her precious secrets.

———————

Word was received several months later through Sheikh Hafiz Wahba that King Ibn Saud was "favorably inclined to this proposal, but that the time was not ripe." In 1948 I again discussed this proposal with Sheikh Hafiz Wahba in Cairo, who was en route from London to Riyadh. Again the King demurred.

34. For general references, see The Middle East, pp. 45-46, 1953; GE, pp. 267-78, 1954; and Dickson. The latter is now a standard reference work on the Beduins of Kuwait and Saudi Arabia and many observations on the Arabs of southern Iraq. For fauna, see GE, p. 272, 1954. For notes, see Field (1951c, pp. 92-93).

35. Quoted from The Middle East, p. 45, 1953. However, GE, p. 267, 1954 the figure of 6,000 square miles is given.

36. Quoted from The Middle East, p. 45, 1953. The figures in 1951 are given in GE, p. 268, 1954, as about 170,000 with 150,000 in Kuwait town.

37. Quoted from GE, pp. 267-68, 1954.

38. Near Hafar al-Batin in Saudi Arabia in June, 1950, I collected a few worked flints of poor quality and technique, indicating the presence of Stone Age man to the south of Kuwait. See Field, 1956b, p. 59.

39. The finest specimens from their collection were presented to the Peabody Museum, Harvard.

40. Jebel Gurain (= the "twin-horned"), so called because of its two low curving peaks, stands at the extreme southern end of Kuwait overlooking the eastern Neutral Zone, which belongs to Kuwait and Saudi Arabia. On the southern and eastern slopes of Jebel Gurain I collected on May 22, 1950 some worked flints of poor quality.

41. On May 21, 1950, during the Peabody Museum-Harvard Expedition, I was guided to these ruins by Dr. R.M.S. Owen, resident geologist of Kuwait Oil Company (Kuoco). We were driven by W.E. Boyd of Kuoco.

42. For data on the Sulubba, see Field (1951b, pp. 29-36). See also "A Handbook of Arabia," Vol. 1, H.M. Stationery Office, London, 1920; Field (1943); Glubb; and Dickson (pp. 515-21).

43. See additional spellings in Field (1951b, p. 29).

44. For historical outline of the Persian Gulf with photographs of some ancient objects found, see Lebkicher, Rentz and Steineke (pp. 25-28). For most recent summary and 53 references, see Robert H. Dyson; also article by Gordon.

45. For the best account of Bahrain, see Belgrave including select Bibliography, pp. 131-32. From this we have drawn freely in the following passages. See also GE, pp. 255-65, 1954. For Iran's claim to the sovereignty of Bahrain (Bahrayn), see Khadduri. For article on Arab dhows with excellent Bibliography, see Bowen.

46. The "Mountain of Smoke" is so called because of the mist and haze which often surrounds the base during the hot summer, thereby making it appear quite lofty.

47. For additional details, see Belgrave (pp. 27-28) and GE, pp. 255-56, 1954.

48. See Government of Bahrain Census, March 3, 1950, pp. 1-15.

49. In a private communication.

50. For description of antiquities, see Belgrave (pp. 58-69). For references, see Cornwall (1943, 1944, 1946b and 1948), Durand and Mackay see additional references, in Belgrave, pp. 131-32. For history of Bahrain Islands, see Belgrave, pp. 76-87.

51. For summary, see Field (1951c, pp. 93-95).

52. See Kuml, Arbog for Jysk Arkaeologisk Selskab, pp. 106-15, Aarhus, 1954. In Danish and English. For description of other Danish Expedition excavations on Bahrain, see articles by Glob, in Kuml, pp. 92-105, 142-53, 164-69, and those by T.G. Bibby, pp. 116-41 and 154-63, Aarhus, 1954. All articles in Kuml are in Danish and English. Attention is called to the discovery of the skeleton of a young camel, with the legs chopped off. Bibby (pp. 140-41) believes this to have been a sacrifice, a custom recorded only by Hassan ibn Thabit at the beginning of the seventh century of our era.

53. During the Peabody Museum-Harvard Expedition, 1950. See Field, 1956b, pp. 51-53.

54. For general references, see The Middle East, p. 44, 1953, and GE, pp. 287-89, 1954. See also Melamid; Persian Gulf Pilot, pp. 8, 191-92, 1942, and Field, 1956b, p. 55. For references to his journey from Salala on the Arabian Sea to Doha with description of southeastern Qatar, see Thomas (1932b). For tribal map, see Field, 1956b, p. 54.

55. Quoted from The Middle East, p. 44. A.J. Wilton, Political Officer in Doha, gave me on May 28, 1950, the same figure quoted for 1951 in GE, p. 287, 1954.

56. Dictated at Dukhan during Peabody Museum-Harvard Expedition, 1950, by blind Sheikh Mansur and his two sons. See also Field (1951c, p. 98, footnote 28).

57. For additional list by Dr. R.V. Browne, IPC geologist, see Field (1951c, p. 98, footnote 28).

58. Quoted from GE, p. 287, 1954.

59. Administrative center; headquarters of M.A. Jacomb, British Political Officer.

60. For a list of Beduin tribes and sub-tribes, see Field, (1951c, pp. 96-97).

61. Subsidiary of Iraq Petroleum Co.

62. During my visit to Umm el-Kahab Wells, northeast of Dukhan, and across to Umm Said, Doha and back via Duhail and Rut al-Faras to Dukhan, I could find no worked flints, although outside a deep (150 feet) cave near Kilometer 67 from Dukhan to Umm Said some flints of poor quality lay scattered on the surface. Dr. R.V. Browne, IPC geologist, informed me that he had never seen any worked flints of Qatar. In addition, Colonel W.E. Browne, former IPC surveyor of Qatar, wrote that he had also never seen any flint tools or man-made flakes on this peninsula.

63. Ruins, probably Portuguese or later, are recorded near Ras Uzairij, on the northeast coast at Az Zubair, Halwan, Al Rebaija, and Fahahil, and at Umm al-Hul between Umm Said and Doha. Along the coast many ruined villages may be seen.

64. For tribal list, see Field (1951c, pp. 96-97). For tribal map, see Field, 1956b, p. 54. At El Afi near Umm Said I measured an Al Manasiri, aged 35: GOL, 188; GB, 141; MFD, 123; Biz.B. 138; Big. B. 111; TFH, 137; UFH, 77; NH, 58; NB, 36; EH, 60; and EB, 30. Skin color, swarthy; hair form curly, texture medium, head hair quantity, double plus, body hair absent, some grayness on head and beard, hair and beard very dark brown or black; eye color dark brown, sclera clear; eyebrow concurrency absent, browridges small, nasal profile straight, tip thickness and alae average; occlusion marked overbite; teeth lost six, wear double plus, caries some, crowding plus; and ear lobe attached, size and protrusion average.

65. See Field (1936).

66. See Field (1951b).

67. See Field (1952b, pp. 96-105 and 118-21).

68. For general references, see GE, pp. 311-15, 1954; The Middle East, p. 43, 1953; Field (1951c, pp. 99-102 and 1956b, pp. 55-57), Melamid, O'Shea, Thesiger (1950b, pp. 137-71), and The Persian Gulf Pilot, pp. 158-82, ninth edition, London Admiralty, 1942. Note: Bertram Thomas crossed from Muscat to Sharja in 1926 by following the coast to Sohar and then due west through the Hajar Mountains and north to the Persian Gulf.

69. For list, see The Middle East, p. 43, 1953 and Field 1951a.

70. The IPC geologists, who surveyed the Trucial Oman Coast from Ras Rakan to Al Arij and south and west to the Qatar Peninsula found no stone implements, no traces of ancient man. This information was conveyed in a private communication.

71. During the Peabody Museum-Harvard Expedition, 1950. See Field, 1951c.

72. For general references, see The Middle East, p. 42, 1953; GE, pp. 278-86 with map and nine references; and Persian Gulf Pilot, p. 7, 1942. Note: in 1926 Bertram Thomas crossed from Muscat to Sharja on Trucial Oman Coast.

73. Excerpted from the Encyclopedia Britannica, fourteenth edition, Vol. 16, p. 785, 1929.

74. Excerpted from Persian Gulf Pilot, p. 7, 1942.

75. Ruus is plural of Ar. Ras = head; cape; projecting point, above or below water.

76. For sketch map of Dhufar and central Qara Mountains, see Thomas (1932b, p. 101). For complete list of fauna collected in Qara Mountains of northern Dhufar, see Thomas (1932b, p. 105) and Appendixes. The Mammals included five hyenas, three foxes, one wolf, two conies, one badger, two tree rats, and two tree bats. For history of Dhufar, see Thomas (1932b, pp. 8-16). In Dhufar (Dhofar), Mahri and on the island of Socotra, Coon (1948b, p. 403 quoting Thomas, 1932b) writes

that pre-Arabic Semitic languages survive. These are Mahri, spoken by the Mahra and Socotrans, and Shahari by the hill-people behind Dhufar. Other early Semitic dialects seem to be affiliated with these two language groups.

77. Quoted from the Encyclopedia Britannica, fourteenth edition, p. 785, 1929.

78. Quoted from GE, p. 280, 1954.

79. In a private communication dated May 3, 1953, Miss Gertrude Caton Thompson called my attention to these axes, one of which Thesiger found, the other he purchased. For their analyses, see Campbell-Smith in GJ, Vol. 98, April, 1947. Miss Caton Thompson bought similar polished nephrite axes in Wadi Amd in the Hadhramaut; for reference, see Caton Thompson, Pl. 61. For recent references, see Field (1955b) and Zeuner (1954).

80. Another megalithic monument stands near El Jidd west of Rutba Wells in western Iraq. A standing Menhir dominates Barda Balkha east of Chemchemal in northeastern Iraq. Dolmens have been found by Pères Jaussen and Savignac in Jordan, principally in the Shobek-Kerak area.

81. See Field (1952a). See also Thomas (1932b).

82. Keith and Krogman (1932, p. 316) gives the following measurements and indices for the Hasik skull: GOL 171.0; GB 137.0; HH 133.5; OH 114.5; UFH 61.0(?); Biz. B. 123.2; NH 47.0; NB 22.8; OW 39.5; OH 32.2; CI 80.12; LHI 76.8; NI 48.5; OI 81.5; and capacity 1365 cc. For profile and view from above, see Thomas (1932b, figs. 7, 9).

83. Krogman, in Thomas (1932b, p. 316) gives the following measurements and indices for the Omani skull: GOL, 162.8; GB 141.5; HH 137.0; OH 116.5; UFH 71.0; Biz. B. 127.0; NH 56.5; NB 24.6; OW 39.02; OH 35.0; CI 86.9; LHI 84.1; NI 43.6; OI 89.7; and capacity 1300 cc.

84. Quoted by Keith and Krogman, in Thomas (1932b, p. 325).

85. See Leys and Joyce.

86. For racial type photographs of an Omani, see Thomas (1932b, figs. 2-3) compared with profiles of an Armenian (fig. 4) and a Madrasi (fig. 5).

87. The Foundation for the Study of Man has recently begun work in Oman. Wendell Phillips writes in a letter dated June 3, 1956 as follows: "When I was in the northern part of the Province of Dhofar, Sultanate of Muscat and Oman in Bait Kathir territory in 1954, I found a flint implement which, I presented to Sultan Said bin Taimur, who very generously presented it to me. This fine specimen (3-1/2 x 1.0 inches) tapers to a point and shows excellent pressure-flaking. If I remember rightly, the area was near the Ducca structure where Cities Service drilled its first test well."

88. Bertram Thomas made his historic journey across the Rub' al Khali from Salala in Dhufar Province of Oman to Doha on the Qatar Peninsula.

89. For large map of the Empty Quarter, see Thomas (1932b). For racial type photographs, see figs. 10-22.

90. This confirms Seligman's earlier work during 1917.

91. Quoted from Thomas (1932b, pp. 325-26). For distribution map, see 1932b, p. 330.

92. Seligman, p. 214.

93. Quoted from Thomas (1932b, p. 329).

94. Note the hyperdolichocephalic Hureida crania from the Hadhramaut attributed to a period about 600 B.C.

95. For general references see The Middle East, pp. 33-40, with map; Encyclopedia Britannica, fourteenth edition, for Aden, Vol. 1, pp. 164-65 and for Hadramaut, Vol. 11, pp. 63-64, 1929, by Philby. For description and historical outline of Hadhramaut, see Sanger (pp. 218-34). For geology, see Little. For description and map, see GE, pp. 235-36, 1954. For references, see Philby (1938) and Thesiger (1946 and 1948-49a-c) and Thomas (1932a). For fauna in the Rub' al Khali, see Thomas (1932b, pp. 236-39 and Appendix II).

96. See Philby, 1928, p. 63.

97. See D. van der Meulen and H. von Wissmann.

98. See Rickards, whom I knew in Iraq; he was interested in archeology and natural history and collected material in Ethiopia and South Arabia. An air accident ended his brilliant career.

99. See Doreen and W.H. Ingrams; many references.

100. See References.

101. See G. Caton Thompson and Elinor W. Gardner.

102. In August, 1950, Major T.A. Altounyan of the Iraq Petroleum Co. led a survey party during December 1949 - January 1950, into the Hadhramaut. He purchased this Spartan bronze figurine during this journey. For a published photograph by Major R.A.B. Hamilton, see Beazley's article in Man, no. 68, 1943. Miss Gertrude Caton Thompson, in a private communication dated May 3, 1953, wrote that this figurine was offered in 1939 to Major Hamilton by a Beduin for 200 rupees. He photographed it. Martin Robertson and Winifred Lamb confirmed that this figurine was Spartan. In London during 1950 Major Altounyan gave me an opportunity to study this superb figurine from Shibam. For recent data, see Berta Segall. See, Ingrams (1938c and Field (1955b).

104. See Huzayyin.

105. On December 15, 1947, during the University of California African Expedition, Huzayyin and I found an open-air site near Kilometer 115 east of Ismailia on the main paved road to Israel. Here on a gravel-covered slope near the western end of Jebel Maghara we collected a number of microlithic flint crescents within a small area, indicating a Mesolithic workshop. These may have been tips for reed shafts serving as arrows. See Field (1948).

106. See Freya Stark.

107. See W.H. Ingrams (1936b).

108. In 1928 I found small obsidian and cherty cores in "Y" trench at Kish during the Field Museum-Oxford University Joint Expedition. Microlithic cores have also been found as far east as the Vindyha Hills of India.

109. See Morant in Caton Thompson (1944, pp. 107-10 and Pls. 46-48).

110. Quoted by Coon (1948a) from L.W.C. Van den Berg, Le Hadhramout et les Colonies arabes dans l'Archipel Indien, Batavia, 1896.

111. See GE, pp. 235-53, 1954; especially 28 references, pp. 252-53. See also Sanger (pp. 213-34).

112. As an anonymous description, in Field (1932, pp. 859-71). See also the excellent racial type photographs.

113. See Ingrams (1938b, pp. 638-51).

114. For general references, see The Middle East, pp. 35-40, 1953; GE, pp. 234-53, 1954. Note two maps by Raisz and 28 references. See also Sanger (pp. 213-34). For historical references, see Lane and Serjeant. See Bibliography with list of Far Eastern sources. For maps, see GSGS 3892 surveyed in 1891-94 and 1901-1904; O.S. 1930, scale one inch to four miles, or 1:253,440.

115. Quoted from The Middle East, p. 37, 1953.

116. In the Museum of Archaeology and Ethnology, Cambridge University.

117. During Field Museum North Arabian Desert Expeditions, 1927, 1928, and 1934.

118. During Peabody Museum-Harvard Expedition, 1950.

119. For general references, see The Middle East, p. 41; GE, pp. 316-329 with 25 references; and Norman E. Crump in Encyclopedia Britannica, fourteenth edition, Vol. 23, pp. 885-86, 1929. For excellent descriptions and photographs of the land and the people, see Clark and Hoogstraal. See also Sanger (pp. 235-79).

120. Quoted from Encyclopedia Britannica, p. 885, 1929. For anthropometric data on the Yemeni Jews, see Weissenberg.

121. The Middle East, p. 41, quoted 3 - 4 million and GE, p. 318 gives figures of 3 - 7 millions.

122. See Sanger (pp. 236-42).

Chapter XI: IRAN

1. A detailed description of the land, a summary of historical references to the peoples from Herodotus to A.D. 1938, a description of the peoples (including the tribes), the physical anthropology of ancient and modern inhabitants, and notes on the Prehistory have been published (Field, 1939, pp. 1-706) together with statistical tables, maps, indexes, and a large Bibliography. Since this volume is readily available, this present section on Iran will be brief and in general be confined to data obtained from 1940-54. The best recent description, including geography and climate, population and socio-economic conditions, environment and sanitation, health services and medical facilities, diseases and Bibliography, is in Simmons, Whayne, Anderson, Horack and Thomas, GE, pp. 179-204, 1954. For a special study on the climates, see Ganji. For general geography and references, see Elwell-Sutton (pp. 6-13). For general descriptions and maps, see Field (1939, pp. 16-18), and Department of State OPA, July, 1952. Additional references have also been published by Ettinghausen (with 1954 Supplement) and Field (1953, 1955a, and 1956). For recent geographical description, see Popov (pp. 2-15). For economic summary and description of Near East Foundation survey of general village life and improvements in the Veramin district, 18 miles southeast of Tehran, see Hedley V. Cooke (pp. 233-58). See also "Report on the Seven-Year Development Plan" by Overseas Consultants Inc., New York, 1949. For economic structure, see Elwell-Sutton (pp. 63-71). For bibliographies on Iran, see Elwell-Sutton (p. 162). For data on tribes of western Iran, see Minorsky (pp. 73-80) with map and Plates. For supplementary Stone Age references, see Crowfoot and de Mecquenem. For additional titles obtained too late to include in References see: (a) Gideon Hadary and Karim Sai, Handbook of Agricultural Statistics of Iran, Bank Melli Iran Press, Tehran, 1949; (b) Iran Ministry of Education, Geography (in Persian), Iran Printing House, Tehran, 1942; (c) Mohammed J. Meimandi-Nejad, "Delimitation and characterization of the natural regions of Iran and application of ecological principles to land use improvement in those regions," M.S. Thesis, pp. 1-100, Catholic University, Washington, 1951; (d) Karim Sai, "L'Iran forestier," Revue du Bois, Vol. 4, no. 11, pp. 3-8, November, 1949 and no. 12, pp. 11-14, December, 1949; and (e) Louis Untereiner, The administrative environment of Iran, pp. 1-100, Center for Advanced Study in the Behavioral Sciences, Stanford, California, 1955.

2. See Persian Gulf Pilot (1942) under Anonymous.

3. See Field (1939, pp. 19-21) and Popov (pp. 15-18).

4. See Field (1939, pp. 22-25) and GE (p. 188), Elwell-Sutton (p. 10).

5. See Field (1939, p. 25). For a detailed description of the qanat system, see Beckett.

6. See Field (1939, pp. 26-28), Schmidt and GE (p. 187). For locust information, see Popov. For list of arthropod vectors, see GE, pp. 185-87; for rodents, pp. 187-88; and for mollusks, p. 188; see also pp. 169-70.

7. Quoted from The Middle East (1953, p. 249). See also Field (1939, pp. 32-34) and Elwell-Sutton (pp. 14-16). For demography, see Mashayekhi, Mead and Hayes (pp. 149-65).

8. See Elwell-Sutton (pp. 16-25).

9. See Elwell-Sutton (pp. 72-81).

10. For historical outline by Sir Denison Ross, see Field (1939, pp. 30-32). See also Elwell-Sutton (pp. 40-56) and for general description, history, economic survey, and Bibliography see The Middle East (1953). For excavations in Azerbaijan, see Burton Brown (1948) and for comparative stratigraphy, see McCown.

11. Geologist and surveyor for the Anglo-Iranian Oil Company. These flints were collected on Christmas day, 1933. The location was Lat. 29° 8′ 7″ N. and Long. 53° 51′ 27″ E. See Field (1939, pp. 552-53).

12. Location Lat. 29° 18´ N. and Long. 52° 45´ E. See Field (1939, p. 553).

13. During Field Museum Anthropological Expedition to the Near East, 1934, (Henry Field, leader and Richard A. Martin, assistant) and accompanied by Donald McCown, Oriental Institute Expedition to Persepolis (Ernst Herzfeld, leader). See Field (1939, pp. 554-56).

14. Professor of Anthropology, University Museum, Philadelphia.

15. Known as Ghar-i-Kamarband, five miles west of Behshahr about 120 feet above the Caspian.

16. Excerpted from Coon (1952a, p. 231).

17. Members included: Henry Field (leader), Robb White, Habibullah Samadi of the Department of Antiquities; Khoresh Shahbaz, U.S. Embassy interpreter; and Yusuf Lazar, animal and plant collector. Transportation facilities were provided by the Iranian Army through the courtesy of the late General Ali Razmara. See Field (1951a, pp. 91-92). See also Field (1951b, p. 15 and 1956b).

18. From the University Museum, Philadelphia, and financed by the American Philosophical Society and with the support of the National Museum of Antiquities in Tehran. The staff included Mrs. Coon, Mr. and Mrs. Louis B. Dupree, Habibullah Samadi and Sohail Azari.

19. This section has been excerpted from Coon (1952b, pp. 179-80). See also Dupree (pp. 250-57) and Archaeology, Vol. 4, no. 2, pp. 116-18.

20. For distribution map of caves and rockshelters, see Field (1951b, p. 15).

21. I suggest the Bam-Kuh-i-Taftan area deserves special study. This high mountain (13,034 feet) must have been a landmark for Paleolithic man. For a description of Kuh-i-Taftan, see Sykes (1897, pp. 586-88 and 1902, pp. 354-55) and Field (1939, pp. 237, 242). Researches should also be conducted between Zahidan along the Makran Coast into the Punjab; this must have an ancient line of migration.

22. See Arne (1935a-b), Field (1939, pp. 257-77), Krogman (1937, 1939 and 1940a-b), Lebzelter, Vallois and Wulsin. Coon's Paleolithic skeletal material remains unpublished.

23. For a demographic study, see Mashayekhi, Mead and Hayes, pp. 149-65. For additional references, see Arutinov and Houssay.

24. During the Peabody Museum-Harvard Expedition to the Near East, 1950. See Field, 1956b.

25. Kurds I are from Zakho in northern Iraq; Kurds II from Rowandiz in northeastern Iraq; Kurds III from Kirkuk and Sulaimaniya; Kurds IV include Kurds I, II, and III; and Kurds V are from northwestern Iran. Lurs I are from the Pusht-i-Kuh and Lurs II from between Khurrumabad and Dorud in central Luristan. The Assyrians were studied in 1934 at Hinaidi Camp near Baghdad. The Chehar Lang of the Bakhtiari tribesmen were examined during April, 1950, in Khuzistan. Kurds I, II, III and IV and Lurs I and Assyrians were obtained during the Field Museum Anthropological Expedition to the Near East, 1934. Kurds V from the Sinneh area of northwestern Iran were recorded at Habbaniya in western Iraq. The Lurs II and the Bakhtiari were also measured during the Peabody Museum-Harvard Expedition to the Near East, 1950. See Field (1951c).

26. Quoted from Field (1951c).

27. See Field (1953b).

28. Calculated in the Statistical Laboratory, Peabody Museum, Harvard.

29. See Field (1939, Pl. 131).

30. Oshanin and Ginzberg told me in Moscow during June, 1945, that they were compiling large series of anthropometric data from the Pamirs and Altai region. We must hope that one day these data with photographs of racial types will be available for comparison.

Chapter XII. AFGHANISTAN

1. For the best description, two maps and medical bibliography, see GE (pp. 163-77); this includes geography and climate, population figures, socio-economic conditions, environment and sanitation, fauna and flora, and health and medical facilities. For map showing position in relation to Iran and Pakistan, see Fortescue-Foulkes (1953). For general references, see Ettinghausen (1952, pp. 39-40, 67, 72 and 83 and 1954 Supplement); and Bibliography No. 56, pp. 9-10, published by Department of State, January 2, 1951. For description of reconnaissance survey by the University Museum, Philadelphia (Rodney S. Young, leader), see Froelich Rainey (pp. 41-56). See also O.R. de Baer, "The Cambridge Expedition to Afghanistan, 1955," JRCAS, Vol. 43, pt. 2, pp. 121-25, April, 1956. For anthropogeographical, zoological and botanical references, see Field (1953, 1955, and 1956).

2. See GE (p. 164) and Stenz.

3. For agricultural development, see Vavilov and Bukinich.

4. See GE (pp. 169-70).

5. See GE (pp. 168-69).

6. See R.E.M. Wheeler (pp. 57-65).

7. See Carleton S. Coon, under Iran.

8. By A.P. Okladnikov.

9. See Davis, Dupree, Fairservis (1950a-b, 1951, 1952 and 1953), Frye and Wheeler.

10. See Bellew, Field (1939), Finn, Garson, Guha, Ripley and Ujfalvy. For data on the Hindu Kush Kafirs, see Herrlich (pp. 51-99). For history of Hazara Mongols, see Bacon (pp. 230-47).

11. Excerpted from Field (1939, pp. 601-602).

12. By Haddon (pp. 22 and 103).

13. For definition, see Haddon (p. 27).

14. Gordon T. Bowles returned in 1937 from a Peabody Museum-Harvard Expedition with measurements and photographs of several thousand individuals from Afghanistan along the southern slopes of the Himalayas to the Shan States of Burma. This valuable material remains unpublished.

15. Quoted in part from Field (1939, pp. 503-504).

16. Excerpted from Field (1939, p. 466 et seq.). For additional measurements and indices, see same reference and de Khanikoff (pp. 133-39).

17. Quoted from Field (1939, p. 601) but see original source for details.

Chapter XIII: BALUCHISTAN

1. Baluchistan was incorporated into West Pakistan on August 15, 1947 when Mohammed Ali Jinnah created this large Moslem State out of former British India. In this study of the easternmost region of our selected area, known as Southwestern Asia, it seemed desirable to indicate cultural and racial relationships into the Indus Valley, where flourished a great civilization contemporaneous with that of Egypt and Mesopotamia. We shall also include data on Ancient Man in India in order to show similar links further east and southeast of Baluchistan. In addition, since this territory adjoining southeastern Iran and southern Afghanistan is relatively little known, we shall include some evidence of the Chalcolithic period in order to present a clearer picture of the ancient and modern dwellers and their cultures. The description of Baluchistan is excerpted from the articles by Sir George MacMunn and Sir Percy Sykes in the Encyclopedia Britannica, fourteenth edition, pp. 5-10, 1929. For other data, see "The Administration Report of the Baluchistan Agency" (Annual) and the District Gazeteers of Baluchistan. For general description, see Curzon, de Cardi, Hedin, Holdrich, McMahon, Pithawalla, Pritchard and Tate (1897 and 1909). For geology, see Blanford and Vredenberg (1901 and 1904). For general bibliographies,

see Guha (1952), Ettinghausen (1952 and 1954 Supplement), and Field (1953, 1955, and 1956).

2. Takht-i-Sulaiman="The Throne of Solomon."

3. West Pakistan includes Sind, Baluchistan, the North-West Frontier Province, western Punjab, the princely State of Bahawalpur and a few other native states. Area, 365,907 square miles. Population in 1951, 75,687,000; these are 80.0 per cent Moslem, remainder Hindu and Sikh. Density per square mile, 206.8. Principal cities: Karachi, the capital, 1,005,000; and Lahore, 849,000. About 450,000 acres under cultivation. Languages: English, Bengali, Punjab, Urdu and Hindi. These data were excerpted from the IPA, pp. 598-99. For economic geography, see Das. During the Peabody Museum - Harvard Expedition in 1955 the Baluchistan States Union (BSU) included Makran, Kalat, Kharan, and Las Bela.

4. For Bibliography of Indian Botany, see Santapau.

5. Excerpted from Encyclopedia Britannica, fourteenth edition, pp. 5-10, 1929. For chronology of prehistoric northwest India, see Piggott (1946, pp. 8-26).

6. Quoted in Field (1939, pp. 54-55).

7. See Dudley Buxton and Rice (p. 84 et seq.). See also Piggott (1943 and 1946).

8. See Frankfort (pp. 40-47).

9. Sir Arthur Keith, in Hall and Woolley, Ur Excavations, Vol. 1, p. 216, Oxford, 1927; also quoted in Field (1939, p. 155).

10. See Haddon and Census of India (1921 et seq.).

11. For Stone Age references, see Piggott (1952, pp. 22-41 with notes and references, pp. 40-41); also for prehistoric and historical culture sequences. See also Zeuner (1950 and 1951) and the excellent account by Sahni who discusses in detail the Stone Age of Europe, India, Pakistan, and Burma. The Bibliography pp. 259-66 is valuable. See also Guha's Bibliography (1952). For special articles, see de Terra and Patterson on the Ice Age and associated human cultures; Sankalia, Subbarao and Deo on the archeological sequence in Central India with map of sites; Sankalia (1953) on the Godvari Paleolithic industry. According to "Indiagram" for March 16, 1954, issued by the Embassy of India, stone tools of a 10,000-year old culture have been discovered in Durgapur, in Burdwan District, West Bengal, by the Archaeological Department of the Government of India; these implements, of various types of quartz, chert, carnelian and rock-crystal, include blades, crescents, points, almond-shaped arrowheads, awls, round and notched scrapers, burins and small axes. For de Terra's "Proto-Neolithic" industry from Choli in Maheshwar area (22°11′ N. and 75° 56′ E.) in Madhya Bharat, see SJA, Vol. 9, no. 4, p. 349; for microliths from Navda Toli on the left bank of the Narmada opposite Maheshwar, see SJA, Vol. 9, no. 4, p. 350; and for Ceylon, see P.E.P. Deranyigala, "Some aspects of the Prehistory of Ceylon, Pt. 3, the Balangoda culture, SZ, Vol. 27, Pt. 1, pp. 125-31 with 13 plates. See Pls. 5-6 for frontal bone and tooth of Homo sapiens balangodensis. This Chapter was written prior to my crossing from Pasni to Quetta, March-April, 1955, during the Peabody Museum-Harvard Expedition. See my forthcoming Report on this reconnaissance survey across Makran and Kalat to be published in Peabody Museum Papers. During the final editorial revision in June, 1956, I received from Dr. A. Gosh, Director-General of Archaeology in New Delhi, the Special Jubilee Number of "Ancient India" no. 9, 1953. Many articles are of special importance especially the following: (a) Indian Archaeology from Jones to Marshall 1784-1905 by Sourindranath Roy; (b) Fifty years of the Archaeological Survey of India by A. Ghosh; (c) Progress in Prehistory by V.D. Krishnaswami; (d) Protohistoric investigation by B.B. Lal; and (e) Exploration of Historical sites by Y.D. Sharma. See also D.H. Gordon, "The pottery industries of the Indo-Iranian border: a restatement and tentative chronology," AI, nos. 10-11, pp. 157-91, 1954-55. This was also received during June, 1956. Another new reference of importance in the same issue

(pp. 1-151) is "Excavation at Hastinapura and other explorations in the Upper Ganga and Sutlej Basins, 1950-52" by B.B. Lal.

12. In four broadcast talks on "Prehistory in India," Zeuner gives a clear summary on each of the following subjects: (a) Archaeology, Prehistory, and Geology; (b) Early Man in Gujerat; (c) soil and climate; and (d) Stone Age Man in India. The student is referred to the following sources, which are given here, because of the difficulty of obtaining this monograph published in Poona. V. Krishaswamy, "Stone Age India," AI, no. 3, pp. 11-49, 1947 and B.B. Lal, "Exploration and excavations: I, Prehistoric and Protohistoric Periods," Archaeology in India, Chapter 2, Ministry of Education, Publication no. 66, Delhi, 1950. See also H.D. Sankalia, "Investigations into Prehistoric Archaeology of Gujerat," Baroda, 1946 and Zeuner (1950). For excavations in Baluchistan, see Stein (1934) and Hargreaves. For New Stone Age see R.E.M. Wheeler, "Brahmagiri and Chandravalli, 1947: Megalithic and other cultures in Mysore State," AI, no. 4, pp. 188-310, 1947-48 and B. Subbarao, "Stone Age Cultures of Bellary," DCDS, no. 7, Poona, 1948. For additional general references, see J. Coggin Brown, Catalogue of Prehistoric Antiquities in the Indian Museum at Calcutta, 1917; L.A. Cammiade and M.C. Burkitt, "Fresh light on the Stone Ages of Southeast India," Antiquity, Vol. 4, pp. 327-39, 1930; R.B. Foote, The Geology of Baroda State, Madras, 1898 and The Foote Collection of Indian Prehistoric and Protohistoric Antiquities with notes on their ages and distribution, Government Press, Madras, 1916; A.S. Gadre, Archaeology in Baroda, 1934-47, State Press, Baroda, 1947; B. Subbarao, Baroda through the Ages, Baroda, 1953; D.H. Gordon, "The Mesolithic industries of India," Man, Vol. 38, no. 19, pp. 21-24, February, 1938; L.A. Krishna Ayer, "The Prehistoric Archaeology of Kerala," Modern Review, pp. 182-90, March, 1946; Panchanan Mitra, "Prehistoric Archaeology in North-West India," AI, no. 1, pp. 8-26, 1946; and Helmut de Terra's references, in Sahni (p. 265). These have been selected from Sahni's Bibliography; attention is called to references on Ceylon by Deranyigala, F. Lewis, N.A. and H.V.V. Noone, H. Parker, J.A. Pole, F. Sarasin and E.J. Wayland; and to references on Burma in Sahni (pp. 138-42 with map of principal Paleolithic and Neolithic sites (fig. 50 on p. 141), and to Hallam L. Movius in TAPS, Vol. 32, pt. 3, pp. 341-92, 1943, and Vol. 38, no. 4, pp. 329-420, 1949.

13. Microliths have been found in the lowest levels at Kish in Iraq, on the surface near Jebel Maghara in northwestern Sinai, in the Hadhramaut, and in the Caucasus, etc. See also under Mesolithic in this Chapter. During the Peabody Museum-Harvard Expedition, 1955, I excavated Microliths from Kapoto rockshelter south of Kalat. Surface microliths were collected on ancient mounds in from north of Panjgur to south of Quetta.

14. See Sahni (pp. 144, 152-54, 166) and Mackay (1939, and previous vols.) and Sir John Marshall. For explorations in Sind, see Majumdar. For excavations: at Chanhu-Daro, see Mackay (1943); at Harappa, see Wheeler and Vats.

15. See Hargreaves, McCown, Piggott (1943, 1946, and 1947) Ross and Stein (1929 and 1931).

16. Excerpted from the article by Sir George MacMunn in "Baluchistan" from the Encyclopedia Britannica, fourteenth edition, p. 7, 1929. See M. Longworth-Dames (1904) and B.S. Guha. For blood groups of peoples of northwest Pakistan, see Chaudri, Ilkin, Mourant, and Walby.

17. Also known as Kej, Katz, or Kash Kaian of Arabic medieval geography, and a part of the ancient Kaini kingdom. The prefix Kej or Kash denoted low-level flats or valleys.

18. Of Tatar origin.

19. Excerpted from Field, (1939, p. 610). See Curzon (Vol. 1, p. 228, and Vol. 2, pp. 258-59, 262-63, 269-70, and 592-94). See Bellew and Longworth-Dames (1904).

20. In Field (1939, pp. 444-84). See also description of racial position and relationships of peoples of Baluchistan to surrounding racial groups and peoples in Field (1939, pp. 445-90) and Cappieri.

21. No attempt has been made to compile all available anthropometric data on India, but some figures from Guha have been tabulated in Field (1939, p. 461 and 479). See also references in Guha (pp. 155 et seq.). For blood groups, see Boyd (p. 171).

During the Peabody Museum-Harvard Expedition to West Pakistan, 1955, I recorded anthropometric data on 275 male Baluchis and Brahuis in Makran and Kalat. Mrs. Field took an excellent series of racial type photographs of this series. The results will appear in Peabody Museum Papers.

For additional information on sites in West Pakistan see, "General Archaeological Map of Western Pakistan Circle Showing Ancient Monuments and Sites" compiled in Lahore by Wali Ullah Khan, August 19, 1948 for the Director-General of Archaeology. Scale one inch = 21.03 miles. This map includes sites attributed to the Prehistoric, Buddhist, Hindu, Mohammedan, and Sikh periods. Two copies are available: one in Peabody Museum-Harvard; the other in my map collection. The original is in the Pakistan Department of Archaeology, Karachi.

Chapter XIV: COMPARATIVE DATA

1. See my "Bibliography, 1926-55" with 409 titles, including 88 microfilms, distributed privately during February, 1956.

2. Published by Carl C. Seltzer, PMP, Vol. 13, no. 13, 1936.

3. The following groups contained nine or less individuals, Ajemis, Iran (2), 161.5, Duhousset; Fellahin, Baiadieh, and Zeinieh, Egypt (4), 162.0, Chantre; Howeitat Beduins, Matarieh, Egypt (8), 162.0, Chantre; Armenians, Iraq (6), 163.07, Smeaton and Field; Dizfulis, Dizful, Iran (9), 163.3, Houssay; Ajemis, Iran (9), 165.0, Chantre; Persians, Iran (5), 165.8, Fedchenko; Gypsies, northern Iraq (6), 166.1, Field; Bakhtiari tribesmen, Khuzistan, Iran (4), 167.0, Gautier; Lurs, Iran (5), 168.0, Houssay; Turkoman Arabs, northern Iraq (6), 168.17, Ehrich; Fellahin, Giza, Egypt, (5), 170.0, Chantre; Osetes, Ellis Island, New York, (7), 170.26, Kennard; Turkoman Kurds, northern Iraq (7), 171.43, Ehrich; Bakhtiari tribesmen, Khuzistan, Iran (3), 171.5, Houssay.

4. In Races of Man, p. 107. London, 1924.

5. Contributions to the Anthropology of Iran, FMNH, Anthropological Series, Vol. 29, Pt. 2, pp. 451-54, 1939.

6. Ibid., pp. 67, 74, 114-15, 157, 286, 390, and 466. See also Fig. 7 on p. 73 where the Armenian type of cradle is shown.

7. The following groups of 168 males, arranged in ascending order, had nine or less individuals or the number was not given: Fellahin (5), Giza, Egypt, 72.68, Chantre; Turkoman Kurds (7), Northern Iraq, 73.29, Ehrich; Lurs (?), Iran 73.57, Houssay; Arabs (6) Giza, Egypt, 73.76, Myers; Howeitat (Huwaitat) Beduins (8), Matarieh, Egypt, 74.21, Chantre; Turkomans (6), northern area, Iraq, 74.45 Kappers; Fellahin (?), Qena, Egypt, 74.48, Craig; Fellahin (?), Giza, Egypt, 74.75, Craig; Fellahin (?), Beheira, Egypt, 75.2, Craig; Fellahin (4), Baiadieh and Zeinieh, Egypt, 75.52, Chantre; Fellahin (?), Dakahlia, 75.69, Craig; Tribal Arabs (8), Iraq, 76.3, Rassam; Gypsies (6), northern Iraq, 77.1, Field; Kurd (1), Caucasus, 77.3, Chantre; Ajemis (?), Iran, 77.74, Chantre; Beduins (7), Mosul Liwa, Iraq, Rassam; Bakhtiari (1), Iran, 78.4, Krischner; Lur (1), Iran, 78.4, Krischner; Bautahari (1), South Arabia, 79.12, Thomas; Turkoman Arabs (6), Iraq, 79.43, Ehrich; Somalis (6), South Arabia, 79.61, Thomas; Arabs (6), Bahrain Island, Persian Gulf, 80.72, Kappers; Osetes (4), Osetia, 80.86; Jews (?), Damascus, Syria, 80.9, Weissenberg;Karachais (5), Caucasus, 81.5, Von Erckert; Brahui

(Sarawán) (?), Baluchistan, 81.5, Haddon; Yafi (5), South Arabia, 81.68, Thomas; Turkomans (?), Iran, 82.0, De Khanikoff; Arabs (?), Yemen, 82.5, Mugnier; Harasi (1), South Arabia, 83.33, Thomas; Bakhtiari (2), Iran, 83.8, Danilov; Plains Osetes (?), Caucasus, 84.2, Bunak; Ansaries (?), Lebanon, 84.43, Kappers; Mountain Jews (?), Caucasus, 84.7; Assyrians (5), Caucasus, 85.0, Von Erckert; Hazara (?), Afghanistan, 85.0, Haddon; Assyrians (5), 85.1, Von Erckert; Omanis (3), 85.18, Thomas; Mountain Jews (4), Daghestan, Caucasus, 85.3, Von Erckert; Alovi (?), Anatolia 85.67, Kappers; Lezghians (3), 85.9, Von Erckert; Tachtadshy Turks (?), Lycia, Turkey, 85.95, Von Luschan; Mashai (1), South Arabia, 86.20, Thomas; Bektashy Turks (?), Lycia, Turkey, 86.5, Von Luschan; Armenians (6), Iraq, 86.6, Smeaton and Field; Mahra (5), South Arabia, 86.67, Thomas; Kurds (5), Urmia, Iran, 86.68, Chantre; Kurds (5), Batumi, Caucasus, 88.1, Chantre; Shahari (9), South Arabia, 88.12, Thomas; Bakhtiari (4), Iran, 89.0, Duhousset; Qara (7), South Arabia, 89.12, Thomas; Bakhtiari (9), Iran, 89.32, Chantre; Al Kathiri (4), South Arabia, 90.32, Thomas; Bakhtiari (1), Iran, 91.0, Krischner; and Bakhtiari (1), Iran, 93.4, Krischner.

TABLE 1: MEASUREMENTS AND INDICES OF CRANIA IN WADI SOLAF, SOUTHWESTERN SINAI

No.	GOL	GB	CI	B-BH	MFD	Biz. B	NPH
1	192	128	66.7	...	107	137	65
2	188	130	69.1	132	95	123	67
3	184	124	67.3	...	97	127	..
4	171	127	74.2	134	90	120	62
5	181	122	67.4	136	88	120	60
6	185	128	69.1	...	103	124	..
7	178	122	68.5	125	90	116	59
8	184	130	70.6	130	96	125	59
9	178	124	69.6	132	92	116	..
10	183	129	70.4	136	93	124	..
11	180	120	66.7	131	90	118	65
12	164	118	71.9	116	82	105	58
13	170	132	77.6	...	97	126	59
14	182	125	68.6	126	93	119	..
15	168	119	70.8	123	87	113	..
16	167	122	73.0	120	89	113	..
17	173	120	69.3	120	90	123	63
18	161	113	70.1	121	80	94	..
19	162	116	71.6	115	80	99	49

TABLE 2: MEASUREMENTS AND INDICES OF CRANIA IN WADI SOLAF, SOUTHWESTERN SINAI

No.	NH	NB	NI	LOH	LOB	LOI
1	44	41	93.1	29	41	70.7
2	48	25	52.0	29	35	82.8
3	56	27	48.2	29	34	85.2
4	47	24	51.0	25	37	67.5
5	48	22	45.8	25	32	78.1
6	58	28	48.2	23	35	65.7
7	49	24	48.9	26	32	81.2
8	47	24	51.0	29	38	76.3
9	48	23	47.9	23	37	62.1
10	51	26	50.9	30	38	78.9
11	53	35	44.2	33	35	94.2
12	46	23	50.2	27	29	93.1
13	52	27	51.9	27	38	71.0
14	55	24	43.6	27	33	81.8
15	50(?)	22	44.0(?)	25	32	78.1
16	47	22	46.8	23	29	79.3
17	49	23	46.9	25	32	78.1
18	..	..	....	..	..	....
19	41	21	51.2	21	30	70.0

TABLE 3: MEASUREMENTS AND INDICES OF CRANIA IN WADI SOLAF, SOUTHWESTERN SINAI

No.	ROH	ROB	F-PI	CM	UFI	C-FI	Z-FI
1	29	40	83.5	.....	47.4	107.0	78.1
2	29	36	73.0	150.0	54.4	94.6	77.2
3	29	34	78.2	.....	....	102.4	76.3
4	24	34	70.8	144.0	51.6	94.4	75.0
5	25	33	72.1	146.3	50.0	98.3	73.3
6	25	35	80.4	.....	....	96.8	83.0
7	26	34	73.7	141.6	50.8	95.0	81.2
8	29	36	73.8	148.0	47.2	96.1	76.8
9	19	34	74.1	144.6	....	93.5	79.3
10	28	35	72.0	149.3	....	96.1	50.9
11	31	32	75.0	143.6	55.0	98.3	76.2
12	29	36	69.4	132.6	55.2	88.9	78.0
13	23	37	73.4	.....	46.8	95.4	76.9
14	27	32	74.4	144.3	....	95.2	78.1
15	22	32	73.1	136.6	....	94.9	76.9
16	26	29	72.9	136.3	....	92.6	78.7
17	29	39(?)	75.0	137.6	51.2	102.5	73.1
18	..	..	70.7	131.6	....	83.1	85.1
19	21	30	68.9	131.0	49.4	85.3	80.8

TABLE 4: ANTHROPOMETRIC DATA ON BEDUINS AND JEBELIYEH IN SINAI

Measurements	No.	Beduins	No.	Jebeliyeh	No.	Towara
Age	148	40.60	73	38.85	..	......
Stature	67	165.72	42	167.01	63	165.80
Head breadth	150	139.72	73	138.64	63	139.18
Head length	150	193.74	73	192.15	63	191.30
Minimum frontal diameter	150	113.78	73	113.50	63	106.85
Bizygomatic diameter	150	132.80	73	133.25	63	129.20
Bigonial diameter	150	109.14	73	109.42	63	97.40
Total facial height	150	120.25	73	121.40	63	117.40
Upper facial height	150	70.95	73	69.65	63	60.56
Nasal height	150	54.86	73	54.34	63	50.18
Nasal breadth	150	36.65	73	35.87	63	39.11
Ear length	142	58.85	72	56.35	..	......
Ear breadth	142	35.33	72	33.59	..	......
Indices						
Cephalic	150	72.35	73	72.24	63	72.95
Fronto-parietal	150	81.22	73	82.21	..	......
Zygo-frontal	150	85.58	73	85.66	..	......
Zygo-gonial	150	82.06	73	82.45	..	......
Total facial	150	91.05	73	91.95	63	91.52
Upper facial	150	53.30	73	52.10	..	......
Nasal	150	66.86	73	66.70	63	78.20
Ear	142	60.50	72	59.80	..	......
Cephalo-facial	150	95.06	73	96.20	..	......
Fronto-gonial	150	96.05	73	96.90	..	......

TABLE 5: CRANIAL MEASUREMENTS AND INDICES OF SKHUL V

Measurements

Head length	192.0
Head breadth	144.0
Basi-bregmatic height	(126.0)
Minimum frontal diameter	100.0
Inter-orbital breadth	(110.0)
Bizygomatic breadth	146.0
Total facial height	130.0
Upper facial height	79.0
Nasal height	(56.0)
Nasal breadth	(52.0)

Indices

Cranial capacity	1518 cc.
Cephalic	75.0
Length-height	65.6
Breadth-height	87.5
Fronto-parietal	69.4
Total facial	89.0
Upper facial	54.1
Zygo-frontal	68.5
Zygo-gonial	67.1
Nasal	57.1

TABLE 6: MEASUREMENTS AND INDICES OF 331 MALES AND 33 FEMALES FROM PALESTINE

Measurements	Males	Females
Stature	168.73	156.72
Sitting height	85.25	80.68
Head length	185.51	177.42
Head breadth	147.46	144.25
Minimum frontal diameter	103.60	102.50
Bizygomatic breadth	136.15	126.51
Bigonial breadth	106.63	97.42
Total facial height	115.94	106.96
Upper facial height	68.32	67.50
Nasal height	46.14	45.99
Nasal breadth	35.13	31.29
Ear height	61.56	57.80
Ear breadth	36.16	34.31

Indices		
Cephalic	79.43	80.77
Fronto-parietal	70.24	70.69
Jugo-frontal	76.19	77.79
Jugo-gonial	76.19	76.29
Total facial	85.40	85.70
Upper facial	50.47	53.08
Nasal	76.88	68.86
Ear	36.16	.....

TABLE 7: MEASUREMENTS AND INDICES OF 135 BEDUINS IN JORDAN

Group	Locality	No.	Stature	Span	SH
Howeitat Beduins	Jazira	70	163.08	173.49	85.00
Beni Sakhr Beduins	Jazira	65	162.78	169.95	83.44

GOL	GB	HH	MFD	Biz. B	Big. B	TFH	UFH
192.42	145.12	123.46	106.22	131.25	105.26	115.10	67.00
189.87	142.51	123.70	104.06	130.60	102.90	120.15	68.90

NH	NB	EH	EB	RSH	CI	TFI	UFI	NI	EI
51.66	33.92	60.39	32.63	51.68	75.51	87.95	50.57	66.34	54.36
52.94	33.38	60.93	32.45	51.18	74.94	91.60	52.85	63.90	53.82

TABLE 8: MEASUREMENTS AND INDICES OF JORDAN TRIBESMEN AND VILLAGERS

Tribe	No.	GOL	GB	CI
Shiab near Sareeh	44	188	145	77.2
Nussour near Es Salt	58	185	143	77.5
Hajayya	13	194	144	74.4
Howeitat (Huwaitat)	49	193	144	74.6
Audat (sub-tribe of Howeitat)	26	186	143	76.9
Beni Hassan	97	186	145	77.7
Beni Sakhr (Sukhr)	13	192	144	74.9
Beni Atiyeh	10	189.8	141	74.1
Adwan near Es Salt	41	187	145	77.6
Nusirat near Irbid	42	184	144	78.1
Batayyni near Irbid	34	186	145	78.2
El-Kaid	45	186	143	77.2
Kutumm (or Shitum)	57	185	144	78.0
Villages				
Tafileh	26	187	145	77.8
Aidoun near Irbid	18	184	145	78.8
Nuaimat near Kerak	54	184	145	78.6
Madeba (Madaba)	47	185	144	78.2
Akaba	13	186	139	74.7
Wadi Musa (District)	16	185	148	77.2
Villagers (Unclassified)	88	187	144	72.0
Totals ...	791	186.94	144.57	77.4

TABLE 9: MEASUREMENTS ON 2,084 MALES IN JORDAN

No.	Group	Locality	Country	No.	Stat.
1	Howeitat Beduins	Jazira	Jordan	70	163.08
2	Beni Sakhr Beduins	Jazira	Jordan	65	162.78
3	Bekaa Villagers	Plain	Lebanon	149	165.42
4	Mitwali (Shia)	Mountains	Lebanon	302	166.96
5	Alouites		Syria	309	166.52
6	Villagers (Sunni)	Hama	Syria	175	163.98
7	Villagers (Christian)	Mhardeh	Syria	157	168.08
8	Villagers (Christian)	Hafar	Syria	93	168.02
9	Villagers (Sunni)	Hidjaneh	Syria	298	164.36
10	Maualy Beduins	Jazira	Syria	176	170.12
11	Akeydat Beduins	Jazira	Syria	120	168.50
12	Rwala Beduins	Jazira	Syria	270	161.89

TABLE 10: MEASUREMENTS ON 2,084 MALES IN JORDAN

No.	Span	SH	GOL	GB	HH	MFD	Biz. B
1	173.49	85.00	192.42	145.12	123.46	106.22	131.25
2	169.95	83.44	189.87	142.51	123.70	104.06	130.60
3	174.32	86.08	177.72	150.64	127.56	106.54	135.26
4	174.72	88.12	176.04	152.82	129.40	108.71	135.34
5	176.00	85.64	178.74	148.50	124.84	109.74	134.86
6	173.74	83.78	184.92	143.78	125.20	109.08	132.52
7	177.32	86.24	184.52	147.06	126.82	108.16	134.08
8	175.41	86.80	189.54	143.35	125.22	106.94	133.07
9	172.86	86.48	184.38	142.54	124.28	103.46	130.34
10	177.54	86.80	190.42	147.06	125.36	111.30	135.91
11	174.94	85.96	191.35	146.14	122.76	110.44	134.58
12		82.69	191.48	143.63		103.78	129.87

TABLE 11: MEASUREMENTS ON 2,084 MALES IN JORDAN

No.	Big. B	TFH	UFH	NH	NB	EH	EB
1	105.26	115.10	67.00	51.66	33.92	60.39	32.63
2	102.90	120.15	68.90	52.94	33.38	60.93	32.45
3	108.50	122.62	70.60	51.42	33.92	60.86	32.78
4	110.21	121.32	70.28	52.58	33.84	61.34	33.08
5	106.78	122.16	71.24	53.94	34.88	61.94	32.06
6	106.68	121.50	69.90	52.60	35.58	61.58	32.74
7	106.71	120.90	69.58	52.86	35.26	63.54	33.34
8	106.02	122.20	70.00	51.66	35.44	63.44	32.78
9	104.22	119.62	69.32	50.70	33.56	60.46	33.16
10	108.10	124.04	73.00	55.42	36.82	62.56	32.26
11	108.04	123.32	71.82	54.66	36.28	62.10	32.74
12	105.53	119.20	69.99	55.11	35.00	60.48	33.12

TABLE 12: INDICES ON 2,084 MALES IN JORDAN

No.	RSH	CI	TFI	UFI	NI	EI
1	51.68	75.51	87.95	50.57	66.34	54.36
2	51.18	74.94	91.60	52.85	63.90	53.82
3	52.00	84.90	90.52	.....	65.72	53.96
4	52.76	87.38	89.64	.....	64.78	54.22
5	51.46	83.24	90.88	.....	65.06	51.90
6	51.18	78.67	91.68	.....	68.20	53.44
7	51.24	79.91	90.18	.....	67.10	52.66
8	52.20	75.89	91.86	.....	69.20	51.66
9	52.60	77.52	91.72	.....	66.68	54.82
10	50.54	77.28	92.34	53.80	66.26	51.71
11	50.54	76.39	91.90	53.40	65.95	52.78
12	51.11	75.00	91.67	53.90	63.73	54.97

TABLE 13: MEASUREMENTS AND INDICES ON 273 JORDAN TRIBESWOMEN AND VILLAGERS

No.	Group	Locality	Country	No.	Stat.	SH
1	Akeydat Beduins	Jazira	Syria	70	153.92	78.78
2	Alouite	Hama	Syria	100	153.56	79.06
3	Mitwali (Shia)	Mountains	Lebanon	103	......	.....

No.	GOL	GB	HH	MFD	Biz. B	Big. B	TFH
1	180.40	139.20	113.00	107.10	123.60	95.30	114.30
2	170.40	146.00	......	102.20	128.40	97.60	115.50
3	169.10	147.80	......	......	......	.....	......

No.	UFH	NH	NB	EH	EB	RSH	CI	TFI	NI
1	68.00	49.50	31.30	.....	.....	51.42	77.14	92.46	63.36
2	62.00	52.10	36.60	57.00	31.00	51.49	85.96	90.04	58.28
3	.....	.....	.....	.....	.....	.....	87.52	.....	.....

TABLE 14: MEASUREMENTS AND INDICES OF 451 LEBANESE MALES

Group	Locality	No.	Stature	Span	SH
Bekaa Villagers	Plain	149	165.42	174.32	86.08
Mitwali (Shia)	Mountains	302	166.96	174.72	88.12

GOL	GB	HH	MFD	Biz. B	Big. B.	TFH	UFH
177.72	150.64	127.56	106.54	135.26	108.50	122.62	70.60
176.04	152.82	129.40	108.71	135.34	110.21	121.32	70.28

NH	NB	EH	EB	RSH	CI	TFI	NI	EI
51.42	33.92	60.86	32.78	52.00	84.90	90.52	65.72	53.96
52.58	33.84	61.34	33.08	52.76	87.38	89.64	64.78	54.22

TABLE 15: MEASUREMENTS AND INDICES OF 1,598 SYRIANS

No.	Group	Locality	No.	Stature
1	Alouite	Hama	309	166.52
2	Villagers (Sunni)	Hama	175	163.98
3	Villagers (Christian)	Mhardeh	157	168.08
4	Villagers (Christian)	Hafar	93	168.02
5	Villagers (Sunni)	Hidjaneh	298	164.36
6	Maualy Beduins	Jazira	176	170.12
7	Akeydat Beduins	Jazira	120	168.50
8	Rwala Beduins	Jazira	270	161.89

No.	Span	SH	GOL	GB	HH	MFD	Biz. B
1	176.00	85.64	178.74	148.50	124.84	109.74	134.86
2	173.74	83.78	184.92	143.78	125.20	109.08	132.52
3	177.32	86.24	184.52	147.06	126.82	108.16	134.08
4	175.41	86.80	189.54	143.35	125.22	106.94	133.07
5	172.86	86.48	184.38	142.54	124.28	103.46	130.34
6	177.54	86.80	190.42	147.06	125.36	111.30	135.91
7	174.94	85.96	191.35	146.14	122.76	110.44	134.58
8	......	82.69	191.48	143.63	......	103.78	129.87

TABLE 15 (Continued)

No.	Big. B	TFH	UFH	NH	NB	EH	EB
1	106.78	122.16	71.24	53.94	34.88	61.94	32.06
2	106.68	121.50	69.90	52.60	35.58	61.58	32.74
3	106.71	120.90	69.58	52.86	35.26	63.54	33.34
4	106.02	122.20	70.00	51.66	35.44	63.44	32.78
5	104.22	119.62	69.32	50.70	33.56	60.46	33.16
6	108.10	124.04	73.00	55.42	36.82	62.56	32.26
7	108.04	123.32	71.82	54.66	36.28	62.10	32.74
8	105.53	119.20	69.99	55.11	35.00	60.48	33.12

No.	RSH	CI	TFI	UFI	NI	EI
1	51.46	83.24	90.88	.....	65.06	51.90
2	51.18	78.67	91.68	.....	68.20	53.44
3	51.24	79.91	90.18	.....	67.10	52.66
4	52.20	75.89	91.86	.....	69.20	51.66
5	52.60	77.52	91.72	.....	66.68	54.82
6	50.54	77.28	92.34	53.80	66.26	51.71
7	50.54	76.39	91.90	53.40	65.95	52.78
8	51.11	75.00	91.67	53.90	63.73	54.97

TABLE 16: AGE DISTRIBUTION OF 36 SYRIAN BEDUINS

Age	No.	Per cent	Age	No.	Per cent
18-19	5	14.0	44-46	4	11.2
20-22	6	16.8	47-49	0	....
23-25	2	5.6	50-52	1	2.8
26-28	0	....	53-55	2	5.6
29-31	3	8.4	56-58	0	....
32-34	1	2.8	59-61	1	2.8
35-37	4	11.2	62-64	0	....
38-40	2	5.6	65-67	2	5.6
41-43	0	....	68-70	3	8.4
			Total......	36	100.8

TABLE 17: DEMOGRAPHY

Sons	No.	Per cent	Daughters	No.	Per cent
None	4	23.53	None	4	23.53
1	7	41.18	1	5	29.41
2	3	17.65	2	5	29.41
3-4	3	17.65	3-4	3	17.65
5-6	0	.....	5-6	0	.....
7+	0	.....	7+	0	.....
Total...	17	100.01	Total...	17	100.00

TABLE 18: HAIR

Color	No.	Per cent
Black	0	.....
Very dark brown	1	7.14
Dark brown	11	78.57
Brown	0	.....
Reddish-brown	0	.....
Light brown	0	.....
Red	0	.....
Black and gray	0	.....
Dark brown and gray	1	7.14
Light brown and gray	0	.....
Gray	1	7.14
White	0	.....
Total...	14	99.99

TABLE 19: EYES

Color	No.	Per cent
Black	0	.....
Dark brown	11	84.62
Blue brown	1	7.69
Blue brown	0	.....
Green brown	0	.....
Green brown	0	.....
Gray brown	0	.....
Blue	1	7.69
Gray	0	.....
Light brown	0	.....
Blue gray	0	.....
Blue green	0	.....
Total...13		100.00

TABLE 20: TEETH

Condition	No.	Per cent
Very bad	0	.....
Bad	1	7.69
Fair	3	23.08
Good	8	61.54
Excellent	1	7.69
Total...	13	100.00

TABLE 21: TATTOOING

	No.	Per cent
None	1	2.63
Some	13	34.21
Extensive	24	63.16
Total...	38	100.00

TABLE 22: MEASUREMENTS AND INDICES OF 37 SYRIAN BEDUINS

Measurements	No.	Range	Mean	S.D.	C.V.
Age	36	17-70	37.41 ± 1.89	16.80 ± 1.34	44.91 ± 3.57
Head length	37	177-202	189.50 ± .68	6.14 ± .48	3.24 ± .25
Head breadth	37	128-153	141.14 ± .66	5.98 ± .47	4.24 ± .33
Minimum frontal diameter	37	102-130	115.74 ± .61	5.54 ± .43	4.79 ± .38
Bizygomatic breadth	37	117-147	134.14 ± .75	6.78 ± .53	5.05 ± .40
Total facial height	37	109-137	124.58 ± .75	6.76 ± .53	5.43 ± .43
Upper facial height	37	66-87	76.22 ± .52	4.72 ± .37	6.19 ± .49
Nasal height	37	50-70	60.50 ± .49	4.40 ± .35	7.27 ± .57
Nasal breadth	37	32-45	37.51 ± .37	3.32 ± .26	8.85 ± .69
Ear length	37	54-73	64.40 ± .50	4.50 ± .35	6.98 ± .55
Ear breadth	37	30-41	34.78 ± .32	2.89 ± .23	8.31 ± .65
Indices					
Cephalic	37	66-82	74.35 ± .39	3.48 ± .27	4.68 ± .37
Fronto-parietal	37	74-102	82.34 ± .57	5.10 ± .40	6.19 ± .49
Facial	37	83-105	92.80 ± .60	5.40 ± .42	5.85 ± .46
Upper facial	37	47-63	56.84 ± .43	3.88 ± .30	6.83 ± .54
Zygo-gonial	37	70-86	77.95 ± .43	3.84 ± .30	4.92 ± .39
Zygo-frontal	37	80-102	86.40 ± .44	4.00 ± .31	4.62 ± .36
Nasal	37	48-80	62.44 ± .81	7.34 ± .58	11.75 ± .92
Ear	36	46-67	54.22 ± .53	4.74 ± .37	8.74 ± .69

TABLE 23: CEPHALIC INDEX OF 375 HITTITE CRANIA

No.	Group	Per cent
41	Subdolichocephals	10.93
47	Mesocephals	12.53
103	Subbrachycephals	27.46
56	Brachycephals	14.93
98	Hyperbrachycephals	26.13
30	Ultrabrachycephals	8.00

TABLE 24: 394 NEOLITHIC CRANIA FROM TURKEY

No.	Site	Period	No.	GOL	GB
1	Kum-Tepe	Neolithic (?)	1	179	148
2	Alishar Hüyük	Proto-Hittite	2	174	144
3	Various	Hittite	6	174	142
4	Various	Seljuk	10	174.3	148.8
5	Various	Ottoman	375	171.3	143.7

No.	Biz. B	NH	NB	CI	FI	NI
1	...	...	...	82.68	...	...
2	...	...	...	82.77	...	...
3	128	47.6	22.5	81.32	50.27	47.03
4	131.7	51.0	25.6	86.51	52.42	48.23
5	...	51.0	24.0	84.07	52.64	47.23

TABLE 25: 2 POST-HITTITE CRANIA FROM KARA HUYUK, ANATOLIA

Measurements	No. 1	No. 2
Head length	190	182
Head breadth	140 (?)	151
Minimum frontal diameter	92.5	98
Bizygomatic diameter	.....	145.5

Indices		
Cephalic	73.68	82.96
Fronto-parietal	66.07	64.90
Zygo-frontal	.....	67.35

TABLE 26: 4 SKELETONS FROM KUM-TEPE NEAR TROY, ANATOLIA

No.	Sex	Group	GOL	GB	MFD	CI	STATURE
3	F	Dolichocephalic	196	140 (?)	99	71.4	155.43
4	F	Dolichocephalic	...	...	..	...	152.09
1	F	Mesocephalic	190 (?)	145 (?)	..	76.31	......
2	M (?)	Brachycephalic	179	145 (?)	96	81.0	160.50

TABLE 27: 3 CRANIA FROM ALISHAR HUYUK, ANATOLIA

No.	Group	GOL	GB	MFD	Biz. B	CI
VIII	Brachycephalic	161.0	140.0	....	96.0	86.95
III	Brachycephalic	202.0 (?)	170.0 (?)	....	....	84.15 (?)
II	Mesocephalic	183.0	140.0	96.0	121.0 (?)	76.50

TABLE 28: MEASUREMENTS AND INDICES ON CHALCOLITHIC SKELETON
FROM BUYUK GULLUCEK, ANATOLIA

Measurements	Centimeters
Head length	187.50
Head breadth	133.00
Minimum frontal diameter	104.00
Basi-bregmatic height	139.00
Horizontal circumference	522.00
Bizygomatic diameter	133.00(?)
Orbital width (left)	39.00
Orbital height (left)	31.00

Indices	
Cephalic	70.93
Basion-bregma length-height	74.13
Basion-bregma heighth-breadth	104.51
Fronto-parietal	78.19
Zygo-frontal	78.19(?)
Orbital	79.48

TABLE 29: 5 CRANIA FROM SEYH HUYUK, ANATOLIA

No.	Sex	GOL	GB	Ba-b	MFD	Biz. B	NH	NB
1	M	195.0	143.0	132.0	97.0	133.0(?)	54.0(?)	27.0(?)
2	M	186.0	134.0	139.0	96.0	130.0(?)	57.0	27.0
3	F	182.0	124.0	131.0	84.0	118.0	47.0	24.0
4	F	189.0(?)	123.0(?)	139.0	86.0	118.0	48.0	24.5
5	F	196.0	133.0	.....	96.5	122.0(?)	54.0	27.5

No.	CI	HL	HW	TFI	UFI	OI	NI
1	73.33	67.69	92.30	88.72(?)	54.88(?)	94.66(?)	50.00(?)
2	72.04	74.73	103.73	92.30(?)	55.00	83.84	47.36
3	68.13	71.97	105.64	93.64	54.23	82.71	51.06
4	65.07(?)	73.54(?)	113.00	93.22	56.77	.....	51.04
5	67.85	.....	......	92.62(?)	59.01	81.39	50.92

TABLE 30: 5 CRANIA FROM KUL-TEPE, ANATOLIA

No.	Sex	GOL	GB	NL	NB	CI	NI
9	M	193.00	143.00	.....	.....	74.09	.....
11	M	192.00	138.00(?)	.....	.....	71.87	.....
12	M	205.00	134.00(?)	50.00(?)	24.00(?)	65.36	48.00(?)
10	F	177.00(?)	140.00(?)	.....	.....	79.09(?)	.....
13	F	187.00	133.00	.....	25.50	71.12	.....

TABLE 31: MEASUREMENTS AND INDICES ON 2,945 MALE TURKS

Group	No.	Stature	CI	Observer
Turks	?	162.2	.....	Weissbach
Turks	?	166.2	.....	Bassanovitch
Bulgaria	42	.....	84.6	Bassanovitch
Turks	137	167.0	84.40	Elsieev
Osmanli	187	.....	81.0	Von Luschan
Cappadocia	120	.....	84.53	Chantre
Anatolia (1916-18)	455	.....	84.19	Hauschild and Wagenseil
Anatolia	272	167.2	.....	Hauschild and Wagenseil
Balkans	300	.....	81.39	Pittard
Balkans	200	.....	82.24	Pittard
Anatolia (1928)	210	171.0	84.78	Pittard
Anatolia (1929)	25	.....	85.01	Kansu
Anatolia (1930-31)	100	167.8	84.19	Kansu
Rumeli (1930-31)	100	167.3	82.57	Kansu
Anatolia and Rumeli (1931-32)	797	166.5	83.5	Kansu

TABLE 32: MEASUREMENTS AND INDICES ON 39,465 MALE TURKS

Group	Area	No.	Stature	GOL	GB	CI
I	Thrace	2651	164.44	181.9	148.8	82.93
II	Bursa-Bilecik	3361	165.17	181.5	153.3	83.07
III	Western Anatolia	3020	164.44	183.6	151.6	82.61
IV	Aegean	3406	164.41	183.1	152.8	83.95
V	Western Anatolia (Interior)	3420	165.09	182.0	153.9	84.53
VI	Central Anatolia	4895	166.80	181.8	155.6	85.41
VII	Northwest Anatolia	4161	164.74	181.0	156.5	86.29
VIII	Southern Anatolia	4766	165.73	184.0	146.8	79.78
IX	Eastern Anatolia	5102	165.02	180.7	150.5	83.28
X	Northeast Anatolia	4683	165.52	183.5	149.5	81.07
I-X	Totals	39,465	165.28	182.3	151.9	83.28

TABLE 33: MEASUREMENTS AND INDICES ON 39,465 MALE TURKS

Measurements	Range	Mean
Stature	164.41-166.80	1652.8
Sitting height	84.06-85.99	847.1
Head length	180.7-184.0	182.3
Head breadth	146.8-156.5	151.9
Minimum frontal diameter	100.7-110.2	108.0
Bizygomatic diameter	136.1-141.6	139.0
Bigonial diameter	102.7-110.3	107.2
Total facial height	120.8-123.2	122.4
Upper facial height	71.0-75.1	73.3
Nasal height	51.4-52.8	52.0
Nasal breadth	32.4-35.0	34.0
Ear length	57.6-62.3	59.9
Ear breadth	32.4-37.6	34.6
Indices		
Cephalic	79.78-86.29	83.28
Fronto-parietal	66.42-73.12	71.25
Zygo-frontal	72.31-80.31	77.57
Zygo-gonial	76.20-80.84	77.54
Total facial	85.74-90.82	87.78
Upper facial	51.19-53.96	52.66
Nasal	61.72-68.01	65.39
Ear	54.44-62.44	59.04

TABLE 34: NASAL PROFILE OF 39,465 MALE TURKS

Area	No.	Convex	Straight	Wavy	Concave
I	2651	52.36	26.71	15.91	5.02
II	3361	35.82	32.26	22.13	9.79
III	3020	21.06	16.75	53.28	8.91
IV	3406	25.93	49.21	15.44	9.42
V	3420	42.02	34.56	14.59	8.83
VI	4895	30.99	42.06	19.15	7.80
VII	4161	26.15	47.18	20.13	6.54
VIII	4766	6.40	24.29	56.43	12.88
IX	5102	57.15	23.13	17.72	2.00
X	4683	19.97	38.86	34.85	6.32
I-X	39,465	31.17	33.82	27.37	7.64

TABLE 35: EYE COLOR OF 39,465 MALE TURKS

Area	No.	Clair	Moyen	Foncé
I	2651	41.23	55.45	3.32
II	3361	35.76	60.82	3.42
III	3020	24.70	72.02	3.28
IV	3406	32.88	43.48	23.64
V	3420	41.81	45.06	13.13
VI	4895	33.89	53.50	12.61
VII	4161	42.20	54.82	2.98
VIII	4766	15.07	82.48	2.45
IX	5102	24.28	73.38	7.68
X	4683	11.66	23.21	65.13
I-X	39,465	29.16	55.56	14.28

TABLE 36: MEASUREMENTS AND INDICES OF 20,263 FEMALE TURKS

Group	Area	No.	Stature	GOL	GB	CI
I	Thrace	2588	151.25	176.2	146.3	83.79
II	Bursa-Bilecik	2459	151.81	175.3	148.2	84.29
III	Western Anatolia	2857	151.90	176.8	144.8	81.53
IV	Aegean	2490	151.97	175.0	146.0	83.56
V	Western Anatolia (Interior)	2273	152.25	175.3	146.3	84.94
VI	Central Anatolia	2424	152.44	175.8	151.8	86.30
VII	Northwest Anatolia	1822	152.33	173.2	150.4	86.92
VIII	Southern Anatolia	628	152.50	176.0	145.8	82.70
IX	Eastern Anatolia	1472	151.68	173.6	143.2	82.43
X	Northeast Anatolia	1250	154.11	176.3	140.8	79.86
I-X	Total	20,263	152.26	175.1	146.7	83.75

TABLE 37: MEASUREMENTS AND INDICES OF 20,263 FEMALE TURKS

Measurements	Range	Mean
Stature	151.25-154.11	152.26
Sitting height	77.99-79.51	78.89
Head length	173.2-176.8	175.1
Head breadth	140.8-151.8	146.7
Minimum frontal diameter	101.1-108.0	104.9
Bizygomatic diameter	128.4-131.9	130.6
Bigonial diameter	96.0-106.4	100.4
Total facial height	110.6-114.0	111.8
Upper facial height	66.8-70.3	68.7
Nasal height	46.6-50.6	48.4
Nasal breadth	30.2-31.4	31.0
Ear length	54.5-58.6	56.8
Ear breadth	30.8-35.5	32.8

Indices		
Cephalic	79.86-86.92	83.75
Fronto-parietal	68.65-74.83	71.50
Zygo-frontal	76.92-83.52	80.14
Zygo-gonial	74.80-80.70	76.77
Total facial	83.65-87.52	85.18
Upper facial	51.36-53.49	52.36
Nasal	60.38-67.00	63.91
Ear	54.80-63.05	58.18

TABLE 38: NASAL PROFILE OF FEMALE TURKS

Area	No.	Convex	Straight	Wavy	Concave
I	2588	39.22	26.27	18.12	16.39
II	2459	16.56	38.47	18.54	26.43
III	2857	14.95	12.36	50.71	21.98
IV	2490	15.06	51.12	17.19	16.63
V	2273	41.75	32.73	10.12	15.40
VI	2424	27.35	51.36	11.02	10.27
VII	1822	13.28	46.82	23.60	16.30
VIII	628	3.50	22.93	59.55	14.02
IX	1472	62.50	20.66	14.33	2.51
X	1250	20.44	37.12	33.28	9.36
I-X	20,263	26.01	34.58	23.35	16.06

TABLE 39: EYE COLOR OF 20,263 FEMALE TURKS

Area	No.	Clair	Moyen	Foncé
I	2588	27.12	64.84	8.04
II	2459	30.95	63.32	5.73
III	2857	17.05	76.79	6.16
IV	2490	29.72	42.17	28.11
V	2273	26.44	50.33	23.23
VI	2424	22.65	50.78	26.57
VII	1822	29.42	65.70	4.88
VIII	628	10.67	85.19	4.14
IX	1472	19.70	72.62	7.68
X	1250	6.80	26.24	66.96
I-X	20,263	23.78	59.14	17.08

TABLE 40: POPULATION AND AREA OF THE CAUCASUS BY REPUBLICS AND REGIONS

Republics and Regions	Population	Area (In sq. km.)
Nakhichevan SSR	121,174	5,988
Abkhazian SSR	251,626	8,381
Adzharistan ASSR	153,998	2,912
South Osetian AR	96,796	4,309
Mountain Karabakh AR	145,763	4,161

TABLE 41: CEPHALIC INDEX OF CRANIA IN THE CAUCASUS

Period, Group or Locality	No.	CI	Observer
Samthavro (Protohistoric)	6	71.55	Chantre
Samthavro (Protohistoric)	10	71.82	Smirnov
Kabarda Kurgans (Scytho-Byzantine)	10	72.35	Antonowitch
Marienfeld (Protohistoric)	4	72.64	Chantre
Koban (Protohistoric)	6	73.71	Chantre
Kislovodsk (Protohistoric)	1	73.77	Chantre
Chmi (Osetia)	8	74.8	Zaborowski
Baksan (Scytho-Byzantine)	1	74.99	Chantre
Natukais (Modern)	20	75.78	Tikhomirov
Redkine-Lager Necropolis (Protohistoric)	1	77.77	Chantre
Osete (? Female)	1	78.82	Bogdanov
Osetes (Dargavskaya Valley)	20	78.90	Field
Shapsugs (Modern)	53	79.03	Tikhomirov
Osetes (Undeformed)	14	80.5	Von Erckert
Chechens of Koban (Modern)	4	80.57	Chantre
Osetes (Undeformed)	9	81.22	Chantre
Osetes (Deformed and Undeformed)	16	81.4	Von Erckert
Georgians of Tiflis (Tbilisi)	7	81.61	Chantre
Osetes (Deformed and Undeformed)	17	83.11	Chantre
Osete	1	83.3	Bogdanov
Chechens of Vladikavkaz (Ordzhonikidze, now Dzhaudzhikau)	1	82.35	Chantre
Abkhazians	27	83.64	Tikhomirov
Lezghian (Modern)	1	83.73	Davis
Armenian of Tiflis (Recent)	1	84.21	Gondati
Osetes (Deformed)	8	85.32	Chantre
Osete (Kobi-Kazbek)	1	86.4	Chantre
Osetes of Koban (Modern)	5	86.48	Chantre
Osetes	2	88.4	Maliev

Total..... 255

TABLE 42: STATURE OF 7,453 MALES IN THE CAUCASUS

Group	Locality	No.	Stature	Observer
Jews	Kubin near Baku	80	162.2	Pantiukhov
Embailuk Nogais		176	162.5	IArkho
Turks	Nukha, Azerbaidzhan	301	162.7	IArkho
Turks	Kakh, Azerbaidzhan	201	162.9	Debets
Edishkul Nogais		145	163.0	IArkho
Jews	Kutais	41	163.0	Pantiukhov
Kara Nogais	Western	188	163.1	IArkho
Kara Nogais	Eastern	156	163.3	Terebinskaia
Turkomans	North Caucasus	302	163.5	IArkho
Jews	Georgia	37	163.6	Weissenberg
Nogais	Khusavyut Region	165	163.8	Terebinskaia
Lezghians		11	164.0	Chantre
Jews		33	164.0	Weissenberg
Jews	Georgia	11	164.1	Chantre

TABLE 42 (Continued)

Group	Locality	No.	Stature	Observer
Turks	Gandzha, Azerbaidzhan	230	164.1	IArkho
Edissan Nogais		146	164.3	IArkho
Jews	Kaitag-Tabasaran	61	164.4	Pantiukhov
Nogais	Terek Region	108	164.6	Levin
Armenians		20	164.6	Weissenberg
Turks	Nakhichevan	151	165.1	Anserov
Yezidis	Yerevan District	20	165.15	Field
Armenians	Tbilisi Province	792	165.2	Deniker
Georgians		900	165.5	Dzhavahov
Kumyks		130	165.9	Debets and Trofimova
Yezidis	Transcaucasia and Anatolia	51	165.99	Field
Armenians		101	166.16	Seltzer
Sarts		54	166.8	Deniker
Balkars		314	166.9	Levin
Turkomans		53	167.0	Deniker
Ersari		125	167.0	Oshanin
Osetes	Gori	258	167.0	Pantiukhov
Armenians		75	167.04	Boas
Armenians		105	167.10	Twarjanowitsch
Armenians		25	167.4	Hrdička
Azerbaidzhanis		288	167.5	Deniker
Karachais		211	167.9	Levin
Uzbeks		120	168.3	Deniker
Kurds	Transcaucasia	300	168.6	Ivanovskii
Osetes	Osetia	30	169.0	Riskine
Tajiks and Galtchas		155	169.2	Deniker
Armenians	Transcaucasia	192	169.4	Deniker
Armenians		239	169.44	Chantre
Osetes (Plains)	North Osetia	67	169.47	Field
Osetes (Irons)	North Osetia	68	169.50	Field
Osetes	Terek	200	169.53	Gilchenko
Osetes (Total)	North Osetia	106	169.77	Field
Osetes (Digors)	North Osetia	38	170.28	Field
Osetes (Mountain)	North Osetia	39	170.31	Field
Osetes		16	171.8	Pantiukhov
Osetes (Non-Enlisted men)		30	171.8	Gilchenko
Osetes (Selected Tall)		20	180.0	Gilchenko

Total... 7,453

TABLE 43: STATURE OF 177 FEMALES IN THE CAUCASUS

Group	Locality	No.	Stature	Observer
Kurds	Transcaucasia	60	152.4	Ivanovskii
Osetes	Osetia	60	157.3	Riskine
Osetes	North Osetia	57	159.39	Field

Total... 177

TABLE 44: STATURE OF 19 MALE AND 2 FEMALE OSETE GROUPS IN THE CAUCASUS

Group	No.	Stature	Observer
Gori	258	164.7	Topinard
Light-eyed	168	168.1	Gilchenko
Blond		168.2	Gilchenko
Light-haired		168.6	Gilchenko
Digors	500	169.0	Riskine
Osetes		169.2	Dzhawachischwili
Digors		169.3	Gilchenko
Kurtatins	67	169.3	Gilchenko
Plains	68	169.47	Field
Irons	200	169.5	Field
Terek		169.53	Gilchenko
Alaghirs		169.6	Gilchenko
North Osetes (Total)	106	169.77	Field
Brunet		170.2	Gilchenko
Digors	38	170.28	Field
Mountain	39	170.31	Field
Osetes	16	171.8	Pantiukhov
Non-Enlisted Men	30	171.8	Gilchenko
Selected Tall (21-25)	20	180.5	Gilchenko
Total...	1,298		

FEMALES

Group	No.	Stature	Observer
Osetes	60	157.3	Riskine
Osetes	47	159.39	Field
Total...	107		

TABLE 45: STATURE OF PEOPLES IN TURKESTAN

Group or Locality	No.	Stature	Observer
Arabs	17	163.7	Maslovskii
Bokara	163	163.71	Oshanin
Vanch	80	164.05	Korovnikov
Arabs	100	165.72	Oshanin
Pendzhikent	279	165.88	Vishnevskii
Iomuds	107	166.34	IArkho
Teke	433	166.39	Oshanin
Arabs	29	166.4	Maslovskii
Chaudirs	200	166.51	IArkho
Kara Kirghiz	74	166.8	Deniker
Pskem Valley and Bokara Region	100	166.8	.....
Tatars (Aralych)	16	169.0	Chantre
Ferghana	200	169.45	IArkho
Tatars (Arkhuri)	15	170.0	Chantre
Gypsies	29	171.9	Deniker
Total...	1,842		

TABLE 46: SITTING HEIGHT OF PEOPLES IN THE CAUCASUS

Group	Locality	No.	SH	Observer
Yezidis	Transcaucasia and Anatolia	51	84.64	Field
Yezidis	Yerevan, Armenia	20	84.70	Field
Osetes (Irons)	North Osetia	68	84.97	Field
Osetes (Plains)	North Osetia	67	85.00	Field
Osetes (Total)	North Osetia	106	85.03	Field
Osetes (Mountain)	North Osetia	39	85.09	Field
Osetes (Digors)	North Osetia	38	85.15	Field
Armenians	Caucasus	98	88.58	Seltzer
Jews	Georgia	19	86.9	Weissenberg
		Total... 274		

TABLE 47: RELATIVE SITTING HEIGHT OF PEOPLES IN THE CAUCASUS

Group	Locality	No.	Stature	Observer
Osetes (Digors)	North Osetia	38	49.92	Field
Osetes (Mountain)	North Osetia	39	50.04	Field
Osetes (Total)	North Osetia	106	50.14	Field
Osetes (Plains)	North Osetia	67	50.20	Field
Osetes (Irons)	North Osetia	68	50.26	Field
Yezidis	Transcaucasia and Anatolia	51	51.00	Field
Yezidis	Yerevan, Armenia	20	51.20	Field
Jews	Georgia	19	53.00	Weissenberg
Armenians	Armenia	98	53.39	Seltzer
		Total... 274		

TABLE 48: HEAD LENGTH OF PEOPLES IN THE CAUCASUS

Group	Locality	No.	GOL	Observer
Turks	Mekha, Azerbaidzhan	301	181.9	IArkho
Nogais	Khasavyut Region	165	182.2	Terebinskaia
Turks	Kakh, Azerbaidzhan	201	183.9	Debets
Kumyks		130	184.6	Debets and Trofimova
Kara Nogais	Eastern	156	184.7	Terebinskaia
Nogais	Terek Region	108	185.8	Levin
Tatars	Kazan	207	186.0	Warushkin
Embailak Nogais		176	186.8	IArkho
Kara Nogais	Western	188	187.1	IArkho
Yezidis	Transcaucasia and Anatolia	49	187.41	Field
Osetes (Mountain)	North Osetia	39	187.68	Field
Balkars		314	187.7	Levin
Osetes (Irons)	North Osetia	67	187.74	Field
Osetes (Total)	North Osetia	105	187.86	Field
Osetes (Plains)	North Osetia	66	187.95	Field
Osetes (Digors)	North Osetia	38	188.04	Field
Osetes (Deformed)	Osetia	82	188.2	Gilchenko
Edissan Nogais		146	188.8	IArkho
Osetes	Osetia	84	189.0	Dzhawachischwili
Kurds	Transcaucasia	30	189.0	Ivanovskii
Karachais		211	189.1	Levin
Edishkul Nogais		145	189.1	IArkho
Osetes	Osetia	200	189.4	Gilchenko
Turks	Gandzha, Azerbaidzhan	230	189.9	IArkho
Osetes	Osetia	300	190.0	Riskine
Turks	Nakhichevan	151	190.0	Anserov
Osetes (Undeformed)	Osetia	118	190.3	Gilchenko
Yezidis	Yerevan, Armenia	20	191.25	Field
Turkomans	North Caucasus	302	192.8	IArkho
Kurds	Transcaucasia	140	193.0	Chantre
Osetes (Tall)	Osetia	20	193.6	Gilchenko
		Total... 4,259		

TABLE 49: HEAD LENGTH OF 154 FEMALES IN THE CAUCASUS

Group	Locality	No.	GOL	Observer
Osetes	Osetia	60	182.0	Riskine
Kurds	Transcaucasia	60	182.0	Ivanovskii
Kurds	Transcaucasia	34	183.0	Chantre
	Total...	154		

TABLE 50: HEAD BREADTH OF PEOPLES IN THE CAUCASUS

Group	Locality	No.	GB	Observer
Turks	Nakhichevan	151	145.0	Anserov
Turks	Gandzha, Azerbaidzhan	230	150.4	IArkho
Yezidis	Transcaucasia and Anatolia	50	150.82	Field
Yezidis	Yerevan, Armenia	20	150.85	Field
Edishkul Nogais		145	152.7	IArkho
Edissan Nogais		146	152.8	IArkho
Turkomans	North Caucasus	302	152.8	IArkho
Nogais	Khasavyurt Region	165	154.2	Terebinaskaia
Osetes	Osetia	170	155.0	Dzhawachischwili
Turks	Mekha, Azerbaidzhan	301	155.0	IArkho
Embailuk Nogais		176	155.4	IArkho
Osetes	Osetia	118	155.6	Gilchenko
Kara Nogais	Eastern	156	155.6	Terebinskaia
Kara Nogais	Western	188	155.7	IArkho
Nogais	Terek Region	108	156.4	Levin
Osetes	Osetia	200	156.5	Gilchenko
Turks	Kakh, Azerbaidzhan	201	156.6	Debets
Osetes (Tall)	Osetia	20	157.4	Gilchenko
Osetes (Deformed)	Osetia	82	157.7	Gilchenko
Osetes (Plains)	North Osetia	66	157.87	Field
Osetes (Total)	North Osetia	105	158.05	Field
Osetes (Digors)	North Osetia	38	158.35	Field
Osetes (Irons)	North Osetia	60	158.98	Field
Osetes (Mountain)	North Osetia	39	160.24	Field
Karachais		211	160.9	Levin
Kumyks		130	161.8	Debets and Trofimova
	Total..	3,355		

TABLE 51: CEPHALIC INDEX OF PEOPLES IN THE CAUCASUS

Group	Locality	No.	CI	Observer
Turkomans		59	75.6	IAvorskii
Turks	Nakhichevan	151	76.1	Anserov
Kurds	Transcaucasia	67	76.2	Chantre
Tatars	Azerbaidzhan	114	76.0	Chantre
Tatars	Azerbaidzhan	207	77.6	Various
Kurds	Transcaucasia	300	77.6	Ivanovskii
Tatars	Aralych	16	77.96	Chantre
Kurds	Transcaucasia	26	78.4	Nasonov
Tatars	Aralych	16	77.96	Chantre
Kurds	Transcaucasia	26	78.4	Nasonov
Kurds	Transcaucasia	140	78.5	Chantre
Tatars	Azerbaidzhan	19	78.83	Chantre
Yezidis	Yerevan, Armenia	20	78.90	Field
Tats	Baku	129	79.2	Deniker
Turks	Gandzha	230	79.3	IArkho
Turkomans	North Caucasus	302	79.3	IArkho
Tatars	Azerbaidzhan	14	79.4	Von Erckert
Kurds	Transcaucasia	30	79.5	Chantre
Tajiks	Norachaine	14	80.11	Chantre

TABLE 51 (Continued)

Group	Locality	No.	CI	Observer
Tajiks	Yerevan, Armenia	17	80.11	Chantre
Osetes (Undeformed)	Osetia	14	80.5	Von Erckert
Yezidis	Georgia	51	80.58	Chantre
Yezidis	Transcaucasia and Anatolia	49	80.58	Field
Osetes	Terek, Osetia	11	80.75	Chantre
Kumyks		130	80.8	Debets and Trofimova
Edishkul Nogais		145	80.9	IArkho
Kalmyks		10	80.9	Von Erckert
Edissan Nogais		146	81.0	IArkho
Osetes	Osetia	16	81.1	Von Erckert
Osetes (Tall)	Osetia	20	81.3	Gilchenko
Osetes	Osetia	16	81.4	Von Erckert
Kurds	Transcaucasia	158	81.42	Chantre
Osetes	Osetia	300	81.5	Riskine
Tatar-Azerbaidzhanis	Lake Goktcha	10	81.6	Chantre
Abazes		11	81.6	Von Erckert
Kalmyks		10	81.7	Chantre
Osetes (Undeformed)	Osetia	118	81.76	Gilchenko
Kurds	Azerbaidzhan	131	81.8	Chantre
Chechens		12	81.9	Von Erckert
Adighe		30	81.9	Von Erckert
Osetes	Osetia	554	81.9	Deniker
Circassians		54	82.05	Kappers
Chechens		10	82.21	Chantre
Osetes	Osetia	200	82.62	Gilchenko
Imeretians		74	82.95	Chantre
Kurds	Transcaucasia	12	83.00	Chantre
Osetes	Osetia	17	83.11	Chantre
Georgians	Georgia	900	83.2	Dzhavahov
Mingrelians	Koban	12	83.22	Chantre
Kara Nogais		188	83.3	IArkho
Embailuk Nogais		176	83.3	IArkho
Georgians	Georgia	43	83.5	Von Erckert
Georgians	Georgia	20	83.55	Chantre
Osetes (Deformed)	Osetia	82	83.79	Gilchenko
Kara Nogais	Eastern	156	84.0	Terebinskaia
Osetes (Plains)	North Osetia	66	84.06	Field
Armenians	Armenia	20	84.1	Weissenberg
Osetes (Digors)	North Osetia	38	84.15	Field
Nogais	Terek Region	108	84.2	Levin
Osetes	Osetia	16	84.6	Pantiukhov
Osetes (Total)	North Osetia	105	84.60	Field
Jews		20	84.7	Weissenberg
Karaims		20	84.8	Weissenberg
Nogais	Khasavyurt Region	165	84.8	Terebinskaia
Osetes (Irons)	North Osetia	67	84.84	Field
Tats	Daghestan	56	84.9	Deniker
Karachais		211	85.1	Levin
Armenians		75	85.11	Boas
Armenians	Tbilisi	25	85.17	Chantre
Jews	Akhaltsikh	18	85.25	Pantiukhov
Armenians	Armenia	30	85.26	Chantre
Turks	Nukha, Azerbaidzhan	301	85.3	IArkho
Turks	Kakh, Azerbaidzhan	201	85.3	Debets
Armenians		25	85.35	Hrdlička
Osetes (Mountain)	North Osetia	39	85.53	Field
Lazes		152	85.6	Deniker
Armenians		341	85.6	Deniker
Armenians	Transcaucasia	278	85.6	Deniker
Armenians		22	85.6	Von Erckert

TABLE 51 (Continued)

Group	Locality	No.	CI	Observer
Armenians (Deformed)	Yerevan, Armenia	10	85.68	Chantre
Armenians	Armenia	297	85.71	Chantre
Armenians	Armenia	292	85.77	Chantre
Armenians		101	85.81	Seltzer
Jews	Georgia	33	85.9	Weissenberg
Armenians		19	86.21	Von Erckert
Armenians	Armenia	318	86.7	Dzhawachischwili
Jews (Mountain)	Daghestan	10	86.7	Von Erckert
Armenians	Armenia	105	86.89	Twarjanowitsch
Armenians	Ghirussi	28	87.29	Chantre
Jews	Kubin	17	87.4	Pantiukhov
Lazes (Deformed)		27	87.48	Chantre
Jews		43	87.5	Pantiukhov
Lezghians		11	87.77	Chantre
Armenians	Yerevan, Armenia	27	91.07	Chantre
	Total...	9,192		

TABLE 52: CEPHALIC INDEX OF 17 OSETE GROUPS

Group	No.	CI	Observer
Osetes	14	80.5	Von Erckert
Terek	11	80.75	Chantre
Osetes	16	81.1	Von Erckert
Selected (Tall)	20	81.3	Gilchenko
Osetes	16	81.4	Von Erckert
Osetes	300	81.5	Riskine
Undeformed	118	81.76	Gilchenko
Osetes	84	81.9	Dzhawachischwili
Osetes	554	81.9	Deniker
Osetes	200	82.62	Gilchenko
Deformed	82	83.79	Gilchenko
Plains	66	84.06	Field
Digors	38	84.15	Field
North Osetes	105	84.60	Field
Osetes (Total)	16	84.6	Pantiukhov
Irons	67	84.84	Field
Mountain	39	85.53	Field
Total...	1,536		

TABLE 53: CEPHALIC INDEX OF 246 FEMALES IN THE CAUCASUS

Group	Locality	No.	CI	Observer
Kurds	Transcaucasia	15	76.4	Chantre
Tatars	Azerbaidzhan	18	76.7	Chantre
Kurds	Transcaucasia	60	77.0	Ivanovskii
Kurds	Transcaucasia	34	77.6	Chantre
Osetes	Osetia	60	81.9	Riskine
Osetes	North Osetia	49	84.6	Field
Karaims		10	85.6	Weissenberg
	Total...	246		

TABLE 54: CEPHALIC INDEX OF PEOPLES IN THE CRIMEA

Group	No.	CI	Observer
Karaims	93	82.9	Adler
Mountain Tatars	180	84.1	Nasonov
Steppe Tatars	200	84.8	Terebinskaia
Mountain Tatars	300	84.8	Terebinskaia
South Coast Tatars	200	85.3	Terebinskaia
Total...	973		

TABLE 55: CEPHALIC INDEX OF PEOPLES IN THE VOLGA REGION

Group	Region	No.	CI	Observer
Mishari Tatars	Chistopol	122	79.1	Trofimova and Debets
Tatars Proper	Chistopol	109	80.2	Trofimova and Debets
Teptiars		112	80.3	Baronov
Kriashen Tatars	Chistopol	121	80.7	Trofimova and Debets
Mishari Tatars	Birsk	149	80.7	Baronov
Bashkirs	Birsk	123	81.4	Baronov
Tatars Proper	Elabuga	146	81.1	Trofimova and Debets
Kriashen Tatars	Elabuga	103	81.9	Trofimova and Debets
Tatars Proper	Kasimov	196	82.2	Trofimova and Debets
Tatars Proper	Arsk	160	82.3	Trofimova and Debets
Bashkirs	Argaiash	131	83.0	Baronov
Karagash Tatars	Astrakhan	158	83.6	Trofimova and Debets
Mishari Tatars	Narovchatsk	175	86.0	Trofimova
	Total...	1,805		

TABLE 56: CEPHALIC INDEX OF PEOPLES IN TURKESTAN

Group	No.	CI	Observer
Iomuds	107	75.16	IArkho
Turkomans	59	75.16	IAvorskii
Teke	51	75.64	IAvorskii
Ersari	125	77.00	Oshanin
Chaudirs	200	77.24	IArkho
Turkomans	23	77.90	Deniker
Arabs	16	82.10	Deniker
Arabs	17	82.10	Maslovskii
Karategin	433	82.77	Oshanin
Vanch	80	83.21	Korovnikov
Shugni (Shakhdara Tribe)	29	83.33	Oshanin
Arabs	29	83.4	Maslovskii
Pskem Valley and Bokhara Region	100	83.57	.....
Bartangi (Iranian Tribe)	13	83.65	Oshanin
Ferghana	200	84.04	IArkho
Shugni (Panj Tribe)	138	84.12	Oshanin
Bokhara	163	84.20	Oshanin
Rushani (Iranian Tribe)	42	84.47	Oshanin
Shugni (Gunt Tribe)	64	85.46	Oshanin
Arabs	100	87.77	Oshanin
Pendzhikent	279	85.84	Vishnevskii
Total...	2,268		

TABLE 57: CEPHALIC INDEX OF PEOPLES IN SOVIET CENTRAL ASIA

Group	Locality	No.	CI	Observer
Iomud Turkomans	Khorezm (Khwarazym)	107	75.2	IArkho
Chaudyr Turkomans	Khorezm	200	77.2	IArkho
Mangyt Uzbeks	Khorezm	80	80.7	IArkho and Libman
Barlas Uzbeks	Turks	100	82.2	Belkina
Kaltai Uzbeks	Turks	100	83.4	Belkina
Uzbeks	Khorezm	100	83.5	IArkho and Libman
Kara Kalpaks	Ferghana	100	83.8	IArkho and Libman
Kirghiz	Ferghana	292	84.0	IArkho
Uzbeks	Karshi (Town)	200	84.1	Oshanin
Kara Kalpaks	Kara Kalpak ASSR	303	84.2	IArkho and Libman
Kypchak Uzbeks	Ferghana	100	84.4	IArkho
Uzbeks (Tribal)	Ferghana	399	84.7	IArkho
Astrakhan	Kazakhstan	105	84.9	Trofimova and Debets
Kirghiz	Tien-Shan	784	85.2	IArkho
Bukhtarma	Kazakhstan	482	85.2	Baronov
Uzbeks	Shakhraziab (Town)	200	85.3	Oshanin
Chuisk	Kazakhstan	120	85.3	IArkho
Malaia	Kazakhstan	466	85.9	Rudenko
Kurama Uzbeks	Ferghana	672	85.9	IArkho
Uigurs		450	87.1	IArkho
	Total...	5,360		

TABLE 58: CEPHALIC INDEX OF PEOPLES IN TANNU TUVA

Group	No.	CI	Observer
Kemchik	124	80.5	IArkho
Seldzhek	40	83.1	Bunak
Tosingal	67	83.2	Bunak
Todzha	57	84.2	Bunak
Total...	288		

TABLE 59: CEPHALIC INDEX OF PEOPLES IN SIBERIA

Group	Locality	No.	CI	Observer
Beltir	Khakass AA	119	79.2	IArkho
Koibal	Khakass AA	41	79.8	IArkho
Shortsi	Khakass AA	119	80.3	IArkho
Kumandin	Oirot AP	99	80.3	IArkho
Yakuts	Siberia	440	80.6	Schreiber
Kyzyl	Khakass AA	128	80.8	IArkho
Teleut	Oirot AP	56	81.0	IArkho
Sagai	Khakass AA	106	82.0	IArkho
Maimalar	Oirot AP	215	82.0	IArkho
Kachin	Khakass AA	207	82.1	IArkho
Tubalar	Oirot AP	203	82.4	IArkho
Yagnobians		21	83.52	Ginzburg
Telengit	Oirot AP	227	84.4	IArkho
Altai-Kizhi	Oirot AP	200	84.5	IArkho
	Total...	2,181		

TABLE 60: MINIMUM FRONTAL DIAMETER OF PEOPLES IN THE CAUCASUS

Group	Locality	No.	MFD	Observer
Osetes	Osetes	16	94.4	Von Erckert
Armenians		101	107.75	Seltzer
Osetes	Osetes	200	111.2	Gilchenko
Yezidis	Transcaucasia and Anatolia	51	113.26	Field
Yezidis	Yerevan, Armenia	20	116.30	Field
Osetes (Plains)	North Osetia	65	117.78	Field
Armenians		75	118.55	Boas
Armenians		105	118.55	Twarjanowitsch
Osetes (Digors)	North Osetia	30	118.70	Field
Osetes (Total)	North Osetia	103	118.78	Field
Osetes (Irons)	North Osetia	65	118.82	Field
Osetes (Mountain)	North Osetia	38	120.06	Field
		Total... 651		

TABLE 61: MINIMUM FRONTAL DIAMETER OF PEOPLES IN TURKESTAN

Group	No.	MFD	Observer
Arabs	29	103.0	Maslovskii
Iomuds	107	104.97	IArkho
Chaudirs	200	107.30	IArkho
Ferghana	200	107.98	IArkho
Arabs	17	109.0	Maslovskii
Total...	553		

TABLE 62: FRONTO-PARIETAL INDEX OF PEOPLES IN THE CAUCASUS

Group	Locality	No.	FPI	Observer
Armenians		101	68.24	Seltzer
Osetes (Mountain)	North Osetia	38	74.41	Field
Osetes (Total)	North Osetia	103	74.62	Field
Osetes (Irons)	North Osetia	65	74.62	Field
Osetes (Digors)	North Osetia	38	74.65	Field
Osetes (Plains)	North Osetia	65	74.74	Field
Armenians		105	75.12	Twarjanowitsch
Armenians		75	75.61	Boas
Yezidis	Transcaucasia and Anatolia	50	76.60	Field
Yezidis	Yerevan, Armenia	20	77.05	Field
		Total... 434		

TABLE 63: BIZYGOMATIC BREADTH OF PEOPLES IN THE CAUCASUS

Group	Locality	No.	Biz. B.	Observer
Armenians		20	136.0	Weissenberg
Turks	Nakhichevan	151	136.0	Anserov
Turks	Mekha, Azerbaidzhan	301	139.1	IArkho
Yezidis	Yerevan, Armenia	20	139.25	Field
Yezidis	Transcaucasia and Anatolia	51	139.55	Field
Turks	Gandzha, Azerbaidzhan	230	139.7	IArkho
Tajiks	Kura Valley	29	139.76	Chantre
Turks	Kakh, Azerbaidzhan	201	140.5	Debets
Armenians		25	140.6	Hrdlička
Armenians	Ghirussi	28	141.0	Chantre
Armenians	Yerevan, Armenia	27	141.0	Chantre
Jews		20	141.0	Weissenberg
Armenians		292	141.6	Chantre
Jews	Georgia	33	142.0	Weissenberg
Kara Nogais	Eastern	156	142.3	Terebinskaia

TABLE 63 (Continued)

Group	Locality	No.	Biz. B.	Observer
Armenians		101	142.84	Seltzer
Georgians	Georgia	900	143.0	Dzhavahov
Lezghians		11	143.0	Chantre
Armenians		75	143.63	Boas
Nogais	Khasavyurt Region	165	143.9	Terebinskaia
Osetes (Digors)	North Osetia	38	143.95	Field
Osetes (Plains)	North Osetia	66	144.20	Field
Osetes (Total)	North Osetia	105	144.30	Field
Osetes (Irons)	North Osetia	67	144.45	Field
Osetes (Mountain)	North Osetia	39	144.45	Field
Osetes	Osetes	136	145.0	Dzhawachischwili
Nogais	Terek Region	108	145.1	Levin
Edissan Nogais		146	145.4	IArkho
Turkomans	North Caucasus	302	145.5	IArkho
Kumyks		130	145.7	Debets and Trofimova
Edishkul Nogais		145	145.8	IArkho
Embailuk Nogais		176	147.4	IArkho
Kara Nogais	Western	188	147.5	IArkho
Karachais		211	147.6	Levin

Total... 4,463

TABLE 64: BIZYGOMATIC BREADTH OF PEOPLES IN TURKESTAN

Group or Locality	No.	Biz. B.	Observer
Teke	51	129.0	IAvorskii
Vanch	80	136.65	Korovnikov
Bokhara	163	138.0	Oshanin
Iomuds	107	138.16	IArkho
Pskem Valley and Bokhara Region	100	140.79	.....
Chaudirs	200	141.82	IArkho
Ferghana	200	143.32	IArkho
Arabs	17	137.0	Maslovskii
Arabs	29	141.0	Maslovskii
Arabs	100	142.1	Oshanin

Total... 1,047

TABLE 65: BIGONIAL BREADTH OF PEOPLES IN THE CAUCASUS

Group	Locality	No.	Big. B.	Observer
Armenians		19	108.63	Von Erckert
Armenians		101	109.94	Seltzer
Armenians		105	112.26	Twarjanowitsch
Yezidis	Transcaucasia and Anatolia	50	114.84	Field
Yezidis	Yerevan, Armenia	19	115.50	Field
Osetes (Irons)	North Osetia	67	116.46	Field
Osetes (Plains)	North Osetia	66	117.06	Field
Osetes (Total)	North Osetia	105	117.50	Field
Osetes (Mountain)	North Osetia	39	118.26	Field
Osetes (Digors)	North Osetia	38	119.38	Field

Total... 380

TABLE 66: BIGONIAL BREADTH OF PEOPLES IN TURKESTAN

Group or Locality	No.	Big. B.	Observer
Iomuds	107	107.89	IArkho
Chaudirs	200	111.58	IArkho
Teke	51	112.00	IAvorskii
Arabs	17	112.00	Maslovskii
Ferghana	200	112.26	IArkho
Arabs	29	118.00	Maslovskii
Total...	604		

TABLE 67: UPPER FACIAL HEIGHT OF PEOPLES IN THE CAUCASUS

Group	Locality	No.	UFH	Observer
Osetes (Plains)	North Osetia	66	70.85	Field
Osetes (Irons)	North Osetia	67	70.95	Field
Osetes (Total)	North Osetia	105	71.05	Field
Osetes (Digors)	North Osetia	38	71.60	Field
Osetes (Mountain)	North Osetia	39	71.75	Field
Yezidis	Transcaucasia and Anatolia	51	74.95	Field
Yezidis	Yerevan, Armenia	20	75.75	Field
Armenians		100	76.61	Seltzer
	Total...	256		

TABLE 68: TOTAL FACIAL HEIGHT OF PEOPLES IN THE CAUCASUS

Group	Locality	No.	TFH	Observer
Armenians		25	120.2	Hrdlička
Armenians		20	122.0	Weissenberg
Osetes (Irons)	North Osetia	67	122.35	Field
Osetes (Plains)	North Osetia	66	122.55	Field
Osetes (Total)	North Osetia	105	123.15	Field
Armenians		19	123.16	Von Erckert
Osetes (Mountain)	North Osetia	39	124.20	Field
Osetes (Digors)	North Osetia	38	124.50	Field
Jews	Daghestan	20	125.0	Weissenberg
Jews	Georgia	33	125.0	Weissenberg
Georgians		900	126.0	Dzhavahov
Yezidis	Transcaucasia and Anatolia	50	127.60	Field
Armenians		100	127.96	Seltzer
Yezidis	Yerevan, Armenia	20	128.25	Field
Armenians		105	130.24	Twarjanowitsch
	Total...	1,377		

TABLE 69: TOTAL FACIAL HEIGHT OF PEOPLES IN TURKESTAN

Group or Locality	No.	TFH	Observer
Vanch	80	115.42	Korovnikov
Pskem Valley and Bokhara Region	100	117.45	.....
Bokhara	163	120.40	Oshanin
Teke	51	122.00	IAvorskii
Arabs	29	122.70	Maslovskii
Arabs	100	124.66	Oshanin
Iomuds	107	130.42	IArkho
Ferghana	200	130.54	IArkho
Chaudirs	200	132.90	IArkho
Total...	1,030		

TABLE 70: TOTAL FACIAL INDEX OF PEOPLES IN THE CAUCASUS

Group	Locality	No.	TFI	Observer
Armenians		25	85.50	Hrdlička
Osetes (Plains)	North Osetia	66	85.50	Field
Osetes (Irons)	North Osetia	67	85.80	Field
Osetes (Total)	North Osetia	105	85.85	Field
Osetes (Mountain)	North Osetia	39	86.50	Field
Armenians		19	86.74	Von Erckert
Osetes (Digors)	North Osetia	38	86.85	Field
Jews	Georgia	33	88.00	Weissenberg
Georgians		900	88.10	Dzhavahov
Jews	Daghestan	20	88.60	Weissenberg
Armenians		20	89.70	Weissenberg
Armenians		100	89.74	Seltzer
Armenians		105	90.79	Twarjanowitsch
Yezidis	Yerevan, Armenia	20	91.50	Field
Yezidis	Transcaucasia and Anatolia	50	91.70	Field
	Total...	1,377		

TABLE 71: NASAL LENGTH OF PEOPLES IN THE CAUCASUS

Group	Locality	No.	NL	Observer
Lezghians		11	51.00	Chantre
Osetes (Irons)	North Osetia	66	52.06	Field
Osetes (Mountain)	North Osetia	39	52.46	Field
Tajiks	Kura Valley	29	52.48	Chantre
Osetes (Total)	North Osetia	104	52.54	Field
Osetes (Plains)	North Osetia	65	52.58	Field
Armenians		25	53.00	Hrdlička
Osetes (Digors)	North Osetia	38	53.38	Field
Armenians		292	53.98	Chantre
Armenians		20	55.00	Weissenberg
Armenians		19	55.79	Von Erckert
Armenians		75	56.28	Boas
Yezidis	Transcaucasia and Anatolia	51	56.50	Field
Jews	Daghestan	20	57.00	Weissenberg
Yezidis	Yerevan, Armenia	20	57.10	Field
Jews	Georgia	33	58.00	Weissenberg
Armenians		101	59.93	Seltzer
Georgians		900	60.00	Dzhavahov
	Total...	1,680		

TABLE 72: NASAL BREADTH OF PEOPLES IN THE CAUCASUS

Group	Locality	No.	NB	Observer
Armenians		105	30.40	Twarjanowitsch
Osetes (Plains)	North Osetia	66	32.78	Field
Armenians		20	33.00	Weissenberg
Osetes (Irons)	North Osetia	67	33.29	Field
Osetes (Total)	North Osetia	105	33.35	Field
Osetes (Digors)	North Osetia	38	33.41	Field
Yezidis	Transcaucasia and Anatolia	51	33.59	Field
Yezidis	Yerevan, Armenia	20	33.95	Field
Jews	Georgia	33	34.00	Weissenberg
Georgians	Georgia	900	34.00	Dzhavahov
Osetes (Mountain)	North Osetia	39	34.31	Field
Jews	Daghestan	20	35.00	Weissenberg
Armenians		25	35.60	Hrdlička
Armenians		292	35.60	Chantre
Armenians		19	35.74	Von Erckert

TABLE 72 (Continued)

Group	Locality	No.	NB	Observer
Tadzhiks (Tajiks)	Kura Valley	29	35.96	Chantre
Lezghians		11	36.00	Chantre
Armenians		75	37.17	Boas
Armenians		101	37.96	Seltzer
		Total... 1,786		

TABLE 73: NASAL INDEX OF PEOPLES IN THE CAUCASUS

Group	Locality	No.	NI	Observer
Georgians	Georgia	900	56.60	Dzhavahov
Jews	Georgia	33	58.60	Weissenberg
Armenians		20	60.00	Weissenberg
Yezidis	Yerevan, Armenia	20	60.30	Field
Armenians		110	60.40	Pantiukhov
Jews	Daghestan	20	61.40	Weissenberg
Yezidis	Transcaucasia and Anatolia	51	61.04	Field
Karaims		20	62.20	Weissenberg
Kurds	Transcaucasia	300	62.30	Ivanovskii
Armenians	Yerevan, Armenia	10	62.35	Chantre
Osetes (Plains)	North Osetia	65	62.62	Field
Osetes (Digors)	North Osetia	38	62.86	Field
Armenians	Tbilisi, Georgia	25	63.50	Chantre
North Osetes (Total)	North Osetia	104	63.58	Field
Armenians		101	63.80	Seltzer
Osetes (Irons)	North Osetia	66	63.98	Field
Armenians		19	64.16	Von Erckert
Tatars	Azerbaidzhan	114	64.20	Chantre
Kurds	Transcaucasia	12	64.40	Chantre
Lazes		27	64.45	Chantre
Osetes (Mountain)	North Osetia	39	65.18	Field
Tatars	Azerbaidzhan	18	65.20	Chantre
Kurds	Transcaucasia	97	65.80	Chantre
Armenians		125	66.00	Pittard
Armenians		75	66.04	Boas
Armenians		292	66.04	Chantre
Tatars	Yerevan, Armenia	17	66.04	Chantre
Tatars	Azerbaidzhan	19	66.04	Chantre
Osetes	Osetia	534	66.50	Deniker
Osetes	Osetia	136	66:50	Dzhawachischwili
Tajiks	Kura Valley	29	66.64	Chantre
Tatars	Aralych	16	66.67	Chantre
Armenians		25	67.17	Hrdlička
Tatars	Arkhuri	15	67.31	Chantre
Lazes		140	67.70	Chantre
Mingrelians		12	67.99	Chantre
Lezghians		11	70.59	Chantre
Osetes		11	74.20	Chantre
Kalmyks		10	75.30	Chantre
		Total... 3,448		

TABLE 74: NASAL INDEX OF FEMALES IN THE CAUCASUS

Group	Locality	No.	NI	Observer
Osetes	North Osetia	47	59.78	Field
Karaims		10	59.00	Weissenberg
Kurds	Transcaucasia	60	62.60	Ivanovskii
Tatars	Azerbaidzhan	18	62.80	Chantre
Kurds	Transcaucasia	15	64.80	Chantre
Kurds	Transcaucasia	34	70.20	Chantre
		Total... 184		

TABLE 75: KISH MALE CRANIA FROM "A" CEMETERY, IRAQ

Measurements	No.	Mean
Head length	25	189.50
Head breadth	25	137.44
Minimum frontal diameter	26	94.69

Index		
Cephalic	24	71.54

TABLE 76: HUMAN REMAINS FROM KISH, IRAQ

Season	Period	Description	Locality
1925-26	Early	Long bones	Cemetery "A"
	Early	Long bones	Inghara South
	Late	Long bones	Mound "W"
	Early	Crania	Cemetery "A"
	Early	Crania	Inghara South
	Late	Crania and long bones	Mound "W"
1927-28	Early	Crania and long bones	Harsagkalemma

TABLE 77: DIFFERENCES AND X P.E.'S OF IRAQ GROUPS

Measurements	Dulaim vs Anaiza diff.	x p.e.	Dulaim vs Total Kish Arabs diff.	x p.e.	Dulaim vs Marsh Arabs diff.	x p.e.
Age	-1.75	1.50	-1.35	1.88	-1.65	2.23
Stature	4.71	4.71	- .63	1.70	.96	2.29
Sitting height	-3.78	4.45	1.56	6.00	-3.72	13.78
Head length	- .18	.18	2.28	4.96	3.78	8.04
Head breadth	3.84	5.19	- .57	1.63	-4.41	11.60
Minimum frontal diameter	2.72	4.32	1.52	5.24	0	0
Bizygomatic breadth	4.75	6.79	5.05	12.62	- .50	1.32
Bigonial breadth	6.28	7.85	3.56	8.90	1.72	4.30
Total facial height	1.00	1.12	1.55	3.60	- .25	.56
Upper facial height	1.30	1.73	-1.45	4.26	1.00	2.78
Nasal height	- .80	1.14	-5.64	18.80	- .12	.35
Nasal breadth	.09	.15	- .72	2.88	- .15	.54
Ear length	1.12	1.62	-4.32	13.50	-1.04	2.81
Ear breadth	.63	1.47	- .90	4.29	2.22	10.09
Indices						
Relative sitting height	-3.60	8.00	1.00	7.14	-2.70	19.29
Cephalic	1.77	2.95	-1.29	5.38	-3.90	15.00
Fronto-parietal	.39	.83	1.53	6.65	2.58	11.73
Zygo-frontal	- .24	.62	-1.80	7.83	.92	4.38
Zygo-gonial	2.31	4.91	.12	.44	2.04	7.56
Facial	-2.35	3.36	-2.30	5.75	.30	.77
Upper facial	- .81	1.59	-3.36	12.44	1.02	3.77
Nasal	- .52	.35	4.52	7.93	- .36	.55
Ear	.48	.64	2.96	7.40	5.00	11.63

TABLE 78: DIFFERENCES AND X P.E.'S OF IRAQ GROUPS

Measurements	Dulaim vs Subba diff.	x p.e.	Dulaim vs Shammar diff.	x p.e.	Dulaim vs Sulubba diff.	x p.e.
Age	-4.30	3.58	-9.25	11.71	-5.15	3.39
Stature	1.44	2.57	1.62	4.26	2.55	2.66
Sitting height	-4.50	13.24	-4.74	18.96	2.82	5.04
Head length	5.04	8.84	-1.68	3.65	1.65	2.06
Head breadth	-4.41	9.59	-1.08	3.09	4.05	5.79
Minimum frontal diameter	-1.56	3.71	.36	1.29	4.20	8.24
Bizygomatic breadth	-1.10	2.12	.30	.79	8.50	12.69
Bigonial breadth	2.00	3.85	1.80	4.62	7.48	12.90
Total facial height	-1.25	1.98	- .95	2.21	2.55	3.23
Upper facial height	-2.60	4.73	- .20	.57	1.90	2.84
Nasal height	-3.92	7.69	-1.20	3.64	- .20	.33
Nasal breadth	- .84	2.33	- .84	3.11	.72	1.80
Ear length	-3.20	6.96	-1.16	3.41	.24	.44
Ear breadth	.90	2.90	- .54	2.45	.87	2.49
Indices						
Relative sitting height	-3.22	18.94	-3.30	23.57	-2.84	10.52
Cephalic	-4.35	12.43	.12	.50	1.65	3.37
Fronto-parietal	1.41	4.86	.27	1.29	1.05	2.39
Zygo-frontal	0	0	.52	2.48	-1.96	4.78
Zygo-gonial	2.34	6.50	1.47	5.65	.78	1.59
Facial	- .15	.29	-1.00	2.63	-3.50	5.22
Upper facial	-1.53	3.92	- .21	.81	-1.50	2.59
Nasal	2.32	3.14	- .80	1.29	1.22	1.11
Ear	4.68	8.83	.32	.76	.96	1.45

TABLE 79: DIFFERENCES AND X P.E.'S OF IRAQ GROUPS

Measurements	Dulaim vs Total Jews diff.	x p.e.	Dulaim vs Turkomans diff.	x p.e.	Anaiza vs Shammar diff.	x p.e.
Age	-5.40	5.51	-7.45	5.78	-7.50	6.41
Stature	3.21	6.42	1.11	1.98	-3.09	3.15
Sitting height	-3.18	9.94	-4.29	11.29	- .96	1.14
Head length	9.99	18.16	4.05	5.26	-1.50	1.56
Head breadth	-6.87	14.93	- .51	.91	-4.92	6.83
Minimum frontal diameter	- .44	1.16	1.24	2.95	-2.36	3.81
Bizygomatic breadth	-2.60	5.78	-1.55	3.23	4.45	6.64
Bigonial breadth	-2.40	5.00	-1.28	2.29	-4.48	5.74
Total facial height	-2.20	3.73	-2.30	3.48	-1.95	2.27
Upper facial height	-1.30	3.33	-1.75	3.37	-1.50	2.05
Nasal height	-2.12	5.58	-1.36	2.67	- .40	.59
Nasal breadth	.51	1.65	-1.29	3.49	- .93	1.60
Ear length	- .92	2.19	-1.72	3.07	-2.28	3.40
Ear breadth	- .48	1.92	- .99	3.41	-1.17	2.79
Indices						
Relative sitting height	-3.16	19.75	-2.96	16.44	.30	.68
Cephalic	-8.01	26.70	-1.65	3.67	-1.65	2.84
Fronto-parietal	3.72	12.40	1.14	3.08	- .12	.26
Zygo-frontal	2.04	5.51	2.20	6.29	.76	2.00
Zygo-gonial	.06	.19	.24	.60	- .84	1.87
Facial	.35	.78	- .65	1.25	1.35	2.01
Upper facial	.24	.83	- .54	1.50	.60	1.20
Nasal	2.88	4.17	- .88	.96	- .28	.19
Ear	.04	.08	.40	.68	- .16	.22

TABLE 80: DIFFERENCES AND X P.E.'S OF IRAQ GROUPS

Measurements	Anaiza vs Sulubba		Total Kish Arabs vs Marsh Arabs		Total Kish Arabs vs Subba	
	diff.	x p.e.	diff.	x p.e.	diff.	x p.e.
Age	-3.40	1.94	- .30	.45	-2.95	2.54
Stature	-2.16	1.64	1.59	4.42	2.07	3.98
Sitting height	6.60	6.73	-5.28	22.00	-6.06	18.36
Head length	1.83	1.58	1.50	4.17	2.76	5.75
Head breadth	.21	.22	-3.84	11.64	-3.84	9.14
Minimum frontal diameter	1.48	1.97	-1.52	5.43	-3.08	7.51
Bizygomatic breadth	3.75	4.31	-5.55	15.86	-6.15	12.06
Bigonial breadth	1.20	1.35	-1.84	4.97	-1.56	3.12
Total facial height	1.55	1.44	-1.80	4.50	-2.80	4.75
Upper facial height	.60	.65	2.45	7.90	-1.15	2.21
Nasal height	.60	.71	5.52	19.03	1.72	3.58
Nasal breadth	.63	.95	.57	2.71	- .12	.40
Ear length	- .88	1.10	3.28	10.58	1.12	2.73
Ear breadth	.24	.47	3.12	16.42	1.80	6.21
Indices						
Relative sitting height	.76	1.55	-3.70	33.64	-4.22	30.14
Cephalic	- .12	.16	-2.61	11.86	-3.06	9.56
Fronto-parietal	.66	1.10	1.05	5.00	- .12	.43
Zygo-frontal	-1.72	3.31	2.72	12.95	1.80	6.43
Zygo-gonial	-1.53	2.47	1.92	7.68	2.22	6.34
Facial	-1.15	1.32	2.60	7.03	2.15	4.39
Upper facial	- .69	.96	4.38	17.52	1.83	4.82
Nasal	1.74	1.02	-4.88	9.96	-2.20	3.67
Ear	.48	.55	2.04	6.00	1.72	3.74

TABLE 81: DIFFERENCES AND X P.E.'S OF IRAQ GROUPS

Measurements	Total Kish Arabs vs Shammar		Total Kish Arabs vs Sulubba		Total Kish Arabs vs Turkomans	
	diff.	x p.e.	diff.	x p.e.	diff.	x p.e.
Age	-7.90	10.97	-3.80	2.57	-6.10	4.88
Stature	2.25	6.82	3.18	3.38	1.74	3.35
Sitting height	-6.30	27.31	1.26	2.29	-5.85	16.25
Head length	-3.96	11.31	- .63	.85	1.77	2.49
Head breadth	- .51	1.70	4.62	6.90	.06	.12
Minimum frontal diameter	-1.16	4.46	2.68	5.36	- .28	.68
Bizygomatic breadth	-4.75	13.19	3.45	5.23	-6.60	14.04
Bigonial breadth	-1.76	4.76	3.92	6.88	-4.84	8.96
Total facial height	-2.50	6.76	1.00	1.32	-3.85	6.11
Upper facial height	1.25	4.17	3.35	5.23	- .30	.62
Nasal height	4.44	16.44	5.44	9.38	4.28	9.11
Nasal breadth	- .12	.63	1.44	4.00	- .57	1.78
Ear length	3.16	11.29	4.56	8.94	2.60	5.00
Ear breadth	.36	1.89	1.77	5.21	- .09	.35
Indices						
Relative sitting height	-4.30	39.09	-3.84	15.36	-3.96	26.40
Cephalic	1.41	7.42	2.94	6.26	- .36	.86
Fronto-parietal	-1.26	6.30	- .48	1.09	- .39	1.08
Zygo-frontal	2.32	11.05	- .16	.39	4.00	11.43
Zygo-gonial	1.35	5.40	.66	1.38	.12	.31
Facial	1.30	3.71	-1.20	1.82	1.65	3.30
Upper facial	3.15	12.60	1.86	3.26	2.82	8.06
Nasal	-5.32	12.09	-3.30	3.30	-5.40	6.67
Ear	-2.64	8.00	-2.00	3.33	-2.56	4.92

TABLE 82: DIFFERENCES AND X P.E.'S OF IRAQ GROUPS

Measurements	Total Kish Arabs vs Total Jews diff.	x p.e.	Marsh Arabs vs Subba diff.	x p.e.	Marsh Arabs vs Shammar diff.	x p.e.
Age	-4.05	4.35	-2.65	2.28	-7.60	10.27
Stature	3.84	8.35	.48	.87	.66	1.74
Sitting height	-4.74	15.80	- .78	2.36	-1.02	4.43
Head length	7.71	16.76	1.26	2.57	-5.46	15.17
Head breadth	-6.30	15.00	0	0	3.33	10.09
Minimum frontal diameter	-1.96	5.44	-1.56	3.80	.36	1.33
Bizygomatic breadth	-7.65	17.79	- .60	1.22	.80	2.42
Bigonial breadth	-5.96	12.96	.28	.57	.08	.22
Total facial height	-3.75	6.81	-1.00	1.64	- .70	1.75
Upper facial height	.15	.44	-3.60	6.67	-1.20	3.64
Nasal height	3.52	10.35	-3.80	7.45	-1.08	3.48
Nasal breadth	1.23	4.92	- .69	2.09	- .69	3.00
Ear length	3.40	9.19	-2.16	4.80	- .12	.36
Ear breadth	.42	1.83	-1.32	4.40	-2.76	13.80
Indices						
Relative sitting height	-4.16	29.71	- .52	3.71	- .60	5.45
Cephalic	-6.72	24.89	- .45	1.32	4.02	19.14
Fronto-parietal	2.19	7.55	-1.17	4.18	-2.31	12.16
Zygo-frontal	3.84	10.38	- .92	3.41	- .40	2.11
Zygo-gonial	- .06	.19	.30	.86	- .57	2.28
Facial	2.65	6.16	- .45	.94	-1.30	3.82
Upper facial	3.60	12.86	-2.55	6.71	-1.23	4.92
Nasal	-1.64	3.04	2.68	3.94	- .44	.80
Ear	-2.92	6.79	- .32	.65	-4.68	12.65

TABLE 83: DIFFERENCES AND X P.E.'S OF IRAQ GROUPS

Measurements	Marsh Arabs vs Sulubba diff.	x p.e.	Marsh Arabs vs Turkomans diff.	x p.e.	Marsh Arabs vs Total Jews diff.	x p.e.
Age	-3.50	2.35	-5.80	4.60	-3.75	3.99
Stature	1.59	1.66	.15	.27	2.25	4.59
Sitting height	6.54	11.89	- .57	1.54	.54	1.74
Head length	-2.13	2.84	.27	.38	6.21	13.21
Head breadth	8.46	12.26	3.90	7.09	-2.46	5.59
Minimum frontal diameter	4.20	8.40	1.24	3.02	- .44	1.19
Bizygomatic breadth	9.00	14.06	-1.05	2.39	-2.10	5.25
Bigonial breadth	5.76	10.29	-3.00	5.56	-4.12	9.16
Total facial height	2.80	3.64	-2.05	3.20	-1.95	3.42
Upper facial height	.90	1.36	-2.75	5.50	-2.30	6.22
Nasal height	- .08	.13	-1.24	2.48	-2.00	5.41
Nasal breadth	.87	2.29	-1.14	3.35	.66	2.36
Ear length	1.28	2.37	- .68	1.24	.12	.29
Ear breadth	-1.35	3.97	-3.21	11.89	-2.70	11.25
Indices						
Relative sitting height	- .14	.56	- .26	1.73	- .46	3.54
Cephalic	5.55	11.56	2.25	5.23	-4.11	14.17
Fronto-parietal	-1.53	3.56	-1.44	4.00	1.14	3.93
Zygo-frontal	-2.88	7.20	1.28	3.76	1.12	3.11
Zygo-gonial	-1.26	2.62	-1.80	4.62	-1.98	6.39
Facial	-3.80	5.85	- .95	1.94	.05	.12
Upper facial	-2.52	4.42	-1.56	4.46	- .78	2.79
Nasal	1.58	1.49	- .52	.59	3.24	5.14
Ear	-4.04	6.52	-4.60	8.36	-4.96	10.55

TABLE 84: DIFFERENCES AND X P.E.'S OF IRAQ GROUPS

Measurements	Subba vs Shammar diff.	x p.e.	Subba vs Sulubba diff.	x p.e.	Subba vs Turkomans diff.	x p.e.
Age	-4.95	4.12	- .85	.48	-3.15	2.01
Stature	.18	.34	1.11	1.09	- .33	.50
Sitting height	- .24	.75	7.32	12.41	.21	.49
Head length	-6.72	14.00	-3.39	4.19	- .99	1.27
Head breadth	3.33	7.93	8.46	11.59	3.90	6.50
Minimum frontal diameter	1.92	4.80	5.76	9.93	2.80	5.49
Bizygomatic breadth	1.40	2.86	9.60	12.97	- .45	.79
Bigonial breadth	- .20	.41	5.48	8.43	-3.28	5.21
Total facial height	.30	.51	3.80	4.27	-1.05	1.35
Upper facial height	2.40	4.53	4.50	5.77	.85	1.31
Nasal height	2.72	5.44	3.72	5.24	2.56	4.06
Nasal breadth	0	0	1.56	3.55	- .45	1.10
Ear length	2.04	4.74	3.44	5.64	1.48	2.43
Ear breadth	-1.44	4.80	- .03	.08	-1.89	5.40
Indices						
Relative sitting height	- .08	.57	.38	1.41	.26	1.44
Cephalic	4.47	13.97	6.00	11.11	2.70	5.51
Fronto-parietal	-1.14	4.22	- .36	.75	- .27	.66
Zygo-frontal	.52	2.00	-1.96	4.45	2.20	5.64
Zygo-gonial	- .87	2.56	-1.56	2.89	-2.10	4.57
Facial	- .85	1.81	-3.35	4.59	- .50	.85
Upper facial	1.32	3.57	.03	.05	.99	2.20
Nasal	-3.12	4.80	-1.10	.99	-3.20	3.40
Ear	-4.36	9.08	-3.72	5.39	-4.28	6.79

TABLE 85: DIFFERENCES AND X P.E.'S OF IRAQ GROUPS

Measurements	Subba vs Yezidis II diff.	x p.e.	Subba vs Total Kurds diff.	x p.e.	Subba vs Assyrians diff.	x p.e.
Age	-3.75	2.72	1.45	1.32	7.70	6.53
Stature	- .15	.24	.12	.24	-4.29	7.15
Sitting height	.24	.65	1.62	5.40	2.97	8.25
Head length	8.85	14.05	5.07	11.27	5.55	10.09
Head breadth	-4.86	8.68	-5.97	14.92	-8.28	14.28
Minimum frontal diameter	1.16	2.32	2.80	7.00	-2.48	5.17
Bizygomatic breadth	-1.70	2.98	-3.10	6.89	-5.40	9.15
Bigonial breadth	-5.56	10.49	-3.96	8.80	-6.32	10.19
Total facial height	-2.65	3.96	.15	.27	-5.00	7.58
Upper facial height	3.30	5.41	.80	1.60	-4.95	8.39
Nasal height	2.12	3.72	2.64	5.62	-6.32	11.70
Nasal breadth	.48	1.33	.66	2.28	.51	1.55
Ear length	.52	.96	1.40	3.50	1.32	2.87
Ear breadth	2.76	7.67	- .39	1.39	.03	.09
Indices						
Relative sitting height	.16	.94	.92	7.08	3.08	19.25
Cephalic	-6.66	16.24	-5.49	17.16	-6.78	15.77
Fronto-parietal	3.36	10.18	4.98	18.44	2.70	8.18
Zygo-frontal	1.84	5.75	3.72	14.31	1.08	3.60
Zygo-gonial	-2.97	7.82	-1.23	3.84	-1.41	3.62
Facial	- .95	1.79	2.30	5.35	- .15	.28
Upper facial	1.44	3.51	1.92	5.49	-1.56	3.71
Nasal	-1.32	1.74	-1.48	2.51	11.60	18.12
Ear	-4.60	8.21	-1.80	4.09	- .92	1.80

TABLE 86: DIFFERENCES AND X P.E.'S OF IRAQ GROUPS

Measurements	Subba vs Total Jews diff.	x p.e.	Shammar vs Sulubba diff.	x p.e.	Shammar vs Turkomans diff.	x p.e.
Age	-1.10	.83	4.10	2.70	1.80	1.40
Stature	1.77	2.85	.93	.99	- .51	.96
Sitting height	1.32	3.47	7.56	14.00	.45	1.29
Head length	4.95	8.68	3.33	4.50	5.73	8.07
Head breadth	-2.46	4.82	5.13	7.66	.57	1.10
Minimum frontal diameter	1.12	2.33	3.84	7.84	.88	2.20
Bizygomatic breadth	-1.50	2.78	8.20	12.62	-1.85	4.11
Bigonial breadth	-4.40	7.86	5.68	10.14	-3.08	5.81
Total facial height	- .95	1.32	3.50	4.61	-1.35	2.14
Upper facial height	1.30	2.32	2.10	3.23	-1.55	3.16
Nasal height	1.80	3.33	1.00	1.69	- .16	.33
Nasal breadth	1.35	3.75	1.56	4.22	- .45	1.32
Ear length	2.28	4.65	1.40	2.69	- .56	1.06
Ear breadth	-1.38	4.31	1.41	4.15	- .45	1.67
Indices						
Relative sitting height	.06	.38	.46	1.84	.34	2.27
Cephalic	-3.66	9.89	1.53	3.26	-1.77	4.21
Fronto-parietal	2.31	6.60	.78	1.81	.87	2.49
Zygo-frontal	2.04	5.10	-2.48	6.20	1.68	4.94
Zygo-gonial	-2.28	5.85	- .69	1.44	-1.23	3.15
Facial	.50	.94	-2.50	3.91	.35	.73
Upper facial	1.77	4.54	-1.29	2.26	- .33	.97
Nasal	.56	.78	2.02	1.96	- .08	.09
Ear	-4.64	8.29	.64	1.05	.08	.15

TABLE 87: DIFFERENCES AND X P.E.'S OF IRAQ GROUPS

Measurements	Shammar vs Total Jews diff.	x p.e.	Sulubba vs Turkomans diff.	x p.e.	Sulubba vs Total Jews diff.	x p.e.
Age	3.85	3.93	-2.30	1.26	- .25	.15
Stature	1.59	3.38	-1.44	1.41	.66	.67
Sitting height	1.56	5.38	-7.11	11.66	-6.00	10.34
Head length	11.67	25.37	2.40	2.50	8.34	10.42
Head breadth	-5.79	13.79	-4.56	5.70	-10.92	14.96
Minimum frontal diameter	- .80	2.22	-2.96	5.10	-4.64	8.44
Bizygomatic breadth	-2.90	7.07	-10.05	14.15	-11.10	16.32
Bigonial breadth	-4.20	9.33	-8.76	12.70	-9.88	15.94
Total facial height	-1.25	2.27	-4.85	5.33	-4.75	5.52
Upper facial height	-1.10	3.06	-3.65	4.87	-3.20	4.78
Nasal height	- .92	2.56	-1.16	1.66	-1.92	3.10
Nasal breadth	1.35	5.00	-2.01	4.47	- .21	.52
Ear length	.24	.63	-1.96	2.84	-1.16	2.00
Ear breadth	.06	.25	-1.86	4.77	-1.35	3.75
Indices						
Relative sitting height	.14	1.00	- .12	.44	- .32	1.23
Cephalic	-8.13	31.27	-3.30	5.50	-9.66	18.94
Fronto-parietal	3.45	12.32	.09	.17	2.67	5.56
Zygo-frontal	1.52	4.34	4.16	8.49	4.00	8.00
Zygo-gonial	-1.41	4.70	- .54	.95	- .72	1.41
Facial	1.35	3.29	2.85	3.90	3.85	5.58
Upper facial	.45	1.67	.96	1.55	1.74	3.00
Nasal	3.68	6.24	-2.10	1.69	1.66	1.54
Ear	- .28	.62	- .56	.76	- .92	1.35

TABLE 88: DIFFERENCES AND X P.E.'S OF IRAQ GROUPS

Measurements	Turkomans vs Yezidis II diff.	x p.e.	Turkomans vs Total Kurds diff.	x p.e.	Turkomans vs Assyrians diff.	x p.e.
Age	- .60	.41	4.60	3.83	10.85	8.48
Stature	.18	.29	.45	.90	-3.96	6.60
Sitting height	.03	.08	1.41	4.15	2.76	7.08
Head length	9.84	12.00	6.06	8.78	6.54	8.61
Head breadth	-8.76	13.69	-9.87	19.35	-12.18	18.45
Minimum frontal diameter	-1.64	3.28	0	0	-5.28	11.00
Bizygomatic breadth	-1.25	2.36	-2.65	6.62	-4.95	8.84
Bigonial breadth	-2.28	4.00	- .68	1.36	-3.04	4.68
Total facial height	-1.60	2.29	1.20	2.00	-3.95	5.64
Upper facial height	2.45	4.22	- .05	.11	-5.80	10.36
Nasal height	- .44	.79	.08	.17	-8.88	16.75
Nasal breadth	.93	2.45	1.11	3.58	.96	2.82
Ear length	- .96	1.52	- .08	.16	- .16	.29
Ear breadth	- .87	2.56	1.50	6.00	1.92	6.40
Indices						
Relative sitting height	- .10	.56	.66	4.71	2.82	17.62
Cephalic	-9.36	19.10	-8.19	19.50	-9.48	18.59
Fronto-parietal	3.63	9.08	5.25	15.00	2.97	7.42
Zygo-frontal	- .36	.95	1.52	4.61	-1.12	3.03
Zygo-gonial	- .87	2.07	.87	2.35	.69	1.60
Facial	- .45	.85	2.80	6.36	.35	.65
Upper facial	.45	1.15	.93	2.91	-2.55	6.38
Nasal	1.88	2.02	1.72	2.12	14.80	17.41
Ear	- .32	.52	2.48	4.86	3.36	5.89

TABLE 89: DIFFERENCES AND X P.E.'S OF IRAQ GROUPS

Measurements	Turkomans vs Total Jews diff.	x p.e.	Yezidis II vs Total Kurds diff.	x p.e.	Yezidis II vs Assyrians diff.	x p.e.
Age	2.05	1.45	5.20	5.53	11.45	11.01
Stature	2.10	3.39	.27	.63	-4.14	7.67
Sitting height	1.11	2.71	1.38	5.31	2.73	8.27
Head length	5.94	7.71	-3.78	7.27	-3.30	5.41
Head breadth	-6.36	10.60	-1.11	2.41	-3.42	5.43
Minimum frontal diameter	-1.68	3.50	1.64	4.32	-3.64	7.91
Bizygomatic breadth	-1.05	2.10	-1.40	3.50	-3.70	6.73
Bigonial breadth	-1.12	1.87	1.60	4.32	- .76	1.36
Total facial height	.10	.13	2.80	6.22	-2.35	4.12
Upper facial height	.45	.87	-2.50	6.25	-8.25	16.18
Nasal height	- .76	1.43	.52	1.41	-8.44	18.76
Nasal breadth	1.80	4.86	.18	.72	.03	.10
Ear length	.80	1.36	.88	2.05	.80	1.67
Ear breadth	.51	1.70	2.37	8.78	2.79	8.72
Indices						
Relative sitting height	- .20	1.18	.76	5.85	2.92	18.25
Cephalic	-6.36	13.83	1.17	3.66	- .12	.28
Fronto-parietal	2.58	6.29	1.62	6.23	- .66	2.00
Zygo-frontal	- .16	.36	1.88	7.52	- .76	2.53
Zygo-gonial	- .18	.42	1.74	6.69	1.56	4.59
Facial	1.00	1.85	3.25	9.03	.80	1.70
Upper facial	.78	2.11	.48	1.78	-3.00	8.33
Nasal	3.76	4.18	- .16	.28	12.92	20.19
Ear	- .36	.59	2.80	6.83	3.68	7.67

TABLE 90: DIFFERENCES AND X P.E.'S OF IRAQ GROUPS

Measurements	Yezidis II vs Total Jews diff.	x p.e.	Total Kurds vs Assyrians diff.	x p.e.	Total Kurds vs Total Jews diff.	x p.e.
Age	2.65	2.21	6.25	10.25	-2.55	2.93
Stature	1.92	3.37	-4.41	11.02	1.65	3.84
Sitting height	1.08	3.09	1.35	5.40	- .30	1.11
Head length	-3.90	6.29	.48	1.14	- .12	.28
Head breadth	2.40	4.29	-2.31	4.71	3.51	8.78
Minimum frontal diameter	- .04	.09	-5.28	15.09	-1.68	4.80
Bizygomatic breadth	.20	.40	-2.30	5.35	1.60	4.44
Bigonial breadth	1.16	2.32	-2.36	4.92	- .44	1.07
Total facial height	1.70	2.70	-5.15	11.70	-1.10	2.12
Upper facial height	-2.00	4.26	-5.75	15.54	.50	1.61
Nasal height	- .32	.71	-8.96	28.00	- .84	2.62
Nasal breadth	.87	2.72	- .15	.79	.69	2.88
Ear length	1.76	3.45	- .08	.26	.88	2.51
Ear breadth	1.38	4.45	.42	1.91	- .99	4.71
Indices						
Relative sitting height	- .10	.62	2.16	18.00	- .86	6.62
Cephalic	3.00	8.11	-1.29	3.69	1.83	7.04
Fronto-parietal	-1.05	3.09	-2.28	8.77	-2.67	9.54
Zygo-frontal	.20	.50	-2.64	11.48	-1.68	4.80
Zygo-gonial	.69	2.03	- .18	.64	-1.05	3.75
Facial	1.45	3.09	-2.45	6.62	-1.80	4.86
Upper facial	.33	1.00	-3.48	12.43	- .15	.62
Nasal	1.88	2.65	13.08	31.14	2.04	3.85
Ear	- .04	.07	.88	2.59	-2.84	6.93

TABLE 91: DIFFERENCES AND X P.E.'S OF IRAQ GROUPS

Measurements	Assyrians vs Total Jews diff.	x p.e.	Total Kurds vs Total Jews diff.	x p.e.
Age	-8.80	9.07	-2.55	2.93
Stature	6.06	11.22	1.65	3.84
Sitting height	-1.65	4.85	- .30	1.11
Head length	- .60	1.11	- .12	.28
Head breadth	5.82	10.03	3.51	8.78
Minimum frontal diameter	3.60	8.18	-1.68	4.80
Bizygomatic breadth	3.90	7.36	1.60	4.44
Bigonial breadth	1.92	3.31	- .44	1.07
Total facial height	4.05	6.53	-1.10	2.12
Upper facial height	6.25	14.20	.50	1.61
Nasal height	8.12	19.80	- .84	2.62
Nasal breadth	.84	3.00	.69	2.88
Ear length	.96	2.29	.88	2.51
Ear breadth	1.41	5.04	- .99	4.71
Indices				
Relative sitting height	-3.02	20.13	- .86	6.62
Cephalic	3.12	8.00	1.83	7.04
Fronto-parietal	- .39	1.15	-2.67	9.54
Zygo-frontal	.96	2.46	-1.68	4.80
Zygo-gonial	- .87	2.49	-1.05	3.75
Facial	.65	1.35	-1.80	4.86
Upper facial	3.33	10.09	- .15	.62
Nasal	-11.04	18.71	2.04	3.85
Ear	-3.72	7.75	-2.84	6.93

TABLE 92: DISPERSION VALUES OF X P.E.'S FOR IRAQ GROUPS

13 Measurements

X P.E.	0-1	1-2	2-3	3-4	4-5	5-6	6+	Totals
Theoretical	6.50	4.20	1.75	0.47	0.08	0.009	0.000+	13
Dulaim vs. Anaiza	2	5	0	0	3	1	2	13
Dulaim vs. Total Kish Arabs	0	2	1	1	3	1	5	13
Dulaim vs. Marsh Arabs	4	1	3	0	1	0	4	13
Dulaim vs. Subba	0	1	4	2	1	0	5	13
Dulaim vs. Shammar	2	1	2	5	2	0	1	13
Dulaim vs. Sulubba	2	1	4	1	0	2	3	13
Dulaim vs. Total Jews	0	3	1	2	0	3	4	13
Dulaim vs. Turkomans	1	1	3	6	0	1	1	13
Anaiza vs. Shammar	1	3	3	3	0	1	2	13
Anaiza vs. Sulubba	5	6	0	0	1	0	1	13
Total Kish Arabs vs. Marsh Arabs	0	0	1	0	4	1	7	13
Total Kish Arabs vs. Subba	1	0	2	3	1	1	5	13
Total Kish Arabs vs. Shammar	1	2	0	0	3	0	7	13
Total Kish Arabs vs. Sulubba	1	1	1	1	1	4	4	13
Total Kish Arabs vs. Turkomans	4	1	1	1	0	1	5	13
Total Kish Arabs vs. Total Jews	1	1	0	0	1	1	9	13
Marsh Arabs vs. Subba	3	2	3	1	2	0	2	13
Marsh Arabs vs. Shammar	2	3	1	3	1	0	3	13
Marsh Arabs vs. Sulubba	1	2	3	2	0	0	5	13
Marsh Arabs vs. Turkomans	2	2	2	3	0	2	2	13
Marsh Arabs vs. Total Jews	1	2	1	1	1	3	4	13
Subba vs. Shammar	5	0	1	0	4	1	2	13
Subba vs. Sulubba	1	1	0	1	2	3	5	13
Subba vs. Turkomans	3	4	1	0	1	3	1	13

TABLE 93: DISPERSION VALUES OF X P.E.'S FOR IRAQ GROUPS

13 Measurements

X P.E.	0-1	1-2	2-3	3-4	4-5	5-6	6+	Totals
Theoretical	6.50	4.20	1.75	0.47	0.08	0.009	0.000+	13
Subba vs. Yezidis II	3	1	2	2	0	1	4	13
Subba vs. Total Kurds	2	2	1	1	0	2	5	13
Subba vs. Assyrians	1	1	1	0	0	1	9	13
Subba vs. Total Jews	0	1	4	3	3	0	2	13
Shammar vs. Sulubba	1	1	1	1	4	0	5	13
Shammar vs. Turkomans	2	5	2	1	1	1	1	13
Shammar vs. Total Jews	2	0	3	2	0	2	4	13
Sulubba vs. Turkomans	0	2	2	0	3	3	3	13
Sulubba vs. Total Jews	2	0	1	2	1	1	6	13
Turkomans vs. Yezidis II	3	1	4	1	2	0	2	13
Turkomans vs. Total Kurds	5	1	1	1	1	0	4	13
Turkomans vs. Assyrians	1	0	1	0	1	1	9	13
Turkomans vs. Total Jews	2	4	2	2	1	0	2	13
Yezidis II vs. Total Kurds	2	1	2	1	2	1	4	13
Yezidis II vs. Assyrians	1	2	0	0	1	2	7	13
Yezidis II vs. Total Jews	3	0	3	3	3	0	1	13
Total Kurds vs. Assyrians	2	2	0	0	2	2	5	13
Total Kurds vs. Total Jews	1	3	4	1	3	0	1	13
Assyrians vs. Total Jews	0	1	1	2	1	1	7	13
Total Kurds vs. Total Jews	1	3	4	1	3	0	1	13

TABLE 94: DISPERSION VALUES OF X P.E.'S FOR IRAQ GROUPS

9 Indices

Theoretical	4.50	2.90	1.21	0.32	0.06	0.006	0.000+	9
Dulaim vs. Anaiza	4	1	1	1	1	0	1	9
Dulaim vs. Total Kish Arabs	1	0	0	0	0	2	6	9
Dulaim vs. Marsh Arabs	2	0	0	1	1	0	5	9
Dulaim vs. Subba	2	0	0	2	1	0	4	9
Dulaim vs. Shammar	3	2	2	0	0	1	1	9
Dulaim vs. Sulubba	0	3	2	1	1	1	1	9
Dulaim vs. Total Jews	4	0	0	0	1	1	3	9
Dulaim vs. Turkomans	3	2	0	2	0	0	2	9
Anaiza vs. Shammar	4	2	3	0	0	0	0	9
Anaiza vs. Sulubba	3	4	1	1	0	0	0	9
Total Kish Arabs vs. Marsh Arabs	0	0	0	0	0	1	8	9
Total Kish Arabs vs. Subba	1	0	0	2	2	0	4	9
Total Kish Arabs vs. Shammar	0	0	0	1	0	1	7	9
Total Kish Arabs vs. Sulubba	1	3	0	3	0	0	2	9
Total Kish Arabs vs. Turkomans	2	1	0	1	1	0	4	9
Total Kish Arabs vs. Total Jews	1	0	0	1	0	0	7	9
Marsh Arabs vs. Subba	3	1	0	3	1	0	1	9
Marsh Arabs vs. Shammar	1	0	2	1	1	1	3	9
Marsh Arabs vs. Sulubba	1	1	1	1	1	1	3	9
Marsh Arabs vs. Turkomans	1	2	0	1	3	1	1	9
Marsh Arabs vs. Total Jews	1	0	1	3	0	1	3	9
Subba vs. Shammar	1	1	2	1	2	0	2	9
Subba vs. Sulubba	3	1	1	0	2	1	1	9
Subba vs. Turkomans	2	1	1	1	1	2	1	9
Subba vs. Yezidis II	1	2	0	1	0	1	4	9
Subba vs. Total Kurds	0	0	1	1	1	2	4	9

TABLE 95: DISPERSION VALUES OF X P.E.'S FOR IRAQ GROUPS

9 Indices

Theoretical	4.50	2.90	1.21	0.32	0.06	0.006	0.000+	9
Subba vs. Assyrians	1	1	0	3	0	0	4	9
Subba vs. Total Jews	3	0	0	0	1	2	3	9
Shammar vs. Sulubba	0	5	1	2	0	0	1	9
Shammar vs. Turkomans	4	0	2	1	2	0	0	9
Shammar vs. Total Jews	1	2	0	1	2	0	3	9
Sulubba vs. Turkomans	4	2	0	1	0	1	1	9
Sulubba vs. Total Jews	0	4	0	1	0	2	2	9
Turkomans vs. Yezidis II	4	1	2	0	0	0	2	9
Turkomans vs. Total Kurds	0	0	3	0	3	0	3	9
Turkomans vs. Assyrians	1	1	0	1	0	1	5	9
Turkomans vs. Total Jews	3	2	1	0	1	0	2	9
Yezidis II vs. Total Kurds	1	1	0	1	0	1	5	9
Yezidis II vs. Assyrians	1	1	2	0	1	0	4	9
Yezidis II vs. Total Jews	3	1	2	2	0	0	1	9
Total Kurds vs. Assyrians	1	0	1	1	0	0	6	9
Total Kurds vs. Total Jews	1	0	0	2	2	0	4	9
Assyrians vs. Total Jews	0	2	2	0	0	0	5	9
Total Kurds vs. Total Jews	1	0	0	2	2	0	4	9

TABLE 96: MEASUREMENTS AND INDICES OF 12 MALES FROM JIDDA, HEJAZ

No.	GOL	GB	CI	MFD	Biz. B.	NH	NB	NI
1	183	146	78.8	108	131	42	39	92.8
2	179	154	86.0	110	135	50	37	74.0
3	175	142	81.1	103	132	50	37	74.0
4	191	144	75.4	105	134	40	37	92.5
5	181	151	83.4	113	136	51	40	78.4
6	195	139	71.3	108	126	60	33	55.0
7	201	153	76.1	111	133	51	40	78.4
8	178	151	84.8	110	136	52	34	65.4
9	198	151	76.3	109	137	52	40	76.9
10	185	144	77.8	111	132	41	37	90.2
11	173	148	85.5	109	130	50	34	68.0
12	192	144	75.0	108	125	51	39	76.5

TABLE 97: MEASUREMENTS AND INDICES OF 45 BEHARNA MALES, BAHRAIN

Measurements	No.	Mean
Age	43	29.90
Head length	44	182.34
Head breadth	44	135.85
Minimum frontal diameter	44	107.45
Bizygomatic breadth	44	124.39
Bigonial breadth	44	102.55
Total facial height	44	119.75
Upper facial height	45	69.10
Nasal height	44	52.55
Nasal breadth	45	34.35
Ear length	45	59.80
Ear breadth	45	33.45
Indices		
Cephalic	44	74.60
Fronto-parietal	44	79.05
Cephalo-facial	44	91.30
Zygo-frontal	44	86.00
Zygo-gonial	44	82.90
Total facial	44	96.20
Upper facial	44	55.85
Nasal	44	65.41
Ear	45	56.65

TABLE 98: MEASUREMENTS AND INDICES OF 3 OMANIS

No.	Age	Stature	GOL	GB	CI
1	21	64-3/4	167	144	86.23
2	26	70	171	148	85.55
3	47	66-1/2	174	144	82.76

TABLE 99: MEASUREMENTS AND INDICES OF 33 SOUTH ARABS

Group	No.	Stature	GOL	GB	CI
Yafi	5	63-1/4	175.10	143.00	81.68
Mashai	1	64-3/4	174.00	150.00	86.20
Mahra	5	66-1/4	168.80	146.20	86.67
Qara	7	66-1/4	164.57	146.57	89.12
Shahari	9	63-1/2	169.77	149.22	88.02
Al Kathiri	4	65-1/2	162.25	146.50	90.32
Bautahari	1	67-1/2	182.00	144.00	79.12
Harasis	1	61-1/2	174.00	145.00	83.33
Total...	33				

TABLE 100: COMPARATIVE HEAD MEASUREMENTS AND CEPHALIC INDICES OF SELECTED GROUPS

Group or Locality	GOL	GB	CI
Muscat	184.35	144.58	78.28
Yemen	180.95	145.50	81.07
Sheher	180.21	145.76	80.92
Somali	191.81	143.19	74.79
Hadendoa	189.97	145.10	76.39
Beni Amer	190.49	142.25	74.70
Tigre	192.10	143.20	74.0
Baij Beduins	191.37	140.26	73.0
Armenians	182.00	155.40	85.38

TABLE 101: MEASUREMENTS AND INDICES OF 15 CRANIA FROM YEMEN

No.	GOL	GB	CI	MFD	Biz. B.	NH	NB	NI
1	164	141	86.0	100	123	45	32	71.1
2	176	148	84.1	101	121	50	31	62.0
3	174	153	87.9	110	135	54	30	55.6
4	173	150	86.7	106	131	45	35	77.8
5	185	145	78.4	101	126	52	39	75.0
6	185	139	75.1	105	121	44	31	70.4
7	173	153	88.4	112	139	50	32	64.0
8	190	145	76.3	101	123	52	31	59.6
9	195	145	74.4	124	135	56	32	57.1
10	174	147	84.5	103	124	52	38	73.1
11	177	150	84.7	105	...	55	37	67.3
12	180	150	83.3	107	...	48	32	66.7
13	177	153	86.4	110	...	50	37	74.0
14	177	146	82.5	109	...	54	34	63.0
15	183	161	88.0	110	138	53	32	60.4
Average	184	156	84.8	110	144	56	36	64.3

TABLE 102: MEASUREMENTS AND INDICES OF 400 YEMENIS

Measurements	No.
Age	33
Stature	164.0
Head length	188
Head breadth	143
Head height	125
Minimum frontal diameter	102
Bizygomatic breadth	132
Bigonial breadth	101
Total facial height	121
Upper facial height	72
Nasal height	56
Nasal breadth	33.5

TABLE 102 (Continued)

Indices	No.
Cephalic	76.0
Upper facial	55.0
Total facial	92.0
Nasal	61.0

TABLE 103: MEASUREMENTS AND INDICES OF MOUNTAIN PEOPLES OF IRAQ AND IRAN

Group	No.	Stature	GOL	GB	CI	NH	NB	NI
Kurds I	133	166.02	181.17	149.95	86.62	54.74	35.00	64.26
Kurds II	234	166.05	181.98	151.96	83.52	54.06	34.97	65.06
Kurds III	230	166.23	179.73	152.53	84.96	53.86	34.49	64.96
Kurds IV	597	166.11	180.93	151.72	83.88	54.14	34.88	64.82
Kurds V	49	167.25	186.10	145.05	78.65	56.40	36.60	64.09
Lurs I	68	163.95	188.02	143.55	76.49	55.45	35.70	64.95
Lurs II	52	168.63	189.99	140.68	74.25	62.22	35.75	57.42
Bakhtiari	147	162.25	183.65	149.65	81.65	55.19	37.10	67.65
Assyrians	106	170.52	180.45	154.03	85.17	63.10	35.03	51.72

TABLE 104: 172 AFGHANS MEASURED BY BOWLES, 1937

Group	Locality	No.
Afghani	Kabul east to Jelabad	50
Afridi	South of Khyber Pass to Tirah Valley	40
Mohmandi	North of Khyber Pass and northeast of Bajaur	42
Pathans, Kattaks, and Bangash	Southwest of Peshawur	40
	Total...	172

TABLE 105: MEASUREMENTS AND INDICES OF 36 MALE AFGHANS

People	No.	Stature	GOL	GB	CI	Observer
Afghans	18	163.8	185.0	157.0	84.9	Matseevskii
Afghans	18	168.1	.....	.....	75.6	Poiarkov
Hazara	..	168.4	.....	.....	85.0	Haddon

TABLE 106: MEASUREMENTS AND INDICES OF 70,485 MALE TURKS IN ANATOLIA

Measurements	Groups	No.
Stature	206	62,367
Sitting height	30	42,467
Head length	84	45,628
Head breadth	85	45,937
Head height	21	2,798
Minimum frontal diameter	46	44,254
Bizyomatic diameter	43	43,720
Bigonial diameter	34	43,247
Total facial height	49	44,793
Upper facial height	45	44,233
Nasal height	47	44,271
Nasal breadth	46	44,211
Ear length	36	43,160
Ear breadth	37	43,382

TABLE 106 (Continued)

Indices	Groups	No.
Relative sitting height	15	2,449
Cephalic	346	70,485
Length-height	20	39,884
Breadth-height	9	419
Fronto-parietal	40	42,004
Zygo-frontal	31	41,430
Total facial	46	44,093
Upper facial	36	42,370
Cephalo-facial	20	2,146
Nasal	44	43,471
Ear	31	42,748
	Total...	966,977

TABLE 107: STATURE OF 206 GROUPS WITH 62,367 MALES

Group	Locality	Country	No.	Stature	Recorder
Jews	Sanaa	Yemen	78	159.4	.....
Sheher Arabs	Aden District	Arabia	31	161.6	Leys and Joyce
Rwala (Ruwalla) Beduins	Jazira	Syria	270	161.89	Shanklin
Jews	Kubin near Baku	Caucasus	80	162.2	Pantiukhov
Bakhtiari Tribesmen	Khuzistan	Iran	147	162.25	Field
Jews II	Sandur	Iraq	47	162.27	Field
Beni Sakhr Beduins	Jazira	Jordan	65	162.78	Shanklin
Arabs		Arabia	133	162.8	Deniker
Anaiza Beduins	Jazira	Iraq	22	162.96	Field
Jews	Kutais	Caucasus	41	163.0	Pantiukhov
Jews		Iran	35	163.0	.....
Fellahin		Egypt	138	163.0	Chantre
Howeitat (Huwaitat) Beduins	Jazira	Jordan	70	163.08	Shanklin
Jews	Georgia	Caucasus	37	163.6	Weissenberg
Fellahin	Farafra Oasis	Egypt	51	163.7	Mitwally
Afghans		Afghanistan	18	163.8	Matseevskii
Fellahin	Kharga Oasis	Egypt	150	163.8	Hrdlička
Fellahin	Kharga Oasis	Egypt	205	163.9	Mitwally
Belbeis	Sharqiya	Egypt	144	163.95	Ammar
Lurs	Khurrumabad	Iran	70	163.95	Field
Villagers (Sunni)	Hama	Syria	175	163.98	Shanklin
Lezghians		Caucasus	11	164.0	Chantre
Jews		Caucasus	33	164.0	Weissenberg
Mountain Jews	Daghestan	Caucasus	20	164.0	.....
Jews	Georgia	Caucasus	11	164.1	Chantre
Jews		Iraq	37	164.1	Weissenberg
Mountain Jews	Daghestan	Caucasus	100	164.2	.....
Fellahin	Baharia Oasis	Egypt	196	164.2	Mitwally
Dehwari		Baluchistan	200	164.25	.....
Arabs		Arabia	29	164.28	Mochi
Villagers (Sunni)	Hidjaneh	Syria	298	164.36	Shanklin
Jews	Kaitag-Tabasaran	Caucasus	61	164.4	Pantiukhov
Turks IV	Aegean Area	Turkey	3406	164.41	.....
Turks I	Thrace	Turkey	2651	164.44	.....
Turks III	Western Anatolia	Turkey	3020	164.44	.....
Total Jews		Iraq	106	164.46	Field and Smeaton
Jews	Aleppo	Syria	10	164.5	
Sayad		Baluchistan	33	164.55	Joyce and Stein
Armenians		Caucasus	20	164.6	Weissenberg
Osetes	Gori	Caucasus	258	164.7	Topinard
Turks VII	Northwest Anatolia	Turkey	4161	164.74	.....

TABLE 107 (Continued)

Group	Locality	Country	No.	Stature	Recorder
Muscatis	Oman	Arabia	31	164.8	Deniker
Arabs	Yemen	Arabia	20	164.8	Leys and Joyce
Villagers	Yezd-i-Khast	Iran	46	164.8	Field
Muscatis	Oman	Arabia	82	164.9	Leys and Joyce
Jews	Isfahan	Iran	86	164.9	Field
Total Egyptians		Egypt	288	165.0	Chantre
Turks IX	Eastern Anatolia	Turkey	5102	165.02	.....
Turks V	Northwest Anatolia (Interior)	Turkey	3420	165.09	.....
Ajemis	Tehran	Iran	108	165.1	Deniker
Sulubba (Sleyb)	Jazira	Iraq	24	165.12	Field
Yezidis	Erivan (Yerevan)	Armenia	20	165.15	Field
Turks II	Bursa-Bilecik	Turkey	3361	165.17	.....
Armenians	Tiflis (Tbilisi) Province	Georgia	792	165.2	Deniker
Total Turks I-X		Turkey	39465	165.28	.....
Villagers (Sunni)	Plain	Lebanon	149	165.42	Shanklin
Villagers	Kinareh	Iran	74	165.5	Field
Georgians	Georgia	Caucasus	900	165.5	Dzhavahov
Fellahin	Dakhla Oasis	Egypt	386	165.5	Mitwally
Turks X	Northeast Anatolia	Turkey	4683	165.52	.....
Fellahin	Sharqiya	Egypt	516	165.54	Craig
Turks	Eastern Anatolia	Turkey	32	165.6	Wagenseil
Druze	Jebel Druze	Syria	181	165.60	Izzeddin
Persians		Iran	154	165.66	Danilov
Beduins	Sinai	Egypt	67	165.72	Field
Jews I	Northern Area	Iraq	58	165.72	Field and Smeaton
Turks VIII	Southern Anatolia	Turkey	4766	165.73	.....
Shammar Negroes	Jazira	Iraq	14	165.76	Field
Towara (Tuarah) Beduins	Sinai	Egypt	63	165.8	Murray
Egyptians	Canal Zone	Egypt	127	165.87	Craig
Total Yezidis	Tbilisi (Tiflis)	Caucasus	51	165.99	Field
Osmanli Turks	Anatolia	Turkey	362	166.0	Deniker
Maaza	Qena and Beni Suef	Egypt	34	166.0	Chantre
Assyrians	Anatolia	Turkey	22	166.0	Chantre
Copts	Luxor	Egypt	96	166.0	Chantre
Copts		Egypt	150	166.0	Chantre
Towara (Tuarah) Beduins	Sinai	Egypt	18	166.0	Chantre
Kurds I	Zakho	Iraq	133	166.02	Field and Smeaton
Kurds II	Rowandiz	Iraq	234	166.05	Field and Smeaton
Shammar Beduins	Northern Jazira	Iraq	272	166.05	Field and Smeaton
Total Kurds	Kurdistan	Iraq	597	166.11	Field and Smeaton
Bektash	Ankara	Anatolia	14	166.14	Crowfoot
Armenians		Caucasus	101	166.16	Seltzer
Subba	Amara Liwa	Iraq	90	166.23	Field and Smeaton
Kurds III	Kirkuk-Sulaimaniya	Iraq	230	166.23	Field and Smeaton
Jews	Damascus	Syria	30	166.3	.....
Faqus	Sharqiya	Egypt	141	166.38	Ammar
Minieh el-Qamh	Sharqiya	Egypt	126	166.38	Ammar
Yezidis	Sheikhan	Iraq	101	166.38	Field and Smeaton
Turks	Brussa	Anatolia	38	166.4	Wagenseil
Turks	Ankara	Anatolia	44	166.5	Wagenseil

TABLE 107 (Continued)

Group	Locality	Country	No.	Stature	Recorder
Alouites		Syria	309	166.52	Shanklin
Fellahin	Sharqiya	Egypt	939	166.52	Ammar
Fellahin	Sharqiya District	Egypt	51	166.52	Ammar
Zaqaziq	Sharqiya	Egypt	288	166.55	Ammar
Turkomans	Northern Area	Iraq	61	166.56	Field
Al bu Muhammad	Amara Liwa	Iraq	200	166.71	Field and Smeaton
Assyrians	Lake Urmia	Iran	33	166.8	Deniker
Turks VI	Central Anatolia	Turkey	4895	166.80	.....
Kafr Saqr	Sharqiya	Egypt	94	166.84	Ammar
Beduins	Jazira	Syria	115	166.86	Huxley
Persians		Iran	204	166.9	Dzhawachischwili
Yezidis	Lake Van	Turkey	22	166.92	Field
Mitwali (Shia)	Mountains	Lebanon	302	166.96	Shanklin
Al Sawaad	Amara Liwa	Iraq	50	166.98	Field and Smeaton
Turks	Konia	Anatolia	44	167.0	Wagenseil
Milanli Kurds	Kurdistan	Anatolia	20	167.0	Chantre
Kurds	Kharput and Erzinghin	Kurdistan	23	167.0	Chantre
Osetes	Gori	Caucasus	258	167.0	Pantiukhov
Jebeliyeh	Sinai	Egypt	42	167.01	Field
Armenians		Caucasus	75	167.04	Boas
Armenians		Caucasus	105	167.10	Twarjanowitsch
Hihya	Sharqiya	Egypt	109	167.13	Ammar
Greek Orthodox		Syria	91	167.16	Huxley
Yezidis	Jebel Sinjar	Iraq	123	167.16	Field and Smeaton
Arabs	An Nasiriya Hospital	Iraq	109	167.17	Smeaton
Syrians		Syria	251	167.19	Seltzer
Pani, Pauni (Pushta)		Baluchistan	100	167.64	.....
Total Turks	Anatolia	Turkey	272	167.2	Wagenseil
Kurds	Kurdistan	Iran	50	167.25	Field
Lebanese	Beirut	Lebanon	164	167.25	Seltzer
Armenians		Caucasus	25	167.4	Hrdlička
Fellahin	Tamiya, Faiyum	Egypt	137	167.46	Field
Azerbaidzhanis	Azerbaidzhan	Caucasus	288	167.5	Deniker
Druze	Jebel Druze	Syria	46	167.55	Huxley
Arabs	Baghdad Hospital	Iraq	21	167.58	Smeaton
Turks	Dardanelles	Anatolia	34	167.6	Wagenseil
Fellahin	Beja	Egypt	223	167.6	Chantre
Maronites		Syria	31	167.61	Huxley
Dulaimi Tribesmen	Haditha	Iraq	136	167.67	Field
Tachtadshy and Bektash	Anatolia	Turkey	50	167.7	Von Luschan
Beduins	Gezira (Jazira)	Egypt	134	167.8	Chantre
Arabs	Gaza	Palestine	78	167.85	Gloor
Biloch		Baluchistan	35	167.89	Joyce and Stein
Turks	Anatolia	Turkey	200	167.92	Hasluck and Morant
Kurds	Kurdistan	Turkey, Armenia, Iran	284	168.0	Chantre
Fellahin	Luxor	Egypt	58	168.0	Chantre
Fellahin	Karnak	Egypt	14	168.0	Chantre
Beduins	Gezira (Jazira)	Egypt	188	168.0	Chantre
Fellahin	Siwa Oasis	Egypt	219	168.0	Mitwally
Ayaideh	Mensaleh and Matarieh	Egypt	25	168.0	Chantre
Moslems		Syria	258	168.0	Huxley
Villagers (Christian)	Hafar	Syria	93	168.02	Shanklin
Villagers (Christian)	Mhardeh	Syria	157	168.08	Shanklin
Afghans		Afghanistan	18	168.1	Poiarkov
Turks	Kastamuni	Anatolia	41	168.1	Wagenseil

TABLE 107 (Continued)

Group	Locality	Country	No.	Stature	Recorder
Baij Beduins	Hilla Liwa	Iraq	35	168.2	Field
Kurds	Kurdistan	Iran	162	168.3	Danilov
Kish Arabs	Hilla Liwa	Iraq	340	168.3	Field
Assyrians	Tiflis (Tbilisi)	Caucasus	11	168.3	.....
Assyrians	Lake Urmia	Iran	11	168.3	Pantiukhov
Faqus	Sharqiya	Egypt	141	168.38	Ammar
Kish Arabs	Hilla Liwa	Iraq	95	168.39	Buxton and Field
Fellahin		Egypt	91	168.4	Chantre
Moslems		Palestine	276	168.48	Gloor
Akeydat Beduins	Jazira	Jordan	120	168.50	Shanklin
Kurds	Lake Goktcha	Transcaucasia	17	168.5	Nasonov
Seistani	Seistan	Baluchistan	25	168.51	Joyce and Stein
Lurs	Pusht-i-Kuh	Iran	52	168.6	Field
Kurds	Lake Goktcha	Transcaucasia	140	168.6	Deniker
Kurds	Kurdistan	Iran	20	168.6	Pantiukhov
Arabs	Hebron	Palestine	115	168.71	Gloor
Arabs	Jerusalem	Palestine	83	168.76	Gloor
Gypsies		Syria	11	168.81	Huxley
Beduins	Western Desert	Egypt	40	168.85	Murray
Assyrians	Habbaniya Camp	Iraq	360	168.89	Field
Turks	Smyrna	Anatolia	39	168.9	Wagenseil
Tatars	Aralych	Caucasus	16	169.0	Chantre
Arabs	Northern Area	Palestine	15	169.16	Gloor
Osetes	Osetia	Caucasus	500	169.2	Dzhawachischwili
Armenians		Transcaucasia	192	169.4	Deniker
Armenians		Transcaucasia	239	169.44	Chantre
Plains Osetes	Osetia	Caucasus	67	169.47	Field
Fellahin	Safed	Palestine	30	169.5	.....
Iron Osetes	Osetia	Caucasus	68	169.50	Field
Osetes	Terek, Osetia	Caucasus	200	169.53	Gilchenko
Azerbaijanis	Azerbaijan	Iran	35	169.6	Danilov
Nusairiyeh (Shia)	Mountains	Syria	25	169.68	Huxley
Turkomans	Aintab Area	Syria	19	169.74	Huxley
North Osetes	Osetia	Caucasus	106	169.77	Field
Tatars	Arkhuri	Caucasus	15	170.0	Chantre
Wulud (Aulad) Ali	Mariut	Egypt	20	170.0	Chantre
Christians		Palestine	55	170.04	Gloor
Maualy Beduins	Jazira	Jordan	176	170.12	Shanklin
Digor Osetes	Osetia	Caucasus	38	170.28	Field
Mountain Osetes	Osetia	Caucasus	39	170.31	Field
Assyrians	Hinaidi Camp	Iraq	106	170.52	Field
Kurds	Kurdistan	Anatolia	48	170.7	Pittard
Kurds		Kurdistan	63	170.7	Deniker
Iranians	Northern Area	Iran	50	170.7	Maslovskii
Osmanli Turks	Anatolia	Turkey	120	171.0	Deniker
Samaritans		Palestine	27	171.07	Szpidbaum
Arabs	Northern Area	Iraq	32	171.28	Ehrich
Iraq Soldiers		Iraq	63	171.63	Buxton and Field
Osetes	Osetia	Caucasus	30	171.8	Gilchenko
Osetes	Osetia	Caucasus	16	171.8	Pantiukhov
Samaritans		Palestine	38	172.26	Huxley
Iraq Soldiers		Iraq	222	172.6	Field
Samaritans	Nablus	Palestine	35	173.0	Huxley
Fellahin	Koraichia	Egypt	10	173.0	Chantre
Harabi	Faiyum	Egypt	29	173.0	Chantre
Samaritans		Palestine	38	173.20	Genna
Arabs	Ramleh	Palestine	30	173.20	Gloor
Jews		Egypt	25	174.4	.....
Lurs	Pusht-i-Kuh	Iran	52	186.6	Field

Total... 62,367

TABLE 108: SITTING HEIGHT OF 57 GROUPS WITH 46,126 MALES

Group	Locality	Country	No.	SH	Recorder
Lurs	Khurrumabad	Iran	69	77.07	Field
Sulubba (Nomads)	Jazira	Iraq	24	81.25	Field
Kish Arabs	Hilla Liwa	Iraq	350	82.51	Field
Rwala (Ruwalla) Beduins	Jazira	Syria	270	82.69	Shanklin
Baij (Beduins)	Hilla Liwa	Iraq	53	83.38	Field
Beni Sakhr Beduins	Jazira	Jordan	65	83.44	Shanklin
Villagers (Sunni)	Hama	Syria	175	83.78	Shanklin
Turks IX	Eastern Anatolia	Turkey	5102	84.06	.....
Dulaimis	Haditha	Iraq	136	84.07	Field
Turks X	Northeast Anatolia	Turkey	4683	84.09	.....
Turks III	Western Anatolia	Turkey	3020	84.23	.....
Total Turks I-X		Turkey	39465	84.71	.....
Kurds	Kurdistan	Iran	50	84.75	Field
Turks VII	Northwest Anatolia	Turkey	4161	84.82	.....
Moslems		Palestine	276	84.84	Gloor
An Nasiriya	An Nasiriya Liwa	Iraq	109	84.98	Smeaton
Turks V	Western Anatolia (Interior)	Turkey	3420	84.98	.....
Howeitat Beduins	Jazira	Jordan	70	85.00	Shanklin
Turks I	Thrace	Turkey	2651	85.00	.....
Iraq Soldiers	.....	Iraq	222	85.09	Field
Turks IV	Aegean Area	Turkey	3406	85.18	.....
Turks VIII	Southern Anatolia	Turkey	4766	85.24	.....
Bakhtiari	Khuzistan	Iran	149	85.51	Field
Assyrians	Total	Iraq	106	85.60	Field
Alouites		Syria	309	85.64	Shanklin
Turks II	Bursa-Bilecik	Turkey	3361	85.79	.....
Akeydat Beduins	Jazira	Syria	120	85.96	Shanklin
Turks VI	Central Anatolia	Turkey	4895	85.99	.....
Bekaa Villagers	Plain	Lebanon	149	86.08	Shanklin
Jews II	Sandur	Iraq	47	86.14	Field
Arabs	Baghdad Hospital	Iraq	21	86.14	Smeaton
Villagers (Christian)	Mhardeh	Syria	157	86.24	Shanklin
Villagers (Sunni)	Hidjaneh	Syria	298	86.48	Shanklin
Kurds III	Kirkuk-Sulaimaniya	Iraq	229	86.68	Field and Smeaton
Villagers (Christian)	Hafar	Syria	93	86.80	Shanklin
Maualy Beduins	Jazira	Syria	176	86.80	Shanklin
Kurds	Total	Iraq	597	86.95	Field and Smeaton
Kurds II	Rowandiz	Iraq	235	87.07	Field and Smeaton
Jews	Total	Iraq	106	87.25	Field and Smeaton
Kurds I	Zakho	Iraq	133	87.25	Field and Smeaton
Christians		Palestine	55	87.32	Gloor
Negroes (Shammar)	Northern Jazira	Iraq	14	87.71	Field
Al bu Muhammad	Amara Liwa	Iraq	219	87.79	Field and Smeaton
Anaiza (Beduins)	Jazira	Iraq	22	87.85	Field
Druze	Jebel Druze	Syria	181	88.00	Izzeddin
Mitwali (Shia)	Mountains	Lebanon	302	88.12	Shanklin
Jews I	Northern Iraq	Iraq	58	88.15	Field and Smeaton
Yezidis	Sheikhan	Iraq	100	88.33	Field and Smeaton
Turkomans	Northern Iraq	Iraq	60	88.36	Field and Smeaton
Yezidis	Combined	Iraq	221	88.45	Field and Smeaton

TABLE 108 (Continued)

Group	Locality	Country	No.	SH	Recorder
Yezidis	Jebel Sinjar	Iraq	121	88.54	Field and Smeaton
Subba	Amara Liwa	Iraq	90	88.57	Field and Smeaton
Al Sawaad	Amara Liwa	Iraq	50	88.78	Field and Smeaton
Shammar (Beduins)	Northern Jazira	Iraq	273	88.81	Field and Smeaton
Turkomans	Northern Iraq	Iraq	31	90.16	Ehrich
Arabs	Kirkuk	Iraq	32	90.22	Ehrich
Samaritans		Palestine	38	93.03	Genna
		Total...	46,126		

TABLE 109: HEAD LENGTH OF 122 GROUPS WITH 49,850 MALES

Group	Locality	Country	No.	GOL	Recorder
Greek Orthodox		Syria	91	167.16	Huxley
Syrians		Syria	251	167.19	Seltzer
Maronites		Syria	31	167.61	Huxley
Turkomans	Aintab Area	Syria	19	169.74	Huxley
Mitwali (Shia)	Mountains	Lebanon	302	176.04	Shanklin
Nusairiyeh (Shia)	Mountains	Syria	25	176.16	Huxley
Yezidis	Sheikhan	Iraq	101	177.15	Field and Smeaton
Bekaa Villagers (Sunni)	Plain	Lebanon	149	177.72	Shanklin
Jews	Baghdad	Iraq	17	177.72	Rassam
Kurds	Mardin	Turkey	12	178.0	Kappers
Alouites		Syria	309	178.74	Shanklin
Druze	Jebel Druze	Syria	46	178.89	Seltzer
Maronites		Syria	31	179.13	Huxley
Kurds	Towns (5)	Iraq	48	179.43	Rassam
Kurds III	Kirkuk-Sulaimaniya	Iraq	230	179.73	Field and Smeaton
Christians	Mosul and Tell Kaif	Iraq	37	180.24	Rassam
Jews II	Sandur	Iraq	47	180.39	Field
Arabs	Baghdad	Iraq	148	180.42	Rassam
Assyrians	Total	Iraq	106	180.45	Field
Turks IX	Eastern Anatolia	Turkey	5102	180.7	.....
Kurds	Total	Iraq	598	180.93	Field and Smeaton
Turks VII	Northwest Anatolia	Turkey	4161	181.0	.....
Druze	Jebel Druze	Syria	181	181.00	Izzeddin
Jews	Total	Iraq	106	181.05	Field and Smeaton
Kurds I	Zakho	Iraq	133	181.17	Field and Smeaton
Assyrians	Habbaniya Camp	Iraq	532	181.21	Field
Kurds	Northern Iraq	Iraq	13	181.31	Ehrich
Turks II	Bursa-Bilecik	Turkey	3361	181.5	.....
Jews I	Northern Iraq	Iraq	59	181.59	Field and Smeaton
Turks VI	Central Anatolia	Turkey	4895	181.8	.....
Turks I	Thrace	Turkey	2651	181.9	.....
Kurds II	Rowandiz	Iraq	235	181.98	Field and Smeaton
Turks V	Western Anatolia (Interior)	Turkey	3420	182.0	.....
Armenians		Lebanon	85	182.0	Kappers
Christians	Baghdad	Iraq	20	182.25	Rassam
Total Turks I-X		Turkey	39465	182.3	.....

TABLE 109 (Continued)

Group	Locality	Country	No.	GOL	Recorder
Beharna	Bahrain Island	Persian Gulf	44	182.34	Field
Arabs	Mosul	Iraq	14	182.5	Kappers
Arabs	Towns (19)	Iraq	39	182.61	Rassam
Lebanese	Beirut	Lebanon	164	183.03	Seltzer
Turks IV	Aegean Area	Turkey	3406	183.1	.....
Turks X	Northeast Anatolia	Turkey	4683	183.5	.....
Turks III	Western Anatolia	Turkey	3020	183.6	.....
Bakhtiari	Khuzistan	Iran	149	183.65	Field
Turkomans	Northern Iraq	Iraq	31	183.87	Ehrich
Villagers	Nuami	Jordan	54	184.0	Shanklin
Villagers	Aidoun	Jordan	18	184.0	Shanklin
Jews	.....	Iraq	37	184.0	Weissenberg
Turks VIII	Southern Anatolia	Turkey	4766	184.0	.....
Villagers (Christians)	Mhardeh	Syria	157	184.52	Shanklin
Villagers (Sunni)	Hama	Syria	175	184.92	Shanklin
Moslems		Syria	258	184.98	Huxley
Beduins	Wadi Musa District	Jordan	16	185.0	Shanklin
Villagers	Kutum	Jordan	57	185.0	Shanklin
Arabs		Palestine	122	185.0	Kappers
Villagers	Madeba	Jordan	47	185.0	Shanklin
Nussour Tribe	Jazira	Jordan	58	185.0	Shanklin
Kurds	Anatolia	Turkey	52	185.0	Kappers
Christians		Palestine	55	185.20	Gloor
Yezidis	Combined	Iraq	224	185.58	Field and Smeaton
Moslems		Palestine	276	185.60	Gloor
El-Kaid Tribe	Jazira	Jordan	45	186	Shanklin
Batayyni Tribe	Jazira	Jordan	34	186	Shanklin
Subba	Amara Liwa	Iraq	90	186.00	Field and Smeaton
Arabs	City-dwellers	Iraq	18	186.0	Kappers
Audat Tribesmen	Jazira	Jordan	26	186.0	Shanklin
Beni Hassan Beduins	Jazira	Jordan	97	186.0	Shanklin
Arabs	Damascus	Syria	44	186.0	Kappers
Kurds	Kurdistan	Iran	49	186.10	Field
Iraq Soldiers	.....	Iraq	222	186.24	Field
Gypsies		Syria	11	186.27	Huxley
Arabs	Aleppo	Syria	13	186.5	Kappers
Turkomans	Northern Iraq	Iraq	60	186.99	Field
Adwan Tribe	Jazira	Jordan	41	187.0	Shanklin
Nusirat Tribe	Jazira	Jordan	42	187.0	Shanklin
Beduins (Unclassified)	Jazira	Jordan	88	187.0	Shanklin
Circassians		Syria	42	187.0	Kappers
Villagers	Tafileh	Jordan	26	187.0	Shanklin
Al Sawaad	Amara Liwa	Iraq	50	187.26	Field and Smeaton
Al bu Muhammad	Amara Liwa	Iraq	221	187.26	Field and Smeaton
Persians		Iran	29	188.0	Kappers
Beduins	Jazira	Syria	50	188.0	Kappers
Kurds	Erzurum	Turkey	32	188.0	Kappers
Shiab Tribesmen	Jazira	Jordan	44	188.0	Shanklin
Lurs	Khurrumabad	Iran	69	188.02	Field
Samaritans	Nablus	Palestine	38	188.28	Huxley
Kish Arabs	Hilla Liwa	Iraq	358	188.76	Field
Nippur Workmen	Afaq (Afej)	Iraq	41	188.85	Field
Samaritans		Palestine	39	188.97	Genna
Beni Atiyeh Beduins	Jazira	Jordan	10	189.0	Shanklin
Persians	Tehran	Iran	18	189.0	Kappers
Beduins	Jazira	Syria	115	189.09	Huxley
Sulubba (Nomads)	Jazira	Iraq	38	189.39	Field

TABLE 109 (Continued)

Group	Locality	Country	No.	GOL	Recorder
Villagers (Christians)	Hafar	Syria	93	189.54	Shanklin
Iraq Soldiers	.....	Iraq	63	189.72	Buxton and Field
Beni Sakhr Beduins	Jazira	Jordan	65	189.87	Shanklin
An Nasiriya	Liwa	Iraq	109	189.88	Smeaton
Arabs	Baghdad	Iraq	18	190.0	Kappers
Kish Arabs	Hilla Liwa	Iraq	100	190.14	Buxton and Field
Maualy Beduins	Jazira	Syria	176	190.42	Shanklin
Arabs	Northern Iraq	Iraq	33	190.44	Ehrich
Egyptians	Canal Zone	Egypt	127	190.61	Craig
Persians	Tabriz	Iran	23	191.0	Kappers
Arabs	Palmyra	Syria	11	191.0	Kappers
Towara (Tuarah) Beduins	Sinai	Egypt	18	191.0	Chantre
Turkomans	Aintab Area	Syria	19	191.04	Huxley
Dulaimis	Haditha	Iraq	136	191.04	Field
Towara Beduins	Sinai	Egypt	63	191.3	Murray
Anaiza (Beduins)	Jazira	Iraq	23	191.22	Field
Baij (Beduins)	Hilla Liwa	Iraq	35	191.31	Field
Akeydat Beduins	Jazira	Syria	120	191.35	Shanklin
Rwala Beduins	Jazira	Syria	270	191.48	Shanklin
Beni Sakhr Beduins	Jazira	Jordan	13	192.0	Shanklin
Jebeliyeh	Sinai	Egypt	73	192.15	Field
Negroes (Shammar)	Northern Jazira	Iraq	14	192.36	Field
Howeitat Beduins	Jazira	Jordan	70	192.42	Shanklin
Yezidis	Jebel Sinjar	Iraq	123	192.48	Field and Smeaton
Shammar (Beduins)	Northern Jazira	Iraq	273	192.72	Field and Smeaton
Arabs	Baghdad Hospital	Iraq	23	193.56	Smeaton
Beduins	Sinai	Egypt	150	193.74	Field
Hajayya Tribesmen	Jazira	Jordan	13	194.0	Shanklin
Kurds	Northern Iraq	Iraq	22	201.0	Chantre

Total... 49,850

TABLE 110: HEAD BREADTH OF 123 GROUPS WITH 50,153 MALES

Group	Locality	Country	No.	GB	Recorder
Beharna	Bahrain Island	Persian Gulf	44	135.85	Field
Sulubba (Nomads)	Jazira	Iraq	37	137.29	Field
Anaiza (Beduins)	Jazira	Iraq	22	137.50	Field
Jebeliyeh	Sinai	Egypt	73	138.64	Field
Villagers	Aqaba	Jordan	13	139.0	Shanklin
Towara (Tuarah) Beduins	Sinai	Egypt	63	139.18	Murray
Beduins	Sinai	Egypt	150	139.72	Field
Baij (Beduins)	Hilla Liwa	Iraq	35	139.93	Field
Towara Beduins	Sinai	Egypt	18	140.0	Chantre
Negroes (Shammar)	Northern Jazira	Iraq	14	140.14	Field
Nippur Workmen	Afaq (Afej)	Iraq	41	140.15	Field
Yezidis	Jebel Sinjar	Iraq	123	140.44	Field and Smeaton
Beni Atiyeh Beduins	Jazira	Jordan	10	141.0	Shanklin
Dulaimis	Haditha	Iraq	136	141.34	Field
Turkomans	Northern Iraq	Iraq	61	141.85	Field
Kish Arabs	Hilla Liwa	Iraq	359	141.91	Field
Jews	Baghdad	Iraq	17	142.18	Rassam
Shammar (Beduins)	Northern Jazira	Iraq	273	142.42	Field and Smeaton
Beni Sakhr Beduins	Jazira	Jordan	65	142.51	Shanklin
Villagers (Sunni)	Hidjaneh	Syria	298	142.54	Shanklin
Kish Arabs	Hilla Liwa	Iraq	100	142.75	Buxton and Field
El-Kaid Tribe	Jazira	Jordan	45	143.0	Shanklin

TABLE 110 (Continued)

Group	Locality	Country	No.	GB	Recorder
Audat Tribe	Jazira	Jordan	26	143.0	Shanklin
Nussour Tribe	Jazira	Jordan	58	143.0	Shanklin
Arabs	Towns (19)	Iraq	39	143.23	Rassam
Villagers (Christians)	Hafar	Syria	93	143.35	Shanklin
Gypsies		Syria	11	143.35	Huxley
Lurs	Khurrumabad	Iran	68	143.55	Field
Rwala Beduins	Jazira	Syria	270	143.63	Shanklin
Iraq Soldiers	.....	Iraq	221	143.71	Field
Villagers (Sunni)	Hama	Syria	175	143.78	Shanklin
Arabs	Baghdad	Iraq	148	143.83	Rassam
Turkomans	Aintab Area	Syria	19	143.89	Huxley
Beduins (Unclassified)	Jazira	Jordan	88	144.0	Shanklin
Nusirat Tribe	Jazira	Jordan	42	144.0	Shanklin
Beni Sakhr Beduins	Jazira	Jordan	13	144.0	Shanklin
Howeitat Beduins	Jazira	Jordan	49	144.0	Shanklin
Hajayya Tribe	Jazira	Jordan	13	144.0	Shanklin
Villagers	Kutum	Jordan	57	144.0	Shanklin
Villagers	Madeba	Jordan	47	144.0	Shanklin
Jews	.....	Iraq	37	144.00	Weissenberg
Iraq Soldiers	.....	Iraq	63	144.34	Buxton and Field
Beduins	Jazira	Syria	115	144.46	Huxley
Villagers	Nuaimi	Jordan	54	145.0	Shanklin
Villagers	Aidoun	Jordan	18	145.0	Shanklin
Villagers	Tafileh	Jordan	26	145.0	Shanklin
Shiab Tribe	Jazira	Jordan	44	145.0	Shanklin
Beni Hassan Beduins	Jazira	Jordan	97	145.0	Shanklin
Adwan Tribe	Jazira	Jordan	41	145.0	Shanklin
Betayyni Tribe	Jazira	Jordan	34	145.0	Shanklin
Arabs	Palmyra	Syria	11	145.0	Kappers
Beduins	Jazira	Syria	50	145.0	Kappers
Kurds	Mardin	Turkey	12	145.0	Kappers
Kurds	Erzurum	Turkey	32	145.0	Kappers
Christians	Baghdad	Iraq	20	145.00	Rassam
Yezidis	Combined	Iraq	224	145.03	Field and Smeaton
Kurds	Kurdistan	Iran	49	145.05	Field
Howeitat Beduins	Jazira	Jordan	70	145.12	Shanklin
Subba	Amara Liwa	Iraq	89	145.75	Field and Smeaton
Al bu Muhammad	Amara Liwa	Iraq	221	145.75	Field and Smeaton
Al Sawaad	Amara Liwa	Iraq	50	145.96	Field and Smeaton
Persians	Tabriz	Iran	23	146.0	Kappers
Turkomans	Northern Iraq	Iraq	31	146.10	Ehrich
Akeydat Beduins	Jazira	Syria	120	146.14	Shanklin
Samaritans	Nablus	Palestine	38	146.17	Huxley
Arabs	Northern Iraq	Iraq	33	146.21	Ehrich
Arabs	Baghdad Hospital	Iraq	23	146.29	Smeaton
Christians	Mosul and Tell Kaif	Iraq	37	146.47	Rassam
Moslems		Palestine	276	146.53	Gloor
Arabs	Canal Zone	Egypt	127	146.53	Craig
Turks VIII	Southern Anatolia	Turkey	4766	146.8	.....
Kurds	Towns (5)	Iraq	48	146.95	Rassam
Kurds	Anatolia	Turkey	52	147.0	Kappers
Villagers (Christians)	Mhardeh	Syria	157	147.06	Shanklin
Maualy Beduins	Jazira	Syria	176	147.06	Shanklin
Moslems		Syria	258	147.28	Huxley
Jews II	Sandur	Iraq	46	147.40	Field

TABLE 110 (Continued)

Group	Locality	Country	No.	GB	Recorder
Villagers	Wadi Musa District	Jordan	16	148	Shanklin
Jews	Total	Iraq	105	148.21	Field and Smeaton
An Nasiriya	Liwa	Iraq	109	148.39	Smeaton
Alouites		Syria	309	148.50	Shanklin
Kurds	Northern Iraq	Iraq	13	148.62	Ehrich
Turks I	Thrace	Turkey	2651	148.8	.....
Jews I	Northern Iraq	Iraq	59	148.81	Field and Smeaton
Persians		Iran	29	149.0	Kappers
Samaritans		Palestine	39	149.30	Genna
Turks X	Northeast Anatolia	Turkey	4683	149.5	.....
Bakhtiari	Khuzistan	Iran	149	149.65	Field
Kurds I	Zakho	Iraq	133	149.95	Field and Smeaton
Persians	Tehran	Iran	18	150.0	Kappers
Arabs		Palestine	122	150.0	Kappers
Turks IX	Eastern Anatolia	Turkey	5102	150.5	.....
Yezidis	Sheikhan	Iraq	101	150.61	Field and Smeaton
Bekaa Villagers (Sunni)	Plain	Lebanon	149	150.64	Shanklin
Arabs	Damascus	Syria	44	151.0	Kappers
Assyrians	Habbaniya Camp	Iraq	532	151.53	Field
Greek Orthodox		Syria	91	151.60	Huxley
Turks III	Western Anatolia	Turkey	3020	151.6	.....
Druze	Jebel Druze	Syria	46	151.72	Seltzer
Kurds	Total	Iraq	597	151.72	Field and Smeaton
Total Turks I-X		Turkey	39465	151.9	.....
Kurds II	Rowandiz	Iraq	234	151.96	Field and Smeaton
Maronites		Syria	31	151.96	Huxley
Arabs	Baghdad	Iraq	18	152.0	Kappers
Arabs	Aleppo	Syria	13	152.0	Kappers
Christians		Palestine	55	152.48	Gloor
Kurds III	Kirkuk-Sulaimaniya	Iraq	230	152.53	Field and Smeaton
Nusairiyah (Shia)	Mountains	Syria	25	152.56	Huxley
Turks IV	Aegean Area	Turkey	3406	152.8	.....
Mitwali (Shia)	Mountains	Lebanon	302	152.82	Shanklin
Arabs	City-dwellers	Iraq	18	153.0	Kappers
Turks II	Bursa-Bilecik	Turkey	3361	153.3	.....
Turks V	Western Anatolia (Interior)	Turkey	3420	153.9	.....
Arabs	Mosul	Iraq	14	154.0	Kappers
Assyrians	Total	Iraq	106	154.03	Field
Circassians		Syria	42	155.0	Kappers
Syrians		Syria	251	155.47	Seltzer
Turks VI	Central Anatolia	Turkey	4895	155.6	.....
Druze	Jebel Druze	Syria	181	156.00	Izzedin
Lebanese	Beirut	Lebanon	164	156.43	Seltzer
Turks VII	Northwest Anatolia	Turkey	4161	156.5	.....
Armenians		Lebanon	85	157.0	Kappers
Kurds	Northern Iraq	Iraq	22	157.0	Chantre

Total... 50,153

TABLE 111: HEAD HEIGHT OF 21 GROUPS WITH 2,798 MALES

Group	Locality	Country	No.	HH	Recorder
Akeydat Beduins	Jazira	Syria	120	122.76	Shanklin
Howeitat Beduins	Jazira	Jordan	70	123.46	Shanklin
Beni Sakhr Beduins	Jazira	Jordan	65	123.70	Shanklin
Villagers (Sunni)	Hidjaneh	Syria	298	124.28	Shanklin
Alouites		Syria	309	124.84	Shanklin
Villagers (Sunni)	Hama	Syria	175	125.20	Shanklin
Villagers (Christian)	Hafar	Syria	93	125.22	Shanklin
Maualy Beduins	Jazira	Syria	176	125.36	Shanklin
Villagers (Christian)	Mhardeh	Syria	157	126.82	Shanklin
Bekaa Villagers (Sunni)	Plain	Lebanon	149	127.56	Shanklin
Syrians		Syria	251	127.77	Seltzer
Mitwali (Shia)	Mountains	Lebanon	302	129.40	Shanklin
Gypsies		Syria	11	130.42	Huxley
Beduins	Jazira	Syria	115	134.50	Huxley
Greek Orthodox		Syria	91	135.10	Huxley
Moslems		Syria	258	136.26	Huxley
Turkomans	Aintab Area	Syria	19	136.54	Huxley
Nusairiyeh (Shia)	Moslems	Syria	25	138.84	Huxley
Druze	Jebel Druze	Syria	46	138.90	Seltzer
Maronites		Syria	30	139.10	Huxley
Samaritans	Nablus	Palestine	38	140.22	Huxley
			Total... 2,798		

TABLE 112: MINIMUM FRONTAL DIAMETER OF 76 GROUPS WITH 48,037 MALES

Group	Locality	Country	No.	MFD	Recorder
Turks III	Western Anatolia	Turkey	3020	100.7	.....
Turkomans	Northern Iraq	Iraq	31	102.9	Ehrich
Moslems		Palestine	276	103.40	Gloor
Beduins	Jazira	Syria	115	103.42	Huxley
Villagers (Sunni)	Hidjaneh	Syria	298	103.46	Shanklin
Samaritans	Nablus	Palestine	38	103.54	Huxley
Rwala Beduins	Jazira	Syria	270	103.78	Shanklin
Howeitat Beduins	Jazira	Jordan	70	104.06	Shanklin
Beni Sakhr Beduins	Jazira	Jordan	65	104.06	Shanklin
Arabs	Northern Iraq	Iraq	33	104.15	Ehrich
An Nasiriya	Liwa	Iraq	109	104.49	Smeaton
Arabs	Baghdad Hospital	Iraq	23	104.58	Smeaton
Christians		Palestine	55	104.59	Gloor
Turkomans	Aintab Area	Syria	19	104.62	Huxley
Gypsies		Syria	11	104.70	Huxley
Greek Orthodox		Syria	91	104.82	Huxley
Moslems		Syria	258	104.86	Huxley
Samaritans	Nablus	Palestine	39	105.28	Genna
Maronites		Syria	31	105.46	Huxley
Kurds	Northern Iraq	Iraq	13	105.69	Ehrich
Nusairiyeh (Shia)	Mountains	Syria	25	105.86	Huxley
Turks VII	Northwest Anatolia	Turkey	4161	106.4	.....
Iraq Soldiers	.....	Iraq	63	106.42	Buxton and Field
Bekaa Villagers (Sunni)	Plain	Lebanon	149	106.54	Shanklin
Turks VIII	Southern Anatolia	Turkey	4766	106.8	.....
Syrians		Syria	251	106.82	Huxley
Towara (Tuarah) Beduins	Sinai	Egypt	63	106.85	Murray
Villagers (Christian)	Hafar	Syria	93	106.94	Shanklin
Druze	Jebel Druze	Syria	46	106.94	Seltzer
Beharna	Bahrain Island	Persian Gulf	44	107.45	Field
Kish Arabs	Hilla Liwa	Iraq	100	107.86	Buxton and Field
Total Turks I-X		Turkey	39465	108.0	.....
Turks VI	Central Anatolia	Turkey	4895	108.0	.....

TABLE 112 (Continued)

Group	Locality	Country	No.	MFD	Recorder
Turks IV	Aegean Area	Turkey	3406	108.1	.....
Villagers (Christian)	Mhardeh	Syria	157	108.16	Shanklin
Mitwali (Shia)	Mountains	Lebanon	302	108.71	Shanklin
Sulubba (Nomads)	Jazira	Iraq	38	108.82	Field
Turks X	Northeast Anatolia	Turkey	4683	109.0	.....
Villagers (Sunni)	Hama	Syria	175	109.08	Shanklin
Turks V	Western Anatolia (Interior)	Turkey	3420	109.2	.....
Turks I	Thrace	Turkey	2651	109.7	.....
Alouites		Syria	309	109.74	Shanklin
Druze	Jebel Druze	Syria	181	110.0	Izzedin
Turks IX	Eastern Anatolia	Turkey	5102	110.2	.....
Anaiza (Beduins)	Jazira	Iraq	22	110.30	Field
Akeydat Beduins	Jazira	Syria	120	110.44	Shanklin
Turks II	Bursa-Bilecik	Turkey	3361	110.7	.....
Baij (Beduins)	Hilla Liwa	Iraq	35	110.86	Field
Maualy Beduins	Jazira	Syria		111.30	Shanklin
Kurds II	Rowandiz	Iraq	235	111.34	Field and Smeaton
Kish Arabs	Hilla Liwa	Iraq	358	111.50	Field
Turkomans	Northern Iraq	Iraq	60	111.78	Field
Kurds	Total	Iraq	598	111.78	Field and Smeaton
Kurds III	Kirkuk-Sulaimaniya	Iraq	230	111.82	Field and Smeaton
Nippur Workmen	Afaq (Afej)	Iraq	41	112.25	Field
Kurds I	Zakho	Iraq	133	112.46	Field and Smeaton
Shammar (Beduins)	Northern Iraq	Iraq	273	112.66	Field and Smeaton
Negroes (Shammar)	Northern Iraq	Iraq	14	112.93	Field
Jews I	Northern Iraq	Iraq	59	113.02	Field and Smeaton
Al bu Muhammad	Amara Liwa	Iraq	221	113.02	Field and Smeaton
Dulaimis	Haditha	Iraq	136	113.02	Field
Yezidis	Jebel Sinjar	Iraq	123	113.22	Field and Smeaton
Yezidis	Combined	Iraq	224	113.34	Field and Smeaton
Yezidis	Sheikhan	Iraq	101	113.42	Field and Smeaton
Jews	Total	Iraq	106	113.46	Field and Smeaton
Jebeliyeh	Sinai	Egypt	73	113.50	Field
Beduins	Sinai	Egypt	150	113.78	Field
Jews II	Sandur	Iraq	47	113.98	Field
Lurs	Khurrumabad	Iran	69	114.05	Field
Kurds	Kurdistan	Iran	49	114.05	Field
Iraq Soldiers	.....	Iraq	221	114.10	Field
Al Sawaad	Amara Liwa	Iraq	50	114.66	Field and Smeaton
Bakhtiari	Khuzistan	Iran	148	115.14	Field
Assyrians	Habbaniya Camp	Iraq	532	115.80	Field
Kurds	Northern Iraq	Iraq	22	116.0	Chantre
Assyrians	Total	Iraq	105	117.06	Field

Total... 48,037

TABLE 113: BIZYGOMATIC BREADTH OF 75 GROUPS WITH 47,628 MALES

Group	Locality	Country	No.	Biz. B	Recorder
Beharna	Bahrain Island	Persian Gulf	44	124.39	Field
Sulubba (Nomads)	Jazira	Iraq	38	126.45	Field
Baij (Beduins)	Hilla Liwa	Iraq	35	128.15	Field
Towara (Tuarah) Beduins	Sinai	Egypt	63	129.2	Murray
Rwala Beduins	Jazira	Syria	270	129.87	Shanklin
Kish Arabs	Hilla Liwa	Iraq	355	129.90	Field
Anaiza (Beduins)	Jazira	Iraq	22	130.20	Field
Nippur Workmen	Afaq (Afej)	Iraq	41	130.30	Field
Villagers (Sunni)	Hidjaneh	Syria	298	130.34	Shanklin
Beni Sakhr Beduins	Jazira	Jordan	65	130.60	Shanklin
Towara Beduins	Sinai	Egypt	18	131.0	Chantre
Howeitat Beduins	Jazira	Jordan	70	131.25	Shanklin
Samaritans	Nablus	Palestine	38	132.15	Huxley
Villagers (Sunni)	Hama	Syria	175	132.54	Shanklin
Beduins	Sinai	Egypt	150	132.8	Field
Villagers (Christian)	Hafar	Syria	93	133.07	Shanklin
Jebeliyeh	Sinai	Egypt	73	133.25	Field
Iraq Soldiers	.....	Iraq	63	133.60	Buxton and Field
Gypsies		Syria	11	133.80	Huxley
Negroes (Shammar)	Northern Jazira	Iraq	14	133.86	Field
	.....	Iraq	221	133.95	Field
Jews	.....	Iraq	37	134.0	Weissenberg
Villagers (Christian)	Mhardeh	Syria	157	134.08	Shanklin
Akeydat Beduins	Jazira	Syria	120	134.58	Shanklin
Shammar (Beduins)	Northern Jazira	Iraq	273	134.65	Field and Smeaton
Turkomans	Northern Iraq	Iraq	31	134.84	Ehrich
Alouites		Syria	309	134.86	Shanklin
Dulaimis	Haditha	Iraq	136	134.95	Field
Kish Arabs	Hilla Liwa	Iraq	100	135.10	Buxton and Field
Bekaa Villagers (Sunni)	Plain	Jordan	149	135.26	Shanklin
Beduins	Jazira	Syria	115	135.30	Huxley
Mitwali (Shia)	Mountains	Lebanon	302	135.34	Shanklin
An Nasiriya	An Nasiriya Liwa	Iraq	109	135.39	Smeaton
Al bu Muhammad	Amara Liwa	Iraq	221	135.45	Field and Smeaton
Turkomans	Aintab Area	Syria	19	135.70	Huxley
Al Sawaad	Amara Liwa	Iraq	50	135.90	Field and Smeaton
Maualy Beduins	Jazira	Syria	176	135.91	Shanklin
Subba	Amara Liwa	Iraq	90	136.05	Field and Smeaton
Turks VIII	Southern Anatolia	Turkey	4766	136.1	.....
Arabs	Baghdad Hospital	Iraq	23	136.15	Smeaton
Jews II	Sandur	Iraq	47	136.15	Field
Kurds	Kurdistan	Iran	49	136.30	Field
Turkomans	Northern Iraq	Iraq	61	136.50	Field
Maronites		Syria	31	137.00	Huxley
Yezidis	Jebel Sinjar	Iraq	123	137.10	Field and Smeaton
Moslems		Syria	258	137.25	Huxley
Greek Orthodox		Syria	91	137.30	Huxley
Turks IX	Eastern Anatolia	Turkey	5102	137.3	.....
Yezidis	Combined	Iraq	224	137.40	Field and Smeaton
Turks III	Western Anatolia	Turkey	3020	137.5	.....
Jews	Total	Iraq	106	137.55	Field and Smeaton
Lurs	Khurrumabad	Iran	67	137.60	Field
Arabs	Northern Iraq	Iraq	33	137.73	Ehrich

TABLE 113 (Continued)

Group	Locality	Country	No.	Biz. B	Recorder
Yezidis	Sheikhan	Iraq	101	137.75	Field and Smeaton
Turks	Thrace	Turkey	2651	138.2	.....
Bakhtiari Tribesmen	Khuzistan	Iran	149	138.24	Field
Kurds	Northern Iraq	Iraq	13	138.38	Ehrich
Turks II	Bursa-Bilecik	Turkey	3361	138.4	.....
Kurds I	Zakho	Iraq	133	138.50	Field and Smeaton
Syrians		Syria	251	138.55	Huxley
Jews I	Northern Iraq	Iraq	59	138.70	Field and Smeaton
Turks IV	Aegean Area	Turkey	3406	138.8	.....
Total Turks I-X		Turkey	39465	139.0	.....
Nusairiyeh (Shia)	Mountains	Syria	25	139.00	Huxley
Kurds	Total	Iraq	598	139.15	Field and Smeaton
Turks X	Northeast Anatolia	Turkey	4683	139.2	.....
Kurds III	Kirkuk-Sulaimaniya	Iraq	230	139.25	Field and Smeaton
Turks V	Western Anatolia (Interior)	Turkey	3420	139.4	.....
Kurds II	Rowandiz	Iraq	235	139.40	Field and Smeaton
Assyrians	Habbaniya Camp	Iraq	532	139.76	Field
Druze	Jebel Druze	Syria	46	140.70	Seltzer
Turks VI	Central Anatolia	Turkey	4895	141.0	.....
Turks VII	Northwest Anatolia	Turkey	4161	141.6	.....
Assyrians	Total	Iraq	105	141.45	Field
Kurds	Northern Iraq	Iraq	22	151.0	Chantre

Total... 47,628

TABLE 114: BIGONIAL BREADTH OF 64 GROUPS WITH 47,088 MALES

Group	Locality	Country	No.	Big. B	Recorder
Arabs	Northern Iraq	Iraq	33	96.00	Ehrich
Towara (Tuarah) Beduins	Sinai	Egypt	163	97.4	Murray
Sulubba (Nomads)	Jazira	Iraq	38	99.18	Field
Anaiza (Beduins)	Jazira	Iraq	22	100.38	Field
Baij (Beduins)	Hilla Liwa	Iraq	35	101.34	Field
Arabs	Baghdad Hospital	Iraq	22	101.70	Smeaton
An Nasiriya	An Nasiriya Liwa	Iraq	109	102.52	Smeaton
Beharna	Bahrain Island	Persian Gulf	44	102.55	Field
Turks II	Bursa-Bilecik	Turkey	3361	102.7	.....
Beni Sakhr Beduins	Jazira	Jordan	65	102.90	Shanklin
Kish Arabs	Hilla Liwa	Iraq	355	103.10	Field
Negroes (Shammar)	Northern Jazira	Iraq	14	103.21	Field
Turkomans	Northern Iraq	Iraq	31	103.81	Ehrich
Villagers (Sunni)	Hidjaneh	Syria	298	104.22	Shanklin
Iraq Soldiers	.....	Iraq	63	104.50	Buxton and Field
Subba	Amara Liwa	Iraq	89	104.66	Field and Smeaton
Samaritans		Palestine	39	104.70	Genna
Shammar (Beduins)	Jazira	Iraq	272	104.86	Field and Smeaton
Al bu Muhammad	Amara Liwa	Iraq	221	104.94	Field and Smeaton
Turks IX	Eastern Anatolia	Turkey	5102	105.0	.....
Kish Arabs	Hilla Liwa	Iraq	100	105.06	Buxton and Field
Howeitat Beduins	Jazira	Jordan	70	105.26	Shanklin

TABLE 114 (Continued)

Group	Locality	Country	No.	Big. B	Recorder
Turks VI	Central Anatolia	Turkey	4895	105.5	.....
Turks VIII	Southern Anatolia	Turkey	4766	105.5	.....
Rwala Beduins	Jazira	Syria	270	105.53	Shanklin
Kurds	Northern Iraq	Iraq	13	105.62	Ehrich
Jews II	Sandur	Iraq	47	105.62	Field
Villagers (Christian)	Hafar	Syria	93	106.02	Shanklin
Nippur Workmen	Afaq (Afej)	Iraq	41	106.40	Field
Moslems		Palestine	276	106.59	Gloor
Dulaimis	Haditha	Iraq	136	106.66	Field
Villagers (Sunni)	Hama	Syria	175	106.68	Shanklin
Turks III	Western Anatolia	Turkey	3029	106.7	.....
Villagers (Christian)	Mhardeh	Syria	157	106.71	Shanklin
Alouites		Syria	309	106.78	Shanklin
Christians		Palestine	55	106.81	Gloor
Total Turks I-X		Turkey	39465	107.2	.....
Iraq Soldiers		Iraq	220	107.10	Field
Kurds I	Zakho	Iraq	133	107.62	Field and Smeaton
Al Sawaad	Amara Liwa	Iraq	50	107.74	Field and Smeaton
Turkomans	Northern Iraq	Iraq	61	107.94	Field
Akeydat Beduins	Jazira	Syria	120	108.04	Shanklin
Maualy Beduins	Jazira	Syria	176	108.10	Shanklin
Turks X	Northeast Anatolia	Turkey	4683	108.2	.....
Kurds II	Rowandiz	Iraq	233	108.26	Field and Smeaton
Bekaa Villagers (Sunni)	Plain	Jordan	149	108.50	Shanklin
Kurds	Total	Iraq	596	108.62	Field and Smeaton
Jews I	Northern Iraq	Iraq	59	108.78	Field and Smeaton
Yezidis	Jebel Sinjar	Iraq	123	108.82	Field and Smeaton
Turks VII	Northwest Anatolia	Turkey	4161	108.9	.....
Druze	Jebel Druze	Syria	181	109.0	Izzedin
Jews	Total	Iraq	106	109.06	Field and Smeaton
Lurs	Khurrumabad	Iran	69	109.30	Field
Turks I	Thrace	Turkey	2651	109.4	.....
Yezidis	Combined	Iraq	224	109.46	Field and Smeaton
Kurds III	Kirkuk-Sulaimaniya	Iraq	230	109.58	Field and Smeaton
Turks IV	Aegean Area	Turkey	3406	109.7	.....
Mitwali (Shia)	Mountains	Lebanon	302	110.21	Shanklin
Yezidis	Sheikhan	Iraq	101	110.22	Field and Smeaton
Turks V	Western Anatolia (Interior)	Turkey	3420	110.3	.....
Bakhtiari Tribesmen	Khuzistan	Iran	149	110.96	Field
Assyrians	Total	Iraq	105	110.98	Field
Kurds	Kurdistan	Iran	49	114.45	Field
Assyrians	Habbaniya Camp	Iraq	532	115.59	Field

Total... 47,088

TABLE 115: UPPER FACIAL HEIGHT OF 72 GROUPS WITH 48,005 MALES

Group	Locality	Country	No.	UFH	Recorder
Towara (Tuarah) Beduins	Sinai	Egypt	63	60.56	Murray
Iraq Soldiers	.....	Iraq	63	66.20	Buxton and Field
Howeitat Beduins	Jazira	Jordan	70	67.00	Shanklin
Kish Arabs	Hilla Liwa	Iraq	100	67.30	Buxton and Field
Nippur Workmen	Afaq (Afej)	Iraq	41	67.60	Field
Moslems		Palestine	276	67.66	Gloor
Beni Sakhr Beduins	Jazira	Jordan	65	68.90	Shanklin
Kurds	Kurdistan	Iran	45	69.10	Field
Beharna	Bahrain Island	Persian Gulf	45	69.10	Field
Villagers (Sunni)	Hidjaneh	Syria	298	69.32	Shanklin
Al Sawaad	Amara Liwa	Iraq	50	69.50	Field and Smeaton
Villagers (Christian)	Mhardeh	Syria	157	69.58	Shanklin
Jebeliyeh	Sinai	Egypt	73	69.65	Field
Sulubba (Nomads)	Jazira	Iraq	38	69.65	Field
Villagers (Sunni)	Hama	Syria	175	69.90	Shanklin
Rwala Beduins	Jazira	Syria	270	69.99	Shanklin
Villagers (Christian)	Hafar	Syria	93	70.00	Shanklin
Anaiza (Beduins)	Jazira	Iraq	23	70.25	Field
Mitwali (Shia)	Mountains	Lebanon	302	70.28	Shanklin
Al bu Muhammad	Amara Liwa	Iraq	221	70.55	Field and Smeaton
Bekaa Villagers (Sunni)	Plain	Lebanon	149	70.60	Shanklin
Beduins	Sinai	Egypt	150	70.95	Field
Turks X	Northeast Anatolia	Turkey	4683	71.0	.....
Alouites		Syria	309	71.24	Shanklin
An Nasiriya	An Nasiriya Liwa	Iraq	109	71.40	Smeaton
Turks IX	Eastern Anatolia	Turkey	5102	71.4	.....
Dulaimis	Haditha	Iraq	136	71.55	Field
Shammar (Beduins)	Northern Jazira	Iraq	273	71.75	Field and Smeaton
Akeydat Beduins	Jazira	Syria	120	71.82	Shanklin
Christians		Palestine	55	72.00	Gloor
Jews II	Sandur	Iraq	47	72.30	Field
Lebanese	Beirut	Lebanon	164	72.50	Seltzer
Turks I	Thrace	Turkey	2651	72.7	.....
Syrians		Syria	251	72.80	Seltzer
Jews	Total	Iraq	106	72.85	Field and Smeaton
Turks VIII	Southern Anatolia	Turkey	4766	72.9	.....
Maualy Beduins	Jazira	Syria	176	73.00	Shanklin
Kish Arabs	Hilla Liwa	Iraq	355	73.00	Field
Negroes (Shammar)	Northern Jazira	Iraq	14	73.07	Field
Kurds III	Kirkuk-Sulaimaniya	Iraq	229	73.20	Field and Smeaton
Jews I	Northern Iraq	Iraq	59	73.25	Field and Smeaton
Kurds I	Zakho	Iraq	133	73.25	Field and Smeaton
Baij (Beduins)	Hilla Liwa	Iraq	35	73.30	Field
Turkomans	Northern Iraq	Iraq	61	73.30	Field
Total Turks I-X		Turkey	39465	73.3	.....
Kurds	Total	Iraq	597	73.35	Field and Smeaton
Yezidis	Sheikhan	Iraq	101	73.35	Field and Smeaton
Lurs	Khurrumabad	Iran	68	73.35	Field
Bakhtiari Tribesmen	Khuzistan	Iran	149	73.58	Field
Kurds II	Rowandiz	Iraq	235	73.60	Field and Smeaton

TABLE 115 (Continued)

Group	Locality	Country	No.	UFH	Recorder
Druze	Jebel Druze	Syria	46	73.65	Seltzer
Turks V	Western Anatolia	Turkey	3420	73.9	.....
Maronites		Syria	31	73.95	Huxley
Turks II	Bursa-Bilecik	Turkey	3361	74.0	.....
Yezidis	Combined	Iraq	224	74.00	Field and Smeaton
Beduins	Jazira	Syria	115	74.05	Huxley
Turks IV	Aegean Area	Turkey	3406	74.1	.....
Iraq Soldiers	.....	Iraq	221	74.15	Field
Subba	Amara Liwa	Iraq	90	74.15	Field and Smeaton
Assyrians	Habbaniya Camp	Iraq	532	74.24	Field
Turks VII	Northwest Anatolia	Turkey	4161	74.4	.....
Moslems		Syria	258	74.60	Huxley
Greek Orthodox		Syria	91	74.65	Huxley
Yezidis	Jebel Sinjar	Iraq	123	74.70	Field and Smeaton
Turks III	Western Anatolia	Turkey	3020	75.1	.....
Turks VI	Central Anatolia	Turkey	4895	75.1	.....
Turkomans	Aintab Area	Syria	19	75.25	Huxley
Arabs	Baghdad Hospital	Iraq	23	75.90	Smeaton
Nusairiyeh (Shia)	Mountains	Syria	25	76.00	Huxley
Kurds	Kurdistan	Iran	49	76.40	Field
Samaritans	Nablus	Palestine	38	78.95	Huxley
Assyrians	Total	Iraq	106	79.10	Field

Total... 48,005

TABLE 116: TOTAL FACIAL HEIGHT OF 80 GROUPS WITH 48,496 MALES

Group	Locality	Country	No.	TFH	Recorder
Kish Arabs	Hilla Liwa	Iraq	100	114.30	Buxton and Field
Howeitat Beduins	Jazira	Jordan	70	115.10	Shanklin
Nippur Workmen	Afaq (Afej)	Iraq	41	115.15	Field
Iraq Soldiers	.....	Iraq	63	115.40	Buxton and Field
Moslems		Palestine	276	115.63	Gloor
Baij (Beduins)	Hilla Liwa	Iraq	35	116.70	Field
Towara (Tuarah) Beduins	Sinai	Egypt	63	117.4	Murray
Christians		Palestine	55	117.50	Gloor
An Nasiriya	An Nasiriya Liwa	Iraq	109	118.30	Smeaton
Greek Orthodox		Syria	91	118.30	Huxley
Sulubba (Nomads)	Jazira	Iraq	38	118.95	Field
Maronites		Syria	31	118.95	Huxley
Rwala Beduins	Jazira	Syria	270	119.20	Shanklin
Villagers (Sunni)	Hidjaneh	Syria	298	119.62	Shanklin
Beduins	Jazira	Syria	115	119.70	Huxley
Beharna	Bahrain Island	Persian Gulf	44	119.75	Field
Kish Arabs	Hilla Liwa	Iraq	354	119.95	Field
Beni Sakhr Beduins	Jazira	Jordan	65	120.15	Shanklin
Beduins	Sinai	Egypt	150	120.25	Field
Druze	Jebel Druze	Syria	46	120.35	Seltzer
Turkomans	Aintab Area	Syria	19	120.40	Huxley
Arabs	Baghdad Hospital	Iraq	22	120.40	Smeaton
Anaiza (Beduins)	Jazira	Iraq	23	120.50	Field
Moslems		Syria	258	120.65	Huxley
Turks II	Bursa-Bilecik	Turkey	3361	120.8	.....
Villagers (Christian)	Mhardeh	Syria	157	120.90	Shanklin
Iraq Soldiers	.....	Iraq	220	121.10	Field
Turks V	Western Anatolia (Interior)	Turkey	3420	121.2	.....

TABLE 116 (Continued)

Group	Locality	Country	No.	TFH	Recorder
Turks I	Thrace	Turkey	2651	121.3	.....
Mitwali (Shia)	Mountains	Lebanon	302	121.32	Shanklin
Jebeliyeh	Sinai	Egypt	73	121.4	Field
Dulaimis	Haditha	Iraq	136	121.50	Field
Villagers (Sunni)	Hama	Syria	175	121.50	Shanklin
Al bu Muhammad	Amara Liwa	Iraq	221	121.75	Field and Smeaton
Turks IX	Eastern Anatolia	Turkey	5102	122.0	.....
Alouites		Syria	309	122.16	Shanklin
Villagers (Christian)	Hafar	Syria	93	122.20	Shanklin
Kurds II	Rowandiz	Iraq	235	122.40	Field and Smeaton
Total Turks I-X		Turkey	39465	122.4	.....
Shammar (Beduins)	Northern Jazira	Iraq	273	122.45	Field and Smeaton
Turks III	Western Anatolia	Turkey	3020	122.5	.....
Kurds	Total	Iraq	598	122.60	Field and Smeaton
Bekaa Villagers (Sunni)	Plain	Lebanon	149	122.62	Shanklin
Kurds III	Kirkuk-Sulaimaniya	Iraq	230	122.65	Field and Smeaton
Subba	Amara Liwa	Iraq	89	122.75	Field and Smeaton
Turks X	Northeast Anatolia	Turkey	4683	122.8	.....
Kurds I	Zakho	Iraq	133	122.85	Field and Smeaton
Syrians		Syria	251	122.90	Seltzer
Turks VI	Central Anatolia	Turkey	4161	122.9	.....
Turks VII	Northwest Anatolia	Turkey	1822	123.0	.....
Negroes (Shammar)	Northern Jazira	Iraq	14	123.07	Field
Al Sawaad	Amara Liwa	Iraq	50	123.10	Field and Smeaton
Jews II	Sandur	Iraq	47	123.30	Field
Akeydat Beduins	Jazira	Syria	120	123.32	Shanklin
Bakhtiari Tribesmen	Khuzistan	Iran	149	123.70	Field and Smeaton
Turkomans	Northern Iraq	Iraq	61	123.80	Field
Samaritans	Nablus	Palestine	38	123.95	Huxley
Jews		Iraq	37	124.0	Weissenberg
Turks VIII	Southern Anatolia	Turkey	4766	124.0	.....
Nusairiyeh (Shia)	Mountains	Syria	25	124.00	Huxley
Maualy Beduins	Jazira	Syria	176	124.04	Shanklin
Jews I	Northern Iraq	Iraq	59	124.05	Field and Smeaton
Lurs	Khurrumabad	Iran	69	124.40	Field
Assyrians	Habbaniya Camp	Iraq	532	124.54	Field
Yezidis	Jebel Sinjar	Iraq	123	124.70	Field and Smeaton
Yezidis	Combined	Iraq	224	125.35	Field and Smeaton
Yezidis	Sheikhan	Iraq	101	125.40	Field and Smeaton
Druze	Jebel Druze	Syria	181	126.00	Izzeddin
Samaritans		Palestine	37	126.95	Genna
Kurds	Northern Iraq	Iraq	13	127.62	Ehrich
Assyrians	Total	Iraq	106	127.75	Field
Turkomans	Northern Iraq	Iraq	31	128.26	Ehrich
Arabs	Northern Iraq	Iraq	33	128.67	Ehrich
Kurds	Kurdistan	Iran	49	128.85	Field
Turks IV	Aegean Area	Turkey	3406	132.2	.....

TABLE 116 (Continued)

Group	Locality	Country	No.	TFH	Recorder
Samaritans		Palestine	39	135.71	Genna
Moslems		Palestine	276	135.76	Gloor
Christians		Palestine	55	138.11	Gloor
		Total...	48,496		

TABLE 117: NASAL HEIGHT OF 78 GROUPS WITH 48,182 MALES

Group	Locality	Country	No.	NH	Recorder
Towara (Tuarah) Beduins	Sinai	Egypt	18	45.0	Chantre
Moslems		Palestine	276	45.50	Gloor
Iraq Soldiers	.....	Iraq	63	46.46	Buxton and Field
Kish Arabs	Hilla Liwa	Iraq	100	47.68	Buxton and Field
Turks V	Western Anatolia (Interior)	Turkey	3420	48.1	.....
Gypsies		Syria	11	49.86	Huxley
Christians		Palestine	55	49.87	Gloor
Kurds	Northern Iraq	Iraq	22	50.0	Chantre
An Nasiriya	An Nasiriya Liwa	Iraq	109	50.10	Smeaton
Towara Beduins	Sinai	Egypt	63	50.18	Murray
Nippur Workmen	Afaq (Afej)	Iraq	41	50.55	Field
Villagers (Sunni)	Hidjaneh	Syria	298	50.70	Shanklin
Turks II	Bursa-Bilecik	Turkey	3361	51.4	.....
Al Sawaad	Amara Liwa	Iraq	49	51.38	Field and Smeaton
Bekaa Villagers (Sunni)	Plain	Lebanon	149	51.42	Shanklin
Turks I	Thrace	Turkey	2651	51.5	.....
Maronites		Syria	31	51.58	Huxley
Turks VIII	Southern Anatolia	Turkey	4766	51.6	.....
Turks IX	Eastern Anatolia	Turkey	5102	51.6	.....
Negroes (Shammar)	Northern Jazira	Iraq	14	51.64	Field
Howeitat Beduins	Jazira	Jordan	70	51.66	Shanklin
Villagers (Christian)	Hafar	Syria	93	51.66	Shanklin
Turks IV	Aegean Area	Turkey	3406	51.9	.....
Total Turks I-X		Turkey	39465	52.0	.....
Turks III	Western Anatolia	Turkey	3020	52.3	.....
Turks VII	Northwest Anatolia	Turkey	4161	52.5	.....
Beharna	Bahrain Island	Persian Gulf	44	52.55	Field
Mitwali (Shia)	Mountains	Lebanon	302	52.58	Shanklin
Villagers (Sunni)	Hama	Syria	175	52.60	Shanklin
Beduins	Jazira	Syria	115	52.70	Huxley
Turks VI	Central Anatolia	Turkey	4895	52.8	.....
Turks X	Northeast Anatolia	Turkey	4683	52.8	.....
Villagers (Christian)	Mhardeh	Syria	157	52.86	Shanklin
Dulaimis	Haditha	Iraq	136	52.86	Field
Beni Sakhr Beduins	Jazira	Jordan	65	52.94	Shanklin
Al bu Muhammad	Amara Liwa	Iraq	220	52.98	Field and Smeaton
Moslems		Syria	258	52.98	Huxley
Druze	Jebel Druze	Syria	46	53.06	Seltzer
Sulubba (Nomads)	Jazira	Iraq	38	53.06	Field
Greek Orthodox		Syria	91	53.10	Huxley
Arabs	Baghdad Hospital	Iraq	23	53.14	Smeaton
Anaiza (Beduins)	Jazira	Iraq	23	53.66	Field
Kurds III	Kirkuk-Sulaimaniya	Iraq	230	53.86	Field and Smeaton
Alouites		Syria	309	53.94	Shanklin
Shammar Beduins	Northern Jazira	Iraq	273	54.06	Field and Smeaton
Kurds II	Rowandiz	Iraq	235	54.06	Field and Smeaton

TABLE 117 (Continued)

Group	Locality	Country	No.	NH	Recorder
Kurds	Total	Iraq	598	54.14	Field and Smeaton
Turkomans	Aintab Area	Syria	19	54.14	Huxley
Turkomans	Northern Iraq	Iraq	61	54.22	Field
Jebeliyeh	Sinai	Egypt	73	54.34	Field
Akeydat Beduins	Jazira	Syria	120	54.66	Shanklin
Yezidis	Sheikhan	Iraq	101	54.66	Field and Smeaton
Kurds I	Zakho	Iraq	133	54.74	Field and Smeaton
Beduins	Sinai	Egypt	150	54.86	Field
Jews II	Sandur	Iraq	47	54.86	Field
Nusairiyeh (Shia)	Mountains	Syria	25	54.94	Huxley
Jews	Total	Iraq	106	54.98	Field and Smeaton
Jews I	Northern Iraq	Iraq	59	55.06	Field and Smeaton
Rwala Beduins	Jazira	Syria	270	55.11	Shanklin
Bakhtiari Tribesmen	Khuzistan	Iran	149	55.19	Field
Syrians		Syria	251	55.22	Seltzer
Samaritans	Nablus	Palestine	38	55.38	Huxley
Maualy Beduins	Jazira	Syria	176	55.42	Shanklin
Lurs	Khurrumabad	Iran	67	55.45	Field
Assyrians	Habbaniya Camp	Iraq	532	55.74	Field
Yezidis	Combined	Iraq	224	55.78	Field and Smeaton
Jews	.....	Iraq	37	56.0	Weissenberg
Druze	Jebel Druze	Syria	181	56.00	Izzedin
Kurds	Kurdistan	Iran	49	56.49	Field
Yezidis	Jebel Sinjar	Iraq	123	56.70	Field and Smeaton
Subba	Amara Liwa	Iraq	90	56.78	Field and Smeaton
Iraq Soldiers	.....	Iraq	221	57.02	Field
Samaritans	Nablus	Palestine	39	57.05	Genna
Kish Arabs	Hilla Liwa	Iraq	358	58.50	Field
Arabs	Northern Iraq	Iraq	33	58.52	Ehrich
Turkomans	Northern Iraq	Iraq	31	58.81	Ehrich
Kurds	Northern Iraq	Iraq	13	58.92	Ehrich
Baij Beduins	Hilla Liwa	Iraq	35	59.90	Field
Assyrians	Total	Iraq	106	63.10	Field

Total... 48,182

TABLE 118: NASAL BREADTH OF 78 GROUPS WITH 48,133 MALES

Group	Locality	Country	No.	NB	Recorder
Turks X	Northeast Anatolia	Turkey	4683	32.4	.....
Jew II	Sandur	Iraq	47	33.29	Field
Beni Sakhr Beduins	Jazira	Jordan	65	33.38	Shanklin
Turks IX	Eastern Anatolia	Turkey	5102	33.4	.....
Iraq Soldiers	.....	Iraq	63	33.47	Buxton and Field
Villagers (Sunni)	Hidjaneh	Syria	298	33.56	Shanklin
Al Sawaad	Amara Liwa	Iraq	49	33.71	Field and Smeaton
Kish Arabs	Hilla Liwa	Iraq	100	33.74	Buxton and Field
Turks VIII	Southern Anatolia	Turkey	4766	33.8	.....
Mitwali (Shia)	Mountains	Lebanon	302	33.84	Shanklin
Jews	Total	Iraq	106	33.89	Field and Smeaton

TABLE 118 (Continued)

Group	Locality	Country	No.	NB	Recorder
Howeitat Beduins	Jazira	Jordan	70	33.92	Shanklin
Bekaa Villagers	Plain	Lebanon	149	33.92	Shanklin
Sulubba (Nomads)	Jazira	Iraq	38	33.98	Field
Jews	.....	Iraq	37	34.0	Weissenberg
Towara Beduins	Sinai	Egypt	18	34.0	Chantre
Total Turks I-X		Turkey	39465	34.0	.....
Turks IV	Aegean Area	Turkey	3406	34.1	.....
Negroes (Shammar)	Northern Jazira	Iraq	14	34.29	Field
Turks VII	Northwest Anatolia	Turkey	4161	34.3	.....
Beharna	Bahrain Island	Persian Gulf	45	34.35	Field
Kurds III	Kirkuk-Sulaimaniya	Iraq	230	34.49	Field and Smeaton
Turks II	Bursa-Bilecik	Turkey	3361	34.5	.....
Turks III	Western Anatolia	Turkey	3020	34.5	.....
Anaiza (Beduins)	Jazira	Iraq	23	34.61	Field
Dulaimis	Haditha	Iraq	136	34.70	Field
Iraq Soldiers	.....	Iraq	222	34.76	Field
Syrians		Syria	251	34.76	Seltzer
Turks I	Thrace	Turkey	2651	34.8	.....
Baij (Beduins)	Hilla Liwa	Iraq	35	34.82	Field
Al bu Muhammad	Amara Liwa	Iraq	220	34.85	Field and Smeaton
Kurds	Total	Iraq	598	34.88	Field and Smeaton
Alouites		Syria	309	34.88	Shanklin
Turks V	Western Anatolia (Interior)	Turkey	3420	34.9	.....
Jews I	Northern Iraq	Iraq	59	34.91	Field and Smeaton
Kurds II	Rowandiz	Iraq	235	34.97	Field and Smeaton
Turks VI	Central Anatolia	Turkey	4895	35.0	.....
Rwala Beduins	Jazira	Syria	270	35.00	Shanklin
Moslems		Palestine	276	35.00	Gloor
Druze	Jebel Druze	Syria	181	35.00	Izzedin
Kurds I	Zakho	Iraq	133	35.00	Field and Smeaton
Turkomans	Northern Iraq	Iraq	31	35.00	Ehrich
Assyrians	Total	Iraq	106	35.03	Field
Yezidis	Sheikhan	Iraq	101	35.06	Field and Smeaton
Yezidis	Combined	Iraq	224	35.12	Field and Smeaton
Kurds	.....	Iraq	13	35.15	Ehrich
Assyrians	Habbaniya Camp	Iraq	532	35.16	Field
Yezidis	Jebel Sinjar	Iraq	123	35.21	Field and Smeaton
Villagers (Christians)	Mhardeh	Syria	157	35.26	Shanklin
Greek Orthodox		Syria	91	35.36	Huxley
Arabs	Northern Iraq	Iraq	33	35.39	Ehrich
Kish Arabs	Hilla Liwa	Iraq	359	35.42	Field
Villagers (Christian)	Hafar	Syria	93	35.44	Shanklin
Subba	Amara Liwa	Iraq	90	35.54	Field and Smeaton
Shammar (Beduins)	Northern Jazira	Iraq	273	35.54	Field
Villagers (Sunni)	Hama	Syria	175	35.58	Shanklin
Lurs	Khurrumabad	Iran	69	35.70	Field
Christians		Palestine	55	35.78	Gloor
Turkomans	Aintab Area	Syria	19	35.78	Huxley
Nippur Workmen	Afaq (Afej)	Iraq	41	35.80	Field

TABLE 118 (Continued)

Group	Locality	Country	No.	NB	Recorder
Nusairiyeh (Shia)	Mountains	Syria	25	35.84	Huxley
Jebeliyeh	Sinai	Egypt	73	35.87	Field
Turkomans	Northern Iraq	Iraq	61	35.99	Field
Akeydat Beduins	Jazira	Syria	120	36.28	Shanklin
Beduins	Jazira	Syria	115	36.41	Huxley
Samaritans		Palestine	39	36.51	Genna
Kurds	Kurdistan	Iran	49	36.60	Field
Beduins	Sinai	Egypt	150	36.65	Field
Gypsies		Syria	11	36.65	Huxley
Moslems		Syria	258	36.71	Huxley
Maronites		Syria	31	36.74	Huxley
Samaritans	Nablus	Palestine	38	36.74	Huxley
Druze	Jebel Druze	Syria	46	36.77	Seltzer
Arabs	Baghdad Hospital	Iraq	22	36.77	Smeaton
Maualy Beduins	Jazira	Syria	176	36.82	Shanklin
An Nasiriya	An Nasiriya Liwa	Iraq	109	37.03	Smeaton
Bakhtiari Tribesmen	Khuzistan	Iran	149	37.10	Field
Kurds	Northern Iraq	Iraq	22	39.0	Chantre

Total... 48,133

TABLE 119: EAR LENGTH OF 62 GROUPS WITH 46,997 MALES

Group	Locality	Country	No.	EL	Recorder
Negroes (Shammar)	Northern Jazira	Iraq	14	35.29	Field
Jebeliyeh	Sinai	Egypt	72	56.35	Field
Anaiza (Beduins)	Jazira	Iraq	23	56.82	Field
Gypsies		Syria	11	57.27	Huxley
Turks V	Western Anatolia (Interior)	Turkey	3420	57.6	.....
Jews II	Sandur	Iraq	47	57.66	Field
Sulubba	Jazira	Iraq	38	57.70	Field and Smeaton
Turks VIII	Southern Anatolia	Turkey	4766	57.7	.....
Dulaimis	Haditha	Iraq	136	57.94	Field
Nippur Workmen	Afaq (Afej)	Iraq	41	58.10	Field
Al Sawaad	Amara Liwa	Iraq	50	58.46	Field and Smeaton
Beduins	Sinai	Egypt	142	58.85	Field
Jews	Total	Iraq	106	58.86	Field and Smeaton
Bakhtiari Tribesmen	Khuzistan	Iran	149	58.90	Field
Turks IV	Aegean Area	Turkey	3406	58.9	.....
Al bu Muhammad	Amara Liwa	Iraq	221	58.98	Field and Smeaton
Shammar (Beduins)	Northern Jazira	Iraq	273	59.10	Field and Smeaton
Kurds II	Rowandiz	Iraq	234	59.38	Field and Smeaton
Beharna	Bahrain Island	Persian Gulf	45	59.50	Field
Turkomans	Northern Iraq	Iraq	61	59.66	Field
Lurs	Khurrumabad	Iran	69	59.70	Field
Kurds	Total	Iraq	598	59.74	Field and Smeaton
Assyrians	Total	Iraq	106	59.82	Field
Iraq Soldiers	.....	Iraq	222	59.82	Field
Jews I	Northern Iraq	Iraq	59	59.82	Field and Smeaton
Total Turks I-X		Turkey	39465	59.9	.....
Kurds III	Kirkuk-Sulaimaniya	Iraq	230	59.94	Field and Smeaton

TABLE 119 (Continued)

Group	Locality	Country	No.	EL	Recorder
Kurds I	Zakho	Iraq	133	60.02	Field and Smeaton
Yezidis	Jebel Sinjar	Iraq	123	60.18	Field and Smeaton
Turks II	Bursa-Bilecik	Turkey	3361	60.3	.....
Yezidis	Combined	Iraq	224	60.38	Field and Smeaton
Beni Sakhr Beduins	Jazira	Jordan	65	60.39	Shanklin
Turks IX	Eastern Anatolia	Turkey	5102	60.4	.....
Villagers (Sunni)	Hidjaneh	Syria	298	60.46	Shanklin
Rwala (Ruwalla) Beduins	Jazira	Syria	270	60.48	Shanklin
Turks VI	Central Anatolia	Turkey	4895	60.5	.....
Turks VII	Northwest Anatolia	Turkey	4161	60.5	.....
Yezidis	Sheikhan	Iraq	101	60.62	Field and Smeaton
Assyrians	Habbaniya Camp	Iraq	532	60.78	Field
Turks I	Thrace	Turkey	2651	60.8	.....
Bekaa Villagers (Sunni)	Plain	Lebanon	149	60.86	Shanklin
Moslems		Palestine	276	60.93	Gloor
Turks X	Northeast Anatolia	Turkey	4683	60.9	.....
Howeitat Beduins	Jazira	Jordan	70	60.93	Shanklin
Subba	Amara Liwa	Iraq	90	61.14	Field and Smeaton
Mitwali (Shia)	Mountains	Lebanon	302	61.34	Shanklin
Villagers (Sunni)	Hama	Syria	175	61.58	Shanklin
Alouites		Syria	309	61.94	Shanklin
Akeydat Beduins	Jazira	Syria	120	62.10	Shanklin
Kish Arabs	Hilla Liwa	Iraq	359	62.26	Field
Turks III	Western Anatolia	Turkey	3020	62.3	.....
Baij Beduins	Hilla Liwa	Iraq	35	62.42	Field
Maualy Beduins	Jazira	Syria	176	62.56	Shanklin
Kurds	Kurdistan	Iran	49	63.35	Field
Villagers (Christian)	Hafar	Syria	93	63.44	Shanklin
An Nasiriya	An Nasiriya Liwa	Iraq	109	63.51	Smeaton
Villagers (Christian)	Mhardeh	Syria	157	63.54	Shanklin
Maronites		Syria	31	63.96	Huxley
Christians		Palestine	55	64.28	Gloor
Arabs	Baghdad Hospital	Iraq	23	65.50	Smeaton
Samaritans		Palestine	39	68.21	Genna

Total... 46,997

TABLE 120: EAR BREADTH OF 62 GROUPS WITH 46,995 MALES

Group	Locality	Country	No.	EB	Recorder
Alouites		Syria	309	32.06	Shanklin
Al bu Muhammad	Amara Iraq	Iraq	221	32.19	Field and Smeaton
Maualy Beduins	Jazira	Syria	176	32.26	Shanklin
Beni Sakhr Beduins	Jazira	Jordan	65	32.45	Shanklin
Howeitat Beduins	Jazira	Jordan	70	32.63	Shanklin
Akeydat Beduins	Jazira	Syria	120	32.74	Shanklin
Villagers (Sunni)	Hama	Syria	175	32.74	Shanklin
Bekaa Villagers (Sunni)	Plain	Lebanon	149	32.78	Shanklin
Villagers (Christian)	Hafar	Syria	93	32.78	Shanklin
Turks IX	Eastern Anatolia	Turkey	5102	33.0	.....
Mitwali (Shia)	Mountains	Lebanon	302	33.08	Shanklin
Rwala (Ruwalla) Beduins	Jazira	Syria	270	33.12	Shanklin
Villagers (Sunni)	Hidjaneh	Syria	298	33.16	Shanklin
Turks VI	Central Anatolia	Turkey	4895	33.3	Field

TABLE 120 (Continued)

Group	Locality	Country	No.	EB	Recorder
Villagers (Christian)	Mhardeh	Syria	157	33.34	Shanklin
Beharna	Bahrain Island	Persian Gulf	45	33.45	Field
Assyrians	Total	Iraq	106	33.48	Field
Subba	Amara Liwa	Iraq	90	33.51	Field and Smeaton
Sulubba (Nomads)	Jazira	Iraq	38	33.54	Field and Smeaton
Al Sawaad	Amara Liwa	Iraq	49	33.54	Field and Smeaton
Jebeliyeh	Sinai	Egypt	72	33.59	Field
Kurds II	Rowandiz	Iraq	234	33.75	Field and Smeaton
Anaiza Beduins	Jazira	Iraq	23	33.78	Field
Turks X	Northeast Anatolia	Turkey	4683	33.8	.....
Kurds	Total	Iraq	598	33.90	Field and Smeaton
Turks VIII	Southern Anatolia	Turkey	4766	33.9	.....
Kurds III	Kirkuk-Sulaimaniya	Iraq	230	33.93	Field and Smeaton
Turks III	Western Anatolia	Turkey	3020	34.0	.....
Kurds I	Zakho	Iraq	133	34.11	Field and Smeaton
Nippur Workmen	Afaq (Afej)	Iraq	41	34.20	Field
Dulaimis	Haditha	Iraq	136	34.41	Field
Arabs	Baghdad Hospital	Iraq	23	34.44	Smeaton
Total Turks I-X		Turkey	39465	34.6	.....
Turks II	Bursa-Bilecik	Turkey	3361	34.8	.....
Jews I	Northern Iraq	Iraq	59	34.89	Field and Smeaton
Jews	Total	Iraq	106	34.89	Field and Smeaton
Jews II	Sandur	Iraq	47	34.92	Field
Shammar Beduins	Northern Jazira	Iraq	273	34.95	Field and Smeaton
Assyrians	Habbaniya Camp	Iraq	532	35.10	Field
Negroes (Shammar)	Northern Jazira	Iraq	14	35.29	Field and Smeaton
Kish Arabs	Hilla Liwa	Iraq	359	35.31	Field
Beduins	Sinai	Egypt	142	35.33	Field
Yezidis	Jebel Sinjar	Iraq	123	35.34	Field and Smeaton
An Nasiriya	An Nasiriya Liwa	Iraq	109	35.39	Smeaton
Turkomans	Northern Iraq	Iraq	61	35.40	Field
Turks IV	Aegean Area	Turkey	3406	35.4	.....
Turks V	Western Anatolia (Interior)	Turkey	3420	35.6	.....
Samaritans		Palestine	39	35.62	Genna
Kurds	Kurdistan	Iran	49	35.65	Field
Moslems		Palestine	276	35.70	Gloor
Yezidis	Combined	Iraq	224	35.76	Field and Smeaton
Iraq Soldiers	.....	Iraq	221	36.06	Field
Lurs	Khurrumabad	Iran	69	36.15	Field
Yezidis	Sheikhan	Iraq	101	36.27	Field and Smeaton
Baij Beduins	Hilla Liwa	Iraq	35	36.51	Field
Bakhtiari Tribesmen	Khuzistan	Iran	149	36.65	Field
Turks VII	Northwest Anatolia	Turkey	4161	36.8	.....
Turks I	Thrace	Turkey	2651	37.6	.....
Christians		Palestine	55	38.31	Gloor

TABLE 120 (Continued)

Group	Locality	Country	No.	EB	Recorder
Lurs	Khurrumabad	Iran	69	47.44	Field
Kurds	Kurdistan	Iran	49	50.44	Field
Bakhtiari Tribesmen	Khuzistan	Iran	146	52.53	Field
		Total...	46,995		

TABLE 121: RELATIVE SITTING HEIGHT 42 GROUPS WITH 6,079 MALES

Group	Locality	Country	No.	RSH	Recorder
Lurs	Khurrumabad	Iran	69	47.44	Field
Kish Arabs	Hilla Liwa	Iraq	342	49.08	Field
Iraq Soldiers	.....	Iraq	222	49.30	Field
Baij Beduins	Hilla Liwa	Iraq	35	49.76	Field
Dulaimis	Haditha	Iraq	136	50.08	Field
Assyrians	Total	Iraq	106	50.22	Field
Kurds	Kurdistan	Iran	50	50.44	Field
Bakhtiari Tribesmen	Khuzistan	Iran	146	50.53	Field
Maualy Beduins	Jazira	Syria	176	50.54	Shanklin
Akeydat Beduins	Jazira	Syria	120	50.54	Shanklin
An Nasiriya	An Nasiriya Liwa	Iraq	109	50.86	Smeaton
Rwala Beduins	Jazira	Syria	270	51.11	Shanklin
Villagers (Sunni)	Hama	Syria	175	51.18	Shanklin
Beni Sakhr Beduins	Jazira	Jordan	65	51.18	Shanklin
Villagers (Christian)	Mhardeh	Syria	157	51.24	Shanklin
Alouites		Syria	309	51.46	Shanklin
Arabs	Baghdad Hospital	Iraq	21	51.46	Smeaton
Howeitat Beduins	Jazira	Jordan	70	51.68	Shanklin
Bekaa Villagers (Sunni)	Plain	Lebanon	149	52.00	Shanklin
Kurds III	Kirkuk-Sulaimaniya	Iraq	229	52.18	Field and Smeaton
Villagers (Christian)	Hafar	Syria	93	52.20	Shanklin
Kurds	Total	Iraq	597	52.38	Field and Smeaton
Kurds II	Rowandiz	Iraq	234	52.46	Field and Smeaton
Arabs	Kirkuk	Iraq	32	52.47	Ehrich
Kurds I	Zakho	Iraq	133	52.54	Field and Smeaton
Villagers (Sunni)	Hidjaneh	Syria	298	52.60	Shanklin
Mitwali (Shia)	Mountains	Lebanon	302	52.76	Shanklin
Al bu Muhammad	Amara Liwa	Iraq	219	52.78	Field and Smeaton
Sulubba (Nomads)	Jazira	Iraq	24	52.92	Field
Negroes (Shammar)	Northern Jazira	Iraq	14	52.92	Field
Yezidis	Jebel Sinjar	Iraq	121	53.00	Field and Smeaton
Turkomans	Northern Iraq	Iraq	60	53.04	Field
Jews II	Sandur	Iraq	47	53.06	Field
Al Sawaad	Amara Liwa	Iraq	50	53.06	Field and Smeaton
Yezidis	Combined	Iraq	221	53.06	Field and Smeaton
Turkomans	Northern Iraq	Iraq	31	53.06	Ehrich
Yezidis	Sheikhan	Iraq	100	53.14	Field and Smeaton
Jews	Total	Iraq	105	53.24	Field and Smeaton
Subba	Amara Liwa	Iraq	90	53.30	Field and Smeaton
Jews I	Northern Iraq	Iraq	58	53.38	Field and Smeaton

TABLE 121 (Continued)

Group	Locality	Country	No.	RSH	Recorder
Shammar Beduins	Northern Jazira	Iraq	272	53.38	Field and Smeaton
Anaiza Beduins	Jazira	Iraq	22	53.68	Field
		Total...	6,079		

TABLE 122: CEPHALIC INDEX OF 348 GROUPS WITH 70,422 MALES

Group	Locality	Country	No.	CI	Recorder
Anaiza Beduins	Jazira	Iraq	23	71.91	Field
Yezidis	Georgia	Caucasus	40	72.2	Goroshchenko
Jebeliyeh	Sinai	Egypt	73	72.24	Field
Beduins	Sinai	Egypt	150	72.35	Field
Sulubba (Sleyb)	Jazira	Iraq	38	72.39	Field and Smeaton
Shammar Negroes	Northern Jazira	Iraq	14	72.65	Field
Harabi	Faiyum and Tripolitan Desert	Egypt	29	72.82	Chantre
Towara (Tuarah) Beduins	Sinai	Egypt	63	72.95	Murray
Yezidis	Jebel Sinjar	Iraq	123	73.05	Field and Smeaton
Villagers	Fidimin, Faiyum	Egypt	306	73.05	Field
Baij Beduins	Hilla Liwa	Iraq	35	73.29	Field
Towara (Tuarah) Beduins	Near Tor, Sinai	Egypt	18	73.3	Chantre
Fellahin	Baharia Oasis	Egypt	196	73.3	Mitwally
Fellahin	Beheira	Egypt	50	73.42	Myers
Villagers	Yezd-i-Khast	Iran	46	73.50	Field
Fellahin	Farafra Oasis	Egypt	51	73.7	Mitwally
Beduins	Western Desert	Egypt	40	73.76	Murray
Fellahin	Faiyum	Egypt	36	73.81	Myers
Beduins	Sinai	Egypt	20	73.87	Eliseieff
Beduins	Gezira (Jazira)	Egypt	134	73.9	Chantre
Shammar Beduins	Northern Jazira	Iraq	273	73.92	Field and Smeaton
Fellahin	Sharqiya	Egypt	20	73.94	Myers
Fellahin	Qena	Egypt	53	73.94	Myers
Beduins	Gezira (Jazira)	Egypt	165	73.96	Chantre
Copts (Soldiers)		Egypt	44	74.0	Myers
Dulaim Tribesmen	Haditha Area	Iraq	136	74.04	Field
Fellahin	Koraichia	Egypt	10	74.09	Chantre
Fellahin	Siwa Oasis	Egypt	221	74.1	Mitwally
Egyptians		Egypt	64	74.1	Myers
Beni Atiyeh Beduins	Jazira	Jordan	10	74.1	Shanklin
Fellahin	Qena and Girga	Egypt	136	74.13	Myers
Fellahin	Menufia	Egypt	91	74.18	Myers
Howeitat (Huwaitat) Beduins	Jazira	Jordan	49	74.2	Shanklin
Copts		Egypt	31	74.21	Chantre
Lurs	Pusht-i-Kuh	Iran	52	74.25	Field
Fellahin	Girga	Egypt	83	74.25	Myers
Moslem Soldiers		Egypt	369	74.26	Myers
Jews	Sanaa	Yemen	78	74.3	.....
Nippur Workmen	Afaq (Afej)	Iraq	41	74.30	Field
Hajayya Tribe	Jazira	Jordan	13	74.4	Shanklin
Ayaideh (Fishermen)	Menzaleh	Egypt	25	74.48	Chantre
Fellahin	Ababdeh	Egypt	81·	74.6	Chantre
Beharna	Bahrain Island	Persian Gulf	44	74.60	Field
Villagers	Aqaba	Jordan	13	74.7	Shanklin
Fellahin		Egypt	127	74.7	Chantre
Fellahin	Luxor	Egypt	58	74.73	Chantre

TABLE 122 (Continued)

Group	Locality	Country	No.	CI	Recorder
Fellahin	Kharga Oasis	Egypt	205	74.8	Mitwally
Fellahin	Kharga Oasis	Egypt	150	74.9	Hrdlicka
Fellahin	Tamiya, Faiyum	Egypt	183	74.91	Field
Beni Sakhr Beduins	Jazira	Jordan	65	74.94	Shanklin
Total		Egypt	288	75.0	Chantre
Fellahin	Dakhla Oasis	Egypt	397	75.0	Mitwally
Maaza	Qena and Beni Suef	Egypt	34	75.0	Chantre
Rwala (Ruwalla) Beduins	Jazira	Syria	270	75.00	Shanklin
Fellahin	Dakahlia	Egypt	109	75.01	Myers
Copts		Egypt	127	75.2	Chantre
Fellahin	Karnak	Egypt	14	75.27	Chantre
Kish Arabs	Hilla Liwa	Iraq	100	75.30	Buxton and Field
Kish Arabs	Hilla Liwa	Iraq	358	75.33	Field
Turkomans	Aintab Area	Syria	19	75.33	Huxley
Arabs	Baghdad Hospital	Iraq	23	75.39	Smeaton
Wulud (Aulad) Ali	Behera in Delta	Egypt	20	75.39	Chantre
Fellahin	Sharqiya	Egypt	515	75.4	Craig
Copts		Egypt	150	75.4	Chantre
Howeitat (Huwaitat) Beduins	Jazira	Jordan	70	75.51	Shanklin
Fellahin		Egypt	138	75.53	Chantre
Copts	Luxor	Egypt	96	75.53	Chantre
Afghans		Afghanistan	18	75.59	Poiarkov
Turkomans	Caspian-Aral Sea	Central Asia	59	75.6	IAvorskii
Turkomans	Northern Area	Iraq	60	75.69	Field and Smeaton
Arabs	Palmyra	Syria	11	75.7	Kappers
Fellahin	Safed	Palestine	30	75.7	Weissenberg
Fellahin	Minieh el-Qamh	Egypt	128	75.77	Ammar
Fellahin	Safed	Palestine	30	75.8	Weissenberg
Villagers (Christian)	Hafar	Syria	93	75.89	Shanklin
Iranians	Azerbaijan	Iran	34	76.0	Deniker
Fellahin	Belbeis	Egypt	144	76.0	Ammar
Egyptians	Canal Zone	Egypt	127	76.18	Craig
Samaritans	Nablus Area	Palestine	20	76.2	Weissenberg
Kurds	Lake Goktcha	Transcaucasia	67	76.2	Chantre
Iraq Soldiers		Iraq	63	76.23	Buxton and Field
Beduins	Jazira	Syria	115	76.29	Huxley
Akeydat Beduins	Jazira	Jordan	120	76.39	Shanklin
Fellahin	Barabra	Egypt	64	76.4	Chantre
Villagers	Kinareh	Iran	73	76.44	Field
Lurs	Khurrumabad	Iran	68	76.49	Field
Seistani	Seistan	Baluchistan	37	76.50	Joyce and Stein
Fellahin	Faqus	Egypt	141	76.56	Ammar
Jews		Iran	14	76.6	Krischner
Persians	Tabriz	Iran	23	76.6	Kappers
Iraq Soldiers		Iraq	221	76.62	Field
Gypsies		Syria	11	76.65	Huxley
Fellahin	Sharqiya District	Egypt	933	76.66	Ammar
Fellahin	Sharqiya	Egypt	51	76.66	Ammar
Fellahin	Zaqaziq	Egypt	288	76.74	Ammar
Khazaal		Jordan	221	76.78	Shanklin
Biloch		Baluchistan	35	76.81	Joyce and Stein
Arabs	Northern Area	Iraq	33	76.85	Ehrich
Audat Tribe	Jazira	Jordan	26	76.9	Shanklin
Fellahin	Jaffa Area	Palestine	32	76.9	Weissenberg
Fellahin	Hihya	Egypt	109	77.0	Ammar
Kurds	Kharput and Erzinghin	Kurdistan	23	77.12	Chantre
Beduins (Unclassified)	Jazira	Jordan	88	77.2	Shanklin
El-Kaid Tribe	Jazira	Jordan	45	77.2	Shanklin

TABLE 122 (Continued)

Group	Locality	Country	No.	CI	Recorder
Shiab Tribe	Jazira	Jordan	44	77.2	Shanklin
Villagers	Wadi Musa District	Jordan	16	77.2	Shanklin
Beduins	Jazira	Syria	107	77.2	Kappers
Sayad		Baluchistan	33	77.21	Joyce and Stein
Samaritans	Nablus	Palestine	27	77.23	Kappers
Fellahin	Kafr Saqr	Egypt	94	77.28	Ammar
Maualy Beduins	Jazira	Jordan	176	77.28	Shanklin
Beduins	Jazira	Syria	50	77.4	Kappers
Jews	Isfahan	Iran	86	77.43	Field
Arabs	Sanaa	Yemen	30	77.47	Atkey
Nussour Tribesmen	Jazira	Jordan	58	77.5	Shanklin
Villagers (Sunni)	Hidjaneh	Syria	298	77.52	Shanklin
Adwan Tribesmen	Jazira	Jordan	41	77.6	Shanklin
Kurds		Transcaucasia	300	77.6	Ivanovskii
Tatars	Azerbaidzhan	Caucasus	207	77.6	Various
Samaritans		Palestine	27	77.64	Szpidbaum
Kurds	Kurdistan	Iran	19	77.68	Danilov
Kurds	Erzerum	Turkey	32	77.7	Kappers
Beni Hassan Beduins	Jazira	Jordan	97	77.7	Shanklin
Villagers	Tafileh	Jordan	26	77.8	Shanklin
Milanli Kurds	Kurdistan	Anatolia	20	77.89	Chantre
Turkomans	Caspian-Aral Sea	Central Asia	23	77.9	Deniker
Samaritans	Nablus	Palestine	38	77.91	Huxley
Al bu Muhammad	Amara Liwa	Iraq	221	77.94	Field and Smeaton
Tatars	Aralych	Caucasus	16	77.96	Chantre
Villagers	Kutum	Jordan	57	78.0	Shanklin
Jews		Iraq	37	78.1	Weissenberg
Nusirat Tribesmen	Jazira	Jordan	42	78.1	Shanklin
Kurds	Kurdistan	Iraq	22	78.11	Chantre
Arabs	An Nasiriya Liwa	Iraq	109	78.19	Smeaton
Batayyni Tribe	Jazira	Jordan	34	78.2	Shanklin
Villagers	Madeba	Jordan	47	78.2	Shanklin
Arabs	City-dwellers	Iraq	39	78.24	Rassam
Omanis	Muscat	Arabia	31	78.28	Leys and Joyce
Al Sawaad	Amara Liwa	Iraq	50	78.30	Field and Smeaton
Subba	Amara Liwa	Iraq	89	78.39	Field and Smeaton
Turks	Novo-Bayazet	Turkey	25	78.4	Nasonov
Kurds		Transcaucasia	26	78.4	Nasonov
Persians		Iran	46	78.4	Danilov
Persians		Iran	168	78.4	Deniker
Villagers	Dizful	Iran	11	78.4	Deniker
Kurds	Airiga	Transcaucasia	25	78.48	Nasonov
Kurds	Azerbaidzhan	Caucasus	140	78.5	Chantre
Kurds		Kurdistan	332	78.5	Deniker
Kurds		Kurdistan and Caucasus	272	78.53	Chantre
Sephardim Jews	Amsterdam, Palestine and Kurdistan	Syria	101	78.6	Kappers
Kurds	Kurdistan	Iran	49	78.65	Field
Villagers (Sunni)	Hama	Syria	175	78.67	Shanklin
Persians		Iran	123	78.7	Various
Lori		Baluchistan	58	78.77	.....
Villagers	Nuaimi	Jordan	54	78.8	Shanklin
Villagers	Aidoun	Jordan	18	78.8	Shanklin
Tatars	Azerbaidzhan	Caucasus	19	78.83	Chantre
Yezidis	Erivan (Yerevan)	Armenia	20	78.90	Field
Moslems		Palestine	276	78.97	Gloor

TABLE 122 (Continued)

Group	Locality	Country	No.	CI	Recorder
Persians	Tehran	Iran	18	79.0	Kappers
Fellahin	Bichariet	Egypt	78	79.0	Chantre
Samaritans		Palestine	39	79.10	Genna
Tats	Baku	Caucasus	129	79.2	Deniker
Arabs	Jidda	Saudi Arabia	12	79.37	Mochi
Tatars	Azerbaidzhan	Caucasus	14	79.4	Von Erckert
Wanechi Pathans		Baluchistan	59	79.42	.....
Turkomans	Northern Area	Iraq	31	79.44	Ehrich
Arabs		Iraq	37	79.5	Chantre
Kurds	Lake Goktcha	Transcaucasia	30	79.5	Chantre
Kurds	Hamadan	Iran	12	79.5	Krischner
Christians	Baghdad	Iraq	20	79.50	Rassam
Kurds	Anatolia	Turkey	52	79.6	Kappers
Persians		Iran	29	79.6	Kappers
Arabs	Baghdad	Iraq	148	79.71	Rassam
Turks VIII	Southern Anatolia	Turkey	4766	79.78	.....
Jews		Iran	35	79.8	.....
Turks	Diarbekir	Turkey	11	79.8	Chantre
Jews	Galilee	Palestine	14	79.80	.....
Villagers (Christian)	Mhardeh	Syria	157	79.91	Shanklin
Jat		Baluchistan	100	79.97	.....
Jews	Damascus	Syria	30	80.0	.....
Persians		Iran	50	80.06	Maslovskii
Arabs	Baghdad	Iraq	18	80.1	Kappers
Tatars	Erivan (Yerevan)	Transcaucasia	17	80.11	Chantre
Tadzhiks (Tajiks)	Norachaine	Caucasus	14	80.11	Chantre
Pani, Pauni (Pushta)		Baluchistan	100	80.28	.....
Jews	Baghdad	Iraq	17	80.28	Rassam
Osetes	Osetia	Caucasus	14	80.5	Von Erckert
Total Yezidis	Georgia	Caucasus	49	80.58	Field
Arabs		Arabia	154	80.7	Deniker
Osetes	Terek	Caucasus	11	80.75	Chantre
Kalmyks		Caucasus	10	80.9	Von Erckert
Sheher Arabs	Near Aden	Arabia	82	80.92	Leys and Joyce
Arabs	Yemen	Arabia	20	81.07	Leys and Joyce
Turks X	Northwest Anatolia	Turkey	4683	81.07	.....
Arabs	City-dwellers	Iraq	18	81.1	Kappers
Osetes	Osetia	Caucasus	16	81.1	Von Erckert
Aschkenazim Jews	Amsterdam, Palestine and Syria		100	81.2	Kappers
Arabs		Palestine	122	81.4	Kappers
Arabs	Aleppo	Syria	13	81.4	Kappers
Osetes	Osetia	Caucasus	16	81.4	Von Erckert
Kurds	Lake Goktcha	Caucasus	158	81.42	Chantre
Christians	Mosul and Tell Kaif	Iraq	37	81.48	Rassam
Arabs	Damascus	Syria	44	81.5	Kappers
Osetes	Georgia	Caucasus	300	81.5	Riskine
Arabs		Arabia	29	81.59	Mochi
Kurds	Mardin	Turkey	12	81.6	Kappers
Arabs	North of Jaffa-Jericho	Palestine	139	81.6	Kappers
Abazek		Caucasus	11	81.6	Von Erckert
Bakhtiari Tribesmen	Khuzistan	Iran	148	81.65	Field
Mir Jat		Baluchistan	48	81.69	.....
Beduins	Jazira	Syria	135	81.7	Kappers
Yezidis	Lake Van	Turkey	20	81.75	Field
Undeformed Osetes	Osetia	Caucasus	118	81.76	Gilchenko
Turks	Brussa	Anatolia	88	81.80	Wagenseil
Dehwari		Baluchistan	200	81.84	.....
Jews II	Sandur	Iraq	47	81.84	Field
Kalandrani		Baluchistan	21	81.87	.....

TABLE 122 (Continued)

Group	Locality	Country	No.	CI	Recorder
Osetes	Osetia	Caucasus	554	81.9	Deniker
Osetes	Osetia	Caucasus	84	81.9	Dzhawachischwili
Adighe		Caucasus	30	81.9	Von Erckert
Chechens		Caucasus	12	81.9	Von Erckert
Arabs	Yemen	Arabia	41	81.9	Deniker
Makrani		Baluchistan	79	81.90	.....
Syrians		Syria	26	82.0	Chantre
Kurds	Northern Area	Iraq	13	82.00	Ehrich
Kurds	City-dwellers	Iraq	48	82.05	Rassam
Total Jews		Iraq	106	82.05	Field and Smeaton
Circassians		Caucasus	54	82.05	Kappers
Chechens		Caucasus	10	82.21	Chantre
Jews I	Northern Area	Iraq	59	82.23	Field and Smeaton
Turks	Anatolia	Turkey	200	82.24	Pittard
Christians		Palestine	55	82.28	Gloor
Turks	Smyrna	Anatolia	60	82.43	Wagenseil
Abazes (Abazin)		Caucasus	23	82.5	Sommier
Cypriots		Cyprus	586	82.54	Buxton
Kurds		Syria and Iraq	35	82.54	Chantre
Arabs	Yemen	Arabia	25	82.56	Mugnier
Arabs	Yemen	Arabia	20	82.56	Bertholon and Chantre
Turks III	Western Anatolia	Turkey	3020	82.61	.....
Kurds I	Zakho	Iraq	133	82.62	Field and Smeaton
Osetes	Osetia	Caucasus	200	82.62	Gilchenko
Jews	Georgia	Caucasus	33	82.9	.....
Turks I	Thrace	Turkey	2651	82.93	.....
Mengal Brahui		Baluchistan	77	82.98	.....
Jews	Aleppo	Syria	10	83.0	.....
Christian Arabs	Mosul	Iraq	58	83.0	Krischner
Turks II	Bursa-Bilecik	Turkey	3361	83.07	.....
Osetes	Osetia	Caucasus	17	83.11	Chantre
Arabs	Yemen	Arabia	16	83.18	Livi
Mingrelians	Georgia	Caucasus	12	83.2	Chantre
Georgians	Georgia	Caucasus	900	83.2	Dzhavahov
Alouites		Syria	309	83.24	Shanklin
Turks IX	Eastern Anatolia	Turkey	5102	83.28	.....
Total Turks I-X		Turkey	39465	83.28	.....
Osetes	Alaghir	Caucasus	14	83.4	.....
Circassians	Georgia	Caucasus	54	83.42	Kappers
Georgians	Georgia	Caucasus	43	83.5	Von Erckert
Circassians		Syria	42	83.5	Kappers
Kurds II	Rowandiz	Iraq	234	83.52	Field and Smeaton
Turks	Konia	Anatolia	66	83.53	Wagenseil
Georgians	Georgia	Caucasus	20	83.55	Chantre
Deformed Osetes	Osetia	Caucasus	82	83.79	Gilchenko
Total Kurds	Kurdistan	Iraq	597	83.88	Field and Smeaton
Turks IV	Aegean Area	Turkey	3406	83.95	.....
Assyrians	Habbaniya Camp	Iraq	532	84.01	Field
Plains Osetes	Osetia	Caucasus	66	84.06	Field
Armenians		Caucasus	20	84.1	Weissenberg
Digor Osetes	North Osetia	Caucasus	38	84.15	Field
Total Turks	Anatolia	Turkey	455	84.19	Wagenseil
Arabs	Mosul	Iraq	14	84.2	Kappers
Turks	Dardanelles	Anatolia	38	84.21	Wagenseil

TABLE 122 (Continued)

Group	Locality	Country	No.	CI	Recorder
Osmanli Turks	Anatolia	Turkey	120	84.33	Chantre
Osmanli Turks	Anatolia	Turkey	131	84.40	Elisieev
Ansaries	Tripoli Area	Lebanon	48	84.43	Chantre
Osmanli Turks	Anatolia	Turkey	16	84.5	Deniker
Kohtan Arabs	Mosul, Baghdad and Basra	Iraq	64	84.50	Kappers
Turks V	Western Anatolia (Interior)	Turkey	3420	84.53	.....
Total North Osetes	Osetia	Caucasus	105	84.60	Field
Osmanli Turks	Ankara and Konia	Anatolia	47	84.61	Kupanic
Turks	Azerbaidzhan	Caucasus	40	84.7	Pantiukhov
Jews		Caucasus	20	84.7	Weissenberg
Osetes	Koban	Caucasus	11	84.78	.....
Iron Osetes	North Osetia	Caucasus	67	84.84	Field
Druze	Jebel Druze	Syria	46	84.84	Seltzer
Afghans		Afghanistan	18	84.86	Matseevskii
Arabs		Lebanon	182	84.88	Kappers
Jews	Georgia	Caucasus	100	84.9	.....
Tats	Daghestan	Caucasus	56	84.9	Deniker
Bekaa Villagers (Sunni)	Plain	Lebanon	149	84.90	Shanklin
Chutta Lok		Baluchistan	33	84.93	.....
Kurds III	Kirkuk-Sulaimaniya	Iraq	230	84.96	Field and Smeaton
Maronites		Syria	31	84.96	Huxley
Yezidis	Sheikhan	Iraq	101	85.05	Field and Smeaton
Mountain Jews	Daghestan	Caucasus	100	85.1	.....
Armenians		Caucasus	75	85.11	Boas
Syrians		Syria	265	85.11	Seltzer
Bilikani Kurds		Kurdistan	30	85.16	Chantre
Total Assyrians	Hinaidi Camp	Iraq	106	85.17	Field
Kurds		Syria	35	85.2	Chantre
Bektash	Ankara	Anatolia	15	85.20	Crowfoot
Armenians		Caucasus	30	85.25	Chantre
Jews	Akhaltsikh	Caucasus	18	85.3	Pantiukhov
Bektash	Lycia	Anatolia	15	85.3	Deniker
Armenians		Caucasus	25	85.35	Hrdlicka
Turks	Eastern Provinces	Anatolia	39	85.35	Wagenseil
Armenians	Beirut and Istanbul	Lebanon and Turkey	97	85.38	Kappers
Turks	Ankara	Anatolia	69	85.38	Wagenseil
Turks VI	Central Anatolia	Turkey	4895	85.41	.....
Mountain Osetes	North Osetia	Caucasus	39	85.53	Field
Mongol Turks	Anatolia	Turkey	10	85.53	Kappers
Armenians		Caucasus	22	85.6	Von Erckert
Armenians		Caucasus	341	85.6	Deniker
Lazes		Caucasus	152	85.6	Deniker
Armenians		Transcaucasia	278	85.6	Deniker
Alouites	Tripoli Area	Lebanon	136	85.66	Kappers
Armenians		Caucasus	297	85.71	Chantre
Lebanese	Beirut	Lebanon	164	85.77	Seltzer
Armenians		Caucasus	292	85.77	Chantre
Armenians		Caucasus	101	85.81	Seltzer
Jews	Georgia	Caucasus	33	85.9	Weissenberg
Chaldeans	Qaraqosh (Karakosh)	Iraq	19	86.01	Kappers
Armenians		Lebanon	85	86.1	Kappers
Armenians		Caucasus	19	86.21	Von Erckert
Turks VII	Northwest Anatolia	Turkey	4161	86.29	.....
Druze	Jebel Druze	Syria	181	86.45	Izzeddin
Nusairiyeh (Shia)	Mountains	Syria	25	86.52	Huxley
Kastamuni Turks	Anatolia	Turkey	95	86.61	Wagenseil

TABLE 122 (Continued)

Group	Locality	Country	No.	CI	Recorder
Sangur		Baluchistan	16	86.64	.....
Mountain Jews	Daghestan	Caucasus	10	86.7	Von Erckert
Armenians		Caucasus	318	86.7	Dzhawachischwili
Armenians		Caucasus	105	86.89	Twarjanowitsch
Assyrians	Lake Urmia Area	Iran	10	87.0	Pantiukhov
Assyrians	Tiflis (Tbilisi)	Caucasus	11	87.0	.....
Assyrians	Mosul	Iraq	39	87.0	Krischner
Bandija		Baluchistan	35	87.00	.....
Turks		Anatolia	200	87.20	Hasluck and Morant
Druze	Jebel Druze	Syria	80	87.26	Kappers
Ghirussi Armenians		Caucasus	28	87.29	Chantre
Mitwali (Shia)	Mountains	Lebanon	302	87.38	Shanklin
Jews	Kubin near Baku	Caucasus	17	87.4	Pantiukhov
Lazes		Caucasus	27	87.48	Chantre
Jews		Transcaucasia	43	87.5	Pantiukhov
Lezghians		Caucasus	11	87.77	Chantre
Bakhtiari Tribesmen	Khuzistan	Iran	20	88.38	Various
Assyrians	Lake Urmia Area	Iran	33	88.70	Deniker
Assyrians	Eastern Anatolia	Turkey	22	89.50	Chantre
Armenians	Erivan (Yerevan)	Transcaucasia	27	91.07	Chantre
		Total...	70,422		

TABLE 123: LENGTH-HEIGHT INDEX OF 20 GROUPS WITH 39,884 MALES

Group	Locality	Country	No.	LHI	Recorder
Howeitat Beduins	Jazira	Jordan	70	64.07	Shanklin
Beni Sakhr Beduins	Jazira	Jordan	65	65.24	Shanklin
Turks VI	Central Anatolia	Turkey	4895	65.40	.....
Turks III	Western Anatolia	Turkey	3020	65.41	.....
Turks II	Bursa-Bilecik	Turkey	3361	66.48	.....
Turks IV	Aegean Area	Turkey	3406	67.52	.....
Turks I	Thrace	Turkey	2651	67.67	.....
Turks VIII	Southern Anatolia	Turkey	4766	67.99	.....
Turks VII	Northwest Anatolia	Turkey	4161	68.39	.....
Total Turks I-X		Turkey	39465	68.87	.....
Gypsies		Syria	11	69.92	Huxley
Beduins	Jazira	Syria	115	71.09	Huxley
Turkomans	Aintab Area	Syria	19	71.15	Huxley
Turks X	Northeast Anatolia	Turkey	4683	71.40	.....
Turks V	Western Anatolia (Interior)	Turkey	3420	73.16	.....
Samaritans	Nablus	Palestine	38	74.39	Huxley
Turks IX	Eastern Anatolia	Turkey	5102	74.76	.....
Druze	Jebel Druze	Syria	46	77.60	Seltzer
Maronites		Syria	30	77.90	Huxley
Nusairiyeh (Shia)	Mountains	Syria	25	79.28	Huxley
		Total...	39,884		

TABLE 124: BREADTH-HEIGHT INDEX OF 9 GROUPS WITH 419 MALES

Group	Locality	Country	No.	BHI	Recorder
Howeitat Beduins	Jazira	Jordan	70	84.98	Shanklin
Beni Sakhr Beduins	Jazira	Jordan	65	86.54	Shanklin
Gypsies		Syria	11	90.92	Huxley
Nusairiyeh (Shia)	Mountains	Syria	25	91.16	Huxley
Maronites		Syria	30	91.79	Huxley
Druze	Jebel Druze	Syria	46	91.79	Seltzer
Beduins	Jazira	Syria	115	93.14	Huxley
Samaritans	Nablus	Palestine	38	95.72	Huxley
Turkomans	Aintab Area	Syria	19	95.78	Huxley
			Total... 419		

TABLE 125: FRONTO-PARIETAL INDEX OF 71 GROUPS WITH 45,871 MALES

Group	Locality	Country	No.	FPI	Recorder
Turks III	Western Anatolia	Turkey	3020	66.42	.....
Turks VII	Northwest Anatolia	Turkey	4161	68.09	.....
Lebanese	Beirut	Lebanon	164	68.56	Seltzer
Christians		Palestine	55	69.13	Gloor
Turks VI	Central Anatolia	Turkey	4898	69.38	.....
Maronites		Syria	31	69.61	Huxley
Nusairiyeh (Shia)	Mountains	Syria	25	69.76	Huxley
Samaritans		Palestine	39	70.20	Genna
Druze	Jebel Druze	Syria	46	70.45	Seltzer
Moslems		Palestine	276	70.50	Gloor
An Nasiriya	An Nasiriya Liwa	Iraq	109	70.51	Smeaton
Turkomans	Northern Iraq	Iraq	31	70.58	Ehrich
Turks V	Western Anatolia (Interior)	Turkey	3420	70.67	.....
Turks IV	Aegean Area	Turkey	3406	70.76	.....
Samaritans	Nablus	Palestine	38	70.96	Huxley
Kurds	Northern Iraq	Iraq	13	71.08	Ehrich
Arabs	Northern Iraq	Iraq	33	71.21	Ehrich
Total Turks I-X		Turkey	39465	71.25	.....
Arabs	Baghdad Hospital	Iraq	23	71.44	Smeaton
Beduins	Jazira	Syria	115	71.56	Huxley
Gypsies		Syria	11	72.19	Huxley
Turkomans	Aintab Area	Syria	19	72.37	Huxley
Turks VIII	Southern Anatolia	Turkey	4766	72.46	.....
Turks II	Bursa-Bilecik	Turkey	3361	72.65	.....
Turks I	Thrace	Turkey	2651	72.85	.....
Beni Sakhr Beduins	Jazira	Jordan	65	72.91	Shanklin
Howeitat Beduins	Jazira	Jordan	70	73.09	Shanklin
Turks X	Northwest Anatolia	Turkey	4683	73.12	.....
Kurds II	Rowandiz	Iraq	234	73.33	Field and Smeaton
Kurds III	Kirkuk-Sulaimaniya	Iraq	230	73.39	Field and Smeaton
Turks IX	Eastern Anatolia	Turkey	5102	73.46	.....
Alouites		Syria	263	73.8	Shanklin
Kurds	Total	Iraq	598	73.81	Field and Smeaton
Kurds	Northern Iraq	Iraq	22	73.89	Chantre
Iraq Soldiers	.....	Iraq	63	73.90	Buxton and Field
Mountain Osetes	North Osetia	Caucasus	38	74.41	Field
Iron Osetes	North Osetia	Caucasus	65	74.62	Field
Osetes	North Osetia	Caucasus	103	74.62	Field
Digor Osetes	North Osetia	Caucasus	38	74.65	Field
Armenians		Caucasus	105	75.12	Twarjanowitsch
Kurds I	Zakho	Iraq	133	75.28	Field and Smeaton

TABLE 125 (Continued)

Group	Locality	Country	No.	FPI	Recorder
Yezidis	Sheikhan	Iraq	101	75.43	Field and Smeaton
Kish Arabs	Hilla Liwa	Iraq	100	75.70	Buxton and Field
Jews I	Northern Iraq	Iraq	59	75.76	Field and Smeaton
Assyrians	Total	Iraq	105	76.09	Field
Assyrians	Habbaniya Camp	Iraq	532	76.40	Field
Yezidis	Lake Van	Anatolia	21	76.42	Field
Jews	Total	Iraq	105	76.48	Field and Smeaton
Yezidis	Transcaucasia and Anatolia		50	76.60	Field
Yezidis	Yerevan (Erivan)	Armenia	20	77.05	Field
Bakhtiari Tribe	Khuzistan	Iran	148	77.14	Field
Jews II	Sandur	Iraq	46	77.44	Field
Al Sawaad	Amara Liwa	Iraq	50	77.86	Field and Smeaton
Al bu Muhammad	Amara Liwa	Iraq	221	77.94	Field and Smeaton
Yezidis	Combined	Iraq	224	78.43	Field and Smeaton
Kish Arabs	Hilla Liwa	Iraq	358	78.67	Field
Kurds	Kurdistan	Iran	49	78.85	Field
Subba	Amara Liwa	Iraq	88	78.89	Field and Smeaton
Beharna	Bahrain Island	Persian Gulf	44	79.05	Field
Turkomans	Northern Iraq	Iraq	60	79.06	Field
Sulubba (Nomads)	Jazira	Iraq	38	79.15	Field
Iraq Soldiers	.....	Iraq	221	79.33	Field
Baij (Beduins)	Hilla Liwa	Iraq	35	79.60	Field
Anaiza (Beduins)	Jazira	Iraq	22	79.81	Field
Lurs	Khurrumabad	Iran	68	79.85	Field
Shammar (Beduins)	Northern Jazira	Iraq	272	79.93	Field and Smeaton
Dulaimis	Haditha	Iraq	136	80.20	Field
Nippur Workmen	Afaq (Afej)	Iraq	41	80.30	Field
Negroes (Shammar)	Northern Jazira	Iraq	14	80.56	Field
Yezidis	Jebel Sinjar	Iraq	123	80.89	Field and Smeaton

Total... 45,871

TABLE 126: CEPHALO-FACIAL INDEX OF 20 GROUPS WITH 2,146 MALES

Group	Locality	Country	No.	CFI	Recorder
Gypsies		Syria	11	78.22	Huxley
Lebanese	Beirut	Lebanon	164	89.15	Seltzer
Maronites		Syria	31	89.87	Huxley
Howeitat Beduins	Jazira	Jordan	70	90.11	Shanklin
Samaritans	Nablus	Palestine	38	90.35	Huxley
Alouites		Syria	309	90.6	Shanklin
Samaritans		Palestine	39	90.60	Genna
Christians		Palestine	55	90.90	Gloor
Beharna	Bahrain Island	Persian Gulf	44	91.30	Field
Nusiriyeh (Shia)	Mountains	Syria	25	91.52	Huxley
Beni Sakhr Beduins	Jazira	Jordan	65	92.09	Shanklin
Bakhtiari Tribesmen	Khuzistan	Iraq	149	92.47	Field
Moslems		Palestine	276	92.56	Gloor
Assyrians	Habbaniya Camp	Iraq	532	92.56	Field
Druze	Jebel Druze	Syria	46	92.72	Field

TABLE 126 (Continued)

Group	Locality	Country	No.	CFI	Recorder
Nippur Workmen	Afaq (Afej)	Iraq	41	92.85	Field
Beduins	Jazira	Syria	115	93.65	Huxley
Kurds	Kurdistan	Iran	49	94.25	Field
Turkomans	Aintab Area	Syria	19	95.15	Huxley
Lurs	Khurrumabad	Iran	68	95.70	Field
		Total...	2,146		

TABLE 127: UPPER FACIAL INDEX OF 66 GROUPS WITH 46,216 MALES

Group	Locality	Country	No.	UFI	Recorder
Iraq Soldiers	.....	Iraq	63	49.34	Buxton and Field
Kish Arabs	Hilla Liwa	Iraq	100	49.55	Buxton and Field
Moslems		Palestine	276	50.03	Gloor
Howeitat Beduins	Jazira	Jordan	70	50.57	Shanklin
Al Sawaad	Amara Liwa	Iraq	50	50.66	Field and Smeaton
Turks X	Northeast Anatolia	Turkey	4683	51.19	.....
Nippur Workmen	Afaq (Afej)	Iraq	41	51.75	Field
Turks IX	Eastern Anatolia	Turkey	5102	52.00	.....
Jebeliyeh	Sinai	Egypt	73	52.1	Field
Al bu Muhammad	Amara Liwa	Iraq	221	52.13	Field and Smeaton
Turks V	Western Anatolia (Interior)	Turkey	3420	52.48	.....
Turks VII	Northwest Anatolia	Turkey	4161	52.54	.....
Alouites		Syria	309	52.6	Shanklin
Kurds III	Kirkuk-Sulaimaniya	Iraq	229	52.61	Field and Smeaton
Druze	Jebel Druze	Syria	46	52.61	Seltzer
Turks I	Thrace	Turkey	2651	52.66	.....
Total Turks I-X		Turkey	39465	52.66	.....
Christians		Palestine	55	52.69	Gloor
Lebanese	Beirut	Lebanon	164	52.70	Seltzer
Kurds	Total	Iraq	597	52.76	Field and Smeaton
Jews I	Northern Iraq	Iraq	59	52.76	Field and Smeaton
An Nasiriya	An Nasiriya Liwa	Iraq	109	52.78	Smeaton
Kurds II	Rowandiz	Iraq	234	52.79	Field and Smeaton
Turks II	Bursa-Bilecik	Turkey	3361	52.82	.....
Lurs	Khurrumabad	Iran	66	52.85	Field
Beni Sakhr Beduins	Jazira	Jordan	65	52.85	Shanklin
Jews	Total	Iraq	106	52.91	Field and Smeaton
Kurds I	Zakho	Iraq	133	52.94	Field and Smeaton
Jews II	Sandur	Iraq	47	53.12	Field
Dulaimis	Haditha	Iraq	136	53.15	Field
Yezidis	Sheikhan	Iraq	101	53.24	Field and Smeaton
Turks VI	Central Anatolia	Turkey	4895	53.26	.....
Bakhtiari Tribesmen	Khuzistan	Iran	149	53.28	Field
Turks IV	Aegean Area	Turkey	3406	53.30	.....
Beduins	Sinai	Egypt	150	53.3	Field
Shammar (Beduins)	Northern Jazira	Iraq	273	53.36	Field and Smeaton
Akeydat Beduins	Jazira	Syria	120	53.40	Shanklin
Turks VIII	Southern Anatolia	Turkey	4766	53.56	.....

TABLE 127 (Continued)

Group	Locality	Country	No.	UFI	Recorder
Turkomans	Northern Iraq	Iraq	61	53.69	Field and Smeaton
Assyrians	Habbaniya Camp	Iraq	532	53.75	Field
Maualy Beduins	Jazira	Syria	176	53.80	Shanklin
Rwala Beduins	Jazira	Syria	270	53.90	Shanklin
Yezidis	Combined	Iraq	224	53.90	Field and Smeaton
Anaiza (Beduins)	Jazira	Iraq	22	53.96	Field
Turks III	Western Anatolia	Turkey	3020	53.96	.....
Maronites		Syria	31	54.44	Huxley
Yezidis	Jebel Sinjar	Iraq	123	54.47	Field and Smeaton
Negroes (Shammar)	Northern Jazira	Iraq	14	54.62	Field
Sulubba (Nomads)	Jazira	Iraq	38	54.65	Field and Smeaton
Subba	Amara Liwa	Iraq	90	54.68	Field and Smeaton
Nusairiyeh (Shia)	Mountains	Syria	25	54.68	Huxley
Beduins	Jazira	Syria	115	54.74	Huxley
Gypsies		Syria	11	54.92	Huxley
Turkomans	Aintab Area	Syria	19	55.37	Huxley
Beharna	Bahrain Island	Persian Gulf	44	55.85	Field
Arabs	Baghdad Hospital	Iraq	23	55.88	Smeaton
Kurds	Kurdistan	Iran	49	55.90	Field
Assyrians	Total	Iraq	105	56.24	Field
Kish Arabs	Hilla Liwa	Iraq	355	56.51	Field
Baij (Beduins)	Hilla Liwa	Iraq	35	57.29	Field
Iraq Soldiers	.....	Iraq	221	57.29	Field
Arabs	Northern Iraq	Iraq	33	57.42	Ehrich
Kurds	Northern Iraq	Iraq	13	57.62	Ehrich
Turkomans	Northern Iraq	Iraq	31	59.10	Ehrich
Samaritans	Nablus	Palestine	38	59.96	Huxley
Gypsies		Syria	11	72.00	Huxley

Total... 46,257

TABLE 128: TOTAL FACIAL INDEX OF 76 GROUPS WITH 47,951 MALES

Group	Locality	Country	No.	TFI	Recorder
Samaritans	Nablus	Palestine	38	76.02	Huxley
Kish Arabs	Hilla Liwa	Iraq	100	84.40	Buxton and Field
Moslems		Palestine	276	85.37	Gloor
Christians		Palestine	55	85.50	Gloor
Druze	Jebel Druze	Syria	46	85.60	Seltzer
Turks V	Western Anatolia (Interior)	Turkey	3420	85.74	.....
Iraq Soldiers	.....	Iraq	63	86.35	Buxton and Field
Greek Orthodox		Syria	91	86.65	Huxley
Turks VII	Northwest Anatolia	Turkey	4161	86.75	.....
Turks VI	Central Anatolia	Turkey	4895	87.16	.....
Maronites		Syria	31	87.30	Huxley
An Nasiriya	An Nasiriya Liwa	Iraq	109	87.46	Smeaton
Turks I	Thrace	Turkey	2651	87.58	.....
Total Turks I-X		Turkey	39465	87.78	.....
Turkomans	Aintab Area	Syria	19	87.80	Huxley
Turks III	Western Anatolia	Turkey	3020	87.86	.....
Kurds II	Rowandiz	Iraq	234	87.95	Field and Smeaton
Howeitat Beduins	Jazira	Jordan	70	87.95	Shanklin

TABLE 128 (Continued)

Group	Locality	Country	No.	TFI	Recorder
Turks IV	Aegean Area	Turkey	3406	88.10	.....
Turks X	Northeast Anatolia	Turkey	4683	88.13	.....
Kurds III	Kirkuk-Sulaimaniya	Iraq	230	88.15	Field and Smeaton
Kurds	Total	Iraq	597	88.20	Field and Smeaton
Turks II	Bursa-Bilecik	Turkey	3361	88.35	.....
Syrians		Syria	251	88.58	Seltzer
Beduins	Jazira	Syria	115	88.60	Huxley
Kurds I	Zakho	Iraq	133	88.70	Field and Smeaton
Nippur Workmen	Afaq (Afej)	Iraq	41	88.70	Field
Turks IX	Eastern Anatolia	Turkey	5102	88.97	.....
Nusairiyeh (Shia)	Mountains	Syria	25	89.40	Huxley
Arabs	Baghdad Hospital	Iraq	22	89.50	Smeaton
Jews I	Northern Iraq	Iraq	59	89.55	Field and Smeaton
Assyrians	Habbaniya Camp	Iraq	531	89.61	Field
Mitwali (Shia)	Mountains	Lebanon	302	89.64	Shanklin
Armenians		Armenia	101	89.74	Seltzer
Bakhtiari Tribesmen	Khuzistan	Iran	149	89.75	Field
Jews	Total	Iraq	106	90.00	Field and Smeaton
Al bu Muhammad	Amara Liwa	Iraq	221	90.05	Field and Smeaton
Villagers (Christian)	Mhardeh	Syria	157	90.18	Shanklin
Dulaimis	Haditha	Iraq	136	90.35	Field
Druze	Jebel Druze	Syria	181	90.40	Izzeddin
Al Sawaad	Amara Liwa	Iraq	50	90.40	Field and Smeaton
Iraq Soldiers	.....	Iraq	221	90.45	Field
Subba	Amara Liwa	Iraq	89	90.50	Field and Smeaton
Bekaa Villagers (Sunni)	Plain	Lebanon	149	90.52	Shanklin
Assyrians	Total	Iraq	105	90.52	Field
Lurs	Khurrumabad	Iran	67	90.75	Field
Turks VIII	Southern Anatolia	Turkey	4766	90.82	.....
Alouites		Syria	309	90.88	Shanklin
Turkomans	Northern Iraq	Iraq	61	91.00	Field
Beduins	Sinai	Egypt	150	91.05	Field
Yezidis	Jebel Sinjar	Iraq	123	91.25	Field and Smeaton
Baij Beduins	Hilla Liwa	Iraq	35	91.30	Field
Shammar Beduins	Northern Jazira	Iraq	273	91.35	Field and Smeaton
Yezidis	Combined	Iraq	224	91.35	Field, and Smeaton
Yezidis	Sheikhan	Iraq	101	91.45	Field and Smeaton
Towara (Tuarah) Beduins	Sinai	Egypt	63	91.52	Murray
Beni Sakhr Beduins	Jazira	Jordan	65	91.60	Shanklin
Rwala Beduins	Jazira	Syria	270	91.67	Shanklin
Villagers (Sunni)	Hama	Syria	175	91.68	Shanklin
Villagers (Sunni)	Hidjaneh	Syria	298	91.72	Shanklin
Villagers (Christian)	Hafar	Syria	93	91.86	Shanklin
Akeydat Beduins	Jazira	Syria	120	91.90	Shanklin
Jebeliyeh	Sinai	Egypt	73	91.95	Field
Negroes (Shammar)	Jazira	Iraq	14	91.97	Field
Jews	Northern Iraq	Iraq	37	92.5	Ehrich
Maualy Beduins	Jazira	Syria	176	92.34	Shanklin

TABLE 128 (Continued)

Group	Locality	Country	No.	TFI	Recorder
Kish Arabs	Hilla Liwa	Iraq	355	92.65	Field
Anaiza (Beduins)	Northern Jazira	Iraq	22	92.70	Field
Arabs	Northern Iraq	Iraq	33	93.36	Ehrich
Jews II	Sandur	Iraq	47	93.40	Field
Sulubba (Nomads)	Jazira	Iraq	38	93.85	Field
Samaritans		Palestine	37	93.97	Genna
Kurds	Kurdistan	Iran	49	94.65	Field
Turkomans	Northern Iraq	Iraq	31	95.03	Ehrich
Beharna	Bahrain Island	Persian Gulf	44	96.20	Field
		Total...	47,951		

TABLE 129: ZYGO-FRONTAL INDEX OF 62 GROUPS WITH 45,300 MALES

Group	Locality	Country	No.	ZFI	Recorder
Turks III	Western Anatolia	Turkey	3020	72.31	.....
Arabs	Northern Iraq	Iraq	33	74.88	Ehrich
Turks VII	Northwest Anatolia	Turkey	4161	75.16	.....
Kurds	Northern Iraq	Iraq	13	76.09	Ehrich
Moslems		Palestine	276	76.16	Gloor
Turkomans	Aintab Area	Syria	19	76.22	Huxley
Christians		Palestine	55	76.32	Gloor
Turkomans	Northern Iraq	Iraq	31	76.32	Ehrich
Druze	Jebel Druze	Syria	46	76.38	Seltzer
Turks VI	Central Anatolia	Turkey	4895	76.51	.....
Beduins	Jazira		115	76.66	Huxley
Kurds	Northern Iraq	Iraq	22	76.82	Chantre
Arabs	Baghdad Hospital	Iraq	23	76.98	Smeaton
An Nasiriya	An Nasiriya Liwa	Iraq	109	77.31	Smeaton
Maronites		Syria	31	77.38	Huxley
Total Turks I-X		Turkey	39465	77.57	.....
Turks V	Western Anatolia (Interior)	Turkey	3420	77.62	.....
Turks IV	Aegean Area	Turkey	3406	77.71	.....
Samaritans		Palestine	39	77.77	Genna
Turks X	Northeast Anatolia	Turkey	4683	77.90	.....
Gypsies		Syria	11	78.22	Huxley
Nusairiyeh (Shia)	Mountains	Syria	25	78.22	Huxley
Turks VIII	Southern Anatolia	Turkey	4766	78.47	.....
Turks I	Thrace	Turkey	2651	79.38	.....
Beni Sakhr Beduins	Jazira	Jordan	65	79.58	Shanklin
Kish Arabs	Hilla Liwa	Iraq	100	79.74	Buxton and Field
Iraq Soldiers	.....	Iraq	63	79.78	Buxton and Field
Kurds II	Rowandiz	Iraq	235	79.82	Field and Smeaton
Turks II	Bursa-Bilecik	Turkey	3361	79.96	.....
Turks IX	Eastern Anatolia	Turkey	5102	80.31	.....
Kurds	Total	Iraq	598	80.46	Field and Smeaton
Kurds III	Kirkuk-Sulaimaniya	Iraq	230	80.58	Field and Smeaton
Howeitat Beduins	Jazira	Jordan	70	80.66	Shanklin
Alouites		Syria	263	81.5	Shanklin
Kurds I	Zakho	Iraq	133	81.38	Field and Smeaton
Jews I	Northern Iraq	Iraq	59	81.78	Field and Smeaton
Turkomans	Northern Iraq	Iraq	60	81.93	Field
Yezidis	Sheikhan	Iraq	101	82.34	Field and Smeaton

TABLE 129 (Continued)

Group	Locality	Country	No.	ZFI	Recorder
Yezidis	Combined	Iraq	224	82.58	Field and Smeaton
Lurs	Khurrumabad	Iran	67	82.65	Field
Jews	Total	Iraq	106	82.74	Field and Smeaton
Yezidis	Jebel Sinjar	Iraq	123	82.78	Field and Smeaton
Assyrians	Total	Iraq	104	83.10	Field
Al bu Muhammad	Amara Liwa	Iraq	221	83.26	Field and Smeaton
Bakhtiari	Khuzistan	Iran	148	83.52	Field
Assyrians	Habbaniya Camp	Iraq	532	83.64	Field
Shammar (Beduins)	Northern Jazira	Iraq	272	83.66	Field and Smeaton
Kurds	Kurdistan	Iran	49	83.75	.....
Jews II	Sandur	Iraq	47	83.98	Field
Al Sawaad	Amara Liwa	Iraq	50	84.14	Field and Smeaton
Dulaimis	Haditha	Iraq	136	84.18	Field
Subba	Amara Liwa	Iraq	88	84.18	Field and Smeaton
Negroes (Shammar)	Northern Jazira	Iraq	14	84.34	Field
Anaiza (Beduins)	Jazira	Iraq	22	84.42	Field
Iraq Soldiers	.....	Iraq	222	84.94	Field
Kish Arabs	Hilla Liwa	Iraq	358	85.98	Field
Beharna	Bahrain Island	Persian Gulf	44	86.00	Field
Sulubba (Nomads)	Jazira	Iraq	38	86.14	Field and Smeaton
Baij (Beduins)	Hilla Liwa	Iraq	35	86.30	Field
Nippur Workmen	Afaq (Afej)	Iraq	41	86.65	Field
Maronites		Syria	31	87.30	Huxley
Samaritans	Nablus	Palestine	38	92.72	Huxley
		Total...	45,300		

TABLE 130: NASAL INDEX OF 80 GROUPS WITH 47,384 MALES

Group	Locality	Country	No.	NI	Recorder
Assyrians	Total	Iraq	106	51.74	Field
Baij (Beduins)	Hilla Liwa	Iraq	35	58.06	Field
Turkomans	Northern Iraq	Iraq	31	59.49	Ehrich
Kurds	Northern Iraq	Iraq	13	59.65	Ehrich
Beduins	Jazira	Syria	115	60.46	Huxley
Jews	.....	Iraq	37	60.7	Weissenberg
Arabs	Northern Iraq	Iraq	33	60.73	Ehrich
Kish Arabs	Hilla Liwa	Iraq	358	61.14	Field
Iraq Soldiers	.....	Iraq	221	61.62	Field
Turks X	Northeast Anatolia	Turkey	4683	61.72	.....
Jews II	Sandur	Iraq	47	61.74	Field
Druze	Jebel Druze	Syria	181	62.60	Izzeddin
Yezidis	Jebel Sinjar	Iraq	123	62.78	Field and Smeaton
Jews	Total	Iraq	106	62.78	Field and Smeaton
Subba	Amara Liwa	Iraq	90	63.34	Field and Smeaton
Jews I	Northern Iraq	Iraq	59	63.62	Field and Smeaton
Yezidis	Combined	Iraq	224	63.62	Field and Smeaton

TABLE 130 (Continued)

Group	Locality	Country	No.	NI	Recorder
Rwala Beduins	Jazira	Syria	270	63.73	Shanklin
Beni Sakhr Beduins	Jazira	Jordan	65	63.90	Shanklin
Kurds	Kurdistan	Iran	49	64.09	Field
Kurds I	Zakho	Iraq	133	64.26	Field and Smeaton
Samaritans		Palestine	39	64.41	Genna
Sulubba (Nomads)	Jazira	Iraq	38	64.44	Field and Smeaton
Yezidis	Shaikhan	Iraq	101	64.66	Field and Smeaton
Mitwali (Shia)	Mountains	Lebanon	302	64.78	Shanklin
Kurds	Total	Iraq	598	64.82	Field and Smeaton
Nusairiyeh (Shia)	Mountains	Syria	25	64.86	Huxley
Lurs	Khurrumabad	Iran	67	64.95	Field
Kurds III	Kirkuk-Sulaimaniya	Iraq	230	64.96	Field and Smeaton
Turks IX	Eastern Anatolia	Turkey	5102	65.05	.....
Kurds II	Rowandiz	Iraq	235	65.06	Shanklin
Alouites		Syria	309	65.06	Shanklin
Assyrians	Habbaniya Camp	Iraq	532	65.08	Field
Turks VII	Northwest Anatolia	Turkey	4161	65.33	.....
Total Turks I-X		Turkey	39465	65.39	.....
Beharna	Bahrain Island	Persian Gulf	44	65.41	Field
Dulaimis	Haditha	Iraq	136	65.66	Field
Bekaa Villagers	Plain	Lebanon	149	65.72	Shanklin
Turks VIII	Southern Anatolia	Turkey	4766	65.89	.....
Akeydat Beduins	Jazira	Syria	120	65.95	Shanklin
Al bu Muhammad	Amara Liwa	Iraq	220	66.02	Field and Smeaton
Turkomans	Aintab Area	Syria	19	66.14	Huxley
Anaiza (Beduins)	Jazira	Iraq	23	66.18	Field
Maualy Beduins	Jazira	Syria	176	66.26	Shanklin
Turks IV	Aegean Area	Turkey	3406	66.27	.....
Turks VI	Central Anatolia	Turkey	4895	66.29	.....
Howeitat Beduins	Jazira	Jordan	70	66.34	Shanklin
Shammar (Beduins)	Northern Jazira	Iraq	276	66.46	Field and Smeaton
Turks III	Western Anatolia	Turkey	3020	66.48	.....
Samaritans	Nablus	Palestine	38	66.54	Huxley
Turkomans	Northern Iraq	Iraq	61	66.54	Field
Villagers (Sunni)	Hidjaneh	Syria	298	66.68	Shanklin
Jebeliyeh	Sinai	Egypt	73	66.7	Field
Beduins	Sinai	Egypt	150	66.86	Field
Al Sawaad	Amara Liwa	Iraq	49	67.06	Field and Smeaton
Villagers (Christian)	Mhardeh	Syria	157	67.12	Shanklin
Bakhtiari Tribe	Khuzistan	Iran	149	67.65	Field
Turks II	Bursa-Bilecik	Turkey	3361	67.65	.....
Turks V	Western Anatolia (Interior)	Turkey	3420	68.01	.....
Turks I	Thrace	Turkey	2651	68.01	.....
Villagers (Sunni)	Hama	Syria	175	68.20	Shanklin
Arabs	Baghdad Hospital	Iraq	22	68.94	Smeaton
Villagers (Christian)	Hafar	Syria	93	69.20	Shanklin
Druze	Jebel Druze	Syria	46	70.54	Seltzer
Nippur Workmen	Afaq (Afej)	Iraq	41	70.84	Field
Kish Arabs	Hilla Liwa	Iraq	100	71.74	Buxton and Field
Maronites		Syria	31	71.82	Huxley
Iraq Soldiers	.....	Iraq	63	72.86	Buxton and Field
Gypsies		Syria	11	73.50	Huxley

TABLE 130 (Continued)

Group	Locality	Country	No.	NI	Recorder
Christians		Palestine	55	73.96	Gloor
An Nasiriya	An Nasiriya Liwa	Iraq	109	74.19	Smeaton
Towara (Tuarah) Beduins	Sinai	Egypt	18	75.55	Chantre
Kurds	Northern Iraq	Iraq	22	78.00	Chantre
Towara Beduins	Sinai	Egypt	63	78.2	Murray
Moslems		Palestine	276	78.26	Gloor
Negroes (Shammar)	Northern Jazira	Iraq	14	80.60	Field
			Total... 47,384		

TABLE 131: EAR INDEX OF 56 GROUPS WITH 46,362 MALES

Group	Locality	Country	No.	EI	Recorder
Al Sawaad	Amara Liwa	Iraq	49	50.02	Field and Smeaton
Villagers (Christian)	Hafar	Syria	93	51.66	Shanklin
Maualy Beduins	Jazira	Syria	176	51.71	Shanklin
Alouite		Syria	309	51.90	Shanklin
Arabs	Baghdad Hospital	Iraq	23	52.58	Smeaton
Villagers (Christian)	Mhardeh	Syria	157	52.66	Shanklin
Akeydat Beduins	Jazira	Syria	120	52.78	Shanklin
Villagers (Sunni)	Hama	Syria	175	53.44	Shanklin
Beni Sakhr Beduins	Jazira	Jordan	65	53.82	Shanklin
Bekaa Villagers (Sunni)	Plain	Lebanon	149	53.96	Shanklin
Mitwali (Shia)	Mountains	Lebanon	302	54.22	Shanklin
Howeitat Beduins	Jazira	Jordan	70	54.36	Shanklin
Turks III	Western Anatolia	Turkey	3020	54.44	.....
Turks IX	Eastern Anatolia	Turkey	5102	54.79	.....
Villagers (Sunni)	Hidjaneh	Syria	298	54.82	Shanklin
Rwala (Ruwalla) Beduins	Jazira	Syria	270	54.97	Shanklin
Subba	Amara Liwa	Iraq	90	55.34	Field and Smeaton
Turks VI	Central Anatolia	Turkey	4895	55.37	.....
Turks X	Northeast Anatolia	Turkey	4683	55.68	.....
An Nasiriya	An Nasiriya Liwa	Iraq	109	55.84	Smeaton
Assyrians	Total	Iraq	106	56.26	Field
Beharna	Bahrain Island	Persian Gulf	45	56.65	Field
Kurds II	Rowandiz	Iraq	234	56.98	Field and Smeaton
Kish Arabs	Hilla Liwa	Iraq	359	57.06	Field
Kurds	Total	Iraq	598	57.14	Field and Smeaton
Kurds III	Kirkuk-Sulaimaniya	Iraq	230	57.18	Field and Smeaton
Kurds I	Zakho	Iraq	133	57.26	Field and Smeaton
Kurds	Kurdistan	Iran	49	57.30	Field
Turks II	Bursa-Bilecik	Turkey	3361	57.69	.....
Yezidis	Jebel Sinjar	Iraq	123	58.98	Field and Smeaton
Total Turks I-X		Turkey	39465	59.04	.....
Sulubba (Nomads)	Jazira	Iraq	38	59.06	Field
Baij Beduins	Hilla Liwa	Iraq	35	59.06	Field
Jews I	Northern Iraq	Iraq	59	59.10	Field and Smeaton
Yezidis	Combined	Iraq	224	59.42	Field and Smeaton
Turks VIII	Southern Anatolia	Turkey	4766	59.44	.....
Anaiza Beduins	Jazira	Iraq	23	59.54	Field

TABLE 131 (Continued)

Group	Locality	Country	No.	EI	Recorder
Turkomans	Northern Iraq	Iraq	61	59.62	Field
Assyrians	Habbaniya Camp	Iraq	532	59.65	Field
Shammar (Beduins)	Northern Jazira	Iraq	273	59.70	Field and Smeaton
Nippur Workmen	Afaq (Afej)	Iraq	41	59.70	Field
Jebeliyeh	Sinai	Egypt	72	59.8	Field
Yezidis	Sheikhan	Iraq	101	59.94	Field and Smeaton
Jews	Total	Iraq	106	59.98	Field and Smeaton
Dulaimis	Haditha	Iraq	136	60.02	Field
Turks IV	Aegean Area	Turkey	3406	60.35	.....
Beduins	Sinai	Egypt	142	60.5	Field
Turks VII	Northwest Anatolia	Turkey	4161	60.86	.....
Iraq Soldiers	.....	Iraq	222	60.94	Field
Jews II	Sandur	Iraq	47	61.06	Field
Lurs	Khurrumabad	Iran	69	61.35	Field
Turks I	Thrace	Turkey	2651	61.97	.....
Turks V	Western Anatolia	Turkey	3420	62.44	.....
Bakhtiari Tribesmen	Khuzistan	Iran	149	62.67	Field
Negroes (Shammar)	Northern Jazira	Iraq	14	74.04	Field

Total... 46,362

TABLE 132: MEASUREMENTS AND INDICES OF 21,981 FEMALE TURKS IN ANATOLIA

Measurement	Group	No.
Stature	35	21,981
Sitting height	17	20,676
Head length	22	20,930
Head breadth	19	20,738
Minimum frontal diameter	16	20,598
Bizygomatic breadth	16	20,597
Bigonial breadth	14	20,558
Upper facial height	16	20,598
Total facial height	16	20,597
Nasal height	16	20,597
Nasal breadth	16	20,598
Ear height	14	20,502
Nasal breadth	13	20,489
Indices		
Cephalic	43	21,538
Fronto-parietal	14	20,428
Zygo-frontal	14	21,056
Upper facial	14	20,428
Total facial	16	20,597
Nasal	16	20,597
Ear	12	20,388

TABLE 133: STATURE OF 35 GROUPS WITH 21,981 FEMALES

Group	Locality	Country	No.	Stat.	Recorder
Jews	Sanaa	Yemen	14	146.7	.....
Jews I	Northern area	Iraq	23	150.90	Smeaton
Total Jews		Iraq	46	151.11	Smeaton
Turks I	Thrace	Turkey	2588	151.25	.....
Jews II	Sandur	Iraq	23	151.29	Smeaton

TABLE 133 (Continued)

Group	Locality	Country	No.	Stat.	Recorder
Assyrians	Habbaniya Camp	Iraq	125	151.61	Field
Turks IX	Eastern Anatolia	Turkey	1472	151.68	.....
Turks II	Bursa-Bilecik	Turkey	2459	151.81	.....
Turks III	Western Anatolia	Turkey	2857	151.90	.....
Turks IV	Aegean Area	Turkey	2490	151.97	.....
Jews	Aleppo	Syria	10	152.1	.....
Beduins	Jazira	Syria	14	152.13	Huxley
Druze	Jebel Druze	Syria	114	152.2	Shanklin and Izzeddin
Turks V	Western Anatolia (Interior)	Turkey	2273	152.25	.....
Total Turks I-X		Turkey	20263	152.26	.....
Turks VIII	Southern Anatolia	Turkey	628	152.33	.....
Turks VII	Northwest Anatolia	Turkey	1822	152.33	.....
Turks VI	Central Anatolia	Turkey	2424	152.44	.....
Subba	Amara Liwa	Iraq	23	152.61	Smeaton
Yezidis	Georgia	Caucasus	40	152.7	Goroshchenko
Total Kurds	Northern Area	Iraq	33	152.70	Smeaton
Sulubba (Sleyb)	Jazira	Iraq	10	153.00	Smeaton
Yezidis	Sheikhan Area	Iraq	24	153.51	Smeaton
Alouites		Syria	100	153.56	Shanklin and Izzeddin
Shammar Beduins	Jazira	Iraq	117	153.66	Smeaton
Aqaidat Beduins	Jazira	Syria	70	153.92	Shanklin and Izzeddin
Turks X	Northeast Anatolia	Turkey	1250	154.11	.....
Turkomans	Northern area	Iraq	29	155.58	Smeaton
Maronites		Syria	19	155.85	Huxley
Yezidis	Jebel Sinjar	Iraq	46	155.94	Smeaton
Arabs	An Nasiriya Liwa	Iraq	26	156.45	Smeaton
Palestinians		Palestine	33	156.72	Gloor
Osetes	Osetia	Caucasus	60	157.3	Riskine
Samaritans		Palestine	44	157.3	Genna
Osetes	North Osetia	Caucasus	47	159.39	Field

Total... 21,981

TABLE 134: SITTING HEIGHT OF 29 GROUPS WITH 21,145 FEMALES

Group	Locality	Country	No.	SH	Recorder
Jews I	Northern Iraq	Iraq	23	77.05	Smeaton
Assyrians	Habbaniya Camp	Iraq	52	77.70	Field
Jews	Total	Iraq	46	77.77	Smeaton
Turks IV	Aegean Area	Turkey	2490	77.99	.....
Turks IX	Eastern Anatolia	Turkey	1472	78.09	.....
Turks III	Western Anatolia	Turkey	2857	78.20	.....
Turks X	Northeastern Anatolia	Turkey	1250	78.39	.....
Jews II	Sandur	Iraq	23	78.49	Smeaton
Aqaidat Beduins	Jazira	Syria	70	78.78	Shanklin and Izzeddin
Total Turks I-X		Turkey	20263	78.89	
Kurds	Total	Iraq	31	78.91	Smeaton
Turks VIII	Southern Anatolia	Turkey	628	79.04	.....
Alouites		Syria	100	79.06	Shanklin and Izzeddin
Turks I	Thrace	Turkey	2588	79.07	.....
Turks V	Western Anatolia (Interior)	Turkey	2273	79.17	.....
Shammar (Beduins)	Jazira	Iraq	117	79.39	Smeaton
Turks II	Bursa-Bilecik	Turkey	2459	79.51	.....

TABLE 134 (Continued)

Group	Locality	Country	No.	SH	Recorder
Yezidis	Sheikhan	Iraq	24	79.63	Smeaton
Yezidis	Combined	Iraq	70	79.64	Smeaton
Yezidis	Jebel Sinjar	Iraq	46	79.66	Smeaton
Turks VI	Central Anatolia	Turkey	2424	79.83	.....
Turks VII	Northwest Anatolia	Turkey	1822	79.84	.....
Subba	Amara Liwa	Iraq	23	79.90	Smeaton
Sulubba (Nomads)	Jazira	Iraq	10	80.20	Smeaton
An Nasiriya	An Nasiriya Liwa	Iraq	26	80.26	Smeaton
Palestinians		Palestine	33	80.68	Gloor
Turkomans	Northern Iraq	Iraq	30	81.49	Smeaton
Druze	Jebel Druze	Syria	114	81.70	Shanklin and Izzeddin
Samaritans		Palestine	44	85.08	Genna
		Total...	21,145		

TABLE 135: HEAD LENGTH OF 35 GROUPS WITH 21,438 FEMALES

Group	Locality	Country	No.	GOL	Recorder
Mitwali (Shia)	Mountains	Lebanon	103	169.10	Shanklin and Izzeddin
Alouites		Syria	100	170.40	Shanklin and Izzeddin
Arabs	Mosul	Iraq	12	170.5	Kappers
Druze	Jebel Druze	Syria	114	171.0	Shanklin and Izzeddin
Yezidis	Sheikhan	Iraq	25	172.08	Smeaton
Jews II	Sandur	Iraq	23	172.17	Smeaton
Jews	Total	Iraq	46	172.44	Smeaton
Jews I	Northern Iraq	Iraq	23	172.71	Smeaton
Turks VII	Northwest Anatolia	Turkey	1822	173.2	.....
Turks IX	Eastern Anatolia	Turkey	1472	173.6	.....
Arabs	Baghdad	Iraq	47	174.00	Rassam
Assyrians	Habbaniya Camp	Iraq	126	174.54	Field
Arabs	Towns (6)	Iraq	18	174.66	Rassam
Turks IV	Aegean Area	Turkey	2490	175.0	.....
Total Turks I-X		Turkey	20263	175.1	.....
Turks II	Bursa-Bilecik	Turkey	2459	175.3	.....
Turks V	Western Anatolia (Interior)	Turkey	2273	175.3	.....
Turks VI	Central Anatolia	Turkey	2424	175.8	.....
Turks VIII	Southern Anatolia	Turkey	628	176.0	.....
Kurds	Total	Iraq	33	176.10	Smeaton
Turks I	Thrace	Turkey	2588	176.2	.....
Turks X	Northeast Anatolia	Turkey	1250	176.3	.....
Maronites		Syria	26	176.43	Huxley
Turks III	Western Anatolia	Turkey	2857	176.8	.....
Armenians	Istanbul	Turkey	25	177.0	Kappers
Palestinians		Palestine	33	177.42	Gloor
Subba	Amara Liwa	Iraq	22	177.81	Smeaton
Turkomans	Northern Iraq	Iraq	30	178.71	Smeaton
Samaritans		Palestine	44	179.64	Shanklin and Izzeddin
Yezidis	Combined	Iraq	71	180.30	Smeaton
Aqaidat Beduins	Jazira	Syria	70	180.40	Shanklin and Izzeddin
An Nasiriya	An Nasiriya Liwa	Iraq	26	181.05	Smeaton
Beduins	Jazira	Syria	14	183.00	Huxley
Shammar (Beduins)	Jazira	Iraq	118	184.20	Smeaton
Yezidis	Jebel Sinjar	Iraq	46	184.77	Smeaton
		Total...	21,438		

TABLE 136: HEAD BREADTH OF 33 GROUPS WITH 21,275 FEMALES

Group	Locality	Country	No.	GB	Recorder
Sulubba (Nomads)	Jazira	Iraq	10	136.00	Smeaton
Yezidis	Jebel Sinjar	Iraq	46	138.01	Smeaton
Aqaidat Beduins	Jazira	Syria	70	139.20	Shanklin
Beduins	Jazira	Syria	14	139.42	Huxley
Shammar Beduins	Jazira	Iraq	118	140.26	Smeaton
Turks X	Northeast Anatolia	Turkey	1250	140.8	.....
An Nasiriya	An Nasiriya Liwa	Iraq	25	140.80	Smeaton
Yezidis	Combined	Iraq	71	140.83	Smeaton
Arabs	Towns (6)	Iraq	18	141.82	Rassam
Arabs	Baghdad	Iraq	47	142.57	Rassam
Turkomans	Northern Iraq	Iraq	30	142.81	Smeaton
Jews II	Sandur	Iraq	23	143.05	Smeaton
Subba	Amara Liwa	Iraq	22	143.08	Smeaton
Turks IX	Eastern Anatolia	Turkey	1472	143.2	.....
Jews	Total	Iraq	46	143.23	Smeaton
Jews I	Northern Iraq	Iraq	23	143.44	Smeaton
Maronites		Syria	26	144.31	Huxley
Turks III	Western Anatolia	Turkey	2857	144.8	.....
Assyrians	Habbaniya Camp	Iraq	125	144.96	Field
Turks VIII	Southern Anatolia	Turkey	628	145.8	.....
Yezidis	Sheikhan	Iraq	25	145.96	Smeaton
Turks IV	Aegean Area	Turkey	2490	146.0	.....
Alouites			100	146.00	Shanklin
Kurds	Total	Iraq	33	146.08	Smeaton
Turks I	Thrace	Turkey	2588	146.3	.....
Turks V	Western Anatolia (Interior)	Turkey	2273	146.3	.....
Total Turks I-X		Turkey	20263	146.7	.....
Mitwali (Shia)	Mountains	Lebanon	103	147.80	Shanklin
Turks II	Bursa-Bilecik	Turkey	2459	148.2	.....
Arabs	Mosul	Iraq	12	150.0	Kappers
Turks VII	Northwest Anatolia	Turkey	1822	150.4	.....
Armenians	Istanbul	Turkey	25	151.0	Kappers
Turks VI	Central Anatolia	Turkey	2424	151.8	.....

Total... 21,275

TABLE 137: MINIMUM FRONTAL DIAMETER OF 28 GROUPS WITH 21,082 FEMALES

Group	Locality	Country	No.	MFD	Recorder
Sulubba (Nomads)	Jazira	Iraq	10	98.90	Smeaton
Yezidis	Jebel Sinjar	Iraq	46	101.02	Smeaton
Yezidis	Combined	Iraq	71	101.02	Smeaton
Yezidis	Sheikhan	Iraq	25	101.06	Smeaton
Turks III	Western Anatolia	Turkey	2857	101.1	.....
Shammar Beduins	Jazira	Iraq	118	101.30	Smeaton
Beduins	Jazira	Syria	14	101.34	Huxley
Maronites		Syria	26	101.74	Huxley
Jews I	Northern Iraq	Iraq	34	101.82	Smeaton
Subba	Amara Liwa	Iraq	23	101.82	Smeaton
An Nasiriya	An Nasiriya Liwa	Iraq	25	102.02	Smeaton
Alouites		Syria	100	102.20	Shanklin
Jews	Total	Iraq	46	102.58	Smeaton
Turkomans	Northern Iraq	Iraq	30	102.90	Smeaton
Turks VII	Northwest Anatolia	Turkey	1822	103.2	.....
Jews II	Sandur	Iraq	23	103.38	Smeaton
Turks VI	Central Anatolia	Turkey	2424	104.4	.....
Turks X	Northeast Anatolia	Turkey	4683	104.6	.....
Turks VIII	Southern Anatolia	Turkey	628	104.8	.....
Total Turks I-X		Turkey	20263	104.9	.....

TABLE 137 (Continued)

Group	Locality	Country	No.	MFD	Recorder
Turks IV	Aegean Area	Turkey	2490	105.1	.....
Turks V	Western Anatolia (Interior)	Turkey	2273	105.4	.....
Turks I	Thrace	Turkey	2588	106.7	.....
Turks IX	Eastern Anatolia	Turkey	1472	106.9	.....
Aqaidat Beduins	Jazira	Syria	70	107.10	Shanklin
Kurds	Total	Iraq	33	107.22	Smeaton
Turks II	Bursa-Bilecik	Turkey	2459	108.0	.....
Assyrians	Habbaniya Camp	Iraq	125	113.20	Field
			Total... 21,082		

TABLE 138: BIZYGOMATIC BREADTH OF 28 GROUPS WITH 20,961 FEMALES

Group	Locality	Country	No.	Biz. B.	Recorder
Sulubba (Nomads)	Jazira	Iraq	10	117.50	Smeaton
Beduins	Jazira	Syria	70	123.60	Shanklin
Beduins	Jazira	Syria	14	124.50	Huxley
Subba	Amara Liwa	Iraq	23	126.55	Smeaton
An Nasiriya	An Nasiriya Liwa	Iraq	26	127.60	Smeaton
Shammar Beduins	Jazira	Iraq	118	127.70	Smeaton
Turks IX	Eastern Anatolia	Turkey	1472	128.4	.....
Alouites		Syria	100	128.40	Shanklin
Turks VIII	Southern Anatolia	Turkey	628	128.5	.....
Maronites		Syria	26	128.75	Huxley
Jews II	Sandur	Iraq	23	129.15	Smeaton
Turks I	Thrace	Turkey	2588	129.7	.....
Jews	Total	Iraq	46	129.75	Smeaton
Turks II	Bursa-Bilecik	Turkey	2459	129.9	.....
Turks X	Northeast Anatolia	Turkey	1250	130.3	.....
Jews I	Northern Iraq	Iraq	23	130.35	Smeaton
Total Turks I-X		Turkey	20263	130.6	.....
Yezidis	Jebel Sinjar	Iraq	46	130.60	Smeaton
Kurds	Total	Iraq	33	130.65	Smeaton
Turkomans	Northern Iraq	Iraq	30	130.65	Smeaton
Turks IV	Aegean Area	Turkey	2490	130.8	.....
Yezidis	Combined	Iraq	71	130.80	Smeaton
Assyrians	Habbaniya Camp	Iraq	124	130.91	Field
Yezidis	Sheikhan	Iraq	25	131.20	Smeaton
Turks VII	Northwest Anatolia	Turkey	1822	131.4	.....
Turks III	Western Anatolia	Turkey	2857	131.5	.....
Turks V	Western Anatolia (Interior)	Turkey	2273	131.6	.....
Turks VI	Central Anatolia	Turkey	2424	131.9	.....
			Total... 20,961		

TABLE 139: BIGONIAL BREADTH OF 24 GROUPS WITH 20,970 FEMALES

Group	Locality	Country	No.	Big. B.	Recorder
Kurds	Total	Iraq	33	94.16	Smeaton
Subba	Amara Liwa	Iraq	22	94.42	Smeaton
Shammar Beduins	Jazira	Iraq	116	94.42	Smeaton
Aqaidat Beduins	Jazira	Syria	70	95.30	Shanklin
Yezidis	Sheikhan	Iraq	25	95.50	Smeaton
Jews I	Northern Iraq	Iraq	24	95.50	Smeaton
Yezidis	Combined	Iraq	70	95.54	Smeaton
Yezidis	Jebel Sinjar	Iraq	45	95.58	Smeaton
Turkomans	Northern Iraq	Iraq	29	95.62	Smeaton
Turks IX	Eastern Anatolia	Turkey	1472	96.0	.....

TABLE 139 (Continued)

Group	Locality	Country	No.	Big. B.	Recorder
Turks VIII	Southern Anatolia	Turkey	628	96.3	.....
An Nasiriya	An Nasiriya Liwa	Iraq	26	96.58	Smeaton
Alouites		Syria	100	97.60	Shanklin
Turks II	Bursa-Bilecik	Turkey	2459	97.7	.....
Jews II	Sandur	Iraq	23	99.14	Smeaton
Turks VI	Central Anatolia	Turkey	2424	99.7	.....
Turks IV	Aegean Area	Turkey	2490	100.2	.....
Total Turks I-X		Turkey	20263	100.4	.....
Turks III	Western Anatolia	Turkey	2857	100.4	.....
Turks VII	Northwest Anatolia	Turkey	1822	100.7	.....
Turks I	Thrace	Turkey	2588	101.0	.....
Turks X	Northeast Anatolia	Turkey	1250	102.3	.....
Turks V	Western Anatolia	Turkey	2273	106.4	.....
Assyrians	Habbaniya Camp	Iraq	125	107.52	Field

Total... 20,970

TABLE 140: UPPER FACIAL HEIGHT OF 27 GROUPS WITH 21,060 FEMALES

Group	Locality	Country	No.	UFH	Recorder
Alouites		Syria	100	62.00	Shanklin
Sulubba (Nomads)	Jazira	Iraq	10	66.00	Smeaton
Jews II	Sandur	Iraq	23	66.15	Smeaton
An Nasiriya	An Nasiriya Liwa	Iraq	26	66.60	Smeaton
Turks X	Northeast Anatolia	Turkey	1250	66.8	.....
Turks VIII	Southern Anatolia	Turkey	628	66.8	.....
Turkomans	Northern Iraq	Iraq	30	67.00	Smeaton
Jews	Total	Iraq	46	67.00	Smeaton
Turks IX	Eastern Anatolia	Turkey	1472	67.2	.....
Yezidis	Sheikhan	Iraq	25	67.20	Smeaton
Turks I	Thrace	Turkey	2588	67.4	.....
Yezidis	Combined	Iraq	71	67.55	Smeaton
Yezidis	Jebel Sinjar	Iraq	46	67.75	Smeaton
Jews I	Northern Iraq	Iraq	23	67.85	Smeaton
Kurds	Total	Iraq	33	67.90	Smeaton
Aqaidat Beduins	Jazira	Syria	70	68.00	Shanklin
Turks II	Bursa-Bilecik	Turkey	2459	68.1	.....
Turks VII	Northwest Anatolia	Turkey	1822	68.4	.....
Shammar Beduins	Jazira	Iraq	116	68.45	Smeaton
Total Turks I-X		Turkey	20263	68.7	.....
Turks V	Western Anatolia (Interior)	Turkey	2273	68.8	.....
Turks IV	Aegean Area	Turkey	2490	69.6	.....
Beduins	Jazira	Syria	14	70.20	Huxley
Turks VI	Central Anatolia	Turkey	4895	70.3	.....
Turks III	Western Anatolia	Turkey	2257	70.3	.....
Maronites		Syria	26	70.45	Huxley
Subba	Amara Liwa	Iraq	23	70.50	Smeaton
Assyrians	Habbaniya Camp	Iraq	125	73.92	Field

Total... 21,060

TABLE 141: TOTAL FACIAL HEIGHT OF 28 GROUPS WITH 20,967 FEMALES

Group	Locality	Country	No.	TFH	Recorder
An Nasiriya	An Nasiriya Liwa	Iraq	25	107.60	Smeaton
Beduins		Syria	14	109.85	Huxley
Turks V	Western Anatolia	Turkey	2273	110.2	.....
Sulubba (Nomads)	Jazira	Iraq	10	110.50	Smeaton
Turkomans	Northern Iraq	Iraq	30	110.50	Smeaton

TABLE 141 (Continued)

Group	Locality	Country	No.	TFH	Recorder
Kurds	Total	Iraq	33	110.50	Smeaton
Turks II	Bursa-Bilecik	Turkey	2459	110.6	.....
Jews II	Sandur	Iraq	23	110.70	Smeaton
Turks I	Thrace	Turkey	2588	111.2	.....
Yezidis	Sheikhan	Iraq	25	111.40	Smeaton
Maronites		Syria	26	111.40	Huxley
Jews	Total	Iraq	46	111.55	Smeaton
Subba	Amara Liwa	Iraq	23	111.55	Smeaton
Turks IX	Eastern Anatolia	Turkey	1472	111.6	.....
Turks VII	Northwestern Anatolia	Turkey	1822	111.7	.....
Turks VIII	Southern Anatolia	Turkey	628	111.7	.....
Total Turks I-X		Turkey	20263	111.8	.....
Yezidis	Combined	Iraq	71	111.85	Smeaton
Yezidis	Jebel Sinjar	Iraq	46	112.10	Smeaton
Turks IV	Aegean Area	Turkey	2490	112.3	.....
Jews I	Northern Iraq	Iraq	23	112.40	Smeaton
Turks III	Western Anatolia	Turkey	2857	112.5	.....
Turks VI	Central Anatolia	Turkey	2424	112.9	.....
Shammar Beduins	Jazira	Iraq	115	112.95	Smeaton
Turks X	Northeast Anatolia	Turkey	1250	114.0	.....
Aqaidat Beduins	Jazira	Syria	70	114.30	Shanklin
Alouites		Syria	100	115.50	Shanklin
Assyrians	Habbaniya Camp	Iraq	124	118.66	Field
		Total...	20,967		

TABLE 142: NASAL HEIGHT OF 28 GROUPS WITH 21,069 FEMALES

Group	Locality	Country	No.	NH	Recorder
Yezidis	Jebel Sinjar	Iraq	46	46.18	Smeaton
An Nasiriya	An Nasiriya Liwa	Iraq	26	46.26	Smeaton
Yezidis	Combined	Iraq	71	46.50	Smeaton
Turks I	Thrace	Turkey	2588	46.6	.....
Turkomans	Northern Iraq	Iraq	30	46.82	Smeaton
Turks VIII	Southern Anatolia	Turkey	628	47.1	.....
Yezidis	Sheikhan	Iraq	25	47.10	Smeaton
Jews II	Sandur	Iraq	23	47.22	Smeaton
Jews	Total	Iraq	47	47.38	Smeaton
Turks II	Bursa-Bilecik	Turkey	2459	47.4	.....
Jews I	Northern Iraq	Iraq	24	47.50	Smeaton
Shammar (Beduins)	Jazira	Iraq	117	47.74	Smeaton
Beduins	Jazira	Syria	14	47.76	Huxley
Turks IX	Eastern Anatolia	Turkey	5102	47.9	.....
Turks IV	Aegean Area	Turkey	2490	48.0	.....
Kurds	Total	Iraq	33	48.06	Smeaton
Total Turks I-X		Turkey	20263	48.4	.....
Turks VII	Northwest Anatolia	Turkey	1822	48.4	.....
Sulubba (Nomads)	Jazira	Iraq	10	48.70	Smeaton
Turks X	Northeast Anatolia	Turkey	1250	49.1	.....
Aqaidat Beduins	Jazira	Syria	70	49.50	Shanklin
Maronites		Syria	26	49.61	Huxley
Turks VI	Central Anatolia	Turkey	2424	49.8	.....
Turks III	Western Anatolia	Turkey	2857	50.6	.....
Subba	Amara Liwa	Iraq	23	51.06	Smeaton
Turks V	Western Anatolia (Interior)	Turkey	2273	51.4	.....
Alouites		Syria	100	52.10	Shanklin
Assyrians	Habbaniya Camp	Iraq	124	54.95	Field
		Total...	21,069		

TABLE 143: NASAL BREADTH OF 28 GROUPS WITH 21,066 FEMALES

Group	Locality	Country	No.	NB	Recorder
Turks III	Western Anatolia	Turkey	3020	30.2	.....
Turks IX	Eastern Anatolia	Turkey	1472	30.5	.....
Turks VII	Northwest Anatolia	Turkey	1822	30.6	.....
Turks V	Western Anatolia (Interior)	Turkey	2273	30.6	.....
Turks X	Northeast Anatolia	Turkey	1250	30.6	.....
Turks VIII	Southern Anatolia	Turkey	628	30.9	.....
Turks IV	Aegean area	Turkey	2490	31.0	.....
Total Turks I-X		Turkey	20263	31.0	.....
Turks VI	Central Anatolia	Turkey	2424	31.2	.....
Aqaidat Beduins	Jazira	Syria	70	31.30	Shanklin
Turks I	Thrace	Turkey	2588	31.4	.....
Sulubba (Nomads)	Jazira	Iraq	10	32.00	Smeaton
Turks II	Bursa-Bilecik	Turkey	2459	32.3	.....
Shammar Beduins	Jazira	Iraq	114	32.48	Smeaton
An Nasiriya	An Nasiriya Liwa	Iraq	25	32.72	Smeaton
Subba	Amara Liwa	Iraq	23	32.90	Smeaton
Maronites		Syria	26	32.93	Huxley
Turkomans	Northern Iraq	Iraq	28	33.29	Smeaton
Kurds	Total	Iraq	32	33.32	Smeaton
Yezidis	Jebel Sinjar	Iraq	46	33.62	Smeaton
Yezidis	Combined	Iraq	71	33.65	Smeaton
Yezidis	Sheikhan	Iraq	25	33.68	Smeaton
Assyrians	Habbaniya Camp	Iraq	125	33.76	Field
Jews II	Sandur	Iraq	23	33.83	Smeaton
Jews	Total	Iraq	47	33.86	Smeaton
Jews I	Northern Iraq	Iraq	24	33.86	Smeaton
Beduins		Syria	14	34.13	Huxley
Alouites		Syria	100	36.60	Shanklin

Total... 21,066

TABLE 144: EAR HEIGHT FOR 24 GROUPS WITH 20,878 FEMALES

Group	Locality	Country	No.	EH	Recorder
Turks V	Western Anatolia (Interior)	Turkey	2273	54.5	.....
Turks VIII	Southern Anatolia	Turkey	628	55.8	.....
Turks IX	Eastern Anatolia	Turkey	1472	55.9	.....
Turks X	Northeast Anatolia	Turkey	1250	56.1	.....
Turks VII	Northwest Anatolia	Turkey	1822	56.7	.....
Total Turks I-X		Turkey	20263	56.8	.....
Turks II	Bursa-Bilecik	Turkey	2459	56.8	.....
Alouites		Syria	100	57.00	Shanklin
Turks I	Thrace	Turkey	2588	57.4	.....
Turks VI	Central Anatolia	Turkey	2424	57.8	.....
Turks IV	Aegean area	Turkey	2490	58.1	.....
Turks III	Western Anatolia	Turkey	2857	58.6	.....
Assyrians	Habbaniya Camp	Iraq	126	59.46	Field
Yezidis	Sheikhan	Iraq	23	59.78	Smeaton
Shammar Beduins	Jazira	Iraq	115	59.82	Smeaton
An Nasiriya	An Nasiriya Liwa	Iraq	26	59.82	Smeaton
Kurds	Total	Iraq	32	59.98	Smeaton
Maronites		Syria	13	60.24	Huxley
Yezidis	Jebel Sinjar	Iraq	46	60.62	Smeaton
Turkomans	Northern Iraq	Iraq	28	60.78	Smeaton
Jews II	Sandur	Iraq	22	61.86	Smeaton
Jews	Total	Iraq	42	61.98	Smeaton
Jews I	Northern Iraq	Iraq	20	62.10	Smeaton
Subba	Amara Liwa	Iraq	22	62.22	Smeaton

Total... 20,878

TABLE 145: EAR BREADTH OF 25 GROUPS WITH 20,960 FEMALES

Group	Locality	Country	No.	EB	Recorder
Turks IX	Eastern Anatolia	Turkey	1472	30.8	.....
Alouites		Syria	100	31.00	Shanklin
Turks VI	Central Anatolia	Turkey	2424	31.6	.....
Yezidis	Jebel Sinjar	Iraq	46	31.83	Smeaton
Turks VIII	Southern Anatolia	Turkey	628	32.1	.....
Kurds	Total	Iraq	33	32.37	Smeaton
Turks II	Bursa-Bilecik	Turkey	2459	32.4	.....
Turkomans	Northern Iraq	Iraq	30	32.40	Smeaton
Yezidis	Combined	Iraq	69	32.43	Smeaton
Shammar Beduins	Jazira	Iraq	115	32.58	Smeaton
Jews II	Sandur	Iraq	23	32.61	Smeaton
Jews	Total	Iraq	47	32.67	Smeaton
Turks III	Western Anatolia	Turkey	2857	32.7	.....
Turks VII	Northwest Anatolia	Turkey	1822	32.7	.....
Turks X	Northeast Anatolia	Turkey	1250	32.7	.....
An Nasiriya	An Nasiriya Liwa	Iraq	26	32.76	Smeaton
Jews I	Northern Iraq	Iraq	24	32.76	Smeaton
Total Turks I-X		Turkey	20263	32.8	.....
Turks IV	Aegean area	Turkey	2490	33.0	.....
Subba	Amara Liwa	Iraq	23	33.39	Smeaton
Turks V	Western Anatolia (Interior)	Turkey	2273	33.5	.....
Yezidis	Sheikhan	Iraq	23	33.66	Smeaton
Assyrians	Habbaniya Camp	Iraq	126	34.98	Field
Turks I	Thrace	Turkey	2588	35.5	.....
		Total...	20,960		

TABLE 146: CEPHALIC INDEX OF 43 GROUPS WITH 21,538 FEMALES

Group	Locality	Country	No.	CI	Recorder
Sulubba (Sleyb)	Jazira	Iraq	10	74.70	Smeaton
Yezidis	Jebel Sinjar	Iraq	46	74.79	Smeaton
Beduins	Jazira	Syria	14	76.08	Huxley
Shammar Beduins	Jazira	Iraq	118	76.23	Smeaton
Kurds	Lake Goktcha	Transcaucasia	15	76.4	Chantre
Jews		Yemen	14	76.7	.....
Kurds	Lake Goktcha	Transcaucasia	60	77.0	Ivanovskii
Aqaidat Beduins	Jazira	Syria	70	77.14	Shanklin
Turkomans		Caucasus	34	77.64	Chantre
An Nasiriya	An Nasiriya Liwa	Iraq	25	77.64	Smeaton
Jews		Iraq	12	78.1	.....
Jews II	Sandur	Iraq	23	78.66	Smeaton
Turkomans	Northern Area	Iraq	30	78.89	Smeaton
Samaritans		Palestine	32	78.97	Kappers
Turks X	Northwest Anatolia	Turkey	1250	79.86	.....
Subba	Amara Liwa	Iraq	22	80.31	Smeaton
Arabs		Iraq	18	81.51	Smeaton
Turks III	Western Anatolia	Turkey	2857	81.53	.....
Maronites		Syria	26	81.81	Huxley
Arabs	Baghdad	Iraq	47	82.20	Smeaton
Turks IX	Eastern Anatolia	Turkey	1472	82.43	.....
Turks VIII	Southern Anatolia	Turkey	628	82.70	.....
Kurds	Kurdistan	Iraq	33	82.74	Smeaton
Assyrians	Habbaniya Camp	Iraq	125	82.96	Field
Total Jews		Iraq	46	83.10	Smeaton
Jews I	Northern Area	Iraq	23	83.10	Smeaton
Turks IV	Aegean Area	Turkey	2490	83.56	.....
Total Turks I-X		Turkey	20263	83.75	.....
Turks I	Thrace	Turkey	2588	83.79	.....

TABLE 146 (Continued)

Group	Locality	Country	No.	CI	Recorder
Turks II	Bursa-Bilecik	Turkey	2459	84.29	.....
North Osetes	Osetia	Caucasus	49	84.60	Field
Turks V	Western Anatolia (Interior)	Turkey	2273	84.94	.....
Kurds		Syria	11	85.2	Chantre
Yezidis	Sheikhan Area	Iraq	25	85.20	Smeaton
Armenians	Istanbul	Turkey	25	85.4	Kappers
Arabs		Lebanon	24	85.40	Kappers
Armenians		Caucasus	44	85.71	Chantre
Armenians	Beirut and Istanbul	Lebanon and Turkey	39	85.72	Kappers
Alouites		Syria	100	85.96	Shanklin
Turks VI	Central Anatolia	Turkey	2424	86.30	.....
Turks VII	Northwest Anatolia	Turkey	1822	86.92	.....
Mitwali (Shia)	Mountains	Lebanon	103	87.52	Shanklin
Arabs	Mosul	Iraq	12	88.1	Kappers
		Total...	21,538		

TABLE 147: FRONTO-PARIETAL INDEX OF 26 GROUPS WITH 21,520 FEMALES

Group	Locality	Country	No.	FPI	Recorder
Turkomans	Northern Iraq	Iraq	30	67.61	Smeaton
Turks VII	Northwest Anatolia	Turkey	1822	68.65	.....
Turks VI	Central Anatolia	Turkey	2424	68.87	.....
Yezidis	Sheikhan	Iraq	25	69.28	Smeaton
Turks III	Western Anatolia	Turkey	2857	70.22	.....
Maronites		Syria	26	70.36	Huxley
Kurds	Total	Iraq	33	70.45	Smeaton
Jews I	Northern Iraq	Iraq	24	70.87	Smeaton
Subba	Amara Liwa	Iraq	23	70.90	Smeaton
Turks V	Western Anatolia (Interior)	Turkey	2273	71.09	.....
Beduins	Jazira	Syria	14	71.29	Huxley
Total Turks I-X		Turkey	20263	71.50	.....
Jews	Total	Iraq	47	71.53	Smeaton
Turks IV	Aegean area	Turkey	2490	71.64	.....
Yezidis	Combined	Iraq	71	72.07	Smeaton
Turks VIII	Southern Anatolia	Turkey	628	72.21	.....
Shammar Beduins	Jazira	Iraq	118	72.22	Smeaton
An Nasiriya	An Nasiriya Liwa	Iraq	24	72.37	Smeaton
Turks I	Thrace	Turkey	2588	72.57	.....
Turks II	Bursa-Bilecik	Turkey	2459	73.15	.....
Sulubba (Nomads)	Jazira	Iraq	10	73.30	Smeaton
Yezidis	Jebel Sinjar	Iraq	46	73.60	Smeaton
Jews II	Sandur	Iraq	23	74.56	Smeaton
Turks X	Northeast Anatolia	Turkey	1250	74.57	.....
Turks IX	Eastern Anatolia	Turkey	1472	74.83	.....
Assyrians	Habbaniya Camp	Iraq	125	78.12	.....
		Total...	21,520		

TABLE 148: ZYGO-FRONTAL INDEX OF 26 GROUPS WITH 21,531 FEMALES

Group	Locality	Country	No.	ZFI	Recorder
Yezidis	Sheikhan	Iraq	25	76.86	Smeaton
Turks III	Western Anatolia	Turkey	2857	76.92	.....
Yezidis	Combined	Iraq	71	77.62	Smeaton
Turkomans	Northern Iraq	Iraq	30	77.90	Smeaton
Turks VII	Northwest Anatolia	Turkey	1822	77.95	.....
Jews I	Northern Iraq	Iraq	24	77.98	Smeaton
Yezidis	Jebel Sinjar	Iraq	46	78.02	Smeaton
Kurds	Total	Iraq	33	78.34	Smeaton
Jews	Total	Iraq	47	78.78	Smeaton
Maronites		Syria	26	79.18	Huxley
Turks VI	Central Anatolia	Turkey	2424	79.46	.....
Shammar Beduins	Jazira	Iraq	118	79.62	Smeaton
Turks IV	Aegean Area	Turkey	2490	80.02	.....
An Nasiriya	An Nasiriya Liwa	Iraq	25	80.06	Smeaton
Turks V	Western Anatolia	Turkey	2273	80.09	.....
Total Turks I-X		Turkey	20263	80.14	.....
Turks X	Northeast Anatolia	Turkey	1250	80.45	.....
Subba	Amara Liwa	Iraq	23	80.82	Smeaton
Beduins	Jazira	Syria	14	81.50	Huxley
Turks VIII	Southern Anatolia	Turkey	628	81.63	.....
Turks I	Thrace	Turkey	2588	82.07	.....
Turks IX	Eastern Anatolia	Turkey	1472	83.25	.....
Turks II	Bursa-Bilecik	Turkey	2459	83.52	.....
Sulubba (Nomads)	Jazira	Iraq	10	84.30	Smeaton
Assyrians	Habbaniya Camp	Iraq	125	86.80	Field

Total... 21,531

TABLE 149: UPPER FACIAL INDEX OF 26 GROUPS WITH 20,892 FEMALES

Group	Locality	Country	No.	UFI	Recorder
Turkomans	Northern Iraq	Iraq	30	50.99	Smeaton
Jews II	Sandur	Iraq	23	51.05	Smeaton
Turks X	Northeast Anatolia	Turkey	1250	51.36	.....
Yezidis	Sheikhan	Iraq	25	51.44	Smeaton
Jews	Total	Iraq	47	51.47	Smeaton
Yezidis	Combined	Iraq	71	51.53	Smeaton
Yezidis	Jebel Sinjar	Iraq	46	51.56	Smeaton
Turks II	Bursa-Bilecik	Turkey	2459	51.70	.....
Turks VII	Northwest Anatolia	Turkey	1822	51.83	.....
Jews I	Northern Iraq	Iraq	24	51.86	Smeaton
An Nasiriya	An Nasiriya Liwa	Iraq	26	51.95	Smeaton
Turks I	Thrace	Turkey	2588	52.08	.....
Kurds	Total	Iraq	33	52.10	Smeaton
Turks V	Western Anatolia (Interior)	Turkey	2273	52.22	.....
Turks IV	Aegean Area	Turkey	2490	52.32	.....
Turks IX	Eastern Anatolia	Turkey	1472	52.33	.....
Total Turks I-X		Turkey	20263	52.36	.....
Turks VIII	Southern Anatolia	Turkey	628	52.70	.....
Turks III	Western Anatolia	Turkey	2857	52.97	.....
Shammar Beduins	Jazira	Iraq	116	53.36	Smeaton
Turks VI	Central Anatolia	Turkey	2424	53.49	.....
Maronites		Syria	26	55.07	Huxley
Sulubba (Nomads)	Jazira	Iraq	10	55.70	Smeaton
Beduins	Jazira	Syria	14	55.79	Huxley
Subba	Amara Liwa	Iraq	23	56.27	Smeaton
Assyrians	Habbaniya Camp	Iraq	125	56.28	Field

Total... 20,892

TABLE 150: TOTAL FACIAL INDEX OF 28 GROUPS WITH 21,070 FEMALES

Group	Locality	Country	No.	TFI	Recorder
Turks V	Western Anatolia (Interior)	Turkey	2273	83.65	.....
Turks II	Bursa-Bilecik	Turkey	2459	83.81	.....
An Nasiriya	An Nasiriya Liwa	Iraq	25	84.20	Smeaton
Turks VII	Northwest Anatolia	Turkey	1822	84.24	.....
Turkomans	Northern Iraq	Iraq	30	84.35	Smeaton
Yezidis	Sheikhan	Iraq	25	84.80	Smeaton
Kurds	Total	Iraq	33	84.90	Smeaton
Turks I	Thrace	Turkey	2588	85.16	.....
Total Turks I-X		Turkey	20263	85.18	.....
Turks IV	Aegean Area	Turkey	2490	85.23	.....
Yezidis	Combined	Iraq	71	85.25	Smeaton
Yezidis	Jebel Sinjar	Iraq	46	85.50	Smeaton
Turks VI	Central Anatolia	Turkey	2424	85.61	.....
Turks III	Western Anatolia	Turkey	2857	85.99	.....
Maronites		Syria	26	86.40	Huxley
Jews I	Northern Iraq	Iraq	24	86.40	Smeaton
Jews	Total	Iraq	47	86.45	Smeaton
Turks IX	Eastern Anatolia	Turkey	1472	86.54	.....
Jews II	Sandur	Iraq	23	86.55	Smeaton
Beduins	Jazira	Syria	14	87.00	Huxley
Turks X	Northeast Anatolia	Turkey	4683	87.46	.....
Turks VIII	Southern Anatolia	Turkey	628	87.52	.....
Subba	Amara Liwa	Iraq	23	88.50	Smeaton
Shammar Beduins	Jazira	Iraq	116	88.60	Smeaton
Alouites		Syria	100	90.04	Shanklin
Assyrians	Habbaniya Camp	Iraq	124	90.99	Field
Aqaidat Beduins	Jazira	Syria	70	92.46	Shanklin
Sulubba (Nomads)	Jazira	Iraq	10	94.50	Smeaton

Total... 21,070

TABLE 151: NASAL INDEX OF 28 GROUPS WITH 21,065 FEMALES

Group	Locality	Country	No.	NI	Recorder
Alouites		Syria	100	58.28	Shanklin
Turks III	Western Anatolia	Turkey	2857	60.38	.....
Assyrians	Habbaniya Camp	Iraq	124	61.84	Field
Turks X	Northeast Anatolia	Turkey	1250	62.79	.....
Aqaidat Beduins	Jazira	Syria	70	63.36	Shanklin
Turks IX	Eastern Anatolia	Turkey	1472	63.67	.....
Total Turks I-X		Turkey	20263	63.91	.....
Turks VII	Northwest Anatolia	Turkey	1822	64.30	.....
Turks V	Western Anatolia (Interior)	Turkey	2273	64.35	.....
Turks VI	Central Anatolia	Turkey	2424	64.92	.....
Turks IV	Aegean Area	Turkey	2490	65.00	.....
Subba	Amara Liwa	Iraq	23	65.66	Smeaton
Turks VIII	Southern Anatolia	Turkey	628	65.98	.....
Turks II	Bursa-Bilecik	Turkey	2459	66.03	.....
Maronites		Syria	26	66.26	Huxley
Sulubba (Nomads)	Jazira	Iraq	10	66.70	Smeaton
Turks I	Thrace	Turkey	2588	67.00	.....
Shammar Beduins	Jazira	Iraq	144	68.66	Smeaton
Kurds	Total	Iraq	32	68.86	Smeaton
Beduins	Jazira	Syria	14	70.34	Huxley
Yezidis	Sheikhan	Iraq	25	71.26	Smeaton
An Nasiriya	An Nasiriya Liwa	Iraq	25	71.26	Smeaton
Turkomans	Northern Iraq	Iraq	28	71.50	Smeaton
Jews II	Sandur	Iraq	23	71.58	Smeaton

TABLE 151 (Continued)

Group	Location	Country	No.	NI	Recorder
Jews	Total	Iraq	47	71.78	Smeaton
Jews I	Northern Iraq	Iraq	24	71.82	Smeaton
Yezidis	Combined	Iraq	71	72.30	Smeaton
Yezidis	Jebel Sinjar	Iraq	46	72.90	Smeaton
		Total...	21,065		

TABLE 152: EAR INDEX OF 23 GROUPS WITH 20,833 FEMALES

Group	Locality	Country	No.	EI	Recorder
Jews I	Northern Iraq	Iraq	20	52.30	Smeaton
Yezidis	Jebel Sinjar	Iraq	46	52.42	Smeaton
Jews	Total	Iraq	42	52.58	Smeaton
Jews II	Sandur	Iraq	22	52.86	Smeaton
Turkomans	Northern Iraq	Iraq	29	53.82	Smeaton
Yezidis	Combined	Iraq	69	53.86	Smeaton
Subba	Amara Liwa	Iraq	22	53.94	Smeaton
Kurds	Total	Iraq	32	54.02	Smeaton
Shammar Beduins	Jazira	Iraq	114	54.62	Smeaton
Turks VI	Central Anatolia	Turkey	2424	54.80	.....
Turks IX	Eastern Anatolia	Turkey	1472	55.09	.....
An Nasiriya	An Nasiriya Liwa	Iraq	26	55.10	Smeaton
Turks III	Western Anatolia	Turkey	2857	56.04	.....
Yezidis	Sheikhan	Iraq	23	56.42	Smeaton
Turks II	Bursa-Bilecik	Turkey	2459	57.31	.....
Turks VIII	Southern Anatolia	Turkey	628	57.68	.....
Total Turks I-X		Turkey	20263	58.18	.....
Turks IV	Aegean Area	Turkey	2490	58.19	.....
Turks X	Northeast Anatolia	Turkey	1250	58.64	.....
Turks VII	Northwest Anatolia	Turkey	1822	58.64	.....
Assyrians	Habbaniya Camp	Iraq	125	59.12	Field
Turks V	Western Anatolia (Interior)	Turkey	2273	61.31	.....
Turks I	Thrace	Turkey	2588	63.05	.....
		Total...	20,833		

ANTHROPOMETRIC DATA

TABLE 153: CEPHALIC INDICES OF LIVING PEOPLES

No.	Place	Group	Sex	No.	CI	Type	Observer	Source
1	Mountains north of Tripoli	Alouites	M	136	85.66	B	Kappers	KAWA, Vol. 33, no. 8, p. 804
2	Mountains north of Tripoli	Ansaries	M and F	48	84.43M; 85.79F	B	Chantre	KAWA, Vol. 33, no. 8, p. 804
3	Jebel Druze	Druze	M	80	87.26	B	Kappers	KAWA, Vol. 33, no. 8, p. 804
4	Lebanon	Lebanese	M	182	84.88	B	Kappers	KAWA, Vol. 33, no. 8, p. 802
			F	24	85.40			
	Syria	Kurds	M	35	85.2	B	Chantre	Biometrika, Vol. 4, p. 165
			F	11	85.2			
5	Beirut and Constantinople	Armenians (mostly students)	M	97	85.38	B	Kappers	KAWA, Vol. 33, no. 8, pp. 794, 802
			F	39	85.72			
6	Aleppo, Hama, Homs, Maalullah, Damascus	Desert border population	M	135	81.7	B	Kappers	KAWA, Vol. 34, no. 1, p. 122
7	District of Palmyra, Aleppo, Selemiye, Deir ez-Zor and Beni Darra	Syrian Beduins	M	107	77.2	M	Kappers	KAWA, Vol. 34, no. 1, pp. 113, 115
8	Near Nablus	Samaritans	M	35	78.1	M	Huxley	KAWA, Vol. 34, no. 1, p. 118
		Samaritans	M	20	76.2	M	Weissenberg	KAWA, Vol. 34, no. 1, p. 118
		Samaritans	M and F	94	77.64M	M	Szpidbaum	KAWA, Vol. 34, no. 1, p. 118
		Samaritans			80.84F	M	Szpidbaum	KAWA, Vol. 34, no. 1, p. 118
		Samaritans	M	27	77.23	M	Kappers	KAWA, Vol. 34, no. 1, p. 118
		Samaritans	F	32	78.97	M	Kappers	KAWA, Vol. 34, no. 1, p. 118
		Children	M and F	25	78.27	M	Kappers	KAWA, Vol. 34, no. 1, p. 118
9	North of Jaffa-Jericho line	Palestinian Arabs	M	139	81.6	B	Kappers	KAWA, Vol. 34, no. 1, p. 121
10	Safed	Palestinian Fellahin	M	30	75.7	M	Weissenberg	KAWA, Vol. 34, no. 1, p. 121
11	Near Jaffa	Palestinian Fellahin	M	32	76.9	M	Weissenberg	KAWA, Vol. 34, no. 1, p. 121
	Amsterdam, Palestine and Syria	Ashkenazim	M	100	81.2	B	Kappers	KAWA, Vol. 34, no. 1, p. 122

ANTHROPOMETRIC DATA

TABLE 153 (Continued)

No.	Place	Group	Sex	No.	CI	Type	Observer	Source
	Amsterdam, Palestine and Syria	Sephardim	M	101	78.6	M	Kappers	KAWA, Vol. 34, no. 1, p. 126
12	Damascus	Jews	M	?	80.9	B	Weissenberg	KAWA, Vol. 34, no. 1, p. 123
13	Near Tor, Sinai	Tuarah (Towara)	M	18	73.3	D	Chantre	JRAI, Vol. 47, p. 215
14	Between Suez and Keneh	Maaza	M	?	75.0	D	Chantre	JRAI, Vol. 47, p. 220
15	Faiyum and Tripolitan Desert	Harabi	M	29	72.82	D	Chantre	JRAI, Vol. 47, p. 226
16	Matarieh	Howeitat	M	8	74.21	D	Chantre	JRAI, Vol. 47, p. 226
17	Menzaleh	Fishermen	M	25	74.48	D	Chantre	JRAI, Vol. 47, p. 226
	Behera in Delta	Aulad Ali	M	20	75.39	D	Chantre	JRAI, Vol. 47, p. 226
	Matarieh, Keneh, Beni Suef, etc.	Arab Beduins	M and F	188	73.96	D	Chantre	1885-1887, p. 307
18	Karakosh (Qaraqosh)	Chaldeans	M and F	19	86.01M 86.17F	B	Kappers	KAWA, Vol. 33, no. 8, p. 806
19	Mosul, Baghdad and Basra	Adnan Arabs	M	38		M	Kappers	KAWA, Vol. 33, no. 8, p. 807
20a	Mosul, Baghdad and Basra	Kohtan Arabs	M and F	64	84.50M 85.14F	B	Kappers	KAWA, Vol. 33, no. 8, p. 807
20b	Tell Kaif and Mosul	Chaldeans	M	178	Peaks 78, 82-3, and 86-7	B	Krischner	KAWA, Vol. 35, no. 2, p. 213
20c	Mosul	Chaldeans	F	19	No curve	B	Krischner	KAWA, Vol. 35, no. 2, p. 213
20d	Chiefly Mosul	Suriani (Assyrians)	M	39	Peak 87	B	Krischner	KAWA, Vol. 35, no. 2, p. 215
20e	Mosul	Suriani (Assyrians)	F	44	Peak 84	B	Krischner	KAWA, Vol. 35, no. 2, p. 215
20f	Mosul	Christian "Arabs"	M	58	Peaks scattered, highest at 83	B	Krischner	KAWA, Vol. 35, no. 2, p. 216
20g	Mosul	Christian "Arabs"	F	124	Peaks 84, 87	B	Krischner	KAWA, Vol. 35, no. 2, p. 216
20h	Mosul	Muslim Arabs	M	225	Peaks 76, 78, 80, 83	B?	Krischner	KAWA, Vol. 35, no. 2, p. 220

TABLE 153 (Continued)

ANTHROPOMETRIC DATA

No.	Place	Group	Sex	No.	CI	Type	Observer	Source
20i	Mosul	Muslim Arabs	F	282	Peaks 80, 82-3	B	Krischner	KAWA, Vol. 35, no. 2, p. 221
20j	Mosul	Kurds	M and F	48	Peaks 84-85.9	B	Krischner	KAWA, Vol. 35, no. 2, p. 223
20k	Mosul and North Persia	Jews	M and F	52	Peaks 83, 88	B	Krischner	KAWA, Vol. 35, no. 2, p. 225
	Bahsany and Bashiqa	Yezidis and Christians	M	69				
	Northern Mesopotamia	Kyzylbash Turks	M	?	Prevailing index 86-87	B	Chantre	KAWA, Vol. 34, no. 8, p. 1087
21	Between Tigris and Euphrates rivers	Baij Arabs	M	38	73.29	D	Field	Thomas, "Arabia Felix," p. 329
22	Kish area	Kish Arabs	M	164	76.61	M	Buxton and Field	JRAI, Vol. 61, p. 111
23	Kish area	Kish Arabs	M	400	75.37	D	Field	Unpublished in 1932
24	Hilla Army Camp	Iraq Army	M	233	76.68	M	Field	Unpublished in 1932
25a	Anatolia	Osmanli Turks	M	131	84.40	B	Elisieff (Chantre)	KAWA, Vol. 34, no. 8, p. 1085
25b	Anatolia	Osmanli Turks	M	120	84.33	B	Chantre	KAWA, Vol. 34, no. 8, p. 1085
	Anatolia	Mongol Turks with epicanthic fold	M	10	85.53	B	Kappers	KAWA, Vol. 34, no. 8, p. 1085
26a	Lycia	Bektashi Turks	M	?	86.5	B	Von Luschan	KAWA, Vol. 34, no. 8, p. 1087
26b	Lycian Anatolia	Tachtadschy Turks	M	?	85.95	B	Von Luschan	KAWA, Vol. 34, no. 8, p. 1087
		Hyperbrachycephalic Turks	M	?	86.35	B	Kappers	KAWA, Vol. 34, no. 8, p. 1087
	Different regions	Armenians	M	297	85.71	B	Chantre	KAWA, Vol. 33, no. 8, p. 792
			F	44	85.71			
27a	Caucasus	Armenians	M	318	86.7	B	Dzhawachischwili	KAWA, Vol. 33, no. 8, p. 794
27b	Caucasus	Abazek	M	11	81.6	B	Von Erckert	Biometrika, Vol. 4, p. 293
27c	Caucasus	Abazin (Abazes)	M	23	82.5	B	Sommier	Biometrika, Vol. 4, p. 293
	Turkey and Persia	Chaldeans	M and F	27	89.5M 88.69F	B	Chantre	KAWA, Vol. 33, no. 8, p. 806

TABLE 153 (Continued)

ANTHROPOMETRIC DATA

No.	Place	Group	Sex	No.	CI	Type	Observer	Source
	Turkey and Persia	Kurds	M	5	86.2	B	Duhousset	KAWA, Vol. 34, no. 4, p. 531
28	Kurdistan and Caucasia	Kurds	M	272	78.53	M	Chantre	KAWA, Vol. 34, no. 4, p. 532
			F	60	?			
29	Karakush, Asia Minor	Kurds	M	115	71.3-78.5	M	Von Luschan	KAWA, Vol. 34, no. 4, p. 532
	Trans-Caucasia, Airiga	Kurds	M	25	78.48	M	Nasonov	KAWA, Vol. 34, no. 4, p. 532
30	Nimrud Dagh	Kurds	M	28	72.3-78.3	M	Von Luschan	KAWA, Vol. 34, no. 4, p. 532
	Sendschirli	Kurds	M	?	74.4-80.9	M	Von Luschan	KAWA, Vol. 34, no. 4, p. 532
31	Batumi	Kurds	M	5	88.1	B	Chantre	KAWA, Vol. 34, no. 4, p. 532
	?	Kurds	M	?	86.49	B	Pittard	KAWA, Vol. 34, no. 4, p. 532
32	Lake Urmia, Iran	Kurds	M	5	86.68	B	Chantre	KAWA, Vol. 34, no. 4, p. 532
33	Diarbekr and Mardin (measured in Damascus)	Kurds	M	106	Peaks 78, 81-82.9	B	Kappers	KAWA, Vol. 34, no. 4, p. 533
34a	Georgia	Osetes	M	17	83.1	B	Chantre	KAWA, Vol. 34, no. 4, p. 534
34b	Georgia	Mingrelians	M	12	83.2	B	Chantre	KAWA, Vol. 34, no. 4, p. 534
34c	Georgia	Georgians	M	?	83.7	B	De Khanikoff	KAWA, Vol. 34, no. 4, p. 534
34d	Georgia	Circassians	M	54	83.42	B	Kappers	KAWA, Vol. 34, no. 4, p. 534
34e	Georgia	Osetes	M	300	81.5	B	Riskine	Biometrika, Vol. 4, p. 295
35a	Transcaucasia	Kurds	M	300	77.6	M	Ivanowskii	Biometrika, Vol. 4, pp. 165, 294
			F	60	77.0			
35b	Transcaucasia	Kurds	M	67	76.2	M	Chantre	Biometrika, Vol. 4, p. 165
			F	15	76.4			
36	Transcaucasia	Jews	M	43	87.5	B	Pantiukhov	Biometrika, Vol. 4, p. 293
37a	All Persia ?	Persians	M	123	78.7	M	Various	Biometrika, Vol. 4, p. 295

TABLE 153 (Continued)

ANTHROPOMETRIC DATA

No.	Place	Group	Sex	No.	CI	Type	Observer	Source
37b	All Persia ?	Persians	M	46	78.4	M	Danilov	Biometrika, Vol. 4, p. 295
38	Azerbaidzhan	Tatars	M	207	77.6	M	Various	Biometrika, Vol. 4, p. 295
	?	Turks	M	40	84.7	B	Pantiukhov	Biometrika, Vol. 4, p. 295
	?	Kurds and Turkomans	M	140	78.5	M	Chantre	Biometrika, Vol. 4, p. 165
			F	34	77.6			
	?	Turkomans	M	6	74.45	D	Kappers	KAWA, Vol. 34, no. 4, p. 537
	Between Caspian and Aral Seas on Persian border	Turkomans	M	59	75.6	M	IAvorskii	KAWA, Vol. 34, no. 4, p. 538
	Between Caspian and Aral Seas on Persian border	Turkomans	M	23	77.9	M	Deniker	KAWA, Vol. 34, no. 4, p. 538
	All Soviet Turkestan ?	Turkomans ?	M	?	85,89	B	Ujfalvy (Ripley)	KAWA, Vol. 34, no. 4, p. 538
39	Persia	Turkomans	M	?	82.0	B	De Khanikoff	KAWA, Vol. 34, no. 4, p. 538
40a	Tabriz	Armenians	M	34	Peaks 83-4 and 86	B	Krischner	KAWA, Vol. 35, no. 2, p. 207
40b	Tabriz	Armenians	F	23	Prevailingly hyper-brachycephalic	B	Krischner	KAWA, Vol. 35, no. 2, p. 207
	Tabriz and other places	Armenians	F	43	Peaks 82-84	B	Krischner	KAWA, Vol. 35, no. 2, p. 207
	New Julfa and Isfahan	Armenians	M	180	Peaks 78, 83-4, 87	B	Krischner	KAWA, Vol. 35, no. 2, p. 210
	New Julfa and Isfahan	Armenians	F	64	Peaks 80, 83, 87-9	B	Krischner	KAWA, Vol. 35, no. 2, p. 210
41	Hamadan	Kurds	M	12	79.5	M	Krischner	KAWA, Vol. 35, no. 2, p. 224
	South Persia	Jews	M	14	76.6	M	Krischner	KAWA, Vol. 35, no. 2, p. 225
	Kermanshah, Kum and Kashan	North Persians	M	318	Peaks 74, 79, 83	?	Krischner	KAWA, Vol. 35, no. 3, p. 399
	Kermanshah, Kum and Kashan	North Persians	F	168	Peaks 74, 79, 83	?	Krischner	KAWA, Vol. 35, no. 3, p. 399

TABLE 153 (Continued)

ANTHROPOMETRIC DATA

No.	Place	Group	Sex	No.	CI	Type	Observer/Kappers	Source
	Two-thirds North Persia, one-third South Persia	Persians	M and F	165	Peaks 74, 78, 83	?		KAWA, Vol. 34, no. 4, pp. 535-7
42	North Persia	Azerbaijan	M	130	Peaks 77-78.9, 81	M	Chantre	KAWA, Vol. 35, no. 3, p. 402
	South of Tehran	Hajemis (Ajemis)	M	?	77.74	M	Chantre	KAWA, Vol. 34, no. 4, p. 539 / KAWA, Vol. 35, no. 3, p. 403
	?	Tajiks	M	41	Peaks 78-79	M	Chantre	KAWA, Vol. 35, no. 3, p. 403
	Isfahan	Persians	M	209	Peaks 75, 78	M	Krischner	KAWA, Vol. 35, no. 3, pp. 405-6
	Isfahan	Persians	F	82	Peak 78	M	Krischner	KAWA, Vol. 35, no. 3, pp. 405-6
	Yezd	Zoroastrians	M and F	119	Peaks 73-	D	Krischner	KAWA, Vol. 35, no. 3, pp. 404-7
	Abadeh	Persians	M and F	63	Peaks 71, 73	D	Krischner	KAWA, Vol. 35, no. 3, p. 408
43	Shiraz, etc.	Southwestern Persians	M	176	Peaks 77, 83	M	Krischner	KAWA, Vol. 35, no. 3, p. 409
44	Luristan	Lurs	M	?	73.57	D	Houssay	KAWA, Vol. 34, no. 4, p. 538
45a	Kermanshah	Bakhtiari	M	4	89.0	B	Duhousset	KAWA, Vol. 34, no. 4, p. 540
45b	Kermanshah	Bakhtiari	M	9	89.32	B	Gauthier (Chantre)	KAWA, Vol. 34, no. 4, p. 540
	Luristan	Bakhtiari and Lurs	M	?	84.5	B	Deniker	KAWA, Vol. 34, no. 4, p. 540
	Luristan	Bakhtiari	M	3	78.4	M	Krischner	KAWA, Vol. 35, no. 3, pp. 408-9
	Luristan				91.0	B		
					93.4	B		
46	Cyprus	Cypriots	M	586	82.54	B	Buxton	JRAI, Vol. 50, p. 205
47	Jidda	Hejazi	M	12	79.37	M	Mochi	JRAI, Vol. 47, p. 220
48a	Yemen	Yemenis	M	16	83.18	B	Livi	JRAI, Vol. 47, p. 217
48b	Yemen	Yemenis	M	20	81.07	B	Leys and Joyce	JRAI, Vol. 47, p. 217

ANTHROPOMETRIC DATA

TABLE 153 (Continued)

No. / 48c	Place / Yemen	Group / Yemenis	Sex / M	No. / 20	CI / 82.56	Type / B	Observer / Bertholon and Chantre	Source / JRAI, Vol. 47, p. 217
48d	Yemen	Yemenis	M	25	82.56	B	Mugnier	Archivio, Vol. 47, p. 203
49	Sana'a, Yemen	Yemenis	M	30	77.47	M	Atkey	JRAI, Vol. 47, p. 217
50	Kordofan	Kababish	M	24	74.29	D	Atkey and Seligman	JRAI, Vol. 43, p. 701
51a	Somaliland	Somali	M	27	74.49	D	Leys and Joyce	JRAI, Vol. 47, p. 217
51b	Somaliland	Somali	M	55	71.4	D	Various	Archivio, Vol. 41, p. 311
51c	Somaliland	Somali	M	25	75.5	D	Puccioni	Archivio, Vol. 41, p. 311
52	Abyssinia (Ethiopia)	Tigre	M	?	74.00	D	Sergi	Thomas, "Arabia Felix," p. 329
53	Eritrea	Beni Amer	M	51	74.70	D	Seligman	JRAI, Vol. 43, p. 601
54	Nubia	Hadendoa	M	54	76.39	M	Seligman	JRAI, Vol. 43, p. 601
55	Nubia	Bisharin	M and F	78	79.00	M	Chantre	JRAI, Vol. 43, p. 601
56	Behind Aden	Sheher	M	82	80.92	B	Leys and Joyce	JRAI, Vol. 47, p. 218
57	South Arabia	Somali	M	6	79.91	B	Thomas	"Arabia Felix," p. 326
	South Arabia	Yafi	M	5	81.68	B	Thomas	"Arabia Felix," p. 326
	South Arabia	Mashai	M	1	86.20	B	Thomas	"Arabia Felix," p. 326
58	South Arabia	Mahra	M	5	86.67	B	Thomas	"Arabia Felix," p. 326
59	South Arabia	Qara	M	7	89.12	B	Thomas	"Arabia Felix," p. 326
60	South Arabia	Shahari	M	9	88.12	B	Thomas	"Arabia Felix," p. 326
61	South Arabia	Al Kathiri	M	4	90.32	B	Thomas	"Arabia Felix," p. 326
	South Arabia	Bautahari	M	1	79.12	M	Thomas	"Arabia Felix," p. 326
	South Arabia	Harasi	M	1	83.33	B	Thomas	"Arabia Felix," p. 326
62	Oman	Omani	M	3	85.18	B	Thomas	"Arabia Felix," p. 326
63	Muscat	Muscati	M	31	78.28	M	Leys and Joyce	JRAI, Vol. 47, p. 218

ANTHROPOMETRIC DATA

TABLE 154: CEPHALIC INDICES OF 51 SERIES OF CRANIA

No.	Place	Group	Sex	No.	CI	Type	Observer	Source
Ia	Sidon	Phoenician, King Tabnith	M	1	77.12	M	Chantre	KAWA, Vol. 34, no. 1, p. 107
1b	Sidon	Phoenician	M	3	76.99	M	Chantre	KAWA, Vol. 34, no. 1, p. 108
1c	Sidon	Phoenician 5th-4th centuries B.C.	M	7	76.07	M	Kappers	KAWA, Vol. 34, no. 1, p. 109
1d	Sidon	Phoenician 5th-4th centuries B.C.	M	8	78.29	M	Kappers	KAWA, Vol. 34, no. 1, p. 109
2a	Sidon	Phoenician ?	F	1	84.23	B	Chantre	KAWA, Vol. 34, no. 1, p. 107
2b	Sidon	Non-Phoenician	M	1	86.11	B	Chantre	KAWA, Vol. 34, no. 1, p. 108
3	Byblos	Phoenician 13th century B.C.	M	1	76.04	M	Kappers	KAWA, Vol. 34, no. 1, p. 108
4a	Palmyra	Palmyrene (Nos. 1-3, II and III) Early centuries A.D.	M	5	73.96	D	.....	KAWA, Vol. 34, no. 1, p. 110
					70.2	D	Blake	JRAI, Vol. 1, pp. 312-20
					76.61	D	Blake	JRAI, Vol. 1, pp. 312-20
					78.26	M	Busk	JRAI, Vol. 4, pp. 360-67
					73.68	D	Busk	JRAI, Vol. 4, pp. 360-67
					71.05	D	Busk	JRAI, Vol. 4, pp. 360-67
4b	Palmyra	Palmyrene Age uncertain	F	1	74.1	D	Seligman	JRAI, Vol. 47, p. 216
4c	Palmyra	Palmyrene	M	6	73.6	D	Seligman	JRAI, Vol. 47, p. 235
5	Palmyra	Palmyrene 2nd-3rd centuries A.D.	M	1	76.40	M	Kappers	KAWA, Vol. 34, no. 1, p. 111
6	Riverbed of Bekaa	Palmyrene type (old) (badly damaged)	M	1	70.0	D	Bergy (Kappers)	KAWA, Vol. 34, no. 1, p. 112
7	Beirut	Recent Semite (not Lebanese)	M	1	73.4	D	Kappers	KAWA, Vol. 34, no. 1, p. 112
	Yabrud	Palestinian	M	6	74.8	D	Seligman	JRAI, Vol. 47, p. 236
8	Megiddo	Jewish 10th century B.C.	M	2	80.45	B	Kappers	KAWA, Vol. 34, no. 1, p. 121
					79.57			
					81.38			

ANTHROPOMETRIC DATA

TABLE 154 (Continued)

No.	Place	Group	Sex	No.	CI	Type	Observer	Source
9	Midian	North Arab 2nd century A.D.	M	1	71.1	D	Seligman	JRAI, Vol. 47, p. 215
10	South of Beersheba	Of considerable age a. Wadi Asluj b. Rekhameh	M F	2	72.65 72.6 72.7	D	Virchow	JRAI, Vol. 47, p. 216
11	Midian and Sinai	North Arab	M	5	69.8	D	Seligman	JRAI, Vol. 47, p. 234
12a	Southern Sinai	Nabataean	M	1	72.0	D	Busk	KAWA, Vol. 34, no. 1, p. 112
12b	Sinai	Arab	M	1	73.6	D	Seligman	KAWA, Vol. 34, no. 1, p. 112
12c	Sinai	Arabs (adult)	M and F	3	69 68 73	D	Giovannozzi	Archivio, Vol. 34, p. 348
13	Sinai	Arabs (adult)	M	2	83 83	B	Giovannozzi	Archivio, Vol. 34, p. 348
14a	Cyprus	Bronze Age crania	M	14	78.61	M	Buxton	JRAI, Vol. 50, p. 205
14b	Cyprus	Total crania	M	24	78.93	M	Buxton	JRAI, Vol. 50, p. 205
15a	Lower Egypt	Ancient Egyptians	M	?	73.0	D	Elliot Smith	KAWA, Vol. 34, no. 8, p. 1092
15b	Lower Egypt	Ancient Egyptians	M	?	75.4	D	Elliot Smith	KAWA, Vol. 34, no. 8, p. 1092
15c	Upper Egypt	Ancient Egyptians	M	?	73.0	D	Elliot Smith	KAWA, Vol. 34, no. 8, p. 1092
	Shellal	New Empire Egyptians	M F	110 113	73.38 73.73	D	Elliot Smith and Wood Jones	Nubian Report, pp. 89-90
	Naqada	Ancient Empire Egyptians	M F	130 169	72.99 74.19	D	Fawcett	Nubian Report, pp. 89-90
	Abusir el-Meleq	Egyptians	M and F	29	68.69-79.77	?	Müller	ADOG, Vol. 2, pp. 310-11
16	Abassieh	Ancient Arab Cemetery	M and F	13	85.3	B	Panceri	JRAI, Vol. 47, p. 230
17	Cairo	?	M	4	76.77 80.1 79.4 70.8	M B M D	Mochi	Archivio, Vol. 37, p. 413

ANTHROPOMETRIC DATA

TABLE 154 (Continued)

No.	Place	Group	Sex	No.	CI	Type	Observer	Source
	Cairo and Tripoli	North African	M	6	73.5	D	Mochi	Archivio, Vol. 37, p. 413
	Menseia, Tripoli	North African	M and F	12	75.3	D		JRAI, Vol. 47, p. 229
	Menseia, Tripoli	?	M	4	85.5	B	Mochi	JRAI, Vol. 47, p. 229
					85.2	B		
					85.3	B		
					86.0	B		
18	Somaliland	Somali	M	10	72.2	D	Puccioni	Archivio, Vol. 41, p. 321
19	Abyssinia	Uallega and Qoram	M	7	73.86	D	De Castro	Archivio, Vol. 41, p. 339
20	Kheybar, Hejaz	Arab	F	1	72.8	D	Huber ?	JRAI, Vol. 47, p. 220
21	Hasik, South Arabia	South Arab	M	1	80.12	B	Thomas	"Arabia Felix," p. 316
22	Oman	Omani	M	1	86.9	B	Keith and Krogman	"Arabia Felix," p. 316
23a	Kish	Cemetery "A," No. 6	M	1	82.08	B	Buxton	"Excavations at Kish," Vol. 1, Appendix, p. 11
23b	Kish	Neo-Babylonian	M	1	81.11	B	Buxton and Rice	JRAI, Vol. 51, p. 109
24a	Kish	Cemetery "A," Nos. 3-5, 7; 3000-2800 B.C.	M	4	68.27	D	Buxton	"Excavations at Kish," Vol. 1, Appendix, p. 11
					66.84	D		
					69.11	D		
					69.43	D		
					67.70	D		
24b	Kish	Cemetery "A"	M	25	71.54	D	Buxton and Rice	JRAI, Vol. 51, p. 110
24c	Jemdet Nasr	4000 B.C.	F	1	60-65	D	Field	JRAS, 1932
24d	Kish	Neo-Babylonian	M	3	69.89	D	Buxton and Rice	JRAI, Vol. 51, p. 109
					70.1	D		
					69.27	D		
					70.41	D		
25	Western Kish	Recent Arab (middle-aged)	F	1	75.8	M	Field	Unpublished
26a	Tell el-Ubaid	Sumerian (early 4th millennium)	M	6	72.6	D	Keith	Hall and Woolley, "Ur Excavations," Vol. 1, p. 220

ANTHROPOMETRIC DATA

TABLE 154 (Continued)

No.	Place	Group	Sex	No.	CI	Type	Observer	Source
26b	Ur	1900-1700 B.C.	M	3	69.8	D	Keith	"Ur Excavations," Vol. I, p. 220
26c	Ur	1900-1700 B.C.	F	3	72.2	D	Keith	"Ur Excavations," Vol. I, p. 220
27	Tell el Ubaid	Sumerian	F	3	77.6	M	Keith	"Ur Excavations," Vol. I, p. 220
28	Yezd and Kerman	Zoroastrian	M	5	70.0	D	De Khanikoff	KAWA, Vol. 35, no. 3, p. 404
29	Asia Minor	Greek Cemetery (3rd century A.D.)	M	15	76.56	M	Zaborowsky	KAWA, Vol. 34, no. 8, p. 1091
30a	Troy	Level III (Pelasgian ?)	M	3	71.1 (mean)	D	Virchow	KAWA, Vol. 34, no. 8, p. 1094
					67.7	D		
					74.3	D		
					71.3	D		
30b	Khanai-Tepe, near Troy	Less ancient than Troy III	M	1	71.5	D	Virchow	KAWA, Vol. 34, no. 8, p. 1094
30c	Ophrynion	500 B.C. ?	M	?	74.5	D	Virchow	KAWA, Vol. 34, no. 8, p. 1094
31	Troy	Level II	F	1	82.5	B	Virchow	KAWA, Vol. 34, no. 8, p. 1094

TABLE 155: GROUPS MEASURED BY KAPPERS

No.	Group	Locality	Country	Sex
1	Arabs		Palestine	M
2	Arabs (Mixed)		Palestine	M
3	Arabs		Palestine	F
4	Arabs	Damascus	Syria	M
5	Arabs	Damascus	Syria	F
6	Arabs	Aleppo	Syria	M
7	Beduins and Arabs	Jazira	Syria	M
8	Arabs	Bahrain Island	Persian Gulf	M
9	Arabs	City-dwellers	Lebanon and Syria	M
10	Arabs		Lebanon	F
11	Arabs (Mixed)		Syria	M
12	Arabs	Tripoli	Lebanon	M
13	Arabs	Malula	Syria	M
14	Alouites	Safitah	Syria	M
15	Moslems	Safitah	Syria	M
16	Alouites	Bishrayeh	Syria	M
17	Circassians		Syria	M
18	Circassians (Mixed)		Syria	M
19	Arabs	Hama and Homs	Syria	M
20	Druze	Jebel Druze	Syria	M
21	Druze	Jebel Druze	Syria	F
22	Armenians		Syria	M
23	Armenians		Syria	F
24	Arabs		Lebanon	M
25	Arabs		Lebanon	F
26	Turks		Turkey	M
27	Turks		Turkey	F
28	Kurds	Anatolia	Turkey	M
29	Arabs	City-dwellers	Iraq	M
30	Arabs (Mixed)		Iraq	M
31	Arabs (Mixed)		Iraq	M
32	Arabs	City-dwellers	Iraq	F
33	Persians	City-dwellers	Iran	M
34	Persians	Tehran and	Iran	F
35	Armenians	Isfahan	Iran	M
36	Sephardim Jews		Iraq	M
37	Sephardim Jews		Iraq	F
38	Sephardim - Ashkenazim Jews		Iraq	M
39	Sephardim - Ashkenazim Jews		Iraq	M
40	Sephardim - Ashkenazim Jews		Iraq	F
41	Ashkenazim Jews		Several	M
42	Ashkenazim Jews		Several	F
43	Jews		Several	M

TABLE 156: MEASUREMENTS AND INDICES RECORDED BY KAPPERS

Group	No.	GOL	No.	GB	No.	HH	No.	LWI	No.	WHI	No.	LHI
1	135	184.3	135	150.3	135	131.4	135	81.6	32	87.2	32	70.2
2	17	180.5	17	153.0	17	134.4	17	85.1	12	87.2	12	74.4
3	4	173.3	4	144.0	4	124.0	4	83.3	4	84.9	4	73.5
4	57	185.2	57	151.4	57	132.8	57	81.9	0	....	0	....
5	7	176.6	7	144.9	7	123.3	7	82.0	0	....	0	....
6	19	186.4	19	152.2	19	132.7	19	81.7	4	86.1	4	71.0
7	86	187.0	86	143.8	86	127.6	86	77.0	14	89.8	14	68.2
8	6	184.5	6	148.7	6	132.8	0	....	0	....	0	....
9	68	186.1	68	157.2	68	133.0	51	84.7	51	84.4	51	71.7
10	3	174.6	3	148.7	3	128.0	3	83.4	3	86.1	3	73.4
11	16	186.9	16	156.7	16	132.9	10	82.2	10	85.6	10	69.6

TABLE 156 (Continued)

Group	No.	GOL	No.	GB	No.	HH	No.	LWI	No.	WHI	No.	LHI
12	23	180.9	23	153.9	23	128.2	23	85.2	6	86.5	6	72.7
13	38	176.7	38	145.0	38	126.4	38	80.0	0	....	0	....
14	74	179.0	74	152.7	74	130.0	74	85.4	2	88.9	2	74.5
15	11	181.1	11	150.4	11	132.0	11	83.1	0	....	0	....
16	28	181.2	28	151.8	28	130.3	28	83.8	0	....	0	....
17	44	185.9	44	155.4	44	130.4	44	83.7	1	84.0	1	86.1
18	8	184.5	8	152.5	8	130.0	8	82.8	1	87.3	1	70.8
19	16	183.8	16	150.0	16	128.9	16	81.8	2	78.3	2	66.2
20	80	178.3	80	155.5	80	128.5	80	87.3	72	82.4	72	71.6
21	2	173.0	2	150.0	2	136.5	2	86.9	0	....	0	....
22	96	183.9	96	156.3	96	132.3	96	86.0	41	83.9	41	72.6
23	34	176.3	34	150.5	34	127.2	34	88.0	5	84.8	5	73.9
24	182	181.7	182	154.9	182	132.6	182	85.4	34	83.7	34	71.7
25	24	174.8	24	149.3	24	125.6	24	86.3	3	85.9	3	73.4
26	83	185.5	83	154.8	83	133.3	83	83.4	0	....	0	....
27	41	178.1	41	149.3	41	125.6	41	83.9	0	....	0	....
28	104	184.1	104	146.3	104	132.0	104	79.2	0	....	0	....
29	73	185.9	73	152.2	73	131.1	73	81.9	26	84.0	26	69.5
30	10	182.3	10	150.2	10	127.4	10	82.7	10	84.94	10	69.36
31	14	187.6	14	152.1	14	130.6	14	81.1	10	85.51	10	99.40
32	19	172.5	19	148.7	19	128.0	19	86.34	0	....	0	....
33	103	188.0	103	149.3	103	131.7	103	79.4	19	86.95	19	69.45
34	6	183.3	6	147.0	6	128.0	6	79.35	0	....	0	....
35	5	187.6	5	150.0	5	129.8	5	80.32	1	81.3	1	73.3
36	101	188.2	101	151.9	64	128.6	101	79.37	27	89.42	27	70.40
37	8	180.0	8	143.2	8	78.79	0	....	0	....	0	....
38	46	189.7	46	150.8	20	127.20	46	79.66	0	....	0	....
39	15	191.2	15	149.2	4	126.25	15	77.67	0	....	0	....
40	7	178.43	7	143.1	2	117.5	7	80.31	0	....	0	....
41	101	187.2	101	151.7	95	125.4	101	81.25	4	81.63	4	....
42	8	181.1	8	148.0	5	122.8	8	81.74	0	....	0	....
43	9	192.7	9	151.7	9	129.3	9	78.64	9	85.0	9	66.57
Total...	1,621